A CATHEDRAL OF CONSTITUTIONAL LAW

BIBLIOTHÈQUE DE LA REVUE D'HISTOIRE ECCLÉSIASTIQUE

VOLUME 112

A Cathedral
of Constitutional Law

Essays on the Earliest Constitutions
of the Order of Preachers
With an English Translation of
Fr Antoninus H. Thomas's 1965 Study

edited by
ANTON MILH O.P. AND MARK BUTAYE O.P.

BREPOLS

© 2023, Brepols Publishers n.v., Turnhout, Belgium.

D/2023/0095/33
ISBN 978-2-503-59334-0
eISBN 978-2-503-59335-7
DOI 10.1484/M.BRHE-EB.5.122437
ISSN 0067-8279

Dedicated to the memory of Fr Mark De Caluwe O.P. (1936-2023),
a pillar of our cathedral of constitutional law.

Table of contents

ANTON MILH O.P. AND
MARK BUTAYE O.P.

Introduction

'It is difficult not to feel a sense of admiration when confronted with this cathedral of constitutional law that is the constitution of the Dominicans', the Belgian sociologist Léo Moulin contended in 1960.[1] He cited a number of reasons for his esteem. For example, he praised the pluricameralism of the Dominican system of government, which requires three successive general chapters to approve a statute before it can be incorporated into the constitutions. He also applauded the corresponding democratic character of the Order, because these three successive chapters are composed of different people, ensuring optimal representation of the brothers. And he mentioned the capacity which this ostensibly ponderous system – chapters are only held every three years – possesses to respond to urgent challenges. If the situation requires, both the Master of the Order and the chapter may temporarily add to or suspend the constitutions through *ordinationes*. Moulin's eulogy of the Dominican constitutions also reflects his critical stance vis-à-vis the political extremism that dominated Europe during the interwar years and its well-known consequences: 'Constitutions that are both linear and complex, subtle and solid, [...] prove to be efficacious and prompt, prudent and bold [...] and are as far removed from the ease of centralised systems as they are from the dangers of anarchy'.[2]

If the constitutions of the Order of Preachers can serve as a critical-constructive mirror to contemporary secular legislative systems, then so much the better, but of course they were composed for a different reason: to organise the Order in such a way as to equip it for its mission. The Fourth Lateran Council (1215) had decreed that new religious institutes could no longer write their own rules, and Dominic and his first brothers therefore adopted the Rule of Augustine. But this did not suffice to shape their life as preachers. As the brothers at the time led a canonical form of life – they were attached to the church of Saint Romanus in Toulouse – they drew inspiration for their *consuetudines* from those

---

1 'Il est difficile de ne pas éprouver un sentiment d'admiration devant cette cathédrale de droit constitutionnel qu'est la législation dominicaine' (Léo Moulin, 'Le pluricaméralisme dans l'Ordre des Frères Prêcheurs', *Res Publica*, 2 (1960) 1, 50-66 (p. 65)).
2 'Constitutions à la fois linéaires et complexes, subtiles et solides, [...] elles s'affirment efficaces et promptes, prudentes et hardies [...] aussi éloignées de la facilité des systèmes centralisateurs que des périls de l'anarchie' (Moulin, 'Le pluricaméralisme...' [see note 1], p. 66). See also id., *Le monde vivant des religieux: Dominicains, Jésuites, Bénédictins...* (Paris: Calmann-Lévy, 1964), ch. 5.

of Prémontré. The resulting text was given force of constitutional law at the 1220 and 1221 chapters, both held in Bologna. Despite their clear Premonstratensian inspiration – large parts of the first *distinctio* in particular were derived literally from the constitutions of Prémontré – the Dominican constitutions from the start reflected the Order's own charism. Dominic left almost no written legacy, but he did attend the chapters of 1220 and 1221 – this fact alone should convince us of the immense importance of the first constitutions. The earliest constitutions contain something of the purpose and form that Dominic gave to his Order: they embody a little of his soul.

Raphaël-Louis Œchslin, the historian of spirituality, has characterised Dominican spirituality as 'incarnated spirituality'. Not in the banal sense that it can only exist if it is actually lived, but because certain specific structures of the Order of Preachers are an essential component of its spirituality: Œchslin mentioned prayer, study, radical poverty and the generous principle of dispensation. A faithful follower of Thomas Aquinas, he compared the relationship between the spirituality and structure of the Order to that between the soul and the body in human beings: they are a single and inseparable whole.[3] The soul, the Order's individuality, is carried by the body, its structures, which in turn are protected by the constitutions. Dominican spirituality can therefore truly be called a 'constitutional spirituality'. Gert Melville has strikingly articulated the extent to which the Dominican constitutions are foundational to the identity of the Order: the constitutions 'stood for a "closed legal system" which really did have the character of a constitution, in a modern sense as well. [...] [C]reated by the communal will of the Order's members, [they] were not only the foundation and legitimization of all organs and instances and not only ensured the validity of the latter's legal and functional actions, but they also symbolized the Order's identity'.[4]

Melville's words, which refer to the Order at its inception, still apply to the Order today. Dominic died in 1221, more than eight centuries ago. But thanks to the constitutions, borne by and itself bearing many successive generations of Dominican brothers, his charism is alive in the Order. The constitutions themselves have become part of the charism of the Order, of the wisdom from which others in the church and in society can draw to meet the challenges they face. It is no coincidence that Pope Francis, in his letter *Praedicator Gratiae* (2021), praised the Order for her 'inclusive form of governance', which he himself described as a '"synodal" process [that] enabled the Order to adapt its life and mission to changing historical contexts while maintaining fraternal communion'.

---

3 See Raphaël-Louis Œchslin, 'Pour une spiritualité dominicaine incarnée', *Vie dominicaine*, 17 (1958), 1-3, 17-21, 33-36 and 49-51 (p. 2).

4 Gert Melville, 'The Dominican *Constitutiones*', in *A Companion to Medieval Rules and Customaries* (Brill's Companions to the Christian Tradition, 93), ed. by Krijn Pansters (Leiden – Boston: Brill, 2020), 253-281 (p. 279).

The Dominican constitutions can thus be a source of inspiration for the church today, as she proceeds along the path of synodality.[5]

Few works of scholarship have been so important for the historical study of the Dominican constitutions as the doctoral dissertation of the Belgian Dominican Antoninus Hendrik Thomas (1915-1996). His thesis, entitled *De oudste constituties van de dominicanen. Voorgeschiedenis, tekst, bronnen, ontstaan en ontwikkeling (1215-1237) – met uitgave van de tekst* ('The Earliest Constitutions of the Dominicans. Antecedents, Text, Sources, Origins and Development (1215-1237) – With an Edition of the Text'), appeared in 1965 as volume 42 of the *Bibliothèque de la Revue d'histoire ecclésiastique*. The notion 'earliest constitutions' deserves some explanation here. The text of the constitutions, as approved by the first two general chapters of the Order in 1220 and 1221, has been lost. Therefore, due to a lack of manuscript tradition, an edition of this earliest approved version of the constitutions is impossible. So what Father Thomas proposes in his dissertation is not a text edition in the strict sense, but rather a scholarly reconstruction with a high degree of probability. Furthermore, Father Thomas has created a confusion of concepts, which was immediately noticed by Father Raymond Creytens in his book review in the *Revue d'histoire ecclésiastique*: this is not an edition (*uitgave van de tekst*), but a reconstruction, and chronologically speaking it does not deal with the earliest constitutions (*oudste constituties*) – because that must have been a provisional and now lost text from the second half of the 1210s – but rather the text approved by the first chapters in the 1220s.[6] Nevertheless, the reconstruction of the text of the earliest constitutions that Father Thomas included in his dissertation remains their 'reference edition' even today, more than half a century after its publication.[7]

The reconstruction itself occupies sixty pages, but Father Thomas's entire dissertation runs to some three hundred additional pages, in which he addresses the text, the sources, the origins and the development of the earliest Dominican constitutions. He wrote in Dutch, and as a result, the fruits of the many years of research that underlay his work have remained largely inaccessible to friars and scholars who do not speak this language. This circumstance inspired the plan to publish an English translation of Thomas's doctoral thesis to mark the eighth centenary of Dominic's *dies natalis* in 2021. Given that 1965 is more than fifty years ago, and Thomas's work therefore necessarily required addition and correction, we decided to bring together a number of experts on the earliest

---

5 Pope Francis, '*Praedicator Gratiae*: Letter of the Holy Father to the Master of
the Order of Preachers for the 8th Centenary of the Death of St. Dominic of
Caleruega', [https://www.op.org/praedicator-gratiae-letter-of-the-holy-father-to-the-master-of-the-order-of-preachers-for-the-8th-centenary-of-the-death-of-st-dominic-of-caleruega/] (accessed 23 July 2022).

6 Raymond Creytens, 'Compte rendu de A.H. Thomas, *De oudste constituties van de dominicanen* [...]', *RHE*, 61 (1966), 862-871.

7 According to Nicole Bériou and Paul-Bernard Hodel, in their *Saint Dominique et l'ordre des frères prêcheurs: Témoignages écrits fin XIIe – XIVe siècle* (Paris: Cerf, 2019), p. 202.

Dominican constitutions and, more widely, the evolution of both ecclesiastical (monastic) and secular law in the Middle Ages to evaluate the achievement of Father Thomas. This expert seminar took place in the Dominican house in Leuven from 30 April to 1 May 2019, and the papers given there have been included in this volume as part 1. References by the authors to passages in Father Thomas's dissertation first give the pages in the original work, and then, in square brackets, the relevant pages in the English translation in part 2 of this volume.

Two esteemed contributors to the current project are sadly no longer with us to witness its completion. A week after the expert seminar was held, Professor Laurent Waelkens was rushed to hospital. This was followed by a year of gruelling treatment, during which he gave impressive testimony to the theological virtues of faith, hope and charity. He died in Leuven on 6 June 2020 at the age of 66. During a visit, he expressed his wish to us that the paper he had presented at the expert seminar should be reworked into an article, notwithstanding his decision to cancel all other scholarly engagements – it was touching proof of Professor Waelkens's commitment to the project. With the help of his wife, Frédérique Waelkens-Donnay, it proved possible to retrieve the digital file of his paper. His student and successor as professor of Roman law and legal history at KU Leuven, Wouter Druwé, was kind enough to supply the references for Waelkens's article and expand it here and there while remaining faithful to the original argument.[8] We owe him a great debt of gratitude for this work.

Less than two months after Professor Waelkens's passing, we received the shocking news of Father Wolfram Hoyer's death in a car accident as he was returning from a sick call. Apart from Simon Tugwell, there have been few other Dominicans in recent decades who have dedicated themselves so intensively to the study of the constitutions and their history as he did. Father Hoyer enthusiastically supported the plan to publish an English translation of Father Thomas's book from the start, all the more so as he remembered the difficulties he had himself when reading it in Dutch, which made him vividly alive to the value of a translation. He sent us his own contribution for this volume a few months before his death. We publish it here in gratitude for his life of fraternal generosity.[9] Due to his untimely death, Father Hoyer was unable to elaborate on certain scholarly intuitions, such as a thorough study of the *consuetudines* of Osma as a source for the Dominican constitutions. We express here our hope that this will be taken up by a future generation of researchers.

---

8 Druwé is the author of a fitting obituary for Waelkens as well as of his academic bibliography: see Wouter Druwé, 'In Memoriam: Laurent Waelkens', *RHE*, 115 (2020), 453-456 and id., 'Academic Bibliography of Laurent Waelkens', *Tijdschrift voor Rechtsgeschiedenis*, 88 (2020), 341-365.

9 See anon., 'P. Wolfram Hoyer OP, 9.6.1969 – 30.7.2020', *Kontakt: Freundesgabe der Dominikaner in Deutschland und Österreich*, 48 (2020-2021), 89 and Viliam Dóci, 'Obituary: Fr. Wolfram Christian Hoyer (*09/06/1969 †30/07/2020)', [https://institutumhistoricum.op.org/necrologio-fr-wolfram-christian-hoyer-op-09-06-1969-30-07-2020/?lang=en] (accessed 27 July 2022).

In the first chapter, *Anton Milh O.P.* (KU Leuven) outlines the development of history writing by Belgian Dominicans in the nineteenth and twentieth centuries. His survey demonstrates that Father Thomas's research on medieval monastic law was situated in a shared interest and a full-blown scholarly tradition. Drawing on a number of cases from the first half of the twentieth century, Milh identifies three tendencies among the Belgian friars historians. First, they increasingly embraced the historical critical method. Second, a network around Dominican history gradually emerged, which also comprised researchers, archivists and librarians beyond the confines of the Order. And finally, the practice of history became institutionalised: the superiors asked brothers to take on certain historical projects and freed them from other responsibilities to do so. This development set the preconditions for the scholarly work of friars such as Gilles Meersseman, and in his wake two young Belgian brothers, Raymond Creytens and Antoninus Thomas. The latter was obviously also strongly influenced by the work of his doctoral supervisor, the Norbertine Father Placide Lefèvre.

The following chapters look anew at a number of sources for the Dominican constitutions identified by Father Thomas. As has been seen, the main source for the first *distinctio* are the thirteenth-century statutes of the Premonstratensian Order.[10] In his contribution, *Herman Janssens O.Praem.* (Abbey of Averbode) surveys the research of the legislation of Prémontré since the seventeenth century, including the manuscripts in question and the corresponding editions. Because it cannot be excluded, and is even to be hoped, that new manuscripts will be discovered in the future that will contain versions of the twelfth- and thirteenth-century *consuetudines* and *statuta* of Prémontré, Janssens concludes with a correlation table with six different redactions from this period. This will allow scholars to quickly determine to what redaction a manuscript belongs.

Alexis Grélois (University of Rouen) then explains why the Friars Preachers used almost nothing from the Cistercian *statuta* for the first *distinctio* of their constitutions. This first *distinctio* deals with the organisation of their daily life, such as prayer times, periods of fasting and silence, the habit et cetera. By as early as the late twelfth century, the legislative corpus of the Cistercians had grown to impressive proportions as it contained a great number of guidelines, both general and specific (even personal). This hindered the spread and implementation of these *statuta*, all the more so as it was the tradition in Cîteaux to hold an annual meeting of all abbots (the *capitulum Cisterciense*, later *conventus abbatum*) which would adopt even more rules. However, the Cistercian form of government, with its frequent chapters and its *definitorium* charged with further developing the decisions of the chapters, did serve as a source of inspiration for the Dominican constitutions, specifically for the second *distinctio*.[11]

10 Cf. Antoninus Hendrik Thomas, *De oudste constituties van de dominicanen: Voorgeschiedenis, tekst, bronnen, ontstaan en ontwikkeling (1215-1237) met uitgave van de tekst* (BRHE, 42) (Leuven: Bureel van de RHE, 1965), pp. 129-157 [pp. 282-306].
11 Cf. Thomas, *De oudste constituties...* [see note 10], pp. 187-199 [pp. 330-340].

Father Thomas pointed in his dissertation to the influence of Bolognese academic circles on the young Order of Preachers, including on its constitutions (for example the adoption of the concept of *nationes*). But readers may notice that Thomas's analysis of the influence of these Bolognese jurists uncharacteristically remains somewhat cursory; we must assume he felt out of his depth when trying to gauge the full extent to which the constitutions were indebted to this source.[12] *Laurent Waelkens* (KU Leuven) expertly fills this lacuna in his contribution, which explains the various legal systems that were in use in Antiquity and the Middle Ages for the collective administration of goods, such as *confraternitas, fiducia* and *possessio*, and assesses their strengths and weaknesses. Mendicant orders such as the Dominicans, who did not wish to amass a stable patrimony but were not willing either to expose themselves to the arbitrariness of the feudal system, found a solution in one particular early-twelfth-century innovation. The foundation of a school for Roman law in Bologna by Countess Matilda of Canossa occasioned the establishment of multiple colleges, which had to be able to own goods if they were to maintain their independence. To ensure that these goods would not at some point be taken from them by the secular ruler and used for other purposes, the school in Bologna and its dependent colleges were granted legal independence. The Dominicans allowed friars to study and teach at the university and were thus integrated into this system. The university of Bologna's exempt status was soon also adopted by other universities in Europe, so that the Dominicans were able to gain a foothold there too. A further development was that in the thirteenth century, cities began to free themselves from their feudal straightjacket by purchasing borough privileges. This permitted the Dominicans to establish houses there, earning them the reputation of being 'urban monks'.

After these discussions of the influence of various great spiritual and/or intellectual traditions – Prémontré, Cîteaux, the Bolognese legal school – on the constitutions, *Wolfram Hoyer O.P.* (Dominican province of Saint Albert of Southern Germany and Austria) examines one specific, material source: the manuscript known as AGOP XIV A4, fols 28^r-47^r, also called the Rodez manuscript or the *codex Ruthenensis*.[13] This manuscript contains the oldest textual tradition of the Dominican constitutions. As Hoyer argues, it is a copy, made between 1280 and 1320, of the revised constitutions commissioned by the 1228 general chapter, supplemented with the decisions of later chapters up to and including that of 1236. In his contribution, Hoyer builds on and complements Dominikus Planzer's palaeographical analysis of AGOP XIV A4, fols 28^r-47^r, particularly with regard to the red 'C' markings in the text. These markings were not ornamental, but they indicate the places where changes were made by the post-1228 chapters. Finally, Hoyer compares the four editions of AGOP XIV A4, fols 28^r-47^r that have so far been published. Whereas Heinrich Suso Denifle (1885) was eager to prove the Premonstratensian – as opposed to the Cistercian – influence on

---

12   Cf. Thomas, *De oudste constituties...* [see note 10], pp. 233-236 [pp. 366-369].
13   Cf. Thomas, *De oudste constituties...* [see note 10], pp. 80-83 and 114-119 [pp. 244-246 and 270-274].

the Dominican constitutions, Pius Mothon, whose 1896 edition was made at the general chapter's request, strove to present the constitutions as the bearer of Dominic's vision for his own Order. Heribert Christian Scheeben (1939) was alert to the complex combination of sources that underlay the Dominican constitutions, but Father Thomas's reconstruction (1965) was the first to give this aspect the weight it merits. 'Thomas not only carried out much deeper research on the background of early Dominican legislation, but his results make it possible to conduct a more detailed analysis and achieve a more precise interpretation of these laws', as Hoyer argues.

Hoyer's appreciation for Father Thomas's work is shared by *Florent Cygler* (University of Nantes), whose contribution offers an overview of what he calls the 'long editorial "journey"' of the medieval Dominican constitutions. After observing that Thomas's reconstruction can now be complemented and corrected on the basis of studies by Bruno Krings (on the *institutiones* of Prémontré) and Simon Tugwell (on the second *distinctio*), he calls for greater scrutiny of the evolution of the Dominican constitutions in the years 1230, 1240 and 1250. Master Raymond of Peñafort, later patron saint of canon lawyers, carried out a thorough revision of the constitutions between 1239 and 1241, not only scrapping the introduction that had been added in 1228 and integrating its content into the body of the constitutions, but also substantially rearranging the text itself. Between 1254 and 1256, Master Humbert of Romans again revised the constitutions, at the general chapter's request, to accommodate the fixing of the liturgy of the Order.[14] These later redactions, particularly Humbert's, have received little attention by comparison with the 'earliest constitutions' (up to 1228), and the many subsequent redactions up to the first printed version of the Dominican constitutions in 1505 have shared in this fate. Cygler argues for an approach to the Dominican constitutions that takes the entire medieval period into consideration and focuses also on 'forgotten' editions.

In the introduction to his dissertation, Father Thomas contended that Jordan of Saxony's *Libellus de principiis Ordinis Praedicatorum* is 'the first, fundamental and most authoritative literary source' for the earliest history of the Order, to which the writings of such authors as Peter Ferrand and Constantine of Orvieto offer little more than hagiographical embellishment.[15] Thomas spoke here as an 'archaeologist' who sought to approach historical truth as closely as possible. But as *Anne Reltgen-Tallon* (University of Picardie Jules Verne) shows in her contribution, the value of these texts lies elsewhere. They are not eyewitnesses, but testimony to how the Order's earliest origins were perceived at a later point in the thirteenth century. Her discussion of the genesis of the Dominican legal system through the eyes of successive annalists demonstrates their tendency to emphasise the originality of the Friars Preachers. One example is the second and third generation of Dominicans' desire to deemphasise the Rule of Augustine.

---

14 Cf. Thomas, *De oudste constituties...* [see note 10], pp. 83-89 [pp. 246-250].
15 Cf. Thomas, *De oudste constituties...* [see note 10], pp. xviii-xix [pp. 163-164].

A project by Hugh of Saint-Cher to draft a fully Dominican set of laws was approved by the pope, but was blocked at the last minute by Master Humbert of Romans, who preferred to retain the Rule that Dominic had chosen on the basis of his own personal history as a canon. Another protagonist of this desire to retreat from the canonical roots of the Order was Constantine of Orvieto, who called the friars' first rules of 1216 *constitutiones*, even though they were *consuetudines* that had been adopted in large part from Prémontré. Another tendency that Reltgen-Tallon has discovered is the propensity to erase the memory of legal disputes during the first years of the Order. Dietrich of Apolda, who wrote in the late thirteenth century, made no mention of the proposal – inspired by the ideal of poverty and humility – to admit lay brothers to positions of authority; a proposal hotly debated and ultimately rejected at the 1220 chapter. But he did include another proposal that sprung from the same ideal, Dominic's request to this chapter to be permitted to resign as the superior of the Order, because it fitted the hagiographical discourse about the founder.

The last chapter similarly addresses the reception of the constitutions. In her contribution, *Anna Zajchowska-Bołtromiuk* (Cardinal Stefan Wyszyński University, Warsaw) examines Heinrich Bitterfeld's *De formatione et reformatione Ordinis Fratrum Praedicatorum*, which was probably written between 1388 and 1390 at Raymond of Capua's request. It is the first treatise that is fully dedicated to the Observant movement, of which Raymond was a protagonist. Bitterfeld believed that the crisis in the Order which he diagnosed at the time resulted from lack of obedience, which in turn was rooted in a mistaken interpretation of certain key passages in the constitutions, such as the proviso that they did not bind *ad culpam*, religious profession and dispensation. Zajchowska shows how Bitterfeld attempted to assign a semi-sacred character to the constitutions by reading them as an application, desired by the *antiqui patres*, of the divine law. In addition, he sought to demonstrate that deliberate mitigation of the constitutions contradicted the very purpose of the religious life, the pursuit of perfection through adherence to the evangelical counsels, and is therefore a mortal sin. Although Bitterfeld was not one of the most radical Observants – John Nider called dispensation a 'licence to hell', and John Dominici regarded the constitutions as the direct expression of the will of the first superior, Dominic, which had to be observed with absolute obedience –, Zajchowska rightly asks whether his approach to observance, rather than reforming the Order, would not have completely transformed it. According to him, the brothers fell into two categories: that of the superiors, to whom the friars owed obedience, and that of the subjects, whose role was limited to passive participation. But this is inconsistent with the Dominican model of government, according to which the brothers in chapter are the highest decision-making body, and whose practice of democratic participation minimises the difference between superior and subject.

Sub Augustini regula mente profecit sedula, tandem virum canonicum auget in apostolicum. For Father Thomas, this antiphon from the office for the feast of Saint

Dominic (*in II nocturno*) aptly summarised not only Dominic's life, but also the constitutions of his Order.[16] The first *distinctio* organises the life of the Friars Preachers according to a canonical-monastic pattern (*virum canonicum…*), but is simultaneously characterised by openness to the apostolic life, to preaching, which is the Order's *raison d'être* (… *auget in apostolicum*). This is developed further in the second *distinctio*. The constitutions' primary objective was to orga-nise the Order, but given that the Order was founded *specialiter ob predicationem et animarum salutem*, the constitutions also reach beyond this and touch the church and the world. The life and work of so many friars can only be properly understood if the charism of Dominic and his first companions is kept in mind as it is enshrined in the constitutions. This is why they merit the enduring attention of researchers, following in the footsteps of Father Thomas and of the scholars who have contributed to this volume. Our gratitude goes out to them, for their enthusiasm and patience in the realisation of this book. We also wish to thank the Dominican province of Saint Thomas Aquinas in Belgium for its generous finan-cial support; Frs Viliam Štefan Dóci and Gianni Festa of the *Institutum Historicum Ordinis Praedicatorum* for their fraternal encouragement; and Chris Vanden Borre and Christine Vande Veire of Brepols Publishers, who contributed so much to bringing this project to completion. Finally, we would like to extend special thanks to Dr. Brian Heffernan, who translated Father Thomas's dissertation. May the fruit of his hard work be useful to many.

---

16 Cf. Thomas, *De oudste constituties…* [see note 10], p. 300 [p. 419].

Sigla

AFP   Archivum Fratrum Praedicatorum
AGOP   Archivum Generale Ordinis Fratrum Praedicatorum
BRHE   Bibliothèque de la Revue d'histoire ecclésiastique
DHGE   Dictionnaire d'histoire et de géographie ecclésiastiques
MOPH   Monumenta Ordinis Fratrum Praedicatorum Historica
RHE   Revue d'histoire ecclésiastique

PART I

———

Essays

ANTON MILH O.P.

Et ut maxima est Historiae necessitas, non minor est utilitas

Belgian Dominican Historians in the 19th and 20th Centuries

The central place that study occupies in Dominican life has caused the *ordo praedicatorum* to be dubbed the *ordo doctorum*. In practice this is often narrowed down to one particular scholarly tradition, that of the *Doctor Angelicus* and his interpreters throughout the centuries. The constitutions of the Order describe Thomas Aquinas as 'optimus magister et exemplar', and they call on the friars to study his writings so that a Thomistic theology can be designed adapted to every new era.[1] Far be it from me to call into question the primacy of Aquinas, but I do observe that this has ensured that the emphasis in the historiography of the intellectual life of the Order has been on philosophy and speculative theology.[2] The study of a discipline such as Church history has, as a result, been somewhat neglected.

Anyone unfamiliar with the historiographical tradition of the Order might be inclined to think that Fr Antoninus Hendrik Thomas's 1965 doctoral dissertation on the earliest constitutions is unique in its kind. It is certainly true that this work is a monument to erudition and scholarly diligence, but a monument, I believe, that must not be viewed in isolation from the work of other Belgian Dominican historians. This chapter addresses trends in the historiographical work of Belgian Dominicans since the restauration of organised Dominican life in the nineteenth century, up to and including the scholarly achievements of Fr Thomas and a number of his fellow friars in the second half of the twentieth century. My aim is not to provide an exhaustive overview, but to demonstrate that Fr Thomas's

1 *Liber Constitutionum et Ordinationum Fratrum Ordinis Praedicatorum iussu Fr. Brunonis Cadoré magistri Ordinis editus* (Rome: Curia generalitia, 2018), n° 82 (p. 34).

2 Examples of this for the Dutch-language context can be found in Marit Monteiro, 'Hoeders van waarheid en waarachtigheid: De Nederlandse dominicanen als vertegenwoordigers van een katholieke intellectuele tegencultuur (1866-1966)', in *Het geloof dat inzicht zoekt: Religieuzen en de wetenschap* (Metamorfosen, 9), ed. by Joep van Gennip and Marie-Antoinette Willemsen (Hilversum: Verloren, 2010), 9-25 and Kees (C.E.M.) Struyker Boudier, *Wijsgerig leven in Nederland en België, 1880-1980*, 8 vols (Nijmegen: Katholiek Studiecentrum; Baarn: Ambo, 1985-1992), II (1986): *De dominicanen*.

A Cathedral of Constitutional Law, éd. par Anton MILH O.P. and Mark BUTAYE O.P., Turnhout, Brepols, 2023 (*Bibliothèque de la Revue d'histoire ecclésiastique*, 112), p. 27-42.
BREPOLS ❧ PUBLISHERS   10.1484/M.BRHE-EB.5.135042

work is exemplary – both as to subject and as to method – of a certain scholarly tradition.

1. Dominican new beginnings in Belgium: a beguine affair?

The Concordat of 1801 restored the freedom of the Church but did not mention the religious orders. For religious this meant the continuation of the difficult situation that had emerged under the French revolutionary regime (1796), with friaries abolished and communities scattered. Religious priests were told, even by Rome, to devote themselves to pastoral work in the dioceses. Thus the Dominican friar Franciscus Ackerman (1770-1847), who had received the habit in 1792, became the parish priest of Saint Elisabeth's ('Great') Beguinage in Ghent in 1809. Three years later, he was sent an assistant, his confrère Pius Braeckman (1764-1847), who had received the habit in 1794. The beguines of the Ghent beguinage had been under the spiritual care of the Dominicans almost from the moment the beguinage was founded in 1233, only a few years after the Dominicans established a friary in the city in 1228.[3]

Belgian independence in 1830 opened new perspectives for a revival of the Order. In the North (now the Netherlands), the old Dominican province of *Germania Inferior* had survived the revolutionary era, paradoxically because of its semi-clandestine existence – the apostolate of the friars consisted of ministering to so-called missionary 'stations'. However, the absence of friaries there (and the ban on founding new religious houses) made the formation of new candidates difficult. The provincial superior Dominicus Raken (1798-1869) attempted to overcome this problem by exercising the right of association enshrined in the new Belgian constitution, a right which made it possible to found religious communities. Ghent seemed to him the ideal location for a house of formation; it would also enable him to concede Ackerman and Braeckman's wish to return to regular conventual life. In the summer of 1835, the Dominicans purchased a building near the Great Beguinage and transformed it into a small noviciate. On 6 December of that year, Ackerman, Braeckman and the Dutchman Raymundus van Zeeland (1797-1845) once again donned the white habit of the Order. During lauds the next morning, five novices received the habit: four Dutchmen and a Belgian. By 1861 the Belgian Dominicans were numerous enough to warrant elevation to the status of a province, which was placed under the patronage of Saint Rose of Lima.[4]

---

3   Gilles Gérard Meersseman, 'Les Frères Prêcheurs et le Mouvement Dévot en Flandre au XIIIe S.', *AFP*, 18 (1948), 69-130 (pp. 81-88). On the spiritual connections between the Dominicans and the beguines, see Stephanus Axters, *Geschiedenis van de vroomheid in de Nederlanden*, 4 vols (Antwerp: De Sikkel, 1950-1960), I (1950): *De vroomheid tot rond het jaar 1300*, pp. 306-335.

4   See Marit Monteiro, *Gods Predikers: Dominicanen in Nederland (1795-2000)* (Hilversum: Verloren, 2008), pp. 50-73 and Ambroos-Maria Bogaerts, *Dominikanen in België, 1835-1958* (Bouwstoffen voor de geschiedenis der dominikanen in de Nederlanden, A) (Brussels: Dominikaans archief, 1969), pp. 29-47.

The first Belgian novice was also the first among the Belgian Dominicans to develop a strong historical interest. Bruno Moulaert (1808-1870) was a priest of the diocese of Ghent before he entered the Order and took the religious name of Bernardus. Moulaert's dedication to the expansion of the Order in Belgium and his many pastoral activities did not prevent him from engaging also in historical research.[5] He visited many archives to do research, collected archival material, and corresponded with surviving members of the old province of *Germania Inferior* in the hope of acquiring documents from them.[6] Moulaert's bibliography contains a significant number of works on seventeenth- and eighteenth-century members of the Order, but his attention to the beguine movement is probably most noteworthy: he published a book on the Great Beguinage in Ghent, left an unpublished manuscript in the archives on the beguinage of Tienen (Tirlemont), and collected a large amount of data on the beguinage of Kortrijk (Courtrai).[7]

Research on the beguines was not a private pursuit just of Moulaert's. His confrères Guilielmus Rommens (1819-1890), Thomas Halflants (1831-1909) and Gustaaf De Ryckere (1839-1907) also took an interest in their history.[8] As an explanation, I would like to suggest that the beguines formed a building block for the reconstruction of Dominican identity in Belgium during the nineteenth century. The new beginnings of Dominican life in Belgium are as much a story of continuity (involving two friars from the old province of *Germania Inferior*, which in a certain way continued to exist in the North) as of discontinuity (there had been no regular communities for three decades). But the ties between the Dominicans and the beguines went all the way back to the thirteenth century, and for the Ghent Great Beguinage, it could even be argued that there was a continuity of six centuries. This makes the beguines a rare constant factor in the history of the Dominicans in the Low Countries and thus an important identity marker.

Incidentally, the ties between the Dominicans and the beguines were stronger than just the provision of spiritual guidance, as is clear from the example of

---

5 On Moulaert, see also Vincent van Caloen, 'Moulaert (Bernard)', in *Biographie Nationale*, 44 vols (Brussels: Bruylant, 1866-1986), XV (1899), col. 303-306 and Kees Schutgens, 'Predikbroeders op de dool: Opheffing van het dominicanenklooster te Sittard (1797-1802) opnieuw in kaart gebracht', in *Dominicanen en dominicanessen in Sittard: Vier eeuwen aanwezigheid*, ed. by Chris Dols, Guus Janssen and Kees Schutgens (Hilversum: Verloren, 2019), 107-134 (pp. 111-114).

6 Emiel Cresens and Ambroos-Maria Bogaerts, *Inventaris van het Dominikaans archief*, 2 vols (Leuven: Dominikaans archief, 1976-1977), I (1976): *Het provinciaal archief*, p. ix.

7 Bernardus Moulaert, *Het Groot-Beggynhof van Gent* (Ghent: Rousseau – Warrie, 1850); id., *De l'Institut des Béguines en Belgique et de son rétablissement en France, avec des nouvelles additions par le P. Moulaert* (Brussels – Leuven: Fonteyn, 1857); KADOC (Leuven), *Dominicanen – Belgische/Vlaamse Provincie Sint-Rosa* (OPSR), 522, 'Aenteekeningen Nopens het Beggynhof van Kortryk', s.d. and 1329.

8 Fr. Th. H. [=Thomas Halflants], 'Le Grand Béguinage de Sainte-Élisabeth à Gand', *L'Année Dominicaine*, 1 (1859-1860), 263-273, 294-299 and 408-412 (the information for this article was provided by Rommens, see p. 412) and Gustaaf De Ryckere, *De heilige Begga en hare wonderbare stichtingen* (Lier: Taymans – Nezy, 1900).

Fr Rommens: a cousin of his became a beguine in 1862.[9] Dominican involvement with the Ghent beguines later found further expression in publications of Frs Lucas Luyts (1898-1979) and Jordanus Piet De Pue (1911-1987).[10] Despite the death of the last beguine in Ghent in 2003, the Dominicans continue to have a pastoral presence in the Great Beguinage.

2. Hagiographical interest

Apart from their attention to the beguines, the nineteenth-century friars seem to have been mainly interested in Dominican saints. In line with my earlier suggestion that the beguines were a Dominican identity marker, I believe that this hagiographical interest was more than just an expression of simple devotion. The renewed start of the Order in Northwest Europe felt somewhat like a reinvention as a result of the discontinuity described above, a reinvention which, moreover, was not without its incidental polemics. Saints' lives helped to enhance the identity of the Order, something which was also realised by the friars in the newly-erected Belgian province. The fact that the lives of saints might foster Dominican vocations will no doubt also have motivated the friar-hagiographers.

As one of the most productive hagiographers, Fr Henri-Marie Iweins (1840-1905) deserves particular mention.[11] Even before joining the Dominicans in 1861, this aristocrat from Ypres had shown evidence of historical interest by publishing a couple of modest historical works. He would retain this interest after joining the Order. Like Moulaert, Iweins actively looked for archival material about the Order, and apart from a history of the Dominican friaries in Ypres and Leuven, he wrote works on a number of Dominican saints.[12]

In 1895, the Belgian friars started a series that would see the publication of Dominican hagiographies on a monthly basis. Four years later, this project developed into a journal, *Sint-Dominicusbode* ('Messenger of Saint Dominic'), with Fr Pius Liekens (1869-1948) as its driving force. Between 1900 and 1906, he

---

9 Rommens held a sermon on this occasion: *Aenspraek door den Eerw. Pater R. Rommens, Predikheer, ter gelegenheid der kleeding van zyne nicht, Maria Cath. Rommens, in het Convent ter Kaerden, op het Groot-Beggynhof, te Gent, den 20 January 1862* (Ghent: Rousseau – Warrie, 1862). On Rommens, see Vincent Van Caloen, 'Rommens (Guillaume)', in *Biographie Nationale...* [see note 5], XIX (1907), col. 927-928.

10 Lucas Luyts, *Het Groot Begijnhof van Sint-Elisabeth in zijn verleden en zijn heden* (Ghent: Dominikanen, 1965), pp. 21-23 and Jordanus Piet De Pue, *Geschiedenis Groot Begijnhof Sint Elisabeth Gent en St. Amandsberg* (Leuven: Paters Dominikanen, 1984), pp. 35-39.

11 On Iweins, see Vincent Van Caloen, *Le Père Henri-Marie Iweins d'Eeckhoutte* (Brussels: Vromant, 1906).

12 Cresens and Bogaerts, *Inventaris...* [see note 6], p. ix. For Iweins's histories of the Dominican friaries in Ypres and Leuven, see Henri-Marie Iweins, *Monographie du couvent des Frères-Prêcheurs à Ypres (1278 à 1797)* (Ypres: Lafonteyne, 1864) and id., *Le couvent des Dominicains de Louvain* (Leuven: Peeters, 1902). For an example of Iweins's hagiographical work, see id., *Le bienheureux Raymond de Capoue, XIIIe maître général des Frères-Prêcheurs* (Leuven: Peeters, 1900).

published four volumes of Dominican hagiographies under the euphonious title of *Bloemen uit Sint-Dominicus' Hof* ('Flowers from Saint Dominic's garden').[13]

Closer examination of these hagiographical writings by Belgian Dominicans at the end of the nineteenth and the beginning of the twentieth century shows that their work took a 'scientific turn'. To illustrate this, I will compare Fr Rommens's biography of Catherine of Siena (1875) with a series of saints' lives by Fr Josephus Arts (1864-1934) published between 1928 and 1931. These publications are particularly well-suited for comparison, because in the introductions to their works both authors specifically discuss the sources and the methods they used. For his biography, Rommens used texts by Catherine's spiritual guide, Raymond of Capua, and her own correspondence. Concerning Raymond, Rommens writes:

> Being sufficiently convinced of his sound judgement, I feel I am allowed to freely follow a writer of such renown and copy his account of what happened, without having to do any further historical research myself to prove him correct. The authority of such a credible author will at the same time offer some insurance against any suspicion of gullibility if some of the stories seem a little naive or artificial.[14]

We can conclude from this quotation that Rommens was rather uncritical in dealing with his sources.

In his *Onze voorbeelden* ('Our examples'), three volumes containing lives of saints,[15] Fr Arts offers a bibliography that is considerably longer than Rommens's: Gérard de Frachet's *Vitae Fratrum*, collections of saints' lives by Seraphinus Razzi, Michele Pio, Johannes Lopez, Jean de Rechac and Friedrich Steill, Thomas Souèges's *Année Dominicaine*, Quétif and Echard's *Scriptores Ordinis* and the *Acta Sanctorum* of the Bollandists.[16] Arts warns his readership against unconditional trust in any source:

> It is a common mistake to show too much confidence in the descriptions of the lives of saints. Quite often, something of the respect for the saints themselves seems to have rubbed off on these pious authors. The fact that people read about the lives of saints without even considering the author, clearly shows that all authors are thought to be excellent historians. [...] It is even an illusion to have blind admiration for the *Acta Sanctorum*, regardless of how worthy of respect it may be, and treat it as if it were the Gospel. We find

---

13 [Albertus De Meyer *et al.*], *De Predikheeren in België: Vijftigste verjaring der Provincie van S. Rosa, 1861-1911* (Antwerp: Sint-Dominicusbode, 1911), pp. 209-210.

14 Guilielmus Rommens, *Geschiedenis van den heilige Catharina van Senen, maagd der Derde-Orde van den heiligen Dominicus (1347-1380)* (Mechelen: Van Velsen, 1876), p. 14.

15 The twenty-three lives of the saints included in the three volumes of *Onze Voorbeelden* only constitute some ten percent of Arts's entire hagiographical work. This publication was prepared at the request of the 1927 Provincial Chapter (*Acta Capituli Provincialis Provinciae S. Rosae in Belgio, diebus 6 maii 1927 et sequentibus in Conventu B.M.V. Annuntiatae Gandavensi celebrati* (Ghent: Veritas, 1927), p. 22).

16 Josephus Arts, *Onze Voorbeelden: Eerste Reeks* (Ghent: Veritas, 1928), pp. xxii-xxvi.

numerous occasions where some strange miracle or questionable revelation is simply validated by saying: 'It is a fact, accepted by the Bollandists'.[17]

Arts believed that a degree of critical distance was advisable in respect of any source. At the same time, this should not degenerate into general scepticism: the authors had had perfectly good reasons in their time to consider something to be true, and it was now up to us to discover these reasons. In doing so, Arts wrote, we should first of all use our common sense.[18] Arts' work must be understood against the background of developments in the Bollandist Society in the second half of the nineteenth and the beginning of the twentieth century. Under the impetus of Charles De Smedt (1833-1911) and especially of his pupil Hippolyte Delehaye (1859-1941), this society began to study the lives of the saints using thorough-going source criticism, what was called *bollandisme moderne*. For Delehaye this meant that his work came under suspicion during the modernist crisis.[19] Arts was well-acquainted with the methods developed by De Smedt and Delehaye, but as far as I have been able to ascertain, his own writings, based on the same methods, escaped adverse attention.

This more historical-critical approach did not mean, however, that hagiography had now become little more than a purely academic exercise. Arts left no doubt about the aim of his work: to become better acquainted with the saints and blesseds of the Order, 'in order to glorify God in the hope of being of benefit to the souls'.[20] The lives of Dominican saints were more than just an instrument *ad intra*, for the exploration of Dominican identity, they were also tools *ad extra*, for the apostolate *ad salutem animarum*. It should be noted though, that even in the 1930s, there was already some scepticism with regard to these written lives of saints as an apostolic instrument. An obituary for Fr Arts commented: 'His lives of the saints testify to his boundless love for the Order, of which he wanted to present all the great figures. Sadly, he did not understand why people were not as eager for the lives of the saints as he was to introduce our Dominican saints and blesseds to them'.[21]

3. Professionalisation and institutionalisation of historical research

The friars-historians managed to attain scholarly credibility during the 1920s and 1930s, although none but one them had actually studied history at university.

---

17 Arts, *Onze Voorbeelden...* [see note 16], p. xxvii.
18 Arts, *Onze Voorbeelden...* [see note 16], pp. xxvii-viii.
19 Robert Godding *et al.*, *Bollandistes: Saints et légendes – Quatre siècles de recherche* (Brussels: Société des Bollandistes, 2007), pp. 133-142.
20 Arts, *Onze Voorbeelden...* [see note 16], p. xxviii.
21 Joannes Dominici Maes, 'In Memoriam Pater Josephus Arts', *De Rozenkrans*, 60 (1934) n° 7, 159-160 (p. 160).

The work of Fr Arts must again be mentioned in this context, especially his two tomes on the Dominicans in Ghent (1913), and on the old Dominican friary of Brussels (1922). In these works, Arts frankly described Dominican life during the Middle Ages and the *Ancien Régime* as a source of inspiration for Dominican life in his own day and age, thus emphasising continuity: 'Évoquer ces souvenirs lointains, c'est vivre avec les membres qui formaient ces familles et auxquels on paye ainsi un juste tribut de reconnaissance, tandis qu'ils nous invitent, en même temps, à aimer cette vie dont ils ont vécu'.[22] In doing so he echoed the views of Fr Bernardus de Jonghe (1676-1749), who had in the early eighteenth century pointed out not just the necessity (*necessitas*), but also the utility (*utilitas*) of the historiography of the Order by and for friars: 'in illa [historia] enim ut in pictura, aut in speculo conspiciuntur gesta praeterita vel praesentia, et majorum exempla posteros ad virtutis semitam efficacius, quam quaevis verba movent'.[23] In the following sections I will give three examples of the professionalisation of historical research done by Dominicans in the first half of the twentieth century, examples that can all three also be regarded as 'institutional' projects, meaning that they were the work of several collaborating friars and were explicitly aimed at serving the Order.

3.1. *The* Spicilegium Sacrum Lovaniense

The book series *Spicilegium Sacrum Lovaniense* was founded immediately after the First World War as a cooperative project between the Catholic University of Leuven and the Jesuit and Dominican theological houses of studies. Its purpose was to study and publish patristic and Christian medieval literature, both from the West and the East. The central Dominican figure in this project was Raymond Martin (1878-1949), an expert on Thomas Aquinas.[24] The early *Spicilegium* volumes suggest that Martin focused mainly on medieval liturgical and theological texts. This was surely to facilitate access to the sources for his own study of Dominican scholastics. He personally edited the works of Robert of Melun (*c.* 1100-1167) in three volumes, as well as a collection of fourteenth-century theological treatises on original sin. Five years after the *disputationes* of Simon of Tournai (*c.* 1131-1201) had been published in *Spicilegium* in 1932, Martin and the German Jesuit Heinrich Weisweiler (1893-1964) added a number of previously

---

22 Josephus Arts, *L'ancien couvent des Dominicains à Bruxelles* (Sint-Amandsberg – Ghent: De Scheemaeker, 1922), p. 1. Cf. id., *De Predikheeren te Gent, 1228-1954* (Ghent: Siffer, 1913), p. 480: '... Providence had protected the two Friars Preachers [Ackerman and Braeckman] whose task it was to forge a link between the past and the future'.

23 Bernardus de Jonghe, *Belgium Dominicanum sive Historia Provinciae Germaniae Inferioris Sacri Ordinis FF. Praedicatorum [...]* (Brussels: Franciscus Foppens, 1719), p. 2.

24 On Martin, see several articles in *Studia Mediaevalia in honorem admodum Reverendi Patris Raymundi Josephi Martin, Ordinis Praedicatorum, S. Theologiae Magistri, LXX^{um} natalem diem agentis*, ed. by Bartholomeus Van Helmond, Simon Brounts and Antoninus Thomas (Bruges: De Tempel, 1948).

unpublished works to the list by the same controversial 'Master Simon'. As regards the patristic texts, it is clear that *Spicilegium* contributed in no small measure to the strong reputation of the Leuven theological faculty in the field of patristics shortly after the Great War.[25]

3.2. The Temmerman case

Another notable example of the professionalisation and institutionalisation of historical research by Belgian Dominicans in the first half of the twentieth century is the *causa* of Fr Antoninus Temmerman. Temmerman was born in 1547 and entered the Order of Preachers in Antwerp at the age of twenty-one. When in 1577 the Calvinists came to power in Antwerp, Catholics found themselves the subject of persecution. The Dominican conventual church, for example, was now reserved for Protestant worship, and the friary was converted into a hospital. Fr Temmerman was one of the few Catholic priests who remained active in the city. In March 1582, William of Orange, the main leader of the Dutch Revolt against the Spanish, came to visit Antwerp. Towards the end of a banquet organised in his honour, William was approached by a young man who tried to shoot him. The attempt failed and William was only lightly injured. The perpetrator, Jauregui, was killed on the spot. He had documents on his person that showed that he was the servant of a Spanish merchant, a first lead in the investigation into this assassination attempt.

During the investigation, it became clear that Fr Temmerman had heard Jauregui's confession only a week before the assassination attempt. Had Jauregui told the latter of his plans? If so, Temmerman could be considered an accessory to the attack. The Spanish merchant who appears to have ordered the attempt had 'left on a business trip' some days beforehand, and managed to evade capture. The same could not be said for his secretary Venero or for Fr Temmerman, who were repeatedly questioned and tortured in the process. Ultimately, Venero admitted to having known about the plans, but he maintained that he had declined to be part of the plot. As for Temmerman, the debate on his involvement would continue for decades: he was accused of having been aware of the plans, having given Jauregui his blessing for the attack 'for the good of the Catholic religion', having granted him absolution for this sin he had yet to commit, and having failed to notify the authorities. This implies that Temmerman must, in the end, have betrayed the seal of confession. Temmerman and Venero were publicly executed by strangulation and then quartered. Their heads were displayed on the walls of the city castle together with that of Jauregui.

The first text to mention Temmerman as a 'martyr for the seal of confession' dates from the early seventeenth century. In the nineteenth century, Frs Moulaert

---

25 Ward De Pril and Johan Leemans, 'Patristics in Belgium around 1911: Universities and Beyond', *Zeitschrift für Antikes Christentum*, 15 (2011), 140-162 (p. 148).

and Iweins collected material on the case. At several provincial chapters, attempts were made to open a *causa* for this 'Belgian John of Nepomuk', but things only really started moving in 1931, when Fr Albertus De Meyer (1881-1971) was commissioned to assemble a dossier 'ad beatificationem et canonisationem Venerabilis Patris Antonini Temmerman, in odium fidei occisi'.[26] To this end, De Meyer had at his disposal the documents collected by a number of Dominicans during the 1920s and 1930s. The oldest document they had managed to find was an anti-Catholic pamphlet from 1582, the year Temmerman was executed.[27] In 1932 De Meyer found the original court documents in the Antwerp city archives, and he published them the following year.[28]

De Meyer believed that Temmerman had not broken the seal of confession, but that the trial documents had been falsified to damage the reputation of the Catholic Church in the person of one unlucky Dominican friar. His study was well-received in the national and international Catholic press.[29] Soon, however, a number of questions were raised. In a counter-expertise, the head of the Belgian State Archives responded that he saw no palaeographic reason whatsoever to assume that any of the case documents had been falsified.[30] Others found inaccuracies in the critical edition of the documents.[31] Moreover, De Meyer, clearly a mercurial character, soon became embroiled in conflict with the archivists both of the city of Antwerp and of the archdiocese of Mechelen (Malines). In 1935 a booklet entitled *Un martyr de la confession* was published, which sought to popularise De Meyer's thesis of falsification of the court documents.[32] It was apparently written by De Meyer, who used the name of his confrère Paul Prignon

---

26 *Acta Capituli Provincialis Provinciae Sanctae Rosae in Belgio, diebus 30 junii 1931 et sequentibus in Conventu B.M.V. Immaculate Conceptae Lovaniensi celebrati* (Ghent: Veritas, 1931), p. 58. For a historical overview of the *causa* of Fr Temmerman, see Archivum Generale Ordinis Praedicatorum (AGOP, Rome), X.34.2, 'De Beatificatione Ven. P. Antonini Temmerman', pp. 6-7.

27 OPSR, 951.4, 'Wat ondergeteekende weet over den Preekheer Pater Antoninus Timmermans die door de ketters te Antwerpen gedood werd in het jaar O.H. 1582, door Pater Antoninus Rutten O.P., klooster van Antwerpen', 2 January 1929 and 'Essai sur le P. Temmerman par le P. Dox', s.d.

28 Albertus De Meyer, *Le procès de l'attentat commis contre Guillaume le Taciturne, prince d'Orange, 18 mars 1582: Étude critique de documents inédits* (Brussels: Éd. Universelle, 1933).

29 For instance in the *Osservatore Romano* of 3 March 1934, where De Meyer's work was called 'un modello di critica storica e un capolavoro di studio critico di documenti'. The Dominican and medievalist Antonin Papillon (1901-1975) congratulated his confrère on his choice of topic, 'auquel vous appliquez votre très sûre méthode historique' (OPSR, 731, Letter from Papillon to De Meyer, 12 December 1933). See also the review in *Analecta Sacri Ordinis Fratrum Praedicatorum*, 42 (1934), 390-392, which adopts De Meyer's thesis and expresses the hope that the Church would recognise Temmerman as a martyr for the seal of confession.

30 OPSR, 951.5, Armand Tihon, 'Rapport d'expertise', 12 July 1935.

31 Jean Gessler, 'Antwerpsche Palaeographica', *Tijdschrift voor Geschiedenis en Folklore*, 1 (1938), 79-83.

32 Paul Prignon d'Onthaine [=Albertus De Meyer], *Un martyr de la confession: Le Père Antonin Temmerman de l'Ordre des Frères-Prêcheurs* (Études Religieuses, 373) (Liège: La Pensée Catholique, 1935).

d'Onthaine (1883-1964) as a pseudonym.[33] Perhaps De Meyer had realised that his personality as well as his work were doing the Temmerman case more harm than good, and he had decided to steer clear of any further trouble.

In 1935, the provincial superior, Jean Massaux (1882-1942), wrote to *postulator generalis* Stefano Lenzetti (1905-1954) to inquire what further steps should be taken in the Temmerman case.[34] The latter in turn sought the advice of the Belgian Dominican Marcolinus Tuyaerts (1878-1948). With regard to De Meyer's study, Tuyaerts answered that the conclusion may have been correct, but that there were two prohibitive objections: De Meyer seems to have been convinced a priori of Temmerman's innocence, and he failed to respect the chronological order of events.[35] The *postulator* used Tuyaerts's criticism in his answer to Massaux. The first step to be taken now was to draft a rigorous historical-critical biography that would demonstrate Temmerman's innocence and that would emphasise not his martyrdom, but the reason for it: 'pro fide et – si possibile est – quidem pro sigillo sacramentali'.[36] Massaux was able to answer the *postulator* that Fr Léon Lotar (1877-1943), a former missionary and amateur historian, had already begun this work.[37]

1937 saw the publication of Lotar's *Le cas du P. Antoine Temmerman: Mémoire sur l'Affaire Jauregui*, in which he re-examined the documents found by De Meyer.[38] In his provisional conclusion, Lotar was more cautious than De Meyer: he no longer considered Temmerman a martyr for the seal of confession but still regarded him as a martyr for the Catholic faith.[39] A reviewer pointed out that Lotar only referred in passing to the work of his confrère De Meyer, mainly in the introduction. He concluded from this that 'even in those circles that are favourably disposed to the memory of the executed monk, it was felt that De Meyer's defence of him had done him more harm than good'.[40] Lotar abandoned De Meyer's theory that the original court documents had been falsified, but did make the case that the trial itself had been invalid as a result of procedural irregularities. Lotar's book received a better reception than De Meyer's, but critics were still only lukewarm in their praise. Moreover, like De Meyer, Lotar had a difficult relationship with the archivists of the city of Antwerp and the archdiocese of Mechelen, so no support could be expected from those quarters. Lotar wrote that the archdiocesan archivist had either not read his study at all, or had not

---

33 See the copy in OPSR, 951.2, on the front page of which Prignon's name has been pasted over by De Meyer's with the comment: 'paru sous le nom du P. Prignon'.

34 AGOP, X.34.7, Letter from Massaux to Lenzetti, 5 February 1935.

35 AGOP, X.34.7, Letter from Tuyaerts to Lenzetti, 13 April 1935.

36 AGOP, X.34.7, Letter from Lenzetti to Massaux, 25 May 1935.

37 AGOP, X.34.7, Letter from Massaux to Lenzetti, 1 June 1935.

38 Léon Lotar, *Le cas du P. Antoine Temmerman: Mémoire sur l'Affaire Jauregui, Anvers, mars 1582* (Brussels: Éd. Universelle, 1937).

39 AGOP, X.34.6, Léon Lotar, 'Le cas du P. Temmerman: Résumé', 5 April 1936.

40 Review by Hans van Werveke, kept in AGOP, X.34.6.

understood it, and that his critical remarks about the *Mémoire* were due to animus against him because he was not a professional historian.[41]

The Second World War halted the Temmerman case. After the war, the new provincial superior Nicolaas Gobert (1908-1985) made inquiries about progress with his Belgian confrère Piet Gils (1913-2001), who at that time was working in Rome as *vice-postulator generalis*. Gils replied that there had never really been a case, because it had never advanced beyond the 'informative stage'. As long as no unambiguous historical conclusion could be reached, the beatification process could not be started.[42] Needless to say De Meyer was less than thrilled with this report. In a final attempt to collect all the sources and offer an unambiguous interpretation, the Belgian Dominicans hired a historian, a layman, who published his findings in 1959. He too concluded that, on the basis of the available source material, Temmerman could neither be regarded as a martyr for the seal of confession, nor as a martyr for the faith.[43] When Fr De Meyer died in 1970, the Temmerman case lost its main champion. At least he was spared the ignominy of the theft of Temmerman's relics from the choir of the conventual church in Antwerp on the night of 29 and 30 December 1974.[44] This was the symbolic end of the Temmerman case, which had in fact fizzled out a long time before.

So what does the Temmerman case tell us about Belgian Dominican historians? First of all, that they had become scholars: they no longer limited themselves to collecting documents, but also performed historical-critical analysis of them. This involved interaction with historians and archivists outside the Order. Secondly, it shows that there was in fact a tradition and a network of Belgian Dominican historians.[45] From the very days of Frs Moulaert and Iweins, friars had been working on the Temmerman case as part of a larger effort to write the history of the old province of *Germania Inferior*. Fr De Meyer was a key figure for the Temmerman affair but also for this wider history of *Germania Inferior*.[46] De Meyer could lay claim to having studied with the famous Professor Alfred

---

41 AGOP, X.34.6, Léon Lotar, 'Correspondance Laenen', s.d. and Letter from Jozef Laenen to Lotar, 2 October 1946, with note by Lotar. See also AGOP, X.34.5, folder containing correspondence between Floris Prims and Lotar.

42 AGOP, X.34.7, Piet Gils, 'Le P.A. Temmerman (deuxième rapport)', 16 September 1946.

43 Emiel Cresens, *De zaak A. Temmerman o.p. (18-28 maart 1582)* (unpublished licentiate thesis, Centrale examencommissie voor het toekennen van academische graden, 1959).

44 At the request of the Dominicans, these relics had been transferred in 1928 from the Church of Saint Paul to their friary (OPSR, 1021, 'Liber Consilii Vicariatus Antverpiensis ad S. Paulum Apostolum 1909-1975', pp. 118-119).

45 Angelus Walz only mentions Frs Moulaert, Arts, Axters and Meersseman as the most important historians of the province of Saint Rose (*Compendium Historiae Ordinis Praedicatorum* (Rome: Angelicum, 1948), p. 627). Stephanus Axters (1901-1977) is one of the Belgian Dominican historians who could unfortunately not be discussed more extensively in this contribution. On Axters, see Rob Faesen and Anton Milh, 'Axters (Gerardus), Stephanus', in *DHGE*, ed. by Luc Courtois *et al.*, 33 vols (Turnhout: Brepols, 1912-), XXXI/fasc. 189b-190 (2018), col. 903-907.

46 Particularly the history of the Observant movement; see Albertus De Meyer, *La congrégation de Hollande ou la réforme dominicaine en territoire bourguignon 1465-1515* (Liège: Soledi, 1946).

Cauchie (1860-1922) in Leuven between 1909 and 1911, and that made him the only friar of his generation to have had any form of academic training in history. In his collection of data, he closely cooperated with Frs Arts and Vincentius Dillen[47] (1878-1952) and later also with Fr Ambrosius-Maria Bogaerts (1908-1989).[48] Although De Meyer's difficult personality – Fr Dillen, his close collaborator, suffered much on account of this – suggests otherwise, he was willing to work with others on this. Thirdly, it is evidence of the institutionalisation of the historical research. Historical research was no longer just a hobby, but friars were specifically charged with it by the province and were given the means to conduct their research.

3.3. *The* Institutum Historicum

The three aspects just mentioned – historical-critical source analysis, a network within and outside the Order, institutionalisation – can also be identified in the involvement of Belgian Dominicans in the *Institutum Historicum* of the Order. Ever since its foundation in 1930, this institute had had a Belgian staff member, Fr Gilles Meersseman (1903-1988). This expert on subjects such as Albert the Great and medieval lay movements published twenty-four articles in *Archivum Fratrum Praedicatorum*, some on the history of the Order of Preachers in Flanders.[49] In 1951 Meersseman was appointed professor of Church history in Fribourg, even though he had no university degree in history. As a staff member of the Historical Institute he was responsible for the study and publication of manuscripts by illustrious Dominicans. At least from 1936 onwards, he was joint editor of the *Dissertationes Historicae* and *Monumenta Historica* series. He also collaborated on the new edition of *Scriptores Ordinis Praedicatorum*.

It is remarkable that Fr De Meyer was called to Rome in 1933 by the Master of the Order, Martin Stanislas Gillet (1876-1951), to study a recently discovered manuscript by Cardinal Cajetan and prepare it for publication.[50] This was probably at Meersseman's suggestion, who knew of his countryman's specialisation in

---

47 Arts, *L'ancien couvent…* [see note 22], p. 4. For the correspondence between De Meyer and Dillen, see OPSR, 824.1 and 824.3. Dillen also published *Een Woord over het Begijnhof van Thienen* (Tienen: Vanhoebroeck-Goidts, 1908), a subject that was at the heart of the work of the first generation of Belgian Dominican historians.

48 In his impressive series *Bouwstoffen voor de geschiedenis der dominikanen in de Nederlanden* (Brussels – Leuven: Dominikaans Archief, 19 vols, 1965-1981) Bogaerts completed the collections created by Dillen and De Meyer.

49 Meersseman's interest in the history of the Dominicans in Flanders was surely not unrelated to his ardent Flemish nationalism. On Meersseman, see also *Gilles Gerard Meersseman O.P.: Una vita per la storia* (I Quaderni dell'Accademia Olimpica, 16), ed. by Ermenegildo Reato (Vicenza: Accademia Olimpica, 1989) and Struyker Boudier, *Wijsgerig leven…* [see note 2], pp. 194-196. The Belgian Dominican Marcolinus Denys (1910-1947), who died at a young age in Rome, is also reported to have contributed to the work of the Historical Institute for a while.

50 OPSR, 718.1, Letter from Gillet to Massaux, 28 November 1933.

sixteenth-century Dominican history. The *Registrum litterarum Fr. Thomae de Vio Caietani* was published in the *Monumenta* series in 1935.[51] As De Meyer clashed with a friar at the Historical Institute, he refused any further cooperation after the publication of his *Registrum*.[52]

In 1939, the friars at the Historical Institute were joined by another Belgian, Fr Raymond Creytens (1911-1997). In 1977 Creytens was even appointed president of the Institute as successor to Fr Thomas Kaeppeli (1900-1984), a role he would keep until 1986. As for his contributions to *Archivum*, with forty-four articles, Creytens is second only to Kaeppeli, who published sixty-one. There is no archival material to confirm it, but one gets the impression that Creytens was the link between the tradition of the Belgian Dominican historians as described so far and Fr Thomas's work.[53] In 1947, Creytens published constitutions in *Archivum* that he had found in a manuscript in The Hague in the Netherlands. He succeeded in establishing that they came from the French Dominican nunnery of Montargis, and he dated them to 1250.[54] A year later, Creytens published a text edition of the constitutions edited by the third Master of the Order, Raymond of Peñafort (1238-1240). The main question that arose was to what extent Raymond was responsible for putting these constitutions in the order they were in, what improvements, if any, he had made to them, and whether he had added anything to them ('ordinatio et correctio et additio'). With the help of the Rodez manuscript – supplemented with the acts of chapters from the 1230s – he was able to more or less reconstruct the 1238 text. Creytens found Raymond's text of 1240 in a manuscript in the city library of Porto. This manuscript had been edited at a later date, but in a way that still showed exactly what had been changed.[55] It is clear from an article from 1951 on Humbert of Romans' commentary on the constitutions as included in the Rodez manuscript that the development of the constitutions remained an interest of his.[56] It was due to this interest that Creytens

---

51 *Registrum litterarum Fr. Thomae de Vio Caietani O.P., Magistri Ordinis 1508-1513* (MOPH, 17), ed. by Albertus De Meyer (Rome: Institutum Historicum Fratrum Praedicatorum, 1935).

52 OPSR, 824.1, Letter from De Meyer to Dillen, 4 April 1935. See also AGOP, XIII.501004, Letter from De Meyer to the Master's assistant, 16 September 1937; Letter from the Master's assistant to Massaux, 21 September 1937; Letter from Massaux to Gillet, 25 September 1937.

53 In Fribourg, Meersseman's pupil Josef Siegwart (1929-2011) developed a similar line of research with his doctoral thesis on *Die Consuetudines des Augustiner-Chorherrenstiftes Marbach im Elsass (12. Jahrhundert)* (Spicilegium Friburgense, 10) (Freiburg: Universitätsverlag, 1965).

54 Raymond Creytens, 'Les constitutions primitives des sœurs dominicaines de Montargis (1250)', *AFP*, 17 (1947), 41-84.

55 Raymond Creytens, 'Les constitutions des frères Prêcheurs dans la rédaction de s. Raymond de Peñafort (1241)', *AFP*, 18 (1948), 5-68.

56 Raymond Creytens, 'Commentaires inédits d'Humbert de Romans sur quelques points des Constitutions dominicaines', *AFP*, 21 (1951), 197-214. On Creytens, see also Guy Bedouelle, 'Le Père Creytens, historien du droit de l'Ordre des Prêcheurs', *Mémoire dominicaine*, n° 13 (1998/2), 233-236 (p. 233) and Simon Tugwell, 'Necrologium: Raymond Michel Creytens OP', *Dominican History Newsletter*, 6 (1997), 8-9.

was invited after the Second Vatican Council to join the commission within the Order that was charged with reviewing the constitutions.

4. Fr Antoninus Hendrik Thomas and the 'earliest constitutions'

Hendrik Thomas was born into a farming family in Merchtem, Brabant, in 1915. After completing his secondary education, he joined the Dominicans in 1934, where he received the religious name of Antoninus. Thomas was ordained a priest in 1942 and completed his studies at the Dominican house of studies in Leuven in 1944. The following year he was permitted to study history at the University of Leuven, where he obtained his licentiate *summa cum laude* in 1947. In 1965, he was awarded a doctoral degree for his study on *De oudste constituties van de dominicanen* ('The earliest constitutions of the Dominicans').[57] Apart from his duties teaching the history of the Order of Preachers both to novices and to professed friars, he was also the editor of *Spicilegium Sacrum Lovaniense* for forty years, and the librarian of the conventual library in Leuven for twenty-five years.[58] In May 1995, he told his prior that the work was becoming too taxing for him, and that he felt he was 'at the end of his tether'.[59] He moved to a nursing home in September 1996 where he died a few days after his arrival.

Thomas did not simply base his text edition of the constitutions on the well-known Rodez manuscript. He believed this manuscript was not 'all-decisive' and that for instance the old legislative texts of the Dominican nuns were often much more useful. Apart from that, he based his reconstruction on a number of sources from outside the Order, like the statute books of the Order of Saint Mary Magdalene and the Penitents of Jesus Christ, and – most importantly – the *consuetudines* of Prémontré. This was entirely in line with the research of his doctoral supervisor, the Norbertine Placide Lefèvre (1892-1978).[60] Lefèvre had started at the university as secretary to Alfred Cauchie and then advanced through the ranks, eventually becoming extraordinary professor. In addition to

---

57 The language in which Fr Thomas's dissertation is written has prevented many researchers from studying this work in detail. Why did he write this study of international importance in his native language, which so few foreigners speak, even though he had a good command of French (as the 'résumé en français' attached to his thesis testifies)? The answer probably lies in the funding of his doctoral studies. His research was financed by the *Stichting Vlaamse Leergangen* in Leuven, which advocated the Dutchification of the university and academic research in Dutch. A related question is why he published his dissertation in the *Bibliothèque de la Revue d'histoire ecclésiastique* (it remains the only Dutch-language volume in this series) and not in *Spicilegium Sacrum Lovaniense*.

58 On Thomas, see also Simon Tugwell, 'Necrologium: Antonien Hendrik Thomas OP', *Dominican History Newsletter*, 6 (1997), 8.

59 OPSR, 949, Letter from Thomas to Joris K. Backeljauw, May 1995.

60 On Placide Lefèvre, see Bernard Ardura, *Prémontrés: Histoire et spiritualité* (Saint-Etienne: CERCOR, 1995), pp. 484-485 and Joseph Coppens, 'Le chanoine Placide Lefèvre, 1892-1978', *Ephemerides Theologicae Lovanienses*, 54 (1978), 235-240.

his activities for the Belgian State Archives, he also involved himself in the historiography of his own order, which resulted among other things in the setting up of the journal *Analecta Praemonstratensia* in 1925. Together with Lefèvre, Thomas published the twelfth-century consuetudinary of the Abbey of Oigny in Burgundy in the *Spicilegium* series in 1976.[61] In articles in *Analecta Praemonstratensia* and *Archivum Fratrum Praedicatorum,* Thomas continued to explore twelfth- and thirteenth-century legal texts of religious orders to obtain a better idea of their similarities and differences.[62]

The most penetrating comment on Thomas's dissertation came from his countryman Fr Creytens. He asked how far Fr Thomas wanted to go back in time in his doctoral research. The term *constitutiones antiquae,* 'earliest constitutions', was traditionally used to indicate the entire legal corpus of the Order before 1237, and not just one text in particular (which would be capable of reconstruction). In his edition, Thomas used texts both from the early 1220s and the early 1230s. In this way he reconstructed a text covering two decades, which therefore 'en tant que tel, n'a jamais existé'.[63] Fr Creytens's remark is pertinent, but does not diminish the value of Fr Thomas's work. This because his dissertation focuses on critically comparing and re-assembling various sources, of both Dominican and non-Dominican origins. In his own words the purpose was not just to acquire 'a deeper knowledge of the earliest legislation of the Dominicans', but also to highlight the relevance of this Dominican legislation in a 'wider perspective' – of both civil and ecclesiastical-canon law.[64] Creytens's comment does not appear to have negatively affected the general appreciation for Thomas's work. Simon Tugwell has called *De oudste constituties van de dominicanen* 'the fundamental study of the earliest Dominican constitutions',[65] and Paul-Bernard Hodel has similarly affirmed that when it comes to the earliest Dominican legislation, 'la meilleure étude reste celle du Père Antoine [*sic*] Henri Thomas'.[66]

---

61 *Le coutumier de l'abbaye d'Oigny en Bourgogne au XIIe siècle: Introduction, texte critique et tables* (Spicilegium Sacrum Lovaniense, 39), ed. by Placide Lefèvre and Antoninus Hendrik Thomas (Leuven: Spicilegium Sacrum Lovaniense, 1976).

62 Antoninus Hendrik Thomas, 'Une version des statuts de Prémontré au début du XIIIe s.', *Analecta Praemonstratensia,* 55 (1979), 153-170; id., 'Un exemplaire glosé des statuts de Prémontré dans le manuscrit Laon 530', *Analecta Praemonstratensia,* 60 (1984), 49-74 and id., 'Les statuts des chanoines du Saint-Sépulchre et leurs rapports avec les constitutions des Dominicains', *AFP,* 48 (1978), 5-22.

63 Raymond Creytens, 'Compte rendu de A.H. Thomas, *De oudste constituties van de dominicanen [...]*', *RHE,* 61 (1966), 862-871 (p. 866).

64 Antoninus Hendrik Thomas, *De oudste constituties van de dominicanen: Voorgeschiedenis, tekst, bronnen, ontstaan en ontwikkeling (1215-1237) met uitgave van de tekst* (BRHE, 42) (Leuven: Bureel van de RHE, 1965), p. xii [p. 158].

65 Tugwell, 'Necrologium'... [see note 58], p. 8.

66 Paul-Bernard Hodel, 'Les constitutions primitives: Un état des lieux', *Mémoire dominicaine,* 13 (1998/2), 37-45 (p. 41); see also *Saint Dominique de l'ordre des frères prêcheurs: Témoignages écrits fin XIIe-XIVe siècle,* ed. by Nicole Bériou and Bernard Hodel, with the collaboration of Gisèle Besson (Paris: Cerf, 2019), pp. 202-203.

5. Conclusion: contextualising Thomas

Fr Thomas's historical study of the constitutions of the Dominicans must be seen in the context of the historiographical tradition of the Belgian province of the Order. When Dominican life restarted in Belgium in the nineteenth century, friars endeavoured to demonstrate and strengthen continuity with Dominican life in the Southern Netherlands during the *Ancien Régime* and even during the Middle Ages. The Ghent beguines, with whom the Dominicans had links dating back to the thirteenth century, proved to be a rewarding object of study. At the end of the nineteenth and the beginning of the twentieth century, the primary interest was in the genre of hagiography. Here, again, historiography was put to a particular use: the lives of Dominican saints served as an apostolic instrument that could be used for recruitment, but also to enhance the profile of the Order internally. Influenced by the Bollandists, Dominican hagiographers began to adopt the methods of historical criticism – especially Fr Josephus Arts. This professionalisation advanced further during the 1920s and 1930s, as three cases show: *Spicilegium Sacrum Lovaniense* (with Fr Raymond Martin as the pivotal figure), the *causa* of Fr Temmerman (with Fr Albertus De Meyer as its greatest champion), and the involvement of Belgian Dominicans such as Gilles Meersseman and Raymond Creytens in the Historical Institute of the Order. Each of these examples also shows further institutionalisation of the historical research. Fr Creytens ultimately passed on his enthusiasm for the constitutions to the younger Fr Thomas, who, under the supervision of the Norbertine Placide Lefèvre, defended his doctoral thesis on this topic in 1965. More than fifty years later the quality of this dissertation is still unanimously acknowledged, which is a homage not only to Fr Thomas, but also to the entire tradition of Belgian Dominican historians that preceded him.

HERMAN JANSSENS O.PRAEM.   _____

État actuel des recherches sur les statuts de l'Ordre de Prémontré aux XIIe et XIIIe siècles[*]

Des recherches furent entreprises tout au long du siècle dernier sur les anciens statuts de l'Ordre de Prémontré. Des archives centralisées de l'Ordre étant inexistantes, les recherches durent se focaliser sur les divers manuscrits conservés dans les abbayes respectives. Ces dernières étaient toutefois fort nombreuses. La plupart d'entre elles avaient été supprimées au cours du dix-huitième, début du dix-neuvième ou même déjà au seizième siècle. Peu d'exemplaires des anciens statuts subsistaient dans les grandes bibliothèques ou dans les archives plus modestes. L'Ordre de Prémontré restauré au dix-neuvième siècle ne possède en outre pas d'institut de recherche centralisé. La connaissance sur la naissance, le contenu et l'évolution des statuts prémontrés ne pouvait donc s'effectuer que lentement. La brève contribution suivante évoque d'abord les principaux auteurs de cette recherche ainsi que leurs publications par ordre chronologique. Ensuite suivra une liste des dix-neuf manuscrits subsistants, contenant les versions successives des statuts ainsi que les diverses éditions du texte. Enfin, nous trouverons un tableau de la concordance des chapitres dans les différentes codifications statutaires.

Il est fort possible que d'autres manuscrits soient retrouvés. Grâce au tableau de la concordance et les éditions du texte mentionnées, on pourra facilement voir à quelle rédaction des statuts ces manuscrits appartiennent.

1. Histoire brève des recherches sur les statuts de l'Ordre de Prémontré

Jean Lepaige († vers 1640 ou 1650)[1], prémontré de l'abbaye de Prémontré, procureur de l'Ordre à la cour du Roi de France et prieur du collège prémontré de Paris, sur base d'un manuscrit de son abbaye, fut le premier à publier en 1633 dans

_____

[*] La traduction de notre texte néerlandais est de Mohan Sawhney de l'abbaye de Grimbergen que nous remercions cordialement.

1 Leo Cyriel Van Dyck, 'Le Paige (Jean)', in *DHGE*, éd. par Luc Courtois *et al.*, 33 t. (Paris : Letouzey et Ané, 1912-), XXXI (2015), col. 809-812 et Placide Lefèvre, 'Une appréciation sur la Bibliotheca

A Cathedral of Constitutional Law, éd. par Anton Milh O.P. and Mark Butaye O.P., Turnhout, Brepols, 2023 (*Bibliothèque de la Revue d'histoire ecclésiastique*, 112), p. 43-60.

BREPOLS ✠ PUBLISHERS   10.1484/M.BRHE-EB.5.135043

son ouvrage *Bibliotheca Praemonstratensis Ordinis* une édition de ce qui à ses yeux étaient les premiers statuts de l'Ordre[2].

Edmond Martène (1654-1739), bénédictin de la Congrégation de Saint-Maur, a publié en 1737 dans son *De antiquis Ecclesiae ritibus* des *Primaria instituta Canonicorum Praemonstratensium*[3]. Il se basait probablement sur un manuscrit du treizième siècle, provenant de l'abbaye de Saint-Victor de Paris.

En 1913, Raphaël Van Waefelghem (1878-1944), prémontré de l'abbaye du Parc lez Leuven, publia les plus anciens statuts de l'Ordre, provenant de l'abbaye de Schäftlarn en Bavière, qu'il faisait remonter à 1135-1143[4].

Sur base de ces textes édités, Hugo Heijman (1890-1962)[5], prémontré de l'abbaye de Berne aux Pays-Bas, défendit en 1925 une thèse de doctorat à l'Université de Fribourg en Suisse, dans laquelle il démontrait que les statuts prémontrés empruntaient beaucoup à la législation cistercienne[6].

Placide Lefèvre (1892-1978)[7], de l'abbaye d'Averbode, professeur extraordinaire de l'Université de Leuven, publia en 1946 les statuts de Prémontré réformés sur les ordres de Grégoire IX (av. 1170-1241) et d'Innocent IV (*c.* 1195-1254), qu'il date aux alentours de 1236-1238[8]. Il a utilisé un manuscrit originaire de l'abbaye d'Heylissem conservé à Averbode et un manuscrit de l'abbaye de Tongerlo[9] qu'il compara aux publications de Van Waefelghem, Martène, Lepaige et les statuts de 1505.

Praemonstratensis de Le Paige par un abbé belge en 1633', *Analecta Praemonstratensia*, 19 (1943), 59-60.

2 'Statvta Primaria Praemonstratensis Ordinis', in Jean Le Paige, *Bibliotheca Praemonstratensis Ordinis* (Paris : Adrian Taupinart, 1633), 784-829 ; réimpression : (Instrumenta Praemonstratensia, 3), 2 t. (Averbode : Praemonstratensia, 1998). Datation (1290) et mention des sources à la page 777.

3 'Primaria instituta Canonicorum Praemonstratensium', in *De antiquis Ecclesiae ritibus*, éd. par Edmond Martène, 4 t. (Anvers : Joannes Baptistæ de la Bry, 1736-1738), III (1737 ; réimpr. Hildesheim, 1967), col. 890-926.

4 Raphaël Van Waefelghem, 'Les premiers statuts de l'Ordre de Prémontré : Le *Clm* 17.174 (XIIᵉ siècle)', *Analectes de l'Ordre de Prémontré*, 9 (1913), 74 p. (pagination spéciale) ; publié également en livre à Leuven, 1913. La publication se base sur un manuscrit de la moitié du douzième siècle provenant de l'abbaye de Schäftlarn : Bayerische Staatsbibliothek (Munich), MS *Clm* 17174, fᵒˢ 11ʳ-39ᵛ.

5 S.n., 'In memoriam [Hugonis Heijman]', *Analecta Praemonstratensia*, 38 (1962), 189-190.

6 Hugo Heijman, 'Untersuchungen über die Praemonstratenser-Gewohnheiten', *Analecta Praemonstratensia*, 2 (1926), 5-32 ; 3 (1927), 5-27 ; 4 (1928), 5-29, 113-131, 225-241 et 351-373.

7 S.n., 'In memoriam Pl. Lefèvre (1892-1978)', *Analecta Praemonstratensia*, 54 (1978), 5-7 ; Wilfried Marcel Grauwen, 'Elenchus operum R.D. Placidi F. Lefèvre, 1908-1978', *Analecta Praemonstratensia*, 54 (1978), 8-30 et Philippe Godding, 'Lefèvre, Fernand', in *Nouvelle biographie nationale*, 15 t. (Bruxelles : Académie royale des sciences, des lettres et des beaux-arts de Belgique, 1988-), IV (1997), 249-250.

8 *Les Statuts de Prémontré réformés sur les ordres de Grégoire IX et d'Innocent IV au XIIIᵉ siècle* (BRHE, 23), éd. par Placide Fernand Lefèvre (Leuven : Bureau de la Revue, 1946).

9 Abbaye d'Averbode (Scherpenheuvel-Zichem), *Archives*, MS IV, 207 ; abbaye de Tongerlo (Westerlo), *Archives*, MS V, 3, fᵒˢ 1ʳ-54ʳ.

Ludo Milis, chercheur à l'Université de Gand, trouva à Oxford un autre exemplaire de la législation prémontrée remontant au début du treizième siècle[10].

En 1976, Placide Lefèvre et le dominicain Antoninus Hendrik Thomas publièrent les statuts des chanoines réguliers d'Oigny[11]. Cette communauté avait beaucoup emprunté à la législation cistercienne. Les auteurs rédigèrent un tableau dans lequel étaient comparées les législations de Oigny, Prémontré, Cîteaux et Arrouaise[12]. Les auteurs doivent beaucoup au Père Jean-Baptiste Van Damme (1914-1990) de l'abbaye trappiste de Westmalle, qui au début des années 1970 a également publié sur *La « Summa Cartae Caritatis » source de constitutions canoniales*[13].

Juste avant de mourir, en 1978, Placide Lefèvre finit une nouvelle édition des *Statuts de Prémontré au milieu du XIIᵉ siècle* basée sur un manuscrit conservé à Munich[14]. L'édition contient en annexe un tableau de la concordance des chapitres dans cinq codifications de Prémontré aux douzième et treizième siècles[15].

En 1979 Antoninus Hendrik Thomas a commenté un manuscrit des statuts prémontrés du début du treizième siècle conservé à Glasgow, provenant d'une abbaye en France[16], et en 1984 d'un texte presque identique à celui de Martène, conservé à Laon[17].

Entretemps Bruno Krings faisait des recherches pour son doctorat sur l'abbaye d'Arnstein. Cette abbaye possédait également un manuscrit des statuts du début du treizième siècle[18]. Grâce à la publication du Père Thomas, il pouvait

---

10 Bodleian Library (Oxford), MS *Ashmole* 1285, fᵒˢ 185ᵛ-196ʳ et Ludo Milis, 'De Premonstratenzer-Wetgeving in de XIIᵉ eeuw : Een nieuwe getuige', *Analecta Praemonstratensia*, 44 (1968), 181-214 et 45 (1969), 5-23.

11 Placide Fernand Lefèvre et Antoninus Hendrik Thomas, *Le coutumier de l'abbaye d'Oigny en Bourgogne au XIIᵉ siècle* (Spicilegium Sacrum Lovaniense, 39) (Leuven : Spicilegium Sacrum Lovaniense, 1976).

12 Lefèvre et Thomas, *Le coutumier...* [voir note 11], pp. xxxviii-xliii.

13 Jean-Baptiste Van Damme, 'La « Summa Cartae Caritatis » source de constitutions canoniales', *Cîteaux : Commentarii cistercienses*, 23 (1972), 5-54. Voir également Jean-Baptiste Van Damme, *Moines – Chanoines – Cîteaux : Influences réciproques*, in *Aureavallis : Mélanges historiques réunis à l'occasion du neuvième centenaire de l'abbaye d'Orval* (Liège : Soledi, 1975), 15-54.

14 Bayerische Staatsbibliothek (Munich), MS *Clm* 7702, fᵒˢ 59ᵛ-92ᵛ et Placide Fernand Lefèvre et Wilfried Marcel Grauwen, *Les statuts de Prémontré au milieu du XIIᵉ siècle* (Bibliotheca Analectorum Praemonstratensium, 12) (Averbode : Praemonstratensia, 1978).

15 Lefèvre et Grauwen, *Les statuts...* [voir note 14], pp. 53-56 : Van Waefelghem (PW), Lefèvre-Grauwen (PG), Martène (MA), Milis (Pmi) et Lefèvre (PL), ainsi que des statuts de l'Ordre du Saint-Sépulcre (SS). Dans ses travaux de comparaison de textes, Lefèvre a ajouté ces sigles à ces textes.

16 Mitchell Library (Glasgow), MS 308892, fᵒˢ 1ʳ-32ʳ et Antoninus Hendrik Thomas, 'Une version des statuts de Prémontré au début du XIIIᵉ siècle', *Analecta Praemonstratensia*, 55 (1979), 153-170.

17 Bibliothèque municipale (Laon), MS 530, pp. 869-922 et Antoninus Hendrik Thomas, 'Un exemplaire glosé des statuts de Prémontré dans le manuscrit Laon 530', *Analecta Praemonstratensia*, 60 (1984), 49-74.

18 Hessisches Hauptstaatsarchiv (Wiesbaden), MS 3004, C17 et Bruno Krings, *Das Prämonstratenserstift Arnstein a.d. Lahn im Mittelalter (1139-1527)* (Veröffentlichungen der Historischen Kommission für

le comparer avec le manuscrit de Glasgow. En 1993, il édita les statuts de 1227 ensemble avec 101 décrets inédits des chapitres généraux, retrouvés dans un ordre chronologique[19].

En l'an 2000, Bruno Krings fit la description d'un manuscrit des statuts, remontant au milieu du douzième siècle[20]. Entretemps Dirk Van de Perre a comparé de nouveau les textes législatifs de Prémontré, Oigny, Cîteaux, et des abbayes des chanoines réguliers de Rolduc et Arrouaise, puisque depuis la parution de la thèse doctorale de Heijman en 1925, beaucoup d'éditions de sources avaient été réalisées du côté cistercien[21].

À la même époque le professeur Gert Melville et ses collaborateurs, spécialement Florent Cygler, ont étudié et comparé ces textes monastiques[22]. Ingrid Ehlers-Kisseler a fait de même une synthèse[23] tandis que le dominicain Simon Tugwell a également étudié la législation prémontrée pour son étude sur les structures de l'Ordre des Prêcheurs en 2001-2002[24]. Il a consulté un manuscrit à Paris qui jusqu'à ce moment-là n'était cité que par le Père Thomas[25].

Nassau, 48) (Wiesbaden : Selbstverlag der Historischen Kommission für Nassau, 1990), pp. 260-261, n° 36.

19 Bruno Krings, 'Das Ordensrecht der Prämonstratenser vom späten 12. Jahrhundert bis zum Jahr 1227 : Der Liber consuetudinem und die Dekrete des Generalkapitels', *Analecta Praemonstratensia*, 69 (1993), 107-242. Ces décrets capitulaires proviennent du manuscrit de Glasgow [voir note 16].

20 Bayerische Staatsbibliothek (Munich), MS *Clm* 1031, f°s 112[r]-141[v] et Bruno Krings, 'Zum Ordensrecht der Prämonstratenser zur Mitte des 12. Jahrhunderts', *Analecta Praemonstratensia*, 76 (2000), 9-28.

21 Dirk Van de Perre, 'Die ältesten Klostergesetzgebungen von Prémontré, Oigny, Cîteaux, Klosterrath und Arrouaise und ihre Beziehungen zueinander', *Analecta Praemonstratensia*, 76 (2000), 29-69.

22 Florent Cygler, 'Ausformung und Kodifizierung des Ordensrechts vom 12. bis zum 14. Jahrhundert : Strukturelle Beobachtungen zu den Cisterziensern, Prämonstratensern, Kartäusern und Cluniazensern', in *De ordine vitae : Zu Normvorstellungen, Organisationsformen und Schriftgebrauch im mittelalterlichen Ordenswesen* (Vita regularis, 1), éd. par Gert Melville (Münster : Lit Verlag, 1996), 6-58 ; voir aussi Jörg Oberste, *Visitation und Ordensorganisation : Formen sozialer Normierung, Kontrolle und Kommunikation bei Cisterziensern, Prämonstratensern und Cluniazensern (12. – frühes 14. Jahrhundert)* (Vita regularis, 2) (Münster : Lit Verlag, 1996) ; Florent Cygler, *Das Generalkapitel im hohen Mittelalter : Cisterzienser, Prämonstratenser, Kartäuser und Cluniazenser* (Vita regularis, 12) (Münster : Lit Verlag, 2002) et id., 'Le chapitre général des prémontrés au Moyen Âge', *Analecta Praemonstratensia*, 81 (2005), 5-34.

23 Ingrid Ehlers-Kisseler, 'Norm und Praxis bei den Prämonstratensern im Hochmittelalter', in *Regula Sancti Augustini : Normative Grundlage differenter Verbände im Mittelalter* (Publikationen der Akademie der Augustiner-Chorherren von Windesheim, 3), éd. par Gert Melville et Anne Müller (Paring : Augustiner-Chorherren-Verlag, 2002), 335-387.

24 Simon Tugwell, 'The Evolution of Dominican Structures of Government : III. The Early Development of the Second Distinction of the Constitutions', *AFP*, 71 (2001), 5-182 et 'IV. Election, Confirmation and "Absolution" of Superiors', *AFP*, 72 (2002), 27-159.

25 Bibliothèque nationale (Paris), MS *lat.* 9752 : statuts du treizième siècle.

Enfin[26], Bruno Krings a effectué une recherche plus systématique sur les manuscrits des statuts prémontrés qui n'avaient pas encore été étudiés. En 2007, il a de nouveau édité des statuts prémontrés des années 1244/46 comparés avec des statuts de 1279. Il a utilisé un manuscrit de Prémontré, conservé dans l'abbaye prémontrée de Wilten à Innsbruck, ainsi que quatre autres[27].

Mentionnons qu'à l'occasion du jubilé des neuf cents ans de l'Ordre de Prémontré, Ulrich Leinsle ainsi que Dominique-Marie Dauzet ont publié des nouvelles synthèses de l'histoire de l'Ordre[28].

2. Vue d'ensemble des manuscrits connus et de leurs éditions

Norbert de Xanten (c. 1075-1134) fut à l'origine dès 1120 d'un nouveau mouvement religieux à Prémontré ; ce mouvement a été suivi dans d'autres endroits, et fut approuvé par le pape Honorius II (1060-1130) en 1126. Il fut toutefois nommé archevêque de Magdebourg peu de temps après. Un « vide institutionnel » était créé de ce fait à Prémontré. Norbert confia en 1128 la direction de ses communautés à d'autres personnes. Des abbés furent choisis dans plusieurs communautés. Ces abbés se réunissaient chaque année sous la direction d'Hugues de Fosses (c. 1087/88-1164), l'abbé de Prémontré. Ils rédigèrent des statuts afin d'éviter que le mouvement ne s'étiole. L'exemple des cisterciens fut adopté tant pour ce qui concerne la structure de « l'Ordre » en naissance, une fédération d'abbayes indépendantes sous l'autorité d'un chapitre général, qu'en ce qui concerne le texte même des statuts, sans toutefois abandonner la profession canoniale ni la règle d'Augustin[29]. Norbert de son côté fonda à partir de 1129 à Magdebourg et dans les environs des communautés qui entretiendraient toujours des relations tendues avec Prémontré.

---

26 Je ne traite pas des *Constitutiones, quae vocantur Ordinis Praemonstratensis, e codice Collegii Sanctae Trinitatis Dublinensis 10810* (Corpus Christianorum : Continuatio Mediaevalis, 216), éd. par Marvin L. Colker (Turnhout : Brepols, 2008) : il ne s'agit pas du tout de statuts prémontrés.

27 Prämonstratenzerstift Wilten (Innsbruck), MS 32 04 05 ; Bibliothèque municipale (Laon), MS 509 ; Bibliothèque municipale (Soissons), MS 97 ; Universitätsbibliothek (Innsbruck), MS 375 ; Bibliothèque nationale (Paris), MS *lat.* 4394 et Bruno Krings, 'Die Statuten des Prämonstratenserordens von 1244/46 und ihre Überarbeitung im Jahr 1279', *Analecta Praemonstratensia*, 83 (2007), 5-127.

28 Ulrich Gottfried Leinsle, *Die Prämonstratenser* (Geschichte der christlichen Orden) (Stuttgart : Kohlhammer, 2020) et Dominique-Marie Dauzet, *L'ordre de Prémontré : Neuf cents ans d'histoire* (Paris : Salvator, 2021).

29 Bonne synthèse et bibliographie abondante dans Cygler, 'Le chapitre général'… [voir note 22], pp. 10-15.

2.1. Les premiers statuts : statuts provisoires

Édition : Raphaël Van Waefelghem, 'Les premiers statuts de l'Ordre de Prémontré : Le *Clm* 17.174 (XIIᵉ siècle)', *Analectes de l'Ordre de Prémontré*, 9 (1913), 74 p. (pagination spéciale) ; publié également en livre à Leuven, 1913. (PW)

> Cette première législation contient 82 chapitres. On ne peut nommer ce texte du terme de statuts, plutôt de coutumes.
>
> Nos 48-49 et 64-73 concernent la législation des convers, nos 74-82 celle des sœurs.
>
> *Publication de* : Bayerische Staatsbibliothek (Munich), MS *Clm* 17174, fᵒˢ 11ʳ-39ᵛ.
>
> *Provenance* : Schäftlarn, milieu du douzième siècle.
>
> Description :
>
> Manuscrit consultable en ligne.
>
> - Van Waefelghem, 'Les premiers statuts'… [voir note 4], pp. 3-5.
> - Elisabeth Klemm, *Die romanischen Handschriften der Bayerischen Staatsbibliothek* (Katalog der illuminierten Handschriften der Bayerischen Staatsbibliothek in München, 3/1-2), 2 t. (Wiesbaden : Reichert, 1980-1988), II (1988) : *Die Bistümer Freising und Augsburg, verschiedene deutsche Provenienzen* (*Textband*, pp. 87-88, n° 108 ; *Tafelband*, p. 74, n° 249).
>
> Van Waefelghem date le texte entre 1135-1143[30], Leo Van Dyck avant 1131[31]. Ce manuscrit de l'abbaye de Schäftlarn en Bavière n'est évidemment pas le manuscrit original de Prémontré mais une copie.

2.2. Les statuts à partir de 1154

Au milieu du douzième siècle, une révision complète des statuts provisoires fut réalisée. Sans modification fondamentale du contenu, le tout fut désormais précédé d'un prologue et divisé en quatre *Distinctiones* concernant 1) la vie quotidienne, 2) les offices claustraux, 3) le droit pénal, 4) l'organisation constitutionnelle de l'Ordre[32].

Ces statuts continuèrent d'évoluer suite aux décisions des chapitres généraux, parfois sous l'influence des autorités ecclésiastiques. Nous parlons d'une nouvelle

---

30 Van Waefelghem, 'Les premiers statuts'… [voir note 4], pp. 5-14.

31 Leo Cyriel Van Dijck, *Les origines du pouvoir de l'abbé général de l'ordre de Prémontré (1120-1177)* (Tongerlo, 1953), pp. 7-9. L'article de Van Dijck, 'Essai sur les sources du droit prémontré primitif concernant les pouvoirs du Dominus Praemonstratensis', *Analecta Praemonstratensia*, 28 (1952), 73-136, reprend le même texte. Pour la datation de PW, voir pp. 86-88. Voir également Van de Perre, 'Die ältesten Klostergesetzgebungen'… [voir note 21], p. 31.

32 Lefèvre et Grauwen, *Les statuts*… [voir note 14], p. vi et Cygler, 'Le chapitre général'… [voir note 22], pp. 8-9.

rédaction lorsque l'ordre des chapitres change ou lorsque des nouveaux chapitres sont ajoutés.

1   *Édition* : *Les statuts de Prémontré au milieu du XIIe siècle* (Bibliotheca Analectorum Praemonstratensium, 12), éd. par Placide Fernand Lefèvre (†) et Wilfried Marcel Grauwen (Averbode : Praemonstratensia, 1978). (PG)
   Publication de[33] :
   a   Bayerische Staatsbibliothek (Munich), MS *Clm* 7702, f°s 59^v-92^v.
      Provenance : chanoines réguliers d'Indersdorf, quinzième siècle.
      Description :
      Manuscrit consultable en ligne.
      Bruno Krings date cette rédaction en 1154/55[34].
      Le manuscrit contient également des *consuetudines* de convers, f°s 92^v-95^r, édités par Trudo Jan Gerits[35].
      -   Carolus Halm, Georgius Thomas et Gulielmus Meyer, *Catalogus codicum latinorum Bibliothecae Regiae Monacensis* (Catalogus codicum manuscriptorum Bibliothecae Regiae Monacensis, 1/1-3 – 4/1-4), 4 t. (Munich : Bibliotheca regia, 1873), I.3 : *Codices num. 5251-8100 complectens* (réimpression Wiesbaden : Harrassowitz, 1968-1969), p. 189, n° 1507.
      -   Lefèvre et Grauwen, *Les statuts...* [voir note 14], p. x.
   b   'Primaria instituta Canonicorum Praemonstratensium', in Edmond Martène, *De antiquis Ecclesiae ritibus*, 4 t. (Anvers : Joannes Baptistæ de la Bry, 1736-1738), III (1737), col. 890-926 (éd. rev. Anvers, 1763-1764, pp. 321-336 ; réimpr. Hildesheim : Georg Olms, 1967). (PM, aussi MA)
      Lefèvre mentionne que Martène a publié :
      Bibliothèque nationale (Paris), MS *lat.* 14762, f°s 223^r-239^r.
      Provenance : chanoines réguliers de Saint-Victor de Paris, treizième siècle[36].
      Description :
      Manuscrit consultable en ligne.
      Bruno Krings date cette version des statuts d'avant 1176[37].
      Après le texte des statuts, ce manuscrit contient quatorze décisions capitulaires, f°s 239^r-240^r[38].
      -   Léopold Delisle, *Inventaire des manuscrits latins conservés à la Bibliothèque Nationale sous les numéros 8823-18613*, 5 t. (Paris : Durand, 1863-1871), III (1869), p. 47.

---

33 Lefèvre et Grauwen, *Les statuts...* [voir note 14], pp. x-xi.
34 Krings, 'Das Ordensrecht'... [voir note 19], pp. 110-111.
35 Trudo Jan Gerits, 'Betekenis en spiritualiteit van de lekebroeders in de middeleeuwse observantie van Prémontré', in *Gedenkboek Orde van Prémontré 1121-1971* (Averbode : Altiora, 1971), 179-196 (pp. 190-192).
36 Lefèvre et Grauwen, *Les statuts...* [voir note 14], pp. x-xi et 57-59.
37 Krings, 'Das Ordensrecht'... [voir note 19], pp. 111-112.
38 Krings, 'Das Ordensrecht'... [voir note 19], pp. 112-113.

c Bodleian Library (Oxford), MS *Ashmole* 1285, f°s 185^v-196^{r39}. (Pmi)
Statuts incomplets.
Provenance : chanoines réguliers de Saint Mary's Overy à Southwark, près
de Londres, treizième siècle.
Description :
Bruno Krings prétend que ce ne sont pas des statuts prémontrés mais la lé-
gislation d'une congrégation de chanoines réguliers non encore identifiée,
empruntée en grande partie à la législation prémontrée[40].
D'autres manuscrits apparentés ont entretemps été découverts:
-   William Henry Black, *A Descriptive, Analytical, and Critical Catalogue
    of the Manuscripts Bequeathed unto the University of Oxford by Elias
    Ashmole* (Oxford : The University Press, 1845), col. 1044-1050.
d Bibliothèque municipale (Laon), MS 530, pp. 869-922.
Provenance : Saint-Martin de Laon, dix-septième siècle.
Description :
Ce manuscrit contient un texte presque identique à l'édition de Martène et
a été abondamment commenté par le Père Thomas[41].
-   *Catalogue général des manuscrits des bibliothèques publiques de France*,
    119 t. (Paris : Plon, 1849-1993), XLI (1903), *Supplément*, II, p. 392 ;
    avec ajouts dans Thomas, 'Un exemplaire glosé'... [voir note 17],
    pp. 50-51.
e Bayerische Staatsbibliothek (Munich), *Clm* 1031, f°s 112^r-141^v.
Provenance : Windberg, milieu du douzième siècle.
Description :
D'après Bruno Krings il s'agit de la même version des statuts comme dans
Clm 7702, donc également de 1154/55, en meilleure version[42].
Le texte des statuts est aussitôt suivi aux f°s 141^v-142^r par vingt-deux
décrets du chapitre général[43].
Suivent ensuite f°s 143^r-146^r des *consuetudines de ordine laicorum* (dix-huit
capitula)[44].
-   Elisabeth Klemm, *Die romanischen Handschriften der Bayerischen Staats-
    bibliothek* (Katalog der illuminierten Handschriften der Bayerischen
    Staatsbibliothek in München, 3/1-2), 2 t. (Wiesbaden : Reichert,
    1980-1988), I (1980) : *Die Bistümer Regensburg, Passau und Salzburg :
    Textband*, pp. 100-101, n° 157. Les statuts ne sont pas mentionnés dans
    la description, l'auteur mentionne uniquement la règle d'Augustin.
-   Krings, 'Zum Ordensrecht'... [voir note 20], pp. 9-11.

---

39 Milis, 'De Premonstratenzer-Wetgeving'... [voir note 10], édition du texte pp. 10-23.
40 Krings, 'Das Ordensrecht'... [voir note 19], pp. 114-118.
41 Thomas, 'Un exemplaire glosé'... [voir note 17], pp. 49-74.
42 Krings, 'Zum Ordensrecht'... [voir note 20], p. 12.
43 Krings, 'Zum Ordensrecht'... [voir note 20], pp. 11 et 15-21.
44 Edité dans Krings, 'Zum Ordensrecht'... [voir note 20], pp. 22-28.

2   *Édition* : Bruno Krings, 'Das Ordensrecht der Prämonstratenser vom späten 12. Jahrhundert bis zum Jahr 1227 : Der Liber consuetudinem und die Dekrete des Generalkapitels', *Analecta Praemonstratensia*, 69 (1993), 107-242. (PK)

Ces statuts sont une évolution des statuts PG[45].

Publication de :

f   Mitchell Library (Glasgow), MS 308892, fᵒˢ 1ʳ-32ʳ. (GL)

Provenance : France, treizième siècle.

Description :

Bruno Krings date cette législation de 1222.

Après les statuts suivent dans le manuscrit, fᵒˢ 32ʳ-47ʳ, 101 décrets de chapitres généraux, de 1180 à 1228[46].

  - Neil R. Ker, *Medieval Manuscripts in British Libraries*, 5 t. (Oxford : Clarendon Press ; New York : The Oxford University Press, 1969-2002), II : *Abbotsford-Keele* (1977), pp. 863-864.
  - Thomas, 'Une version'... [voir note 16], pp. 156-157. Copie de la description de Neil Ker et commentaire.
  - Krings, 'Das Ordensrecht'... [voir note 19], pp. 119-122.

g   Hessisches Hauptstaatsarchiv (Wiesbaden), MS 3004, C17.

Même texte que le manuscrit de Glasgow, incomplet.

Provenance : Arnstein, 1228/29.

Description :

Bruno Krings date cette version des statuts de 1227[47].

  - Krings, *Das Prämonstratenserstift Arnstein...* [voir note 18], pp. 260-261, n° 36[48].

3   *Édition* : *Les Statuts de Prémontré réformés sur les ordres de Grégoire IX et d'Innocent IV au XIIIᵉ siècle* (BRHE, 23), éd. par Placide Fernand Lefèvre (Leuven : Bureau de la Revue, 1946). (PL)

En 1232, le pape Grégoire IX décréta une série de décisions concernant l'Ordre de Prémontré. Elles furent acceptées dans l'Ordre en 1234 et ajoutées aux statuts. Placide Lefèvre parla d'une nouvelle rédaction des statuts qu'il date aux alentours de 1236-1238[49]. Ces statuts contiennent à nouveau la législation des convers (IV,10) et des sœurs (IV,11-12).

Publication rédigée à partir de :

h   Abbaye d'Averbode (Scherpenheuvel-Zichem), *Archives*, MS IV, 207, fᵒˢ 3ʳ-77ᵛ.

Provenance : Heylissem, 1579.

Description :

---

45 Thomas, 'Une version'... [voir note 16], pp. 155-170.
46 Edité dans Krings, 'Das Ordensrecht'... [voir note 19], pp. 131-133 et 195-230.
47 Krings, 'Das Ordensrecht'... [voir note 19], pp. 124-125.
48 Information complémentaire dans Krings, 'Das Ordensrecht'... [voir note 19], pp. 122-125.
49 Lefèvre, *Les Statuts...* [voir note 8], pp. xiv-xix.

Placide Lefèvre date cette version des statuts de 1236-1238[50].
-    Lefèvre, *Les Statuts...* [voir note 8], p. xxvi, n. 1.
i   Abbaye de Tongerlo (Westerlo), *Archives*, MS V, 3, f°s 1^r-54^r.
Provenance : Tongerlo, quatorzième siècle.
Description :
Placide Lefèvre date la version des statuts dans ce manuscrit en 1245 ou 1247[51].
Ajouter :
-    Jan Corthouts, *Inventaris van de handschriften in het abdijarchief te Tongerlo* (Bibliotheca Analectorum Praemonstratensium, 17) (Tongerlo, 1987), pp. 2-3, n° 4[52].
j   Bibliothèque nationale (Paris), MS *lat.* 9752, f°s 1^v-26^r.
Le texte des statuts est incomplet.
Provenance : Wedinghausen, treizième siècle.
Description :
Manuscrit consultable en ligne.
-    Léopold Delisle, *Inventaire des manuscrits latins conservés à la Bibliothèque Nationale sous les numéros 8823-18613*, 5 t. (Paris : Durand, 1863-1871), I (1863), p. 48.
-    Pour ajouts supplémentaires voir : Antoninus Hendrik Thomas, *De oudste constituties van de dominicanen : Voorgeschiedenis, tekst, bronnen, ontstaan en ontwikkeling (1215-1237) met uitgave van de tekst* (BRHE, 42) (Leuven : Bureel van de RHE, 1965), pp. 130-131 [pp. 282-283][53].
k   Bibliothèque municipale (Nancy), MS 1772 (997), pp. 691-729.
Provenance : Transcription en 1725 d'un exemplaire ancien de l'abbaye de Santa Maria de la Vid, par José Esteban de Noriega (1684-1739).
Description :
-    *Catalogue général des manuscrits des bibliothèques publiques de France*, 119 t. (Paris : Plon, 1849-1993), XLVI (1924), p. 384.
-    Voir aussi Thomas, 'Une version'... [voir note 16], p. 155, n. 9.
l   Bibliothèque municipale (Nancy), MS 1775 (1000), f°s 87-121.
Provenance : Transcription en 1725 d'un exemplaire ancien de l'abbaye de Santa Maria de la Vid, par José Esteban de Noriega.
Description :
-    *Catalogue général des manuscrits des bibliothèques publiques de France*, 119 t. (Paris : Plon, 1849-1993), XLVI (1924), pp. 384-385.
-    Voir aussi Thomas, 'Une version'... [voir note 16], pp. 154-155, n. 9.

50 Lefèvre, *Les Statuts...* [voir note 8], p. xxvii, n. 4.
51 Lefèvre, *Les Statuts...* [voir note 8], p. xxvii.
52 Voir aussi Lefèvre, *Les Statuts...* [voir note 8], p. xxvi, n. 2.
53 Voir aussi Thomas, 'Une version'... [voir note 16], pp. 154-155, n. 8 ; Tugwell, 'The Evolution III'... [voir note 24], pp. 5 et 98 et id., 'The Evolution IV'... [voir note 24], pp. 27 et 36.

m   Bibliothèque Alpha (Liège), MS 279.
   Statuts incomplets.
   Provenance : Averbode, 1415.
   Description :
   - Marcel Grandjean, *Bibliothèque de l'Université de Liège : Catalogue des manuscrits* (Liège : Vaillant – Carmanne, 1875), p. 193.
   - Ajouts précieux dans Krings, 'Die Statuten'... [voir note 27], p. 15, n. 33.

4   *Édition* : Bruno Krings, 'Die Statuten des Prämonstratenserordens von 1244/46 und ihre Über-arbeitung im Jahr 1279', *Analecta Praemonstratensia*, 83 (2007), 5-127. (1246)
   Après de violentes protestations du chapitre général, le pape Innocent IV adoucit les mesures de son prédécesseur. Le chapitre général adapta donc à nouveau les statuts en 1246.
   Manuscrits utilisés :
   n   Prämonstratenserstift Wilten (Innsbruck), MS 32 04 05, fᵒˢ 1ʳ-60ᵛ.
      Provenance : Prémontré, après 1246.
      Description :
      - Gabriele Kompatscher Gufler *et al.*, *Katalog der mittelalterlichen Handschriften der Bibliothek des Prämonstratenser Chorherrenstiftes Wilten* (Österreichischen Akademie der Wissenschaften – Philosophisch-Historische Klasse : Denkschriften, 425 ; Veröffentlichungen der Kommission für Schrift- und Buchwesen des Mittelalters, II, 10) (Vienne : Österreichische Akademie der Wissenschaften, 2012), pp. 134-140 (texte de Claudia Schretter).
      - Krings, 'Die Statuten'... [voir note 27], pp. 10-12.
   o   Bibliothèque municipale (Laon), MS 509, fᵒˢ 1ʳ- 60ʳ.
      Provenance : Prémontré, après 1279.
      Description :
      - *Catalogue général des manuscrits des bibliothèques publiques de France*, 119 t. (Paris : Plon, 1849-1993), XLI (1903), *Supplément*, II, p. 388.
      - Ajouts dans Krings, 'Die Statuten'... [voir note 27], p. 13.
   p   Bibliothèque municipale (Soissons), MS 97, fᵒˢ 45ʳ-69ᵛ.
      Provenance : inconnue, après 1279.
      Description :
      - *Catalogue général des manuscrits des bibliothèques publiques de France*, 119 t. (Paris : Plon, 1849-1993), III (1885), p. 94.
      - Ajouts importants dans Krings, 'Die Statuten'... [voir note 27], pp. 13-14.
   q   Universitätsbibliothek (Innsbruck), MS 375, fᵒˢ 1ʳ-70ʳ.
      Provenance : Wilten, 1417.
      Description :
      - Walter Neuhauser et Lav Šubarić, *Katalog der Handschriften der Universitätsbibliothek Innsbruck* (Österreichischen Akademie der

Wissenschaften – Philosophisch-Historische Klasse : Denkschriften, 327 ; Veröffentlichungen der Kommission für Schrift- und Buchwesen des Mittelalters, II, 4.4), 9 t. (Vienne, Österreichische Akademie der Wissenschaften : 1987-2015), IV (2005) : *Cod. 301-400*, pp. 338-340.

- Krings, 'Die Statuten'... [voir note 27], pp. 14-16.

r   Bibliothèque nationale (Paris), MS *lat.* 4394, f°s 123^r-181^r.

Le manuscrit ne contient que la troisième et quatrième distinction des statuts, les autres parties furent perdues. Le texte est très proche de celui de Laon (o).

Provenance : Saint-Martin à Laon, après 1279.

Description :

Consultable en ligne.

- *Catalogus codicum manuscriptorum bibliothecæ regiæ*, 4 t. (Paris : Imprimerie royale, 1739-1744), III.3 (1744), p. 587.
- Krings, 'Die Statuten'... [voir note 27], p. 16.

5   *Édition* : Jean Le Paige, *Bibliotheca Praemonstratensis Ordinis* (Paris : Adrian Taupinart 1633), pp. 784-829. (1290)

Jean Lepaige publia en premier les anciens statuts prémontrés. Il data cette édition de l'année 1290. Placide Lefèvre fit remarquer que cette édition n'était pas exempte d'erreurs. Dans l'appareil critique de son édition (PL), il renvoya au texte corrigé par lui à partir de quelques manuscrits conservés[54]. Beaucoup de versions de manuscrits conservés des statuts prémontrés donnent cette version.

Après 1290 suivent à nouveau toute une série de décisions capitulaires au contenu législatif. Elles furent rassemblées dans une distinction séparée en 1322, la cinquième, et ajoutées aux statuts. Il s'agit d'un prologue et de dix-sept numéros, souvent des ajouts ou des changements de la législation existante. Trudo Jan Gerits y consacra une thèse de licence[55]. En 1505 parurent les premiers statuts imprimés des prémontrés, divisés à nouveau en quatre distinctions.

---

54 Lefèvre, *Les Statuts*... [voir note 8], pp. xxiv-xxvi.

55 Le texte a été publié par Le Paige, *Bibliotheca*... [voir note 2], pp. 832-840. Il compte dix-neuf chapitres. Cf. Trudo Jan Gerits, *De evolutie van de premonstratenzer wetgeving van 1290 tot 1322* (thèse de licence inédite, KU Leuven, 1964). Voir aussi Cygler, 'Ausformung'... [voir note 22], p. 21.

3. Tableau de la concordance des chapitres dans les différentes codifications statutaires de Prémontré aux XIIᵉ et XIIIᵉ siècles

Elaborée d'après Lefèvre, *Les Statuts...* [voir note 8], pp. 146-151 et Lefèvre et Grauwen, *Les statuts...* [voir note 14], pp. 54-56.

	PW	PG	PK	PL	1246	1290
Prologus		✓	✓	✓	✓	✓
Prima distinctio						
De sacramento altaris	(58)	(III,5)	(III,5)	(III,11)	1	1
De matutinis		1	1	1	2	2
De prima et missis post primam		2	2	2	3	3
De privatis confessionibus		3	3	3	4	4
De capitulo		4	4	4	5	5
Qualiter se habeant fratres in estate	19	5	5	5	6	6
Qualiter se habeant fratres in hyeme	20	6	6	6	7	7
Quando ministri maioris misse indui debeant		7	7			
De labore	35	8	8	7	8	8
Quomodo se habeant fratres tempore lectionis	36	9	9	8	9	9
De refectione	37	10	10	9	10	10
Quomodo se habeant fratres post vesperas	38	11	11	8	9	9
De hiis qui voluerint bibere extra horam	39	12	12	9	10	10
De victu	(30)	(IV,12)	(IV,12)	10	11	11
De collatione		13	13	11	12	12
Quomodo se habeant fratres post completorium	40	14	14	12	13	13
Quas officinas ingredi liceat	41	15	15	13	14	14

	PW	PG	PK	PL	1246	1290
De noviciis probandis/ recipiendis	32-34	16	16	14	15	15
Qui et quando debeant ordinari			17	15	16	16
De dirigendis in via *et silentio observando*	42	17	18	16	17	17
De infirmis extra chorum	44					
De infirmis qui non sunt in infirmitorio	46	18	19	17		
De infirmis qui sunt in infirmitorio	45	19	20	18	18	18
De minutione	61	20	21	19	19	19
De rasura		(IV,15)	(IV,15)	20	20	20
Secunda distinctio						
De abbate	1	1	1	1	1	1
De priore	2	2	2	2	2	2
De subpriore	3	3	3	3	3	3
De circatore	4	4	4	4	4	4
De cantore et succentore	5	5	5	5	5	5
De hebdomadario invitatorii	15	6	6	6	6	6
De armario et solatio eius	14	7	7	7	7	7
De sacrista et solatio eius	6	8	8	8	8	8
De magistro novitiorum	7	9	9	9	9	9
De cellerario/provisore exteriorum	8	10	10	10	10	10
De cellerario et solatio eius	9	11	11	11	11	11
De vestiario et solatio eius	11	12	12	12	12	12
De vestitu		(IV,14)	(IV,14)	13	13	13
De servitore infirmorum	10	13	13	14	14	14

	PW	PG	PK	PL	1246	1290
De hospitali fratre	12	14	14	15	15	15
De hospitalitate				16	16	16
De portario et solatio eius	13	15	15	17	17	17
De mense lectore	16	16	16	18	18	18
De mandato hospitum	17					
De communi mandato	18	17	17	19	19	19
Tertia distinctio						
De levioribus culpis			54	1	1	1
De mediis culpis			55	2	2	2
De gravi culpa			56	3	3	3
De graviori culpa			57	4	4	11
De graviori culpa						4
De tempore et modo gravioris culpe						5
Quid faciendum sit si quid de Sacramento dominici Corporis alicubi ceciderit			58	5	5	11
Item de graviori culpa			59	6	6	4
De conspiratoribus				7	7	6
De infamatoribus				8	7	6
De percussoribus						7
De hiis qui apostataverint			53	9	8	8
De fratribus emittendis						(IV,15)
De gravissima culpa			60	10	9	9
De crimine effornicationis						10
De incarcerandis						(IV,16)
Quando debeant fratres communiter ad pacem ire			47			
Quomodo supervenientes et transmissi fratres loquantur			50			

	PW	PG	PK	PL	1246	1290
Quomodo fratres loquantur parentibus et nunciis supervenientibus			51			
De hiis qui murmuraverint			52			
Quarta distinctio						
De annuo colloquio/capitulo	26	1	1	1	1	1
De hiis qui non interfuerint annuo colloquio/capitulo	27	2	2	1	1	1
De construendis abbatiis	21	3	3	2	2	2
Ut nemo recipiat ad aliam abbatiam ire volentem	24	4	4			
De pennuria abbatis	28	5	5	2	2	2
Que lex sit inter abbatias que se genuerunt	25	6	6	3	3	3
De appellationibus						4
In quibus requirendis est assensus patris abbatis, et de permutationibus faciendis				4	4	5
De annuis circatoribus		7	7	7	7	8
De visitationibus et inquisitionibus faciendis, et qualiter moneri debeat prelatus				8	8	9
De electione abbatum		8	8	6	6	7
Que lex sit inter abbatias que se non genuerunt	29	9	9	5	5	6
De unitate abbatiarum	22	10	10	2	2	2
Quos libros non liceat habere diversos	23	11	11	2	2	2
De victu	30	12	12	(I,10)	(I,11)	(I,11)

	PW	PG	PK	PL	1246	1290
Quibus diebus vescimur quadragesimali cibo	31	13	13	(I,10)	(I,11)	(I,11)
De vestitu		14	14	(II,13)	(II,13)	(II,13)
De rasura et tonsura		15	15	(I,20)	(I,20)	(I,20)
Que non expediat nos habere	43	16	16	9	9	10
De conversis et de hiis que licet eis addiscere, et de orationibus eorumdem				10	10	11
De receptis sororibus				11	11	12
De non recipiendis sororibus				12	12	13
Ne mulieres intrent officinas canonicorum				13	13	14
De generali excommunicatione				14	14	15
De fratribus emittendis				15	(III,9)	(III,9)
De incarcerandis				16	(III,11)	(III,11)
De pueris in baptismate non levandis				17	15	16
De canonicis et conversis qui prelatis secularibus et principibus accommodantur				18	16	17
De custodia sigilli conventus, pecunie proprie et aliene				19	17	18
De transeuntibus ad alium Ordinem				20	18	19
De canonicis parrochialibus				21	19	20
De servientibus abbatum				22	20	21
De culpis incertis et penis earum				23	21	22

	PW	PG	PK	PL	1246	1290
De non revelandis secretis Ordinis nostri				24	22	23
De his qui conqueruntur aliis personis quam de Ordine (1294)						24

ALEXIS GRÉLOIS

Les cisterciens et l'essor de la pratique statutaire, des origines au début du XIVe siècle

1. Ordres nouveaux et pratique statutaire

L'une des particularités saillantes du mouvement canonial et du « nouveau monachisme » contemporains de la Réforme grégorienne est l'apparition d'un nouveau mode de régulation des communautés laissant une part décisive à l'écrit. Bien entendu, il existait auparavant des textes normatifs comme la *Règle* de Benoît de Nursie composée au sixième siècle ou la *Concordancia regularum* de Benoît d'Aniane publiée en 816 ; ces règles étaient également précisées par des coutumes qui furent parfois mises par écrit : nous connaissons ainsi trois versions du coutumier de Cluny[1]. Cependant, le respect des usages au sein de la communauté reposait fondamentalement sur leur transmission par les paroles, par les gestes et surtout par l'imitation ; lorsqu'un monastère adoptait les pratiques d'un autre, leur introduction pouvait justifier la rédaction d'un coutumier, mais elle dépendait principalement de l'enseignement dispensé en personne par le ou les réformateurs (que ce soit dans la maison à réformer ou dans l'abbaye servant de modèle)[2].

De leur côté, les chanoines réguliers et les moines réformés apparus au tournant du douzième siècle revendiquèrent un retour au sens littéral de la règle, qu'il s'agît des Évangiles pour un Étienne de Muret[3], d'une des versions de ce qu'on appelle communément la *Règle* d'Augustin pour les chanoines réguliers ou les hospitaliers, ou du texte bénédictin pour les moines. Ce changement témoignait d'une inflexion en faveur de la textualité de la règle au détriment de l'oralité de

---

1 *From Dead of Night to End of Day : The Medieval Customs of Cluny / Du cœur de la nuit à la fin du jour : Les coutumes clunisiennes au Moyen Âge* (Disciplina Monastica, 3), éd. par Susan Boynton et Isabelle Cochelin (Turnhout : Brepols, 2005).

2 Voir par exemple Dominique Iogna-Prat, *Ordonner et exclure : Cluny et la société chrétienne face à l'hérésie, au judaïsme et à l'islam, 1000-1150* (Collection historique) (Paris : Aubier, 1998), pp. 61-63.

3 Jean Becquet, *Études grandmontaines* (Mémoires & documents sur le Bas-Limousin, 22) (Ussel : Musée du Pays d'Ussel, 1998), p. 5.

A Cathedral of Constitutional Law, éd. par Anton MILH O.P. and Mark BUTAYE O.P., Turnhout, Brepols, 2023 (*Bibliothèque de la Revue d'histoire ecclésiastique*, 112), p. 61-72.
BREPOLS ❧ PUBLISHERS   10.1484/M.BRHE-EB.5.135044

la coutume, suspectée de favoriser déformations, mitigations et dénaturation[4]. Ce nouveau rapport aux textes normatifs est l'une des facettes de la « révolution de l'écrit »[5].

Non contents de vouloir revenir au texte de la règle, les religieux réformés se distinguèrent aussi de leurs prédécesseurs en mettant par écrit leur normes au moment où ils les produisaient : comme l'a superbement montré Florent Cygler, les statuts « précisent et complètent à la fois les dispositions de la règle et celles des coutumiers, mais de manière prospective. Contrairement à la règle, ils ne préexistent pas nécessairement à [...] l'établissement de la communauté claustrale ; à la différence des coutumiers, ils ne fixent pas *a posteriori* des us de vie déjà implantés ; bien au contraire : constamment, ils en édictent de nouveaux ou révisent les anciens »[6]. Cette mise à l'écrit donna naissance à des textes de natures diverses, parmi lesquels il convient d'accorder une attention particulière à des décisions prises en chapitre appelées *capitula* ou *statuta*.

Lors de sa tournée en France en 1119-1120, le pape Calixte II approuva deux séries de textes de ce type : le 1er septembre (oralement) puis le 15 du même mois (par écrit) pour Fontevraud et le 23 décembre pour Cîteaux. Dans le premier cas, il s'agissait, selon Jacques Dalarun, des *Capitula regularia magistri Roberti*, c'est-à-dire deux séries de statuts destinés à réglementer la vie des moniales et des frères du monastère double institué par Robert d'Arbrissel, la première série concernant les moniales étant complétée par quelques statuts dus à la première abbesse, Pétronille de Chemillé[7]. Dans le second cas, le pape confirma la *Charte de charité* organisant les relations entre les abbés liés au Nouveau Monastère, ainsi que quelques statuts, sur lesquels nous reviendrons bientôt[8].

Les statuts cisterciens et les institutions qu'ils mettaient en place furent rapidement imités par d'autres ordres naissants, notamment les chanoines réguliers de Prémontré et d'Arrouaise qui reprirent de larges extraits du résumé de la *Charte*

4 Giles Constable, *The Reformation of the Twelfth Century* (Cambridge : Cambridge University Press, 1996), pp. 145-146.

5 Pour une présentation problématisée de cette notion, voir Paul Bertrand, 'À propos de la révolution de l'écrit (Xe-XIIIe siècles) : Considérations inactuelles', *Médiévales*, 54 (2009), 75-92.

6 Florent Cygler, 'Règle, coutumiers et statuts (Ve-XIIIe siècles) : Brèves considérations historico-typologiques', in *La vie quotidienne des moines et chanoines réguliers au Moyen Âge et Temps modernes* (Travaux du L.A.R.H.C.O.R.), éd. par Marek Derwich, 2 t. (Wrocław : Institut d'histoire de l'Université de Wrocław, 1995), I, 31-49 (à la p. 34).

7 Jacques Dalarun, 'Capitula regularia magistri Roberti : de Fontevraud au Paraclet', *Comptes-rendus des séances de l'Académie des Inscriptions et Belles-Lettres*, 147 (2003), 1601-1636 et id., 'Les plus anciens statuts de Fontevraud', in *Robert d'Arbrissel et la vie religieuse dans l'Ouest de la France* (Disciplina monastica, 1), éd. par id. (Turnhout : Brepols, 2004), 139-172.

8 Sur ce point, je me permets de renvoyer à Alexis Grélois, 'Genèse et évolution de la Charte de charité cistercienne au XIIe siècle', in *La Charte de charité, 1119-2019 : Un document pour préserver l'unité entre communautés* (Cerf Patrimoines), éd. par Éric Delaissé (Paris : Cerf, 2020), 43-68 (aux pp. 48-49).

de charité et des premiers statuts cisterciens dans leurs coutumiers primitifs[9] ; il en fut de même pour les ordres religieux militaires[10]. Florent Cygler a souligné le rôle joué par la promulgation de statuts dans l'institutionnalisation des nouveaux ordres religieux, notamment lorsqu'il s'agit de donner de la consistance à des groupements lâches ou menacés de dissolution, comme Prémontré dans les années 1130 ou La Chartreuse dans la seconde moitié du douzième siècle[11]. La pratique de la réglementation par promulgation de statuts fut donc rapidement imitée dans d'autres institutions, parfois anciennes : il est bien connu que Pierre le Vénérable répliqua aux critiques visant Cluny par la promulgation d'une longue série de statuts entre 1132 et 1146[12].

2. La production statutaire chez les cisterciens

En plus d'avoir été les principaux initiateurs de ce type de réglementation, les cisterciens se distinguent des autres ordres ou institutions régulières semblables par l'ampleur de leur production statutaire. L'édition des statuts des origines à 1787 publiée entre 1933 et 1941 par le trappiste Joseph-Marie Canivez compte sept forts volumes (huit avec les indices)[13]. Focalisée sur le seul douzième siècle (plus l'année 1201), la nouvelle édition d'un autre trappiste, le grand liturgiste Chrysogonus Waddell, publiée en 2002, compte pour sa part 928 pages[14].

L'importance de ce corpus s'explique par trois facteurs. Le premier tient aux circonstances de promulgation de ces statuts, lors de chapitres annuels réunissant en principe tous les supérieurs des monastères masculins membres de l'Ordre. Le véritable fondateur de celui-ci, Étienne Harding, qui redoutait de perdre le contrôle sur les maisons fondées par ses disciples, fit reconnaître par le pape le 23 décembre 1119 la *Charte de charité* et une série de statuts qui visaient à

---

9   Voir l'excellente mise au point de Dirk Van de Perre, 'Die ältesten Klostergesetzgebungen von Prémontré, Oigny, Cîteaux, Klosterrath und Arrouaise und ihre Beziehungen zueinander', *Analecta Praemonstratensia*, 76 (2000), 29-69.

10 Voir par exemple Alain Demurger, *Les templiers : Une chevalerie chrétienne au Moyen Âge* (Points Histoire, 404) (Paris : Le Seuil, 2008), pp. 56-66 et 73-74.

11 Florent Cygler, *Das Generalkapitel im hohen Mittelalter : Cistercienzer, Prämonstratenser, Kartäuser und Cluniazenser* (Vita regularis, 12) (Münster : Lit Verlag, 2002) et id., 'Le Chapitre général des Prémontrés au Moyen Âge', *Analecta Praemonstratensia*, 81 (2005), 5-34.

12 *Statuts, chapitres généraux et visites de l'ordre de Cluny*, éd. par Gaston Charvin, 9 t. (Paris : De Boccard, 1965-1982), I (1965), pp. 20-40 et Giles Constable, *The Abbey of Cluny : A Collection of Essays to Mark the Eleven-Hundredth Anniversary of Its Foundation* (Vita regularis, 43) (Münster : Lit Verlag, 2010), pp. 307-311.

13 *Statuta capitulorum generalium Ordinis Cisterciensis ab anno 1116 ad annum 1786* (BRHE, 9-14B), éd. par Joseph-Marie Canivez, 8 t. (Leuven : Revue d'histoire ecclésiastique, 1933-1941).

14 *Twelfth-Century Statutes from the Cistercian General Chapter* (Cîteaux – Commentarii cistercienses : Studia et documenta, 12), éd. par Chrysogonus Waddell (Brecht : Cîteaux, 2002).

assurer le maintien de l'unanimité au sein de la congrégation naissante grâce à l'uniformité de l'observance[15].

De plus, les abbés devaient se rendre chaque année à Cîteaux pour assister au chapitre des moines (*capitulum Cisterciense*). Dans un premier temps, encore en 1119-1120, les abbés n'y avaient qu'une voix délibérative et devaient se soumettre aux décisions prises par Étienne Harding et ses moines. Dans un second temps, les abbés prirent le contrôle de ces assemblées, d'ailleurs parfois appelées « réunion des abbés » (*conventus abbatum*), au détriment des moines de Cîteaux qui avaient été exclus des débats[16]. Ce changement est parfois situé après la résignation ou la mort d'Harding (datées communément de 1133 et 1134 respectivement), mais l'analyse de la *Charte de charité* montre qu'il remonte aux années 1120[17]. Notons au passage que l'expression « chapitre général » ne se généralisa chez les cisterciens que vers le milieu du douzième siècle[18].

Quoi qu'il en soit, la fréquence annuelle de ces réunions ne souffrit aucune exception avant la fin du quatorzième siècle, période au cours de laquelle la conjonction de la guerre de Cent Ans, des épidémies de peste et des divisions créées au sein de l'Ordre par le Grand Schisme semble bien avoir empêché la tenue des réunions pendant quelques années[19]. Mais dans l'ensemble, la fréquence annuelle des chapitres généraux favorisa la production d'un important corpus, alors que chez les clunisiens, aucun statut ne semble avoir été promulgué par un abbé entre Pierre le Vénérable et Hugues V en 1200[20].

Chez les cisterciens, le corpus statutaire s'accrut encore à partir de 1190[21]. Ce fut en effet à cette époque que le chapitre général prit l'habitude de désigner une commission d'abbés chargée de mettre en forme et de publier ses décisions, le définitoire[22]. L'importance de ces commissions est prouvée par les conflits récurrents au cours du treizième siècle[23] que leur nomination suscita entre les

---

15 La dernière édition de la bulle *Ad hoc in apostolice* se trouve dans *Narrative and Legislative Texts from Early Cîteaux* (Cîteaux – Commentarii cistercienses : Studia et documenta, 9), éd. par Chrysogonus Waddell (Brecht : Cîteaux, 1999), pp. 295-296.

16 Grélois, 'Genèse et évolution'... [voir note 8], pp. 54-55.

17 Grélois, 'Genèse et évolution'... [voir note 8], p. 61.

18 Grélois, 'Genèse et évolution'... [voir note 8], pp. 55, 60 et 63.

19 Alexis Grélois, 'Tradition and Transmission : What Is the Significance of the Cistercian General Chapters' Statutes ? (Twelfth to Fourteenth Centuries)', in *Shaping Stability : The Normation and Formation of Religious Life in the Middle Ages* (Disciplina Monastica, 11), éd. par Krijn Pansters et Abraham Plunkett-Latimer (Turnhout : Brepols, 2016), 205-216 (aux pp. 209 et 211).

20 Charvin, *Statuts*... [voir note 12], p. 40.

21 Grélois, 'Tradition and Transmission'... [voir note 19], p. 210.

22 Bernard Lucet, 'Questions proposées au chapitre de Cîteaux au XIIIᵉ siècle', in *Sous la Règle de saint Benoît : Structures monastiques et sociétés en France du Moyen Âge à l'époque moderne* (Centre de recherches d'histoire et de philologie de la IVᵉ Section de l'École pratique des Hautes Études, 47) (Genève : Droz, 1982), 75-88.

23 Jean-Berthold Mahn, *L'ordre cistercien et son gouvernement des origines au milieu du XIIIᵉ siècle (1098-1265)* (Bibliothèque des écoles françaises d'Athènes et de Rome, 161) (Paris : De Boccard, ²1951), pp. 229-238 ; Jean-Baptiste Van Damme, 'Les pouvoirs de l'abbé de Cîteaux aux XIIᵉ et

abbés de Cîteaux et les « premiers abbés », les chefs des quatre premières abbayes fondées par Cîteaux, qui jouissaient de prérogatives particulières.

Le deuxième facteur expliquant l'importance du corpus statutaire cistercien est la diversité des décisions ainsi désignées par les moines blancs. Alors que les statuts cluniens, prémontrés ou chartreux ne continrent longtemps (au moins dans leurs versions parvenues jusqu'à nous) que des règles de portée générale (liturgiques ou économiques par exemple)[24], les collections de *statuta* cisterciens comportent aussi des décisions concernant des abbayes particulières et même des individus à partir de 1190[25]. Sont donc regroupés sous l'appellation générique de *statuta* des textes de natures et de portées très diverses : en employant des catégories anachroniques, on pourrait parler de textes constitutionnels, législatifs, réglementaires et judiciaires, à la fois civils et pénaux.

Dès la fin du douzième siècle, les *statuta* les plus nombreux servirent à désigner des commissions d'abbés chargées d'arbitrer les litiges entre les monastères de l'Ordre ou d'enquêter à leur sujet, notamment en cas d'incorporation de nouvelles communautés. Ces délégations donnaient lieu à la production d'actes écrits qui n'ont été conservés que de façon très partielle : les délégués recevaient une charte généralement scellée par les abbés de Cîteaux et des premières filles (comme la plupart des notifications des décisions du chapitre général) et les arbitrages étaient scellés par les abbés délégués et par les parties concernées[26].

Ce ne fut que tardivement que l'on se soucia d'ordonner les statuts de façon systématique par catégories. Dans la documentation conservée, le recueil des *statuta* de 1344 fait pour l'abbaye de Clairvaux est le premier à distinguer ainsi les *commissiones, petitiones, relationes, punitiones, citationes, orationes pro vivis* et *orationes pro defunctis*[27]. Ce ne fut qu'au quinzième siècle que les statuts conservés à Cîteaux adoptèrent systématiquement ce type d'organisation[28].

Enfin, le dernier facteur expliquant l'importance du corpus statutaire cistercien tient à leur enregistrement et à leur conservation de façon systématique à partir de la fin du douzième siècle – le parallèle avec les correspondances pontificales ou les archives capétiennes méritant d'être relevé[29].

XIIIe siècle', *Analecta Cisterciensia*, 24 (1968), 60-85 et Guido Cariboni, *Il nostro ordine è la Carità : Cistercensi nei secoli XII e XIII* (Milan : Vita e Pensiero, 2011), pp. 93-126.

24 Cygler, 'Le Chapitre général'… [voir note 11], pp. 5-7.
25 Waddell, *Twelfth-Century Statutes*… [voir note 14], p. 193.
26 Citons le plus ancien exemple attesté : l'arbitrage rendu en juillet 1191 entre les abbayes de Grandselve et de Boulbonne (Claude Devic et Joseph Vaissete, *Histoire générale de Languedoc avec des notes et les pièces justificatives*, 16 t. (Toulouse : Édouard Privat, 1872-1904), VIII (1879), col. 1891) à la suite du chapitre général de 1190 (Waddell, *Twelfth-Century Statutes*… [voir note 14], p. 206).
27 Canivez, *Statuta capitulorum generalium*… [voir note 13], III (1935) : *1262-1400*, pp. 474-501.
28 Canivez, *Statuta capitulorum generalium*… [voir note 13], IV (1936) : *1401-1456*, pp. 530-561 (1443 et 1444).
29 *L'art médiéval du registre : Chancelleries royales et princières* (Études et rencontres de l'École des chartes, 51), éd. par Olivier Guyotjeannin (Paris : École nationale des chartes, 2018) (voir notamment les contributions de James Baldwin, Werner Maleczek et Nicholas Vincent).

3. Les collections cisterciennes de *statuta*

Les éditions de Martène en 1717[30] puis de Canivez ont tendu à occulter la complexité de la tradition manuscrite des *statuta* cisterciens. Celle-ci commença à être prise en considération avec la redécouverte au cours du vingtième siècle des « textes primitifs » de l'Ordre. L'aboutissement de cet effort fut la monumentale édition des statuts antérieurs à 1202 par le père Waddell publiée en 2002, qui eut l'immense mérite de ne pas chercher à compiler toutes les collections existantes pour produire un *Urtext* soi-disant original et exhaustif ; au contraire, Waddell donna une édition scientifique de chacune des traditions manuscrites qu'il avait identifiée (quatorze en tout). Une telle démarche serait utile pour les siècles suivants, mais elle représenterait un effort considérable et l'on peut se contenter pour l'heure d'utiliser l'édition de Canivez, à condition toutefois de tenir compte de son apparat critique et de ne pas considérer que cette publication renferme la totalité des statuts jamais promulgués, les découvertes dans les fonds d'archives des abbayes étant également à prendre en compte.

Canivez avait distingué trois types de collections de statuts : les *collectiones plenissimæ* rassemblant (supposément) tous les statuts promulgués une année donnée, les *collectiones breves* ne comportant que les décisions les plus importantes, tandis que les *collectiones brevissimæ* ne conservaient que les décisions de portée générale[31]. L'analyse de la tradition manuscrite montre que les deux premiers types n'étaient conservés qu'à Cîteaux et Clairvaux (dont les collections, hélas mal conservées, semblent d'ailleurs avoir été plus précises que celle de Cîteaux)[32]. Les autres abbayes de l'Ordre se contentaient de collections de statuts de portée générale[33].

L'étude de la tradition manuscrite montre aussi que les collections de statuts rangés par année qui ont tant suscité l'attention des historiens ne représentent qu'une infime partie de la documentation. Pour le douzième siècle, on ne dispose de ce type de séries que pour les années 1157-1161 (*collectio brevis*)[34], les années 1180-1189 (*idem*)[35] et à partir de 1190 (*collectio completissima*)[36].

Pour l'essentiel, les statuts étaient accessibles grâce à des compilations. Si nous n'avons pas de certitude sur le contenu exact des statuts approuvés par Calixte II en 1119, nous disposons de plusieurs compilations réalisées au cours du douzième siècle. La plus ancienne est probablement formée par les vingt *Capitula* clôturant un résumé des usages cisterciens comportant aussi l'*Exordium*

---

30 *Thesaurus novus anecdotorum*, éd. par Edmond Martene et Ursin Durand, 5 t. (Paris : Sumptibus Bibliopolarum Parisiensium, 1707-1750), III (1717) : *Chronica varia*, col. 1243-1646.

31 Canivez, *Statuta capitulorum generalium*... [voir note 13], I (1933) : *1116-1120*, p. xvi.

32 Grélois, 'Tradition and Transmission'... [voir note 19], pp. 213-214.

33 Grélois, 'Tradition and Transmission'... [voir note 19], pp. 208-209.

34 Cette collection n'est connue que par le manuscrit École de médecine (Montpellier), H 322 ; éd. dans Waddell, *Twelfth-Century Statutes*... [voir note 14], pp. 67-75.

35 Waddell, *Twelfth-Century Statutes*... [voir note 14], pp. 86-162.

36 Waddell, *Twelfth-Century Statutes*... [voir note 14], pp. 193-501 (jusqu'en 1201).

Cisterciense et la *Summa cartæ caritatis*, réalisée au plus tard en 1130[37]. Une liste de douze statuts, contenue dans le manuscrit Bibliothèque nationale de France (BnF, Paris), *lat.* 12169, constitue un autre exemple de codification précoce des décisions statutaires – Waddell voulait y voir les plus anciens statuts annuels conservés, mais leur portée générale et leur ordonnancement fragilisent cette hypothèse[38].

La compilation la plus répandue est appelée *Instituta capituli generalis*, qui avait été datée erronément de 1134 au dix-septième siècle par Angel Manrique[39], erreur reprise par Canivez[40] ; l'expression « statuts de 1134 » est hélas toujours fréquemment employée, notamment par les historiens de l'art. Cette collection est en fait connue par trois versions[41]. Selon Waddell, la première, comportant 87 statuts, aurait été réalisée à l'occasion des nombreuses incorporations opérées par le chapitre général de 1147[42], ce qui est vraisemblable. La deuxième, en 83 chapitres, aurait été diffusée après la décision par le chapitre général de 1152 d'interdire toute nouvelle fondation au sein de l'Ordre. Ce statut[43] n'est cependant attesté que dans la troisième version des *Instituta*, comptant 92 statuts. Celle-ci se trouve notamment dans le manuscrit Dijon 114, copié au plus tard en 1186 pour servir d'*exemplar* de référence de la liturgie cistercienne[44]. Dans presque tous les manuscrits, cette collection est précédée par un sommaire qui précise que ses dix

---

37 Le Père Waddell a publié deux fois son édition des *Capitula* : *Narrative and Legislative Texts...* [voir note 15], pp. 186-191 et id., *Twelfth-Century Statutes...* [voir note 14], pp. 512-516. Sur la datation de l'ensemble *Exordium Cistercii – Summa cartæ caritatis – Capitula*, voir Grélois, 'Genèse et évolution'... [voir note 8], p. 61.

38 Waddell, *Narrative and Legislative Texts...* [voir note 15], pp. 301-302 et id., *Twelfth-Century Statutes...* [voir note 14], p. 56. Ces douze statuts se trouvaient initialement à la fin du coutumier cistercien, les *Ecclesiastica officia*. Waddell les a curieusement placés en tête de sa recension des « collections annuelles », alors qu'ils ne présentent aucun élément de datation ; ils auraient donc dû être placés parmi les « collections systématiques », avant les *Capitula*. La comparaison faite par Waddell (*Narrative and Legislative Texts...* [voir note 15], pp. 303-310 et *Twelfth-Century Statutes...* [voir note 14], pp. 57-64) tend en effet à démontrer que cette collection serait antérieure à la plus ancienne version connue actuellement des *Ecclesiastica officia*, figurant dans le manuscrit Trente 1711 (*Les 'Ecclesiastica officia' cisterciens du XIIᵉ siècle : Texte latin selon les manuscrits édités de Trente 1711, Ljubljana 31 et Dijon 114 – Version française* (Documentation cistercienne, 22), éd. par Danièle Choisselet et Placide Vernet (Reiningue : Documentation cistercienne, 1989)). Il faut toutefois noter que le sixième statut du manuscrit BnF, *lat.* 12169 utilise l'expression relativement tardive « chapitre général » là où les *Instituta* (XXXIII) parlent du « chapitre des abbés de Cîteaux » (sur ces expressions, voir *supra* note 18 et le texte).

39 Ángel Manrique, *Cisterciensium seu verius ecclesiasticorum annalium a condito Cistercio...*, 4 t. (Lyon : Boissat – Anisson, 1642-1659), I (1642), pp. 271-272 (avec une édition des *Instituta*, pp. 272-282).

40 Canivez, *Statuta capitulorum generalium...* [voir note 13], I, pp. 12-33.

41 Voir leur présentation et le détail de leur contenu dans Waddell, *Twelfth-Century Statutes...* [voir note 14], pp. 520-537.

42 Waddell, *Twelfth-Century Statutes...* [voir note 14], pp. 517-519.

43 Waddell, *Narrative and Legislative Texts...* [voir note 15], p. 364 et id., *Twelfth-Century Statutes...* [voir note 14], pp. 560-561.

44 Sur ce manuscrit, voir Waddell, *Narrative and Legislative Texts...* [voir note 15], pp. 37-39 et id., *Twelfth-Century Statutes...* [voir note 14], pp. 529-531.

premiers statuts avaient été institués pour l'essentiel par les premiers moines de Cîteaux ou tirés de la *Charte de charité*[45]. Il pourrait donc s'agir au moins en partie des statuts approuvés par Calixte II en 1119.

Même si les *Instituta* furent donc complétés jusque vers 1180, un chapitre général avait décidé, sans doute en 1179 selon Waddell, de compiler les statuts promulgués depuis la mort de saint Bernard, en fait depuis 1157, le travail étant confié à une commission composée des abbés de Cîteaux, des premières filles et de sept autres monastères[46]. Cette collection[47] s'est vu assigner à tort la date de 1157 par Canivez[48]. L'existence de deux collections de statuts contemporaines et donc potentiellement concurrentes reste à expliquer.

4. Des statuts annuels aux codifications

L'étude de la tradition montre que la plupart des collections annuelles de statuts se trouvent dans les manuscrits à la suite de compilations et qu'elles furent copiées au fur et à mesure des années, jusqu'à ce qu'une nouvelle compilation paraisse et rende caduque la précédente[49]. En effet, les statuts de portée générale avaient souvent vocation à amender des ouvrages normatifs déjà existants, qu'il s'agisse des livres liturgiques, du coutumier (*Ecclesiastica Officia*)[50] ou encore des *Usages des convers*[51]. Contrairement aux historiens, les moines n'avaient pas besoin de conserver la trace de toutes les affaires dont les chapitres généraux avaient pu traiter[52]. Même à Cîteaux, la collection *plenissima* présentait des lacunes depuis au moins le dix-septième siècle[53].

Cependant, les compilations produites au douzième siècle souffraient d'un gros défaut qui en compliquait le maniement. Si l'on peut distinguer *grosso modo* un classement dans les *Capitula* et dans la collection du manuscrit *lat.* 12169 de la BnF, ce n'est vraiment pas le cas dans les *Instituta*, les décisions ayant

45 *Huc usque capitula de institutione primorum monachorum Cisterciensium et de Carta caritatis fere omnia sunt sumpta* (Waddell, *Narrative and Legislative Texts...* [voir note 15], p. 320 et id., *Twelfth-Century Statutes...* [voir note 14], p. 532).

46 Waddell, *Twelfth-Century Statutes...* [voir note 14], pp. 569-570. La date de 1179 a été déduite par Waddell du fait que l'existence d'une collection de statuts datés commençant en 1180.

47 Son texte a été édité dans Waddell, *Twelfth-Century Statutes...* [voir note 14], pp. 572-606.

48 Canivez, *Statuta capitulorum generalium...* [voir note 13], I, pp. 60-68.

49 Grélois, 'Tradition and Transmission'... [voir note 19], p. 208 ; pour les périodes ultérieures, citons par exemple le manuscrit Médiathèque Louis-Aragon (Le Mans), 357, qui rassemble les statuts promulgués de 1290 à 1309 à la suite du *Libellus antiquarum definitionum* de 1289 (Canivez, *Statuta capitulorum generalium...* [voir note 13], III, p. ix).

50 Les *'Ecclesiastica officia'...* [voir note 38].

51 Les *capitula* XXI et XXII ont été repris dans le chapitre XIII des *Usus conversorum* (*Cistercian Lay Brothers : Twelfth-Century Usages with Related Texts*, éd. par Chrysogonus Waddell (Cîteaux –Commentarii cistercienses : Studia et documenta, 10) (Brecht : Cîteaux, 2000), p. 71).

52 Grélois, 'Tradition and Transmission'... [voir note 19], p. 212.

53 Grélois, 'Tradition and Transmission'... [voir note 19], p. 210.

peut-être été laissées dans l'ordre de leur promulgation (Waddell y identifiait des strates correspondant aux principaux abbés de Cîteaux)[54]. Pourtant, les *Instituta* comportaient entre 83 et 92 statuts selon les versions. Le même défaut affectait la compilation réalisée vers 1179, pourtant riche de 64 statuts. Il était donc nécessaire de parcourir l'ensemble du corpus pour y trouver un texte précis. Pour remédier à cette situation, il s'avéra nécessaire de rassembler les statuts existants de façon ordonnée, autrement dit de procéder à une codification systématique.

Grâce aux travaux menés par Bernard Lucet dans les années 1960-1970[55], nous sommes bien renseignés sur les quatre premières entreprises de ce type. La première vit très certainement le jour à l'initiative de l'abbé de Cîteaux Arnaud Amalric, le futur chef de la croisade des Albigeois, et fut réalisée en 1202. Le chapitre général de 1204 ordonna à tous les abbés de se procurer au plus vite le *Libellus definitionum*, autrement dit le recueil des décisions entérinées par le définitoire[56]. De façon significative, l'ouvrage s'ouvre par une préface expliquant la façon dont il devait être utilisé[57], en s'aidant de la division du recueil en quinze *distinctiones* :

1   Construction et mobilier des abbayes, églises, granges et autres édifices.
2   Dédicaces, ordinations et bénédictions.
3   Office.
4   Privilèges et immunité.
5   Chapitre général.
6   Chapitre des coulpes et punitions.
7   Visites régulières, autorité de l'abbé-père, élections et destitutions.
8   Officiers.
9   Voyages.
10 Qui peut être admis licitement, vivant ou mort.
11 Ce que l'on peut avoir, donner, concéder et si l'on peut mettre à gage.
12 Vente et achat.
13 Nourriture et vêtement.
14 Convers.
15 Divers – cette section devait être consacrée aux moniales à partir de 1237.

En effet, la codification de 1202 fut amendée à trois reprises, en 1220, 1237 et 1257. Dans les deux derniers cas, des *statuta* précisent le processus de rédaction, confié d'abord à une commission de quatre puis cinq abbés, qui devaient présenter leur travail aux abbés de Cîteaux et de ses premières filles ; ceux-ci devaient

---

54 Waddell, *Narrative and Legislative Texts…* [voir note 15], p. 299.
55 *La codification cistercienne de 1202 et son évolution ultérieure* (Bibliotheca Cisterciensis, 2), éd. par Bernard Lucet (Rome : Editiones cisterciences, 1964) ; id., 'L'ère des grandes codifications cisterciennes (1202-1350)', in *Études d'histoire du droit canonique dédiées à Gabriel le Bras*, 2 t. (Paris : Sirey, 1965), I, 249-262 ; *Les codifications cisterciennes de 1237 et de 1257* (Sources de l'histoire médiévale publiées par l'IRHT, 9), éd. par id. (Paris : CNRS, 1977).
56 Canivez, *Statuta capitulorum generalium…* [voir note 13], I, p. 296.
57 Lucet, *La codification cistercienne…* [voir note 55], p. 25.

ensuite transmettre leur version aux définiteurs, avant présentation au chapitre général[58].

Malheureusement, les codifications postérieures (*Libellus antiquarum definitionum* compilé en 1289, actualisé légèrement en 1316, complété en 1350 par le *Libellus novellarum definitionum*) n'ont pas fait l'objet d'éditions scientifiques et il faut contenter d'une publication du dix-septième siècle[59].

5. Conclusion

Au début du douzième siècle, les cisterciens furent donc les premiers à utiliser les *statuta* comme outils de régulation de leur Ordre en formation. Ils fournirent ainsi un modèle pour la plupart des nouvelles institutions régulières, notamment pour les prémontrés. Par la suite, la production foisonnante de statuts engendrée par les réunions régulières du chapitre général donna naissance à un corpus textuel qui fait aujourd'hui les délices des historiens (au risque d'en survaloriser l'intérêt) mais qui était une source de complication pour les abbés. En effet, à la fin du douzième siècle, chaque monastère cistercien devait en principe posséder, en plus des manuscrits liturgiques et de l'exemplaire de la *Règle* prévus dans les *Capitula*[60], la *Charte de charité*, parfois précédée par l'histoire des débuts de l'Ordre (*Exordium Cistercii* ou *Exordium parvum*), le coutumier (*Ecclesiastica officia*), les *Usages* propres aux convers, sans oublier une compilation des décisions des chapitres généraux (*Capitula* puis *Instituta*), complétée par les décisions des dernières réunions. Les codifications réalisées à partir de 1202 eurent le mérite de mettre en ordre les *Instituta* et de les actualiser, mais elles furent elles aussi rapidement frappées de caducité du fait de la production continue de statuts par les chapitres généraux ; par ailleurs, elles n'avaient vocation à remplacer qu'une petite partie du corpus normatif des cisterciens. Au contraire, les prémontrés s'étaient dotés dès 1130 environ de statuts ordonnés, de portée générale[61]. Il est donc compréhensible que les dominicains se soient tournés vers leur exemple

---

58 Canivez, *Statuta capitulorum generalium...* [voir note 13], II (1934) : *1221-1261*, pp. 131, 141 et 424.

59 *Nomasticon Cisterciense, seu Antiquiores ordinis Cisterciensis constitutiones...*, éd. par Julien Paris, (Paris : Alliot, 1664), pp. 482-582 et 616-662 ; réimpr. *Nomasticon Cisterciense seu antiquiores ordinis Cisterciensis Constitutiones a R. P. D. Juliano Paris, Fulcardimontis abbate collectæ ac notis et observationibus adornatæ...*, éd. par Hugues Séjalon (Solesmes : E typographeo sancti Petri, 1892), pp. 366-470 et 497-536.

60 *Capitula*, X : *Quos libros non liceat habere diuersos* (Waddell, *Narrative and Legislative Texts...* [voir note 15], p. 187 et id., *Twelfth-Century Statutes...* [voir note 14], p. 513).

61 Bruno Krings, 'Das Ordensrecht der Prämonstratenser vom späten 12. Jahrhundert bis zum Jahr 1227 : Der Liber consuetudinum und die Dekrete des Generalkapitels', *Analecta Praemonstratensia*, 69 (1993), 107-242 et id., 'Zum Ordensrecht der Prämonstratenser bis zur Mitte des 12. Jahrhunderts', *Analecta Praemonstratensia*, 76 (2000), 9-28.

pour rédiger la première distinction de leurs premières constitutions, même si les usages relatifs aux chapitres et aux définiteurs empruntèrent beaucoup aux cisterciens[62]. Le choix par les frères prêcheurs du modèle prémontré s'explique donc autant par des raisons d'identité canoniale que pour des motifs pratiques.

---

62 Antoninus Hendrik Thomas, *De oudste constituties van de dominicanen : Voorgeschiedenis, tekst, bronnen, ontstaan en ontwikkeling (1215-1237) met uitgave van de tekst* (BRHE, 42) (Leuven : Bureel van de RHE, 1965), en particulier pp. 187-199 [pp. 330-340] sur les emprunts aux cisterciens.

LAURENT WAELKENS †
ET WOUTER DRUWÉ

Les dominicains, les collèges et les universités[*]

Une pauvreté savante au XIIIe siècle

De la lecture des constitutions dites « primitives » de l'Ordre des Prêcheurs éditées par le Père Antoninus Hendrik Thomas, émane leur caractère juridique. Dans ces dernières, on peut déceler en outre, et ceci est à souligner, comment ces constitutions ont été rédigées dans le style juridique de l'École bolonaise de la période entre Azzon (*c.* 1200) et Raymond de Peñafort (*c.* 1230). Dans l'organisation première des frères prêcheurs, une place importante fut donnée à des éléments juridiques, comme la notion de *culpa* qui y fut redéfinie plusieurs fois[1]. Mais, à quoi bon tous ces éléments juridiques dans une société qui se voulait théologique, scientifique et sociale ? Afin de resituer les premières constitutions dans l'esprit du temps, nous retournerons plusieurs fois dans l'Antiquité, toutefois en espérant de ne pas submerger le lecteur par trop de détails.

Dès leur fondation les dominicains ont souhaité vivre dans la pauvreté, désir difficile à accorder avec une vie de travail qui a l'ambition de perdurer et d'améliorer le monde. Dans cette situation il ne suffisait pas d'être pauvre, il leur fallait organiser un patrimoine collectif. Comment ont-ils organisé l'achat et l'entretien de résidences, comment ont-ils construit des églises et comment ont-ils financé la vie de tous les jours au treizième siècle, tout en respectant les exigences du

---

[*] Une version antérieure de cette contribution a été écrite et présentée par Laurent Waelkens, professeur émérite de droit romain à la KU Leuven, lors d'une réunion d'experts du 30 avril au 2 mai 2019 au couvent des dominicains à Leuven, autour de l'ouvrage du dominicain Antoninus Hendrik Thomas sur les anciennes constitutions. Peu de jours après cette intervention, le professeur Waelkens a été hospitalisé pour une cure de longue durée. Il est malheureusement décédé le 6 juin 2020. Sur la demande de ce dernier, Wouter Druwé, son successeur comme professeur de droit romain et d'histoire du droit à la KU Leuven, a complété la présente contribution, en incluant des notes de bas de page et en réécrivant certains passages, toujours néanmoins en restant fidèle à la thèse que le professeur Waelkens a voulu exprimer. Cette contribution a aussi bénéficié du conseil linguistique de Mme Frédérique Waelkens-Donnay.

1 Voir : Antoninus Hendrik Thomas, *De oudste constituties van de dominicanen : Voorgeschiedenis, tekst, bronnen, ontstaan en ontwikkeling (1215-1237) met uitgave van de tekst* (BRHE, 42) (Leuven : Bureel van de RHE, 1965), pp. 133-134 [pp. 285-286] et 331-339 [p. 423] (dist. 1, cap. 21-25).

A Cathedral of Constitutional Law, éd. par Anton MILH O.P. and Mark BUTAYE O.P., Turnhout, Brepols, 2023 (*Bibliothèque de la Revue d'histoire ecclésiastique*, 112), p. 73-86.
BREPOLS ❧ PUBLISHERS   10.1484/M.BRHE-EB.5.135045

fondateur ? Pour bien illustrer le sujet, nous aimerions expliquer comment les couvents et les groupements religieux géraient leur patrimoine avant le treizième siècle et quels étaient les nouveaux moyens créés à l'époque de saint Dominique. Ce n'est pas un hasard si l'Ordre des Prêcheurs s'est développé aux alentours des premières universités.

1. La gestion de biens collectifs dans l'Antiquité romaine et au Moyen Âge

Pour bien comprendre une réalité du treizième siècle, nous retournons donc à l'Antiquité romaine. Le droit romain, en Occident dans sa version latine et en Orient dans sa version grecque, n'a jamais cessé d'influencer les sociétés postérieures, voire de conditionner leur pensée. Comment les premiers groupements religieux chrétiens ont-ils géré leurs biens communs et comment pouvait-on en général gérer des biens susceptibles de servir au bien commun d'un groupement ou d'une association ?

1.1. La confraternité

Une première formule a été celle de la confraternité, qui était basée sur la famille (*familia*). Dans l'Antiquité, la famille n'était pas constituée d'office par la cohabitation ni par le mariage d'un couple, elle était voulue et décidée séparément de l'union personnelle[2]. Tout homme libre et toute femme libre pouvaient se constituer une famille, avec un patrimoine séparé, et pouvaient organiser des échanges de biens à partir de cette famille qui était une structure de patrimoine et de responsabilités, une structure d'avoirs et d'obligations[3]. Plusieurs hommes libres pouvaient ainsi également décider de mettre leurs biens en commun – en utilisant la technique de l'*adrogatio*[4] – et de se constituer une *familia* dans un but religieux. Ils devenaient ainsi comme des frères dans une confraternité : il n'y avait plus qu'un patrimoine commun, avec un seul gérant des biens mis en commun, seul le *paterfamilias* se trouvait confronté aux créditeurs et organisait la gestion du temporel.

---

2 Pour une discussion des différentes formes de cohabitation en Antiquité et de leur survivance au Moyen Âge, voir : Laurent Waelkens, 'Medieval Family and Marriage Law : From Actions of Status to Legal Doctrine', in *The Creation of the Ius Commune : From Casus to Regula*, éd. par John W. Cairns et Paul J. du Plessis (Edinburgh : Edinburgh University Press, 2010), 103-125.

3 Sur la *familia* romaine voir : Laurent Waelkens, *Amne adverso : Roman Legal Heritage in European Culture* (Leuven : Leuven University Press, 2015), pp. 193-200.

4 Selon les *Institutes* de Justinien (1, 11, 4), cette technique avait néanmoins comme condition que l'*adrogans* (celui qui deviendrait le seul *paterfamilias* des familles fusionnées) ait au moins 18 ans de plus que l'*adrogatus*.

Dans la sphère religieuse, la *familia papalis* et la *familia episcopalis* (d'une façon analogue à la *familia Caesaris*) semblent avoir été de ce type : durant le temps d'une papauté ou d'un épiscopat, l'entourage immédiat du pape et des évêques étaient censés vivre comme *familiares*, dans une sorte de confraternité avec leur patron[5]. Leurs revenus tombaient alors dans la communauté des biens papaux ou épiscopaux. On ne pouvait les citer en justice, le pape ou l'évêque étant présumé seul responsable pour les obligations de son entourage dans l'exercice de ses fonctions. La famille des papes et évêques a prouvé son utilité, mais comportait un grand inconvénient car lors de la mort du titulaire ou du déplacement d'un évêque, cette confraternité cessait d'exister.

Au Moyen Âge, la confraternité (ou le confrèrement) laïque se retrouve encore couramment, mais dans la littérature on ne trouve pas d'exemples où cette formule est appliquée à un prieuré ou un couvent[6]. En effet, deux éléments caractéristiques de la confraternité antique la rendaient peu pratique pour les dominicains. En premier lieu les confrères n'avaient aucun contrôle sur la gestion et la destination des biens et surtout, la famille – et donc la confraternité – était dissoute par la mort du *paterfamilias*. En l'absence d'un testament, mêmes les biens d'origine commune se trouvant dans ses avoirs partaient chez ses héritiers personnels. La confraternité était une bonne formule pour travailler ensemble, mais ne permettait pas de construire un avenir.

1.2. La fiducie

Une deuxième formule était nettement plus adaptée à la formation de patrimoines susceptibles de servir les destins des communautés chrétiennes : la *fiducia*, en anglais le *trust*, en allemand le *Treuhand*, en néerlandais le *hoede*. La base de cette institution est simple. Deux personnes font un *pactum fiduciae*. L'un cède des biens à l'autre, mais l'autre doit respecter le but de la cession formulée dans le pacte de fiducie. Bien qu'il ne nous reste que peu de textes antiques sur la fiducie, il semble probable que le but du *pactum fiduciae* ait pu être n'importe lequel, par exemple « investir dans des appartements, construire un silo, participer dans

---

5 Voir, par exemple, sur la *familia* des évêques d'Augsbourg et de Worms aux dixième et onzième siècles : Ludolf Kuchenbuch, 'Abschied von der Grundherrschaft : Ein Prüfgang durch das ostfränkisch-deutsche Reich', *Zeitschrift der Savigny-Stiftung – Germanistische Abteilung*, 121 (2004), 1-99 (pp. 18-22 et 40-52).

6 Voir, sur l'affrèrement, le confrèrement ou la confraternité laïque en France au Moyen Âge : Jean-François Poudret, 'Vie communautaire et séparation : Confrontation de la pratique médiévale et du droit savant', *Revue historique de droit français et étranger*, 74 (1996), 199-220. Il s'agissait par exemple d'une vie en commun qui résultait de l'indivision prolongée entre les héritiers, ou d'une poursuite de la vie commune entre père et fils nonobstant le mariage de celui-ci, mais aussi de véritables contrats d'affrèrement (*affreramentum* ou *affrareschatio*). Parfois, cette forme d'affrèrement est comparée à une *societas generalis omnium bonorum* de droit romain.

le capital d'un magasin »[7]. Si le fiduciaire ne fait pas ce qui a été entendu avec le fiduciant, ce dernier – ou ses successeurs – pouvaient le citer en justice pour voir appliquer le pacte de fiducie. Il est néanmoins important de souligner que l'*actio fiduciae* restait une *actio in personam*, sans caractère réel. Néanmoins, la *fiducia* se maintenait après la mort du fiduciaire. En cas d'un tel décès, les comptes fiduciaires passaient aux ayant droits prévus dans le *pactum fiduciae*. Si de son côté le fiduciaire avait des sommes ou des biens à exiger, il le faisait avec l'*actio fiduciae contraria*[8].

1.3. La fiducie au service des évêques

Depuis l'Antiquité tardive, la fiducie a été d'une grande importance pour les églises, car elle a aussi servi pour les donations pieuses (souvent *mortis causa*)[9]. Par des dons ou des legs, des chrétiens transmettaient aux évêques des biens immobiliers en fiducie, les destinant précisément à l'enseignement, à l'hospitalité, aux prisonniers, aux pauvres, aux malades.

Certains évêques géraient ces biens avec un tel soin, qu'on leur confiait même des biens fiduciaires qui ne leur étaient pas expressément alloués. Dans le *Code* de Justinien nous lisons comment l'évêque de Rome reçut du tribunal des biens qui dans des testaments avaient été légués « aux pauvres » et « aux prisonniers » sans qu'il fût mis dans le testament que l'évêque de Rome en était l'héritier[10]. Il

---

7 Lors du processus de la codification justinienne, les références à la *fiducia* comme forme de sûreté réelle ont été supprimées. Dans le *Corpus iuris civilis* de Justinien, la *fiducia* n'apparaît que rarement, et toujours dans le sens d'une « fiducia cum amico, quo tutius nostrae res apud eum essent ». Dans ce dernier cas, le but de la *fiducia* était surtout un dépôt (*depositum*). Voir par exemple : *Digeste* de Justinien (*Dig.*) 39, 6, 42. Voir aussi : David Johnston, 'Trusts and Trust-like Devices in Roman Law', in *Itinera Fiduciae : Trust and Treuhand in Historical Perspective* (Comparative Studies in Continental and Anglo-American Legal History, 19), éd. par Richard Helmholz et Reinhard Zimmermann (Berlin : Duncker und Humblot, 1998), 45-56. Néanmoins, l'idée d'une fiducie subsistait.

8 Waelkens, *Amne adverso...* [voir note 3], pp. 248-249. Sur la *fiducia* en droit romain antique, voir par exemple : Gijsbert Noordraven, *De Fiducia in het Romeinse recht* (Arnhem : Gouda Quint, 1988) ; Max Kaser, *Das römische Privatrecht*, 2 t. (Munich : Beck, ²1971-1975), I (1971) : *Das altrömische, das vorklassische und klassische Recht*, pp. 133-134, 415, 460-463.

9 Sur la *Fortleben* de la *donatio mortis causa* au Haut Moyen Âge, voir : Harald Siems, 'Von den *piae causae* zu den Xenodochien', in *Itinera Fiduciae...* [voir note 7], 57-84. Voir aussi, sur l'importance des donations pieuses aux dixième et onzième siècles : Eliana Magnani, 'Transforming Things and Persons : The Gift *pro anima* in the Eleventh and Twelfth Centuries', in *Negotiating the Gift : Premodern Figurations of Exchange* (Veröffentlichungen des Max-Planck-Instituts für Geschichte, 188), éd. par Gadi Algazi, Valentin Groebner et Bernhard Jussen (Göttingen : Vandenhoeck und Ruprecht, 2003), 269-284. Et, sur la conception de ces donations pieuses en Occident et dans l'Empire byzantin : Annick Peters-Custot, 'Les donations pieuses dans l'Italie méridionale normande : *quid* du don/contre-don dans une terre influencée par l'héritage culturel et juridique byzantin ?', in *Ius commune graeco-romanum : Essays in Honour of Prof. Dr. Laurent Waelkens* (Iuris Scripta Historica, 30), éd. par Wouter Druwé, Wim Decock, Paolo Angelini et Matthias Castelein (Leuven : Peeters, 2019), 109-128.

10 *Code* de Justinien (*Cod.*) 6, 48, 26.

suffisait qu'au moment de la division du testament il sache garantir la destination des biens. Si un évêque tenait un compte en faveur des prisonniers qui était contrôlable et semblait fonctionner sérieusement, les tribunaux n'avaient aucun impédiment pour lui accorder ce qu'un *de cujus* avait destiné dans son testament aux prisonniers. Au sixième siècle les œuvres des évêques étaient tellement bien structurées, que l'empereur et la juridiction suprême leur attribuèrent en fiducie tous les biens dont la destination touchait quelque peu leur action. Dans les *Novelles* de Justinien on découvre un testament qui contenait une donation « au Christ ». L'évêque du lieu exigea cette somme du successeur universel, mais ce dernier prétendît que l'évêque n'était pas le Christ. Le juge donna pourtant raison à l'évêque[11]. Dans une autre sentence une donation à un saint devait être rendue à une institution de bienfaisance dans la région qui portait le nom de ce saint[12]. Nous lisons même un cas où dans un legs « aux pauvres » il est expressément stipulé qu'il ne pouvait être confié à l'évêque. Le juge impérial l'a néanmoins attribué à ce dernier parce que les avocats des héritiers ne surent présenter une meilleure solution. Au moins les biens serviraient au but auquel ils avaient été désignés[13].

Les évêques qui géraient ces biens en fiducie, devaient faire attention à ne pas mêler des comptes. En cas de conflit, la gestion des biens épiscopaux était contrôlée par les tribunaux impériaux[14]. Ils ne pouvaient évidemment pas léguer ces biens à leurs propres parents. Dans ces mêmes textes juridiques de Constantinople nous trouvons même des décisions plus générales selon lesquelles les donations pieuses ne pouvaient retourner au domaine privé[15]. Chez nous ces décisions étaient reprises dans les ordonnances de Charlemagne (747/748-814) et de Louis le Pieux (778-840)[16]. Dorénavant des donations pieuses resteraient jusqu'à la fin des temps dans la mainmorte.

1.4. Les aléas de la fiducie au Moyen Âge

Si ce système a si bien fonctionné dans l'Empire, pourquoi n'a-t-il pas pu être repris par les dominicains au treizième siècle ? Au premier Moyen Âge, il y a une évolution qui, dans beaucoup de régions occidentales, a rendu impossible la fiducie des biens ecclésiastiques. Au premier siècle, l'empereur Auguste

---

11 *Novelles* de Justinien (*Nov.*) 131, 9*pr.*

12 *Nov.* 131, 9, 1.

13 *Nov.* 131, 11.

14 Dans de différentes décisions citées au titre *De episcopis et clericis* du *Code* de Justinien (1, 3), les empereurs ont averti les évêques que leurs comptes seraient contrôlés.

15 Voir, par exemple : *Cod.* 1, 3, 41 (42), 5 ; *Nov.* 7, 1-2.

16 Ainsi, Louis le Pieux a promulgué la *Novelle* de Justinien 7, 1-2, dans son royaume. Voir aussi : Adolphe de Watteville, 'Préface', in *Législation charitable ou Recueil des lois, arrêtés, décrets, ordonnances royales* (Paris : Librairie de jurisprudence de Cotillon, ²1847), i-xv (pp. iii-iv) et Pierre Petot, 'L'origine de la mainmorte servile', *Revue historique de droit français et étranger*, 19 (1940-1941), 275-309 (pp. 276-278).

(63 av. J.-C. - 14 apr. J.-C.) ramena d'Égypte une nouvelle technique de gestion des terres agricoles. En Égypte, toutes les terres appartenaient en principe au pharaon, qui les concédait au plus offrant. Auguste reprit cette façon de penser dans ses provinces impériales, notamment en Orient[17]. Après lui, tous les empereurs ont appliqué cette technique dans l'Empire d'Orient, sauf dans la province de Constantinople, la nouvelle Rome. Leur administration allouait les terres aux paysans en concession, c'est-à-dire dans un statut précaire, et en posant des conditions d'exploitation. Si les concessionnaires (souvent appelés *coloni*) ne respectaient pas les conditions, la concession pouvait être annulée et la terre allouée à autrui[18]. Dans l'Empire d'Occident, dont beaucoup de provinces sont restées sous le contrôle du Sénat jusqu'au troisième siècle, la tradition fut différente. On y considérait que tout citoyen pouvait acquérir des terres en pleine propriété, qu'il en devenait le *dominus* et le transmettait ensuite librement à qui il voulait[19].

Au moment où ils ont été coupés politiquement de Rome, beaucoup de princes occidentaux se considérèrent les successeurs de l'empereur d'Occident et continuèrent à utiliser le droit romain[20]. Mais il est incroyable de constater avec quelle vitesse des évolutions juridiques provenant d'Italie, voire d'Orient, gagnèrent le Nord. À partir du sixième siècle en Gaule et en Rhénanie, trois siècles plus tard jusqu'en Scandinavie, on reprit l'idée orientale que l'empereur est le propriétaire ultime des terres agricoles et ne les cède qu'en concession. La version occidentale de ces concessions deviendrait le droit féodal[21]. Le seul prince – en principe le juge suprême – alloue des terres et les destine, normalement au profit de sa politique, dans la plupart des cas au profit de ses guerres. Et l'idée de la donation pieuse devant servir à jamais aux causes sociales ? Les princes prétendent simplement que le domaine public aussi appartient à ce monde de bienfaisance et qu'ils peuvent attribuer les bénéfices de ces biens aussi bien à la guerre qu'aux œuvres des évêques.

Dans ce raisonnement la fiducie des terres accordés aux évêques devient illégale : la destination des terres appartient au prince et lorsqu'un évêque meurt ou qu'il est déplacé, ses terres doivent revenir au prince local. En Occident,

---

17 Voir : Waelkens, *Amne adverso…* [voir note 3], pp. 53-56.

18 Cette technique juridique des concessions survivait dans l'Empire d'Orient. Voir, par exemple : Alan Harvey, *Economic Expansion in the Byzantine Empire, 900-1200* (Cambridge : Cambridge University Press, 1989), pp. 46-47 ; Jacques Lefort, 'Rural Economy and Social Relations in the Countryside', *Dumbarton Oaks Papers*, 47 (1993), 101-113 (pp. 106-107) et Mapia Mataiqy, 'Conceding Land to Small Peasants-Paroikoi during the Palaiologan Period', *Byzantin Symmeikta*, 24 (2014), 111-127 (p. 127).

19 Kaser, *Das römische Privatrecht…* [voir note 8], II (1975) : *Die nachklassischen Entwicklungen*, pp. 250-251.

20 Voir, par exemple : Detlef Liebs, *Römische Jurisprudenz in Gallien (2. bis 8. Jahrhundert)* (Freiburger Rechtsgeschichtliche Abhandlungen – Neue Folge, 38) (Berlin : Duncker und Humblot, 2002) et Dietrich Claude, 'Niedergang, Renaissance und Ende der Präfekturverwaltung im Westen des römischen Reichs (5.-8. Jh.)', *Zeitschrift der Savigny-Stiftung für Rechtsgeschichte – Germanistische Abteilung*, 114 (1997), 352-379.

21 Waelkens, *Amne adverso…* [voir note 3], pp. 86-89.

beaucoup de tribunaux jugeaient que la fiducie était un droit féodal réservé au souverain. Dans certaines régions on y ajouta que les évêques ne se battaient pas et que dès lors ils ne pouvaient accéder au droit civil. Les anciennes libertés romaines n'étaient qu'accordées aux guerriers. Les églises, qui ne s'engagent ni dans la guerre ni dans l'ost, n'ont donc pas la *libertas* nécessaire à la tenure des terres. Entre le septième et le neuvième siècle, d'après la région, la fiducie accordée aux évêques disparut et beaucoup d'évêques se mirent au service du prince afin d'obtenir un champ d'action minimal pour leurs œuvres sous la forme de bénéfices[22].

1.5. La possession

Et pourtant, pendant que les évêques se soumettaient aux princes pour s'assurer des revenus, les abbayes, d'abord de saint Colomban (540-615) et ensuite celles des bénédictins rassemblèrent des terres sans fin. Pour expliquer leur façon de travailler, il faut rejoindre à nouveau l'Empire romain et découvrir la façon dont les biens des communes romaines étaient administrés.

Dans la République et l'Empire romains, il n'existait pas de patrimoine communal *stricto sensu*. Les habitants d'un municipe élisaient un conseil communal et ensuite le conseil communal nommait un receveur. Tant que le nouveau conseil n'était pas installé, l'ancien continuait de fonctionner. Si un membre du conseil mourait, le conseil subsistait et élisait simplement un nouveau membre. La commune était donc immortelle[23]. Ce que la majorité du conseil avait décidé était censé être décidé par tous et le receveur devait s'y tenir[24]. Si le conseil avait voté une taxe, le trésorier l'exigeait de chaque contribuable et plaçait l'argent sur un compte de sa propre *familia*, mais un compte destiné à la commune. Si le conseil municipal décidait d'agrandir la maison communale, le receveur communal payait de cet argent qu'il trouvait dans sa *familia*, dans son patrimoine, mais sur un compte destiné exclusivement à la commune. Tant qu'il respectait les procédures d'entrées et de sorties d'argent, il était couvert. S'il commettait des irrégularités, le gouverneur provincial pouvait intervenir et affecter les comptes. Tant que lui aussi respectait les procédures, il était couvert aussi. À la fin de chaque administration, l'ancien magistrat municipal était obligé de se tenir à la

---

22 Laurent Waelkens, '*Libertas ecclesiae* herbekeken', in *Recht in geschiedenis : Een bundel bijdragen over de rechtsgeschiedenis van de middeleeuwen tot de hedendaagse tijd*, éd. par Vivian Boulpaep *et al.* (Leuven : Davidsfonds, 2006), 497-504, avec comme source principale : Brigitte Szabó-Bechstein, *Libertas Ecclesiae : Ein Schlüsselbegriff des Investiturstreits und seine Vorgeschichte, 4.-11. Jahrhundert* (Studi gregoriani per la storia della 'libertas ecclesiae', 12) (Rome : Libreria Ateneo Salesiano, 1985).

23 *Dig.* 3, 4, 7, 2 (Ulpianus X ad edictum).

24 *Dig.* 50, 1, 19 (Scaevola I quaestionum) : « Quod maior pars curiae effecit, pro eo habetur, ac si omnes egerint. »

disposition de la justice pour répondre aux éventuelles plaintes[25]. Mais on peut se demander à qui appartenait l'argent qui se trouvait sur le compte et à qui appartenait la maison communale. Au milieu du deuxième siècle, le juriste Gaius (*c.* 110-180) donnait une réponse simple : à l'*universitas*, à l'universalité, sans que cette universalité jouisse elle-même d'une personnalité juridique[26]. Si les procédures étaient respectées et que personne ne pouvait être citée en justice, la question du patrimoine était sans importance. Voilà donc une institution – le municipe – qui était immortelle et pouvait disposer de biens à jamais.

Des abbayes se sont inspirées de cette procédure communale. Les membres de celles-ci appointaient un chapitre qui était compétent pour leurs finances, la *curia*, qui fonctionnait comme un conseil communal. Si un membre agissait en public, il engageait l'abbaye pour autant qu'il se conforma aux procédures convenues. S'il mourait, ses compétences retournaient chez les autres membres de la *curia*. À la mort d'un *curialis* il n'y avait donc pas de contrôle judiciaire comme sur une succession – tout continuait comme avant[27]. Ainsi du côté de la gestion du patrimoine, l'abbaye devenait immortelle. Les biens acquis appartenaient à l'*universitas*. Personne ne devait s'en inquiéter. On ne s'inquiétait pas de savoir si l'abbaye avait le statut d'une fondation ou d'une personnalité juridique – tant qu'elle respectait ses procédures, sa situation était protégée par les tribunaux.

Pendant le premier Moyen Âge et à l'époque de la querelle des investitures les abbayes ont cependant été également confrontées au problème du *dominium* princier sur les terres agricoles. Le problème se révéla moins urgent que dans le cas des évêques, dont chaque succession nécessitait l'agrément des juges du prince local. Les abbayes détenaient de grands domaines et dans beaucoup de régions les princes prétendirent que les droits ultimes sur ces terres leur revenaient, que les abbayes étaient donc redevables envers le prince[28]. La réponse collective doit avoir été que les abbayes n'avaient rien à faire avec le droit de succession, puisqu'elles étaient immortelles, qu'elles ne détenaient pas leurs terres en fiducie et qu'elles ne les revendiquaient pas devant les tribunaux. Elles les détenaient en possession (*possessio*) et dès lors elles n'avaient rien à faire avec le *dominium* ultime du prince.

---

25 Voir, pour un exemple de statuts communaux avec des dispositions pareilles : Julián González et Michael H. Crawford, 'The Lex Irnitana : A New Copy of the Flavian Municipal Law', *The Journal of Roman Studies*, 76 (1986), 147-243.

26 *Institutiones Gai* 2, 11 : « Quae publicae sunt, nullius videntur in bonis esse; ipsius enim universitatis esse creduntur. »

27 *Edictum Theoderici regis Italiae* (Università degli studi di Camerino – Istituto giuridico. Testi per esercitazioni, 4/1), éd. par Pier Luigi Falaschi (Milan : Giuffrè, 1966), n° 27 : « Curialis si sine successore intestatus defecerit. »

28 Szabó-Bechstein, *Libertas Ecclesiae...* [voir note 22].

Mais qu'est-ce donc une possession[29] ? Elle provient également de la procédure romaine et ne peut être confondue avec le *dominium* ou la propriété. Si
deux hommes avaient un conflit au sujet d'un terrain et qu'ils le soumettaient
au juge, lors de leur première comparution le juge se devait d'accorder le terrain
provisoirement à l'un des deux. Cette attribution provisoire, c'était la possession :
l'un des deux pouvait rester assis sur le terrain, *potest sedere*. Si l'autre n'était
pas d'accord avec cette attribution provisoire, il devait intenter la procédure de
revendication contre le possesseur, ce qui le conduisait chez un juge du fond qui
analysait la question de fond en comble avant de se prononcer définitivement.
Il y avait cependant des temps de prescription à respecter. On ne pouvait obtenir une décision de possession que si on avait amené son conflit dans l'année
devant le juge[30]. Ensuite si on voulait mettre en doute la solution provisoire du
premier juge, il fallait réagir à temps. Ce temps était de dix ans en matière de
biens immobiliers. Celui qui n'avait pas réagi dans les dix ans contre l'attribution
d'une possession, ne pouvait plus la mettre en doute[31]. La possession devenait
permanente. Le bénéficiaire n'en était pour autant pas devenu *dominus*. Il était
possesseur, mais par la prescription sa possession était devenue intouchable[32]. La
question du *dominium* ne se posait plus.

Voilà ce que les abbayes pouvaient invoquer au Moyen Âge face aux princes.
Elles se considéraient comme des possesseurs de leurs terres et étaient convaincues que personne ne pouvait les en déloger. Leurs *curiae* étaient immortelles, les
règles de succession ne s'appliquaient pas à elles. Elles tombaient en dehors de
la féodalité. À aucun moment, les princes ou leurs juges n'étaient censés pouvoir
intervenir. Néanmoins, sur un point cette argumentation risquait d'être assez
faible. En effet, en droit romain l'établissement d'une *possessio* nécessitait une
décision d'un juge impérial. La majorité des abbayes ne disposait pas d'une telle
décision, même ancienne. C'est pourquoi elles développèrent un autre raisonnement pour suppléer l'argumentation basée sur la *possessio*. Ce raisonnement
supplémentaire était fondé sur la *custodia*, une tenure en droit romain dont
le titulaire était responsable pour toute perte ou tout dommage[33]. Selon cette
argumentation, ceux qui voulaient contester la *custodia* des abbayes, devaient
obtenir la possession auprès des juges princiers, mais le droit romain stipulait un
délai strict de forclusion d'une année. Par conséquent, tous ces délais étaient déjà
échus. Et si après un an et un jour plus personne ne pouvait demander une mise
en possession, on pourrait conclure que les abbayes elles-mêmes tenaient cette
possession. Ainsi les abbayes ont traversé l'époque des investitures et la féodalité

---

29 Sur la *possessio* en droit romain, voir : Waelkens, *Amne adverso...* [voir note 3], pp. 278-286 ; Kaser,
Das römische Privatrecht... [voir note 8], I, pp. 387-389 (sur la relation entre la possession et les
décisions provisoires, *interdicta*) et pp. 396-400 (sur la protection possessoire).

30 Voir : *Institutiones Gai* 4, 150 et *Dig.* 43, 31, 1pr.

31 *Cod.* 7, 35, 7 (Dioclétien et Maximien, 294).

32 Voir, sur le caractère de la *praescriptio longi temporis* comme une *exceptio* : Kaser, *Das römische
Privatrecht...* [voir note 8], I, pp. 424-425.

33 Kaser, *Das römische Privatrecht...* [voir note 8], I, pp. 506-509.

sans grand risque de perdre leurs biens. Leurs terres n'étaient – en principe – pas soumises à la féodalité, elles étaient allodiales, et donc insaisissables sans violence armée – et la plupart des princes médiévaux avaient horreur de la violence armée contre le clergé.

Grâce en partie à cette autonomie juridique du système féodal, beaucoup d'abbayes accumulèrent de nombreuses possessions. Cette manière notamment de vivre de ses biens choqua saint Dominique. Néanmoins, au début du douzième siècle il n'y avait toujours pas d'autre choix : ou bien les abbayes géraient librement des fortunes, ou bien leurs biens étaient en fiduciaire et étaient tôt ou tard détournés par les princes.

2. La double juridiction

Une première solution se dessina en 1122 dans le concordat de Worms, conclu entre l'empereur Henri V (1086-1125) et le pape Calixte II (1060-1124) et qui distingua dorénavant deux juridictions distinctes, celle de l'empereur et celle du pape. Gratien, professeur de droit canonique (*magister*) à Bologne, et les premiers décrétistes essayèrent de définir les droits de l'Église dans cette nouvelle situation. La première version du *Décret* de Gratien – probablement écrite dans les années 1130 – semble avoir été une longue plaidoirie pour une justice autonome ecclésiastique[34]. De 1125 à 1150 des juristes ont probablement ajouté 240 textes au *Code* de Justinien qui concernaient la compétence des églises[35]. Une chose restait cependant inaltérée dans la vision des princes : la fiducie restait féodale et était donc encore soumise aux tribunaux impériaux – ou aux tribunaux féodaux délégués. Des canonistes comme Gratien († av. 1179) ou Huguccio de Pise (*c.* 1140-1210) ont cherché à défendre les biens ecclésiastiques, et en effet, dès le douzième siècle les canonistes ont obtenu dans plusieurs régions que les bénéfices des biens fiscaux au profit de l'Église, donc la recette des anciens biens épiscopaux saisis par les princes, seraient alloués par la justice ecclésiastique. Néanmoins, la fiducie en restait exclue, jusqu'en 1158, l'année de la Diète de Roncaglia.

Vers 1100 la dame la plus riche de l'Occident, la comtesse Mathilde de Canossa (*c.* 1046-1115), fonda une école à Bologne. On y étudierait le droit romain.

---

34 Laurent Waelkens, 'Le Décret de Gratien : ouvrage scientifique ou plaidoirie d'un canoniste face à l'ordre impérial ?', in *Recto ordine procedit magister : Liber amicorum E.C. Coppens* (Iuris Scripta Historica, 28), éd. par Jan Hallebeek, Louis Berkvens, Georges Martyn et Paul Nève (Bruxelles : KVAB, 2012). Bien sûr, le *Décret* de Gratien a aussi fonctionné comme un manuel pour l'éducation canonistique : Péter Erdö, *Geschichte der Wissenschaft vom kanonischen Recht : Eine Einführung* (Kirchenrechtliche Bibliothek, 4), éd. par Ludger Müller (Berlin : Lit Verlag, 2006), pp. 49-51 et Joseph Goering, 'The Scholastic Turn (1100-1500) : Penitential Theology and Law in the Schools', in *A New History of Penance* (Brill's Companion to the Christian Tradition, 14), éd. par Abigail Firey (Leiden : Brill, 2008), 219-237.

35 Laurent Waelkens, 'L'hérésie des premiers titres du Code de Justinien : Une hypothèse sur la rédaction tardive de C. 1,1-13', *Revue d'histoire du droit*, 79 (2011), 253-296.

Cette idée de l'étude du droit fut bien accueillie partout. Beaucoup des grands vassaux de l'empereur envoyèrent des gens de leur administration à Bologne. Des dizaines de grands seigneurs voulaient y fonder des nations ou collèges, des logis pour leurs ressortissants. Le seul moyen de financement durable était de nouveau la mise à disposition de fermes ou de terres agricoles dont les fruits alimenteraient les nations, mais alors resurgit le vieux problème des terres destinées. Comment garantir qu'après vingt ans, ou lors d'un procès, ou avec une théorie sur le caractère féodal de la fiducie, les juges impériaux ne puissent saisir ces terres ? La question a été largement débattue entre l'empereur et ses grands vassaux en 1158, à la Diète de Roncaglia. À la fin, la Diète obtint que l'empereur Frédérique Barberousse (1122-1190) délégua à l'université de Bologne sa propre justice impériale sur tout ce qui concerne l'école de droit de Bologne[36]. Dorénavant les professeurs et les étudiants immatriculés ne seraient plus soumis qu'à la justice de leur école. Tout comme ses vassaux l'empereur trouvait important que le droit romain fût étudié de façon approfondie. Pour ces raisons, tous les grands vassaux investirent dans leurs nations, et bien selon la vieille formule romaine de la fiducie. Ils donnèrent des terres en fiducie aux directeurs des nations, avec le but de rendre possible les études de droit d'un certain nombre de leurs ressortissants. À Bologne le nouveau tribunal de l'école de droit aurait bien eu tort de ne pas garantir à ces bienfaiteurs que leurs biens engagés ne seraient jamais considérés comme des biens féodaux. Dans sa jurisprudence autonome, le tribunal de l'école de droit réintroduisait la fiducie romaine sous sa forme originale : avec des biens destinés à un but précis et des donateurs qui avaient le contrôle sur le bon usage des moyens.

Les premiers professeurs de droit se mettaient en association avec leurs étudiants. Ils formaient des petites *societates* avec six ou sept étudiants et décidaient librement des tarifs qu'ils leur imposaient. Afin de faire baisser les prix, les collèges commencèrent à discuter les prix des cours avec les professeurs. Ils approchèrent d'abord individuellement des professeurs, mais après quelque temps les professeurs s'associèrent eux aussi pour mieux discuter avec les collèges. L'organisation de ce groupe des professeurs était basée sur celle des communes romaines. Ils avaient une assemblée qui prenait des décisions, un recteur qui discutait au nom du groupe des professeurs et un receveur qui exécutait les décisions, qui recevait l'argent des collèges et le distribuait entre les professeurs. L'argent que les collèges payaient, appartenait à l'*universitas*, comme dans l'Antiquité. Néanmoins, au douzième siècle cette *universitas* ne fut plus considérée comme une abstraction, mais à Bologne devint le nom de l'association des *scholares*, l'*universitas scholarum*. Pendant cinquante ans il subsista deux universités côte à côte, mais au treizième siècle elles fusionnèrent en une entité, une seule université.

Dans un cours de droit bolonais, rapporté dans la *Glose* d'Accurse (*c.* 1182-1263), nous trouvons un passage sur les problèmes que les collèges

---

36 Authentica *'Habita'* post *Cod.* 4, 13.

eurent pour assurer leur pérennité, surtout en cas du décès du dernier directeur d'un collège[37]. La question se posait notamment de savoir si les biens fiduciaires qui se trouvaient dans son patrimoine partaient à ses héritiers propres ou au fisc. On remarque que la question a tourmenté les universitaires, puisque le professeur qui répond dans la *Glose* se base sur une théorie formulée par le professeur local Moïse de Ravenne († apr. 1157), qui enseignait dans les années 1140, donc bien avant Roncaglia, et qui avait proposé que ces biens appartiennent au bâtiment du collège. D'autres, comme Jean Bassian († 1197), argumentaient qu'après le décès du dernier directeur, les biens du collège ne se trouvaient dans aucun patrimoine – comme une *hereditas iacens* – en attendant la nomination rétroactive d'un nouveau gérant. Lorsqu'une personne mourait, comme le dernier gérant d'un collège, les revenus et les frais de la succession restaient théoriquement chez lui jusqu'à la division de la succession – et ensuite devenaient le *dominium* des héritiers avec effet rétroactif jusqu'à sa mort. Pendant des mois les biens pouvaient donc appartenir à un mort, qui était considéré comme une personne fictive. Cette notion fut utilisée pour la première fois explicitement par Sinibaldo dei Fieschi (1195-1254), le futur Innocent IV (r. 1243-1254)[38]. Bref, il suffisait donc d'inscrire dans les statuts des collèges que leurs gérants auraient cette position d'une personne fictive dans le cas où un collège se trouvait sans gérants. Jusqu'au partage et à l'attribution à un nouveau gérant, les biens appartiendraient à la personne fictive du gérant décédé.

---

37 Gl. '*Nomen universitatis*' ad *Dig.* 3, 4, 7, 2 : « Item quid si nullus omnino remansit? Respondit Ioannes [Bassianum] solutum esse collegium: et res in nullius bonis sunt, sicut et hereditariae: sed tamen si postea auctoritate domini papae, vel eius ad quem spectat cura eiusdem collegii, instituatur aliquis in eodem collegio, iuris artificio fingitur istius fuisse, ut (...), licet quidem archiepiscopus Moyses ipsos parietes possidere dixerit etiam durante collegio: quod durissimum est dicere, et contra legem videtur, ut (...). Verum tamen id esse videtur, ut nullo modo dicantur esse ullius, scilicet ab tempore quo solutum est collegium: sed ipso iure sint fisco vel papae quaesita, ut (...), et hoc quantum ad dominium: secus quantum ad possessionem, ut (...). Posset tamen pro Moyse allegari quod plerunque dicitur Ecclesia ipse locus parietibus circundatus, et etiam consecratus: et alias dicitur Ecclesia ius habere, et possidere, et vindicare, ut (...). Unde videtur quod talis locus siue parietes possideant etiam durante collegio: et vindicent per praelatos tanquam quilibet priuatus per procuratorem vel colonum. »

38 Sinibaldo dei Fieschi, *Commentaria super libros quinque Decretalium* (ici : l'édition Frankfurt-am-Main, 1570), ad X 2, 20, 57, *Praesentium*, n° 5 : « (...) quia cum collegium in causa universitatis fungatur una persona ». Voir aussi : Adriana Campitelli, '« Cum collegium in causa Universitatis fingatur una persona » : Riflessioni sul commento di Sinibaldo dei Fieschi (c. praesentium, de testibus et attestationibus, 57 X, 2, 20) – La persona giuridica collegiale in diritto romano e canonico', in « *Aequitas romana ed aequitas canonica* » : *Atti del III Colloquio (Roma 24-26 aprile 1980) e del IV Colloquio (Roma 13-14 maggio 1981) 'Diritto romano – diritto canonico'*, éd. par Tarcisio Bertone et Oddo Bucci (Vatican : Libreria Editrice Vaticana – Libreria Editrice Lateranense, 1990), 125-131.

3. Conclusion

Voilà donc ce que saint Dominique trouva à Bologne au début du treizième siècle : une entière liberté de gérer des biens avec des contrôles possibles par la justice. À Toulouse il avait vu l'insécurité et l'instabilité d'une confraternité, à Bologne il trouvait le cadre juridique pour réaliser de façon stable son ordre mendiant. Seulement, il fallait devenir collège faisant partie de l'université. Il fallait envoyer des étudiants à la faculté de droit canon ou à la nouvelle faculté de théologie et adopter le ton juridique des juristes de Bologne dans les premières constitutions. Une fois que les prédicateurs eurent à Bologne leur juriste Raymond de Peñafort (1175-1275), tous ces problèmes fondirent comme de la glace au soleil : ils avaient pignon sur rue à Bologne.

Mais comment commencer une fondation ailleurs ? Les autres universités naissantes avaient également besoin d'un cadre juridique sûr pour financer les études. À Paris, le roi refusait de donner l'autonomie juridique à l'université. Là l'université a trouvé une solution en se mettant sous la juridiction de l'évêque faisant appel au concordat de Worms. Elle a eu raison du roi, même si le pape a dû promettre de ne jamais organiser des cours de droit romain dans cette institution contrôlée par l'Église, ce que Honorius III (c. 1148-1227) a fait dans la bulle *Super speculam* en 1219[39]. L'université devenait entièrement autonome du roi et les dominicains obtenaient la possibilité de fonder un nouveau collège avec les mêmes garanties de pérennité qu'à Bologne, cette fois-ci sous la juridiction de l'évêque. La même chose se passa en Angleterre : en 1244, Oxford obtenait la juridiction pour juger souverainement dans ses murs, comme Bologne ; Cambridge était protégé par la jurisprudence de l'évêque d'Ely, comme Paris[40]. Leuven en 1425 obtint aussi une cour rectorale entièrement indépendante des princes[41].

Mais alors, les dominicains ne pourraient-ils fonctionner qu'au sein de quartiers universitaires ? Pour réaliser les rêves de saint Dominique, les dominicains deviendraient-ils à jamais dépendants des universités ayant leur propre justice ? Non, dans le courant du treizième siècle le mouvement communal prit son essor. Des villes entières rachetèrent la justice à leur prince, selon différentes formules de justice basse, moyenne ou haute. En lisant bien les chartes et les privilèges des villes, les dominicains trouvèrent de plus en plus de villes libres où ils pouvaient appliquer leurs constitutions sans danger de saisies féodales. Les campagnes leurs restèrent cependant fermées. À cause du cadre juridique et du modèle bolonais,

---

39 Voir, sur l'historiographie concernant cette bulle : Jacques Krynen, 'La réception du droit romain en France : Encore la bulle *Super speculam*', *Revue d'histoire des facultés de droit et de la science juridique*, 28 (2008), 227-262.

40 James A. Brundage, 'The Bar of the Ely Consistory Court in the Fourteenth Century : Advocates, Proctors, and Others', *Journal of Ecclesiastical History*, 43 (1992), 541-560.

41 Sur la cour rectorale de Leuven, voir : Carl Vandenghoer, *De rectorale rechtbank van de oude Leuvense universiteit (1425-1797)* (Verhandelingen van de Koninklijke Academie voor Wetenschappen, Letteren en Schone Kunsten van België – Klasse der Letteren, 124) (Bruxelles : Koninklijke Academie voor Wetenschappen, Letteren en Schone Kunsten van België, 1987).

l'Ordre a donc été associé dès le départ aux universités et s'est vu obligé de se cantonner dans les grandes villes. Voici démontré pourquoi on retrouve dans les premières constitutions de l'Ordre des Prêcheurs le langage juridique des années 1200-1230 de l'université de Bologne.

WOLFRAM HOYER O.P. † _____

A Manuscript and Its Editions

AGOP XIV A4, folios 28ʳ-47ʳ

1. The importance of AGOP XIV A4, fols 28ʳ-47ʳ as a historical source for Dominican proper law

In dealing with the early decades of Dominican proper law, namely the twenty-three years between the papal confirmation of the Order of Preachers in 1216 and the second reedition of the friars' constitutions by Master of the Order Raymond of Peñafort (1175-1275) in 1239, the historian faces two major problems. The first is the scarceness of contemporary sources. Although popes, bishops and princes in those years issued numerous charters and certificates to protect and promote the Order and its members, these documents remain silent on Dominican laws. Even the bull *Religiosam vitam eligentibus*, by which Pope Honorius III (*c.* 1150-1227) on 22 December 1216 took prior Dominic (*c.* 1170-1221) and his companions at Saint Romanus in Toulouse under the protection of Saint Peter, only states that they lived as canons following the *Rule* of Augustine, but gives no further details on their constitutions.[1] The only narrative source of the time that mentions Dominican legal topics, the so-called *Libellus* of Jordan of Saxony (*c.* 1190-1237), a chronicle of the beginnings of the Order of Preachers, gives a few hints on the origin of some Dominican laws, but Jordan's intention was more to glorify Saint Dominic and the first friars than to explain the content and the development of their institutional regulations.[2] In theory, the best sources for this issue should be the acts of the general chapters which the friars began to celebrate from 1220 onwards, as these assemblies were and still are the legislative body of the Order of Preachers. Nineteen of them were held between 1220 and 1239; only the meeting of 1237 was cancelled due to the sudden death of Master Jordan of Saxony. All of them added to Dominican proper law. Unfortunately,

---

1 '[…] in primis siquidem statuentes ut ordo canonicus, qui secundum Deum et beati Augustini regulam in eadem ecclesia institutus esse dinoscitur, perpetuis ibidem temporibus inviolabiliter observetur' (*Monumenta diplomatica sancti Dominici* (MOPH, 25), ed. by Vladimir J. Koudelka (Rome: Institutum Historicum Fratrum Praedicatorum, 1966), p. 73; full text of the bull: pp. 73-76).

2 The Latin text of the *Libellus de principiis Ordinis Praedicatorum* is edited in: *Monumenta historica sancti patris nostri Dominici* (MOPH, 16) (Rome: Institutum Historicum Fratrum Praedicatorum, 1935), pp. 25-88.

A Cathedral of Constitutional Law, éd. par Anton MILH O.P. and Mark BUTAYE O.P., Turnhout, Brepols, 2023 (*Bibliothèque de la Revue d'histoire ecclésiastique*, 112), p. 87-102.
BREPOLS ❦ PUBLISHERS   10.1484/M.BRHE-EB.5.135046

their acts have been passed down to us only very fragmentarily. Most of them were already lost at the beginning of the fourteenth century, when Bernard Gui (*c.* 1261-1331) in 1305 collected all the textual morsels of legislative decisions issued by general chapters that he could still find.[3] So in practice, the fragments of these acts that we have today merely give us some additional data, but not much more.

The reason for this scarceness of contemporary sources lies in the second major problem: as they are subject to change, the laws of the Order were and are time-dependent. Only the *Rule* of Augustine enjoys the status of a canonised text, with a wording fixed by tradition and by the pre-eminence of its author, whereas a norm introduced by a general chapter can be confirmed, abrogated or changed by decision of a following general chapter: in the beginning simply by every following one, from 1225 or 1228 onwards by introduction at and approbation and confirmation by three consecutive general chapters.[4] Not that Dominican legal texts are ephemeral by nature; at least, no more or less so than modern laws. However, newer laws could and do supersede older ones and texts with older norms become expendable. Consequently, with the progress of legal development, the parchment or paper on which these norms were written down also became expendable items and they were thrown away or used for something else.

The bulk of our knowledge of the Dominican constitutions prior to 1239 derives from one text conserved in one single manuscript. This text was written down on fols 28^r to 47^r of a manuscript codex that today is kept in the archive of the general curia of the Order of Preachers in Rome, the *Archivum Generale Ordinis Praedicatorum* (AGOP), under the inventory number XIV A4. The text

---

3   According to Gui's introductory words to his collection: 'Ab anno Domini MCCXX usque ad annum eiusdem Domini benedicti MCCXL de actis capitulorum generalium pauca que potui reperire inferius annotavi. Ab anno Domini MCCXL usque ad annum Domini MCCCV quo hec scripsi, habentur inferius complecius recollecta, quibusdam tamen exceptis, pro quibus suo tempore si occurrerit recolligendis et complendis, spacia vacua locis suis dimittantur' (*Acta capitulorum generalium ordinis Praedicatorum 1: ab anno 1220 usque ad annum 1303 iussu reverendissimi patris fratris Andreae Frühwirth magistri generalis* (MOPH, 3), ed. by Benedictus Maria Reichert (Rome: In Domo Generalitia; Stuttgart: Apud Jos. Roth. Bibliopolam, 1898), p. 1). Gui's work is still the basis for the edition of the acts of the Dominican general chapters from 1220 to 1844 that is in current use, namely in MOPH 3, 4 and 8-16, Rome et al., 1898-1904.

4   Due to the lack of sources it is a matter of debate when exactly the so-called three-chapter rule was introduced. The law in question is mentioned in the so-called primitive constitutions, dist. 2, cap. 6: 'Et ut multitudo constitutionum vitetur, prohibemus ne aliquid de cetero statuatur, nisi per duo capitula continua fuerit approbatum. Et tunc in tertio capitulo immediate sequente poterit confirmari vel deleri, sive per priores provinciales sive per alios diffinitores, ubicumque illud tertium capitulum teneatur' (quoted after Antoninus Hendrik Thomas, *De oudste constituties van de dominicanen: Voorgeschiedenis, tekst, bronnen, ontstaan en ontwikkeling (1215-1237) met uitgave van de tekst* (BRHE, 42) (Leuven: Bureel van de RHE, 1965), p. 344 [p. 423]). Thomas dates it to the year 1228. Simon Tugwell suggests it was introduced by the general chapter of 1226 (in: 'The Evolution of Dominican Structures of Government: III. The Early Development of the Second Distinction of the Constitutions', *AFP*, 71 (2001), 5-182 (pp. 60-67)).

has three parts: a prologue introduces the constitutions that are organised into two main bodies, so-called distinctions, with the first distinction primarily addressing Dominican life in a local religious community, its liturgical obligations and its offices of governance and administration, and the second distinction mostly dealing with everything that had to be administrated or institutionalised above the convent level, that is the provinces and the Order as such, their chapters and offices, but also the organisation of and formation in Dominican houses of studies or the office of preacher. The prologue is preceded by an introduction, a preamble, that is not part of Dominican legislation, but recounts how the general chapter of 1228 in Paris, under Master Jordan of Saxony, reedited the friars' constitutions. Furthermore, there is an introductory rubric, explaining the content of the text:

> Iste sunt constituciones prime ordinis fratrum predicatorum, que erant tempore magistri Iordanis, beati Dominici immediate successoris, ex quibus formauit et ordinauit constituciones alias, que nunc habentur frater Raimundus de Penna Forti magister ordinis tercius.[5]

From this introductory rubric, to be more precise, from the words *constituciones prime*, derives the name by which this source is commonly called: the primitive constitutions. But this designation is wrong: historically, the first or earliest Dominican constitutions were those submitted to the papal curia in 1216, when Saint Dominic applied for papal approval of his newly founded order, an application that resulted in the already mentioned bull *Religiosam vitam eligentibus*. Unfortunately, these constitutions – truly the first – have since been lost. The text of AGOP XIV A4, fols 28^r-47^r is merely the oldest surviving textual form of the Dominican constitutions – the result of a thorough redaction or rewriting of these laws undertaken by the general chapter of 1228. Therefore the text is more appropriately called either the first reedition of the Dominican friars' constitutions or the Dominican friars' constitutions under Jordan of Saxony.

For a modern reader, the medieval Latin term *constitutiones* may be misleading. It does not mean a constitution in the sense of the fundamental political or legal principles by which an entity is governed, but simply one of the four types of norms in Dominican legislation – the others being *ordinationes* (instructions), *admonitiones* (admonitions) and *declarationes* (explanations), with *constitutiones* (laws) indicating the norms that were generally valid and binding. This means that the text of AGOP XIV A4, fols 28^r-47^r does not represent the entire body of Dominican proper law. Furthermore, it includes not only the legal output of the general chapter of 1228, but also changes made by the following general chapters up to 1236. But we know from fragments of some acts of these general chapters that the text of AGOP XIV A4, fols 28^r-47^r does not include all of the constitutions issued by them. This means that the other historical sources on the friars' proper law before 1239 are not irrelevant. Due to the influence of early

---

5 AGOP, MS XIV A4, fol. 28^r.

Dominican laws on other religious orders or entities, such as the Dominican nuns, the Magdalene sisters or the Sack friars, their texts must also be taken into consideration. By consequence, every attempt at editing the early friars' constitutions will always lead to patchwork.

Because of its pre-eminence as a source, AGOP XIV A4, fols 28^r-47^r has been of interest to modern scholarly historiography from its very beginning. As early as 1719 the codex and the text of the constitutions were mentioned by Jacques Échard (1644-1724) in the first volume of his work on *Scriptores Ordinis Praedicatorum*, as being part of the library of the convent in Rodez in southern France.[6] Some years later, the book was sent to Rome to Antoninus Brémond (1692-1755), a Dominican historian who was Master of the Order from 1748 until his death seven years later. In 1885, the Dominican historian Heinrich Suso Denifle (1844-1905) published the first edition of AGOP XIV A4, fols 28^r-47^r.[7] A few years later, in 1896, a second edition was published anonymously in the official journal of the Order of Preachers – it is known, however, that the editor was Pius Mothon (1849-1929).[8] In 1939, Heribert Christian Scheeben (1890-1968) published his own edition.[9] Antoninus Hendrik Thomas's (1915-1996) dissertation followed in 1965. Thomas made use of all three preceding editions.

Before we can evaluate these scholarly appraisals of AGOP XIV A4, fols 28^r-47^r, we will have to take a closer look at the original manuscript.

2. Palaeographical observations on AGOP XIV A4, fols 28^r-47^r

Many researchers, such as Pius Mothon, Dominicus Planzer, Antoninus Hendrik Thomas or Simon Tugwell, call AGOP XIV A4 the *codex Rutenensis* or the codex

---

6 *Scriptores ordinis Praedicatorum recensiti, notisque historicis et criticis illustrati [...] Inchoavit reverendus pater frater Jacobus Quetif [...], absolvit Jacobus Echard*, 2 vols (Paris: Ballard, 1719-1721), I (1719), p. 88, n° 4: 'Hoc manuscriptus in membraneum etiamnum apud nostros Ruthenenses servari me monuit reverendus admodum pater Melchior Thomas de Lermite ceu a se visum, dum provinciae Tolosanae praefectus visitationes suas obiret. Opus jam rarum, ex quo beatus Raimundus tertius ordinis magister licet idem tamen ratione composuit'.

7 'Die Constitutionen des Prediger-Ordens vom Jahr 1228', ed. by Heinrich Suso Denifle, in *Archiv für Litteratur- und Kirchengeschichte des Mittelalters*, ed. by id. and Franz Ehrle, 7 vols (Berlin: Weidmann; Freiburg: Herder, 1885-1900), I (1885), 165-227.

8 'Vetera monumenta legislativa sacri ordinis Praedicatorum ex saeculo a nativitate Christi tertio decimo, ordinis primo', [ed. by Pius Mothon,] *Analecta Sacri Ordinis Fratrum Praedicatorum*, 4 (1896), 610-648. Mothon is identified as the editor by Dominicus Planzer, 'De codice Ruthenensi miscellaneo in tabulario ordinis Praedicatorum asservato', *AFP*, 5 (1935), 5-123 (pp. 20-21).

9 *Die Konstitutionen des Predigerordens unter Jordan von Sachsen* (Quellen und Forschungen zur Geschichte des Dominikanerordens in Deutschland, 38), ed. by Heribert Christian Scheeben (Cologne: Albertus-Magnus-Verlag; Leipzig: Harrassowitz, 1939).

of Rodez.[10] This name is true insofar as this book was originally part of the library of the Dominican convent of Rodez in southern France before it was sent to Rome. But another book of manuscripts was also sent from Rodez to the archive of the general curia, a volume which today carries the inventory number AGOP XIV A3 and which contains some works by Bernard Gui, especially his collection of the fragments of the acts of the early general chapters. Because of its provenance, this AGOP XIV A3 is also called the codex of Rodez, for example by Benedictus Reichert (1868-1917).[11] To prevent all misunderstanding, it seems wiser to call the book containing the constitutions only by its current inventory number, AGOP XIV A4.

AGOP XIV A4 consists of six different main parts, with most of them having indices and appendices. It contains hundreds of bulls and charters in full text copy or as *regesta*, several juridical texts in full, for example some by Hermann of Minden († after 1299), a collection of texts by Cardinal-Bishop John Marsicano of Tusculum (*c.* 1050-1119) or the *Determinatio compendiosa de iurisdictione imperii* by Bartholomew of Lucca (*c.* 1236-1327) and – what interests us most – on fols 28^r-47^r a copy of the constitutions of the Dominican friars, followed on fols 49^r-57^r by the constitutions of the Dominican nuns. Dominicus Planzer published a detailed codicological description of the whole collective manuscript, so there is no need to repeat his results here.[12] On the whole, most of the texts collected in AGOP XIV A4 have to do with laws issued by Pope Boniface VIII (1235-1303) or with their juridical consequences – with the exception of the texts containing the constitutions of the Dominican friars and nuns, as these were both already outdated and obsolete at the time of that pontiff. Rather these two texts were copied into and/or included in the manuscript collection for documentary reasons, as witnesses of what the Dominican constitutions had once looked like. The text of the friars' constitutions is the second main part of the whole collection of AGOP XIV A4, written on the fols 28-47 in two sexternions, from which three leaves were cut off (between the current fols 47 and 48). We do not know if these leaves that were cut off were empty or not. However, all the indications are that there was no loss of text.

This is what codicological research can tell us; palaeographical analysis of fols 28^r-47^r can yield further results. I will address only the most important results here, both to correct Planzer on a number of points and to furnish more information. The friars' constitutions were written in a single column of text, surrounded by a generous free outer frame. The number of lines varies between 29 and 31 for each folio, with fol. 47^r having eleven lines only. The text column was written in

---

10 Cf. Mothon, 'Vetera monumenta legislativa'... [see note 8], p. 620 *passim*; Planzer, 'De codice Ruthenensi'... [see note 8], p. 5 *passim*; Thomas, *De oudste constituties*... [see note 4], p. 80 [p. 244] *passim*: 'codex Rutenensis' or p. 82 [p. 245] *passim*: 'het handschrift van Rodez' and Tugwell, 'The Evolution'... [see note 4], p. 6 *passim*: 'the Rodez manuscript'.

11 In Reichert, *Acta capitulorum*... [see note 3], pp. ix-x.

12 Planzer, 'De codice Ruthenensi'... [see note 8].

black ink by a single writer, who also wrote headlines over each folio that read 'Constitutiones antique ordinis fratrum predicatorum'. As orthographical signs, this writer used dots for commas or final points and a kind of colon that also functions as a modern colon or comma. The form of his letters shows that he learned to write in the last decades of the thirteenth century or at least that he was used to write in the *textualis* style of those years. There are influences of the subsequent development of handwriting after 1300, too, but he did not write in the style of a typical *bastarda*. Therefore, I would like to suggest that he wrote his text between 1280 and 1320 – Planzer and Scheeben dated this handwriting to the middle of the fourteenth century.[13]

The writer of the text column left empty spaces at the end of the last line of the preceding chapter and/or at the end of the first line of the subsequent chapter for the titles or headlines of the chapters of the constitutions. Another writer wrote the headlines into these blank spaces with red ink. These headlines only differ from the text column by their colour, not by their height or ornamental decoration. This rubricist also wrote the earlier mentioned introductory rubric, and in addition turned many letters in the text column into capital letters by adding short strokes in red ink to them. This was meant as a reading aid, as the writer of the text column was quite erratic in his style of capitalisation. The handwriting of the rubricist can also be found in the nuns' constitutions, where he wrote the headlines, too – so both texts came from the same *scriptorium* and were produced more or less at the same time. As the characteristics of the rubricist's handwriting look the same as the those of the text writer –showing elements of the writing styles both before and after 1300, but not yet the typical features of a *bastarda* – his work must equally be dated between 1280 and 1320.

The beginning of each chapter of the friars' constitutions is marked by initials that are two or three lines high in red or blue ink. They are not decorated much and they are of low artistic value. It is impossible to date these initials due to the primitive form of the letters. They could have been written much later than the text column or the headlines. But apart from their simple design, they nevertheless represent a certain artistic or calligraphic effort. In other parts of AGOP XIV A4, texts appear without initials, although space was left free for these. It seems reasonable to assume, therefore, that the initials in the friars' constitutions were written at the same time as the text column and the rubrics. The writer of the initials may also have produced another feature of AGOP XIV A4, fols 28^r-47^r: supralinear majuscule 'C' letters with a second vertical stroke next to the arched stem of the body of the letter, sometimes slightly crossing both ends of the arch. These C letters or C signs appear in the same red or blue ink of the initials that were written into the blank spaces left free by the writer of the text column, and they fulfil a practical function that will be revealed later.

---

13 Cf. Planzer, 'De codice Ruthenensi'... [see note 8], p. 10 and Scheeben, *Die Konstitutionen*... [see note 9], p. 11.

The text column and the headlines have not remained untouched, but they were corrected by two hands. Most of these corrections come from a writer who can be called corrector 1. Using a very fine pen and a black, but pale ink, he corrected several single words in the text column and on four occasions the order of words. He also corrected one headline, which indicates that he worked after the rubricist. Because of the width of the pen and the colour of the ink, some further interventions can also be attributed to corrector 1: sometimes the writer of the text column did not properly separate the words within in the line. Nor did he hyphenate divided words at the end of lines – and some of his word divisions are unconventional (like 'C-istercienses', 'a-liquatenus', 'recl-udentibus'). So to aid reading, corrector 1 furnished many small pen strokes within lines to indicate the correct word separation and also hyphens at the end of lines, but he did not do this systematically and nor are his corrections without errors. Furthermore, corrector 1 marked the minuscule letter 'i' supralinearly with a short pen stroke, as the writer of the text column did not put dots or strokes on the stems of this letter, meaning that originally all combinations of 'i' plus 'n', plus 'm' or plus 'u' were difficult to read. All these improvements, the division or separation of words and the strokes on the letter 'i' show how thoroughly corrector 1 revised the text. He left very few letters written in his handwriting, so it is impossible to date his work. Nevertheless, the same argument applies here as for the writing of the initials: corrector 1 put great effort into the text, so it is reasonable to think that he worked at the same time as the writers of the text column, the rubrics and the initials. A second corrector also made adjustments to AGOP XIV A4, fols 28^r-47^r (corrector 2), but he only emended the letters of two words, using a pen with a different width and a darker black ink than corrector 1. Nothing more can be said about him.

Four margins appear on the folios. Three of these came from the same pen, ink and handwriting: on fols 31^r and 36^v each, this writer added a short piece of text to the text column. He also repeated the text of the introductory rubric at the bottom of fol. 28^r, but not without making a mistake. This last margin serves as a librarian's note – it is the only library note in the whole codex AGOP XIV A4. Unlike the text column and the rubrics, the handwriting of these three margins does not show any signs of the writing style that was fashionable before 1300, but belongs clearly to the fourteenth century. The three margins were thus written later – the 1330s seems a good suggestion.

A fourth margin was added to fol. 29^v by one of the two writers who can be identified by name: Planzer tells us that it was the same writer who furnished one of the paginations and identifies him as Antoninus Brémond.[14] In this location, in the middle of the chapter 'De matutinis' that introduces the regulations on the convent's daily chapter meeting, next to 'Intrante conventu', Brémond added the words 'De capitulo quotidiano'. It seems that he thought that a headline was

---

14 Cf. Planzer, 'De codice Ruthenensi'… [see note 8], p. 17, footnote 3.

missing here. The word 'Intrante' is indeed marked by an initial, which normally indicates the beginning of a new chapter in AGOP XIV A4, fols 28^r-47^r. Also, in 1239 Raymond of Peñafort in fact did cut the long chapter 'De matutinis' into two halves directly before 'Intrante conventu' and put the second half with the regulations on the conventual chapter into the second distinction, with the laws on provincial and general chapters. This was the form of the constitutions Brémond knew in his own age. But apart from the initial at the word 'Intrante', no other evidence in AGOP XIV A4, fols 28^r-47^r supports the idea that a headline is in fact missing here: the text itself continues smoothly. There are no words like 'statuimus' that normally mark the beginning of a new law. The daily chapter was part of the conventual liturgy every morning. The headline would have had to have been missed by the text writer, who left no blank space for it, by the rubricist, who did not write it down, and by corrector 1, who did not introduce it. Furthermore, there is one other example of an initial without headline, on fol. 46^r. In this location, many of the so-called *extravagantes* were collected, that is, a series of singular laws that were not part of any of the constitutions' chapters and that were passed as laws after the general structure of the text of the constitutions was fixed in 1228. So in AGOP XIV A4, fols 28^r-47^r an initial does not necessarily introduce a chapter of the constitutions, but it was also used to introduce certain paragraphs. This means that there is no headline missing on fol. 29^v.

Fols 28^r to 47^r equally contain catchwords and one *reclamans*, seemingly written by more than one writer. Moreover, there are two systems of foliation, written by two different hands: in the eighteenth century, Brémond paginated AGOP XIV A4, fols 28^r-47^r, writing the number on each page in ink (with fol. 28^r = p. 55 and fol. 49^r = p. 96). As Brémond's pagination did not include some folios at the beginning and at the end of the volume, Dominicus Planzer in the twentieth century added a new foliation in pencil. So Planzer became the second writer on AGOP XIV A4, fols 28^r-47^r who can be identified by name. All the other writers who left traces on the folios between the fourteenth and the twentieth century remain anonymous.

Six of them worked on or with the text of the constitutions proper. Paleographically, the writing of two of these, namely the writer of the text column and the rubricist, can be directly dated to the years between 1280 and 1320. The huge effort of the writer of the initials and of corrector 1, which seems justifiable only if they worked around the same time as the writer of the text column and the rubricist, means that we can indirectly also date their work to this time. The margins, pagination/foliation, the catchwords and the *reclamans* are of no great importance for our purpose. In summary, it can be said that AGOP XIV A4, fols 28^r-47^r was written in the decades around the year 1300. It is surely no coincidence that the text of the constitutions of Master Jordan of Saxony (and that of the nuns) was written down at the same time, when Bernard Gui made his collection on Dominican legislation, and that the two manuscripts AGOP XIV A4 (containing the constitutions of Master Jordan) and AGOP XIV A3 (with the collection of the acts of the general chapters) came from the same convent of Rodez.

3. The date of composition of the text

So we now know when the text was written down. But when was it composed? The text itself does not answer this question: the only explicit date it gives is the year 1228, which is mentioned in the preamble. But the preamble's story about the revision work of the general chapter of 1228 could also have been told later, for example in the fourteenth century. Unfortunately, few of the palaeographic observations can help with the dating of the composition: certainly, the text on AGOP XIV A4, fols 28^r-47^r itself is a copy – to be more precise, a fair copy of an already existing text. Although its calligraphic or artistic value is limited, the chief writers did put a lot of effort in its production. The spaces that the writer of the text column left blank for the initials, headlines and the C signs mentioned above generally fit them perfectly; the extensive work of corrector 1 – including changing the order of words – seems to have been possible only if there were an original text which could be followed as a template. Nevertheless, the text of this template could easily have been composed shortly before the production of the manuscript pages itself, that is, in the decades around the year 1300.

There is, however, one design feature that provides a strong argument for dating the original template to the first half of the thirteenth century: the C signs. Apart from their alternating colour, they have no decorative function. They are not regularly distributed across the text. Some chapters of the constitutions have none, like the chapter 'De leuioribus culpis' (fols 34^{r-v}), which is seventy-one lines long. In the chapter 'De graui culpa' (fols 35^{r-v}), which is 28 lines long, there are only two, and in the chapter 'De grauiori culpa' (fols 36^r-37^r), which is sixty-nine lines long, there are five. The already mentioned so-called *extravagantes* between the chapter 'De edificiis' and the rule of the lay friars (fols 46^{r-v}) contain eleven C signs in thirty-two lines. Some of these signs introduce norms with a different content to the regulations that come before. Many others, however, introduce regulations that complement or specify laws with the same content. Nor do they generally separate laws from each other, as there are many constitutions without them, but they separate some. Three of the C signs were actually put into the text later, as corrections (fols 29^{r-v} and 38^v). They were written in black ink and were crammed into the lines. All in all, the C signs are intended as markers of an interpolation or a caesura in the text – interpolations that were present in its original template, perhaps as corrections, replacements of an older text by a new one, margins or other later revisions.

We do not know what these revisions in the original template looked like, but we can see what the C signs in AGOP XIV A4, fols 28^r-47^r indicate: our record of the acts of the early general chapters is fragmentary, but we know of thirty-one introductions or changes to constitutions issued by the general chapter of Paris in 1236.[15] The texts of seventeen of these are to be found in AGOP XIV A4, fols 28^r-47^r, including one in a margin. Most of these seventeen decisions are introduced by a C sign. The few that lack such a sign either stand at the beginning of a chapter of the constitutions or change only the wording of a phrase and therefore did not require explicit indication. This proves the practical function of the C signs, namely to mark changes to the text made by general chapters after 1228.

So we can say that although AGOP XIV A4, fols 28^r-47^r was written down in the decades between 1280 and 1320, it is a copy of a text of the second reedition of the Dominican friars' constitutions of 1228, into which some constitutional decisions issued by the general chapters between 1229 and 1236 were incorporated. Several of these later incorporations are marked by C signs. Even if our record of the acts of the early general chapters is scrappy, we know that only fifty percent of the decisions of the general chapter of 1236 were included in AGOP XIV A4, fols 28^r-47^r. So the manuscript does not give a comprehensive representation of the status of the Dominican friars' constitutions after 1228. However, the decisions incorporated are included word for word. Although AGOP XIV A4, fols 28^r-47^r is incomplete as a historical source, it is nevertheless a reliable one.

4. The four editions of AGOP XIV A4, fols 28^r-47^r

Having described the most important characteristics of the manuscript of AGOP XIV A4, fols 28^r-47^r, we can now answer the question as to how the four editors mentioned above treated this text in their works. There is no need to go into every detail here; we will focus instead on a number of features.

From the point of view of loyalty to the manuscript, Mothon's edition is much closer to AGOP XIV A4, fols 28^r-47^r than are the other three. All four editors standardised orthography and punctuation, but Mothon did so only moderately. None of them reproduced the C signs. But apart from these commonalities, the editions differ from each other as the different interests of the editors left deep traces.

Heinrich Suso Denifle's aim was to reconstruct the text of the constitutions in the form it had been given by the general chapter of 1228,[16] as he wanted

---

15 Cf. Reichert, *Acta capitulorum...* [see note 3], pp. 6-10.

16 'Ich muss sehr bedauern, dass die Constitutionen vom Jahr 1228 nur in einer Handschrift auf uns gekommen sind, da diese viel zu wünschen übrig lässt. Der Schreiber derselben nahm nämlich in dieselbe nicht wenige Bestimmungen aus dem im Jahr 1236 zu Paris gefeierten *Capitulum generalissimum* auf, ohne dies irgendwo zu bemerken. Wie er dazu kam, lässt sich unschwer erklären. In seiner Vorlage wurden nämlich die neuen Vorschriften an den Rand geschrieben und die abrogierten Bestimmungen eventuell im Text durchgestrichen. [...] Die Herstellung des ursprünglichen Textes war deshalb mit nicht wenigen Schwierigkeiten verbunden. Durchaus ist es mir nicht gelungen, da ich einige Male nicht wissen konnte, was früher im Texte stand' (Denifle, 'Die Constitutionen'... [see note 7], pp. 167-168).

to prove that Saint Dominic used the institutions of the Premonstratensians as a basis for the laws of his own new order.[17] This idea came from Master of the Order Humbert of Romans (c. 1194-1277).[18] As a consequence, Denifle rejected the thesis that the Cistercian laws had been a major influence on the Dominican constitutions.[19] In the footnotes, Denifle consistently points out every Premonstratensian legal parallel to the Dominican norms. He does not explain that the text is a copy from the beginning of the fourteenth century, gives no description of the physical characteristics of the manuscript and does not speak of the different writer's hands, the extensive correction work, the pagination or foliation or the C signs. In the margins of his edition, he numbers the chapters of the constitutions in Arabic numerals, with the first distinction numbering twenty-five chapters and the second thirty-seven. As he accepts Brémond's title 'De capitulo quotidiano', Denifle divides the chapter 'De matutinis' in two, albeit with an explicit explanation in the footnote.[20] Apart from his intention to prove the Premonstratensian foundation of the Dominican constitutions, Denifle does not speak about the guidelines that governed his editorial work; they only become evident if one knows the original manuscript, especially Denifle's emendations or his treatment of the margins.

Pius Mothon does not seem to have known Denifle's edition. His motivation for editing AGOP XIV A4, fols 28^r-47^r was provided by the general chapter of 1895 in Ávila, which ordered the Master of the Order to institute a commission of scholars for the revision of all legal documents and texts concerning the Order of Preachers.[21] With explicit reference to this,[22] a series of editions of *vetera monumenta legislativa* was launched in 1896 in the official journal of the order, the *Analecta Sacri Ordinis Praedicatorum*, beginning with the *Rule* of Augustine[23] and continuing with AGOP XIV A4, fols 28^r-47^r (called *Liber consuetudinum* or *consuetudinarius*); other texts followed. It is not fully clear whether Mothon prepared his edition directly from the manuscript or primarily from a transcription that

---

17 'St. Dominicus hat den Statuten seines Ordens jene der Praemonstratenser zu Grunde gelegt. Den Beweis liefern zunächst die unten publicierten Constitutionen aus dem Jahr 1228. [...] Ich habe unten in den Anmerkungen durchweg die Nachweise geliefert' (Denifle, 'Die Constitutionen'... [see note 7], pp. 172-173).

18 Cf. Denifle, 'Die Constitutionen'... [see note 7], p. 173. Neither Humbert and Denifle waste any thought on the question whether the Premonstratensian norms might have been borrowed by the author(s) of the Dominican constitutions not directly, but indirectly through the acceptance of the legal customs of Osma.

19 Cf. Denifle, 'Die Constitutionen'... [see note 7], p. 174, footnote 1.

20 'Die Ueberschrift wurde im Cod. erst nachträglich dazu gesetzt' (Denifle, 'Die Constitutionen'... [see note 7], p. 196, footnote 1).

21 Cf. *Acta capituli generalis diffinitorum sacri ordinis Praedicatorum Abulae in conventu sancti Thomae Aquinatis celebrati in festo Pentecostes die prima Junii et sequentibus anno Domini 1895* (Rome: Typis Vaticanis, 1895), p. 138.

22 Cf. Mothon, 'Vetera monumenta legislativa'... [see note 8], p. 610.

23 In Mothon, 'Vetera monumenta legislativa'... [see note 8], pp. 610-616 (introduction) and pp. 616-619 (edition of the text from the so-called prototype of Master Humbert of Romans).

Marie-Xavier Faucher (1843-1930) had made in 1873.[24] Nevertheless, Mothon briefly describes the codex AGOP XIV A4 and mentions that it originated from Rodez, but does not speak about the physical characteristics of the text on fols 28[r]-47[r] (no remarks on the writers, the corrections or the C signs etc.).[25] Nor does he explain that the text was a copy made around 1300. Capitalisation, orthography and punctuation are only moderately standardised. For easier quotation, Mothon numbers the chapters of the constitutions in Roman numerals, beginning anew in each distinction, with the first distinction numbering XXIV and the second distinction XXXVII chapters. But Mothon explicitly explains in a footnote that these numerals do not appear in the original manuscript.[26] Although Mothon leaves the chapter 'De matutinis' intact, he numbers the *extravagantes* in the second distinction with the numeral XXXVI as a separate chapter, albeit with a comment in a footnote that the manuscript itself does not do so.[27] Of the margins on AGOP XIV A4, fols 28[v], 31[r] and 36[v], Mothon only accepts the one on fol. 31[r] (directly in his text), but not the other two and not the one of Brémond on fol. 29[v]. Furthermore, Mothon's edition does not mention pagination or foliation in the manuscript. Like Denifle, Mothon never speaks about his editorial guidelines, but as he indicates his emendations in square brackets or mentions every intervention explicitly in the footnotes, his changes are easier to identify. In his extensive annotations, Mothon attempts to show whether, and if so, to what extent single norms in this oldest surviving text of the Dominican constitutions can be traced back to Saint Dominic himself.

Heribert Christian Scheeben completed his edition in the year 1934, but only published it in 1939, unchanged, as he states.[28] He used Denifle's and Mothon's works, but not Planzer's codicological analysis.[29] He therefore gives a similar short description in the introduction himself: Scheeben tells us that AGOP XIV A4 contains copies of both the friars' and the nuns' constitutions and states that the friars' text was written around 1350 and the nuns' in the first half of the fourteenth century, but without giving reasons for this dating. He concludes from the fact that the handwriting of the constitutions of the friars does not recur anywhere throughout the codex that fols 28[r]-47[r] originally came from another book and that they were only bound together later with the rest of AGOP XIV A4. He also refers to the headlines, the introductory rubric and

---

24 Cf. Planzer, 'De codice Ruthenensi'... [see note 8], pp. 20-21.

25 Cf. Mothon, 'Vetera monumenta legislativa'... [see note 8], p. 620.

26 'In codice originali Rutenensi numeri capitulorum non indicantur sed tantum proponuntur tituli. Numeros addidimus, ad commoditatem lectoris, pro citationum capitulorum a nobis in posterum referendis' (Mothon, 'Vetera monumenta legislativa'... [see note 8], p. 623, footnote 2).

27 'Hoc capitulum in codice Rutenensi absque titulo reperitur; ac de extravagantibus habetur' (Mothon, 'Vetera monumenta legislativa'... [see note 8], p. 647, footnote 1).

28 Cf. Scheeben, *Die Konstitutionen*... [see note 9], p. 7.

29 He actually announces Planzer's works in his introduction and reports later in a footnote that it had been published in the meantime (cf. Scheeben, *Die Konstitutionen*... [see note 9], p. 11 and footnote 2 on the same page).

the titles of the chapters of the constitutions, and he speaks about the margins.[30] In his attempt to date the template of the copy in AGOP XIV A4, fols 28^r-47^r, Scheeben explains that several constitutions issued by the general chapter of 1236 are missing in the text, but that norms issued in 1241 and 1242 were included. He concludes that the template as such was written in 1242, but that the main bulk of the constitutions it contained came from the time of Master Jordan of Saxony.[31] Scheeben adverts to his main point of interest only indirectly: he mentions explicitly that Mothon's edition lacks any attempt to date or explain the different layers that are visible in the text, something that he discusses extensively and remedies thoroughly himself by dating every single constitution or groups of them.[32] Scheeben presents only a selection of the editorial guidelines he used (for example giving numbers to paragraphs of the constitutions or correcting obvious mistakes in the manuscript), but in fact he extensively standardised orthography, capitalisation and punctuation.[33] All emendations are indicated by round or square brackets, with the original wording of AGOP XIV A4, fols 28^r-47^r moved to the footnotes. Following Mothon, Scheeben numbers the chapters of the constitutions with Roman numerals, with the first distinction numbering XXV, the second distinction numbering XXXVIII chapters. Furthermore, he sub-divides some lines or phrases in many chapters in Arabic numerals, according to the chronological stratification he wants to prove. Thus some of the chapters have no such subdivision (for example in the first distinction the short ones on 'De mulieribus non intromittendis' or 'De refectione', or the long one on 'De magistro novitiorum'), whereas some have many (for example in the first distinction 'De levioribus culpis' or 'De gravi culpa'). The reason for numbering XXV chapters in the first distinction is the fact that Scheeben accepts Brémond's alleged division of the chapter 'De matutinis'. In the second distinction, Scheeben also assigns a Roman numeral to the *extravagantes* (XXXVI) and to the confirmation of the choir office that follows the rule on the lay friars (XXXVIII). All the margins are either tacitly incorporated into the text or are, again silently, omitted. Scheeben also never mentions the C signs. All these numerous interventions and prolific corrections – both those openly announced and those performed tacitly – prove that Scheeben's work is not an edition of an existing text, but an attempt to reconstruct the form of the Dominican friars' constitutions prior to the reedition of 1239. Scheeben relies heavily on this reedition.[34] The use of Raymond's work is also the reason why Scheeben postulates that the text of AGOP XIV A4 in five places includes decisions of general chapters up to 1242. There is no room

---

30 Cf. Scheeben, *Die Konstitutionen…* [see note 9], p. 11.

31 Cf. Scheeben, *Die Konstitutionen…* [see note 9], p. 12.

32 'Auch hat er [Mothon] nicht versucht, die Schichten, die sich ganz deutlich in dem vorliegenden Text abheben, zu scheiden und eine Erklärung für diese Schichten zu geben' (Scheeben, *Die Konstitutionen…* [see note 9], p. 13). Neither did Denifle by the way.

33 Cf. Scheeben, *Die Konstitutionen…* [see note 9], p. 17.

34 'Wo der Text [of AGOP XIV A4, fols 28^r-47^r] unklar war, habe ich die Redaktion Raymunds oder die Akten der Generalkapitel herangezogen' (Scheeben, *Die Konstitutionen…* [see note 9], p. 17).

here to discuss this in detail.[35] Suffice it to say that Scheeben overlooked the fact
that the Dominican legislative process did not stop in 1239, but that the general
chapters after 1240 continued to change the text of the constitutions. Indeed, the
last changes made in the text of AGOP XIV A4, fols 28^r-47^r can be attributed to
the general chapter of 1236.

Antoninus Hendrik Thomas worked on AGOP XIV A4, fols 28^r-47^r within
the scope of his dissertation on 'de oudste constituties van de dominicanen', their
historical background, origin and development. Even if he presents a text of the
constitutions at the end of his book, this text is not an edition of an existing
document, but a reconstruction of the historical Dominican laws prior to 1239
– Thomas speaks explicitly of a 'reconstructie van de tekst'.[36] He obtains this by
introducing most of the textual witnesses he discusses in his doctoral thesis into
the text of AGOP XIV A4, fols 28^r-47^r: the constitutions of the Dominican and
the Magdalene nuns, Raymond's reedition, the text given in Humbert's prototype
and the constitutions of the Sack friars. As Thomas tries to honour all these
sources by making them visible in his reconstruction, his text of the constitutions
is a monument the many possibilities of modern typography: in principle there
are two different systems of annotation, but as the counting of text lines starts
again with every chapter, some pages show four annotation systems. The edited
words are presented in six different type sizes, beginning with *typis romanis maioribus* and ending with *typis cursivis minoribus maiore intervalli distinctis*; sometimes
single words are presented in two different type sizes.[37] There are several types
of brackets and sometimes two text columns for presentation of an older and a
younger version of a text. As he had to juggle very different text sources, Thomas
had no other option than to extensively standardise orthography, capitalisation
and punctuation. As he was not editing an existing manuscript but reconstructing
a text, he could not take the physical features of AGOP XIV A4, fols 28^r-47^r into
consideration, including the C signs. He, too, numbers the chapters of the constitutions with Arabic numerals, with the first distinction numbering twenty-five
chapters – Thomas accepts the division of the chapter 'De matutinis', but gave
the second half the title 'De capitulo', with a footnote indicating the wording of
Brémond's margin[38] – and the second distinction thirty-seven chapters. Finally,
Thomas did not leave the so-called *extravagantes* as they were, but moved them
to different parts of the text, where he either thought they would fit or where

---

35 There was no edition of Raymond's text at the time of Scheeben's edition of AGOP XIV A4,
     fols 28^r-47^r. This was prepared by Raymond Creytens: 'Les constitutions des frères Prêcheurs dans
     la rédaction de s. Raymond de Peñafort (1241)', *AFP*, 18 (1948), 5-68. All Scheeben had at his
     disposal was a reconstruction by Heinrich Suso Denifle: 'Die Constitutionen des Predigerordens in
     der Redaktion Raimunds von Penafort', in *Archiv...* [see note 7], I, 530-564. A weighing of priority of
     historical rank of the two reconstructions (Denife's and Scheeben's) would lead us too far away from
     our task.
36 Thomas, *De oudste constituties...* [see note 4], p. 111 [p. 268].
37 Thomas, *De oudste constituties...* [see note 4], p. 305 [p. 423].
38 Thomas, *De oudste constituties...* [see note 4], p. 314 [p. 423].

Raymond of Peñafort put them. The margins received the same treatment. It is possible to find traces of AGOP XIV A4, fols 28^r-47^r in Thomas's reconstruction, but only by studying the annotations closely.

In sum we can say the following. Denifle wanted to show the influence of the Premonstratensian institutions as a major source for early Dominican proper law. Mothon's annotations focus very much on what he thought was the will of Saint Dominic, made explicit by the constitutions. Scheeben's aim was to show and identify the different historical layers of the constitutions, the Premonstratensian influence and the issues of the different general chapters. Thomas broadened the horizon with his extensive presentation of the development of monastic law in general and the Dominican legislation in detail, and with the various different influences on the early Dominican constitutions that he identified: general canon law, the canons of the Fourth Lateran Council, the *consuetudines* of the canons of Osma, the Premonstratensian institutions, the Cistercian institutions, civil law and academic customs. Thomas not only carried out much deeper research on the background of early Dominican legislation, but his results make it possible to conduct a more detailed analysis and achieve a more precise interpretation of these laws. Nevertheless, the results of our palaeographical analysis and the different experiments of the four existing editions show that the history of scholarly treatment of AGOP XIV A4 has surely not come to an end yet and that many more things can still be learned.

FLORENT CYGLER

Les constitutions dominicaines au Moyen Âge

Histoire et perspectives éditoriales

L'*opus maior* d'Antoninus Hendrik Thomas, *De oudste constituties van de dominica-nen*, constitue, depuis sa parution dans la « Bibliothèque de la Revue d'histoire ecclésiastique » en 1965, un jalon de marque et un incontournable repère dans une longue « aventure » éditoriale qui a débuté à la fin du dix-neuvième siècle : celle de l'édition critique du texte des constitutions dominicaines, dans lesquelles se cristallise le *ius particulare* de l'Ordre, produites au Moyen Âge[1]. Plus d'un siècle plus tard, cette « aventure » se poursuit, et le monument d'érudition qu'est le travail du Père Thomas continue d'y occuper une place centrale. Ainsi, en 2001, dans une imposante étude critique ayant pour but premier de (re)dater avec précision chacune des dispositions des articles de la seconde distinction et des *extravagantes* des « primitive constitutions », Simon Tugwell en a révisé l'édition que le Père Thomas avait donnée[2]. Un an plus tard, Wolfram Hoyer a livré une traduction allemande du texte des « ältesten Konstitutionen » édité par le Père Thomas, laquelle tient compte des corrections proposées par le Père Tugwell[3].

---

1 Voir, outre les vues d'ensemble quelque peu datées de Raymond Creytens, 'Costituzioni domenicane', in *Dizionario degli istituti di perfezione*, éd. par Giancarlo Rocca, 10 t. (Rome : Edizioni Paoline, 1974-2003), III (1976), col. 183-198 (plus particulièrement col. 183-190) et de Raymond M. Louis, 'Histoire du texte des constitutions dominicaines', *AFP*, 6 (1936), 334-350, qui vont au-delà du seul Moyen Âge, Markus Bitterlich, *Statuten mittelalterlicher Ordensgemeinschaften : Strategien normative Stabilisierung mittels statutarischer Gesetzgebung am Beispiel der Zisterzienser, Prämonstratenser, Dominikaner und Franziskaner* (Diss. phil. (dactyl.), TU Dresden, 2015), pp. 289-294 ; Florent Cygler, 'Le *ius particulare* dominicain au XIIIe siècle : prise de vue', in *Regulae – Consuetudines – Statuta : Studi sulle fonti normative degli ordini religiosi nei secoli centrali del Medioevo. Atti del I e del II Seminario internazionale di studio del Centro italo-tesdesco di storia comparata degli ordini religiosi (Bari/Noci/Lecce, 26-27 ottobre 2002 / Castiglione delle Stivere, 23-24 maggio 2003)* (Vita regularis, 25), éd. par Cristina Andenna et Gert Melville (Münster : Lit Verlag, 2005), 445-459 et Paul-Bernard Hodel, 'Les constitutions primitives : Un état des lieux', *Mémoire dominicaine*, 13 (1998/2), 37-45.
2 Simon Tugwell, 'The Evolution of Dominican Structures of Government : III. The Early Development of the Second Distinction of the Constitutions', *AFP*, 71 (2001), 5-182.
3 *Jordan von Sachsen – Ordensmeister, Geschichtsschreiber, Beter : Eine Textsammlung* (Dominikanische Quellen und Zeugnisse, 3), éd. par Wolfram Hoyer (Leipzig : Benno, 2002), pp. 244-297 (voir aussi pp. 204-230, pour une présentation et mise en perspective introductives et actualisées). – À cette date, une traduction italienne du texte édité par le Père Thomas existait déjà : Pietro Lippini,

A Cathedral of Constitutional Law, éd. par Anton MILH O.P. and Mark BUTAYE O.P., Turnhout, Brepols, 2023 (*Bibliothèque de la Revue d'histoire ecclésiastique*, 112), p. 103-112.
BREPOLS ❧ PUBLISHERS   10.1484/M.BRHE-EB.5.135047

Enfin, un travail similaire de traduction complète, en français cette fois, du texte des « constitutions anciennes » est paru fin 2019 dans une anthologie d'une ampleur proprement inédite (plus de 1700 pages) réunissant de très nombreux et divers « témoignages écrits » médiévaux sur saint Dominique établie par Nicole Bériou et Paul-Bernard Hodel avec l'aide de Gisèle Besson[4].

C'est de cette « aventure éditoriale » qu'il sera ici brièvement question ; seront abordés les points suivants : ses étapes, la persistance de quelques problèmes et, en guise de conclusion, les défis éditoriaux qui pourraient aujourd'hui encore être relevés.

In principio, pour ainsi dire, est un manuscrit unique en son genre : l'imposant et fameux *Codex Ruthenensis miscellaneus* (*Archivum Generale Ordinis Praedicatorum* (AGOP, Rome), MS XIV A4), qui compile de très nombreux textes différents datant principalement du quatorzième siècle et dont Dominikus Planzer a donné une description complète en 1935[5]. Parmi ces textes figure celui des *constituciones prime ordinis fratrum Predicatorum, que erant tempore magistri Jordanis,..., ex quibus formavit et ordinavit constitutiones alias que nunc habentur, frater Raymundus de Pennaforti,...*[6] comprenant un préambule, un prologue, deux parties thématiques appelées « distinctions » (*distinctiones*) subdivisées en respectivement 25 et 36/37[7] chapitres portant titres et une série d'*extravagantes*. Heinrich Denifle, après l'avoir repéré, en livra une première édition (partielle) en 1885[8], Pie Mothon une seconde dix ans plus tard (1896)[9] et Heribert Christian Scheeben une autre en 1939[10]. Pour le Père Denifle et Scheeben, ce texte était celui des constitutions en vigueur sous Jourdain de Saxe (1222-1237). Le premier estima même que sa quasi-totalité avait été composée en 1228 et ignora pour cette raison les dispositions ultérieures, notamment celles datant du chapitre généralissime de 1236. Le Père Mothon et Scheeben, en revanche, en firent l'édition complète,

---

La vita quotidiana di un convento medievale : Gli ambienti, le regole, l'orario e le mansioni dei Frati Domenicani del tredicesimo secolo (Attendite ad petram, 5) (Bologne : Edizioni Studio Domenicano, 1990), pp. 361-414.

4 *Saint Dominique de l'ordre des frères prêcheurs : Témoignages écrits, fin XIIe-XIVe siècle*, éd. par Nicole Bériou et Bernard Hodel, avec la collaboration de Gisèle Besson (Paris : Cerf, 2019), pp. 199-263.

5 Dominikus Planzer, 'De codice Ruthenensis miscellaneo in Tabulario Ordinis Praedicatorum asservato', *AFP*, 5 (1935), 5-123. – Sur ce manuscrit, voir aussi la contribution de Wolfram Hoyer au présent volume.

6 Planzer, 'De codice Ruthenensis'... [voir note 5], p. 29.

7 Le 37e chapitre de la seconde distinction est la très courte *Regula fratrum nostrorum conversorum*, soit un texte à part.

8 'Die Constitutionen des Prediger-Ordens vom Jahr 1228', éd. par Heinrich Suso Denifle, in *Archiv für Litteratur- und Kirchengeschichte des Mittelalters*, éd. par id. et Franz Ehrle, 7 t. (Berlin : Weidmann ; Freiburg : Herder, 1885-1900), I (1885), 165-227.

9 'Vetera monumenta legislativa sacri ordinis Praedicatorum ex saeculo a nativitate Christi tertio decimo, ordinis primo', [éd. par Pie Mothon,] *Analecta Sacri Ordinis Praedicatorum*, 4 (1896), 610-648 (réimpr. séparée : *Constitutiones primaevae s. ordinis Praedicatorum*, Fiesole, 1962).

10 *Die Konstitutionen des Predigerordens unter Jordan von Sachsen* (Quellen und Forschungen zur Geschichte des Dominikanerordens in Deutschland, 38), éd. par Heribert Christian Scheeben (Cologne : Albertus-Magnus-Verlag ; Leipzig : Harrassowitz, 1939).

reconnaissant et soulignant par ailleurs dans leurs observations de critique interne sa dépendance marquée des statuts des chanoines prémontrés dans sa première distinction[11]. Enfin, à compter de la fin des années 1930, les études originales menées sur Dominique et la naissance de l'Ordre des frères prêcheurs, dans le sillage de celles de son maître, Pierre Mandonnet, par Marie-Humbert Vicaire le conduisirent à observer, comme l'avait déjà fait Scheeben, que les anciennes constitutions telles que notées dans le *Ruthenensis* avaient été progressivement rédigées, en l'occurrence selon lui entre (1215-)1216 et 1236(-1237), avec pour étapes marquantes l'adoption, en 1216 après le concile de Latran IV, de la *Règle* de saint Augustin augmentée d'*arctiores consuetudines* par la communauté de Saint-Romain de Toulouse[12], les deux premiers chapitres généraux réunis et présidés en 1220 et 1221 par Dominique à Bologne et les deux chapitres généralissimes convoqués en 1228 et 1236 à Paris par son successeur à la tête de l'Ordre, Jourdain de Saxe[13]. Le texte du *Ruthenensis* est en effet, de toute évidence, un texte extrêmement stratifié en tous ses éléments ; il présente, pour reprendre les métaphores botanique et textile employées par le Père Hoyer dans l'introduction à sa traduction, comme des « cernes annuelles de croissance » (« Jahresringe »[14]) et, ainsi, constitue comme une « couverture en patchwork » (« Patchworkdecke »[15]).

C'est en partant notamment de ce constat que le Père Thomas entreprit de faire du texte des anciennes constitutions une nouvelle édition critique[16], laquelle éclipse par son ampleur et sa minutie – et en toute conséquence remplace – toutes les précédentes et reste jusqu'à aujourd'hui l'édition de référence : le profond travail de critique textuelle en trois chapitres et la solide introduction historique en un chapitre qui le précède (« De voorgeschiedenis : Kloosterlijke wetgeving tot het begin van de XIIIe eeuw ») occupent presque les trois quarts de

---

11 Sur les statuts prémontrés et ladite dépendance, voir le clair aperçu donné par Herman Janssens dans ce volume.

12 'Libellus de principiis ord. Praedicatorum auctore Iordano de Saxonia', éd. par Heribert Christian Scheeben, in *Monumenta historica sancti patris nostri Dominici (fasc. II)* (MOPH, 16) (Rome : Institutum Historicum Fratrum Praedicatorum, 1935), 1-88 (ici p. 46 (§ 42)).

13 Pierre Mandonnet, *Saint Dominique : L'idée, l'homme et l'œuvre. Augmenté de notes et d'études critiques par Marie-Humbert Vicaire et Reginald Ladner*, 2 t. (Paris : Desclée De Brouwer, 1937-1938), II (1938) : *Perspectives*, pp. 203-239 (« La législation des prêcheurs »), plus particulièrement jusqu'à la p. 230, et pp. 273-292 (« Les institutions des prêcheurs (1220 et 1221-1227) : Essai des restitution »). – Dans le cadre desdites études, le Père Vicaire avait aussi établi une première traduction française du texte du *Ruthenensis* : Marie-Humbert Vicaire, *Saint Dominique de Caleruega d'après les documents du XIIIe siècle* (Paris : Cerf, 1955), pp. 139-184.

14 Hoyer, *Jordan von Sachsen*... [voir note 3], pp. 206 et 222.

15 Hoyer, *Jordan von Sachsen*... [voir note 3], p. 208.

16 Antoninus Hendrik Thomas, *De oudste constituties van de dominicanen : Voorgeschiedenis, tekst, bronnen, ontstaan en ontwikkeling (1215-1237) met uitgave van de tekst* (BRHE, 42) (Leuven : Bureel van de RHE, 1965), pp. v-xxi (« Inleiding ») [pp. 153-165].

l'étude, soit 292 pages[17] ; l'édition proprement dite, placée en annexe (« Textus constitutionum antiquarum o.p. »), fait quant à elle une soixantaine de pages[18].

Pour établir son texte, le Père Thomas a utilisé plus de témoins que ses prédécesseurs : si le texte du *Ruthenensis* continue de lui servir de base, il en compare, pour parfois les corriger, les leçons à celles d'autres textes proches des anciennes constitutions, contemporains ou de peu postérieurs, à savoir les consti-tutions révisées par le Maître de l'Ordre Raymond de Peñafort (1238-1240), promulguées par les chapitres généraux de 1239-1241[19], celles des sœurs domini-caines telles que transmises par les *Institutiones* de Saint-Sixte et les *Constitutiones* des pénitentes de sainte Marie-Madeleine, ainsi que celles des frères sachets[20]. Il s'est aussi préoccupé d'en déterminer les sources, distinguant pour chacune des deux distinctions des sources directes ou principales (ainsi les coutumes de Prémontré pour la première et la législation du IVe concile du Latran de 1215 pour la seconde) d'une part, « secondaires » d'autre part[21]. Enfin, il s'est efforcé d'en dater les différentes dispositions[22]. Le résultat de ces investigations critiques poussées est la reconstitution d'un texte – différent de celui du *Ruthenensis*, que parfois elle réagence et complète – censé contenir la législation primitive de l'Ordre telle qu'elle devait être en vigueur en 1236(-1237), juste avant la révision de Raymond de Peñafort. Raymond Creytens, dans la longue recension, parfois critique, qu'il fit, dès après sa parution, de l'étude du Père Thomas dans la *Revue d'histoire ecclésiastique*[23], tout en estimant que celui-ci devait être « très proche de l'original »[24], ne manqua toutefois pas de justement relever qu'« en tant que tel, [il n'avait] jamais existé »[25]. Mais n'était-ce peut-être pas déjà le cas, de toute façon, du texte du *Ruthenensis* lui-même ?

Après la publication du livre du Père Thomas, seules deux études, assez récentes et donc aussi bien postérieures, vinrent l'actualiser, la première plutôt indirectement, la seconde de front. En 1993, Bruno Krings publia une version inédite des *Institutiones patrum Praemonstratensis ordinis* datant des années 1220[26] – version dont le Père Thomas, qui ne disposait encore que de celles de la

17 Thomas, *De oudste constituties...* [voir note 16], respectivement pp. 79-292 et 1-78 [pp. 243-412 and 183-241].

18 Thomas, *De oudste constituties...* [voir note 16], pp. 304-369 [pp. 423].

19 Sur cette révision, voir encore *infra*.

20 Thomas, *De oudste constituties...* [voir note 16], pp. 79-124 : « De tekst » [pp. 243-278].

21 Thomas, *De oudste constituties...* [voir note 16], pp. 125-238 : « De bronnen » [pp. 279-370].

22 Thomas, *De oudste constituties...* [voir note 16], pp. 239-292 : « Ontstaan en ontwikkeling » [pp. 371-412].

23 Raymond Creytens, 'Compte rendu de A.H. Thomas, *De oudste constituties van de dominicanen [...]*', *RHE*, 61 (1966), 862-871.

24 Creytens, 'Compte rendu'... [voir note 23], p. 868.

25 Creytens, 'Compte rendu'... [voir note 23], p. 867.

26 Bruno Krings, 'Das Ordensrecht der Prämonstratenser vom späten 12. Jahrhundert bis zum Jahr 1227 : Der Liber consuetudinum und die Dekrete des Generalkapitels', *Analecta Praemonstratensia*, 69 (1993), 107-242.

seconde moitié du douzième siècle et de la fin de la décennie 1230[27], avait émis
l'hypothèse de l'existence, sans toutefois avoir pu, du moins dans un premier
temps, l'étayer[28]. Et, comme déjà précisé, le Père Tugwell reprit en 2001, pour
la seule seconde distinction des constitutions, l'édition du Père Thomas : outre
corriger, préciser ou confirmer certaines datations proposées par ce dernier et
exclure des témoins utilisables pour ce faire, parce que jugées trop tardives, les
constitutions des sachets, son travail rétablit l'ordre qu'ont les chapitres dans
le *Ruthenensis* et les subdivise en sous-unités textuelles, certaines d'entre elles
n'étant, de son propre aveu, que des « conjectural reconstructions of earlier
versions of some constitutions »[29].

Cette intense et longue activité éditoriale autour du texte du *Ruthenensis*, qui
culmine avec *De oudste constituties…*, ne devrait cependant pas faire perdre de
vue que les prêcheurs ont continué de produire des recueils de leurs constitutions
au Moyen Âge. Le premier d'entre eux a déjà été évoqué deux fois : il s'agit
des *correctio et ordinacio et additio constitutionum* effectuées entre 1239 et 1241[30]
par Raymond de Peñafort, qui était aussi comme l'on sait un éminent canoniste.
Le second est la correction de la « lettre de la règle » opérée entre 1254 et
1256[31] par Humbert de Romans (1254-1263) dans le cadre de la fixation de la
liturgie de l'Ordre à la demande du chapitre général de 1254[32]. Contrairement
aux anciennes constitutions, si tant est qu'elles aient jamais été coulées en un
seul texte entre 1216/1220 et 1236, ces deux versions ultérieures peuvent tout

---

27 Respectivement : 'Primaria instituta Canonicorum Praemonstratensium', in *De antiquis Ecclesiae
ritibus*, éd. par Edmond Martène, 4 t. (Anvers : Joannes Baptistæ de la Bry, 1736-1738), III (1737 ;
réimpr. : Hildesheim, 1967), col. 890-926 et *Les Statuts de Prémontré réformés sur les ordres de
Grégoire IX et d'Innocent IV au XIIIe siècle* (BRHE, 23), éd. par Placide Fernand Lefèvre (Leuven :
Bureau de la Revue, 1946).

28 Cf. notamment Thomas, *De oudste constituties…* [voir note 16], p. 131 [p. 283] : « Wel zou
men, met het oog op de hier voorgenomen bronnenstudie, graag beschikken over de tekst die
aan de dominicanen, vermoedelijk rond 1215-1220, rechtstreeks als voorbeeld heeft gediend. »
Presque quinze ans plus tard, il signalait toutefois une telle version ultérieure, que Bruno Krings
put ensuite exploiter : id., 'Une version des statuts de Prémontré au début du XIIIe siècle', *Analecta
Praemonstratensia*, 55 (1979), 153-170.

29 Tugwell, 'The Evolution'… [voir n. 3], p. 9. Ainsi l'édition (par ailleurs souvent marginalement
tronquée) donnée en annexe (pp. 160-182), n'en est toutefois au mieux qu'indirectement :
conformément au propos de l'étude et au titre de l'annexe (p. 160 : « The text of PC II : a résumé of
its development ») , les textes ou leurs éléments, qu'ils aient été amendés ou pas, y sont (ré)ordonnés
dans l'ordre chronologique de leurs années d'adoption tel qu'établi par le Père Tugwell et ne peuvent
donc pas être toujours lus de façon continue.

30 *Acta capitulorum generalium ordinis Praedicatorum 1 : ab anno 1220 usque ad annum 1303 iussu
reverendissimi patris fratris Andreae Frühwirth magistri generalis* (MOPH, 3), éd. par Benedictus Maria
Reichert (Rome : In Domo Generalitia ; Stuttgart : Apud Jos. Roth. Bibliopolam, 1898), pp. 11
(1239), 13 (1240) et 18 (1241). La formule citée est celle de la *confirmatio* de 1241.

31 Reichert, *Acta capitulorum…* [voir note 30], pp. 68 (1254), 73 (1255) et 78 (1256).

32 Reichert, *Acta capitulorum…* [voir note 30], p. 68 : *Committimus magistro ordinis totam ordinacionem
ecclesiastici officii, diurni quam nocturni, et eorum que ad hoc pertinent, et correctionem librorum
ccclesiasticorum, et quod corrigat litteram regule.*

à fait être qualifiées d'officielles dans la mesure où elles avaient été validées par le chapitre général. Le texte mis au point par Humbert est le plus anciennement documenté. Il est transmis par seulement deux autres manuscrits ; la version légèrement actualisée par quelques *extravagantes* donnée par le plus connu des deux, appelé *Prototype*, qui est un manuscrit liturgique (AGOP, MS XIV L1), a été éditée en 1897-1898[33]. Le texte de Raymond, quant à lui, est longtemps resté sans support manuscrit connu. Quatre ans après la première édition du texte du *Ruthenensis* par ses soins, le Père Denifle essaya, en 1889, de le reconstituer pour ainsi dire *ex nihilo* en expurgeant la version d'Humbert des constitutions adoptées entre 1242 et 1256 que celle-ci contenait[34] – une méthode certes pratique et non dénuée de logique, mais aussi simpliste, car elle ne tenait pas compte du fait que la version d'Humbert pouvait aussi avoir modifié ou remplacé certains passages de celle de Raymond. En 1948, le Père Creytens en publia une édition fondée sur un (seul) témoin, qu'il avait localisé dans un *codex miscellaneus* augustinien provenant de Coïmbre (Portugal)[35]. Le *Liber* de Raymond est particulièrement important car il marque un tournant, non seulement parce qu'en effet, d'une part, il révisait les anciennes constitutions par suppression ou modification de certaines de leurs dispositions (*correctio*) ou, d'autre part, les actualisait aussi en y apportant quelques ajouts (*additio*), mais encore et surtout parce qu'il remaniait profondément leur agencement. Ainsi, le préambule ajouté en 1228 fut supprimé, ses contenus étant « fondus » dans le corps du texte, et le nombre de chapitres dans chaque distinction plus ou moins notablement réduit (20 contre auparavant 25 dans la première et seulement 15 contre auparavant 36/37 dans la seconde). Par ailleurs, l'ordre des différents chapitres dans chaque distinction, bien peu systématique, fut modifié de telle sorte qu'apparaissent nettement des sous-parties thématiquement cohérentes – au nombre de quatre dans chaque distinction – sous lesquelles ranger un ou plusieurs chapitres[36]. Ce nouvel agencement en un

---

33 'Liber Constitutionum Ordinis Fratrum Praedicatorum (iuxta codicem prototypum B. Humberti in Archivo Generali Ordinis Romae asservatum)', [éd. par Pie Mothon,] *Analecta Sacri Ordinis Fratrum Praedicatorum*, 5 (1897), 26-60, 98-122 et 162-181.

34 'Die Constitutionen des Predigerordens in der Redaction Raimunds von Peñafort', éd. par Heinrich Suso Denifle, in *Archiv...* [voir note 8], V (1889), 530-564.

35 'Les constitutions des frères prêcheurs dans la rédaction de s. Raymond de Peñafort (1241)', éd. par Raymond Creytens, *AFP*, 18 (1948), 5-68.

36 Cf. le sommaire noté à la suite du prologue, Creytens, 'Les constitutions'... [voir note 35], p. 30 :
Prima distinctio continet : I. De officio ecclesie. – II. De inclinationibus. – III. De suffragiis mortuorum. – IV. De ieiuniis. – V. De cibo. – VI. De collatione. – VII. De infirmis. – VIII. De minutione. – IX. De lectis. – X. De vestitu. – XI. De rasura. – XII. De silentio. – XIII. De recipiendis. – XIV. De novitiis et eorum instructione. – XV. De professione. – XVI. De levi culpa. – XVII. De gravi culpa. – XVIII. De graviori culpa. – XIX. De gravissima culpa. – XX. De apostatis.
Secunda distinctio continet : I. De domibus concedendis et construendis. – II. De electione prioris conventualis et institutione subprioris. – III. De electione prioris provincialis. – IV. De electione magistri. – V. De electione diffinitorum capituli provincialis et generalis. – VI. De capitulo cotidiano. – VII. De capitulo provinciali. – VIII. De capitulo generali. – IX. De solempni celebratione capituli. – X. De capitulo generalissimo. – XI. De visitatoribus. – XII. De predicatoribus. – XIII. De itinerantibus. – XIV. De

prologue et deux distinctions de respectivement 20 et 15 chapitres pouvant être regroupés en 2x4 sous-parties fut alors « gelé » (Gert Melville)[37] : tous les textes postérieurs, à commencer par celui d'Humbert, le suivent. Raymond de Peñafort a donc initié la standardisation thématique du texte des constitutions de l'Ordre.

D'autres versions, plus jeunes et moins connues, existent, dont deux qui couvrent en gros la période allant de la seconde moitié du treizième au milieu du quatorzième siècle, voire un peu au-delà, soit tout de même au moins un siècle d'évolution législative contre seulement au mieux quarante ans (1216-1256) pour les trois précédentes (en fait seulement trente, compte tenu du fait que la transmission régulière et à peu près complète des actes des chapitres généraux ne commence qu'en 1236). Georgina R. Galbraith a édité l'une en 1925, en annexe de son étude sur *The Constitution of the Dominican Order*[38], et l'historien de l'art William Hood a publié l'édition de l'autre par les soins de Crispin C. Robinson en 1993 en annexe de son livre sur les fresques de Fra Angelico au couvent Saint-Marc de Florence[39]. Ces deux dernières éditions ne sont toutefois pas critiques ; il s'agit de simples transcriptions[40].

Il reste par ailleurs un petit nombre de versions manuscrites (une dizaine), majoritairement du quatorzième siècle, elles ni éditées, ni transcrites, ni même collationnées, dont le Père Hodel a donné une liste en 1998 dans son « état des lieux » consacré aux « constitutions primitives »[41], lequel n'a depuis guère

---

studentibus. – XV. De conversis. Les sous-parties thématiques identifiables sont ainsi : 1) *spiritualia* (I-III), 2) vie quotidienne (IV-XII), 3) entrée dans l'Ordre (XIII-XV) et 4) code pénal (XVI-XX) pour la première distinction et 1) maisons (I), 2) supérieurs et définiteurs (II-V), 3) chapitres (VI-X) et 4) charges et états particuliers (XI-XV) pour la seconde.

37 Gert Melville, 'Die Rechtsordnung der Dominikaner in der Spanne von *constituciones* und *admoniciones* : Ein Beitrag zum Vergleich mittelalterlicher Ordensverfassungen', in *Grundlagen des Rechts : Festschrift für Peter Landau zum 65. Geburtstag* (Rechts- und Staatswissenschaftliche Veröffentlichungen der Görres-Gesellschaft – Neue Folge, 91), éd. par Richard Henry Helmholz *et al.* (Paderborn : Schöningh, 2000), 579-604 (repris in Gert Melville, *Frommer Eifer und methodischer Betrieb : Beiträge zum mittelalterlichen Mönchtum*, éd. par Cristina Andenna et Mirko Breitenstein (Cologne : Böhlau, 2014), 295-322), ici p. 589 : « So bedurfte es auch nach einer kurzen Anlaufsphase seit 1228 nur einer einzigen redaktionellen Gesamtüberarbeitung der Konstitutionen, die von Raimundus de Peñaforte… durchgeführt und auf dem Generalkapitel von 1241 angenommen wurde – die aber zugleich das strikt gegliederte Textraster der Rechtssätze gleichsam *einfror*, so daß einer künftigen Rechtsfortschreibung jegliche darüber hinaus führende materielle Erweiterung versagt blieb. »

38 Georgina R. Galbraith, *The Constitution of the Dominican Order, 1216 to 1360* (Publications of the University of Manchester, 170 – Historical Series, 44) (Manchester : The University Press, 1925), pp. 203-253. – Le manuscrit Add 23935 (British Library, Londres), dont provient le texte édité par Galbraith (f°s 572^r-579^v), est aussi le second manuscrit connu, rapidement signalé *supra*, nous ayant transmis le texte d'Humbert de Romans (f°s 74^v-80^v).

39 'The Dominican Constitutions', éd. par Crispin C. Robinson, in William Hood, *Fra Angelico at San Marco* (New Haven – Londres : Yale University Press, 1993), 279-290.

40 La traduction anglaise par le Père Tugwell du texte transcrit par Robinson (Robinson, 'The Dominican Constitutions'… [voir note 39], pp. 290-301) est néanmoins accompagnée de notes (pp. 323-326) en grande partie critiques.

41 Hodel, 'Les constitutions primitives'… [voir note 1], p. 40.

changé. Ainsi la tradition éditoriale des constitutions dominicaines médiévales reste-t-elle aujourd'hui encore plus qu'hier déséquilibrée et donc quelque peu insatisfaisante :

- L'attention des éditeurs et critiques, presque tous dominicains, s'est surtout concentrée (et se concentre encore !) sur les anciennes constitutions, qui non seulement ont été plusieurs fois éditées, mais encore ont bénéficié du travail critique à ce jour le plus abouti et le plus récent, celui du Père Thomas.
- A *contrario*, les versions ultérieures des constitutions médiévales, en particulier celles d'Humbert de Romans et les suivantes, ont été et restent négligées. Leurs éditions, quand elles existent, outre être souvent difficiles d'accès et d'utilisation, sont datées ou insuffisantes. L'exemple du texte d'Humbert est à cet égard sans doute le plus parlant : sa seule édition existante, fondée sur un seul manuscrit (sur deux), est toujours celle donnée à la fin du dix-neuvième siècle en trois parties dans les *Analecta Sacri Ordinis Fratrum Praedicatorum*[42].

Il résulte de cette situation éditoriale une sorte de distorsion ou réduction temporelle et historique : la législation dominicaine médiévale aurait été pour l'essentiel élaborée – et presque comme figée – dans la première moitié du treizième siècle. Mais le Moyen Âge s'étend jusqu'au tout début du seizième siècle – moment où parut (en 1505) la toute première édition imprimée (et en même temps révisée) du texte des constitutions, que le Maître de l'Ordre d'alors, Vincent Bandello (1501-1506), avait longuement préparée.

Certes[43], la lenteur à dessein prudente d'un processus législatif précisément centré sur la révision continue des dispositions constitutionnelles en trois lectures successives (*inchoatio*, *approbatio* et *confirmatio*) par trois chapitres généraux différents a préservé avec quelque succès les prêcheurs du danger de l'« inflation constitutionnelle » (*multitudo constitutionum*)[44] et fait que le texte des constitutions est resté (relativement) bref, alors que la législation statutaire d'autres ordres religieux ne cessait d'enfler au fil du temps, souvent dans d'importantes proportions (les exemples cistercien ou, surtout, cartusien sont à cet égard particulièrement significatifs)[45]. Certes, il est aussi peu discutable que les

---

42 Voir *supra*, note 33.

43 Sur les points qui suivent, voir la très commode, complète et récente synthèse, accompagnée de nombreuses références, de Gert Melville, 'The Dominican *Constitutiones*', in *Companion to Medieval Rules and Customaries* (Brill's Companions to the Christian Tradition, 93), éd. par Krijn Pansters (Leiden : Brill, 2020), 253-281.

44 Thomas, *De oudste constituties...* [voir note 16], p. 344 (II, 6) [p. 423].

45 Cf. brièvement Florent Cygler, 'Ausformung und Kodifizierung des Ordensrechts im 12. und 13. Jahrhundert : Strukturelle Beobachtungen zu den Cisterziensern, Prämonstratensern, Kartäusern und Cluniazensern', in *De ordine vitae : Zu Normvorstellungen, Organisationsformen und Schriftgebrauch im mittelalterlichen Ordenswesen* (Vita regularis, 1), éd. par Gert Melville (Münster : Lit Verlag, 1996), 7-58 ; id., '« Unité des cœurs » et « uniformité des mœurs » au défi de l'espace et du temps : les statuts des ordres religieux au Moyen Âge', in *Enfermements II : Règles et dérèglements en milieu clos (IVe-XIXe siècle)* (Homme et société, 49), éd. par Isabelle Heullant-Donat *et al.*, (Paris : Publications de la Sorbonne, 2015), 171-188.

éléments structurels qui font leur originalité[46], plus particulièrement dans la seconde distinction, étaient tous en place au plus tard en 1236(-1237) – notamment : dispense et « principe de la loi purement pénale », système administratif à trois niveaux (local, provincial et général) et régime de gouvernement à la fois traditionnellement autoritaire et plus modernement démocratique, rationalisme et fonctionnalisme poussés dictés par la *ratio* du *finis Ordinis* de la prédication (et des études qui y préparent).

Estimer, comme par exemple encore récemment le Père Hoyer, que « ... nach 1236 wurden die Konstitutionen von den Generalkapiteln praktisch nicht mehr verändert »[47] serait cependant exagéré : une rapide comparaison, pour un même chapitre des constitutions, entre les leçons du texte d'Humbert et celles par exemple du texte retranscrit par Georgina R. Galbraith est suffisante pour s'apercevoir que, reformulations et ajouts aidant, les changements ont été dans certains cas considérables. Et que dire des quantités avec le temps accrues d'*admonitiones* et autres *declarationes* par lesquelles les chapitres généraux, année après année, entendaient façonner l'application des constitutions à plus ou moins court ou long terme[48] ?

Autant dire et parier que l'« aventure éditoriale » des constitutions dominicaines au Moyen Âge n'est assurément pas terminée tant il reste(rait) à faire en termes d'éventuels projets éditoriaux. Le Père Hodcl en a déjà suggéré deux[49] :

– « faire l'historique des Constitutions » à l'aide des actes des chapitres généraux, sur une durée plus ou moins longue[50] ;
– collationner les manuscrits inédits des constitutions.

D'autres de plus ou moins grande ampleur restent envisageables – par exemple : l'édition critique du texte transcrit par Galbraith ou, à l'instar de ce qui s'est fait récemment pour les constitutions des frères mineurs[51] ou celles des carmes[52], l'agrégation, idéalement actualisée, des éditions déjà existantes[53].

---

46 Cf. aussi Florent Cygler, 'L'originalité des « constitutions primitives » dominicaines', in *L'origine dell'Ordine dei Predicatori e l'Università di Bologna* (Philosophia, 32 = Divus Thomas : Commentarium de philosophia et theologia, 3ᵉ sér., 44/2 [109/2]), éd. par Giovanni Bertuzzi (Bologne : Edizioni Studio Domenicano, 2006), 57-80.

47 Hoyer, *Jordan von Sachsen...* [voir note 3], p. 223 sv.

48 Voir Melville, 'Die Rechtsordnung'... [voir note 37], *passim*.

49 Hodel, 'Les constitutions primitives'... [voir note 1], p. 43.

50 Le Père Hodel signale que ce travail a déjà été en partie fait par André Duval, mais est resté inédit.

51 *Constitutiones generales ordinis fratrum minorum* (Analecta Franciscana, 13 et 17 = Analecta Franciscana : Documenta et studia, 1 et 5), éd. par Cesare Censi et Georges Mailleux, 2 t. (Grottaferrata : Quaracchi, 2007-2010), I (2007) : *Saeculum XIII* et II (2010) : *Saeculum XIV/1*.

52 *Corpus constitutionum ordinis fratrum beatissimae virginis Mariae de Monte Carmelo*, éd. par Edison R. L. Tinambunan et Emanuele Boaga, 4 t. (Rome : Edizioni Carmelitane, 2011-2016), I (2011) : *1281-1456*.

53 L'Istituto storico domenicano de Rome a piloté, par le biais du Père Hoyer, un tel projet au tout début des années 2000, qui prit la forme d'un CD-Rom accompagné d'un livret d'une trentaine

de pages faisant office de mode d'emploi : *Constitutiones et Acta Capitulorum Generalium Ordinis Fratrum Praedicatorum 1232-2001* (Berlin : Directmedia, 2002). Mais, outre de nombreuses erreurs ou approximations, n'y ont été reprises, pour le Moyen Âge, que les constitutions d'Humbert de Romans, cependant que les actes des chapitres généraux ont été privés de leur apparat critique.

ANNE RELTGEN-TALLON

La première législation dominicaine dans les récits fondateurs de la mémoire de l'Ordre

Dans sa thèse consacrée à l'histoire de la sainteté en Occident aux derniers siècles du Moyen Âge, André Vauchez avançait l'idée que le modèle de perfection religieuse incarné par les prêcheurs au treizième siècle procédait bien plus de la fidélité à une règle que de l'imitation d'une personne[1]. Bien entendu, c'était là une manière de parler, puisque les dominicains n'ont jamais eu de règle propre. Il s'agissait donc plutôt de souligner l'importante nuance qui les distingue, du point de vue du culte du fondateur, de leurs homologues franciscains et de reprendre ainsi une dénonciation déjà classique du parallèle trompeur souvent dressé entre les fondateurs des deux principaux ordres mendiants[2]. Toutefois, une quarantaine d'années s'est écoulée depuis lors, marquée par de très abondants travaux consacrés à l'histoire des débuts de l'Ordre des Prêcheurs en général[3] et de son développement institutionnel en particulier[4], dans le sillage du courant

---

1   André Vauchez, *La sainteté en Occident aux derniers siècles du Moyen Âge, d'après les procès de canonisation et les documents hagiographiques* (Bibliothèque des Écoles françaises d'Athènes et de Rome, 241) (Rome : École française de Rome, 1988²), p. 391.

2   Voir à ce sujet l'article de référence de Kaspar Elm, 'Franziskus und Dominikus : Wirkungen und Antriebskräfte zweier Ordensstifter', *Saeculum*, 23 (1972), 127-147.

3   Entre autres importantes étapes de ce renouvellement historiographique, on citera bien sûr la thèse fondamentale de Luigi Canetti, *L'invenzione della memoria : Il culto e l'immagine di Domenico nella storia dei primi frati Predicatori* (Biblioteca di Medioevo latino, 19) (Spolète : Centro italiano di studi sull' alto Medioevo, 1996) ; mais aussi une série de volumes collectifs : *I frati Predicatori nel Duecento* (Quaderni di Storia religiosa, 3) (Vérone : Cierre, 1996) ; *L'ordre des Prêcheurs et son histoire en France méridionale* (Cahiers de Fanjeaux, 36) (Toulouse : Privat, 2001) ; *Domenico di Caleruega e la nascità dell'ordine dei frati Predicatori : Atti del XLI Convegno storico internazionale, Todi, 10-12 ottobre 2004* (Spolète : Centro italiano di studi sull' alto Medioevo, 2005) ; et enfin, tout récemment, le volume de traduction en français des sources médiévales relatives à saint Dominique et aux débuts de l'Ordre : *Saint Dominique de l'ordre des frères prêcheurs : Témoignages écrits fin XIIᵉ – XIVᵉ siècle*, éd. par Nicole Bériou et Bernard Hodel, avec la collaboration de Gisèle Besson (Paris : Cerf, 2019), où se trouvent synthétisés les acquis de tous les travaux récents ayant permis de renouveler la connaissance de ce corpus complexe.

4   Parmi les meilleures études récentes sur le sujet, voir en particulier Florent Cygler, 'Zur Funktionalität der dominikanischen Verfassung im Mittelalter', in *Die Bettelorden im Aufbau : Beiträge zu Institutionalisierungsprozessen im mittelalterlichen Religiosentum* (Vita regularis, 11), éd. par Gert

A Cathedral of Constitutional Law, éd. par Anton Milh O.P. and Mark Butaye O.P., Turnhout, Brepols, 2023 (*Bibliothèque de la Revue d'histoire ecclésiastique*, 112), p. 113-130.
BREPOLS ❧ PUBLISHERS   10.1484/M.BRHE-EB.5.135048

initié par l'historiographie allemande sur la question de l'institutionnalisation des expériences religieuses[5]. Un tel *aggiornamento* ne permettrait sans doute plus aujourd'hui à l'historien de la sainteté de s'exprimer dans les mêmes termes qu'autrefois.

Par ailleurs, sans pour autant contester le bien-fondé de cette intuition sans doute assez juste d'une identité dominicaine résidant fondamentalement dans la législation de l'Ordre, on ne peut qu'être frappé par l'apparent contraste qu'elle fait avec la faible place de l'activité législative des premières générations de prêcheurs dans la tradition historiographique dominicaine, où la conservation même des principaux textes fait défaut. Comme chacun le sait, il existe un unique manuscrit des constitutions « primitives »[6] (comme d'ailleurs pour la mise à jour opérée par Raymond de Peñafort entre 1236 et 1241)[7]. Ce manuscrit est du reste en piètre état et présente ce qui est sans doute un état de celles-ci en 1236, mais copié près d'un siècle plus tard[8], sans que l'on sache très bien si c'est d'après un témoin plus ancien ou s'il s'agit d'un travail de reconstitution animé par un esprit quelque peu « antiquaire »[9] – du même type que celui par lequel Bernard Gui entreprit, à peu près à la même époque, de restituer, au moins en substance, les actes des chapitres généraux les plus anciens, lesquels ne nous sont connus, eux aussi, que grâce à cette initiative[10].

Melville et Jörg Oberste (Berlin – Münster : Lit Verlag, 1999), 385-428; John Van Engen, 'From Canons to Preachers : A Revolution in Medieval Governance', in *Domenico di Caleruega...* [voir note 3], 261-295 ; et, surtout, l'importante série d'articles de Simon Tugwell, 'The Evolution of Dominican Structures of Government', *AFP*, 69 (1999), 5-60 ; 70 (2000), 5-109 ; 71 (2001), 5-182 ; 72 (2002), 26-159 et 75 (2005), 29-94.

5   Voir à ce sujet la synthèse de Gert Melville, 'The Institutionalization of Religious Orders (Twelfth and Thirteenth Centuries)', in *The Cambridge History of Medieval Monasticism in the Latin West*, éd. par Alison Beach et Isabelle Cochelin, 2 t. (Cambridge : Cambridge University Press, 2020), II : *The High and late Middle Ages*, 783-802.

6   Archivum Generale Ordinis Fratrum Praedicatorum (Rome), MS XIV A4, f°s 28[r]-47[r] : il s'agit du fameux manuscrit de Rodez, où le texte des anciennes constitutions fut découvert et édité pour la première fois par Heinrich Suso Denifle: 'Die Constitutionen des Prediger-Ordens vom Jahr 1228', in *Archiv für Litteratur- und Kirchengeschichte des Mittelalters*, éd. par id. et Franz Ehrle, 7 t. (Berlin : Weidmann ; Freiburg : Herder, 1885-1900), I (1885), 165-227.

7   Cf. Raymond Creytens, 'Les constitutions des frères Prêcheurs dans la rédaction de s. Raymond de Peñafort (1241)', *AFP*, 18 (1948), 5-68.

8   Cf. Antoninus Hendrik Thomas, *De oudste constituties van de dominicanen : Voorgeschiedenis, tekst, bronnen, ontstaan en ontwikkeling (1215-1237) met uitgave van de tekst* (BRHE, 42) (Leuven : Bureel van de RHE, 1965), pp. 80-83 [pp. 244-246].

9   Comme le suggère Tugwell, 'The Evolution... I : The First and Last Abbot' [voir note 4], *AFP*, 69 (1999), 5-60 (p. 45).

10   Voir l'introduction à l'édition de référence : *Acta capitulorum generalium ordinis Praedicatorum 1 : ab anno 1220 usque ad annum 1303 iussu reverendissimi patris fratris Andreae Frühwirth magistri generalis* (MOPH, 3), éd. par Benedictus Maria Reichert (Rome : In Domo Generalitia ; Stuttgart : Apud Jos. Roth. Bibliopolam, 1898), p. vii.

Le texte fondateur de la mémoire dominicaine lui-même, le très important *Libellus de principiis Ordinis Praedicatorum* de Jourdain de Saxe[11], successeur de saint Dominique à la tête de l'Ordre, n'a été conservé que dans de très rares manuscrits (quatre connus dont deux sont perdus)[12]. Tant il est vrai que les premières générations de prêcheurs étaient peu enclines à la conservation des traces du passé et, au contraire, cultivaient un pragmatisme qui leur faisait détruire ou laisser de côté les textes désormais jugés obsolètes[13] – ce qui fut le cas de l'œuvre de Jourdain de Saxe dès lors que, après avoir servi de première *Vie* liturgique de saint Dominique, elle fut remplacée, sans doute à partir de 1238[14], par la nouvelle légende rédigée par le frère espagnol Pierre Ferrand[15].

Ce genre de texte pouvait cependant parfois trouver une seconde vie dans le remploi qui en était fait par la suite : en témoigne le caractère extrêmement répétitif de la littérature hagiographique consacrée au saint fondateur chez les dominicains du treizième siècle, au sein de laquelle les variantes sont souvent infimes. C'est ainsi que le *Libellus* de Jourdain de Saxe a continué, longtemps après avoir cessé d'être copié en tant que tel, de circuler en substance, demeurant par conséquent la source principale, quoique parfois indirecte, de tous les textes consacrés ultérieurement, chez les prêcheurs, à la glorieuse geste des origines[16]. Et parce qu'il ne s'agissait pas seulement d'une *Vie* de saint Dominique, mais aussi d'une chronique des débuts de l'Ordre[17], c'est également à lui que remonte toute la tradition relative à l'histoire de l'élaboration progressive d'une législation proprement dominicaine.

1. Le chapitre toulousain de 1216

Cette histoire, selon Jourdain de Saxe, commence en 1216, après le retour de Dominique et de l'évêque Foulque de Toulouse du concile du Latran, à la

---

11 Jourdain de Saxe, *Libellus de principiis Ordinis Praedicatorum*, éd. par Heribert Christian Scheeben, in *Monumenta historica sancti patris nostri Dominici* (MOPH, 16) (Rome : Institutum Historicum Fratrum Praedicatorum, 1935), 25-88 (Bériou et Hodel, *Saint Dominique...* [voir note 3], pp. 605-672).

12 Cf. Bériou et Hodel, *Saint Dominique...* [voir note 3], pp. 603-604.

13 Voir à ce sujet les remarques de Van Engen, 'From Canons to Preachers...' [voir note 4], p. 268.

14 Comme l'a montré Simon Tugwell, *The So-Called "Encyclical" on the Translation of Saint Dominic Ascribed to Jordan of Saxony : A Study in Early Dominican Hagiography* (Dissertatio ad lauream, Oxford, 1987), pp. 48-51.

15 Simon Tugwell, *Petri Ferrandi legenda sancti Dominici* (MOPH, 32) (Rome : Institutum Historicum Fratrum Praedicatorum, 2015), pp. 264-381 pour l'édition du texte (Bériou et Hodel, *Saint Dominique...* [voir note 3], pp. 797-857).

16 Selon Canetti, *L'invenzione...* [voir note 3], p. 332, il constitue encore les deux tiers de la légende de Pierre Ferrand, elle-même base de toutes les suivantes.

17 Ce caractère un peu hybride du texte, qui tient à la fois de l'hagiographie et de l'historiographie, a été relevé depuis longtemps déjà par Christopher Nugent Lawrence Brooke, 'Saint Dominic and His First Biographer', *Transactions of the Royal Historical Society*, 5e série, 17 (1967), 23-40.

faveur duquel les deux hommes avaient demandé au pape la confirmation de leur congrégation de prédicateurs permanents contre l'hérésie et s'étaient vu imposer par celui-ci un certain nombre de conditions, dont le choix d'une règle déjà approuvée. Voici en effet les termes dans lesquels le *Libellus* relate cet épisode :

> Aussi, après la célébration du concile, ils rentrèrent et firent connaître aux frères la parole du seigneur pape ; ils choisirent bientôt la règle du bienheureux Augustin, prédicateur excellent, puisqu'ils allaient devenir eux-mêmes des prédicateurs ; ils adoptèrent en outre pour leur usage quelques coutumes plus strictes sur la nourriture et les jeûnes, sur les lits et les lainages. Ils se proposèrent également et instituèrent de ne pas avoir de possessions, afin de ne pas entraver l'office de la prédication par le souci des choses terrestres, mais de recevoir seulement les revenus dont ils pourraient tirer ce qui leur serait nécessaire pour vivre[18].

Ce passage appelle plusieurs remarques. On notera, tout d'abord, le commentaire qui suit la mention de l'adoption de la règle d'Augustin : bien qu'il semble anodin à première vue, on peut toutefois se demander, à la réflexion, quel pouvait être le motif d'une telle tentative de justification d'un choix qui, pourtant, devait sembler assez naturel compte tenu des origines canoniales de Dominique de Caleruega[19]. Peut-être après tout n'était-il pas perçu comme tel par Jourdain de Saxe, qui avait rejoint les rangs des prêcheurs à une époque où leur transformation en un nouvel ordre religieux à part entière était déjà largement entamée[20] et où les raisons du choix d'une règle généralement plutôt associée au monde des chanoines réguliers paraissaient désormais moins claires[21]. Cela expliquerait aussi

---

18 Bériou et Hodel, *Saint Dominique…* [voir note 3], pp. 630-631. Texte latin : « Itaque celebrato concilio revertentes, verbo domini pape fratribus publicato, mox beati Augustini, predicatoris egregii, ipsi futuri predicatores regulam elegerunt, quasdam sibi super hec in victu et ieiuniis, in lectis et laneis arctiores consuetudines assumentes. Proposuerunt etiam et instituerunt possessiones non habere, ne predicationis impediretur officium sollicitudine terrenorum, sed tantum reditus *eis adhuc habere complacuit* (*recipere unde possent sibi in victui necessariis providere*) » (Jourdain de Saxe, *Libellus…* [voir note 11], p. 46). En italiques et entre parenthèses figure une variante signalée en note dans l'édition de Heribert Christian Scheeben mais retenue pour l'établissement du texte par Simon Tugwell dans sa nouvelle édition provisoire, qui a été utilisée par Nicole Bériou et Bernard Hodel pour leur traduction française.

19 Voir à ce sujet Marie-Humbert Vicaire, 'Saint Dominique, chanoine d'Osma', *AFP*, 63 (1993), 5-41 ; Lázaro Sastre Varas, 'El obispo Diego de Acebes y el Cabildo de la catedral de Osma : Raíces espirituales de Santo Domingo de Guzmán', in *Domenico di Caleruega…* [voir note 3], 91-129 et Adeline Rucquoi, *Dominicus Hispanus : Ochocientos años de la orden de predicadores* (Valladolid : Junta de Castilla y León, 2016), pp. 48-66.

20 Selon son propre témoignage (Jourdain de Saxe, *Libellus…* [voir note 11], pp. 54-62 et Bériou et Hodel, *Saint Dominique…* [voir note 3], pp. 642-652), il est une recrue parisienne de Réginald d'Orléans, lui-même arrivé au couvent Saint-Jacques fin novembre 1219 (cf. Marie-Humbert Vicaire, *Histoire de Saint Dominique*, 2 t. (Paris : Cerf, 1982), II : *Au cœur de l'Eglise*, p. 171).

21 Sur le tournant qu'ont représenté les années 1217-1220 dans l'histoire de l'Ordre, voir les réflexions de Grado Merlo, 'Gli inizi dell'ordine dei frati predicatori : Spunti per una riconsiderazione', *Rivista di storia e letteratura religiosa*, 31 (1995), 415-441.

la présentation inhabituelle qui est faite ici d'Augustin comme étant avant tout un grand prédicateur. Cet effort pour rapprocher son image de ce qui constitue la vocation première des fils de saint Dominique pourrait très bien traduire un certain sentiment d'incompréhension, de la part d'une recrue de fraîche date, face à des choix faits antérieurement, dans un contexte de maturation du projet dominicain qui, pour autant, n'était pas encore tout à fait alors ce qu'il devait devenir par la suite.

L'autre point sur lequel il convient d'attirer l'attention est la mention, présente dans ce passage du *Libellus*, de l'adoption de quelques coutumes plus strictes en sus de la règle d'Augustin. L'existence, en effet, d'un premier noyau plus ancien que les autres dans le texte des premières constitutions dominicaines, assez largement emprunté aux coutumes de Prémontré, a été établie depuis longtemps[22] ; mais l'idée, généralement admise[23], que celui-ci remonte à la phase législative initiale de 1216 repose en réalité sur le seul témoignage de Jourdain de Saxe. Et ces considérations sont également valables pour ce qui concerne l'histoire de l'adoption progressive du principe de la mendicité par les dominicains : c'est à nouveau le seul récit du *Libellus* qui permet d'établir que les années 1216 à 1220 ont été marquées chez ces derniers par la pratique d'une pauvreté qui n'était pas encore intégrale, mais consistait dans le simple refus de la possession foncière[24].

L'insistance de Jourdain sur ce point est compréhensible, puisqu'à l'époque où il écrit cette partie du *Libellus*[25], le principe de la mendicité vient tout juste d'être adopté (ou est en passe de l'être), lors du premier chapitre général de 1220, auquel il lui a précisément été donné d'assister[26]. Elle ne prend donc tout son sens que rétrospectivement, dans la suite de son texte, lorsqu'est évoquée la décision dudit chapitre[27]. Toutefois, la tradition ultérieure l'a conservée alors

22 Déjà le Maître Humbert de Romans la relevait dans son commentaire sur les constitutions, au début des années 1260 (bien qu'une première version de ce texte ait sans doute été rédigée entre 1248 et 1252 ; cf. Simon Tugwell, *Humberti de Romanis Legendae sancti Dominici* (MOPH, 30) (Rome : Institutum Historicum Fratrum Praedicatorum, 2008), pp. 287-294) : « Notandum est quod constitutiones Praemonstratensium omnino eodem modo incipiunt, et ex hoc elicitur, quod verum est, quod constitutiones nostrae extractae sunt ab illorum constitutionibus, cum ipsi nos praecesserint : et hoc iustum fuit » (Humbert de Romans, 'Expositio super Constitutiones Fratrum Praedicatorum', in *B. Humberti de Romanis opera de vita regulari*, éd. par Joachim Joseph Berthier, 2 t. (Rome : Befani, 1888-1889), II (1889), p. 2). Voir à ce sujet Thomas, *De oudste constituties...* [voir note 8], p. 127 [p. 280].

23 À la suite de Pierre Mandonnet, *Saint Dominique : L'idée, l'homme et l'œuvre, augmenté de notes et d'études critiques par Marie-Humbert Vicaire et Reginald Ladner*, 2 t. (Paris : Desclée De Brouwer, 1937), II : *Perspectives*, pp. 210-230.

24 Certaines dépositions de témoins au procès en canonisation de saint Dominique vont dans le même sens, mais sans donner les mêmes éléments de datation : cf. *infra*.

25 C'est-à-dire au plus tard en 1221, selon la datation désormais largement admise de Simon Tugwell, 'Notes on the Life of Saint Dominic : V. The Dating of Jordan's Libellus', *AFP*, 68 (1998), 5-33.

26 Selon son propre témoignage : cf. Jourdain de Saxe, *Libellus...* [voir note 11], p. 66 (Bériou et Hodel, *Saint Dominique...* [voir note 3], p. 656).

27 Jourdain de Saxe, *Libellus...* [voir note 11], p. 66 (Bériou et Hodel, *Saint Dominique...* [voir note 3], p. 656).

même qu'elle supprimait, dans son souci d'expurger le *Libellus* de tout élément historiographique pour le transformer en une véritable hagiographie, l'évocation des décisions adoptées en 1220 : c'est le cas, notamment, dans la première véritable *Vie* de saint Dominique qui en fut extraite par Pierre Ferrand[28].

Cette incohérence, quoique minime, n'a pas échappé à l'auteur la première révision de son texte, commandée par le Maître de l'Ordre Jean de Wildeshausen et approuvée pour l'usage liturgique dans l'ensemble de l'Ordre par le chapitre général de 1248 : Constantin d'Orvieto, qui devait devenir évêque de sa cité dès 1250[29]. Voici en effet la façon dont celui-ci remanie le récit du chapitre toulousain de 1216 :

> Aussi, afin de ne pas entraver l'office de la prédication auquel ils devaient se consacrer de tous leurs efforts, se proposèrent-ils dès ce moment de renoncer complètement aux possessions terrestres et aux revenus, ce qui par la suite, lors du premier chapitre général célébré à Bologne, fut, dans le désir comme dans les faits, mis à exécution pour toujours par le biais d'une constitution irrévocable[30].

Cette réécriture des faits n'est pas anodine. Elle consiste non seulement à rétablir ce qui avait été évacué de la légende précédente, celle de Pierre Ferrand, à savoir l'adoption de la mendicité en sus de la renonciation aux possessions foncières par le refus de tout autre type de revenu, mais aussi à la faire remonter à l'année 1216, la décision du chapitre de 1220 apparaissant ici comme une confirmation purement formelle. S'agit-il d'une simple approximation, de la part d'un frère ayant un peu de mal à comprendre les subtilités de l'évolution institutionnelle de l'Ordre à l'époque de sa genèse, ou bien d'une véritable tentative pour supprimer ce qui apparaissait peut-être comme un hiatus dans cette histoire ? Le doute est permis, si l'on prend en compte les autres ajouts apportés par Constantin d'Orvieto au texte de Pierre Ferrand.

En effet, c'est chez Constantin que l'on voit apparaître également pour la première fois le terme de « constitutions » pour décrire la législation de 1216, dans le passage déjà cité comme dans celui qui le précède presque immédiatement :

> Bientôt, après avoir invoqué l'Esprit-Saint, ils choisirent à l'unanimité la règle du bienheureux Augustin, docteur et prédicateur excellent, puisqu'ils allaient devenir eux-mêmes des prédicateurs autant de fait que de nom, en adoptant

---

28 Tugwell, *Petri Ferrandi legenda...* [voir note 15], pp. 314-315 (Bériou et Hodel, *Saint Dominique...* [voir note 3], pp. 824-825).

29 Cf. Canetti, *L'invenzione...* [voir note 3], pp. 404-406.

30 Bériou et Hodel, *Saint Dominique...* [voir note 3], p. 888. Texte latin : « Quapropter ne predicationis, cui summopere debebant intendere, impediretur officium, proposuerunt, ex tunc terrenas possessiones et reddidus prorsus abiicere, quod postmodum in primo capitulo generali Bononie celebrato affectu pariter et effectu per constitutionem immobilem perpetue fuit exsecutioni mandatum » (Constantin d'Orvieto, 'Legenda sancti Dominici', in *Monumenta historica...* [voir note 11], p. 303).

toutefois quelques coutumes de vie plus strictes qu'ils décidèrent d'observer sous la forme de constitutions[31].

Cette fois, il ne peut s'agir que d'un ajout délibéré et mûrement réfléchi : le texte de Constantin, en effet, fait ici écho à la décision du chapitre général de 1249 qui abolit l'usage du terme de « livre de coutumes », à propos de la législation dominicaine, au profit de celui de « constitutions »[32]. Sans doute cette décision est-elle un tout petit peu postérieure à la rédaction de la légende de Constantin et ne l'a-t-elle donc pas directement influencée ; mais une telle convergence traduit très certainement les débats internes à l'Ordre dans ces années-là.

Car le sens de la décision de 1249, qui s'inscrit dans tout un train de mesures législatives comparables[33], est parfaitement clair : il s'agit, à l'évidence, de rompre avec un vocabulaire rappelant de façon trop manifeste les origines canoniales des prêcheurs pour mieux affirmer la singularité du propos de vie dominicain. La fin des années 1240 voit effectivement se développer au sein de l'Ordre tout un courant de contestation de l'usage de la règle d'Augustin, de plus en plus perçue comme un carcan imposé par la législation de Latran IV alors que la vocation des prêcheurs était sensiblement différente et que sa réalisation pleine et entière ne pouvait que difficilement être atteinte à l'intérieur de ce cadre contraignant[34] : d'où les ajustements permanents réalisés par les chapitres généraux et l'adoption précoce d'un très large principe de dispense[35], formulé dès le préambule du texte des anciennes constitutions[36]. Un quart de siècle plus tard, cependant, certains

---

31 Bériou et Hodel, *Saint Dominique...* [voir note 3], p. 887. Texte latin : « Qui mox invocato spiritu sancto regulam beati Augustini, doctoris et predicatoris egregii, ipsi pariter re et nomine predicatores futuri unanimiter elegerunt, quasdam quidem arctioris vite consuetudines, quas sibi per formam constitutionum observandas statuerant, insuper assumentes » (Constantin d'Orvieto, 'Legenda'... [voir note 30], p. 302).

32 Reichert, *Acta capitulorum generalium...* [voir note 10], p. 43 : « Ubi dicitur in constitutionibus, librum autem istum quem consuetudinarium appellamus, deleatur istud, quem librum consuetudinarium appellamus, et dicatur sic, librum autem istum diligenter conscripsimus ».

33 Cf. Van Engen, 'From Canons to Preachers'... [voir note 4], p. 262.

34 Ce point a été soulevé depuis longtemps et a même été à l'origine de tout un débat historiographique sur la question du soutien ou au contraire des réticences d'Innocent III face au projet qui lui fut soumis en 1215 par Dominique et Foulque de Toulouse : voir à ce sujet l'excellent résumé de Simon Tugwell, 'Notes on the Life of Saint Dominic : I. Dominic and His Popes', *AFP*, 65 (1995), 5-53, pp. 16-17 et 20-21.

35 Sans équivalent dans l'histoire des ordres religieux contemporains : cf. Tugwell, 'Notes on the Life... I' [voir note 34], p. 20 ; Cygler, 'Zur Funktionalität'... [voir note 4], pp. 400-405 et Van Engen, 'From Canons to Preachers'... [voir note 4], pp. 290-291.

36 Sans doute en 1228 et sur l'intervention du Maître Jourdain de Saxe en personne (cf. Van Engen, 'From Canons to Preachers'... [voir note 4], pp. 290-291) : « Ad hec tamen in conventu suo prelatus dispensandi cum fratribus habeat potestatem, cum sibi aliquando videbitur expedire, in hiis precipue, que studium vel predicationem vel animarum fructum videbuntur impedire, cum ordo noster specialiter ob predicationem et animarum salutem ab initio noscatur institutus fuisse, et studium nostrum ad hoc principaliter ardenterque summo opere debeat intendere, ut proximorum animabus possimus utiles esse » (dans Thomas, *De oudste constituties...* [voir note 8], p. 311 [p. 423] ; Bériou et Hodel, *Saint Dominique...* [voir note 3], p. 207).

prêcheurs, et non des moindres, commençaient à aspirer à une mise en ordre de leur législation. Le cardinal Hugues de Saint-Cher, en particulier, s'efforça alors de porter le projet d'un vaste chantier de réécriture d'une règle proprement dominicaine à partir des différents éléments jusqu'alors épars de cette législation, à savoir la règle d'Augustin, mais également les constitutions qui, à cette époque, étaient encore celles mises à jour par Raymond de Peñafort[37], et, enfin, les actes des chapitres généraux[38]. Ce projet fut d'ailleurs approuvé dans un premier temps par le pape Alexandre IV, en 1255[39], sous réserve toutefois de l'accord du Maître de l'Ordre, Humbert de Romans[40]. Et c'est précisément parce que celui-ci fit défaut que le projet fut abandonné.

Humbert, en effet, était pour sa part profondément attaché à la règle d'Augustin et s'était déjà attelé, avant son élection comme Maître en 1254, et probablement de son propre chef[41], à la rédaction du célèbre commentaire qu'il lui a consacré et qui en constitue une véritable défense et illustration[42]. Sans doute sa visée était-elle cependant essentiellement pragmatique : l'une des principales vertus de la règle d'Augustin résidait en effet, selon lui, dans sa souplesse même, qui lui permettait de coexister harmonieusement avec la pratique législative régulière des chapitres généraux ; la rédaction d'une nouvelle règle aurait à l'inverse risqué, à ses yeux, de figer une législation dominicaine encore en devenir en ce milieu du treizième siècle[43]. Or, significativement, on trouve l'expression d'une idée assez proche sous la plume de Constantin d'Orvieto, qui commente en ces termes les décisions du chapitre toulousain de 1216 :

> En cela, le père qui organisait avec prévoyance les débuts de son Ordre, sans dédain pour les traces des Pères qui l'avaient précédé, tint un juste milieu, si bien que *les fils qui naîtraient et se lèveraient* (Ps 77,6) y auraient une mesure de la perfection requise sur laquelle ils pourraient s'établir, et que n'y manquerait pas la possibilité de monter plus haut par un progrès continuel, n'ignorant pas qu'il est écrit : *Le sentier des justes avance comme une lumière resplendissante,*

---

37 Cf. Raymond-Marie Louis, 'Histoire du texte des Constitutions dominicaines', *AFP*, 6 (1936), 334-350 (p. 336) : la nouvelle révision qui eut lieu sous le généralat d'Humbert de Romans ne fut initiée qu'en 1254, en même temps que la réforme liturgique de l'Ordre, lors du chapitre général de Buda qui vit également l'élection d'Humbert (Reichert, *Acta capitulorum generalium...* [voir note 10], p. 68 : « Committimus magistro ordinis, totam ordinacionem ecclesiastici officii, diurni quam nocturni, et eorum que ad hoc pertinent, et correctionem librorum ecclesiasticorum, et quod corrigat litteram regule »).

38 Cf. Van Engen, 'From Canons to Preachers'... [voir note 4], p. 270.

39 Le texte a été édité dans Mandonnet, *Saint Dominique...* [voir note 23], II, p. 269.

40 Voir à ce sujet les remarques de Van Engen, 'From Canons to Preachers'... [voir note 4], pp. 274-275.

41 Van Engen, 'From Canons to Preachers'... [voir note 4], p. 271.

42 C'est l'intention qu'il exprime clairement en introduction à son commentaire : « Cogitanti mihi de sermone qui exiit inter fratres de regula beati Augustini noto vobis, et timenti ne forte sermo huiusmodi aliquibus vestrorum esset occasio minoris devotionis ad ipsam » (Humbert de Romans, 'Expositio regule beati Augustini', in Berthier, *B. Humberti de Romanis opera...* [voir note 22], I, p. 43).

43 Cf. Van Engen, 'From Canons to Preachers'... [voir note 4], pp. 271-274.

et va croissant jusqu'à la perfection du plein jour (Pr 4,18). Cela avait été fort bien réfléchi, pour éviter que, si (Dominique) tendait aussitôt démesurément vers les sommets, ceux qui viendraient par la suite fussent contraints de reculer plutôt que d'aller de l'avant et qu'ainsi ce reproche de l'Evangile fût à bon droit formulé contre eux : *Cet homme a commencé à édifier et n'a pas pu achever* (Lc 14,30)[44].

Pour autant, ce passage disparaît de la révision de la légende de saint Dominique opérée dans le cadre de la réforme liturgique de l'Ordre menée à bien sous le généralat d'Humbert de Romans[45]. Sans doute apparaissait-il comme une digression un peu inutile dans un texte à vocation essentiellement hagiographique ; à moins qu'il n'ait semblé attirer maladroitement l'attention, dans sa tentative pour justifier un choix initial critiqué par certains de ses contemporains, à savoir celui de la règle d'Augustin, sur ce qui pouvait apparaître comme des tâtonnements un peu laborieux dans les débuts de l'histoire de l'Ordre, voire de véritables obstacles dans le déroulement du projet dominicain. La légende de Constantin d'Orvieto, en effet, était également celle où apparaissait pour la première fois le thème du songe d'Innocent III lors duquel était révélée à ce dernier l'excellence du nouvel Ordre dont Dominique de Caleruega et l'évêque Foulque de Toulouse envisageaient la fondation[46], épisode qui était présenté comme la réponse divine à son hésitation, voire à ses réticences face à leur demande d'approbation, seules explications logiques aux conditions qu'il leur imposa ensuite[47]. Sans doute les auteurs de la légende dite d'Humbert de Romans avaient-ils donc avant tout le souci d'essayer d'atténuer toute impression de débuts difficiles ou heurtés dans l'histoire de la genèse de l'Ordre. Ils ont ainsi supprimé le commentaire relatif à la pertinence du choix de la règle d'Augustin ; en revanche, ils ont conservé la version de Constantin d'Orvieto quant à l'adoption du principe de mendicité[48] qui, à l'inverse, allait plutôt dans le sens souhaité en gommant toute impression de

---

44 Bériou et Hodel, *Saint Dominique…* [voir note 3], p. 888. Texte latin : « In quo pater providus circa ordinis sui componenda primordia precedentium patrum non dedignatus vestigia sic medium tenuit, ut eis, *qui nascerentur et exsurgerent* (Ps 77,6), filiis et in quo starent modus debite perfectionis adesset, et quo possent ascendere per profectum continuum non deesset, non ignorans quod scriptum est : *Iustorum semita quasi lux splendens procedit et crescit usque ad perfectum diem* (Pr 4,18). Et hoc satis consulte, ne dum se statim in altum supra modum extenderet, succedentes in posterum retrocedere potius quam procedere cogerentur, sicque merito contra ipsos iuxta evangelicum illud improperium diceretur : *Iste homo cepit edificare et non potuit consummare* (Lc 14,30) » (Constantin d'Orvieto, *Legenda…* [voir note 30], pp. 302-303).

45 Tugwell, *Humberti de Romanis Legendae…* [voir note 22], p. 475 pour le passage concernant le chapitre toulousain de 1216.

46 Constantin d'Orvieto, *Legenda…* [voir note 30], pp. 301-302 (Bériou et Hodel, *Saint Dominique…* [voir note 3], p. 885-886).

47 Voir l'analyse de Tugwell, 'Notes on the Life… I' [voir note 34], pp. 9-11.

48 « Proposuerunt autem ex tunc, ne predicationis impediretur officium, a se terrenas possessiones abicere, quod postmodum in primo capitulo generali ordinis quod celebratum fuit Bononie anno domini .m.cc.xx. affectu pariter et effectu per constitutionem perpetue fuit executioni mandatum » (Tugwell, *Humberti de Romanis Legendae…* [voir note 22], p. 475).

rupture, donnant ainsi, au contraire, l'impression d'une parfaite linéarité dans le développement du projet dominicain.

2. L'élection d'un abbé en 1217

D'autres passages du *Libellus* que le paragraphe relatif aux décisions de 1216 ont également fait l'objet de réinterprétations ultérieures témoignant d'une certaine incompréhension des modalités de la construction institutionnelle de l'Ordre dans les premières années de son existence. C'est le cas, en particulier, de celui qui évoque l'élection d'un abbé au moment de la décision de la dispersion des frères de Toulouse en 1217 :

> Par ailleurs, il [Dominique] jugea bon qu'ils élisent pour eux-mêmes un frère comme abbé, qui les dirigeât tous par son autorité, comme étant leur supérieur et leur chef ; cependant ce qui relevait de la correction de ce dernier, il se le réserva pour lui-même. Frère Matthieu fut élu canoniquement comme abbé. Il fut dans cet ordre le premier et le dernier à être appelé abbé, car par la suite les frères décidèrent qu'en marque d'humilité celui qui serait à leur tête serait appelé non pas « abbé », mais « maître » de l'ordre[49].

Comme l'a montré Simon Tugwell[50], cette formulation donne à penser qu'aux yeux de Jourdain, l'élection de frère Matthieu signifiait la désignation de ce dernier comme supérieur de l'Ordre, ce qui était sans doute assez cohérent avec sa vision de frère parisien pour qui le couvent Saint-Jacques était clairement la tête d'une nouvelle congrégation religieuse et, par conséquent, son supérieur celui de l'ensemble des prêcheurs. Il ne lui restait donc ensuite qu'à rendre compte du changement du titre d'abbé en celui de maître, ce qu'il expliquait par la recherche de l'humilité ; mais en aucun cas il n'était question, chez lui, d'un quelconque changement institutionnel dans l'histoire de l'Ordre.

Or, cette dernière hypothèse est tout de même la seule qui permette de rendre compte de certaines contradictions apparentes dans les débuts de celle-ci, comme par exemple le fait que saint Dominique ait manifestement continué à se comporter en supérieur de l'ensemble de la congrégation en train de se transformer en nouvel ordre religieux alors même qu'un autre que lui avait été élu abbé. Cela ne peut en effet s'expliquer que si ce dernier titre renvoyait plutôt au projet de fondation d'une « province » française, vraisemblablement sur

---

49 Bériou et Hodel, *Saint Dominique*... [voir note 3], pp. 633-634. Texte latin : « Visum est autem ei bonum, ut aliquem sibi fratrem in abbatem eligerent, cuius auctoritate ceteri regerentur, ut maioris et capitis, cuius tamen correctionem ipse sibi retinuit. Et electus est frater Mattheus canonice in abbatem. Ipse in hoc ordine primus atque novissimus abbas appellatus est, quia postmodum placuit fratribus, ut ob humilitatis insinuationem is, qui preesset, non abbas, sed magister ordinis diceretur » (Jourdain de Saxe, *Libellus*... [voir note 11], p. 48).

50 Sur ce point comme pour l'ensemble de ce paragraphe, voir Tugwell, 'The Evolution... I' [voir note 9].

le modèle cistercien, avec une maison-mère dont le supérieur porterait le titre d'abbé (Matthieu, en effet, devait prendre la tête du groupe de frères envoyés de Toulouse à Paris en 1217). Mais la législation dominicaine évolua ensuite dans un sens qui rendit ce titre caduc, si bien que Matthieu fut tout à la fois, comme le souligne Jourdain, le premier et le dernier abbé de l'Ordre. Pour autant, la disparition du titre d'abbé ne s'explique pas par l'apparition de celui de maître, qui ne remplace pas le précédent. Simplement, c'est là la perception des faits de Jourdain de Saxe découvrant l'existence d'un « maître » de l'Ordre à l'occasion du chapitre général de 1220, en la personne de saint Dominique, sans soupçonner toutefois que ce dernier porte ce titre depuis un certain temps déjà.

Il en va naturellement différemment chez Pierre Ferrand qui, quant à lui, écrit presque vingt ans plus tard, à une époque où il est désormais parfaitement clair que saint Dominique n'a jamais cessé de diriger le nouvel Ordre des frères prêcheurs. Aussi l'auteur de sa première *Vie* donne-t-il une version quelque peu différente des faits, en mettant l'élection de frère Matthieu en rapport avec le projet qu'aurait alors caressé le saint de partir en mission auprès des Sarrasins, ce qui aurait nécessité de prendre des dispositions particulières pour le gouvernement de l'Ordre en son absence[51]. Cela dit, une telle interprétation revient tout de même elle aussi à considérer que c'est bien le gouvernement de l'Ordre qui a été remis à frère Matthieu avec sa nouvelle charge d'abbé ; par conséquent, pour expliquer le passage du titre d'abbé à celui de maître par la suite, Pierre Ferrand se contente de reprendre la version des faits donnée par Jourdain, à savoir le motif de l'humilité. Il y ajoute cependant l'adoption, à peu près contemporaine selon lui (c'est-à-dire datant d'environ 1220), du vocabulaire définitif pour désigner les prélatures inférieures au sein de l'Ordre, ce qui permet sans doute à ses yeux de mieux expliquer le changement de vocable pour désigner le supérieur de l'ensemble des prêcheurs en le replaçant dans le contexte plus large d'un travail de définition de l'ensemble des structures de gouvernement chez les dominicains :

> Par la suite les frères décidèrent en effet que pour marquer l'humilité, celui qui serait à la tête de l'ordre tout entier serait appelé non pas « abbé » mais « maître de l'ordre » et que tous les autres prélats inférieurs seraient désignés par les termes de « prieurs » ou « sous-prieurs »[52].

Il est aujourd'hui à peu près établi que saint Dominique a effectivement caressé l'idée de partir en mission, et cela peut-être dès 1217, mais avec l'idée de ne réaliser ce projet que deux ans plus tard, et sans lui assigner encore le but d'œuvrer

---

51 Tugwell, *Petri Ferrandi legenda...* [voir note 15], pp. 318-319 (Bériou et Hodel, *Saint Dominique...* [voir note 3], p. 827).

52 Bériou et Hodel, *Saint Dominique...* [voir note 3], pp. 827-828. Texte latin : « Placuit namque postmodum fratribus ut insinuande humilitatis gratia qui toti preesset ordini non abbas sed magister ordinis diceretur, ceteri vero inferiores prelati priorum vel suppriorum vocabulo censerentur » (Tugwell, *Petri Ferrandi legenda...* [voir note 15], p. 319).

à la conversion des Sarrasins[53]. Le lien suggéré par Pierre Ferrand entre ce projet et l'élection d'un abbé à la tête de l'Ordre est donc probablement une erreur. Mais celle-ci révèle un véritable effort de sa part pour essayer de reconstituer le déroulement des faits, ce qui témoigne une nouvelle fois de ce que celui-ci n'était sans doute déjà plus très lisible, dès son époque, aux yeux d'un certain nombre de prêcheurs. Par ailleurs, cette tentative de reconstitution l'amène également à opérer un rapprochement entre l'apparition du titre de maître et celui de l'ensemble du vocabulaire désignant les supérieurs de l'Ordre, en situant les deux choses autour de 1220, moyennant quoi il est sans doute, cette fois, assez proche de la vérité. Mais cela suggère tout de même qu'il ne comprenait pas très bien les raisons de ce qu'il considérait, à la suite de Jourdain, comme la transformation du titre d'abbé en celui de maître et qu'il s'efforçait par conséquent de le rattacher à un travail plus large de fixation de la nomenclature. Ce faisant, il a attiré l'attention sur cet aspect de la législation du chapitre général de 1220 et a ainsi inspiré à son successeur dans l'œuvre de construction de la légende de saint Dominique, Constantin d'Orvieto, le commentaire suivant :

> Par la suite en effet, les frères décidèrent que celui qui serait à la tête de l'ordre tout entier serait appelé non pas abbé mais « maître » de l'ordre, et que tous les autres prélats inférieurs seraient désignés par les termes – communs aux religieux – de « prieurs » et de « sous-prieurs », *se gardant* bien évidemment sur toute chose, selon l'Apôtre, d'*innovations en paroles*, sinon *impies*[54], du moins outrancières[55].

Une fois de plus, les glissements par rapport aux textes antérieurs sont ici tout à la fois minimes mais néanmoins suggestifs. La version élaborée par Pierre Ferrand pour expliquer l'élection de frère Matthieu est désormais complètement adoptée, mais celle de l'abandon du titre d'abbé au motif de l'humilité est en revanche laissée de côté, soit qu'elle ne paraisse plus très convaincante, soit qu'elle semble devenue inutile, comme si l'adoption d'une nouvelle terminologie était, avec le recul, considérée comme une évolution inéluctable et nécessaire dans l'histoire de l'Ordre. Aussi l'effort de justification porte-t-il désormais sur les autres titres existant en son sein, qui apparaissent manifestement comme quelque peu entachés d'archaïsme et d'une certaine absence d'originalité : ne peut-on voir là un autre signe de l'aspiration de certains prêcheurs, au milieu du treizième siècle, à mieux se détacher de leurs origines canoniales afin d'affirmer une identité

---

53 Cf. Simon Tugwell, 'Notes on the Life of Saint Dominic : II. Plans and Travels 1218-1219', *AFP*, 65 (1995), 53-169 (pp. 84-85) en particulier; et id., 'Notes on the Life of Saint Dominic : VI. Dominic Would-Be Missionary', *AFP*, 68 (1998), 33-116 (pp. 63-72).

54 Allusion à 1 Tim 6,20.

55 Bériou et Hodel, *Saint Dominique...* [voir note 3], p. 890. Texte latin : « Placuit namque postmodum fratribus, ut qui toti preesset ordini, non abbas sed magister ordinis diceretur, ceteri vero inferiores prelati, prior et supprior, communi scilicet religiosorum vocabulo censerentur, devitantes nimirum iuxta apostolum etsi non profanas superstitiosas, tamen vocum in omnibus novitates » (Constantin d'Orvieto, *Legenda...* [voir note 30], p. 305).

qui leur appartienne en propre ? Cela expliquerait sans doute pourquoi ce passage a été supprimé, comme d'autres, dans la légende remaniée sous le généralat d'Humbert de Romans[56]. Il n'en demeure pas moins très révélateur de toutes les interrogations qui ont pu traverser l'Ordre dans les mêmes années.

3. Les deux premiers chapitres généraux

Le dernier passage qui, dans le *Libellus* de Jourdain de Saxe, évoque l'histoire du développement institutionnel de l'Ordre est celui qui traite des deux premiers chapitres généraux. Il porte la marque très nette d'un récit d'expérience personnelle plus que d'un souci d'exhaustivité.

C'est ainsi que Jourdain commence par insister sur le caractère inouï de sa propre participation au chapitre de 1220 alors qu'il n'avait rejoint les rangs de l'Ordre que depuis à peine deux mois, puis sur celui de sa nomination comme provincial de Lombardie l'année suivante, au bout d'un an seulement passé dans l'Ordre des frères prêcheurs, lors d'un second chapitre bolonais auquel il n'avait pourtant pas participé. Mais, au passage, il nous apprend tout de même aussi qu'il s'agissait de la première nomination d'un provincial de Lombardie et que, par ailleurs, un certain frère Gilbert fut alors envoyé en Angleterre à la tête d'un groupe de frères, avec le titre de prieur[57]. C'est de là que vient l'idée, généralement reçue dans la tradition dominicaine, que la division de l'Ordre en provinces prit forme à l'occasion de ce second chapitre général ; mais c'est seulement sous la plume de Bernard Gui qu'elle s'exprime clairement pour la première fois, d'une façon encore quelque peu hésitante d'ailleurs[58].

Jourdain de Saxe est certes un peu plus disert sur le chapitre de 1220. Toutefois, même à son propos, il insiste surtout sur celles des décisions adoptées à cette occasion qui étaient susceptibles d'intéresser directement le frère du couvent parisien qu'il était : à savoir, tout d'abord, celle d'organiser des chapitres généraux annuels se tenant alternativement à Paris et à Bologne, qui se trouvaient ainsi consacrées comme les deux maisons-mères du nouvel Ordre ; et, d'autre part, l'adoption, déjà évoquée plus haut, de la mendicité, qui suivait de peu une

---

56 Qui rétablit d'ailleurs également, au passage, la référence à l'humilité à propos de l'adoption du titre de « maître » : « Placuit namque postmodum fratribus insinuande humilitatis gratia ut qui toti preesset ordini non abbas sed magister ordinis diceretur » (Tugwell, *Humberti de Romanis Legendae…* [voir note 22]).

57 Jourdain de Saxe, *Libellus…* [voir note 11], p. 67 (Bériou et Hodel, *Saint Dominique…* [voir note 3], pp. 656-657).

58 Dans son *Traité sur les trois degrés des prélats dans l'ordre des Prêcheurs* : « Ce que je crois plutôt mais je n'en ai pas trouvé la pleine certitude » (Bériou et Hodel, *Saint Dominique…* [voir note 3], p. 1192). Texte latin : « Quod magis estimo sed certitudinem plenariam non inveni » (Simon Tugwell, *Bernardi Guidonis scripta de sancto Dominico* (MOPH, 27) (Rome : Institutum Historicum Fratrum Praedicatorum, 1998), p. 102).

décision analogue du couvent Saint-Jacques[59]. Le reste de la matière abordée en 1220 au-delà de ces deux décisions n'est pas totalement passé sous silence dans le *Libellus*, qui laisse même transparaître son importance tout en demeurant, cependant, très allusif : « Plusieurs autres constitutions y furent faites aussi, qui sont encore observées aujourd'hui »[60]. C'est traiter bien rapidement de ce qui fut l'un des principaux temps forts de l'élaboration de la législation dominicaine primitive, alors même que Jourdain disposait, pour le faire, d'une information de première main.

Les hagiographes ultérieurs au sein de l'Ordre, cependant, n'ont pas toujours donné beaucoup plus de détails sur le sujet, même lorsqu'ils se sont efforcés de compléter ce qui était déjà connu des débuts de l'histoire des prêcheurs. Ce fut le cas, en particulier, du frère thuringien Thierry d'Apolda, auteur à l'extrême fin du treizième siècle, sur mandat de ses supérieurs, d'une nouvelle *Vie* de saint Dominique se présentant comme une compilation des légendes antérieures et de sources nouvelles[61]. Parmi celles-ci figuraient, en bonne place, les dépositions des frères du couvent de Bologne lors du procès en canonisation de 1233, jusqu'alors laissées de côté par ce type de littérature. Ces témoignages permirent en particulier à Thierry d'Apolda d'enrichir le récit concernant les dernières années de la vie du saint. Cependant, à propos de l'épisode décisif que fut le premier chapitre général, il ne retint, comme ajout à la légende de saint Dominique, que la proposition de démission de ce dernier, suivie de son refus par le chapitre et de la décision de celui-ci de se doter, pendant toute sa durée, de définiteurs qui seraient investis de tous les pouvoirs en matière législative et disciplinaire[62]. Sa source était ici la déposition des frères Venturino de Vérone et Rodolphe de Faenza[63], sans doute retenue sur ce point par l'hagiographe en tant que preuve supplémentaire de l'humilité et, par conséquent, de la sainteté de Dominique.

Il est vrai aussi que cet épisode est le seul à être explicitement mis en rapport, dans les actes du procès, avec le chapitre de 1220. Cependant, d'autres témoignages font clairement référence à certaines des décisions qui y furent adoptées,

59 Cf. Vicaire, *Histoire de saint Dominique*... [voir note 20], II, p. 176.

60 Bériou et Hodel, *Saint Dominique*... [voir note 3], p. 657. Texte latin : « Alia quoque plura ibi constituta sunt, que usque hodie observantur » (Jourdain de Saxe, *Libellus*... [voir note 11], p. 67).

61 Sur l'auteur comme sur sa légende de saint Dominique, voir Simon Tugwell, 'The Nine Ways of Prayer of St. Dominic : A Textual Study and a Critical Edition', *Mediaeval Studies*, 47 (1985), 1-124 (plus spécialement pp. 13-22).

62 Thierry d'Apolda, 'Libellus de vita et obitu et miraculis sancti Dominici et de ordine quem instituit', *Acta Sanctorum*, 1 (1867), 558-628 (p. 590) : « Cumque cessionem ispius nequaquam Fratres admittere acquiescerent, decrevit ex eorum beneplacito, ut deinceps statuerentur diffinitores, qui haberent potestatem super ipsum et totum Capitulum diffiniendi, statuendi, ordinandi, donec duraret Capitulum, salva imposterum reverentia magistrali. Ad extirpandas etiam vitiorum frutices, et plantanda virtutum germina, statutum est ab illis sanctis patribus, ut singulis annis generalia Capitula celebrarentur ».

63 *Acta canonizationis s. Dominici*, éd. par Angelus Walz, in *Monumenta historica sancti patris nostri Dominici* (MOPH, 16) (Rome : Institutum Historicum Fratrum Praedicatorum, 1935), pp. 124 et 151 (Bériou et Hodel, *Saint Dominique*... [voir note 3], pp. 700 et 730).

ou simplement envisagées, sans, pour autant, être repris par Thierry d'Apolda. Par exemple, les discussions évoquées par Jean de Navarre à propos du rôle respectif des frères clercs et des convers dans l'administration de l'Ordre[64], qui ne peuvent guère se comprendre qu'en lien avec une réflexion plus générale sur la question de la possession des biens et remontent donc forcément, par conséquent, au chapitre de 1220[65] ; et, plus encore, ce que le témoignage de ce frère nous fait savoir quant à l'adoption progressive de la pauvreté au sein de l'Ordre, soulignant, en particulier, le rôle déterminant de Dominique dans le processus – mais également, il est vrai, la difficulté de la tâche et les résistances multiples auxquelles elle se heurta :

> Item, il a dit que, comme l'ordre des Prêcheurs avait des bourgs fortifiés et de nombreuses possessions dans ces régions, qu'ils portaient de l'argent en chemin avec eux, allaient à cheval et revêtaient des surplis, ce frère Dominique travailla à faire en sorte que les frères de cet ordre abandonnent et méprisent toutes choses temporelles, s'attachent à la pauvreté, n'aillent pas à cheval, vivent d'aumônes et *ne portent rien en chemin avec eux* (Lc 9,3)[66].

On peut donc imaginer que l'une des raisons pour lesquelles la tradition hagiographique n'a pas retenu ces éléments, pourtant propres à ajouter à l'exaltation du saint fondateur, résidait une fois de plus dans la volonté de gommer tout ce qui pouvait donner l'impression d'une genèse difficile, voire de simples tâtonnements dans les débuts de l'histoire institutionnelle de l'Ordre. Dans cette perspective, mieux valait ne pas évoquer une proposition de gouvernement par les convers qui fut finalement rejetée ni, a fortiori, une conversion à la mendicité qui suscita, semble-t-il, bien des remous.

Cela dit, on peut aussi se demander si ce n'est pas avant tout parce qu'il accorde un rôle trop important à Dominique dans le processus qui mena à l'adoption de la pauvreté intégrale par les prêcheurs que le témoignage de Jean de Navarre est laissé de côté par Thierry d'Apolda. C'est du moins ce que suggère le fait qu'il laisse également de côté celles des autres dépositions au procès en canonisation qui, quoique de façon moins complète, et détaillant par conséquent

---

64 Walz, *Acta canonizationis...* [voir note 63], pp. 144-145 (Bériou et Hodel, *Saint Dominique...* [voir note 3], p. 722).

65 De plus, l'évocation du précédent grandmontain pour justifier le refus, par les frères clercs, de se voir soumis à l'autorité des convers quant aux questions administratives donne à penser que la discussion a lieu peu après la seconde grande crise qui secoue Grandmont à ce sujet entre 1217 et 1219 (selon le témoignage de Jacques de Vitry, *Historia occidentalis* (Spicilegium Friburgense, 17), éd. par John Frederick Hinnebusch (Fribourg : Presses universitaires de Fribourg, 1972), pp. 124-127).

66 Bériou et Hodel, *Saint Dominique...* [voir note 3], pp. 721-722. Texte latin : « Item dixit, quod cum ordo predicatorum haberet castra et possessiones multas in partibus supradictis, pecuniam portarent in via secum et equitarent et superpellicia deferrent, prefatus frater Dominicus laboravit et fecit, quod fratres ipsius ordinis dimitterent et contemnerent omnia temporalia, et insisterent paupertati, et non equitarent, et viverent de elemosinis et nichil secum in via portarent » (Walz, *Acta canonizationis...* [voir note 63], p. 144).

beaucoup moins les divers obstacles rencontrés, vont dans le même sens que celle de Jean de Navarre. On peut évoquer ici, par exemple, celle d'Etienne de Lombardie :

> Item, il a dit que, de même qu'il avait aimé la pauvreté pour lui, il l'a aimée aussi pour ses frères. Donc, il leur ordonna de porter de piètres vêtements et de ne jamais emporter d'argent en chemin, mais partout de vivre d'aumônes. Et cela, il l'a fait écrire dans sa règle[67].

Cette dernière phrase est lourde de sens : elle nous apprend que, en cette année 1233 qui vit se dérouler le procès en canonisation, la législation de 1220 apparaissait, aux frères de Bologne, comme la véritable « règle » de leur Ordre, bien que celui-ci, en réalité, n'en possédât point en propre ; et que, par ailleurs, cette législation était pour eux entièrement imputable à Dominique – et non seulement, donc, l'adoption du principe de mendicité. Étienne, d'ailleurs, avait précédemment employé une expression très comparable à propos d'un autre point de cette législation :

> Item, il a dit que son habitude était de toujours parler de Dieu ou avec Dieu dans la maison, hors de la maison et en chemin. Il y incitait les frères et l'a aussi établi dans ses constitutions[68].

Le terme de « constitutions » employé ici, et sans doute plus exact, est néanmoins manifestement interchangeable avec celui de « règle » employé plus loin, et sert à nouveau à désigner l'ensemble des décisions adoptées lors du chapitre fondateur de 1220 comme la véritable législation propre de l'Ordre ; d'autre part, celle-ci est clairement considérée comme l'œuvre de Dominique en personne. Or, cette approche est également celle des deux témoins bolonais qui ont déposé après Etienne de Lombardie, à savoir Paul de Venise et Frugerio de Penna, qui s'expriment dans des termes très proches à propos de chacun des deux points qui viennent d'être évoqués. Ainsi Paul de Venise dit-il, à propos de l'obligation de ne parler que de Dieu ou avec Dieu, que saint Dominique « l'a fait écrire dans la règle des frères Prêcheurs »[69] ; et, sur la question de la pauvreté, qu'il « a établi dans ses constitutions que les possessions ne devaient pas être reçues dans l'ordre »[70].

---

67 Bériou et Hodel, *Saint Dominique...* [voir note 3], p. 736. Texte latin : « Item dixit quod sicut amaverat paupertem in se, sic amavit eam in fratribus suis. Unde iniunxit eis, ut vilibus vestibus uterentur et in via pecuniam numquam portarent, sed ubique de elemosinis viverent. Et hoc fecit in regula sua scribi » (Walz, *Acta canonizationis...* [voir note 63], p. 157).

68 Bériou et Hodel, *Saint Dominique...* [voir note 3], p. 734. Texte latin : « Item dixit, quod consuetudo sua erat, ut de Deo vel cum Deo semper in domo et extra domum et in via loqueretur. Et ad hoc idem hortabatur fratres, et etiam in constitutionibus suis posuit » (Walz, *Acta canonizationis...* [voir note 63], p. 155).

69 Bériou et Hodel, *Saint Dominique...* [voir note 3], p. 741. Texte latin : « Et in regula fratrum predicatorum hoc scribi fecit » (Walz, *Acta canonizationis...* [voir note 63], p. 161).

70 Bériou et Hodel, *Saint Dominique...* [voir note 3], p. 741. Texte latin : « Et posuit in constitutionibus suis, ne possessiones reciperentur in ordine » (Walz, *Acta canonizationis...* [voir note 63], p. 161).

Quant à Frugerio de Penna, il dit également à propos de la première obligation :
« Cela, il le fit mettre dans la règle des frères Prêcheurs »[71] ; et, sur l'interdiction
des possessions et l'obligation de vivre exclusivement de l'aumône : « Et cela, il l'a
fait écrire dans la règle des frères »[72].

Bien entendu, cette convergence, sur ces deux points, s'explique très certainement par la méthode employée par les enquêteurs nommés pour recueillir les
témoignages sur la sainteté de Dominique auprès des frères de Bologne, à l'aide
d'un questionnaire élaboré au fur et à mesure des dépositions et soumis ensuite
aux témoins interrogés ultérieurement[73]. Il n'en demeure pas moins que, dans
ce cas précis, les deux qui sont venus après Jean de Navarre ont confirmé ses
dires, aussi bien sur les deux décisions qu'il présentait comme insérées dans la
législation de 1220 que sur le processus législatif en lui-même et, plus encore
peut-être, sur sa perception treize ans plus tard par les frères de Bologne. Très
clairement, la législation adoptée lors du premier chapitre général était, dans leur
esprit, l'œuvre de Dominique ; et, non moins clairement, elle était considérée par
eux comme la véritable « règle » du nouvel Ordre, comme le montre l'emploi de
ce terme aux côtés de celui de « constitutions » pour la désigner.

On conçoit aisément, dès lors, qu'une telle sacralisation ait pu apparaître
dangereuse aux générations dominicaines ultérieures, soucieuses, comme on l'a
vu précédemment, de préserver la possibilité d'une constante adaptation de cette
« règle » aux nécessités nouvelles et, par conséquent, de la maintenir sous la
forme de « constitutions » susceptibles d'être mises à jour au fil des ans. Dans
cette perspective, la paternité du fondateur en personne était sans doute plus
une gêne qu'une garantie et mieux valait, probablement, la passer quelque peu
sous silence, malgré tout son potentiel hagiographique, plutôt que de prendre le
risque, en la mettant en exergue, de se lier les mains pour l'avenir. En cette fin du
treizième siècle où écrivait, par exemple, un Thierry d'Apolda, le précédent des dé-
chirements traversés par la famille franciscaine sur la question de la fidélité à une
règle voulue par le fondateur en personne ne constituait-il pas un avertissement
redoutable ?

Ainsi l'étude de la façon dont s'est transmis le souvenir des premiers temps
forts de l'histoire institutionnelle de l'Ordre à travers la construction d'une mémoire dominicaine au cours du treizième siècle est-elle riche d'enseignements sur
les débats qui ont continué d'agiter les prêcheurs, bien au-delà de leurs premières
années d'existence, au sujet de leur législation. Peut-être contribue-t-elle aussi, ce
faisant, à expliquer en partie la mauvaise conservation des textes les plus anciens
signalée en introduction : toute réécriture de l'histoire, aussi minime soit-elle,
ne s'accompagne-t-elle pas nécessairement de la destruction des témoignages

---

71 Bériou et Hodel, *Saint Dominique…* [voir note 3], p. 746. Texte latin : « Et hoc in fratrum
predicatorum regula fecit poni » (Walz, *Acta canonizationis…* [voir note 63], p. 165).

72 Bériou et Hodel, *Saint Dominique…* [voir note 3], p. 747. Texte latin : « Et hoc in fratrum regula fecit
scribi » (Walz, *Acta canonizationis…* [voir note 63], p. 166).

73 Cf. Marie-Humbert Vicaire, *Saint Dominique : La Vie apostolique* (Paris : Cerf, 1965), pp. 23-25.

susceptibles de l'infirmer[74] ? Cela n'en donne naturellement que plus de valeur encore aux rares documents ayant malgré tout réussi à traverser les siècles jusqu'à nous, même lorsqu'il s'agissait déjà, à l'époque où ils furent composés, d'œuvres de reconstitution, comme c'est très probablement le cas pour le texte des « constitutions primitives » de l'Ordre des frères prêcheurs[75].

---

74 Comme l'a bien montré, entre autres, le bel ouvrage de Patrick J. Geary, *Phantoms of Remembrance : Memory and Oblivion at the End of the First Millenium* (Princeton (NJ) : Princeton University Press, 1994).

75 Un texte « qui, en tant que tel, n'a jamais existé », selon la formule de Raymond Creytens dans sa recension de l'édition de Thomas dans la *RHE*, 61 (1966), 862-871 (p. 866).

ANNA ZAJCHOWSKA-BOŁTROMIUK

Reformatio or deformatio?[*]

The First Observant Friars and the Dominican constitutions in the Light of Henry of Bitterfeld's Treatise on Reform of the Order

Having found many friars who zealously intend to return to regular observances in the form as given to us by the holy father Dominic and later maintained by his holy successors... I gave an order... that in each province... of the Order there be at least one convent where the observances will be strictly followed according to the form and wording of our constitutions... Let those gathered be assigned to this convent, where, as had been said, our constitutions will be strictly followed and regular observances maintained in the manner described in these constitutions.[1]

It is with these words that Raymond of Capua, Master of the Order of Preachers, outlined his project of reform in an initiating decree of 1390.[2] In spite of the

---

* This article was written as part of grant n° UMO-2018/31/B/HS3/01196 ('Henry of Bitterfeld and the Observant Reform of the Order of Preachers: Critical edition of the *De formatione et reformatione Ordinis Fratrum Praedicatorum*') financed by the National Science Centre, Poland.

1 '[...] inventis quampluribus fratribus, qui ferventer desiderant reduci ad primam formam observantiae regularis, per beatissimum patrem nostrum Dominicum inchoatam, et per Sanctos sucessores eius postomodum consummatam [...] Decrevi [...], quod in qualibet provincia saepe dicti Ordinis sit ad minus unus conventus, *in quo regularis observantia teneatur ad unguem iuxta nostrarum Constitutionum tenorem et formam*. [...] Illos, quos invenerit, assignet in dicto Conventu, *in quo servetur ad unguem, ut dictum est, tenor Constitutionum nostrarum et observantia regularis, sicut in ipsis Constitutionibus est expressa* [...]' (*Beati Raymundi Capuani, XXIII magistri generalis Ordinis Praedicatorum Opuscula et litterae*, ed. by Hyacinthe-Marie Cormier (Rome: Ex typographia polyglotta, 1895), pp. 54-55).

2 Observant reform of the orders, including the Dominican Order, is enjoying growing scholarly interest, as can be seen in a number of recent publications, such as: A Companion to Observant Reform in the Late Middle Ages and Beyond (Brill's Companions to the Christian Tradition, 59), ed. by James D. Mixson and Bert Roest (Leiden: Brill, 2018); Anne Huijbers, *Zealots for Souls:*

A Cathedral of Constitutional Law, éd. par Anton MILH O.P. and Mark BUTAYE O.P., Turnhout, Brepols, 2023 (*Bibliothèque de la Revue d'histoire ecclésiastique*, 112), p. 131-150.

BREPOLS ❧ PUBLISHERS   10.1484/M.BRHE-EB.5.135049

fact that most researchers today recognise that at Raymond's time arguments were developed advocating change rather than any specific actions undertaken,[3] and that Raymond's decree led to the establishment of only a few convents with strict observance in Italy and in the German provinces, the project of reform was immediately met with violent opposition from a number of the friars.

Opponents of reform, in response to the call to meticulously follow the observances as stipulated in the Rule of Augustine, and above all in the Order's constitutions, indicated that although the solutions outlined by the reformers were well within the limits of the law, they nevertheless unjustifiably excluded other interpretations of the same.[4] The accusations could of course be regarded as a reaction by depraved friars, who were not planning to give up their lifestyle and yield to the rigours of reform. However, when we take into account the specific character of the Dominican constitutions and the way they understand monastic obedience, it will transpire that 'conventual' friars – as the Observants called their adversaries – were not entirely without reason.

Raymond of Capua characterised the actions he was introducing as a reform, or – as he himself defined it – as a return to the initial form of the Order as described in the Rule and the constitutions.[5] Is this indeed what they were? Did the Observants really bring the Order back to the form intended by Saint Dominic and his immediate successors? Or maybe the implementation of the demands advanced by the reformers and the acceptance of their interpretation of the constitutions ultimately led to vital structural and legislative changes, thus constituting a 'deformation' rather than a reform? These are the questions I will attempt to answer on the basis of an analysis of Henry of Bitterfeld's treatise *De formatione et reformatione Ordinis Fratrum Praedicatorum*, the first work entirely dedicated to Dominican Observant reform, which presents its theoretical assump-

---

Dominican Narratives of Self-Understanding during Observant Reforms, c. 1388-1517 (Quellen und Forschungen zur Geschichte des Dominikanerordens – Neue Folge, 22) (Berlin – Boston: De Gruyter, 2018); and James D. Mixson, Poverty's Proprietors: Ownership and Mortal Sin at the Origins of the Observant Movement (Studies in the History of Christian Traditions, 143) (Leiden: Brill, 2009). A summary of current research of the Observant movements can be found in Michele Lodone, 'Riforme e osservanze tra XIV e XVI secolo', *Mélanges de l'École française de Rome*, 130 (2018), 267-278.

3 Cf. Michael Vargas, 'Weak Obedience, Undisciplined Friars, and Failed Reforms in the Medieval Order of Preachers', *Viator*, 42 (2011), 283-307 (p. 306).

4 Cf. Raymond Creytens, 'Raphaël de Pornassio O.P. († 1467): Vie et Œuvres II – Les écrits relatifs à l'histoire dominicaine', *AFP*, 50 (1980), 117-166 (p. 127).

5 'Reformationis vocabulum, proprie dicat primae formae ressumptionem. [...] Dum Ordinem visitarem, inventis quampluribus fratribus, qui fervente desiderant *reducere ad primam formam observantiae regularis*, per Beatissimum Patrem nostrum Dominicum inchoatam [...] *decrevi...*' (Cormier, *B. Raymundi Capuani...*, p. 54 [see note 1]).

tions.[6] The text was likely composed at the request of Raymond of Capua between 1388 and 1390, so still prior to the issuing of the decree that initiated the reform.[7]

The body of this chapter consists of five parts. The first addresses how obedience and the place of the law in the regular life are understood in the Dominican constitutions. The second demonstrates how Henry of Bitterfeld represented this issue in his treatise, and the next three parts outline the Observant interpretation of the provisions that led to the biggest controversy in the dispute between the reformers and the conventual friars – on the formula of religious profession, on the principle that the constitutions are binding on pain of a penance, not on pain of sin, and on dispensation.

1. Dominican constitutions and the vow of obedience

The lawmakers who created the Dominican constitutions decided to break with the monastic model of obedience of which the Cistercian monks had become an icon in the twelfth century. The founding of the Cistercians was a response to the decline of monastic discipline in Benedictine abbeys, and their primary 'battle cry' was the diligent following of all observances; their entire legislation was subordinated to this. The Cistercians were heirs to the many centuries of monastic tradition which saw in the regular life a sure path to salvation and the subjugation of sinful human nature.[8] Their way of thinking about the observances ascribed to these an exceptionally high importance, so that every breach of them was treated as at least a venial sin. This was discussed by Bernard of Clairvaux in his treatise *De dispensatione et praecepto*, which Bitterfeld very extensively cites.[9]

---

6 The most comprehensive and still valid article on Bitterfeld is by Vladimir J. Koudelka, 'Heinrich Bitterfeld: Professor an der Universität Prag', *AFP*, 23 (1953), 5-65. A summary of the literature on Bitterfeld was prepared by Pavel Černuška in the introduction to his edition of Bitterfeld's texts on the Eucharist: Henry of Bitterfeld, *Eucharistické texty* (Pontes Pragenses, 44), ed. by Pavel Černuška (Brno: L. Marek, 2006), pp. 52-72.

7 Vladimir Koudelka has proposed a very precise date of composition of the treatise, but I believe on insufficient grounds. He interprets the passage of the treatise which mentions the flourishing Jewish state that fell due to the sins of its inhabitants as an allusion to the pogrom of the Jews in Prague in the spring of 1389. Such an identification seems to me to be an overinterpretation, as it is much more likely that Bitterfeld meant the Roman conquest of Judea (cf. Koudelka, 'Heinrich Bitterfeld'... [see note 6], pp. 19-20).

8 Cf. Simon Tugwell, 'Introduction', in *Early Dominicans: Selected Writings* (Classics of Western Spirituality), ed. by Simon Tugwell (New York: Paulist Press, 1982), 1-48, pp. 20-21. On the development of Cistercian legislation, see Emilia Jamroziak, 'Cistercian Customaries', in *A Companion to Medieval Rules and Customaries* (Brill's Companions to the Christian Tradition, 93), ed. by Krijn Pansters (Leiden – Boston: Brill, 2020), 77-102.

9 Cf. Florent Cygler, 'Une nouvelle conception de la culpabilité chez les réguliers: Humbert de Romans, les Dominicains et le "principe de la loi purement pénale" au XIIIᵉ siècle', in *La culpabilité* (Cahiers de l'Institut d'anthropologie juridique, 6), ed. by Jacqueline Hoareau-Dodinau and Pascal Texier (Limoges: PULIM, 2001), 387-401 (p. 389).

The Dominicans, though they modelled their legislation on the Premonstratensians, who in turn had adopted theirs from the Cistercians, extensively modified it, introducing a number of innovative legal solutions. The most important are: insistence on the purely penal character of the constitutions, the formula of religious profession, and the rules on granting dispensation.[10]

First of all, when enacting the constitutions, the friars decided that the constitutions should not bind the friars in conscience. The purely penal character of the Dominican law meant that friars who did not abide by any provision could be penalised, but – beside exceptions specified in the constitutions – did not commit a sin. Moreover, the constitutions include an option to be dispensed from the observance of any provision should this constitute an obstacle to preaching the Gospel. This approach to the binding force of the law, one which was far from rigorous, was reflected in the formula of Dominican profession. The friars vowed obedience to God, Saint Dominic and the Master of the Order in line with the Rule and the constitutions, but not to the Rule and constitutions themselves. The result of this was that the Dominican law lacked supernatural sanction. The Dominican approach to law, and in particular the observances it contained, stemmed from the specific character of the life designed by Saint Dominic and his successors, which was a life of preaching combined with contemplation. For the Dominicans, preaching was a priority, and nothing, not even observances, must stand in its way.[11]

This approach to observances that we notice in the Order of Preachers and that was new compared to the monastic tradition, was founded upon a new concept of humanity and the role of law in social life. While the monks saw in monastic observances a way to tame evil human nature, which would inevitably fall into sin if left to its own devices, Saint Dominic believed in the friars' sincere pursuit of the good, and saw the law as – at the most – a teacher on the path to perfection.[12] He wanted the friars to follow the guidance of the constitutions not out of fear of committing sin, but in the freedom of their conscience, guided by the desire for the good. At the same time, he warned the friars against a pharisaic attitude towards observances, so that diligent adherence to the law would not become a goal in itself, thus destroying a living love of God and of people, with freedom being the condition for this love.[13]

The Dominicans realised how exceptional their solution was and what controversies it might entail.[14] At the same time, they had strong legal and theological arguments to stand by it. Firstly, Humbert of Romans emphasised that as there are two laws – the divine law and the human law –, there are also two arenas

---

10 Cf. Vargas, 'Weak obedience'... [see note 3], p. 288.

11 Cf. Tugwell, 'Introduction'... [see note 8], p. 22.

12 Cf. Tugwell, 'Introduction'... [see note 8], p. 23 and Pierre Raffin, 'La tradition dominicaine de l'obéissance religieuse', La Vie Spirituelle, 65 (1985) n° 663, 39-50, p. 47.

13 Cf. Tugwell, 'Introduction'... [see note 8], p. 21.

14 Cf. Cygler, 'Une nouvelle conception'... [see note 9], p. 389.

in which human beings bear the consequences of violating those laws. If you break the divine law, you are accountable to God; if you break the human law you are accountable to other human beings. The first kind of infraction involves committing sin, the second involves incurring a penance.[15] This was supported by the belief, developed on theological grounds, that only the divine law has power to bind the human conscience.

Thomas Aquinas maintained that human beings should first listen to their conscience and can only choose to surrender to the will of their superiors on the basis of their free decision.[16] He added that obedience to another human being could extend to external deeds only, and this exclusively in the scope limited by the nature of the superior's authority.[17] The same applies, in his opinion, to the law of the religious orders. This cannot unconditionally bind the human conscience, as this would cancel the possibility of making a free choice. Thomas explains that if the rule were to bind religious in conscience in such a way that they could never or almost never violate it without the risk of committing a mortal sin, entering the Order would entail a greater danger of damnation than living in the world, as it creates greater opportunity for sin. This is why, as Thomas further explains, the lawmakers formulated the religious profession in such a way that the duty of obedience to the rule was an assistance rather than an obstacle on the path to salvation. At the same time he calls the Order of Preachers the order which has 'the most careful and secure form of profession' which binds the friars to observe only those regulations of the rule which are expressed in it in the form of precepts (*praeceptum*), or those which are given this rank by a superior. Within this perspective, as Thomas writes further, the superior is like a living rule ('Est autem praelatus quasi quaedam regula animata'), in whose hands rest the interpretation and usage of the legal regulations.[18] Thus, the friar does not profess

---

15 Cf. Cygler, 'Une nouvelle conception'... [see note 9], p. 395.

16 'Deus reliquit hominem in manu consilii sui, non quia liceat ei facere omne quod velit, sed quia ad id quod faciendum est non cogitur necessitate naturae, sicut creaturae irrationales, sed libera electione ex proprio consilio procedente. Et sicut ad alia facienda debet procedere proprio consilio, ita etiam ad hoc quod obediat suis superioribus, [...] quod *dum alienae voci humiliter subdimur, nosmetipsos in corde superamus*' (Thomas Aquinas, *Summa theologiae* II-II, q. 104, a. 1, ad 1).

17 Cf. Thomas Aquinas, *Summa theologiae* II-II, q. 104, a. 5, ad 3. Thomas's notion of conscience as the most important agency that judges human actions is the source of his notion of obedience. However, there is no place here to discuss this in detail.

18 'Respondeo. Dicendum, quod nihil est peccatum mortale monacho vel religioso cuicumque, per se loquendo, quod non sit peccatum mortale alteri, nisi sit contrarium ei ad quod se voto professionis obligavit; per accidens tamen, ut ratione scandali vel alicuius huiusmodi, posset aliquid ei esse peccatum quod non esset alii peccatum. Est ergo considerandum quid sit illud ad quod religiosus voto professionis se adstringit. Et si quidem religiosus profitendo voveret se regulam servaturum, videretur se obligare voto ad singula quae continentur in regula; religionis status esset religiosis in laqueum et sic, contra quodlibet eorum agendo, peccaret mortaliter: et ex hoc sequeretur quod peccati mortalis, quod vix aut nunquam possent declinare. Sancti ergo patres qui ordines instituerunt, nolentes hominibus iniicere damnationis laqueum, sed magis viam salutis, ordinaverunt talem professionis formam in qua periculum esse non posset; sicut in ordine fratrum praedicatorum est cautissima et securissima forma profitendi qua non promittit servare regulam, sed obedientiam

obedience to the dead letter of law, even if these were written by the highest authority of the founder of the Order, but to a living human being, who can use this law as a tool, without treating its dutiful observance as a goal in itself.

This novel approach to observances and to the vow of obedience contained in the Dominican constitutions was a challenge to the Observants, who demanded faithful observance of the law and claimed that in doing so they were following in the footsteps of Saint Dominic and the ancient fathers. It is no accident then that the issue of how this must be interpreted appears in the writings of many Dominican Observants. It is also present in Bitterfeld's treatise, whose central subject is the law and its role in the reform of the Order.

2. The law and the reform of the Order of Preachers as understood by Henry of Bitterfeld

Bitterfeld chose a citation from Ezekiel (7:26) as *verba thematis* for the prologue of his work: 'Lex peribit a sacerdote et consilium a senioribus'. This sentence serves as a point of departure for deliberations on the role of law in the history of human communities. The author begins by stating that each human community is governed by a double law – the divine law (the *lex* in the Ezekiel quote) and the human law (the *consilium*).[19] The divine law can be of a double kind. It encompasses the universal law of nature (*lex naturae*) and particular laws that

---

secundum regulam: unde ex voto obligantur ad servanda ea quae ponuntur in regula tanquam praecepta, et quae praelatus secundum tenorem regulae sibi praecipere voluerit. Cetera vero quae non continentur in regula sub praecepto, non cadunt directe sub voto: unde ea praetermittens non peccat mortaliter. Beatus vero Benedictus statuit monachum profiteri non quidem observare regulam, sed quod profitens promittit conversionem morum suorum secundum regulam: hoc est dictu, ut secundum regulam dirigat mores suos: contra quod facit, si vel ea quae sunt praecepta in regula, transgrediatur, vel etiam contemnat regulam, secundum eam dirigere actus suos omnino recusans. Non autem omnia quae in regula continentur, sunt praecepta: quaedam enim sunt monitiones sive consilia; quaedam vero ordinationes sive statuta quaedam, ut quod post completorium nemo loquatur. Huiusmodi autem statuta quae in regula continentur, non habent vim praecepti; sicut nec praelatus statuens aliquid, intendit semper ad peccatum mortale obligare per praeceptum. Est autem praelatus quasi quaedam regula animata; unde stultum esset putare quod monachus frangens silentium post completorium peccaret mortaliter, nisi forte faceret hoc contra praeceptum praelati, vel ex contemptu regulae. Abstinere autem a carnibus non ponitur in regula beati Benedicti ut praeceptum, sed ut statutum quoddam; unde monachus comedens carnes, non ex hoc ipso peccat mortaliter, nisi in casu propter inobedientiam vel contemptum' (Thomas Aquinas, *Quaestiones quodlibetales* I, q. 9, a. 4, resp.).

19 'Ab exordio mundi in qualibet republica semper humana uita fuit duplici iudicio regulanda, scilicet iudicio Dei et hominum' (Henry of Bitterfeld, *Tractatus de formatione et reformatione Ordinis Fratrum Praedicatorum* [henceforth quoted as *Tractatus*], fol. 267ʳ. All quotes from Bitterfeld's treatise are from the critical edition of the text I am preparing. The footnotes refer to folio numbers from the manuscript of the University Library (Staatsbibliothek) in Eichstätt (MS 709, fols 267ʳ-299ʳ), one of two manuscripts containing the whole text of *De formatione*. The other manuscript, preserved in Vienna (Domin. 44/266), was heavily edited over time.

concern only certain groups of people (*lex disciplinae*).[20] This differentiation is not Bitterfeld's original idea, but was most probably borrowed from Thomas Aquinas, who introduced it in his *Super sententiis magistri Petri Lombardi*.[21]

All the regulations of the divine law have one goal, according to Bitterfeld: to guide people towards salvation.[22] The role of human law, on the other hand, is to adjust the requirements of the eternal law to the specific situations of human life and to adjudicate on moral doubts for which there is no answer in revelation.[23] This is why each human community needs both the eternal divine law, which constitutes a general framework, and the human law, which is variable in time.[24]

Knowledge of both laws is, in Bitterfeld's opinion, the basis for building social hierarchy, including the Church's hierarchy. Thus, there is a place in it for priests (*sacerdotes*), who know the divine law, and sages (*sapientes*), who are responsible for the establishment and preservation of human laws, and finally, for subjects (*subditi*), whose duty is to obey the other two.[25] If one of these elements is missing, or malfunctions, the community experiences a crisis.[26]

Bitterfeld then applies this model of the functioning of law to his own religious order. Although he does not say it directly, we can conjecture that, in his opinion, in the case of the Dominican friars, the *consilium*, established by the sages, whom he refers to as *antiqui patres*, constitute the regulations of the Order: the Rule of Augustine and the constitutions. In his opinion, the source of the crisis in the

---

20 'Iudicium quidem Dei nobis innotuit per legem nature et discipline, sicut et probatur ex mandatis primis parentibus insertis et expressis. Similiter et tempore legis, quando moralia precepta promulgando fuerunt renouata et hiis cerimonialia superaddita, ut essent quedam nature, tamquam omnibus communia, quedam discipline ad obedienciam probandam quorundam singulariter instituta' (*Tractatus...* [see note 19], fol. 267ʳ).

21 'Si dicatur, quod peccatum mortale distinguitur a veniali, quia mortale est contra praeceptum, veniale praeter praeceptum; contra. In hoc differunt praecepta *legis disciplinae* a praeceptis legis naturalis, quod praecepta legis disciplinae prohibent ea quae non sunt mala nisi quia prohibita; praecepta vero legis naturalis prohibent ea quae sunt prohibita quia mala. Ergo in his quae lege naturali prohibentur, distinctio mali non sumitur ex prohibitione legis, sed potius ex ipsa natura actus' (Thomas Aquinas, *Super sententiis magistri Petri Lombardi*, lib. 2, d. 42, q. 1, a. 4, arg. 3).

22 'Discurrentibus igitur legem Dei nichil occurrit, quod sine racione efficaci uideatur edictum, quin humane uite proficeret ad salutem' (*Tractatus...* [see note 19], fol. 267ʳ).

23 'Insuper humana uita fuit eciam hominum iudicio regulanda per racionis inuencionem et experienciam, ut donum Dei ex hominibus commendabile redderetur, quando dictamen recte racionis sapienter ueritatem uite patefaceret pluribus abumbratam. Et hoc est consilium, quod in preceptis nature tamquam correlarium latitat inferendum. Sic enim legi Dei racionis inuencio seu lex humana uidetur adiuncta, si quod lege Dei non exprimatur, quid agendum sit, ad consilium sapientis recurratur' (*Tractatus...* [see note 19], fol. 267ʳ).

24 'Debent concurrere lex sacerdotis et consilium seniorum pro reipublice cuiuslibet consumata salute' (*Tractatus...* [see note 19], fol. 267ᵛ).

25 'Dedit igitur Deus legem populo, sed principaliter sacerdoti, uoluit et esse consilium, sed singulariter in seniore, ut ab hiis ordinarie proflueret in inferiores, sicut ungentum, quod descendit prius in barbam Aaron, demum in oram uestimenti eius' (*Tractatus...* [see note 19], fol. 267ᵛ).

26 'Sic in Ecclesia propter peccata populi auferentur boni principes, religiosi doctores, consiliarii prudentes. Consurgit puer contra senem nullusque ordo honoratur sanctusque status Ecclesie confunditur' (*Tractatus...* [see note 19], fol. 268ʳ).

Order was that each rank of the hierarchy was lacking people who adequately fulfilled their duties to the law, the superiors and sages who knew the law, and obedient subjects: 'Iam omne caput langwidum et omne cor merens a planta pedis usque ad uerticem non est in eo sanitas, quia prelati sine uita, doctores sine sciencia et fratres inferiores sine obediencia'.[27]

The diagnosis obviously gives rise to a proposed remedy for the crisis, and this remedy is to return to adherence to the law. In the conclusion of the prologue to his treatise, Bitterfeld declares that he is ready to be the first to submit to this: 'corrigibilem me offerens, prompta uoluntate redigi desiderans in obseruanciam regule secundum antiquos mores patrum et ordinis professionem'.[28] And in the opening to the fourth part of his work, the commentary on the prologue to the constitutions, he takes adherence to the constitutions as a touchstone of the success of the reform: 'Quapropter <ad> [scripsi ad sensum, AZB] emenda-cionem tocius nostre conuersacionis satis necessarium uidetur materiam nostre Constitucionis ponderare, ut appareat singularius quantum a rectis limitibus de uia nos abduxerant, si uiam rectam mensurare uelimus'.[29]

Bitterfeld realised that the constitutions were subject to various interpreta-tions, and that his opponents were ready to use them against the work of reform: 'bella contra iustos excitabunt tamquam contra salutis inimicos per infamiam, su-surracionem, conspiracionem et falsam interpretacionem eciam erga seculares'.[30] He deals in his treatise with what he believes is the false interpretation of key sti-pulations in the constitutions, more or less openly disputing his opponents' views. The essential question concerning the observances, a question that emerged in the context of religious vows and became a divisive issue between proponents and opponents of the reform, was whether the profession of these vows obliged friars to observe the constitutions, and if so, to what extent.

3. The formula of profession

The question as to whether the Dominican profession obliges friars to observe the Rule and the constitutions emerged at the very beginning of the Order's existence, in the thirteenth-century *Questiones circa statuta ordinis Predicatorum*, which Raymond Creytens ascribed to Humbert of Romans.[31] The presence of this issue in Humbert's work was most certainly the result of the dispute that took

27 *Tractatus…* [see note 19], fol. 268ᵛ.
28 *Tractatus…* [see note 19], fol. 269ᵛ.
29 *Tractatus…* [see note 19], fol. 295ᵛ.
30 *Tractatus…* [see note 19], fol. 290ʳ.
31 Cf. Raymond Creytens, 'Commentaires inédits d'Humbert de Romans sur quelques points des Constitutions dominicaines', *AFP*, 21 (1951), 197-214 (p. 202). For more on the specific character of the Dominican vows, see for example Marie-Humbert Vicaire, 'Relecture des origines dominicaines: Le vœu de notre profession', *Mémoire Dominicaine*, n° 4 (1994), 207-224.

place within the Order in the late thirteenth century, which demonstrates that the answer to this question was not at all unequivocal.[32]

In order to understand Bitterfeld's standpoint on this issue it is necessary to go back to the very beginning of the treatise. Its first part is devoted to the theory of regular life, its definition and substance, and the meaning of particular vows. These reflections, seemingly disconnected from the main issue discussed in the treatise, constitute an inseparable foundation for his entire argument. Bitterfeld lists three definitions of regular life, and devotes most attention to the third, which he believes to express the essence of the consecrated life in the most accurate way. In doing so, he quotes Thomas Aquinas (though without providing the source). He states that religious are a class of people who are bound by the vows of poverty, chastity and obedience, who have decided to devote their entire lives to the service to God, renouncing all sin.[33] And later on, he sums up, following in Aquinas' footsteps, saying that the regular life means pursuing perfection in love. This practice is realised through fulfilment of the three religious vows.[34]

These assumptions have far-reaching consequences for Bitterfeld's standpoint in the dispute over the understanding of the role of law and the scope of the binding force of the constitutions. First, they allow Bitterfeld to argue against those who state that the friars are allowed to do everything that was not forbidden by the Rule and constitutions. In Bitterfeld's opinion, this statement is false as it ignores the assumptions adopted by the lawmakers regarding the level of moral development of the friars. Based on the assertion that the friars' goal, arising out of the very essence of their vocation, is to pursue perfection in love, Bitterfeld emphasises that when they enter the Order, the friars should be free from any mortal sin, and moreover, should avoid anything that might lead them into committing mortal sin. This means that they should be ready to renounce things that are allowed to people who live outside the Order.[35]

Second, on the basis of these assumptions, Bitterfeld answers the doubt as to whether friars who vow obedience only are obliged to also obey all the other vows. Bitterfeld notices that if the vows of poverty, chastity and obedience belong to the non-negotiable essence of regular life, then even if friars directly vow

---

32 Cf. Creytens, 'Commentaires inédits'... [see note 31], p. 203.

33 'Tercio modo sumitur stricte et anthonomastice et dictur status solempnis professionis quoad tria uota principalia, scilicet paupertatis, castitatis et obediencie. Quia tales sic se obligantes totam uitam suam mancipant diuinis obsequiis sibi peccati maculam aufferentes' (*Tractatus...* [see note 19], fol. 269ʳ).

34 'Ideo dicit sanctus Thomas, quod status religionis est exercicium siue disciplina, quo quis exercetur ad perfeccionem caritatis. Ex quo apparet, quod religio, ut hic sumitur, est in consiliis, quia illa ordinantur ad perfeccionem caritatis, ut apparebit in sequentibus, quoad tria predicta' (*Tractatus...* [see note 19], fol. 269ʳ).

35 'Religio presupponit totam uitam moralem et euitacionem omnium peccatorum mortalium, quia et hoc requiritur ad caritatem, quam presupponit, ut dictum est. Non ergo licet religioso, quod layco, ut puta pompose incedere, criminari proximum, inebriari. Et miror quorundam fatuitatem, qui putant sibi pene omnia licere, que Constitucione et Regula expresse non prohibentur' (*Tractatus...* [see note 19], fol. 270ʳ).

obedience only, they make profession of this 'according to the Rule', and thus indirectly they also bind themselves to observe poverty and chastity.[36]

Third, for Bitterfeld, the assumptions he adopts concerning the definition of the regular life give rise to the view that if the three Evangelical counsels of obedience, poverty and chastity constitute the right path for the friars to achieve perfect love, then all the observances which are directly related to their fulfilment must be absolutely observed. A further consequence is that the link with an individual religious vow becomes the criterion of the degree of binding force of the stipulations of the constitutions. The part of the treatise dedicated to chastity, and later the passage that explains that the constitutions bind the friars on pain of a penance, not of sin, contains a more precise development of this issue. Bitterfeld notes, referring to Peter Paludanus, that not all stipulations are linked in the same way to the fulfilment of each vow. Some of them are directly presented as appertaining to the fulfilment of one of the vows, while others have only an indirect link to individual vows. Obedience to the former is non-negotiable, while the latter can be observed less rigorously.[37]

The degree to which the various stipulations had binding force had already been discussed by Humbert of Romans in his *Questiones circa statuta ordinis Predicatorum*, which referred in this context to the example of the divine law, which – according to Humbert – was similarly binding to different degrees.[38] Humbert in turn at least partially derived this thought from Saint Bernard, the difference being that Humbert added to the categories of commandments that Bernard listed as 'binding on pain of light sin' a new category of commandments that could be broken without committing any sin at all.[39] The degrees to which religious vows were binding was also discussed by John Dominici, another Dominican

---

36 'Secundum dubium est, utrum ex professione nostra conuincimur uouere castitatem et uidetur, quod non, quia solum promittimus obedienciam, sicut patet ex forma in Constitucione nostra contenta: "Ego frater" etc. [...] Respondetur, quod votum est duplex. Vnum explicitum, aliud est interpretatum. Primum est obediencia, que uocaliter promittitur. Secundum est paupertas et castitas, que "Regula" sunt annexa et principaliter eam constituents' (*Tractatus...* [see note 19], fol. 282ᵛ).

37 'Ex quo apparet, quod contenta in "Constitucione" et "Regula" non equaliter ex professione inducunt obligacionem, quia silencium non tantum obligat, sicut castitas, quia non ad transgressionem uoti sicut patet. Et sic dicit Petrus de Palude q. 1[...], quod directe quis obligat se ad intencionem prelati, indirecte ad "Regulam" et magis ad forcia et minus ad minora' (*Tractatus...* [see note 19], fol. 282ᵛ); 'sed Petrus de Palude scripsit magistro Hugoni determinando quinque questiones. In prima questione dicit soluendo primum argumentum, quod tria sunt in nostra "Constitucione", que principaliter scilicet obligant nos ad mortale, sicut quod est contra paupertatem castitatem et obedienciam, aliqua, que sunt proxime hiis subordinata, in quibus secundum intencionem prelatorum peccamus uenialiter, in aliis autem, que sunt quasi per accidens, solum penaliter' (*Tractatus...* [see note 19], fol. 298ʳ).

38 Cf. Creytens, 'Commentaires inédits'... *[see note 31]*, p. 206; Cygler, 'Une nouvelle conception'... [see note 9], pp. 396-397.

39 Cf. Cygler, 'Une nouvelle conception'... [see note 9], p. 398.

Observant of Bitterfeld's generation, who divided the constitutional regulations into *consilia, mandata* and *praecepta*.[40]

The opponents of the Observants, when referring to the question of duties arising from the religious profession, pointed to the stipulation that the constitutions were binding on pain of a penance, not of sin. This solution, which, as I said, had been a distinguishing feature of Dominican law in comparison to the law in force in other religious communities, posed quite an interpretational challenge for the Observants. It is no surprise, then, that Bitterfeld dedicated an extensive part of his treatise to it.

4. The penal character of the Dominican constitutions

The provision on the purely penal character of the constitutions is one of the six doctrines that Bitterfeld discusses in the last part of his treatise – the commentary on the prologue of the constitutions. It is interesting that this part was referred to in the prologue to the treatise as 'causas speciales circa materiam nostre professionis', as if Bitterfeld identified the content of the constitutions that he was discussing with the formula of religious profession.[41]

Already in the introduction to his discussion of the 'doctrine' of the penal character of the constitutions, Bitterfeld notes that many scholars (*doctores*) have raised doubts as to whether this stipulation could be defended.[42] He describes two arguments they used. First, everybody who violates the constitutions commits at least venial sin (*peccatum veniale*), otherwise such a person could not be called a criminal (*transgressor*). Second, if the violation of the law incurred a penance only, and did not involve any transgression against virtue, this would mean that the regulation itself would have a tyrannical character, as it was not there to serve the protection of any value. And because it is impossible to admit such an assumption, given that, as Bitterfeld states following Aristotle, the goal of any lawmaker is to achieve a certain virtue, it must be true that everyone

---

40 Cf. Raymond Creytens, 'L'obligation des Constitutions dominicaines d'après le B. Jean Dominici o.p.', *AFP*, 23 (1953), 195-235 (p. 199).

41 *Tractatus…* [see note 19], fol. 268ᵛ.

42 'Sed quomodo hoc stare possit satis dubitabile est aput multos doctores' (*Tractatus…* [see note 19], fol. 297ᵛ). For more on the penal character of the Dominican constitutions, see Florent Cygler and Gert Melville, 'Augustinusregel und dominikanische Konstitutionen aus der Sicht Humberts de Romanis', in *Regula sancti Augustini: Normative Grundlage differenter Verbände im Mittelalter* (Publikationen der Akademie der Augustiner-Chorherren von Windesheim, 3), ed. by Gert Melville and Anne Müller (Paring: Augustiner-Chorherren-Verlag, 2002), 419-454; Gert Melville, 'Gehorsam und ungehorsam als Verhaltensformen: Zu pragmatischen Beobachtungen und Deutungen Humberts de Romanis O.P.', in *Obedientia: Zu Formen und Grenzen von Macht und Unterordnung im mittelalterlichen Religiosentum* (Vita Regularis, 27), ed. by id. and Sébastien Barret (Münster: Lit Verlag, 2005), 181-204.

who violates any stipulation transgresses against the virtue in question, and thus commits at least venial sin.[43]

In response to these doubts, Bitterfeld refers to the solution proposed by Henry of Ghent, who said that if the lawmaker's intent was to introduce a regulation which did not expose those who violated it to sin, such a violation would indeed only entail punishment, and not sin. This situation refers to those provisions which regulate morally neutral issues, such as violation of silence after Compline.[44] In Henry of Ghent's argument the category of 'the lawmaker's intent' is striking. It is this intent, and not the literal wording of the stipulation, that religious should take into account when interpreting any specific provision. The necessity to examine the lawmaker's intent behind any regulation also appears in the context of a discussion of dispensation. Bitterfeld notes that the friars who abuse this instead of profiting from their membership of the Order, become worse than if they had remained in the world, as they do not follow the 'intent of the fathers expressed in the "constitutions"'.[45]

Having addressed the essential part of the 'doctrine' he is commenting on, Bitterfeld proceeds to discuss the two exceptions it contains, when, according to the lawmaker, the principle of the constitutions binding only on pain of a penance does not apply, that is, the superior's precept and contempt (*contemptus*). Bitterfeld discusses the first exception very briefly, stating that it occurs when a religious violates any regulation of the constitutions in spite of having received a specific precept (*praeceptum*) to observe it from his superior.[46] Bitterfeld has more to say on the issue of obedience to superiors when discussing the vow of obedience in the first part of the treatise. One of the questions he poses there is whether religious profession obliges friars to observe all the precepts of the superior, as long as they do not violate moral principles ('si in omnibus licitis

---

43 'Primo, quia transgressor peccat ad minus contra obedienciam, alias transgressor non esset. Igitur ad minus uidetur, quod uenialiter peccet. Secundo, quia statutum, quod solum attendit penam, est tyrannicum, igitur oportet, ut quod intencio legislatoris tendat ad uirtutem ex 10 Ethicorum. Hanc autem obmittere uel transgredi est peccare contra uirtutem inesse debitam. Igitur est culpa' (*Tractatus...* [see note 19], fols 297ᵛ-298ʳ).

44 'Statutum est duplex: penale et legale. Si esset legale et penale ut non loqui post completorium, sed si quis loquatur, dicat septem Pater noster, tunc non potest esse sine culpa. Si autem est penale et non habet legale nisi ut materiale, tunc obligat solum ad penam, ut quicumque loquetur post completorium, dicat septem Pater noster nisi propter contemptum, sed hoc est per accidens. Si autem consideremus intencionem statuentis, ut per penam inducat, ne omnino fiat illud, propter cuius transgressionem instituitur et tunc illud de natura sua malum est. Et sic semper est culpa. Si autem de actu indifferenti ita, quod non intendit, ne omnino fiat, sed ne temerarie fiat, sicut loqui post completorium. Si ex racionabili causa quis loquatur, meretur solam penam, qua punitur sine culpa, non sine causa' (*Tractatus...* [see note 19], fol. 298ʳ).

45 'Pauci proficiunt ex religione, sed magis sunt peiores, quam dum fuerant seculares, quia intencionem patrum in "Constitucionibus" positam non prosequuntur debito exercicio caritatis et religionis racione peruerse dispensacionis negligentes' (*Tractatus...* [see note 19], fol. 298ʳ).

46 'Si sibi precipitur a prelato, quod regula non precipit uel "Constitucio", peccat transgrediendo contra obedienciam et sic frangere silencium in casu, si prelatus prohiberet, sub precepto esset mortale' (*Tractatus...* [see note 19], fol. 298ʳ).

teneamur prelatis nostris obedire ex professione?').[47] In answering this question, he states that the authority of superiors over friars is limited by the regulations of the Rule and the constitutions. He adds, however, that it is not only about the stipulations themselves in their literal wording, but also about the intent behind the wording, including, first of all, the concern about communal life.[48] In this approach, the constitutions seem to act primarily as a limitation on the authority of superiors, and only secondarily on their subjects' freedom.

Raymond of Capua was inclined to make regular use of the stipulation concerning the superior's precept which obliged the friars to observe the constitutions. In one of his letters, he writes that as the superior of the entire Order he could issue a precept to all the friars to observe the constitutions, and, by virtue of the vow of obedience, they would be obliged to listen to him.[49] Raymond's and Henry's contemporary, John Dominici, the Italian reformer of the Order, attempted in his turn to harden the meaning of the doctrine in question on the penal character of the Dominican law stating that the friars made a vow of obedience to Saint Dominic, whose will is written into the constitutions. Thus, when a friar does not observe the constitutions, he violates the precept of the superior, thus violating the vow of obedience.[50] If this interpretation is correct, the entire provision on the penal character of the law would have to be treated as void, as it is impossible to find a case in which this *praeceptum* of Saint Dominic would not be binding.

Bitterfeld's thought, on the other hand, seems to take an entirely different route. He bases his own interpretation of this contentious regulation – an interpretation which allowed him, despite everything, to insist that the friars must obey the constitutions – on the second exception, contempt for the law. Quoting Aquinas, Bitterfeld states that contempt for the constitutions occurs when a friar violates them as a result of having neglected the pursuit of perfection.[51] And this

---

47 *Tractatus...* [see note 19], fol. 285ʳ.

48 'Solum in hiis debet esse obediencia, que sunt in "Regula" contenta subintelligendo "Constitucionem" et consimilia, secundum que fit professio. Sic tamen, quod non solum, que directe sunt in "Regula", sed intellecta et supposita, scilicet sine quibus uita communis seruari non potest, ut mutuum obsequium, determinacio penarum, eciam si expresse in regula non sanctirentur. Et illa opinio pene tenetur ab omnibus' (*Tractatus...* [see note 19], fols 285ʳ-285ᵛ).

49 'An ego, seu quicumque rector unius religionis debeam sive debeat operam efficacem dare, quod subditi servent suam Regulam, vel non: ad nichilum valet officium nostrum; si autem dicunt, quod sic, ergo non essem reprehendendus, etsi omnes cogerem ad servandum ea, quae scripta sunt tam in Regula, quam in Constitutionibus nostris, ipsique indubitanter ex voto suae professionis mihi tenentur effectualiter obedire; et si non facerent, venirent contra votum solemne suae Professionis. Sic enim omnes, et singuli sunt profesi, obedire videlicet magistro OFP, et sucessoribus eius secundum regulam beati Augustini et Constitutiones FP usque ad mortem' (Cormier, *Beati Raymundi...* [see note 1], p. 91).

50 Creytens, 'L'obligation'... [see note 40], pp. 198 and 203. Raphaël of Pornassio was among those who used this argument by John Dominici, see id., 'Raphaël de Pornassio'... [see note 4], p. 124.

51 'Religiosus non tenetur esse perfectus, sed tendere ad perfeccionem. Tendere autem ad perfeccionem est adhibere studium secundum professionem regule. Qui autem habitum tendendi perdit, conformari regule contempnit' (*Tractatus...* [see note 19], fol. 298ᵛ).

while the pursuit of perfection constitutes the main purpose of regular life, which can be realised through the three vows. Thus, when a friar neglects this pursuit, deviating from the path laid out by the constitutions and the Rule, he commits mortal sin. This does not occur when the cause of the violation of the stipulations is human frailty, such as lust or anger, even if such a violation takes place on multiple occasions.[52] This does not mean, however, that a friar may commit such a violation without any consequences. Apart from the penalty such behaviour entails, the guilty friar is at risk of disregarding the regulations, thus falling into mortal sin.[53] Persistent violations of the constitutions, including those resulting from human frailty, may evolve into a bad habit, which can subsequently spread among friars, causing a crisis for the entire community.[54] The issue of a custom which – to the detriment of the Order – evolves into a binding principle is a typical element of the dispute between Observants and their opponents, as the 'custom-based' argument was used by all – not just Dominican – proponents of the easing of monastic discipline.[55]

Bitterfeld gives no summary of his deliberations on the passage of the consti-tutions in question. However, it is clear on the basis of his arguments that he believed that the principle that the constitutions are binding on pain of a penance, not of sin, only refers to friars who pursue perfection through loving God, and who happen to violate the regulations occasionally, solely as a result of their own frailty, or who, in justified cases, conclude that the lawmaker's intent is better served by bypassing the letter of the law.

In an attempt to reinterpret the provision on the purely penal character of the constitutions, Bitterfeld – like other Observants – indirectly questioned one of the foundations of the Dominican understanding of regular life. The penal nature of the Dominican constitutions, the sources of which, according to Gilles Meersseman, most probably derived from the law of the communes, was of vital importance to Dominican identity and had far-reaching consequences for the structure of the community.[56] As in Italian cities, which were the first to introduce purely penal law, the central monarchic power of the pope or the emperor was replaced by collective government by the inhabitants. Similarly, in the Order of

---

52 'Quando autem e conuerso, propter aliquam causam particularem, puta concupiscenciam uel iram, non peccat ex contemptu eciam si frequenter fiat' (*Tractatus...* [see note 19], fol. 298ᵛ).

53 'Sed frequencia ex disposicione ducit ad contemptum' (*Tractatus...* [see note 19], fol. 298ᵛ).

54 'Quintum est quod caueri debeat, quod peccatum non fiat tam generale, ut omnes inficiat, ne et tunc pro lege habeatur prauitatem consuetudinem estimentes' (*Tractatus...* [see note 19], fol. 294ᵛ); 'Sic in proposito propter assiduitatem peccandi prauos mores bonos estimamus, cum magis usum uel abusum approbemus. Vnde Seneca libro *De beata* uita in principio: Argumentum pessimi, turba. Queramus, quod optimum perfectum, non quid usitatissimum. Et sequitur: Nulla res maioribus malis implicatur, quam que ad rumorem componitur. Et sequitur concludendo: Quod hoc ex multitudine peccancium procedit, que incorrigibilis est' (*Tractatus...* [see note 19], fol. 289ᵛ).

55 Cf. Mixson, *Poverty's Proprietors...* [see note 2], p. 41.

56 Cf. Gilles Gérard Meersseman, 'La loi purement pénale d'après les statuts des confréries médiévales', in *Mélanges Joseph de Ghellinck, S.J.* (Museum Lessianum – Section historique, 13-14), 2 vols, (Gembloux: Duculot, 1951), II, 975-1002 (p. 976).

Preachers the hierarchical monastic structure, headed by an abbot elected for life, was replaced by collective government, with a central role for general chapters which had the power to make changes to the constitutions.[57] Superiors of all ranks were selected by the chapters for a specific period of time, after which they left their offices to become one of the *subditi*.[58] In this model of governing a community, the division into superiors (*praelati*) and subjects (*subditi*) became blurred. The Master of the Order, the prior provincial, or the local prior, as John Dominici, among others, outlined, are only representatives of the conventual, provincial and general chapters and are subject to these, executing the guidelines they have enacted.[59] Importantly, both the *subditi* and the *praelati* participate in this law-making process.[60] Nor can the superior – as Humbert of Romans in *De vita regulari* already pointed out – make any decision of great importance without consulting the community.[61]

The Observant path to reform of the Order involved changing this approach to the law by placing emphasis on the absolute duty of observance, and it would inevitably have led to changes in the structure of the Order. And indeed, in the course of the reform, in addition to the priors provincial, who were elected for a specific term, nominated superiors emerged – the vicars general.[62] This tendency to abandon the collective model of government of the Order which was linked to the penal character of the law is also visible in how the proponents of Observant reform describe the religious community. It can also be seen in Bitterfeld's writing, as he makes a very strict distinction between superiors and subjects in his treatise. For example, in the second part of *De formatione*, he lists four offences that can be committed by each group, and in part three he provides appropriate remedies. He also ascribes a different role to each group in the reform of the Order. The former are described as active participants, and the latter as passive participants.[63]

Bitterfeld apparently shares the belief of the Order's lawmakers that the law they were enacting was purely human in character, a belief which found expression in the principle that the constitutions were binding on pain of a penance, not

---

57 Cf. Vargas, 'Weak obedience'... [see note 3], pp. 293 and 301. For more on various models of commune life in the Dominican context, see Raffin, 'La tradition dominicaine'... [see note 12], pp. 40-42.

58 Cf. Raffin, 'La tradition dominicaine'... [see note 12], p. 44.

59 Cf. Creytens, 'L'obligation'... [see note 40], p. 201 and Raffin, 'La tradition dominicaine'... [see note 12], p. 44.

60 On this subject, see Gert Melville, 'The Fixed and the Fluid: Observations on the Rational Bases of Dominican Constitution and Organization in the Middle Ages', in *Making and Breaking the Rules: Discussion, Implementation, and Consequences of Dominican Legislation* (Studies of the German Historical Institute, London), ed. by Cornelia Linde (Oxford: Oxford University Press, 2018), 19-35 (esp. pp. 24-27 and 31-32).

61 Cf. Raffin, 'La tradition dominicaine'... [see note 12], p. 45.

62 Cf. Vargas, 'Weak obedience'... [see note 3], p. 301.

63 'De modo igitur potest triplex questio formari. Prima si subito reformacio fieri debeat, an paulatim. Secunda per quos actiue et passiue' (*Tractatus*... [see note 19], fol. 290ʳ).

of sin. In the previously discussed deliberations on the double character of the law that is in force in human communities, there is, after all, a place for *consilium*. Bitterfeld certainly classifies the Dominican constitutions among this category of laws. However, it is important to look at how the author speaks of statutory law. In his opinion, as he himself emphasises, this is a *corrolarium* to the divine law, and it cannot exist without that law.[64] Thus, though it is a human law, it is not entirely 'secular'. It is further sacralised by the fact that it was enacted by *antiqui patres*, who enjoyed unquestioned authority. Each attempt at negating this law was a challenge to the will of the ancient fathers, which should always be treated as an undisputable point of reference. This respectful attitude that Bitterfeld has towards the constitutions can be seen very clearly in his thinking on dispensation.

5. Dispensation

Bitterfeld discusses the issue of dispensation in three places in his treatise: in the diagnosis of the causes of crisis, in a presentation of remedies, and finally in his commentary on the prologue, which concludes the treatise. In the second of these parts, Bitterfeld offers a systematic exposition of dispensation. He begins with a definition, stating that dispensation is an interpretation or 'relaxation' (*relaxatio*) of the law.[65] Bitterfeld gives a similar definition of dispensation in his commentary on the prologue to the constitutions, stating that the use of dispensation constitutes an interpretation of the law or relaxation of its rigour.[66] Shortly thereafter, he adds, following Thomas Aquinas, that it can also be understood as an adjustment of general principles to individual cases.[67] Next, he presents two conditions for the appropriate use of dispensation. In his opinion, these conditions are that the person who grants the dispensation must have the right to do so, and must have a justified reason for doing so.[68] The only good reason for granting dispensation is the common good (*utilitas communis*). The commentary to the prologue gives an example of such a situation, when he writes that the reason why dispensation had been written into the constitutions was to facilitate study for friars, which, viewed in a wider perspective, serves the Order's apostolate of preaching, which in turn

---

64 'Insuper humana uita fuit eciam hominum iudicio regulanda per racionis inuencionem et experienciam, ut donum Dei ex hominibus commendabile redderetur, quando dictamen recte racionis sapienter ueritatem uite patefaceret pluribus abumbratam. Et hoc est consilium, quod in preceptis nature, tamquam correlarium, latitat inferendum. Sic enim legi Dei racionis inuencio seu lex humana uidetur adiuncta, si quod lege Dei non exprimatur, quid agendum sit, ad consilium sapientis recurratur' (*Tractatus...* [see note 19], fol. 267ʳ).
65 'Est autem dispensacio iuris interpretacio uel iuris relaxacio' (*Tractatus...* [see note 19], fol. 293ᵛ).
66 'Dispensare, id est legem interpretari uel rigorem diminuere' (*Tractatus...* [see note 19], fol. 297ᵛ).
67 'Dispensacio est commensuracio communis ad singula' (*Tractatus...* [see note 19], fol. 293ᵛ).
68 'Nota quod ad dispensandum duo requiruntur: auctoritas et causa. Sine altero horum non est dispensacio' (*Tractatus...* [see note 19], fol. 294ʳ).

serves the salvation of souls: 'Deinde exprimitur causa dispensandi, quia racione studii, propter quod saluti animarum debeamus prouidere'.[69]

According to Bitterfeld, every time the superior grants dispensation, he should bear in mind that the will of the *antiqui patres*, which is contained in the constitutions, is more important than his own judgment and that he should follow his own judgment only when he is convinced that this is what the lawmakers would have desired.[70] It could also happen, as Bitterfeld writes in his commentary to the prologue, that situations occur which were not anticipated by the lawmakers, and these cases may also allow for the use of dispensation.[71] Such an approach guarantees that this would not be a violation of the law.[72] If any of these conditions is not met, the granting of dispensation becomes a threat to the Order, as it covers all kinds of abuse under the appearance of legality: 'legis transgressio, "Regule" corrupcio, "Constitucionum" exinanicio, totum uocatur iam dispensacio'.[73] It leads to the moral downfall of the friars, who, instead of pursuing perfection in love, become worse than they had been, as they do not benefit from the guidelines provided by the fathers of the Order as written into the law.[74]

Dispensation had been universally known in the Church, but the Dominicans extended its use to a degree that was previously unknown. While the device was intended to allow for human frailty in the monastic communities, for Dominicans it was supposed to facilitate the pursuit of the main purpose of the Order: the preaching of the Word of God. Jordan of Saxony mentioned in this context that there was no provision in the constitutions that a friar could not be dispensed from.[75] The reformers of the Order, like Bitterfeld, saw in dispensation first of all a source of abuse. In order to undermine its force, John Dominici claimed that the privilege of using dispensation did not belong to priors,[76] and the representative of the next generation of reformers, Johannes Nider, defined dispensation as 'a licence to enter hell'.[77]

The Observants, in their reaction to the abuse of dispensation, reminded their opponents of the objective it was initially supposed to serve: to facilitate study, which could then become the basis for preaching. It is noteworthy, however, that

---

69 *Tractatus...* [see note 19], fol. 297ᵛ.
70 'Prelatus sentencias patrum sue semper preponere debet uoluntati, nisi uerisimile sit in tali causa legislatores hec non intendisse' (*Tractatus...* [see note 19], fol. 293ᵛ).
71 'Quidam casus eueniunt, super quibus intencio legislatoris non ferebatur, ut presumitur, ideo tunc habet dispensare' (*Tractatus...* [see note 19], fol. 297ᵛ).
72 'Videtur ergo, quando dispensacio iuris ei non contrarietur, licita sit. Dum uero non obseruetur, plurima mala presto proueniunt' (*Tractatus...* [see note 19], fol. 294ᵛ).
73 *Tractatus...* [see note 19], fol. 287ᵛ.
74 'Pauci proficiunt ex religione, sed magis sunt peiores, quam dum fuerant seculares, quia intencionem patrum in "Constitucionibus" positam non prosequuntur debito exercicio caritatis et religionis racione peruerse dispensacionis negligentes' (*Tractatus...* [see note 19], fol. 289ʳ).
75 Cf. Melville, 'The Fixed and the Fluid'... [see note 60], p. 33.
76 Cf. Creytens, 'Raphaël de Pornassio'... [see note 4], p. 126.
77 Michael D. Bailey, *Battling demons: Witchcraft, Heresy and Reform in the Late Middle Ages* (Pennsylvania: Pennsylvania State University Press, 2003), p. 83.

Bitterfeld practically nowhere in his treatise mentions the main mission of the Order. The topic of preaching appears at the beginning of the treatise, where Bitterfeld describes various types of orders, identifying the Dominicans as the most perfect one, which combines the contemplative life with preaching, but even there he emphasises that contemplation should always have precedence over preaching and the latter should never stand in the way of the former. He returns to the issue of the mission of the Order once at the end of the treatise, where he admits that the entire legislation of the Order is subject to the goal of preaching: 'Ideo in comparacione ad officium predicacionis tota nostra Constitucio et uita regularis habet, ut patet de diuino officio, de ieiunio etc.'[78] However, the text does not contain a single remark on how the crisis of the Order affected the effectiveness of the friars' preaching, or how they should preach the Gospel so as to follow in the footsteps of the 'ancient fathers'. Bitterfeld seems to treat Dominicans as friars whose gravest offence is to neglect the communal life.

6. Conclusion

A reading of Bitterfeld's treatise allows us to reconstruct the standpoint of the author as regards the place of the constitutions in Dominican life. This standpoint is based on a few preliminary assumptions: (1) each friar is obliged, by virtue of the religious vows, to incessantly pursue perfection; (2) the constitutions are the written will of the Order's lawmakers, referred to as *antiqui patres*, including Saint Dominic, to whom the friars vow their obedience; (3) the interpreter of the stipulations of the constitutions should always ask himself what the lawmaker's intent could have been in drawing up the provision in question and is bound to fulfil that intent.

It arises from these assumptions that: (1) each friar who neglects the pursuit of perfection, holds the constitutions, which serve the achievement of this purpose, in contempt, and thus his behaviour fulfils the criterion for the second case in which the purely penal character of the constitutions is suspended; (2) as observances bring about the realisation of the main purpose of the Order to various degrees (some directly, others indirectly), the degree to which they are binding also differs; (3) the will of the lawmakers expressed in the constitutions always takes precedence over the will of individual friars, and dispensation should therefore only be given in exceptional cases.

In the light of these findings, Bitterfeld appears as a moderately radical reformer compared to some of the contemporary supporters of observance. However, no matter how far the radicalism of the Observants went in espousing a tougher approach to Dominican law, we see that the accusations of their opponents were not entirely groundless. The main motto of the reform – the return of the

---

78 *Tractatus...* [see note 19], fol. 299ʳ.

Dominicans to faithful observance of the monastic regulations, that is, the Rule of Augustine and the constitutions of the Order – paradoxically contradicted the intent of the makers of these regulations (despite the fact that the Observants referred frequently to this intent), as these had not demanded at all that the laws they made should be always observed with absolute diligence.

While the Observants did not change the legislation, as analyses of their writings demonstrate, they sought to impose their interpretation of the Dominican law. The very manner in which the theoreticians of Dominican reform spoke about the law indicates that they were assigning a new role to it. Placing an emphasis on the authority of the lawmakers of the constitutions amounted to giving them semi-sacral character, which blurred the clear distinction between the divine law, which is binding in conscience, and human law, which functions only on pain of a penance. Casuistic attempts to bypass the provision on the constitutions' purely penal character, for example by extending the scope of the binding nature of exceptions to this principle while at the same time limiting the possibilities of dispensation, replaced the pragmatic approach of Saint Dominic and his early friars, who regarded the law as the means to realising their mission to preach and not as a restrictive system of norms, by conservative rigorism. A further consequence was that it shifted the Dominican way of life towards a monastic model, in which the main purpose was not effective preaching, but the communal life and the personal perfection of the friars.

Michael Vargas has advanced the hypothesis that the crisis of the Order was not ultimately due to external factors, as is usually assumed, but to how Saint Dominic and his brethren understood obedience. He has also added that if this assumption is true, then the only way to reform the Order was to change its legislation, and as a result the structure and the model of life.[79] This hypothesis finds confirmation in the analysis of texts that promoted reform, as well as in the subsequent practical implementation of reform, including the appointment of nominated, unelected, vicars general, and the increasingly frequent issuing by the chapters of prescriptions with the rank of a precept instead of counsels or admonitions.[80]

Dominican Observants were convinced that the programme they were implementing was a reform, a return to the initial form, which they understood as

---

79 Cf. Vargas, 'Weak obedience'… [see note 3], p. 297.
80 As Vargas has noted, in the fourteenth century, as the crisis began and the first attempts at reform were made, general chapters gradually began to change the character of the resolutions and precepts they issued, which could, in line with the procedure stipulated by the constitutions, become law if they were confirmed by three subsequent chapters. In the first decades of the Order's existence, all the resolutions of the general chapters and the circular letters by the Masters of the Order begin with such words as: *admonemus, monemus* and *volumus*. As such, they had the character of spiritual advice, and were not precepts. In the course of the fourteenth century, the verb *praecepimus* replaced these other words. According to Vargas, this was a way to use the formula of the precept (*praeceptum*) in relation to these resolutions, which is one of the two exceptions in which the constitutions are binding on pain of sin (cf. Vargas, *Weak obedience*… [see note 3], p. 290).

adherence to the monastic regulations. However, the tougher discipline in the Order, the use of interpretations which neutralised the stipulations that gave superiors room for manoeuvre and the alignment of the legislative framework with the real needs of the community and individual friars, contradicted the intent of the lawmakers. Perhaps indeed the solutions they were proposing, and which soon brought about structural changes, were the only way to lead the Order out of the crisis. Perhaps the model developed by Saint Dominic and the first generation of Dominican friars was no longer fit for purpose once the Order had grown from a small community of zealous friars into an international organisation that enjoyed enormous prestige within the Church and society, whose members were not always guided by pure motivation when they entered its ranks. Maybe to save the Order there was no need so much to re-form it as to give it an entirely new form, adjusted to the new reality, de-forming the Order as it existed before. Even if the Observants reached this conclusion, they did not express this view anywhere. In fact, much to the contrary, they went to great effort to prove that their activities served no other purpose than to restore the constitutions and the Rule of Augustine to their rightful place.

PART II

_____

Antoninus Hendrik Thomas O.P.
The Earliest Constitutions of the Dominicans
Antecedents, Text, Sources, Origins and Development (1215-1237)
With an Edition of the Text

Original Dutch edition published in Leuven in 1965
Translated into English by Brian Heffernan

Introduction

When Dominic de Guzman, a canon regular of the cathedral of Osma in Old Castile, after nine years of wearisome missionary work in the heretical region around Fanjeaux in Southern France, retired to the urban area of Toulouse and founded a society of diocesan preachers, he laid the foundations of a religious order. Like Francis of Assisi's fraternity, this order represented a successful attempt to capture and harmoniously converge two spiritual trends of his day into a single institute: the desire for the religious life and for the apostolate. The members of the new foundation were recognised by the bishop as his official helpers in pastoral ministry, and were partially supported by revenue of the diocese. On their journeys through the area where they exercised their apostolate, they practised the evangelical poverty which had been the rule of life – as early as 1206 – of the group of papal missionaries to which Dominic had belonged. After they established themselves near the church of Saint Romanus in 1216, Pope Honorius III approved their canonical form of communal life on the basis of the rule of Augustine, as well as their apostolic mission. The dispersal of these religious during disturbances in the autumn of 1217 gave rise to a first series of foundations, first in Paris and Madrid, subsequently also in other big cities in France, Spain, Italy and Germany. When the founder died in 1221, the order counted some thirty houses. This rapid expansion went hand in hand with the beginning of internal organisation, the setting up of a suitable governing structure, and the drawing up of legislation which defined the religious customs and the structure of the order.

A study of the earliest laws of the Dominicans stands within the context of the great number of publications that have, for some decades now, been dedicated to the history of the medieval legislation of religious orders. For many religious orders, the earliest constitutions are among the most important, and in some cases, least accessible, historical sources. Written by the founder or his immediate successors, they preserve the original inspiration of the institute, and contain the authentic guidelines that were intended to regulate the lives of its members. The various rules and *consuetudines* that have been handed down to the present day testify to the unceasing solicitude of past generations to find new and adapted forms for the communal experience of the Christian ideal of perfection. Although they were intended primarily for a limited group, these monastic legislative texts bear the imprint of their times and their environment, and they contain similarities with the life and organisation of other ecclesiastical and secular communities. Thus, they often include valuable information on everyday practices, social and economic structures and legal relations within the society in which they emerged. The legislation of religious institutes is rightly regarded as an important aspect of medieval associational life, and is entitled to its fair share in the lively interest that this part of historical research has engendered.

Publications addressing the history of monastic institutes that have appeared since the beginning of the twentieth century are quite numerous. General or specific directories, some of which have since been expanded or have seen second editions, list the most important source material and contain more or less extensive historical surveys of the legislation and structure of the various monastic communities.[1] Certain extremely valuable studies deal exclusively or partially with the constitutional history of a particular order or abbey.[2] Various monastic constitutions have been studied, and, to the extent that this was possible, critical editions have been published.[3] Thanks to systematic study of the contemporary documents, it has proven possible to bring many problems concerning the canons regular closer to resolution, and we now have a more accurate view of the origins and evolution of the canonical reform, the history of the rule, and the genesis and connections between the legislative texts that were used in the various religious

---

1 M. Heimbucher, *Die Orden und Kongregationen der katholischen Kirche*, 2 vols, which first appeared in 1895-1896, is imperfect and incomplete in many respects, but is still frequently consulted. The third edition appeared in Paderborn in 1933-1934. – With regard to special directories, the following titles could be mentioned: L. H. Cottineau, *Répertoire topo-bibliographique des abbayes et prieurés*, 2 vols, Mâcon, 1935-1936; D. Beaunier – J. M. Besse, *Abbayes et prieurés de l'ancienne France*, 12 vols, Ligugé-Paris, 1905-1941; *Monasticon belge*, begun under U. Berlière, vol. I, Maredsous, 1890, vol. II, Maredsous-Liège, 1928-1955, vol. III, 1, Liège, 1960; M. Schoengen, *Monasticon Batavum*, 3 vols, Amsterdam, 1941-1942; N. Backmund, *Monasticon Praemonstratense*, 3 vols, Straubing, 1949-1956.

2 See for instance R. Molitor, *Aus der Rechtsgeschichte benediktinischer Verbände*, 3 vols, Münster, 1928-1933; Ph. Schmitz, *Histoire de l'ordre de saint Benoît*, vol. 1, Maredsous, 1942 (Livre III, *Histoire constitutionnelle*, pp. 251-356); J.-B. Mahn, *L'ordre cistercien et son gouvernement des origines au milieu du XIIIᵉ siècle (1098-1265)*, Paris, 1945; C. Bock, *Les codifications du droit cistercien*, Westmalle, 1956. For the Franciscans, see the bibliography included in H. Boehmer, *Analekten zur Geschichte des Franciscus von Assisi*, 3ʳᵈ edition by C. Andresen, Tübingen, 1961, pp. VII-XI.

3 For the Benedictines, see for instance B. Albers, *Consuetudines monasticae*, 5 vols, Stuttgart-Vienna, 1900-1912, which includes the legislative texts of many abbeys and congregations; for the Cistercians see J. Turk, *Charta caritatis prior*, in *Analecta S. Ordinis Cisterciensis*, vol. I, 1945, pp. 11-61; B. Griesser, *Die Ecclesiastica officia Cisterciensis Ordinis des Cod. 1711 von Trient*, ibid., vol. XII, 1956, pp. 153-288; for the Carthusians see A. De Meyer – J. M. De Smet, *Guigo's Consuetudines van de eerste Kartuizers* (Mededelingen van de Koninklijke Vlaamse Academie voor Wetenschappen, Letteren en Schone Kunsten van België, Klasse der Letteren, vol. XIII, no. 6), Brussels, 1951; for the Premonstratensians see R. Van Waefelghem, *Les premiers statuts de Prémontré* (reprint from *Analectes de Prémontré*, vol. IX), Leuven, 1913; H. Heijman, *Untersuchungen über die Praemonstratenser-Gewohnheiten*, in *Analecta Praemonstratensia*, vols II-IV, 1926-1928; Pl. F. Lefèvre, *Les statuts de Prémontré réformés sur les ordres de Grégoire IX et d'Innocent IV au XIIIᵉ siècle* (Bibliothèque de la Revue d'histoire ecclésiastique, vol. 23), Leuven, 1946; for the Crosiers see A. van de Pasch, *De tekst van de constituties der Kruisheren van 1248*, in *Bulletin de la Commission royale d'histoire*, vol. CXVII, 1952, pp. 1-95.

communities.[4] In the space of twenty years, the renewed study of the sources of Cistercian monastic law has yielded unsuspected results and has led to new insights, which have in many cases confirmed or corrected previous views.[5] The medieval non-monastic religious movements, too, have become the subject of original and illuminating studies.[6] Few institutes have escaped this historical interest. For most of them, the state of research is now far advanced; for others there is at least a firm basis thanks to the discovery of new documents.

The legislation of the Dominicans has similarly received a great deal of attention ever since the publication of the earliest text of their constitutions by H. Denifle in 1885.[7] Beginning in 1903, A. Mortier published his extensive history of the masters general, several pages of which are dedicated to the constitutions.[8] 1921 saw the publication of a study by P. Mandonnet on Saint Dominic and his work as founder and first organiser of the order.[9] This book was later revised and complemented with new critical studies by M. H. Vicaire and R. Ladner.[10] In 1927, H. C. Scheeben wrote the first modern biography of Dominic.[11] Scheeben captivatingly, if a little idiosyncratically, sketched the apostolic figure of the saint against the background of the ecclesiastical conditions and religious movements of his time, and also highlighted his originality as founder of the order. In his important *Compendium*, A. Walz devoted a number of sections to the legislation and institutions of the order throughout the various periods.[12] In 1936, R.-M. Louis published a brief outline of the history of the Dominican

---

4 See for this Ch. Dereine's articles in the bibliography, and the work of J. C. Dickinson, *The Origins of the Austin Canons and their Introduction into England*, London, 1950.

5 The edition by J. Turk, *Charta caritatis prior* (see *supra*, note 3) was soon followed by other studies and editions, including by J. A. Lefèvre and J.-B. Van Damme (for further details see the bibliography).

6 See for instance H. Grundmann, *Religiöse Bewegungen im Mittelalter. Untersuchungen über die geschichtlichen Zusammenhänge zwischen der Ketzerei, den Bettelorden und der religiösen Frauenbewegung im 12. und 13. Jahrhundert und über die geschichtlichen Grundlagen der deutschen Mystik* (Historische Studien, vol. 267), Berlin, 1935. In the anastatic reprint of this work (1961), the author included an appendix (pp. 487-524): *Ordensgründungen und Ketzersekten im 12. Jhdt.* See also A. Mens, *Oorsprong en betekenis van de Nederlandse Begijnen- en Begardenbeweging* (Verhandelingen van de Koninklijke Vlaamse Academie voor Wetenschappen, Letteren en Schone Kunsten van België, Klasse der Letteren, vol. IX, no. 7), Antwerp, 1947; E. Werner, *Pauperes Christi. Studien zu sozial-religiösen Bewegungen im Zeitalter des Reformpapsttums*, Leipzig, 1956.

7 H. Denifle, *Die Constitutionen des Predigerordens vom Jahre 1228*, in *Archiv für Literatur- und Kirchengeschichte des Mittelalters*, vol. I, 1885, pp. 165-227.

8 A. Mortier, *Histoire des maîtres généraux de l'ordre des Frères Prêcheurs*, 8 vols, Paris, 1903-1920.

9 P. Mandonnet, *Saint Dominique. L'idée, l'homme et l'œuvre*, Ghent, 1921.

10 Published under the same title, Paris, s.a. [1937].

11 H. C. Scheeben, *Der heilige Dominikus*, Freiburg im Breisgau, 1927.

12 A. Walz, *Compendium historiae Ordinis Praedicatorum*, Rome, 1930. A second edition appeared in 1948.

constitutions.[13] The institutes that have, since the end of the previous century, taken up the task of studying and publishing critical editions of the sources have also made an important contribution. Several volumes of the *Monumenta Ordinis Fratrum Praedicatorum historica*, begun in 1896 by B. M. Reichert and continued by the *Institutum historicum O.P.* in Rome, contain the first lives, the canonisation documents and bulls concerning Dominic, the old chronicles of the order and the general and provincial chapters.[14] The *Archivum Fratrum Praedicatorum* has since 1931 regularly published text editions and studies on the history of the Dominicans.[15] The *Quellen und Forschungen zur Geschichte des Dominikanerordens in Deutschland* series, founded by P. von Loë in 1907,[16] and *Archiv der deutschen Dominikaner*, which has appeared since 1937, similarly include studies that are of interest for the life and legislation of the order as a whole. A number of aspects of its administrative organisation have attracted the attention of outsiders, who addressed these topics in separate studies.[17] The masterly outcome of years of study by M. H. Vicaire appeared in 1957, not only throwing light on Dominic's life and apostolic work, but also offering interesting expositions on the structure and first legislation of the order.[18]

Among the publications on the history of the Dominicans, there are a number that have dealt more specifically with the legislation of the order. H. Denifle preceded his edition of the earliest constitutions, which he believed dated from 1228, with a number of reflections on the meaning of certain customs and institutions.[19] G. R. Galbraith, in her work, meticulously described and dissected the structure and governing bodies of the order, its "constitution", which she characterised

---

13 R.-M. Louis, *Histoire du texte des constitutions dominicaines*, in *Archivum Fratrum Praedicatorum*, vol. VI, 1936, pp. 334-350.

14 In vol. XVI, 1935: *Libellus de principiis Ordinis Praedicatorum* by Jordan of Saxony and the *Legendae* compiled by Peter Ferrand, Constantinus of Orvieto and Humbert of Romans; in vol. XV, 1933: *Historia diplomatica sancti Dominici*; in vol. III, 1898: *Acta capitulorum generalium Ordinis Praedicatorum*, vol. I; in vol. XXII, 1951: the *Epistulae* by Jordan of Saxony.

15 The following could be mentioned in relation to the thirteenth century: D. Planzer, *De codice Ruthenensi miscellaneo in tabulario Ordinis Praedicatorum asservato* (vol. V, 1935, pp. 5-123); H. C. Scheeben, *De bullario quodam Ordinis Praedicatorum saeculi XIII* (vol. VI, 1936, pp. 217-266); id., *Dominikaner oder Innozentianer* (vol. XIX, 1939, pp. 237-297).

16 Among the works that are of general importance for the history of the order are vol. 35: H. C. Scheeben, *Beiträge zur Geschichte Jordans von Sachsen*, Vechta-Leipzig, 1938; vol. 38: Id., *Die Konstitutionen des Predigerordens unter Jordan von Sachsen*, Cologne-Leipzig, 1939.

17 E. Barker, *The Dominican Order and Convocation*, Oxford, 1913; H. P. Tunmore, *The Dominican Order and Parliament*, in *The Catholic Historical Review*, vol. XXVI, 1941, pp. 479-489; L. Moulin, *Les formes du gouvernement local et provincial dans les ordres religieux*, in *Revue internationale des sciences administratives*, vol. XXI, 1955, pp. 31-57; id., *Le pluricaméralisme dans l'ordre des Frères Prêcheurs*, in *Res publica*, vol. II, 1960, pp. 50-66.

18 M. H. Vicaire, *Histoire de saint Dominique*, 2 vols, Paris. This author previously published a number of noteworthy works: *Fondation, approbation, confirmation de l'ordre des Frères Prêcheurs*, in *Revue d'histoire ecclésiastique*, vol. XLVII, 1952, pp. 123-141 and 586-603; *Saint Dominique de Caleruega d'après les documents du XIII° siècle*, Paris, 1955.

19 H. Denifle, *Die Constitutionen*, pp. 168-193.

as "efficient, intricate and surprisingly modern".[20] She identified the main stages in the evolution of the legislation, institutions and offices during the thirteenth century, and also attempted to highlight the heritage of monastic tradition in the organisation of the Dominicans in addition to its original elements. An appendix to her work contained the early fourteenth-century text of the constitutions. H. C. Scheeben defended more trenchantly defined positions in various places in his biography of Dominic.[21] According to him, the process of drawing up of constitutions proper to the order only began after the founder's death (1221), at the general chapter of 1222, so that the *Constitutiones antiquae* must in fact be dated to Jordan of Saxony's generalate. But in the introduction to his own edition of the text, he corrected his previous view and expressed his modified opinion that the rules on observance and a number of stipulations on the government of the order had been written down as early as 1220.[22] Following in the footsteps of P. Mandonnet, M. H. Vicaire concluded after critical enquiries that not only had the first *distinctio* (the *consuetudines*) been edited by or under Dominic's influence, but the origin of this part must be dated to the first years of the order, that is, 1215-1216.[23] This author has also defended opinions on the further evolution of the legislation that are considerably at odds with H. C. Scheeben's.

The strongly diverging conclusions that these two authoritative historians have reached have strengthened us in our conviction that there are still many problems in relation to the origin and development of the earliest constitutions of the Dominicans for which no satisfactory solution has so far been reached. There are other issues still that await thorough investigation or treatment. First and foremost, we lack an edition of the text that can withstand the test of criticism. Editors have hitherto limited themselves to consulting single manuscripts and publishing these as faithfully as possible. The study of the sources has not progressed beyond pointing out the passages derived from the Premonstratensians.[24] A number of authors have, it is true, suggested the possibility and likelihood of literary or substantive affinity with the statutes of other orders, but without further enquiry.[25] A comparative study, along the lines of what has been done

---

20 G. R. Galbraith, *The Constitution of the Dominican Order*, Manchester, 1925, p. 1.
21 H. C. Scheeben, *Der heilige Dominikus*, pp. 316-317, 372-373.
22 H. C. Scheeben, *Die Konstitutionen des Predigerordens*, pp. 12-13, 18-21.
23 P. Mandonnet – M. H. Vicaire, *Saint Dominique*, vol. II, pp. 210-230.
24 See the editions of the text by H. Denifle (cf. *supra*, note 7) and H. C. Scheeben (cf. *supra*, note 16), in the footnotes.
25 H. C. Scheeben, *Die Konstitutionen des Predigerordens*, p. 34: "Es lassen sich aber in den Konstitutionen noch weitere Einflüsse nachweisen." See also P. Mandonnet – M. H. Vicaire, *Saint Dominique*, vol. II, p. 236, footnote 103, p. 259, footnote 46.

for the *Consuetudines* of Prémontré[26] and of the Carthusians,[27] is also desirable, possible and profitable for the constitutions of the Dominicans.

The absence of full, systematic studies of the earliest legislation of the Dominicans and the feasibility of acquiring greater clarity on the basis of the available documents have largely determined the choice and definition of our subject matter. The chronological limitation (1215-1237) arises from the fact that most issues in relation to the constitutional history of the Dominicans relate precisely to this period. During these two decades, the contours of the legislation and the organisation of the order were developed under the leadership of the first two masters general, Dominic and Jordan of Saxony. The revision of the constitutions by Raymond of Peñafort, the third master general (1238-1240), consisted mainly of arranging previously adopted laws in a more logical order. Nor was the schema of his codification fundamentally altered by the textual revision under Humbert of Romans (1254-1256), or by the many new editions that have appeared up to the beginning of the twentieth century. Moreover, the history of the legislation is easier to follow from 1239 onwards on the basis of the reports of the general chapters, the most important ordinances of which were preserved. As a rule, our study will limit itself to the earliest constitutions, and will successively examine their historical environment, text, affinity with other statutes, and development. From time to time, attention will be given to the origins and meaning of various customs and institutions, so as to underline more clearly the dependence or originality of the Dominican constitutions, as the case may be.

Although the primary aim of our study is to acquire deeper knowledge of the earliest constitutions of the Dominicans, it is not without wider significance. Religious institutes occupied a prominent place in the context of medieval society. Their organisation was frequently influenced or imitated by civic or ecclesiastical communities. The mendicant orders were founded at the beginning of the thirteenth century, a period of intensive practice of canon law and of great flourishing of religious and civic associational life. The close connections between these two types of associations have been amply accentuated by authoritative historians.[28] Attention has repeatedly been focused specifically on the Dominican Order in this context. The German historian A. Hauck has characterised its organisation as one of the most successful of the Middle Ages.[29] Its constitutions served, for instance,

---

26 H. Heijman, *Untersuchungen über die Praemonstratenser-Gewohnheiten.*

27 A. De Meyer – J. M. De Smet, *Guigo's* Consuetudines *van de eerste Kartuizers*, pp. 65-91: "De genesis van de *Consuetudines*".

28 See for instance P. Mandonnet – M. H. Vicaire, *Saint Dominique*, vol. II, pp. 235-238; G. De Lagarde, *Individualisme et corporatisme au moyen âge*, in *L'organisation corporative du moyen âge à la fin de l'ancien régime* (Études présentées à la Commission internationale pour l'histoire des assemblées d'états, vol. II) (Université de Louvain. Recueil de travaux publiés par les membres des Conférences d'histoire et de philologie, 2nd series, vol. 44), Leuven, 1937, p. 14.

29 "Man irrt wohl nicht, wenn man sie als das Vollkommenste bezeichnet, was das Mittelalter in Hinsicht auf die Verfassungsbildung mönchischer Korporationen hervorgebracht hat"

as an example for other religious orders and fraternities, and were, to a greater or lesser extent, adopted, particularly by the Crosiers,[30] Servites,[31] Friars of the Penitence of Jesus Christ,[32] Carmelites,[33] Franciscans,[34] Mercedarians,[35] Augustinians[36] and by a number of hospitaller institutes.[37] Its structure, which remains largely intact today, lives on in those of modern orders and congregations.[38]

The sources that can be consulted for the history of the Dominican constitutions have now, for the most part, been published. The investigative resourcefulness and perseverance that drove researchers such as J. Quétif and J. Échard,[39] H. Denifle, B. M. Reichert and F. Balme in previous centuries, and subsequently, the members of the Historical Institute of the order in Rome and others, to systematically examine countless archives and libraries in many countries, assures us that no important document has been overlooked. It is true that valuable material that is important for the history of individual houses and provinces has since been discovered in many archives, but this has added little to the legal history of the order as a whole during the first two decades of its existence. Further critical research

---

(*Kirchengeschichte Deutschlands*, vol. IV, Berlin-Leipzig, 1954[8], p. 409). In a recent study, L. Moulin writes, "Il est difficile de ne pas éprouver un sentiment d'admiration devant cette cathédrale du droit constitutionnel qu'est la législation dominicaine" (*Le pluricaméralisme dans l'ordre des Frères Prêcheurs*, in *Res publica*, vol. II, 1960, p. 65).

30 W. Sangers, *De oudste constituties der Kruisherenorde*, in *Miscellanea L. Van der Essen*, vol. I, Brussels, 1947, pp. 315-327; A. van de Pasch, *De tekst van de constituties der Kruisheren van 1248*, in *Bulletin de la Commission royale d'histoire*, vol. CXVII, 1952, pp. 1-95, with an edition of the text on pp. 42-95.

31 *Constitutiones antiquae Fratrum Servorum sanctae Mariae*, in *Monumenta Ordinis Servorum sanctae Mariae*, vol. I, 1897, pp. 27-54, where the footnotes indicate the passages derived from the Dominican constitutions.

32 See for this also pp. 260-267.

33 See Melchior a S. Maria, *Carmelitarum regula et ordo decursu XIII saeculi*, in *Ephemerides Carmeliticae*, vol. II, 1948, pp. 51-64.

34 See F. Ehrle, *Die ältesten Redactionen der Generalconstitutionen des Franziskanerordens*, in *Archiv für Literatur- und Kirchengeschichte des Mittelalters*, vol. VI, 1892, pp. 25, 115-116, 124-125, 136-137. For the similarity between the texts, see P. Mandonnet – M. H. Vicaire, *Saint Dominique*, vol. II, pp. 250, 258, 260.

35 See P. Mandonnet – M. H. Vicaire, *op. cit.*, vol. II, pp. 252-253.

36 See P. Mandonnet – M. H. Vicaire, *op. cit.*, vol. II, pp. 251.

37 See L. Le Grand, *Statuts d'hôtels-Dieu et de léproseries*, Paris, 1906, pp. XX-XXII, 61-96, 143, 154, 172, 178. For the influence of the Dominican constitutions on the rule of the English anchoresses (*Ancren Riwle*), see V. MacNabb, *The Authorship of the Ancren Riwle*, in *Archivum Fratrum Praedicatorum*, vol. IV, 1934, pp. 49-74. For the German Order, see M. Perlbach, *Die Statuten des deutschen Ordens*, Halle, 1890, pp. XXXVII, L, 120-121.

38 According to E. Barker, *The Dominican Order and Convocation*, pp. 43-44, 74-75, the organisation of the Dominican Order possibly influenced the English representative system. Even after 1230, Dominicans were entrusted with the task of drafting legislation for various cities in Northern Italy (see *Acta canonizationis S. Dominici. Processus Bononiensis* (Monumenta Ordinis Fratrum Praedicatorum historica, vol. XVI), Rome, 1935, no. 39, pp. 158-159).

39 Cf. R. Creytens, *L'œuvre bibliographique d'Échard, ses sources et leur valeur*, in *Archivum Fratrum Praedicatorum*, vol. XIV, 1944, pp. 43-71.

has, however, demonstrated that certain accepted opinions on the authenticity and dating of some documents are untenable, and errors of transcription and interpretation have been corrected. The attempts that we have personally undertaken to supplement the documentary basis did not produce any significant results. Neither the consultation of a considerable number of catalogues of domestic and foreign manuscript collections, nor the enquiries carried out on the spot by helpful persons have added much to the relevant material. It must be assumed that new important discoveries will be the result of chance rather than systematic research.

The documentary material consists of the various types of sources that are relevant for the legal history of a medieval religious order. It exceeds in magnitude the material that is extant for most other orders. The constitutions of the Dominicans were constantly evolving, both as regards their content, form and wording. But their general structure and outline remained largely unchanged during Jordan of Saxony's generalate (1222-1237). After a first edition by H. Denifle in 1885,[40] they were published on three further occasions, each time according to the Rodez manuscript, which dates from the beginning of the fourteenth century.[41] The revision and *ordinatio* of the text approved by the chapters of 1239-1241 have been ascribed to Raymond of Peñafort, the third master general (1238-1240). The original version was found by R. Creytens and published in 1948.[42] A new revision was undertaken by order of the general chapter of 1254, under the leadership of Humbert of Romans, who was elected master general that same year.[43] The text was submitted to the chapter of 1256 and officially adopted.[44] It appeared in print for the first time towards the end of the nineteenth century.[45] As the constitutions form not only the main source for, but also the subject of our study, there is no need to address them further here.

The development of the legislation can be followed in detail by consulting the acts of the general chapters. Every year, this central governing body of the order devoted a large part of its activities to revising and supplementing the constitutions. Unfortunately, the reports of the chapters have been preserved *in extenso* only from 1236 onwards, and we have but fragments from the immediately preceding years. The only edition of these was published in 1898 by

---

40 Cf. *supra*, footnote 7.

41 In *Analecta sacri Ordinis Fratrum Praedicatorum*, vol. II, 1895-1896, pp. 621-648; by L. G. Alonso Getino, *El Liber consuetudinum*, in *La Ciencia Tomista*, vol. XIII, 1916, pp. 210-244; H. C. Scheeben, *Die Konstitutionen des Predigerordens unter Jordan von Sachsen*, pp. 48-80; partially by M. Gelabert – J. M. Milagro, *Santo Domingo de Guzmán*, Madrid, 1947, pp. 864-906.

42 R. Creytens, *Les constitutions des Frères Prêcheurs dans la rédaction de s. Raymond de Peñafort*, in *Archivum Fratrum Praedicatorum*, vol. XVIII, 1948, pp. 29-68.

43 See F. Heintke, *Humbert von Romans, der fünfte Ordensmeister der Dominikaner* (Historische Studien, vol. 222), Berlin, 1933, vol. 53, 71-73.

44 *Acta capitulorum generalium Ordinis Praedicatorum*, vol. I (cf. footnote 46), pp. 73, 78, 84.

45 *Liber constitutionum Ordinis Fratrum Praedicatorum*, in *Analecta sacri Ordinis Fratrum Praedicatorum*, vol. III, 1897-1898, pp. 26-60, 98-122, 162-181.

B. M. Reichert.[46] It was based on Bernard Gui's collection as it appears in an early fourteenth-century manuscript in the city library of Bordeaux, not only because this was the oldest extant collection, but also because it was compiled by someone whose name alone is a pledge of earnestness and meticulousness.[47] Bernard used the *rotuli*, the sheets on which the chapter members recorded the decisions so as to transmit them to their provinces or houses. He also clearly indicated what he had been able to discover concerning the first period of the order. And whenever documentary sources were lacking, he did not fail to state so clearly.[48] His collection also appears to have served as a prototype for all other copies that are still known, except for that of Florence.[49]

Countless papal bulls permit us to follow the evolution of the directives issued for the Dominicans by the curia. The bulls and letters issued at the time of the foundation and during the following years give precise definitions of the purpose, form of life and activities of the order. The documents from the time after Dominic's death (1221) usually deal with privileges concerning the cure of souls, decisions on community life and rules for relations with the diocesan clergy and other bodies. Most of these bulls have been published extensively in the *Bullarium Ordinis Praedicatorum*,[50] which may not be perfect from the perspective of textual criticism and diplomatics, but which, as the first collection of this kind, has provided a great service. It can be supplemented by A. Potthast's *Regesta*[51] and by the data from the registers of the papal chancery, which were published by V. Ligiez.[52] Dominic's full *chartularium*, including private legal documents, was compiled by F. Balme and contains 136 documents.[53] The editor marred his work, however, with all too extensive and often ill-founded comments. A new edition, itself not entirely free of errors either, was published by M. H. Laurent in 1933, and indicates no fewer than 153 documents.[54] It has the appropriate diplomatic

---

46 *Acta capitulorum generalium Ordinis Praedicatorum*, vol. I (Monumenta Ordinis Fratrum Praedicatorum historica, vol. III), Rome-Stuttgart, 1898.

47 For the technical details, see the editor's introduction, pp. V-XIII.

48 Bernard begins his text as follows: "Ab anno Domini 1220 usque ad annum eiusdem Domini benedicti 1240, de actis capitulorum generalium pauca quae potui reperire, inferius annotavi. Ab anno vero Domini 1240 usque ad annum Domini 1305, quo haec scripsi, habentur inferius completius recollecta, quibusdam tamen exceptis, pro quibus suo tempore, si occurrerit, recolligendis et complendis, spacia vacua locis suis inferius dimittantur" (*ed. cit.*, p. 1).

49 *Ed. cit.*, pp. IX-X.

50 *Bullarium Ordinis Praedicatorum*, ed. Th. Ripoll – A. Bremond, 8 vols, Rome, 1729-1740.

51 *Regesta Pontificum Romanorum inde ab anno post Christum natum MCXCVIII ad annum MCCCIV*, ed. A. Potthast, vol. I, Berlin, 1874.

52 *Regesta Pontificum Romanorum pro sacro Ordine Praedicatorum*, in *Analecta sacri Ordinis Fratrum Praedicatorum*, vol. III, 1897-1898, *passim*; *Epitome bullarii Ordinis Praedicatorum, ibid.*, vol. IV, 1899-1900, *passim*.

53 F. Balme – P. Lelaidier – J. Collomb, *Cartulaire ou histoire diplomatique de saint Dominique*, 3 vols, Paris, 1893-1901.

54 *Historia diplomatica S. Dominici*, ed. M. H. Laurent (Monumenta Ordinis Fratrum Praedicatorum historica, vol. XV), Paris, 1933.

apparatus, with meticulous source references and sober bibliographical details relating to the persons and places mentioned.

The proceedings of the informative processes held in preparation for the canonisation of Dominic also to some degree belong to the archival source base.[55] The witnesses heard during the sessions held in Bologna from 6 to 17 August 1233[56] were members of the order. Their statements focused primarily on the activities of the founder during the last years of his life (1215-1221). The persons who were heard afterwards in Toulouse,[57] mainly non-Dominicans, testified primarily about his work as apostolic preacher in Southern France from 1206 to 1215. All these witnesses had to swear an oath before they were heard, so that their sincerity cannot reasonably be doubted. Similarly, there are clear guarantees of their competence. Most had personally known the founder of the order and had even lived with him for a considerable length of time. They were interviewed according to a predetermined scheme that was devised to obtain as precise information as possible about the virtues of this candidate for sainthood. It is true that they emphasised mainly the positive and favourable sides of his character. Their testimonies paint the picture of a morally sound person who was the recipient of many graces, but do not present a sublimated hagiography. On occasion they even mention his less realistic plans and the resistance which these encountered.[58] Their answers bring to light a number of valuable details concerning Dominic's views and work as an administrator, and his personal contribution to the drafting of the legislation.

The literary sources on the earliest legal history of the Dominicans are few in number, but those that exist are all the more important. The earliest lives of Dominic have all been studied and published in critical editions. The lion's share of attention must go to the *Libellus de principiis Ordinis Praedicatorum*, compiled by Jordan of Saxony in 1232-1233, ten years after the founder's death.[59] Although this work was written with a view to the forthcoming canonisation (1234), it nevertheless, and by contrast with contemporary hagiographical customs, gives

---

55 *Acta canonizationis S. Dominici*, ed. A. Walz (Monumenta Ordinis Fratrum Praedicatorum historica, vol. XVI), Rome, 1935, pp. 123-194.

56 *Ed. cit.*, pp. 123-167.

57 *Ed. cit.*, pp. 176-187. The date of the interviews is not given. The letter addressed by the main committee in Bologna to the subcommittee in Toulouse to begin the process is dated 19 August 1233 (pp. 169-172). – For Gregory IX's bull of canonisation see pp. 190-194.

58 His plan to entrust the *conversi* with the administration of temporal goods was not accepted (*ed. cit.*, no. 26). Nor was his request to be discharged from his post as master general (*ibid.*, no. 33).

59 Jordan of Saxony, *Libellus de principiis Ordinis Praedicatorum*, ed. H. C. Scheeben (Monumenta Ordinis Fratrum Praedicatorum historica, vol. XVI), pp. 25-88. The edition of the Bollandists (*Acta Sanctorum*, vol. XXXV (*Augusti tomus primus*), pp. 541-555), which is based on the Osma manuscript, adds a number of miracles (pp. 554-555, nos. 88-95) that occurred after Dominic's death. H. C. Scheeben did not include this part, but he did include the message of the translation (pp. 82-88, nos. 121-130) which is lacking in the Bollandists' edition.

remarkably little attention to miraculous events in Dominic's life.[60] According to his own testimony, the author's main purpose was to meet his fellow friars' demands for as accurate an historical account as possible of the founding and first years of the order. As the second master general, who had personally known and lived with Dominic, Jordan was well-equipped for his task. For the facts that he had not personally witnessed, he consulted the *primitivi fratres*, the first members of the order. A number of details appear to justify the view that he also used written documents, so that he must equally be regarded as one of the earliest historians of the order.[61] His chronicle is truly the first, fundamental and most authoritative literary source on the earliest history of the Dominicans.[62] The authors of the later *legendae*, such as Peter Ferrand, Constantinus of Orvieto and Humbert of Romans, often literally depend upon him.[63] The details that they added are limited in scope and clearly betray the intention to embellish the narrative, according to hagiographical traditions, to provide edifying reading material for the choir and the refectory.[64]

Humbert of Romans occupies a place of his own as a witness to the evolution of the institutions of the Dominicans during the thirteenth century.[65] Elected master general in 1254, he resigned his charge in 1263, but went on to write a number of valuable commentaries on the rule of Augustine and the constitutions

---

60 For conclusions on the circumstances of the edition, the value of the work etc., see the introduction to both editions and B. Altaner, *Der hl. Dominikus. Untersuchungen und Texte* (Breslauer Studien zur historischen Theologie, vol. 2), Breslau, 1922, pp. 4-19. This question was investigated more closely in a thesis for the licentiate in Philosophy and Letters (History), written by our confrere C. M. Hinderyckx, *Kritische studie van het* Libellus de principiis Ordinis Praedicatorum *door Jordaan van Saksen* (1963).

61 Jordan is very sober with facts about Dominic's life and work before the foundation of the order (1203-1215: see nos. 14-37). His account of the occasion for and the beginning of the mission in Southern France (1206-1207) is similar to Peter of Vaux-de-Cernay, *Hystoria Albigensis*, ed. P. Guébin – E. Lyon, vol. I, Paris, 1926 (it is instructive to compare Jordan, nos. 17 and 28 with Peter, nos. 20 and 48). It is not possible to prove that Jordan was immediately and literally indebted to Peter, who wrote his work c. 1215 (cf. P. Mandonnet – M. H. Vicaire, *Saint Dominique*, vol. I, pp. 143-150). Jordan's account contains a number of inaccuracies for the period 1206-1207 (cf. M. H. Vicaire, *Saint Dominique en 1207*, in *Archivum Fratrum Praedicatorum*, vol. XXIII, 1953, pp. 337-338). He was in possession of many details concerning the foundation of the first community in Toulouse in 1215 (Jordan, nos. 38-39) and the organisation of the house near the church of Saint Romanus (nos. 43-44), details which he perhaps not only received from the *primitivi fratres*, but also derived immediately from written sources. The reader has the impression that he was simply recording the content of the documents (compare his text in the numbers cited with M. H. Laurent, *Historia diplomatica S. Dominici*, nos. 60-61, 70, 74).

62 B. Altaner, *Der hl. Dominikus*, p. 19, calls the *Libellus* "das grundlegende erste und wichtigste Werk zur Geschichte der Anfänge des Dominikanerordens".

63 *Legenda sancti Dominici*, by Peter Ferrand, Constantinus of Orvieto and Humbert of Romans (Monumenta Ordinis Fratrum Praedicatorum historica, vol. XVI), pp. 209-260, 286-352, 369-433 respectively, edited by M. H. Laurent, H. C. Scheeben and A. Walz respectively. Constantinus and Humbert also often depend on Peter Ferrand.

64 Humbert's *Legenda* is even divided into *lectiones*.

65 See for his life and work F. Heintke, *Humbert von Romans*.

of the order,[66] as well as lengthy expositions on the vows and the offices of the order.[67] His works may not be official norms, but they do share in the authority ascribed to their author, even after his resignation. Even if he had not explicitly appealed to his competence, these writings would have provided proof of his administrative experience. At the behest of the general chapter, he began a review of the office and the legislation immediately after being elected master general. To this end, he thoroughly studied the statutes of both the older and more recent religious orders. He was, therefore, well-prepared to speak authoritatively about the Dominican organisation's own place in the history of the religious life.[68] Admittedly, his writings in many places are ascetical literature rather than legal commentaries, and they include a wealth of scriptural passages. Nor can it be denied that he shows a tendency in some passages to interpret and impose his own personal views. However, his works also contain precious information about the origin and development of the constitutions, the tasks of officers and the various government organs as they were stipulated at that time by law and custom. In this sense, his writings must be regarded as a valuable source.[69]

In order to acquaint ourselves more fully with the text and history of the constitutions of other orders, we have consulted a rather extensive series of sources and works. Our endeavours would have been considerably expedited if we had been able to use reliable editions and recent monographs on the ecclesiastical, religious and secular communities before and during the thirteenth century. In fact, in the case of certain institutes, we had to content ourselves with outdated and incomplete textual editions. The legislation of other orders is available partly in critical, and partly in less perfect editions, and we did not have the possibility, in respect of the latter, to compare them with the manuscripts upon which they are based. It was not feasible to fill every lacuna in this field by personal research, as this would have meant doing for the other institutes what we were intending to do only for the Dominicans. We are well aware that this relative lack of clarity on the historical context is also likely to obscure insight into the meaning of certain Dominican texts and institutions, and to leave us somewhat in the dark as to the true character of their relationship to other communities. The medieval religious institutions are so intimately linked that they should all be studied together if we are to acquire adequate insight into the legislation and organisation

---

66 *Expositio Regulae beati Augustini*, ed. J. J. Berthier, in Humbert of Romans, *Opera de vita regulari*, vol. I, Rome, 1888, pp. 43-633; *Expositio super Constitutiones Fratrum Praedicatorum, ed. cit.*, vol. II, pp. 1-178.

67 *Expositio de tribus votis substantialibus religionis, ed. cit.*, vol. I, pp. 1-41; *Instructiones de officiis Ordinis, ed. cit.*, vol. II, pp. 179-369.

68 "... ut ex experientia quam habuit in multis et variis negotiis ordinis et ex tantarum auctoritate religionum, securius diffiniret de iis quae ad religionis naturam pertinere noscuntur" (*Expositio super Constitutiones, ed. cit.*, p. 2).

69 It is not clear from the editor's introduction that the text was critically examined to an adequate standard. Not all manuscripts were consulted and there are almost no references to variants.

of each institute separately. The incomplete and relative character of some of our conclusions finds a partial explanation in this circumstance.

The description of the subject and the nature of the content justify the division of our text into four chapters. The first chapter is intended as an introduction, which outlines the legal history of historical religious institutes. This overview gives us the opportunity to describe the legal environment in which the Dominican constitutions emerged, and at the same time to familiarise ourselves with the many legislative texts that will be consulted during the study of the sources. The second chapter examines the text of the constitutions, compares it with other legislative texts of Dominican origin, and, as far as possible, offers a reconstruction of this text in its original form. A third chapter is devoted to the study of the sources. The text and a number of Dominican customs are compared there with other religious constitutions and documents of other institutes which directly influenced them, or at least show a literary or substantive affinity with them. The fourth chapter uses the results of the two preceding enquiries, in conjunction with internal criticism and data from other sources on the history of the order, to describe the specific origin and development of the constitutions.

In completing this doctoral dissertation, it is our happy duty to thank all who contributed. In the first place, our thanks go to the Very Rev. Father L. Camerlynck, S.T.M., Prior Provincial of the Flemish Dominicans, and to his predecessor, the Very Rev. Father N. Gobert. Our training in the historical sciences was due almost entirely to the professors of the University of Leuven, especially to the late Canon A. De Meyer, S.T.M., *Jonkheer* Dr L. van der Essen, Dr E. Lousse and Dr J. A. Van Houtte. We are particularly obliged to our dedicated supervisor, Canon Prof. Pl. Lefèvre, O.Praem., S.T.M., and Professors Canon Dr J. M. De Smet, Canon G. Fransen, S.T.M., and M. Cappuyns, O.S.B., S.T.M., who made many critical comments and offered useful advice, as well as to Canon Prof. R. Aubert, S.T.M., who was willing to include this work in the *Bibliothèque de la Revue d'histoire ecclésiastique.*

We are pleased also to mention our confreres R. Creytens of the Historical Institute of the Dominicans in Rome, Dr S. P. Wolfs in Nijmegen, and C. M. Hinderynckx in Leuven, whose useful comments on more than one occasion enabled us to correct our text. We extend thanks also to all who facilitated the publication of this dissertation. Among them, I would like to mention Mrs L. Thomas-De Vos and Mrs M. De Vos-Thomas, who both patiently devoted their time to making the manuscript ready for publication. It would be very gratifying to me, lastly, if the Board of *Vlaamse Leergangen* and of the International Institute for Theoretical Sciences, who gave generous financial support, were to regard this book as a token of gratitude.

Abbreviations and sigla

A = *Acta C.G.*	*Acta capitulorum generalium Ordinis Praedicatorum*, vol. I
Anal. O.P.	*Analecta sacri Ordinis Fratrum Praedicatorum*
Arch. F.P.	*Archivum Fratrum Praedicatorum*
Bull. O.P.	*Bullarium Ordinis Praedicatorum*
C	*Constitutiones antique Ordinis Fratrum Predicatorum*, according to the Rodez MS (Rome, Arch. Gen. O.P., Cod. XIV A 4, pp. 55-93)
CA	*Constitutiones antique Ordinis Fratrum Predicatorum*, according to the critical edition in Appendix I
DHGE	*Dictionnaire d'histoire et de géographie ecclésiastiques*
Hystoria Albigensis	Peter of Vaux-de-Cernay, *Hystoria Albigensis*
Inst.	*Institutiones sororum S. Sixti de Urbe*
Laurent	*Historia diplomatica S. Dominici*
LTK	*Lexikon für Theologie und Kirche*
M	*Constitutiones Sororum S. Marie Magdalene*
Mansi	*Sacrorum conciliorum nova et amplissima collectio*
MGH	*Monumenta Germaniae historica*
MOPH	*Monumenta Ordinis Fratrum Praedicatorum historica*
OM	*Ordo monasterii*
Pa	*Institutiones Patrum Praemonstratensium* (12th century), ed. E. Martène
Pb	*Institutiones patrum Premonstratensis Ordinis* (13th century), ed. Pl. F. Lefèvre
PL	*Patrologia latina*, ed. J.-P. Migne
Proc. Bon.	*Processus Bononiensis: Acta canonizationis S. Dominici*, pp. 123-167
Proc. Tolos.	*Processus Tolosanus: Acta canonizationis S. Dominici*, pp. 176-187
QF	*Quellen und Forschungen zur Geschichte des Dominikanerordens in Deutschland*
R	*Constitutiones Ordinis Fratrum Predicatorum* (1241), ed. R. Creytens
RA	*Regula Augustini*
RHE	*Revue d'histoire ecclésiastique*
S	*Constitutiones Fratrum de Penitentia Iesu Christi* (*Saccatorum*)

Bibliography

I. Sources

A. Archival sources

1. Manuscripts

London, British Museum, *Cottonian Collection*, Cod. Nero A XII, 13, fol. 155^r-174^r: *Constitutiones Fratrum de Penitentia Iesu Christi*.

Osma, Biblioteca Capitular, MS. 96, fol. 1^r-41^r: *Statuta ecclesie Oxomensis per dominum Petrum de Montoya eiusdem ecclesie episcopum edita*.

Paris, Bibliothèque Nationale, *ms. lat.* 1233, fol. 1^v-32^v: [*Liber ordinis S. Rufi*].

Paris, Bibliothèque Nationale, *ms. lat.* 9752, fol. 1^v-25^v: *Institutiones patrum Premonstratensis Ordinis*.

Paris, Bibliothèque Nationale, *ms. lat.* 14762, fol. 223^r-240^r: *Institutiones Patrum Premonstratensium*.

Paris, Bibliothèque Ste-Geneviève, MSS. 1636, 1637, 1646: [*Liber ordinis S. Victoris*].

Paris, Bibliothèque Ste-Geneviève, MS. 2972, fol. 6^r-31^v: *Constitutiones Ordinis Vallis-Scholarium*.

Porto, Bibliotheca Publica Municipal, MS. 101, fol. 86^r-115^v: *Constitutiones Ordinis Fratrum Predicatorum*.

Rome, Archivio Generalizio O.P., Cod. XIV A 4, pp. 55-93: *Constitutiones antique Ordinis Fratrum Predicatorum*.

Vich, Museo Episcopal, MS. 149 (unfoliated), pp. 13-25: [*Consuetudines canonicorum S. Ioannis in dioecesi Vicensi Ordinis S. Rufi*].

Vienna, Nationalbibliothek, *Cod. lat.* 4724, fol. 311^r-317^r: *Institutiones Ordinis monialium S. Sixti de Urbe*; – fol. 320^r-328^r: *Constitutiones Sororum S. Marie Magdalene*.

2. Published editions

Acta canonizationis S. Dominici, ed. A. Walz, in MOPH, vol. XVI (Monumenta historica S. P. N. Dominici, vol. II), Rome, 1935, pp. 123-194.

Acta capitulorum generalium Ordinis Praedicatorum, vol. I, ed. B. M. Reichter, in MOPH, vol. III, Rome, 1898.

Acta Pontificum Romanorum inedita, ed. J. von Pflugk-Harttung, 3 vols, Tübingen-Stuttgart, 1881-1886.

B. Albers, *Consuetudines monasticae*, 5 vols, Stuttgart-Vienna, 1900-1912.

E. Amort, *Vetus disciplina canonicorum saecularium et regularium*, Venice, 1747.

Antiquae constitutiones coenobii S. Petri-Montis ordinis canonicorum regularium S. Augustini dioecesis Metensis, ed. C. L. Hugo, *Sacrae antiquitatis monumenta*, vol. II, pp. 425-438.

Antiquae constitutiones et quaedam decreta capitulorum generalium Ordinis Vallis-Caulium, ed. E. Martène – U. Durand, *Thesaurus novus*, vol. IV, col. 1651-1670.

Antiquae consuetudines canonicorum regularium insignis monasterii S. Victoris Parisiensis, ed.
  E. Martène, *De antiquis Ecclesiae ritibus*, vol. III, pp. 252-291.

*Antiquae consuetudines canonicorum regularium monasterii S. Iacobi de Monteforti in dioecesi
  Macloviensi*, ed. E. Martène – U. Durand, *Thesaurus novus*, vol. IV, col. 1215-1230.

Antiquae consuetudines Oignacensis monasterii, ed. E. Martène, *De antiquis Ecclesiae ritibus*,
  vol. III, pp. 340-344.

Antiquiores consuetudines Cluniacensis monasterii, ed. L. d'Achery, *Spicilegium*, vol. I,
  pp. 641-703; – PL, vol. 149, col. 635-778.

L. Auvray, *Les registres de Grégoire IX* (Bibliothèque des Écoles françaises d'Athènes et de
  Rome, 2nd series, vol. 9), 4 vols, Paris, 1896-1955.

F. Balme – P. Lelaidier – J. Collomb, *Cartulaire ou histoire diplomatique de saint Dominique*,
  3 vols, Paris, 1893-1901.

F. Balme – C. Paban – J. Collomb, *Raymundiana seu documenta quae pertinent ad S.
  Raymundi de Pennaforti vitam et scripta* (MOPH, vol. VI), Rome-Stuttgart, 1898-1901.

H. Boehmer, *Analekten zur Geschichte des Franciscus von Assisi (Sammlung ausgewählter
  kirchen- und dogmengeschichtlicher Quellenschriften*, new series, vol. 4), 3rd ed. by
  C. Andresen, Tübingen, 1961.

Bullarium Ordinis Fratrum Praedicatorum, ed. Th. Ripoll – A. Bremond, 8 vols, Rome,
  1729-1740.

*Bullarium Romanum (Bullarum, diplomatum et privilegiorum sanctorum Romanorum
  Pontificum Taurinensis editio)*, 3 vols, Turin, 1857-1859.

A. Carrier de Belleuse, *Coutumier du XIe siècle de l'ordre de St-Ruf en usage à la cathédrale de
  Maguelone* (Études et documents sur l'ordre de St-Ruf, vol. 8), Sherbrooke, Que., 1950.

Constitutiones antiquae Fratrum Servorum S. Mariae, in *Monumenta Ordinis Servorum S.
  Mariae*, vol. I, 1897, pp. 5-52.

Constitutiones antique Ordinis Fratrum Predicatorum, ed. in *Anal. O.P.*, vol. II, 1895-1896,
  pp. 621-648; – L. G. Alonso Getino, in *La Ciencia Tomista*, vol. XIII, 1916, pp. 210-244;
  – H. C. Scheeben, *Die Konstitutionen des Predigerordens unter Jordan von Sachsen*,
  pp. 48-80.

Constitutiones Fratrum de Penitentia Iesu Christi, ed. G. M. Giacomozzi, *L'Ordine della
  Penitenza di Gesù Cristo*, pp. 73-113.

Constitutiones Ordinis Fratrum Predicatorum (1241), ed. R. Creytens, *Les constitutions des
  Frères Prêcheurs dans la rédaction de s. Raymond de Peñafort*, in *Arch. F.P.*, vol. XVIII,
  1948, pp. 28-68. – See also H. Denifle, *Die Constitutionen des Predigerordens in der
  Redaction Raimunds von Peñafort*, pp. 533-564.

Constitutiones Ordinis Fratrum Predicatorum (1256), ed. in *Anal. O.P.*, vol. III, 1897-1898,
  pp. 31-60, 98-122, 162-181.

Constitutiones Ordinis Vallis-Scholarium, ed. E. Martène – U. Durand, *Voyage littéraire*, vol. I,
  Paris, 1717, pp. 114-134.

Constitutiones particulares monasterii canonicorum regularium S. Dionysii Remensis, ed.
  E. Martène, *De antiquis Ecclesiae ritibus*, vol. III, pp. 297-302.

Constitutiones Portuenses, see *Regula canonicae institutionis ... a B. Petro de Honestis
  conscriptae*.

Constitutiones sororum Ordinis Predicatorum, ed. in *Anal. O.P.*, vol. III, 1897-1898,
    pp. 338-348. – See also *Consuetudines sororum monasterii beati Dominici de Monte-Argi*.

Constitutiones Sororum S. Marie Magdalene, ed. A. Simon, *L'ordre des Pénitentes de Ste Marie-Madeleine en Allemagne au XIIIe siècle*, pp. 155-169.

Consuetudines Carthusienses, see *Consuetudines domini Guigonis prioris Carthusiae*.

Consuetudines Casinenses, see *Ordo Casinensis*.

Consuetudines Cluniacenses antiquiores, ed. B. Albers, *Consuetudines monasticae*, vol. II,
    pp. 1-61. – See also *Antiquiores consuetudines Cluniacensis monasterii*.

Consuetudines domini Guigonis prioris Carthusiae, ed. L. Holstenius – M. Brockie, *Codex regularum*, vol. II, pp. 312-332; – PL, vol. 153, col. 635-759.

Consuetudines Einsidlenses, ed. B. Albers, *Consuetudines monasticae*, vol. V, pp. 73-110.

Consuetudines Farfenses, ed. B. Albers, *Consuetudines monasticae*, vol. I, pp. 1-206.

Consuetudines Floriacenses, ed. B. Albers, *Consuetudines monasticae*, vol. V, pp. 137-151.

Consuetudines Fructuarienses, ed. B. Albers, *Consuetudines monasticae*, vol. IV, pp. 9-191.

Consuetudines Hirsaugienses, ed. in PL, vol. 150, col. 927-1146.

Consuetudines Marbacenses, ed. E. Martène, *De antiquis Ecclesiae ritibus*, vol. III,
    pp. 303-320.

Consuetudines monasteriorum Germaniae, ed. B. Albers, *Consuetudines monasticae*, vol. V,
    pp. 7-69.

Consuetudines monasticae, see B. Albers.

Consuetudines S. Benigni Divionensis, ed. L. Chomton, *Histoire de l'église Saint-Bénigne de Dijon*, Dijon, 1900, pp. 348-441.

Consuetudines sororum monasterii beati Dominici de Monte-Argi, ed. R. Creytens, *Les constitutions primitives des sœurs dominicaines de Montargis*, in *Arch. F.P.*, vol. XVII,
    1947, pp. 67-83.

Consuetudines Vallymbrosanae, ed. B. Albers, *Consuetudines monasticae*, vol. IV, pp. 223-262.

Corpus iuris canonici, ed. A. L. Richter, 2nd ed. by A. Friedberg, 2 vols, Leipzig, 1879-1881.

Corpus iuris civilis, ed. P. Krueger, Th. Mommsen, R. Schoell and G. Kroll, 3 vols, anastatic reprint, Berlin, 1928-1929.

R. Creytens, *Les constitutions des Frères Prêcheurs dans la rédaction de s. Raymond de Peñafort (1241)*, in *Arch. F.P.*, vol. XVIII, 1948, pp. 5-68.

――――, *Les constitutions primitives des sœurs dominicaines de Montargis*, in *Arch. F.P.*,
    vol. XVII, 1947, pp. 41-84.

――――, *Le „Directoire" du* Codex Ruthenensis *conservé aux Archives générales des Frères Prêcheurs*, in *Arch. F.P.*, vol. XXVI, 1956, pp. 98-126.

――――, *L'ordinaire des Frères Prêcheurs au moyen âge*, in *Arch. F.P.*, vol. XXIV, 1954,
    pp. 108-188.

L. d'Achery, *Spicilegium sive collectio veterum aliquot scriptorum, qui in Galliae bibliothecis delituerant*, 2nd ed. by L. Fr. J. de la Barre, 3 vols, Paris, 1723.

H. de Curzon, *La règle du Temple*, Paris, 1886.

J. Delaville Le Roulx, *Cartulaire général de l'ordre des Hospitaliers de Saint-Jean de Jérusalem (1100-1310)*, 4 vols, Paris, 1894-1906.

H. Denifle, *Die Constitutionen des Predigerordens vom Jahre 1228*, in *Archiv für Literatur- und Kirchengeschichte des Mittelalters*, vol. I, 1885, pp. 165-227.

————, *Die Constitutionen des Predigerordens in der Redaction Raimunds von Peñafort*, in *Archiv für Literatur- und Kirchengeschichte des Mittelalters*, vol. V, 1889, pp. 530-564.

C. Douais, *Acta capitulorum provincialium Ordinis Fratrum Praedicatorum*, Toulouse, 1894.

R. Duellius, *Miscellaneorum, quae ex codicibus MSS. collegit, libri duo*, Vienna-Graz, 1723-1724.

W. Dugdale, *Monasticon Anglicanum*, new ed. by J. Caley, H. Ellis and B. Bandinel, 6 vols, London, 1817-1830.

Ecclesiastica officia Cisterciensis Ordinis (c. 1130-1135), ed. B. Griesser, *Die Ecclesiastica officia Cisterciensis Ordinis des Cod. 1711 von Trient*, in *Analecta S. Ordinis Cisterciensis*, vol. XII, 1956, pp. 179- 280.

Ecclesiastica officia Cisterciensis Ordinis (c. 1183-1188), ed. Ph. Guignard, *Les monuments primitifs de la règle cistercienne*, pp. 87-245.

Ecclesiastica officia Cisterciensis Ordinis (c. 1150), ed. C. Noschitzka, *Codex manuscriptus 31 Bibliothecae Universitatis Labacensis*, in *Analecta S. Ordinis Cisterciensis*, vol. VI, 1950, pp. 38-124.

Expositio quattuor magistrorum super Regulam Fratrum Minorum (1241-1242). Accedit eiusdem Regulae textus cum fontibus et locis parallelis (Storia e letteratura. Raccolta di studi e testi, vol. 30), ed. L. Oliger, Rome, 1950.

Gallia christiana in provincias ecclesiasticas distributa, 16 vols, Paris, 1716- 1865.

Ph. Guignard, *Les monuments primitifs de la règle cistercienne*, Dijon, 1878.

M. Herrgott, *Vetus disciplina monastica*, Paris, 1726.

Historia diplomatica S. Dominici, ed. M. H. Laurent, in MOPH, vol. XV (Monumenta historica S. P. N. Dominici, vol. I), Paris, 1933.

L. Holstenius – M. Brockie, *Codex regularum monasticarum et canonicarum*, 6 vols, Augsburg, 1759.

Honorii III Romani Pontificis opera omnia (Medii aevi Bibliotheca patristica, 1st series, vols 1-5), ed. C. A. Horoy, 5 vols, Paris, 1879-1882.

C. L. Hugo, *Sacrae antiquitatis monumenta historica, dogmatica, diplomatica*, 2 vols, Étival, 1725-1731.

Initia consuetudinis Benedictinae (Corpus consuetudinum monasticarum, vol. I), ed. K. Hallinger, Siegburg, 1963.

Institutiones Patrum Praemonstratensium, ed. E. Martène, *De antiquis Ecclesiae ritibus*, vol. III, pp. 323-336.

Institutiones patrum Premonstratensis Ordinis, ed. Pl. F. Lefèvre, *Les statuts de Prémontré réformés sur les ordres de Grégoire IX et d'Innocent IV au XIIIᵉ siècle*, pp. 1-126.

Institutiones sororum Sancti Sixti de Urbe, ed. A. Simon, *L'ordre des Pénitentes de Sᵗᵉ Marie-Madeleine en Allemagne au XIIIᵉ siècle*, pp. 143-153.

A. F. La Cava, *Liber Regulae S. Spiritus*, Milan, 1947.

Pl. F. Lefèvre, *Les statuts de Prémontré réformés sur les ordres de Grégoire IX et d'Innocent IV au XIIIᵉ siècle* (Bibliothèque de la Revue d'histoire ecclésiastique, vol. 23), Leuven, 1946.

L. Le Grand, *Statuts d'hôtels-Dieu et de léproseries* (Collection de textes pour servir à l'étude et à l'enseignement de l'histoire), Paris, 1901.

V. Ligiez, *Epitome bullarii Ordinis Praedicatorum*, in *Anal. O.P.*, vol. IV, 1899-1900,
　　pp. 48-63, 108-128, 250-256, 373-384, 494-512.

———, *Regesta Romanorum Pontificum pro S. Ordine Fratrum Praedicatorum*, in *Anal. O.P.*,
　　vol. III, 1897-1898, pp. 183-188, 246-251, 307-315, 368-380, 436-444, 485-508,
　　566-572, 614-635.

Litterae encyclicae magistrorum generalium Ordinis Praedicatorum, ed. B. M. Reichert, in
　　MOPH, vol. V, Rome, 1900.

R. J. Loenertz, *Archives de Prouille*, in *Arch. F.P.*, vol. XXIV, 1954, pp. 5-49.

———, *Documents pour servir à l'histoire de la province dominicaine de Grèce*, in *Arch. F.P.*,
　　vol. XIV, 1944, pp. 72-115.

E. Martène, *De antiquis Ecclesiae ritibus*, 4 vols, Antwerp, 1763-1764.

———, U. Durand, *Thesaurus novus anecdotorum*, 5 vols, Paris, 1717.

Id., *Veterum scriptorum et monumentorum historicorum, dogmaticorum, moralium amplissima
　　collectio*, 9 vols, Paris, 1724-1739.

P.-Th. Masetti, *Monumenta et antiquitates veteris disciplinae Ordinis Praedicatorum ab anno
　　1216 ad 1348 praesertim in Romana provincia*, 2 vols, Rome, 1864.

G. G. Meersseman, *Dossier de l'ordre de la Pénitence au XIIIe siècle* (Spicilegium Friburgense,
　　vol. 7), Fribourg (Switzerland), 1961.

Memoriale propositi, ed. H. Boehmer, *Analekten zur Geschichte des Franciscus von Assisi*,
　　pp. 49-56; – G. G. Meersseman, *Dossier de l'ordre de la Pénitence au XIIIe siècle*,
　　pp. 92-112.

Nomasticon Cisterciense, see J. Paris.

Ordinarium iuxta ritum sacri Ordinis Fratrum Praedicatorum, ed. F. M. Guerrini, Rome,
　　[1921].

Ordo Casinensis I, dictus Ordo regulans, ed. T. Leccisotti – K. Hallinger – M. Wegener, in
　　Initia consuetudinis Benedictinae, pp. 101-104.

Ordo Casinensis II, dictus Ordo officii, ed. T. Leccisotti, in *Initia consuetudinis Benedictinae*,
　　pp. 113-123.

Ordo monasterii, ed. D. De Bruyne, *La première règle de saint Benoît*, in Revue bénédictine,
　　vol. XLII, 1930, pp. 318-319; – R. Arbesmann – W. Hümpfner, *Iordani de Saxonia Liber
　　Vitasfratrum* (Cassiciacum, vol. 1), New York, 1943, pp. 488-493.

J. Paris, *Nomasticon Cisterciense seu antiquiores Ordinis Cisterciensis constitutiones*, new ed. by
　　H. Sejalon, Solesmes, 1892.

G. Penco, *S. Benedicti Regula. Introduzione, testo, apparati e commento* (Biblioteca di studi
　　superiori, vol. 39), Florence, 1958.

J. J. Percin, *Monumenta conventus Tolosani Ordinis Fratrum Praedicatorum primi*, Toulouse,
　　1693.

M. Perlbach, *Die Statuten des deutschen Ordens*, Halle, 1890.

Peter the Venerable, *Statuta congregationis Cluniacensis*, ed. in PL, vol. 189, col. 1025-1048.

D. Planzer, *De codice Ruthenensi miscellaneo in tabulario Ordinis Praedicatorum asservato*, in
　　Arch. F.P., vol. V, 1935, pp. 5-123.

Propositum Bernardi Primi, ed. in PL, vol. 216, col. 289-293, 648-650; – G. G. Meersseman,
　　Dossier de l'ordre de la Pénitence au XIIIe siècle, pp. 284-286, 288-289.

Propositum Humiliatorum, ed. H. Tiraboschi, *Vetera Humiliatorum monumenta*, vol. II,
   pp. 128-134; – G. G. Meersseman, *Dossier de l'ordre de la Pénitence au XIIIᵉ siècle*,
   pp. 276-282.

Propositum Pauperum Catholicorum, ed. in PL, vol. 215, col. 1512-1513; – G. G.
   Meersseman, *Dossier de l'ordre de la Pénitence au XIIIᵉ siècle*, pp. 282-284.

Regesta Honorii Papae III, ed. P. Pressutti, 2 vols, Rome, 1888-1892.

*Regesta Pontificum Romanorum ab condita Ecclesia ad annum post Christum natum
   MCXCVIII*, ed. Ph. Jaffé, 2ⁿᵈ ed. by G. Wattenbach, S. Loewenfeld, F. Kaltenbrunner
   and P. Ewald, 2 vols, Leipzig, 1885 1888.

*Regesta Pontificum Romanorum inde ab anno post Christum natum MCXCVIII ad annum
   MCCCIV*, ed. A. Potthast, 2 vols, Berlin, 1874-1875.

Regula bullata S. Francisci, ed. H. Boehmer, *Analekten zur Geschichte des Franciscus von
   Assisi*, pp. 20-24.

Regula canonicae institutionis sive Constitutiones Portuenses a B. Petro de Honestis conscriptae,
   ed. E. Amort, *Vetus disciplina canonicorum*, pp. 338-382; – PL, vol. 163, col. 703-748.

Regula canonicorum, ed. Ch.-J. Hefele – H. Leclercq, *Histoire des conciles*, vol. V, Paris, 1912,
   pp. 95-98.

Regula Hospitalis S. Spiritus, ed. A. F. La Cava, *Liber Regulae S. Spiritus*, pp. 111-209.

Regula Humiliatorum, ed. L. Zazoni, *Gli Umiliati*, pp. 352-370.

Regula militum Hospitalis Sancti Ioannis Hierosolymitani, ed. L. Holstenius – M. Brockie,
   Codex regularum, vol. II, pp. 445-449; – J. Delaville Le Roulx, *Cartulaire général de
   l'ordre des Hospitaliers de Saint-Jean de Jérusalem*, vol. I, pp. 62-68.

Regula Ordinis SS. Trinitatis seu Redemptionis captivorum, in L. Holstenius – M. Brockie,
   Codex regularum, vol. III, pp. 3-11; – PL, vol. 214, col. 445-449.

Regula pauperum commilitonum Christi Templique Salomonici, ed. Mansi, vol. XXI,
   col. 359-372.

Regulae Ordinis Sempringensis sive Gilbertinorum canonicorum, ed. L. Holstenius –
   M. Brockie, *Codex regularum*, vol. II, pp. 467-536; – W. Dugdale, *Monasticon
   Anglicanum*, vol. II, pp. XXIX-XCIX.

Regula Petri de Honestis, see *Regula canonicae institutionis … a B. Petro de Honestis
   conscriptae.*

Regula prima S. Francisci, ed. H. Boehmer, *Analekten zur Geschichte des Franciscus von Assisi*,
   pp. 1-18.

Regula S. Augustini, ed. R. Arbesmann – W. Hümpfner, *Iordani de Saxonia Liber
   Vitasfratrum* (Cassiciacum, vol. 1), New York, 1943, pp. 494-504.

Regula S. Benedicti, ed. G. Penco, *S. Benedicti Regula* (Biblioteca di studi superiori, vol. 39),
   Florence, 1958; – R. Hanslik, *Benedicti Regula* (Corpus Scriptorum ecclesiasticorum
   latinorum, vol. 75), Vienna, 1960.

Regula S. Francisci, see *Regula prima* and *Regula bullata.*

Regula secunda, see *Ordo monasterii.*

Regula tertia, see *Regula S. Augustini.*

Sacrorum conciliorum nova et amplissima collectio, ed. J. D. Mansi, anastatic reprint, Graz,
   1960-1961.

H. C. Scheeben, *Accessiones ad historiam Romanae provinciae saeculo XIII*, in *Arch. F.P.*, vol. IV, 1934, pp. 99-140.

———, *De bullario quodam Ordinis Praedicatorum saeculi XIII*, in *Arch. F.P.*, vol. VI, 1936, pp. 217-266.

———, *Die Konstitutionen des Predigerordens unter Jordan von Sachsen* (QF, vol. 38), Cologne-Leipzig, 1939.

Statuta canonicorum regularium Ordinis S^{mi} Sepulchri, monasterii S. Crucis, prope Galoppiam, Liège, 1745.

Statuta capitulorum generalium Ordinis Cisterciensis ab anno 1116 ad annum 1786 (Bibliothèque de la Revue d'histoire ecclésiastique, vols 9-14), ed. J.-M. Canivez, 8 vols, Leuven, 1933-1941.

Statuta congregationis Cluniacensis, see Peter the Venerable.

Statuta Murbacensia, ed. B. Albers, *Consuetudines monasticae*, vol. III, pp. 79-93.

Statuta Ordinis Premonstratensis, ed. R. Van Waefelghem, *Les premiers statuts de l'ordre de Prémontré*, pp. 16-67.

H. Tiraboschi, *Vetera Humiliatorum monumenta*, 3 vols, Milan, 1766-1768.

Usus Cistercienses, see *Ecclesiastica officia Cisterciensis Ordinis*.

Usus conversorum Ordinis Cisterciensis, ed. J. A. Lefèvre, *L'évolution des Usus conversorum de Cîteaux*, in *Collectanea Ordinis Cisterciensium Reformatorum*, vol. XVII, 1955, pp. 85-97.

J.-B. Van Damme, *Documenta pro Cisterciensis Ordinis historiae ac iuris studio*, Westmalle, 1959.

R. Van Waefelghem, *Les premiers statuts de l'ordre de Prémontré* (reprint from *Analectes de Prémontré*, vol. IX), Leuven, 1913.

Vetera Hyreevallis statuta, ed. C. L. Hugo, *Sacrae antiquitatis monumenta*, vol. I, pp. 135-144.

P. von Loë, *Statistisches über die Ordensprovinz Teutonia* (QF, vol. I), Leipzig, 1907.

B. Literary sources

Bernard Gui, *De fundatione et prioribus conventuum provinciarum Tolosanae et Provinciae Ordinis Praedicatorum*, ed. P. A. Amargier, in MOPH, vol. XXIV, Rome, 1961.

———, *Tractatus de tribus gradibus praelatorum in Ordine Praedicatorum*, ed. E. Martène – U. Durand, *Veterum scriptorum… amplissima collectio*, vol. VI, col. 397-436.

Brevis historia Ordinis Fratrum Praedicatorum auctore anonymo, ed. E. Martène – U. Durand, *Veterum scriptorum… amplissima collectio*, vol. VI, col. 331-344.

Brevissima chronica magistrorum generalium Ordinis Praedicatorum, ed. E. Martène – U. Durand, *Veterum scriptorum… amplissima collectio*, vol. VI, col. 344-396.

Chronica Ordinis [*Praedicatorum*], see Galvano Fiamma, Gerard of Frachet and Peter Ferrand.

Constantinus of Orvieto, *Legenda S. Dominici*, ed. H. C. Scheeben, in MOPH, vol. XVI (Monumenta historica S. P. N. Dominici, vol. II), Rome, 1935, pp. 286-352.

R. Creytens, *L'instruction des novices dominicains au XIIIe siècle d'après le ms. Toulouse 418*, in *Arch. F.P.*, vol. XX, 1950, pp. 114-193.

Dietrich of Apolda, *Vita S. Dominici*, ed. in *Acta Sanctorum*, vol. XXXV (*Augusti tomus primus*), Paris-Rome, 1867, pp. 558-628.

Galvano Fiamma, *Chronica maior Ordinis Praedicatorum*, ed. G. Odetto, *La Cronaca maggiore dell'Ordine domenicano di Galvano Fiamma*, in *Arch. F.P.*, vol. X, 1940, pp. 319-370.

——, *Chronica Ordinis Fratrum Praedicatorum*, ed. B. M. Reichert, in MOPH, vol. II, Rome-Stuttgart, 1897, pp. 1-111.

[Gerard of Frachet], *Chronica Ordinis (prior)*, ed. B. M. Reichert, in MOPH, vol. I, Leuven, 1896, pp. 321-338.

Gerard of Frachet, *Vitae fratrum Ordinis Praedicatorum*, ed. B. M. Reichert, in MOPH, vol. I, Leuven, 1896, pp. 1-320.

Humbert of Romans, *Expositio super Constitutiones Fratrum Praedicatorum*, ed. J. J. Berthier, in *Humberti de Romanis opera de vita regulari*, vol. II, Rome, 1889, pp. 1-178.

——, *Expositio Regulae beati Augustini*, ed. J. J. Berthier, in *Humberti de Romanis opera de vita regulari*, vol. I, Rome, 1888, pp. 43-633.

——, *Instructiones de officiis Ordinis*, ed. J. J. Berthier, in *Humberti de Romanis opera de vita regulari*, vol. II, Rome, 1889, pp. 179-369.

——, *Legenda S. Dominici*, ed. A. Walz, in MOPH, vol. XVI (Monumenta historica S. P. N. Dominici, vol. II), Rome, 1935, pp. 369-423.

——, *Opera de vita regulari*, ed. J. J. Berthier, 2 vols, Rome, 1888-1889.

Jordan of Saxony, *Epistulae*, ed. A. Walz, in MOPH, vol. XXIII, Rome, 1951.

——, *Libellus de principiis Ordinis Predicatorum*, ed. H. C. Scheeben, in MOPH, vol. XVI, Rome, 1935, pp. 25-88.

R. J. Loenertz, *Une ancienne chronique des provinciaux dominicains de Pologne*, in *Arch. F.P.*, vol. XXI, 1951, pp. 5-50.

G. Odetto, *La Cronaca maggiore dell'Ordine domenicano di Galvano Fiamma. Frammenti editi*, in *Arch. F.P.*, vol. X, 1940, pp. 297-373.

[Peter Ferrand], *Chronica Ordinis (posterior)*, ed. B. M. Reichert, in MOPH, vol. I, Leuven, 1896, pp. 321-337; – MOPH, vol. VII, Rome, 1904, pp. 1-11.

Peter Ferrand, *Legenda S. Dominici*, ed. M. H. Laurent, in MOPH, vol. XVI (Monumenta historica S. P. N. Dominici, vol. II), Rome, 1935, pp. 209-260.

Peter of Vaux-de-Cernay, *Hystoria Albigensis* (Société de l'histoire de France, vols 412, 422, 442), ed. P. Guébin – E. Lyon, 3 vols, Paris, 1926-1939.

J. Quétif – J. Échard, *Scriptores Ordinis Praedicatorum*, 2 vols, Paris, 1719-1721.

Stephen of Salagnac – Bernard Gui, *De quatuor in quibus Deus Praedicatorum Ordinem insignivit*, ed. Th. Kaeppeli, in MOPH, vol. XXII, Rome, 1949.

Tractatus de approbatione Ordinis Fratrum Praedicatorum, ed. Th. Kaeppeli, in *Arch. F.P.*, vol. VI, 1936, pp. 144-160.

A. Walz, *Die* Miracula beati Dominici *der Schwester Cäcilia. Einleitung und Text*, in *Miscellanea Pio Paschini. Studi di storia ecclesiastica* (Lateranum, new series, vol. XIV, vols 1-4), vol. I, Rome, 1948, pp. 293-326.

II. Scholarly works

L. G. Alonso Getino, *Capitulos provinciales y priores provinciales de la Orden de Santo Domingo en España*, in *La Ciencia Tomista*, vol. XIII, 1916, pp. 67-96, 210-244.

B. Altaner, *Der Armutsgedanke beim hl. Dominikus*, in *Theologie und Glaube*, vol. XI, 1919, pp. 404-427.

——, *Zur Beurteilung der Persönlichkeit und der Entwicklung der Ordensidee des hl. Dominikus*, in *Zeitschrift für Kirchengeschichte*, vol. XLVI, 1928, pp. 396-407.

——, *Die Beziehungen des hl. Dominikus zum hl. Franziskus von Assisi*, in *Franziskanische Studien*, vol. IX, 1922, pp. 1-28.

——, *Die Briefe Jordans von Sachsen, des zweiten Dominikanergenerals (1222-1237). Text und Untersuchungen. Zugleich ein Beitrag zur Geschichte der Frömmigkeit im 13. Jahrhundert*, (QF, vol. 20), Leipzig, 1925.

——, *Die Dominikanermissionen des 13. Jahrhunderts* (Breslauer Studien zur historischen Theologie, vol. 3), Habelschwerdt, 1924.

——, *Der hl. Dominikus. Untersuchungen und Texte* (Breslauer Studien zur historischen Theologie, vol. 2), Breslau, 1922.

M. Ambraziejutè, *Studien über die Johanniter-Regel*, Fribourg (Switzerland), 1929.

E. Barker, *The Dominican Order and Convocation. A Study of the Growth of Representation in the Church during the Thirteenth Century*, Oxford, 1913.

R. F. Bennett, *The Early Dominicans. Studies in Thirteenth-Century Dominican History*, Cambridge, 1937.

W. R. Bonniwell, *A History of the Dominican Liturgy*, New York, 1945[2].

C. Capelle, *Le vœu d'obéissance des origines au XIIe siècle. Étude juridique* (Bibliothèque d'histoire du droit et du droit romain, vol. 2), Paris, 1959.

V. Carro, *Santo Domingo de Guzmán, fundador de la primera orden universitaria, apostólica y misionera*, in *La Ciencia Tomista*, vol. LXX, 1946, pp. 5-81, 282-329.

M. D. Chapotin, *Histoire des dominicains de la province de France*, Paris, 1898.

F. Chatillon, *Etiam… (Animadversiones Augustinianae)*, § V: *En marge du Décret de Gratien et des Constitutions de l'ordre des Frères Prêcheurs*, in *Revue du moyen âge latin*, vol. IX, 1953, pp. 307-341.

M. D. Chenu, *Réformes de structure en chrétienté*, in *Économie et humanisme*, vol. V, 1946, pp. 85-98.

L. Chomton, *Histoire de l'église Saint-Bénigne de Dijon*, Dijon, 1900.

M. P. Coenegracht, *De kloosterwetgeving van de Brabantse Witte Vrouwen*, in *Ons Geestelijk Erf*, vol. XXXIV, 1960, pp. 337-373.

L. H. Cottineau, *Répertoire topo-bibliographique des abbayes et prieurés*, 2 vols, Mâcon, 1935-1936.

O. Decker, *Die Stellung des Predigerordens zu den Dominikanerinnen (1207-1267)* (QF, vol. 31), Vechta-Leipzig, 1935.

A. De Meyer – J. M. De Smet, *Guigo's* Consuetudines *van de eerste Kartuizers* (Mededelingen van de Koninklijke Vlaamse Academie voor Wetenschappen, Letteren en Schone Kunsten van België, Klasse der Letteren, vol. XIII, no. 6), Brussels, 1951.

H. Denifle, *Die Entstehung der Universitäten des Mittelalters bis 1400*, Berlin, 1885.

Ch. Dereine, *Chanoines*, art. in DHGE, vol. XII, 1953, col. 353-404.

————, *Coutumiers et ordinaires de chanoines réguliers*, in *Scriptorium*, vol. V, 1951, pp. 107-113.

————, *Les coutumiers de Saint-Quentin de Beauvais et de Springiersbach*, in RHE, vol. XLIII, 1948, pp. 411-442.

————, *Saint-Ruf et ses coutumes aux XIᵉ et XIIᵉ siècles*, in *Revue bénédictine*, vol. LIX, 1949, pp. 161-182.

————, *Vie commune, règle de saint Augustin et chanoines réguliers au XIᵉ siècle*, in RHE, vol. XLI, 1946, pp. 365-406.

J. C. Dickinson, *The Origins of the Austin Canons and their Introduction into England*, London, 1950.

E. Feyaerts, *De evolutie van het predikatierecht der religieuzen*, in *Studia catholica*, vol. XXV, 1950, pp. 177-190, 225-240.

G. R. Galbraith, *The Constitution of the Dominican Order 1216 to 1360* (Publications of the University of Manchester. Historical Series, vol. 44), Manchester, 1925.

J. Gallén, *La province de Dacie de l'ordre des Frères Prêcheurs*, vol. I: *Histoire Générale jusqu'au Grand Schisme* (Institutum historicum FF. Praedicatorum. Dissertationes historicae, vol. 12), Helsinki, 1946.

M. Gelabert – J. M. Milagro, *Santo Domingo de Guzmán visto por sus contemporáneos* (Biblioteca de Autores Cristianos, vol. 22), Madrid, 1947.

G. M. Giacomozzi, *L'Ordine della Penitenza di Gesù Cristo* (Scrinium historiale, vol. 2), Rome, 1962.

F. Gosse, *Histoire de l'abbaye et de l'ancienne congrégation des chanoines réguliers d'Arrouaise*, Lille, 1786.

H. Grundmann, *Religiöse Bewegungen im Mittelalter. Untersuchungen über die geschichtlichen Zusammenhänge zwischen der Ketzerei, den Bettelorden und der religiösen Frauenbewegung im 12. und 13. Jahrhundert und über die geschichtlichen Grundlagen der deutschen Mystik* (Historische Studien, vol. 297), Berlin, 1935.

J. Guiraud, *Saint Dominique et la fondation du monastère de Prouille*, in *Revue historique*, vol. LXIV, 1897, pp. 224-257.

W. Gumbley, *A List of the English Provincial Priors*, in *English Historical Review*, vol. XXXIII, 1918, pp. 243-251.

H. Heijman, *Untersuchungen über die Praemonstratenser-Gewohnheiten*, in *Analecta Praemonstratensia*, vol. II, 1926, pp. 5-32; vol. III, 1927, pp. 5-27; vol. IV, 1928, pp. 5-29, 113-131, 225-241, 351-373.

M. Heimbucher, *Die Orden und Kongregationen der katholischen Kirche*, 2 vols, Paderborn, 1933-1934³.

F. Heintke, *Humbert von Romans, der fünfte Ordensmeister der Dominikaner* (Historische Studien, vol. 222), Berlin, 1933.

L. Hertling, *Kanoniker, Augustinerregel und Augustinerorden*, in *Zeitschrift für katholische Theologie*, vol. LIV, 1930, pp. 335-369.

W. A. Hinnebusch, *The Early Dominicans and Unsacerdotalism*, in *Medievalia et humanistica*, vol. IV, 1946, pp. 62-70.

———, *The Early English Friars Preachers* (Institutum historicum FF. Praedicatorum. Dissertationes historicae, vol. 14), Rome, 1951.

———, *The Personnel of the Early English Dominican Province*, in *The Catholic Historical Review*, vol. XXIX, 1943, p. 247.

J. Hourlier, *Le chapitre général jusqu'au moment du Grand Schisme. Origines, développement. Étude juridique* (Thèse de la Faculté de droit de Paris), Paris, 1936.

Vl. J. Koudelka, *Le "monasterium Tempuli" et la fondation dominicaine de San Sisto*, in *Arch. F.P.*, vol. XXXI, 1961, pp. 5-81.

———, *Notes sur le cartulaire de S. Dominique*, in *Arch. F.P.*, vol. XXVIII, 1958, pp. 92-114; vol. XXXIII, 1963, pp. 89-120; vol. XXXIV, 1964, pp. 5-44.

R. Ladner, *L'Ordo Praedicatorum avant l'ordre des Prêcheurs*, in P. Mandonnet – M. H. Vicaire, *Saint Dominique*, vol. II, pp. 11-68.

H. C. Lambermond, *Der Armutsgedanke des hl. Dominikus und seines Ordens*, Zwolle, 1926.

M. H. Laurent, *S. Dominique à Rome en 1221. Un document inédit*, in *Arch. F.P.*, vol. XX, 1950, pp. 325-329.

M. H. Lavocat, *Les observances monastiques. I. La collation*, in *L'Année dominicaine*, vol. LX, 1924, pp. 62-70.

Pl. Lefèvre, *Prémontré, ses origines, sa première liturgie, les relations de son code législatif avec Cîteaux et les chanoines du Saint-Sépulcre de Jérusalem*, in *Analecta Praemonstratensia*, vol. XXV, 1949, pp. 96-103.

A. G. Little, *The Administrative Divisions of the Mendicant Orders in England*, in *English Historical Review*, vol. XXXIV, 1919, pp. 205-209.

———, *The Mendicant Orders*, in *Cambridge Medieval History*, vol. VI, Cambridge, 1936, pp. 727-762.

———, *Provincial Priors and Vicars of the English Dominicans*, in *English Historical Review*, vol. XXXIII, 1918, pp. 496-497.

R.-M. Louis, *Histoire du texte des constitutions dominicaines*, in *Arch. F.P.*, vol. VI, 1936, pp. 334-350.

J.-B. Mahn, *L'ordre cistercien et son gouvernement des origines au milieu du XIIIe siècle (1098-1265)*, Paris, 1945.

Th. Malvenda, *Annalium sacri Ordinis Praedicatorum centuria prima*, Naples, 1627.

Th. M. Mamachi – Fr. M. Pollidori – V. M. Badetti – H. D. Cristianopoli, *Annalium Ordinis Praedicatorum volumen primum*, Rome, 1756.

P. Mandonnet, *Saint Dominique. L'idée, l'homme et l'œuvre*, Ghent, 1921.

——— – M. H. Vicaire, *Saint Dominique. L'idée, l'homme et l'œuvre*, 2 vols, Paris, [1937].

G. Meersseman, *L'architecture dominicaine au XIIIe siècle. Législation et pratique*, in *Arch. F.P.*, vol. XVI, 1946, pp. 136-190.

———, *Les débuts de l'ordre des Frères Prêcheurs dans le comté de Flandre (1224-1280)*, in *Arch. F.P.*, vol. XVII, 1947, pp. 5-40.

————, *La loi purement pénale d'après les statuts des confréries médiévales*, in *Mélanges J. de Ghellinck* (Museum Lessianum. Section historique, vol. 14), Gembloux, 1951, vol. II, pp. 975-1002.

A. Mens, *Oorsprong en betekenis van de Nederlandse Begijnen- en Begardenbeweging. Vergelijkende studie: XIIᵉ-XIIIᵉ eeuw* (Verhandelingen van de Koninklijke Vlaamse Academie voor Wetenschappen, Letteren en Schone Kunsten van België, Klasse der Letteren, vol. IX, no. 7), Antwerp, 1947.

L.-R. Misserey, *Chapitres de religieux*, art. in *Dictionnaire de droit canonique*, vol. III, 1942, col. 595-610.

A. Mortier, *Histoire des maîtres généraux de l'ordre des Frères Prêcheurs*, 8 vols, Paris, 1903-1920.

L. Moulin, *Les formes du gouvernement local et provincial dans les ordres religieux*, in *Revue internationale des sciences administratives*, vol. XXI, 1955, pp. 31-57.

————, *Le pluricaméralisme dans l'ordre des Frères Prêcheurs*, in *Res publica*, vol. II, 1960, pp. 50-66.

Ph. Mulhern, *The Early Dominican Laybrother*, Washington, 1944.

M. Peuchmaurd, *Mission canonique et prédication*, in *Recherches de théologie ancienne et médiévale*, vol. XXX, 1963, pp. 251-276.

J. B. Pierron, *Die katholischen Armen. Ein Beitrag zur Entstehungsgeschichte der Bettelorden mit Berücksichtigung der Humiliaten und der Wiedervereinigten Lombarden*, Freiburg im Breisgau, 1911.

M. Plasschaert, *De origine officii superioris provincialis*, in *Ephemerides Theologicae Lovanienses*, vol. XXXIV, 1958, pp. 330-356.

H. Prutz, *Die geistlichen Ritterorden. Ihre Stellung zur kirchlichen, politischen, gesellschaftlichen und wirtschaftlichen Entwicklung des Mittelalters*, Berlin, 1908.

H. Rashdall, *The Universities of Europe in the Middle Ages*, new ed. by F. M. Powicke and A. B. Embden, 3 vols, Oxford, [1936].

B. M. Reichert, *Feier und Geschäftsordnung der Provinzialkapitel des Dominikanerordens im 13. Jahrhundert*, in *Römische Quartalschrift für christliche Altertumskünde und Kirchengeschichte*, vol. XVII, 1903, pp. 101-140; vol. XXI, 1907, pp. 48-50.

L. Rousseau, *De ecclesiastico officio Fratrum Praedicatorum secundum ordinationem venerabilis magistri Humberti de Romanis*, in *Anal. O.P.*, vol. XVII, 1925-1926, pp. 711-730, 744-766, 813-825; vol. XVIII, 1927-1928, pp. 104-120, 142-163, 193-203, 252-273.

G. M. Ruf, *De relatione inter capitulum generale et magistrum generalem in Ordine Fratrum Praedicatorum (1216-1501)*, Augsburg, 1958.

H. C. Scheeben, *Die Anfänge des zweiten Ordens des hl. Dominikus*, in *Arch. F.P.*, vol. II, 1932, pp. 284-315.

————, *Beiträge zur Geschichte Jordans von Sachsen* (QF, vol. 35), Vechta-Leipzig, 1938.

————, *Dominikaner oder Innozentianer*, in *Arch. F.P.*, vol. IX, 1939, pp. 237-297.

————, *Der heilige Dominikus*, Freiburg im Breisgau, 1927.

————, *Der literarische Nachlass Jordans von Sachsen*, in *Historisches Jahrbuch*, vol. LI, 1931, pp. 56-71.

————, *Prediger und Generalprediger im Dominikanerorden des 13. Jahrhunderts*, in *Arch. F.P.*, vol. XXXI, 1961, pp. 112-141.

G. Schreiber, *Gemeinschaften des Mittelalters. Recht und Verfassung, Kult und Frömmigkeit* (Gesammelte Abhandlungen, vol. 1), Münster, 1948.

————, *Kurie und Kloster im 12. Jahrhundert. Studien zur Privilegierung, Verfassung und besonders zum Eigenkirchenwesen der vorfranziskanischen Orden, vornehmlich auf Grund der Papsturkunden von Paschalis II bis auf Lucius III (1091-1181)* (Kirchenrechtliche Abhandlungen, vols 65-68), 2 vols, Stuttgart, 1910.

J. Siegwart, *Die Chorherren- und Chorfrauengemeinschaften in der deutschsprachigen Schweiz vom VI. Jahrhundert bis 1160. Mit einem Überblick über die deutsche Kanonikerreform des X. und XI. Jahrhunderts* (Studia Friburgensia, new series, vol. 30), Fribourg (Switzerland), 1962.

A. Simon, *L'ordre des Pénitentes de Ste Marie-Madeieine en Allemagne au XIIIe siècle*, Fribourg (Switzerland), 1918.

L. Spätling, *De apostolicis, pseudoapostolis, apostolinis. Dissertatio ad diversos vitae apostolicae conceptus saeculorum decursu elucidandos*, Munich, 1947.

M. Tangl, *Die päpstlichen Kanzleiordnungen von 1200-1500*, Innsbruck, 1894.

I.M. Tonneau, *L'obligation* ad poenam *des constitutions dominicaines*, in *Revue des sciences philos, et théol.*, vol. XXIV, 1935, pp. 107-115.

H. P. Tunmore, *The Dominican Order and Parliament. An Unsolved Problem in the History of Representation*, in *The Catholic Historical Review*, vol. XXVI, 1941, pp. 479-489.

I. J. van de Westelaken, *Premonstratenzer wetgeving, 1120-1165*, in *Analecta Praemonstratensia*, vol. XXXVIII, 1962, pp. 7-42.

F. Van Ortroy, *Pierre Ferrand O.P. et les premiers biographes de S. Dominique, fondateur de l'ordre des Frères Prêcheurs*, in *Analecta Bollandiana*, vol. XXX, 1911, pp. 27-87.

M. H. Vicaire, *La bulle de confirmation des Prêcheurs*, in RHE, vol. XLVII, 1952, pp. 176-192.

————, *Dominique (Saint)*, art. in DHGE, vol. XIV, 1960, col. 592-608.

————, *L'évangélisme des premiers Frères Prêcheurs*, in *La vie spirituelle*, vol. LXXVI, 1947, pp. 264-277.

————, *Fondation, approbation, confirmation de l'ordre des Prêcheurs*, in RHE, vol. XLVII, 1952, pp. 123-141, 586-603.

————, *Histoire de saint Dominique*, 2 vols, Paris, 1957.

————, *L'imitation des apôtres. Moines, chanoines et mendiants (IVe-XIIIe siècles)*, Paris, 1963.

————, *Saint Dominique de Caleruega d'après les documents du XIIIe siècle*, Paris, 1955.

————, *Saint Dominique en 1201*, in *Arch. F.P.*, vol. XXIII, 1953, pp. 335-345.

La vita comune del clero nei secoli XI e XII. Atti della Settimana di studio: Mendola, settembre 1959 (Pubblicazioni dell'Università cattolica del S. Cuore, 3rd series, vols 2-3. – Miscellanea del Centro di studi medioevali, vol. 3), 2 vols, Milan, 1962.

A. Walz, *Compendium historiae Ordinis Praedicatorum*, Rome, 1948^2.

————, *"Magne Pater Augustine". Dominikanisches zur Regel des hl. Augustinus*, in *Angelicum*, vol. XXXI, 1954, pp. 213-231.

E. Werner, *Pauperes Christi. Studien zu sozial-religiösen Bewegungen im Zeitalter des Reformpapsttums*, Leipzig, 1956.

L. Zanoni, *Gli Umiliati nei loro rapporti con l'eresia, l'industria della lana ed i comuni nei secoli XII e XIII sulla scorta di documenti inediti* (Bibliotheca historica Italica, 2nd series, vol. 2), Milan, 1911.

CHAPTER I

Antecedents

Monastic legislation up to the beginning of the thirteenth century

Ever since the emergence of cenobitic life in the course of the fourth century, dozens of monastic founders and legislators have repeated, commented on, supplemented and amended the evangelical guidelines for spiritual perfection with almost inexhaustible diversity. In the long series of monastic rules and legal codes, the constitutions of the Dominicans occupy a place all their own. Their content and form were determined not only by the founder and his immediate successors as rulers of the order, but also by the special circumstances that occasioned the foundation. At the same time, however, Dominican legislation was indebted to the monastic and canonical traditions, and it thus adopted customs and rules that, in some cases, date back to the earliest times of the monastic life. To provide clearer insight into the origins and meaning of Dominican legislation, this chapter will give an overview of the development of monastic law up to the beginning of the thirteenth century.

The first section will examine the earliest documents of monastic legislation: the *consuetudines* or writings which recorded the traditional customs of the monks and canons regular. Then we will address the *statuta* or legal codes in which some monastic institutes recorded the special norms and principles that were to regulate the religious' way of live and activity in the future. A third section will look at a particular genre of guidelines for religious community life: the *propositum conversationis*, which a number of originally non-monastic societies that emerged from the apostolic movement at the beginning of the thirteenth century imposed upon their members as a rule of life. Afterwards, we will discuss the foundation of the Dominicans and the origins of their legislation.

Section I. *Consuetudines* of monks and canons

The community life of religious was initially based upon a rule, that is, a collection of spiritual guidelines and disciplinary rules that had usually been drawn up or collected by a single person. The rules of Saint Benedict for monks and Saint Augustine for canons were particularly widely known and disseminated in the West. The need to further explain or supplement certain points in these monastic rules led to the emergence of various *consuetudines*, a word which refers both to the normative customs themselves and to the usages of the monks and canons regular as recorded in writing.

After Pachomius († 346), the first organiser and legislator of the cenobitic life, many monastic founders in the East and the West left a *regula*. The names of Basil († 379), Martin of Tours († 397), Cassian († 434), Caesarius of Arles († 542), Columbanus († 615) and Isidore of Seville († 636) are well known in this context.[1] In North Africa, Augustine, the bishop of Hippo († 430), was the great promoter of the communal life for clerics.[2] His admonitions were regarded as having the force of law also in communities of women.[3] Beginning in the sixth century, most older rules were superseded by Saint Benedict's *Regula monasteriorum*, which was soon received everywhere in the West as the ideal legal code, due to its healthy spiritual guidelines which are closely aligned with Sacred Scripture and tradition, its sense of moderation and balance with regard to asceticism and observances, and its clearly formulated principles on the organisation and government of the community.[4] In the course of the eleventh century, the *Regula S. Augustini* gained new currency, but initially only in cathedral chapters or in communities composed primarily of clerics.[5] But at that time, the rules were no longer the only legislative text that were to be observed in the monasteries that accepted them as the fundamental law. They had been supplemented by all kinds of unwritten and written customs and usages known as *consuetudines*. Even the rule of Benedict, which contains quite detailed guidelines for the horarium, liturgical prayer and discipline, required supplementation and adaptation according

---

1 For the origins of the various rules and their editions, see for instance M. Heimbucher, *Die Orden und Kongregationen der katholischen Kirche*, vol. I, pp. 61-153; E. Dekkers – A. Gaar, *Clavis Patrum latinorum* (*Sacris erudiri*, vol. III), Steenbrugge, 1961², pp. 407-417, including critical details.

2 Augustine's biographer had the following to say about the foundation of the community at Hippo (after 391): "Factusque presbyter, monasterium intra ecclesiam mox instituit et cum Dei servis vivere coepit secundum regulam sub sanctis apostolis constitutam" (Possidius, *Vita S. Augustini*, c. 5, ed. M. Pellegrino, *Possidio: Vita di S. Agostino. Introduzione, testo critico, versione e note*, Rome, [1955], p. 52). See also A. Zumkeller, *Das Mönchtum des heiligen Augustinus* (Cassiciacum, vol. 11), Würzburg, 1950, pp. 46-211; A. Manrique, *La vida monástica en San Agustín. Enchiridion histórico-doctrinal y regla*, El Escorial-Salamanca, 1959.

3 Augustine's letter to a community of women (*Epist. 211*) was published by A. Goldbacher, in *S. Aureli Augustini Hipponensis episcopi epistulae*, vol. IV (Corpus Scriptorum ecclesiasticorum latinorum, vol. 57), Vienna-Leipzig, 1911, pp. 356-371. For critical details on these guidelines for sisters, see E. Dekkers – A. Gaar, *Clavis Patrum lat.*, no. 1839 c.

4 The *Regula* was possibly compiled c. 529: see E. Dekkers – A. Gaar, *Clavis Patrum lat.*, no. 1852; Ph. Schmitz, art. *Bénédictine (Règle)*, in *Dictionnaire de droit canonique*, vol. II, 1937, col. 297-298. Recent editions include: G. Penco, *S. Benedicti Regula. Introduzione, testo, apparati e commento* (Biblioteca di studi superiori, vol. 39), Florence, 1958; R. Hanslik, *Benedicti Regula* (Corpus Script. eccles. lat., vol. 75), Vienna, 1960. There is as yet no unanimity on its relation to the *Regula Magistri* (ed. in PL, vol. 88, col. 943-1052 and H. Vanderhoven – F. Masai – P. B. Corbett, *Aux sources du monachisme bénédictin*. I. *La Règle du Maître. Édition diplomatique des manuscrits latins 12205 et 12634 de Paris* (Les Publications de Scriptorium, vol. 3), Brussels-Paris-Antwerp-Amsterdam, 1953, pp. 125-317), which appears to have been compiled at a later date, but which contains much older texts. Cf. E. Dekkers – A. Gaar, *Clavis Patrum lat.*, no. 1858.

5 On this, see Ch. Dereine, *Vie commune, règle de saint Augustin et chanoines réguliers au XIᵉ siècle*, in RHE, vol. XLI, 1946, pp. 365-406. See also *infra*, pp. 188-190.

to the circumstances of time and place, as, incidentally, the legislator himself had foreseen.[6]

§ 1. *Monastic* consuetudines

One indication that communities had their own convictions and customs can be found as early as the eighth century in commentaries on the rule of Saint Benedict, that is, writings containing personally inflected explanations of the text. The diverging interpretations proposed in relation to certain points appear to reflect the existence, even at this early stage, of diverging practices. Thus, Paul the Deacon's commentary not only offers a reasoned explanation of the rule, but also gives a concrete image of Benedictine monastic life in one specific community, perhaps Civate in Lombardy.[7] His work acquired the status of an almost classic example and it inspired many commentators down the centuries. In parallel with commentaries on the rule, collections of the particular customs of abbeys were compiled. As foundations spread over time and across space, the links between motherhouse and daughter house became looser, giving rise to divergences in the observance of the rule. Monte Cassino possessed its own *consuetudines* as early as the eighth century, and they were certainly written down before the beginning of the ninth century.[8]

In the tenth and eleventh centuries, Benedictine monastic life was dominated and led by Cluny.[9] Since its foundation in 909, this Burgundian abbey had been exempt from all secular jurisdiction and placed under the *tuitio* of the Holy See. Thanks to this privileged legal position, it was able to develop its own internal community life unimpeded, and moreover take the lead in a powerful external reform movement. Dozens of abbeys submitted to its authority, thus creating a monastic empire which stretched across all of France and a great part of England, Germany, Italy and Spain. Under the direction of eminent abbots, who usually enjoyed long terms of office, its customs were recorded and introduced

---

6 To give a number of examples: "Quod si aut loci necessitas vel labor aut ardor aestatis amplius poposcerit, in arbitrio prioris consistat..." (*Reg. S. Ben.*, c. 40); "Vestimenta fratribus secundum locorum qualitatem, ubi habitant, vel aerum temperiem dentur..." (c. 55); "...ordinet, si melius aliter iudicaverit" (c. 18).

7 Ph. Schmitz, art. *Bénédictine (Règle)*, in *Dict. de droit canon.*, vol. II, 1937, col. 306. Similarly, Benedict of Aniane's *Concordia regularum* (PL, vol. 103, col. 703-1380) is in fact a commentary on the rule.

8 Parts of these *consuetudines* were published by B. Albers, *Consuetudines monasticae*, vol. III, pp. 14-18, 19-23. For a number of elucidations on this, see T. Leccisotti, *A proposito di antiche consuetudini cassinesi*, in *Benedictina*, vol. X, 1956, pp. 329-338. The first part of the *Corpus consuetudinum monasticarum*, under the title *Initia consuetudinis Benedictinae*, contains a great number of texts of *consuetudines, ordines* and other writings concerning monastic legislation from the eighth and ninth centuries (ed. K. Hallinger, Siegburg, 1963).

9 See for instance G. de Valous, *Le monachisme clunisien des origines au XVᵉ siècle. Vie intérieure des monastères et organisation de l'ordre* (Archives de la France monastique, vols. 39-40), 2 vols., Ligugé, 1935. For a bibliography, see Id., art. *Cluny*, in DHGE, vol. XIII, 1956, col. 169-174; J. Leclercq, *Pour une histoire de la vie à Cluny*, in RHE, vol. LVII, 1962, pp. 385-408, 783-812.

in the many abbeys, priories and *cellae* of the *ordo*. The oldest *consuetudines* that are extant were written down under the Abbots Majolus (964-994) and Odilo (996-1030).[10] A later redaction, from 1042-1043, became more commonly known as the *Consuetudines Farfenses*[11] after the name of the Italian abbey of Farfa which adopted them. The customs from the years 1079-1087[12] were introduced in Germany by Hirsau.[13] The *Consuetudines monasteriorum Germaniae*[14] of the tenth and eleventh centuries were influenced more by the Lotharingian reforms.[15] The *Consuetudines* of Fruttuaria,[16] in Italy, were akin to the earliest monastic customs of Cluny and in their turn influenced the *Consuetudines* of Saint Benignus of Dijon, handed down to us in a redaction from the twelfth-thirteenth century.[17]

The *consuetudines* of Cluny moreover formed the foundation for the customs observed in a number of eleventh-century foundations which strove to restore Benedictine monastic life to its original pristine state and attempted to observe the rule of Saint Benedict according to the letter. It was perhaps due to the influence of the Eastern hermit movement, which always also had Western supporters, that the leaders of new communities placed full emphasis on solitude, poverty and frugality, on manual labour as a form of asceticism and a means to earn one's living according to the example of the apostles.[18] In 1027, Saint Romuald, abbot

---

10 For the history of the *consuetudines*, see for instance G. de Valous, *Le monachisme clunisien*, vol. I, pp. 19-21; H. R. Philippeau, *Pour l'histoire de la coutume à Cluny*, in *Revue Mabillon*, vol. XLIV, 1954, pp. 141-151. The text of the *Consuetudines Cluniacenses antiquiores* has been published by B. Albers, *Consuetudines monasticae*, vol. II, pp. 1-61.

11 Ed. B. Albers, *Consuetudines monasticae*, vol. I, pp. 1-206. The edition in PL, vol. 150, col. 1192-1300, under the title *Disciplina Farfensis* is incomplete.

12 *Antiquiores consuetudines Cluniacenses*, ed. in PL, vol. 149, col. 643-778. They are attributed to Ulrich, the first monk of Cluny, later of Hirsau, who wrote them down at the request of Abbot William of Hirsau. The *Consuetudines* themselves were compiled, also c. 1080, at Cluny by the monk Bernard: see H. R. Philippeau, *Pour l'histoire de la coutume à Cluny*, pp. 142-147. The text was published by M. Herrgott, *Vetus disciplina monastica*, pp. 134-364. For an overview of the *consuetudines* from this period, see K. Hallinger, *Klunys Brauche zur Zeit Hugos des Grossen (1049-1109)*, in *Zeitschrift der Savigny-Stiftung für Rechtswissenschaft, Kanonistische Abteilung*, vol. XLV, 1959, pp. 99-140; J. Leclercq, *Pour une histoire de la vie à Cluny* (cf. note 9), pp. 385-407.

13 *Consuetudines Hirsaugienses*, ed. in PL, vol. 150, col. 927-1146.

14 Ed. B. Albers, *Consuetudines monasticae*, vol. V, pp. 3-9. These *Consuetudines* from the late tenth or early eleventh century possibly originated in the abbey of Trier or Gorze. The *Consuetudines Einsidlenses* (*ibid.*, pp. 73-110) were compiled in the eleventh century.

15 By contrast with what used to be the prevailing view, the customs of the Lotharingian type originated largely independently of Cluny: see the extensive study by K. Hallinger, *Gorze – Kluny* (Studia Anselmiana, vols. 22-25), 2 vols., Rome, 1950-1951.

16 The *Consuetudines Fructuarienses*, compiled towards the end of the eleventh century, were published by B. Albers, *Consuetudines monasticae*, vol. IV, pp. 1-191.

17 Ed. L. Chomton, *Histoire de l'église Saint-Bénigne de Dijon*, pp. 348-441.

18 On the resurgence of eremitism in the eleventh century, see for instance J. B. Mahn, *L'ordre cistercien et son gouvernement des origines au milieu du XIIIᵉ siècle (1098-1265)*, pp. 26-35. A. Mens, *Oorsprong en betekenis van de Nederlandse Begijnen- en Begardenbeweging*, pp. 66-89 has similarly pointed to the influence of Eastern eremitism. A conference organised by the University of Milan in Passa della Mendola, in September 1962, was dedicated to the study of eremitism in the eleventh and twelfth

of Saint Apollinaris in Ravenna, established himself together with a number of hermits in Camaldoli, near Arezzo.[19] The customs of the community that emerged there were written down around 1082 by Rudolf, and later supplemented by the Priors Placid and Martin.[20] The *consuetudines* of Vallombrosa, founded near Florence in 1030 by John Gualbert, are extant in a twelfth-century redaction.[21] In France, Bruno of Cologne, together with several companions, withdrew to the Grande Chartreuse (1084). Their *consuetudines* were recorded by Guigo, the fifth prior, in 1116.[22] Around 1073, Stephen of Thiers established himself in a hermitage near Muret, in the Auvergne, from which the Order of Grandmont later arose.[23] The rule that is ascribed to him[24] possibly reflects his views and regulations, but was apparently first redacted by Stephen of Lisiac (1139-1163), who also recorded the customs.[25]

The ideal of a more secluded cenobitic life similarly inspired the founders of Cîteaux to leave the abbey of Molesme and withdraw into solitude.[26] Of their

---

centuries. For an overview of the papers presented there, see E. Mikkers, *Eremitical Life in Western Europe during the XIth and XIIth centuries*, in *Cîteaux*, vol. XIV, 1963, pp. 44-54.

19 See for instance A. des Mazis, art. *Camaldoli* and *Camaldules (Ordre des)* in DHGE, vol. XI, 1949, esp. col. 509-518; A. Pagnini, *Storia dei Benedittini camaldolesi, cenobiti, eremiti, monache ed oblati*, Sassoferrato, 1949.

20 Rudolf's *Liber eremiticae regulae* was published by J. B. Mittarelli – A. Costadoni, *Annales Camaldulenses*, vol. III, Venice, 1758, Appendix, col. 512-543. For Placid's *Constitutiones novae* (1188), see *ibid.*, vol. IV, Venice, 1759, pp. 127-129. The *Constitutiones Camaldulensis Ordinis (ibid.*, vol. VI, Venice, 1760, Appendix, col. 1-65) are a new redaction of both previous codes, undertaken under the direction of Prior Martin III (1253).

21 Ed. B. Albers, *Consuetudines monasticae*, vol. IV, pp. 223-262. Cf. Id., *Die ältesten* Consuetudines *von Vallombrosa*, in *Revue bénédictine*, vol. XXVIII, 1911, pp. 432-436. For the connection with the Cistercians, see R. Duvernay, *Cîteaux, Vallombreuse et Étienne Harding*, in *Analecta S. Ordinis Cisterciensis*, vol. VIII, 1952, pp. 379-495.

22 *Consuetudines domini Guigonis prioris Carthusiae*, ed. L. Holstenius – M. Brockie, *Codex regularum*, vol. II, pp. 312-332; PL, vol. 153, col. 635-759. On the origin of the foundation and the *consuetudines*, see L. Ray, art. *Chartreux (Règle des)*, in *Dict. de droit canon.*, vol. III, 1943, col. 632-635; A. De Meyer – J. M. De Smet, *Guigo's* Consuetudines *van de eerste Kartuizers*, pp. 7-25. For the date of the redaction, see *ibid.*, pp. 13-14.

23 On the foundation and history of the customs, see especially the series of articles by J. Becquet, in *Revue Mabillon*, 1952 and later (cf. *infra*).

24 *Regula S. Stephani Grandimontensis*, ed. in PL, vol. 204, col. 1135-1162 (according to Clement III's bull from the year 1188). Cf. J. Becquet, *La règle de Grandmont*, in *Bulletin de la Société archéologique et historique du Limousin*, vol. LXXXVII, pp. 1-36.

25 See J. Becquet, *Recherches sur les Institutions religieuses de l'ordre de Grandmont au moyen âge*, in *Revue Mabillon*, vol. XLII, 1952, pp. 31-42; Id., *L'Institution, premier coutumier de l'ordre de Grandmont*, *ibid.*, vol. XLVI, 1956, pp. 15-32.

26 Numerous and important studies have appeared over the last two decades on the origins and legislation of Cîteaux. For the foundation and earliest customs, see for instance J.-B. Mahn, *L'ordre cistercien et son gouvernement*, pp. 40-59; J.-M. Canivez, art. *Cîteaux*, in DHGE, vol. XII, 1953, esp. col. 852-856. On the origin and development of the legislation, see for instance the studies and text editions by J. Turk, in *Analecta S. Ordinis Cisterciensis* (esp. vols I, 1945; IV, 1948) and J. A. Lefèvre, in *Collectanea Ordinis Cisterciensium Reformatorum* (esp. vols. XVI, 1954; XVII, 1955) and other journals. Cf. F. Masai, *Les études cisterciennes de J. A. Lefèvre*, in *Scriptorium*, vol. XI, 1957, pp. 119-123.

former Benedictine environment, they retained the traditional framework of the monastic customs of life.[27] But to safeguard literal observance of the rule of Saint Benedict, they introduced a new way of life in their *novum monasterium*, characterised by strict seclusion, austerity in the liturgical services, more perfect poverty and the practice of manual labour. The first legislators formulated uniformity in the interpretation of the rule and in respect of monastic observances as the fundamental principle and requirement for any abbey that sought admission to their *ordo*.[28] The oldest documents describe not only the relations between abbeys, but also the communal monastic form of life.[29] The first full description of the liturgical and monastic customs can be found in the *Consuetudines* from 1130-1135.[30]

§ 2. *Canonical* consuetudines

The necessity of having additional *consuetudines* became even more evident in the institutes of canons which adopted the shorter and less detailed rule of Saint Augustine during the course of the eleventh and twelfth centuries.[31] Like the

---

A good *status quaestionis* of the problem and an assessment of recent publications can be found in A. d'Herblay, *Le problème des origines cisterciennes*, in RHE, vol. L, 1955, pp. 158-164. Later studies have criticised the views of J. A. Lefèvre and other authors and have advanced new opinions, see for instance J. Winandy, *Les origines de Cîteaux et les travaux de M. Lefèvre*, in *Revue bénéd.*, vol. LXVII, 1957, pp. 49-76; J.-B. Van Damme, *Autour des origines cisterciennes*, in *Collectanea Ord. Cist. Ref.*, vol. XX, 1958, pp. 37-60, 153-168, 374-390; Ch. Dereine, *La fondation de Cîteaux d'après l'*Exordium Cistercii *et l'*Exordium parvum, in *Cîteaux*, vol. X, 1959, pp. 125-139.

27 Recent research has shown that the first Cistercians relied heavily on the Benedictine tradition with regard to monastic customs, especially Cluny and Vallombrosa. See on this B. Schneider, *Cîteaux und die benediktinische Tradition. Die Quellenfrage des* Liber Usuum *im Lichte der* Consuetudines monasticae, Rome, 1961.

28 "Nunc vero volumus illisque precipimus ut regulam beati Benedicti per omnia observent sicuti in novo monasterio observatur: non alium inducant sensum in lectione sancte regule, ..." According to J. Turk (*Charta caritatis prior*, in *Analecta S. Ord. Cist.*, vol. I, 1945, pp. 41-43, 53), this text is part of the *Carta caritatis* of 1119. According to J. A. Lefèvre (*La véritable* Carta caritatis *primitive et son évolution (1114-1119)*, in *Collectanea Ord. Cist. Ref.*, vol. XVI, 1954, p. 28), it is part of the primitive *Carta caritatis* of 1114. This latter contention has been refuted by J.-B. Van Damme, *Autour des origines cisterciennes*, in *Collectanea Ord. Cist. Ref.*, vol. XX, 1958, pp. 46-50.

29 See for instance, *Exordium parvum* (1119) and *Exordium Cisterciense* with the accompanying *Capitula*, ed. J.-B. Van Damme, *Documenta, pro Cisterciensis Ordinis historiae ac iuris studio*, Westmalle, 1959, pp. 13-14, 21-28 respectively. According to J. A. Lefèvre, *La véritable constitution cistercienne de 1119*, in *Collectanea Ord. Cist. Ref.*, vol. XVI, 1954, pp. 77-104 (text at pp. 100-104), these *Capitula* date from 1119. According to J.-B. Van Damme, *Autour des origines cisterciennes, ibid.*, vol. XX, 1958, pp. 51-60, the *Summa cartae caritatis*, together with the *Exordium Cisterciense* and the *Capitula* perhaps date from the years 1123-1124.

30 Ed. B. Griesser, *Die Ecclesiastica officia Cisterciensis Ordinis des Cod. 1711 von Trient*, in *Analecta S. Ord. Cist.*, vol. XII, 1956, pp. 179-280.

31 For the reform movement and its various aspects, see the synthetic studies by L. Hertling, *Kanoniker, Augustinusregel und Augustinerorden*, in *Zeitschrift für katholische Theologie*, vol. LIV, 1930, pp. 335-369; Ch. Dereine, *Vie commune, règle de saint Augustin et chanoines réguliers au XIe siècle*, in RHE, vol. XLI,

new monastic orders, many clerical communities were animated by the desire to organise their communal life according to the earliest norms and examples. Dozens of chapters attached to cathedrals and collegiate churches reintroduced the strict *vita communis*, and this was confirmed by popes and bishops.[32] A return to the tradition of the primitive church and to the apostolic form of life is often presented as the motive that inspired this reform.[33] Originally, the customs of the reformed communities were based on the decrees of councils and on the church fathers.[34] But from the second half of the eleventh century onwards, the rule of Saint Augustine increasingly came to the fore.[35]

The designation *regula beati Augustini* in documents connected to the reform of communities of canons does not always refer to the same text. Like the expressions *institutiones, statuta, decreta beati Augustini*, it could sometimes refer to his *Sermones de vita et moribus clericorum*, passages from his *Confessiones* and from the *Vita S. Augustini* by Possidius.[36] Some manuscripts contain only the guidelines in the letter that Augustine wrote for a convent of women (EA = *Epistula Augustini*), albeit adapted for use in a community of men (RA = *Regula Augustini*).[37]

1946, pp. 365-406; Id., art. *Chanoines*, in DHGE, vol. XII, 1953, esp. col. 375-386; J. C. Dickinson, *The Origins of the Austin Canons and their Introduction into England.*

32 The article by Ch. Dereine, *Vie commune*, pp. 366-385, quoted above, mentions 144 communities that adopted the communal life before 1100.

33 On the canons of Saint John the Baptist in Florence: "... ad instar primitivae ecclesiae communiter viventes, regulam sanctorum Patrum observant" (quoted in Ch. Dereine, *Vie commune*, pp. 372-373, no. 42); in Senlis (c. 1072): "... mundo renuntiantes, regularem, id est sanctorum Apostolorum et beati Augustini quae scripta est, vitam canonice amplectentes" (*ibid.*, pp. 376, no. 70); in Toulouse (1077): "... communis omnibus secundum apostolicae institutionis formam victus sit et vestitus..." (*ibid.*, p. 378, no. 84); in Narbonne (1090): "... institutionem regularium clericorum secundum vitam apostolicam communiter conversantium..." (*ibid.*, p. 381, no. 113). See also nos. 38, 110, 117. The *vita apostolica* was similarly presented as an ideal by the Council of Rome in 1059: "Et rogantes monemus, ut ad apostolicam, communem scilicet, vitam, summopere pervenire studeant" (can. 4, in Mansi, vol. XIX, col. 898). On the significance of the *vita apostolica* as the guiding idea of the reform, see Ch. Dereine, *La* vita apostolica *dans l'ordre canonial du IX° au XI° siècle*, in *Revue Mabillon*, vol. LI, 1961, pp. 47-53; M. H. Vicaire, *L'imitation des apôtres*, pp. 53-66.

34 For the meaning of the expressions *decreta Patrum, instituta, institutiones beati Augustini, Gregorii, Hieronymi et coeterorum Patrum* etc., see Ch. Dereine, *Vie commune*, pp. 391-402.

35 The title *regula beati Augustini* first appears in the letter in which Alexander II approved the communal life of the canons at Reims (Ch. Dereine, *Vie commune*, p. 375, no. 61; see also nos. 80, 108, 110, 115, 122, 123, 126, 129, 130, 136, 138).

36 Ch. Dereine, *Vie commune*, p. 394.

37 For an edition of the *Epistula 211*, see *supra*, p. 184, note 3. The text of the *Regula Augustini* (*Regula tertia, Regula ad servos Dei*) was published by D. De Bruyne, *La première règle de saint Benoît*, in *Revue bénéd.*, vol. XLII, 1930, pp. 320-326 and by R. Arbesmann – W. Hümpfner, *Iordani de Saxonia Liber Vitasfratrum* (Cassiciacum, vol. 1), New York, 1943, pp. 494-504. In an unpublished work, W. Hümpfner corrected his 1943 edition of the text in a number of places: see A. Zumkeller, *Zur handschriftlichen Überlieferung und ursprünglichen Textgestalt der Augustinusregel*, in *Augustiniana*, vol. XI, 1961, pp. 432-433. The problem of the authenticity of the *Regula Augustini* has occasioned a great number of studies and animated much debate over the last three decades. An overview of the various opinions can be found in U. Dominguez-del-Val, *La regla de San Agustin y los últimos estudios*, in *Revista espanola de teologia*, vol. XVII, 1957, pp. 482-529; M. B. Hackett, *The Rule of*

Elsewhere, RA was preceded by a short text usually known to scholars as the *Ordo monasterii* (OM) or *Regula secunda*,[38] a monastic set of regulations which indicated the various obligations and exercises of the horarium, including liturgical prayer, manual labour, time for reading and meals, silence and poverty. This *ordo*, which was perhaps composed towards the end of the fifth century in Italy or Africa, formed a single whole with the text of the *Regula*, which only contained general rules and exhortations in relation to the monastic life.[39] As it explicitly highlighted the *vita apostolica* as the ideal,[40] it was often regarded as the work of Augustine, who in his day had been the great protagonist of the communal life according to the example of the apostles.[41] Having been accepted on the bishop of Hippo's authority by a number of institutes as their programme for life, the OM soon proved unsuited for literal observance, particularly due to its stipulations regarding the liturgy and its strict rules on fasting, and it had to be abandoned. Gradually, the text disappeared entirely or partially from the manuscripts, so that only RA remained as the rule of Saint Augustine.[42]

The two texts of rules ascribed to Augustine each served as the basis for different types of canonical monastic customs. The institutes that had adopted RA and the traditional patristic texts as their fundamental law observed the rules on

---

St. Augustine and Recent Criticism, in *The Tagastan*, vol. XX, 1958, pp. 43-50. The opinion that only the female version (EA) is an authentic work by Augustine and that the rule for men (RA) must be regarded as a later adaptation and transposition is currently the prevailing one. And yet even in recent years, authors, particularly from the Augustinian Order, have continued to present arguments for the authenticity of the *Regula*, so that the issue does not appear to have been resolved in a generally accepted and definitive fashion. Cf. E. Dekkers – A. Gaar, *Clavis Patrum lat.*, no. 1839 c.

38 The title *Regula secunda* is due to the fact that the *Regula consensoria* (PL, vol. 32, col. 1447-1450 and vol. 66, col. 993-996) was also regarded as a work by Augustine and was called the *Regula prima* (cf. E. Dekkers – A. Gaar, *Clavis Patrum lat.*, no. 1872). The text of the *Regula secunda* or *Ordo monasterii* (OM) was published by D. De Bruyne, *La première règle de saint Benoit*, in *Revue bénéd.*, vol. XLII, 1930, pp. 318-319; R. Arbesmann – W. Hümpfner, *Iordani de Saxonia Liber Vitasfratrum*, pp. 488-493. Cf. A. Casamassa, *Note sulla* Regula secunda S. Augustini, in *Sanctus Augustinus vitae spiritualis magister*, vol. I, Rome, 1958, pp. 357-389.

39 For the manuscripts that contain all or part of OM, see Ch. Dereine, *Enquête sur la règle de saint Augustin*, in *Scriptorium*, vol. II, 1948, pp. 28-36; A. Zumkeller, *Zur handschriftlichen Überlieferung und ursprünglichen Textgestalt der Augustinusregel*, in *Augustiniana*, vol. XI, 1961, pp. 425-433, which mentions approximately a hundred manuscripts that predate 1200.

40 "Apostolicam enim vitam optamus vivere" (*edit. cit.*, see *supra*, note 38).

41 Cf. E. Dekkers – A. Gaar, *Clavis Patrum lat.*, no. 1839 c. Following P. Mandonnet – M. H. Vicaire, *Saint Dominique*, vol. II, pp. 120-148, a number of recent writers have also attributed the OM to Augustine, for example W. Hümpfner, *Die Mönchsregel des heiligen Augustinus*, in *Augustinus Magister*, vol. I, Paris, 1954, pp. 241-254. According to M. Verheijen, *Remarques sur le style de la* Regula secunda *de saint Augustin. Son rédacteur*, in *Augustinus Magister, ibid.*, pp. 255-263, this rule was drawn up by Alypius and confirmed by Augustine.

42 P. Mandonnet, who regarded OM as the real rule and RA as a mere commentary, characterised the omission of OM as a "décapitation universelle" of the rule (P. Mandonnet – M. H. Vicaire, *Saint Dominique*, vol. II, pp. 151-162). Occasionally, only parts of OM were omitted. Cf. also, especially with regard to Prémontré, Ch. Dereine, *Enquête sur la règle de saint Augustin*, in *Scriptorium*, vol. II, 1948, p. 33.

the communal life, but did not otherwise diverge from the conventional views and customs concerning the ascetical obligations of the clergy. Their organisation of life and legislation has therefore been called the *ordo antiquus* in the literature.[43] This tendency continued in many communities even after 1100. Among the most authoritative representatives of this moderate strand were the canons of Saint-Ruf, an abbey founded near Avignon in 1039 that soon became the centre of an order with houses spread across various territories in France and Spain.[44] As early as the second half of the eleventh century, their customs had become so renowned and appreciated that they were not only adopted by canons but also influenced several foundations of hermits. Yet few copies appear to be extant today. Abbot Lietbert's *Ordinarium*, compiled between 1100 and 1110, gives a description of the liturgical ceremonies throughout the year and also contains a number of rules in relation to monastic discipline and the acceptance and profession of novices.[45] The *Consuetudines* of Las Abadesas (Barcelona) are less complete when it comes to liturgical services, but they do provide a better view of the customs of Saint-Ruf in the course of the thirteenth century.[46] After the *Regula S. Augustini*, divided into chapters, they contain part of the *Regula secunda* (OM), the *Regula consensoria* and a list of the most important obligations that the rule of Saint Augustine imposes upon the canons.[47] This is followed by a description of monastic customs, containing a number of texts derived from the works of church fathers and older rules for canons.[48]

Similarly, in Northern France and in the German lands, most communities of canons preferred a moderately strict monastic way of life according to the *ordo antiquus*. The customs of Saint Quentin in Beauvais, adopted mainly by the founder and first abbot, Ivo of Chartres, around 1070, were written down

---

43 Cf. Ch. Dereine, art. *Chanoines*, col. 387-389.

44 On the abbey and *ordo* of Saint-Ruf, see A. Carrier de Belleuse, *Abbayes et prieurés de l'ordre de Saint-Ruf* (Études et documents sur l'ordre de Saint-Ruf, vol. 1), Romans, 1936; Ch. Dereine, *Saint-Ruf et ses coutumes aux XIᵉ et XIIᵉ siècles*, in *Revue bénéd.*, vol. LIX, 1949, pp. 159-182.

45 The text has been handed down in two manuscripts but as yet remains unpublished: see Ch. Dereine, *Saint-Ruf et ses coutumes*, pp. 164-165. The manuscript in the Bibliothèque Nationale in Paris (*ms. lat.* 1233, from the twelfth/thirteenth century) does not contain the whole text. It begins with Advent (fol. 1ᵛ: "Notum sit omnibus ut semper a V. Kal. decembris…") and ends on fol. 32ᵛ with texts from the office of Saint Mary Magdalene and the Annunciation. In between there are rules for the formation of novices, profession and religious discipline: "Qualiter canonicus recipiatur…" (fol. 25ʳ); "De silentio…" (fol. 28ᵛ). The text of the *Ordinarium* continues on fol. 29ʳ: "De mandato in cena Domini".

46 The *Consuetudines* have been handed down in MS. 149 (non-foliated) of the Museo Episcopal of Vich (Spain). For a description and the content of this manuscript, see Ch. Dereine, *Saint-Ruf et ses coutumes*, pp. 175-179. Cf. J. Leclercq, *Documents pour l'histoire des chanoines réguliers*, in RHE, vol. XLIV, 1949, p. 561. The *consuetudines* of various chapters in other cities in the vicinity partially contained the same texts: *ibid.*, pp. 561-565.

47 The text of OM only begins at "Nemo sibi vendicet aliquid proprium…" (p. 11) and thus omits the rules on strict fasting and the liturgical office. For the *Regula consensoria*, see *supra*, p. 190, note 38.

48 Various passages from the *Institutio canonicorum* of the Council of Aachen (816) were copied literally.

by one of his successors, possibly between 1120 and 1140.[49] Their moderation with regard to observance also made them popular in other foundations.[50] The *Consuetudines* of Marbach in the diocese of Basle, which date from the first half of the twelfth century, are in large measure dependent on Saint-Ruf[51] and in their turn influenced the customs of Rottenbuch.[52] The *Consuetudines* of the abbey of Saint-Pierremont in the diocese of Metz belonged to the same strand.[53]

While the traditional customs remained in force in most cathedral chapters, certain foundations of eremitical origins desired to base the communal life upon an *institutio* that would rival the austerity of the monastic life.[54] This ascetical tendency became even stronger when the *Ordo monasterii* was recognised as an authentically Augustinian text. The intention to restore the pure tradition motivated the founders of Springiersbach (diocese of Trier) and Prémontré (diocese of Laon) to observe the guidelines of this *ordo* to the letter.[55] Manual labour, strict fasting and silence were regarded as integral elements of the canonical life. Not only the strict *vita communis*, but also the conscious effort to lead a sober life, as well as the more perfect practice of poverty – for instance by wearing woollen rather than linen clothes – were regarded as requirements of the *vita apostolica*, which always remained the ideal. The stricter observance (*ordo novus*) also found

---

49 Ch. Dereine, *Les coutumiers de Saint-Quentin de Beauvais et de Springiersbach*, in RHE, vol. XLIII, 1948, pp. 417-421, with the text of the prologue on pp. 433-437.

50 J. C. Dickinson, *The Origins of the Austin Canons*, pp. 110-111 discusses the influence of certain foundations in England.

51 See J. Siegwart, *Die Chorherren- und Chorfrauengemeinschaften in der deutschsprachigen Schweiz vom VI. Jahrhundert bis 1160. Mit einem Überblick über die deutsche Kanonikerreform des X. und XI. Jahrhunderts*, pp. 263-270. F.-A. Goehlinger, *Histoire de l'abbaye de Marbach*, Colmar, 1954, which we were unable to consult, possibly also discusses the customs. The *Consuetudines* were published by E. Amort, *Vetus disciplina canonicorum*, pp. 383-432; E. Martène, *De antiquis Ecclesiae ritibus*, vol. III, pp. 306-320. The text will probably be published again in the forthcoming work by J. Siegwart, *Die* Consuetudines *der Regularkanoniker von Marbach und Springiersbach* (Spicilegium Friburgense). On the indebtedness of the *Consuetudines Marbacenses* to Saint-Ruf, see Ch. Dereine, *Saint-Ruf et ses coutumes*, pp. 176-179.

52 Ch. Dereine, *Les chanoines réguliers dans l'ancienne province ecclésiastique de Salzbourg*, in RHE, vol. LV, 1960, p. 904.

53 On this foundation, see Ch. Dereine, art. *Chanoines*, col. 389. The text of the *Consuetudines* was published under the title *Antiquae constitutiones coenobii Sancti Petri-Montis ordinis canonicorum regularium sancti Augustini, dioecesis Metensis*, in C. L. Hugo, *Sacrae antiquitatis monumenta*, vol. II, pp. 425-438.

54 Ch. Dereine, art. *Chanoines*, col. 389-390.

55 For Springiersbach, see Ch. Dereine, *Les coutumiers de Saint-Quentin de Beauvais et de Springiersbach*, pp. 417-421, including the text of part of the *Consuetudines* on pp. 437-440. The *Ordo monasterii* was observed there up to 1118. – For Prémontré, see Id., *Le premier ordo de Prémontré*, in *Revue bénéd.*, vol. LVIII, 1948, pp. 84-92. The strict customs of the first Premonstratensians (1120-1126) were not derived from the monastic *consuetudines*. They were prescribed in the *Ordo monasterii*, which Norbert introduced as rule: see I. J. van de Westelaken, *Premonstratenzer wetgeving (1120-1165)*, in *Anal. Praem.*, vol. XXXVIII, 1962, pp. 5-12.

supporters beyond Springiersbach and Prémontré, and it posed an acute dilemma of conscience for the leaders of some communities.[56]

The falling into desuetude of the *Ordo monasterii* had not weakened the ascetical tendency among canons regular. The new *consuetudines* that replaced the pseudo-Augustinian text testify to the same rigorism. On the advice of Pope Gelasius II, the canons of Springiersbach relinquished certain ill-adapted liturgical customs and somewhat alleviated the austerity of their monastic discipline.[57] Yet total abstinence from meat, strict fasting, manual labour and constant silence continued to be seen as essential requirements of the apostolic life, and they were prescribed by the *Consuetudines* that Provost Richard drafted just after 1125.[58] Similarly, Prémontré soon had to give up the *Ordo monasterii*, which Norbert had adopted as the legislative text.[59] The customs were written down before 1135 under the leadership of Hugh of Fosse, the second abbot.[60] They follow the example of the *arctior consuetudo* of the canonical life, but, unlike Springiersbach, they are greatly dependent on the monastic tradition, especially that of the Cistercians, from which they derive many texts.[61] An extensive and thoroughly

---

56 The canons of Chaumouzey (Épinal) could only be dissuaded from joining the *ordo novus* by Pontius of Saint-Ruf and Bishop Walter of Maguelone. See the text of two letters in Ch. Dereine, art. *Chaumouzey*, in DHGE, vol. XII, 1953, col. 598. The wearing of woollen garments and stricter rules concerning silence and fasting were introduced in Rolduc in the first quarter of the twelfth century: see Ch. Dereine, *Les chanoines réguliers au diocèse de Liège avant saint Norbert* (Académie Royale de Belgique, Classe des Lettres et des Sciences morales et politiques, Mémoires, vol. XLVII, 1), Brussels, 1952, pp. 188-193; Id., art. *Chanoines*, col. 390.

57 See the pope's letter in P. Mandonnet – M. H. Vicaire, *Saint Dominique*, vol. II, pp. 154-155. Cf. Ch. Dereine, *Les coutumiers de Saint-Quentin de Beauvais et de Springiersbach*, pp. 422-423.

58 Richard had a very strong influence on the life of the community from 1115 to 1150. For the origins of the *Consuetudines*, see Ch. Dereine, *Les coutumiers de Saint-Quentin de Beauvais et de Springiersbach*, pp. 425-432. A few pages of the text according to a twelfth-century manuscript from Vienna appear on pp. 437-440. They contain no fewer than five quotations from the *Ordo monasterii*, which Richard believed to have been written by Augustine.

59 Cf. *supra*, p. 192, note 55; Ch. Dereine, art. *Chanoines*, col. 390. As early as 1134, the OM was omitted from some manuscripts of Prémontré: see L. C. Van Dijck, *Un Ordo monasterii non amputé dans un ms. de Prémontré*, in *Analecta Praem.*, vol. XXXIV, 1958, pp. 5-12.

60 See R. Van Waefelghem, *Les premiers statuts de l'ordre de Prémontré* (offprint from *Analectes de Prémontré*, vol. IX), Leuven, 1913, pp. 12-14. The text appears on pp. 15-67. Like H. Heijman, *Untersuchungen über die Praemonstratenser-Gewohnheiten*, in *Analecta Praem.*, vol. IV, 1928, pp. 5-29, I. J. van de Westelaken, *Premonstratenzer wetgeving*, pp. 17-26 is convinced that these *Consuetudines* are not the earliest. According to him, they were compiled only after 1140. The earliest statutes, the text of which is now lost, supposedly date from before 1131. Cf. B. Griesser, *Die Ecclesiastica officia Cisterciensis Ordinis des Cod. 1711 von Trient*, in *Analecta S. Ord. Cist.*, vol. XII, 1956, pp. 162, 167-169; J.-B. Van Damme, *Genèse des Instituta generalis capituli*, in *Cîteaux*, vol. XII, 1961, pp. 50-51, 54, note 62.

61 Cf. H. Heijman, *Untersuchungen über die Praemonstratenser-Gewohnheiten*, in *Analecta Praem.*, vol. II, 1926, pp. 5-26. There is also indebtedness to Cluny (*ibid.*, vol. III, 1927, pp. 5-27). Cf. also L. C. Van Dijck, *Essai sur les sources du droit prémontré primitif concernant les pouvoirs du Dominus Praemonstratensis*, ibid., vol. XXVIII, 1952, pp. 73-136; J. A. Lefèvre, *A propos des sources de la législation primitive de Prémontré*, ibid., vol. XXX, 1954, pp. 12-19. For the influence of the monastic

adapted version of the *Institutiones Praemonstratenses* dates from the second half of the twelfth century.[62] It was in large part copied literally from the statutes of the canons of the Holy Sepulchre, an order which originated from a community of priests in Jerusalem and which had spread across Europe from Palestine in the course of the twelfth century.[63]

Following the example of Springiersbach and Prémontré, other abbeys and congregations of canons joined the new observance and expanded or reformed their *consuetudines*. The typical elements of the *ordo novus* can be found in Oigny, in the diocese of Autun, founded shortly after 1100 by a group of hermits. The statutes prescribed not only strict poverty and communal life, but also required the *rigor abstinentiae*, as well as manual labour, constant silence and the wearing of woollen clothes.[64] The same ascetical tendency also characterised the way of life followed in Hérival, a community of hermit origins that had emerged in the diocese of Toul around 1070. Its customs were codified around 1135.[65] The abbey of Arrouaise, in the diocese of Arras, founded in 1090, initially remained loyal to the *ordo antiquus*. But from 1125, discipline at the abbey was noticeably tightened

---

consuetudines on certain communities of canons, see J. C. Dickinson, *The Origins of the Austin Canons*, pp. 72-81.

62 Ed. E. Martène, *De antiquis Ecclesiae ritibus*, vol. III, pp. 323-336. This edition is based on the only known manuscript that contains this text, Paris, Bibl. Nat., *ms. lat.* 14762, fol. 223^r-240^r, as F. Balme, *Cartulaire de saint Dominique*, vol. II, p. 427, note 2, already observed. E. Martène's text is in fact identical to that of the manuscript in question and even includes a number of its errors. In the chapter *De dirigendis in via* (dist. I, c. 17), both texts have: "Egredientes fratres ad *missam* silentium teneant…" (on fol. 228^r in the manuscript; on p. 328 in the edition), whereas the correct text is: "…ad mensam…" (see the earliest *Consuetudines*, in the edition quoted above by R. Van Waefelghem, p. 44; in the statutes of the thirteenth century, ed. Pl. F. Lefèvre, *Les statuts de Prémontré réformés sur les ordres de Grégoire IX et d'Innocent IV au XIIIe siècle*, p. 29). Other similar cases are mentioned in I. J. van de Westelaken, *Premonstratenzer wetgeving*, pp. 33-35.

63 For the origin of this order, see for instance M. Hereswitha (Sister), *De vrouwenkloosters van het Heilig Graf in het prinsbisdom Luik*, Leuven, 1941, pp. 3-5; G. Tessier, *Les débuts de l'ordre du St-Sépulcre en Espagne*, in *Bibliothèque de l'École des chartes*, vol. CXVI, 1958, pp. 5-28. The legislation was published in *Statuta canonicorum regularium Ordinis S^{mi} Sepulchri, monasterii S. Crucis, prope Galoppiam*, Liège, 1745. These statutes were perhaps influenced by the *Institutiones Praemonstratenses* from the second half of the twelfth century (ed. E. Martène, see previous footnote): cf. Pl. Lefèvre, *Prémontré, ses origines, sa première liturgie, les relations de son code législatif avec Cîteaux et les chanoines du Saint-Sépulcre de Jérusalem*, in *Analecta Praem.*, vol. XXV, 1949, pp. 96-103.

64 Ch. Dereine, art. *Chanoines*, col. 384, 389; Id., *Coutumiers et ordinaires de chanoines réguliers*, in *Scriptorium*, vol. V, 1951, p. 110. The prologue to the *Consuetudines* of Oigny appears in an article by the same author, *Les coutumiers de Saint-Quentin de Beauvais et de Springiersbach*, pp. 440-441.

65 The foundation of the community under the aegis of the priest Engibald, who had come to Hérival in 1070, perhaps dates to 1082: A. Galli, *Les origines du prieuré Notre-Dame d'Hérival*, in *Revue Mabillon*, vol. XLIX, 1959, pp. 1-7. The *Consuetudines*, drawn up during Prior Constantinus's term of office, after 1120, were published under the title *Vetera Hyreevallis statuta*, by C. L. Hugo, *Sacrae antiquitatis monumenta*, vol. I, pp. 135-144. For the sources (the rule of Benedict and perhaps also the rule of Columbanus), see A. Galli, *art. cit.*, pp. 18-34.

under the influence of the Premonstratensians and possibly also the Cistercians.[66] Saint Victor in Paris, a centre of theological science, united intense study with the demands of a monastic way of life. The constitutions, compiled under the Abbot Gilduin (1113-1155), were also introduced in the houses of the congregation outside France and moreover influenced other abbeys.[67] The *Consuetudines* of Montfort in the diocese of Saint-Malo date from the mid-twelfth century.[68] The tendency towards collective seclusion and asceticism continued and inspired new foundations. In 1199, a number of professors from Paris withdrew to the solitude of Val-des-Écoliers, in the diocese of Langres, where they established an abbey which soon became the centre of an order with numerous daughter houses.[69] They derived much from the Victorines for their legislation, which was drawn up in the early thirteenth century.[70]

§ 3. Content and structure

Later historians and editors understood *consuetudines* to mean not just the customs that represented the observance of the rule in the various abbeys, but also, and primarily, the writings in which these customs were recorded.[71] Just as in

---

66 F. Gosse, *Histoire de l'abbaye et de l'ancienne congrégation des chanoines réguliers d'Arrouaise*, Lille, 1786, pp. 10-32. The earliest text of the statutes appears to have been lost. A thirteenth-century redaction is discussed and partially published on pp. 169-187. On the relationship with Prémontré and Cîteaux, see H. Heijman, *Untersuchungen über die Praemonstratenser-Gewohnheiten*, in *Analecta Praem.*, vol. IV, 1928, pp. 232-241; P. Vermeer, *De invloed van de* Carta caritatis *van Cîteaux op de statuten van Arrouaise*, in *Studia catholica*, vol. XXVIII, 1953, pp. 105-114; Id., *St. Bernard en de orden der reguliere kanunniken van Prémontré, St. Victor en Arrouaise*, in *Sint Bernardus van Clairvaux*, Achel, 1953, pp. 55-64; G. de Beaufort, *La Charte de charité cistercienne et son évolution*, in RHE, vol. XLIX, 1954, pp. 395-396.

67 See for instance *Gallia christiana*, vol. VII, col. 656-665; LTK, vol. X, 1938, col. 620-621; M. Fourrier-Bonnard, *Histoire de l'abbaye royale et de l'ordre des chanoines réguliers de Saint-Victor de Paris*, 2 vols., Paris, 1904-1908; M. Heimbucher, *Die Orden und Kongregationen*, vol. I, pp. 413-416. The text of the *Consuetudines* was published by E. Martène, *De antiquis Ecclesiae ritibus*, vol. III, pp. 252-291.

68 *Antiquae consuetudines canonicorum regidarium Sancti Iacobi de Monteforti, in dioecesi Macloviensi*, ed. E. Martène – U. Durand, *Thesaurus novus*, vol. IV, col. 1215-1230. Cf. Ch. Dereine, *Coutumiers et ordinaires de chanoines réguliers*, p. 113.

69 *Gallia christiana*, vol. IV, col. 777-778; L. H. Cottineau, *Répertoire topo-bibliographique des abbayes et prieurés*, vol. II, col. 3257-3258. Cf. *Gallia christiana, tomo cit.*, Instrumenta, col. 1199-1200, which also contains the letter by William, bishop of Langres, who approved the foundation in September 1215 "... sub regula beati Augustini ... more fratrum beati Victoris Parisiensis...".

70 *Constitutiones Ordinis Vallis-Scholarium*, ed. E. Martène – U. Durand, *Voyage littéraire*, vol. I, Paris, 1717, pp. 114-134.

71 See *supra*, pp. 185-186, the many collections of Benedictine monastic customs that were published under the title of *Consuetudines*. But it must be borne in mind that this title often did not appear in the old manuscripts themselves but was added by modern editors. On the use and meaning of these names see the information in L. Prosdocimi, *A proposito della terminologia e della natura giuridica delle norme monastiche e canonicali nei secoli XI e XII*, in *La vita comune del clero nei secoli XI e XII*, vol. II, Milan, 1962, pp. 1-8.

classical literature and in the legal texts from the Roman and medieval periods,[72] in the monastic context, too, *consuetudo* initially referred more to customs as distinct from written legal stipulations, or simply to the communal form of life or observance.[73] Both meanings have persisted and, in many cases, they are closely connected, so that it is not always entirely clear whether the word refers to written or unwritten norms.[74] Guigo, the first person to record the customs of the Carthusians, presented his work as a description of the *consuetudines domus nostrae*,[75] by which he meant the customs or normative practices themselves rather than their written record.[76] The title *consuetudines* was apparently already an umbrella term and meant something like legal code.[77] This meaning is even more clearly to the

---

72 For the various meanings, see for instance A. Forcellini, *Lexicon totius latinitatis*, vol. I, Padua, 1940; *Thesaurus linguae latinae*, vol. IV, Leipzig, 1906-1909, v° *Consuetudo* in both. See also A. Van Hove, *De consuetudine* (Commentarium Lovaniense in Codicem iuris canonici, vol. I, 3), Mechelen, 1933, pp. 4-5. In Justinian's legislation the following text is important: "Inveterata consuetudo pro lege non immerito custoditur, et hoc est ius quod dicitur moribus constititum" (*Digesta*, lib. I, t. 3, § 32, in *Corpus iuris civilis*, p. 34). For the meaning of *consuetudo* in medieval texts, see for instance C. Du Cange, *Glossarium mediae et infimae latinitatis*, vol. III; J. F. Niermeyer, *Mediae latinitatis lexicon minus*, vol. III, Leiden, 1956. For canon law, cf. *Decretales Gregorii IX*, lib. I, tit. IX, *De consuetudine* (*Corpus iuris canonici*, vol. II, col. 36-41); see also following pages, such as col. 563, 654, 910. Cf. also A. Van Hove, *op. cit.*, pp. 31-34 (*Decretum Gratiani* and decretists), pp. 35-37 (*Decretales* by Gregory IX); W. Plöchl, *Geschichte des Kirchenrechts*, vol. I, Vienna-Munich, [1960], pp. 128-129, 303. For the meaning of "compulsory performance" (*praestatio, pensitatio quae ex consuetudine debetur*), cf. C. Du Cange, *op. cit.*; J. F. Niermeyer, *op. cit.*

73 For the meaning of "custom", it suffices to refer to a number of texts: "…quaedam ibi secundum auctoritatem regulae, quaedam vero usu et consuetudine prolata sunt, quae consuetudo, si aliquo vitio corrupta non fuerit, pro lege regulari inculpate retineri poterit" (*Statuta Murbacensia*, ed. B. Albers, *Consuetudines monasticae*, vol. III, p. 79 ; cf. also p. 93); "Consuetudines autem ubi invente fuerint noxia, …" (*Capitula de inspiciendis monasteriis*, c. 4, ed. A. Boretius, in MGH, *Legum sectio II: Capitularia regum Francorum*, vol. I, Hanover, 1883, p. 322); "…ut certius ex scripto quam ex consuetudine habeatis, quid vos sequi conveniat" (Peter Abelard, *Epist. 8*, in PL, vol. 178, col. 257). – For the meaning of "way of life, observance": *De hiemali consuetudine* (*Consuetudines* of Trier, title of chapter 1; ed. B. Albers, *ibid.*, vol. V, p. 7) ; "…qualiter vivere sub unius vinculo caritatis et consuetudinis debeant…" (*Consuetudines Vallymbrosanae*, prol., ed. B. Albers, *ibid.*, vol. IV, p. 223); "…omnium monasteriorum salubris una consuetudo…" (Ardo Smaragdus, *Vita S. Benedicti abbatis Ananiensis*, ed. G. Waitz, in MGH, *Scriptores*, vol. XV, Leipzig, 1925, p. 215); "…communis regularium fratrum consuetudo…" (letter by Pope Gelasius II to the canons of Springiersbach, 11 August 1118, ed. P. Mandonnet – M. H. Vicaire, *Saint Dominique*, vol. II, p. 155).

74 In one passage of the *Consuetudines Einsidlenses*, *consuetudines* could mean either "customs" or "customs recorded in writing": "…ab antiquis beati Benedicti regulae amatoribus per temporum vices constitutae sunt consuetudines de omnibus omnino rebus…" (B. Albers, *Consuetudines monasticae*, vol. V, p. 73). In another passage, it possibly refers to written regulations: "…post Tertiam capitulum adeant … et, sermone a priore audito, recitentur consuetudines illorum dierum" (p. 90).

75 *Consuetudines domini Guigonis*, prol., in PL, vol. 153, col. 636-637.

76 *Consuetudines*, c. 19: "…consuetudinem quam … multum inolevisse dolemus…"; c. 41: "…quae consuetudo et abstinentiam tollit…"; c. 42: "…quae ad monachorum pertinent consuetudines…".

77 "Incipit prologus consuetudinum…". This title was apparently added not by Guigo himself but by the copyist.

fore in the proceedings of the general chapters.[78] A further development in the usage of this term can be found among the Premonstratensians, who called their legislation *Liber consuetudinum* or "book of customs" in the second half of the twelfth century.[79]

In accordance with their intention to supplement or interpret certain points of the rule, Benedictine *consuetudines* are thoroughly similar to each other as regards content and structure well into the twelfth century, some diverging formulations on details notwithstanding. A great number of these writings consist almost exclusively of an *ordinarium*, a codex of the rubrics for liturgical ceremonies according to the various days and times of the liturgical year.[80] In other texts, the *ordo* covers the first part only, followed by rules relating to other monastic exercises.[81] These parts, too, are usually drafted according to the same scheme, and they provide a description of the acts and obligations of the community and the individual monks during the monastic day, week or year. All texts contain guidelines for the horarium with its various exercises, such as labour, prayer and meals, hours of sleep, care of the sick, the entry and profession of novices, penitential customs such as fasting, abstinence and silence. In a number of cases, this is followed by stipulations on the election and responsibilities of the superiors and the *officiales* of lower rank.[82] The same content and structure can be found in the earliest legal texts of the canons regular, which are incidentally often derived from the monastic

---

78 The general chapter of 1259 expressed itself as follows: "Item, secunda die et tertia, leguntur fratribus Consuetudines post capitulum monachorum" (*Statuta antiqua Ordinis Cartusiensis*, vol. I, c. 14, Neuville-sous-Montreuil, s.a., p. 106). Cf. *ibid.*, vol. I, c. 1, p. 204: "Et quamvis in Consuetudinibus Domni Guigonis … quaedam mutata sint, statuit tamen idem Capitulum, quod eaedem Consuetudines in singulis Domibus nostri Ordinis ex integro quantum ad litteram sine mutatione aliqua habeantur…".

79 *Institutiones Praemonstratenses*, prol.: "…librum istum, quem librum consuetudinum vocamus, diligenter conscripsimus…" (ed. E. Martène, *De antiquis Ecclesiae ritibus*, vol. III, p. 323).

80 To this type belong the *Consuetudines* of Saint-Vanne at Verdun and of Fleury (ed. B. Albers, *Consuetudines monasticae*, vol. V, pp. 113-133 and 137-151 respectively), of Vallombrosa (*ibid.*, vol. IV, pp. 223-262) and the *Regularis concordia* (PL, vol. 137, col. 475-502).

81 This scheme appears in the *Antiquiores consuetudines Cluniacenses* (cf. *supra*, p. 186, note 12), the content of which is described as follows (PL, vol. 149, col. 643): "Pars autem prima est de opere divino, et quod maxime fit in ecclesia per annum universum; secunda, de eruditione novitiorum [it is in fact about monastic exercises]; tertia de obedientiis" [it is actually about the abbey's *officiales*]. The same is the case for the Consuetudines of Farfa (ed. B. Albers, Consuetudines monasticae, vol. I, pp. 1-206) and Fruttuaria (*ibid.*, vol. IV, pp. 1-191) and of the Carthusians (PL, vol. 153, col. 635-759). In the case of the Cistercians, both the monastic discipline and the liturgical customs are described under the title *Ecclesiastica officia* (see *supra*, p. 8, note 30). In the case of the Benedictines in Dijon, the *Ordinarium* is the second part (c. 53-71), following the regular customs (c. 1-52). See the list of chapters in L. Chomton, *Histoire de l'église Saint-Bénigne de Dijon*, pp. 346-347. Cf. also *Decreta Lanfranci* (PL, vol. 150, col. 443-516). An exception are the *Consuetudines Hirsaugienses* (PL, vol. 150, col. 927-1146). The first part deals with novices and the regular life, the second with the *officiales* and the superiors. The series of chapters on the *culpae* and penalties is striking (lib. II, c. 3-11).

82 Stipulations about superiors and functionaries appear in *Consuetudines Farfenses*, lib. II, c. 5, 18-21, 43-49 (B. Albers, *Consuetudines monasticae*, vol. I, pp. 143, 158-161, 176-184); in *Antiquiores*

customs.[83] But as early as the mid-twelfth century, the Premonstratensians collected most chapters relating to the liturgical offices in a separate *Liber ordinarius*.[84]

The *consuetudines* of monks and canons also represented their own literary genre due to their form. Initially, they did not resemble legal or normative texts. As records of monastic customs that had become established in practice, they long retained their descriptive, concrete style, with verbs in the indicative rather than the imperative mood. The *Antiquiores consuetudines Cluniacenses* were composed as a story in which Ulrich of Cluny gives Abbot William of Hirsau a description of the customs in his Burgundian abbey with regard to the liturgy, the monastic exercises and the government of the community.[85] Their compilers appear to have been motivated more by a desire to paint as accurate a picture as possible of the customs in the abbey rather than to issue rules for the regulation of community life. The monks appear in these texts as living and acting persons rather than as subjects upon whom demands are imposed. One typical case are the *Consuetudines* of the Carthusians. They are written in the form of a letter in which the writer, Guigo, the fifth prior of the Grande Chartreuse, mostly in the first-person plural, describes the daily life of the monks and takes his readers on a guided tour, as it were, of his monastery.[86] Other *consuetudines* are written mainly in the subjunctive mood, but do not usually contain abstract terms or expressions, either in the *ordinarium* or in the parts that deal with day-to-day life in the monastery.[87]

---

consuetudines *Cluniacenses* (see previous note); in *Consuetudines Fructuarienses* (see previous note); in *Consuetudines Carthusienses*, c. 15-18, 30, 32, 37-38, 46-50, 62-64 (PL, vol. 153, col. 661-743).

83 We are acquainted with the earliest customs of the canons of Saint-Ruf through the *Ordinarium* of Lietbert (see *supra*, p. 191, note 45). The customs of Saint-Victor in Paris were described as *Liber ordinis* in the twelfth century (Paris, Bibl. Ste-Geneviève, MSS. 1636 and 1637). In Schäftlarn's manuscript, the earliest legislation of Prémontré still bore the title *Liber ordinarius* (R. Van Waefelghem, *Les premiers statuts de Prémontré*, p. 2).

84 Pl. F. Lefèvre, *L'ordinaire de Prémontré d'après des manuscrits du XIIe et du XIIIe siècle* (Bibliothèque de la Revue d'histoire ecclésiastique, vol. 22), Leuven, 1941, pp. XVI-XVII. Four chapters (vol. I, c. 1-4) continued to be part of the *Consuetudines* in the twelfth and thirteenth centuries: cf. Id., *Les statuts de Prémontré*, p. 146.

85 Cf. *supra*, p. 186, note 12. In his letter to William of Hirsau, Ulrich mentions the occasion for the writing down of the *consuetudines* of Cluny: "Quod pravitati meae iniunxistis, de hoc videre potestis me non fuisse negligentem; habetis enim consuetudines monasterii nostri, quas collectas utcumque notavi, quantum ego scire potui et recordari" (PL, vol. 149, col. 638). In the *prooemium*: "Interim erat ei [Willelmo] mecum sermo assiduus, imo, quantum fieri potuit, pene continuus, de consuetudinibus ecclesiae nostrae, ..." (col. 643).

86 In the *prologus*, Guigo greets the addressees and in the usual fashion declares his lack of authority: "Et nos, ... dignos minime putabamus" (PL, vol. 153, col. 637-638). On occasion he also indicates a shift to another subject: "Sed haec hactenus; nunc cetera prosequamur" (col. 659-660). On these *Consuetudines* as letter and as legal code, see A. De Meyer – J. M. De Smet, *Guigo's Consuetudines van de eerste Kartuizers*, pp. 7-25.

87 See for instance *Regularis concordia* (*supra*, note 80); *Decreta Lanfranci* (*supra*, note 81); *Consuetudines Farfenses* (*supra*, p. 186, note 11); also the *Ecclesiastica officia* of the Cistercians (*supra*, note 30). On the *Liber usuum* of Cîteaux as a legal code, see B. Schneider, *Cîteaux und die benediktinische Tradition*, Rome, 1961, p. 111.

Unlike the rules, the *consuetudines* were not regarded as absolutely fixed law, although in some cases they were effectively treated as texts *ne varietur* for a considerable period of time. They usually derived their normative force not from the personal authority of their compilers, who were not always known by name, but from the fact that they were the written record of monastic customs that had been shaped and affirmed by a venerable tradition of *patres antiquiores* or *seniores*.[88] The person whose name was normally associated with the redaction of certain consuetudinaries usually did no more than record and hand down what had, by observance in practice for one or more generations, acquired force of law. In fact, for long periods in the history of most abbeys, we are aware of only one redaction of the *consuetudines*.[89] The desire to frequently edit and adapt certain parts of the text appears to have been alien to monasticism in the High Middle Ages. Only in the twelfth century did certain orders adopt a more flexible attitude. The earliest-known *usus* of the Cistercians, compiled in 1130-1135, were supplemented around 1150 and in the years 1183-1188.[90] Similarly, the Premonstratensians extensively expanded and thoroughly revised their earliest legislation, dating from the first decade of the twelfth century, after a few decades.[91]

Most monastic and canonical *consuetudines* lack any stipulations concerning the cure of souls. This topic was treated at length only in writings that belong more to the genre of polemical literature.[92] In fact, even in the early Middle Ages

---

88 *Consuetudines Einsidlenses*: "...ab antiquis beati Benedicti regule amatoribus per temporum vices constitute sunt consuetudines de omnibus omnino rebus..." (ed. B. Albers, *Consuetudines monasticae*, vol. V, p. 73). The *seniores* were also authorised to interpret the *consuetudines*: "Si de aliqua consuetudine dubitatur, quidquid ille communi seniorum consilio ibidem definivit, de coetero quasi pro lege habeatur" (*Consuetudines Hirsaugienses*, lib. II, c. 4, published in PL, vol. 150, col. 1042). Changes to certain customs also required the approval of soberminded counsellors: "...quaedam in pristinis usibus, certae utilitatis causa monente, mutavi ... Feci tamen hoc non solo arbitrio, sed, iuxta Regulae praeceptum, quorundam Deum timentium ac sapientium fratrum consilio. Feci hoc tandem capituli universalis consensu" (Peter the Venerable, *Statuta congregationis Cluniacensis*, in PL, vol. 189, col. 1025-1026). On the binding force of the *consuetudines,* especially for the Carthusians, see A. De Meyer – J. M. De Smet, *Guigo's* Consuetudines *van de eerste Kartuizers*, pp. 20-22.

89 Redactions at intervals of less than fifty years are known only for the *Consuetudines* of Cluny in the tenth and eleventh centuries; elsewhere the intervals were longer. In the case of the Carthusians, the *Consuetudines domini Guigonis* (1116) were only replaced by the *Statuta antiqua* in 1259: see A. De Meyer – J. M. De Smet, *op. cit.*, p. 16.

90 The text of the *Ecclesiastica officia* from the mid-twelfth century was published by C. Noschitzka, *Codex manuscriptus 31 Bibliothecae Universitatis Labacensis*, in *Analecta S. Ord. Cist.*, vol. VI, 1950, pp. 38-124. The *Consuetudines* from the last quarter of the twelfth century were published by Ph. Guignard, *Les monuments primitifs de la règle cistercienne*, Dijon, 1878, pp. 87-245. For precise details on the chronology, see J. A. Lefèvre, *L'évolution des* Usus conversorum *de Cîteaux*, in *Collectanea Ord. Cist. Ref.*, vol. XVII, 1955, pp. 80-84.

91 See *supra*, p. 194, with footnote 62.

92 The following treatises can be mentioned: Rupert of Deutz, *Altercatio monachi et clerici, quod liceat monacho praedicare* (PL, vol. 170, col. 537-542); *De vita vere apostolica* (*ibid.*, col. 637), a work not by Rupert of Deutz, but perhaps by the mysterious monk and writer Honorius Augustodunensis (c. 1080 – c. 1137), like the *Quaestio utrum liceat monachis praedicare* (ed. J. Endres, *Honorius Augustodunensis*, Kempten, 1906, pp. 145-150). Cf. H. Menhardt, *Der Nachlass des Honorius*

some monks dedicated themselves to the apostolate, either as missionaries, parish ministers or itinerant preachers.[93] But they never regarded the exercise of specifically priestly ministry as an integral part of their *institutio*. Authoritative writers believed that for monks, the imitation of the apostles consisted in the practice of communal life with its obligations of charity, poverty and strict discipline.[94] Nor does it appear that the exercise of the *cura animarum* was an essential plank in the programme of canonical reforms, although it was occasionally promoted by these reforms.[95] The canons regular based their attitude to this issue not on general principles, but rather on accidental factors and circumstances. In fact, they ministered to many parish churches, especially in the twelfth century, and they can be called the "classic pastoral ministers of the Middle Ages".[96] The idea that the *canonici regulares* had, by their profession, withdrawn from the world was even used as an argument to assign priestly ministries to the canons by preference.[97] But some superiors declined any form of the apostolate as an impediment to the repose of the contemplative life.[98] The few institutes whose legislative texts mention ministry in parish churches did not view preaching as a mission of the institute.[99]

Augustodunensis, in *Zeitschrift für deutsches Altertum und deutsche Literatur*, vol. LXXXIX, 1958-1959, pp. 23-69, especially pp. 58-60, 67-69.

93 See Ph. Hofmeister, *Mönchtum und Seelsorge bis zum 13. Jahrhundert*, in *Studien und Mitteilungen zur Geschichte des Benediktiner-Ordens und seiner Zweige*, vol. LXV, 1953-1954, pp. 209-273; U. Berlière, *L'exercice du ministère paroissial par les moines dans le haut moyen âge*, in *Revue bénéd.*, vol. XXXIX, 1927, pp. 227-250; pp. 244-245 contains a list of Benedictine preachers from the tenth to the twelfth centuries. Cf. Id., *L'exercice du ministère paroissial par les moines du XIIᵉ au XVIIᵉ siècle, ibid.*, pp. 340-364; M. Peuchmaurd, *Mission canonique et prédication*, in *Recherches de théol. anc. et méd.*, vol. XXX, 1963, pp. 251-276.

94 See J. Leclercq, *La vie parfaite*, Turnhout, 1948, especially ch. III, *La vie apostolique*, pp. 82-105. Cf. Id., *Études sur le vocabulaire monastique du moyen âge* (Studia Anselmiana, vol. 48), Rome, 1961, especially pp. 7-28. In an excursus, *La vie apostolique des moines*, the author argues that, for monks, the *vita apostolica* consisted of "le fait de pratiquer les vertus de détachement et de concorde dont les Apôtres avaient donné l'exemple" (p. 38). Cf. also M. D. Chenu, *Moines, clercs, laïcs au carrefour de la vie évangélique (XIIᵉ siècle)*, in RHE, vol. XLIX, 1954, especially pp. 60-69.

95 See for instance J. Dickinson, *The Origins of the Austin Canons*, pp. 220-245; Ch. Dereine, art. *Chanoines*, col. 391-395.

96 G. Schreiber, *Kurie und Kloster*, vol. II, p. 45.

97 Ivo of Chartres believed that the canons regular had greater authority than others with regard to the cure of souls. He wrote about the decision of the bishop of Limoges, who had banned regular clergy from parish ministry: "Qui rectius quidem fecisset, si omnes sacerdotes ad regularem vitam invitasset, quam regulariter viventes a Dominicarum ovium custodia penitus removisset" (*Epist. 69*, in PL, vol. 162, col. 88-89). Cf. *Epist. 213 (ibid.*, p. 216).

98 See a number of examples in Ch. Dereine, art. *Chanoines*, col. 392-393.

99 The Premonstratensian statutes of the thirteenth century dedicated only one chapter to parish ministry: dist. IV, c. 21, *De canonicis parrochialibus* (ed. Pl. F. Lefèvre, *Les statuts de Prémontré*, p. 123). Furthermore, they mention preaching only twice, but on each occasion in the sense of *predicatio pro questu* (pp. 43, 90).

Like civic communities, medieval monastic institutions, too, assigned ample space in their legislation to customary law. The Benedictine *consuetudines* were created because of the desire to record the familiar customs that supplemented the rule of Saint Benedict in certain abbeys for posterity and give them force of law. Most monastic consuetudinaries that have been preserved were compiled between the tenth and the twelfth centuries and came from influential centres of reform, like Cluny, Gorze and Cîteaux, whence they spread to far-flung regions. The canons regular, who initially based their way of life on the guidelines of councils and church fathers, from the twelfth century onwards similarly began to organise their communal life according to the traditional monastic customs. In most communities, the texts known as *Regula beati Augustini* were supplemented or replaced by *consuetudines* that were often directly derived from the monastic tradition. Despite various differences in the order and phrasing of various rules, all these consuetudinaries are strikingly similar as far as content, structure and style are concerned. Of course, they are only the written record of a communal way of life dedicated primarily to liturgical celebration, ascetical practice and manual labour.

Section II. Monastic *statuta* and legal codes

The respect that medieval religious had for their traditional customs and for the writings in which these were handed down, did not lead to rigidity in the legislative field. In addition to the guidelines that they might receive from higher authorities, primarily popes, councils and bishops, most abbeys and orders had other means to safeguard the integrity of observance, either by repeating prior rules and demanding their strict application, or by issuing new ordinances and adapting to changed circumstances. Such measures could be issued by single individuals or by a collective authority, and in some cases they were long preserved and observed as additional norms for the monastic life.

§ 1. The statutes of monks and canons

The disciplinary writings associated with the monastic reforms of the eighth and ninth centuries drafted or inspired by Benedict of Aniane, the leader of this movement, can be regarded as the earliest representatives of this new genre of legislation.[100] The *Statuta Murbacensia*, probably issued in August 816, are a recapitulation of the main decrees of the synod held that year in Aachen.[101] The *Capitulare monasticum* contains the decisions taken by the assembly of abbots

---

100 On Benedict of Aniane and his reform, see J. Semmler, art. *Benedikt von Aniane*, in LTK, vol. II, 1958, col. 179-180, including literature.

101 Ed. B. Albers, *Consuetudines monasticae*, vol. III, pp. 79-93. By contrast with prevailing views, these *Statuta* appear to have been the work neither of Haito of Reichenau, nor of Sintpert of Augsburg. We do not know the name of the author, an abbot-bishop. For this issue, see J. Semmler, *Zur*

after the council of 817 to restore monastic discipline.[102] The *Statuta congregationis Cluniacensis* contain the changes that Peter the Venerable made to the liturgical and monastic customs of Cluny.[103]

Various kinds of *statuta* were similarly issued for canons. Before the *Regula S. Augustini* became popular again in the eleventh century, the communities of canons possessed their own legislation in the form of the *Regula canonicorum* of Bishop Chrodegang of Metz († 766).[104] The *Institutio canonicorum*,[105] drawn up by the Council of Aachen in 816, was intended as a moderate programme that would be adopted everywhere. But the upheaval that reigned in the Carolingian Empire after the death of Louis the Pious thwarted the realisation of this plan. Yet the rule of Aachen continued to be used in some dioceses into the eleventh century. A late-eleventh century *Regula canonicorum*[106] ascribed to Gregory VII was less widespread. Around 1115, Peter de Honestis compiled a rule for the canons of S. Maria in Portu in Ravenna, of which he was the founder and first prior.[107]

Legislation through *statuta* became a common procedure in some orders in the twelfth century. Since 1113-1114, the annual general chapters of the abbots in Cîteaux further expanded the original core of Cistercian legislation.[108] In 1119,

---

handschriftlichen Überlieferung und Verfasserschaft der Statuta Murbacensia, in *Jahrbuch für das Bistum Mainz*, vol. VIII, 1958-1960, pp. 273-285.

102 The text was published by A. Boretius, in MGH, *Legum sectio II: Capitularia regum Francorum*, vol. I, Hanover, 1883, pp. 344-349; B. Albers, *Consuetudines monasticae*, vol. III, pp. 115-144. For *statuta* from the same period, cf. A. E. Verhulst – J. Semmler, *Les statuts d'Adalhard de Corbie de l'an 822*, in *Le moyen âge*, vol. LXVIII, 1962, pp. 91-124, 233-269.

103 Published in PL, vol. 189, col. 1025-1048.

104 The *Regula* was written between 753 and 755, possibly in 754 (E. Morhain, *Origine et histoire de la Regula canonicorum de saint Chrodegang*, in *Miscellanea Pio Paschini*, vol. I, Rome, 1948, p. 179). For the two reviews (PL, vol. 189, col. 1057-1096 and 1097-1120), see LTK, vol. II, 1958, col. 781-784. The original text was edited by J. B. Pelt, *Études sur la cathédrale de Metz. La liturgie*, vol. I, Metz, 1936, pp. 6-28.

105 Published in PL, vol. 105, col. 815-934; A. Werminghoff, in MGH, *Legum sectio III: Concilia*, section II: *Concilia aevi Karolini*, vol. I, Hanover-Leipzig, 1906, pp. 312-421. On the history and meaning of the *Institutio canonicorum*, see J. Siegwart, *Die Chorherren- und Chorfrauengemeinschaften in der deutschsprachigen Schweiz*, pp. 120-128.

106 Ed. Ch.-J. Hefele – H. Leclercq, *Histoire des conciles*, vol. V, Paris, 1912, pp. 95-98. This *Regula* was not drawn up by Gregory VII, but was compiled around 1080 by an anonymous author on the basis of older documents: see Ch. Dereine, *La prétendue règle de Grégoire VII pour chanoines réguliers*, in *Revue bénéd.*, vol. LXXI, 1961, pp. 108-118; C. D. Fonsega, *La cosidetta „Regola di Gregorio VII" per i canonici regulari*, in *Rivista di storia della Chiesa in Italia*, vol. XVI, 1962, pp. 135-136. On the influence of this rule, see Ch. Dereine, *L'influence de la règle de Grégoire VII*, in RHE, vol. XLIII, 1948, pp. 512-514.

107 *Regula canonicae institutionis sive Constitutiones Portuenses a B. Petro de Honestis conscriptae*, ed. E. Amort, *Vetus disciplina canonicorum*, pp. 338-382; PL, vol. 163, col. 703-748.

108 Recent research has demonstrated that a primitive *Carta caritatis* existed even before 1199. But opinions differ as to its content. According to J. A. Lefèvre, *La véritable* Carta caritatis *primitive et son évolution (1114-1119)*, in *Collectanea Ord. Cist. Ref.*, vol. XVI, 1954, pp. 5-29, the earliest text contained the chapters 1-3 of the so-called *Carta caritatis prior*: see the text in the quoted work, pp. 27-28. This view is supported by J. Winandy, *Les origines de Cîteaux et les travaux de M. Lefèvre*, in *Revue bénéd.*, vol. LXVII, 1957, pp. 52-53. An alternative opinion is that the *Carta caritatis* existed

the *Carta caritatis* was approved by Pope Callixtus II, together with a series of additional statutes.[109] The ordinances of the chapters held in the following years were collected in the *Instituta generalis capituli,* which were submitted to the pope for approval in 1152.[110] The rules in this collection were subsequently changed on numerous occasions until they reached their definitive form towards the end of the twelfth century.[111] A new collection of statutes was compiled in the early thirteenth century and promulgated by the general chapter of 1204 as *Libellus definitionum.*[112]

The Cistercians thus had a double series of legal stipulations. The rule, the *Carta caritatis* and the *Ecclesiastica officia* or *Usus* were regarded in principle as the unchangeable monuments of the legislation of their order.[113] The statutes of the general chapters, by contrast, were of course subject to change and adjustment,[114] although the main ordinances were assembled over the years in collections which the legislators also intended to have final authority. The two categories continued to exist alongside each other and no attempts were ever made to join them together into a single code. The decisions of the annual chapters were in due course inserted into the *Consuetudines.* But the first rule regarding the supplementation

---

from 1113, but consisted only of the first chapter of the *Carta caritatis prior*: see J.-B. Van Damme, *Autour des origines cisterciennes,* in *Collectanea Ord. Cist. Ref.,* vol. XX, 1958, pp. 40-46; Id., *Formation de la constitution cistercienne. Esquisse historique,* in *Studia monastica,* vol. IV, 1962, pp. 131-133.

109 See J. Turk, *Charta caritatis prior,* in *Analecta S. Ord. Cist.,* vol. I, 1945, pp. 11-61, with an edition of the text on pp. 53-56. J.-B. Van Damme, *Autour des origines cisterciennes,* pp. 153-168. According to J. A. Lefèvre, *La véritable constitution cistercienne de 1119,* in *Collectanea Ord. Cist. Ref.,* vol. XVI, 1954, pp. 77-104, the file that was approved in 1119 contained the *Exordium Cistercii,* the *Summa cartae caritatis* and a series of *Statuta.* He believes the so-called *Carta caritatis prior* is of a later date (before 1151). The most recent studies on the development of Cistercian legislation appear to support the traditional views against J.A. Lefèvre's theory.

110 See J. A. Lefèvre, *Pour une nouvelle datation des* Instituta generalis capituli apud Cistercium, in *Collectanea Ord. Cist. Ref.,* vol. XVI, 1954, pp. 241-266; especially J.-B. Van Damme, *Genèse des* Instituta generalis capituli, in *Cîteaux,* vol. XII, 1961, pp. 28-60, where the various ordinances are dated in groups (1114-1151).

111 C. Bock, *Les codifications du droit cistercien,* Westmalle, [1956] (collection of a series of articles in *Collectanea Ord. Cist. Ref.* published between 1947 and 1955), p. 23; J. A. Lefèvre – B. Lucet, *Les codifications cisterciennes aux XIIᵉ et XIIIᵉ siècles d'après les traditions manuscrites,* in *Analecta S. Ord. Cist.,* vol. XV, 1959, pp. 3-22; J.-B. Van Damme, *La constitution cistercienne de 1165,* in *Analecta S. Ord. Cist.,* vol. XIX, 1963, pp. 51-104.

112 *Statuta capitulorum generalium Ordinis Cisterciensis,* vol. I, p. 296. Cf. C. Bock, *Les codifications du droit cistercien,* pp. 25-27.

113 A proviso must be made here with respect to the *Carta caritatis,* which was in fact subjected to emendations and additions at least until 1165, when it acquired its definitive form: see *supra,* p. 202, with footnotes 108-109, and especially J.-B. Van Damme, *La constitution cistercienne de 1165* (cf. note 111), pp. 51-104.

114 This has been described correctly as "…ce droit cistercien traditionnel, essentiellement mouvant et qui mettra plus d'un demi-siècle à se fixer définitivement" (J. A. Lefèvre, *La véritable* Carta caritatis *primitive et son évolution (1114-1119),* in *Collectanea Ord. Cist. Ref.,* vol. XVI, 1954, p. 14); J.-B. Van Damme, *Genèse des* Instituta generalis capituli (cf. note 110), pp. 28-60.

and improvement of the *Liber usuum* appeared only in 1177.[115] The revised text was completed between 1183 and 1188 and was thenceforth in use as *textus typicus*.[116]

The Premonstratensians went one step further in the direction of regular codification of the legislation of their order. Following the example of the Cistercians, they also held an annual general chapter, which issued *statuta*.[117] They similarly began to adapt and supplement their legislative texts at an early stage. The *Consuetudines* from the second half of the twelfth century specifically reserved space for new ordinances.[118] Several texts can easily be identified as chapter decisions.[119] A later redaction, dating from the first half of the thirteenth century, was even announced in the prologue as *Liber institutionum capituli generalis*.[120] Thus, the Premonstratensians established a close connection between the two forms of legislation, and they were perhaps the first to merge *consuetudines* and *statuta* into a single code.

§ 2. The statutes of military orders and charitable societies

The institutes that, from the first half of the twelfth century onwards, dedicated themselves to all manner of service to their neighbour necessarily had to draft most of their statutes themselves to articulate their goals and their way of life. The hospitaller and military orders emerged from small societies in the Holy Land.[121] Their members, mostly laity, devoted themselves to the care of the

---

115 *Statuta cap. gen. Ord. Cist.*, vol. I, p. 85.

116 See *supra*, p. 199, note 90.

117 For the organisation and activity of the general chapter, see *Institut. Praem.*, dist. IV, c. 1, *De annuo colloquio* (in the twelfth-century text, ed. E. Martène, *De antiquis Ecclesiae ritibus*, vol. III, p. 334); *De annuo capitulo* (in the thirteenth-century text, ed. Pl. F. Lefèvre, *Les statuts de Prémontré*, pp. 84-91).

118 "In hac quarta distinctione, quaedam, quae in generali capitulo communi consilio pro conservatione ordinis sunt posita, possunt reperiri" (*Institut. Praem.*, prol., ed. E. Martène, *De antiquis Ecclesiae ritibus*, vol. III, p. 323).

119 "Communi assensu patrum statutum est…" (vol. IV, c. 1); "Attendentes…, statuimus ut…" (d. IV, c. 12). Vol. IV is followed by twelve *statuta* by general chapters of the twelfth century that are not dated more specifically (*ed. cit.*, pp. 335-336). In 1198, Innocent III recalled an earlier ordinance by the chapter: "Olim in communi capitulo statuistis…" (quoted in Pl. F. Lefèvre, *Les statuts de Prémontré*, p. 114, note 1).

120 "Eapropter, librum istum, quem librum institutionum capituli generalis vocamus, conscripsimus diligenter…" (Pl. F. Lefèvre, *op. cit.*, p. 1). The editor also indicates which texts were interpolated by a general chapter: pp. 41, 42, 53, 58, 75, 113, 114, 117, 120, 122. The following must be added to this list: "Statutum est autem…" (p. 100); "Statuimus etiam…" (p. 105); "…statuimus quod fratres…" (p. 123); "Statuimus ut…" (p. 125).

121 On these institutes, see for instance H. Prutz, *Die geistlichen Ritterorden. Ihre Stellung zur kirchlichen, politischen, gesellschaftlichen und wirtschaftlichen Entwicklung des Mittelalters*; R. Foreville – J. Rousset de Pina, *Du premier concile de Latran à l'avènement d'Innocent III* (Histoire de l'Église depuis les origines jusqu'à nos jours, ed. A. Fliche – V. Martin – J.-B. Durosselle – E. Jarry, vol. IX, 2), [Paris], 1953, pp. 307-317; J. Leclercq – F. Vandenbroucke – L. Bouyer, *Histoire de la spiritualité chrétienne*, vol. II: *La spiritualité du moyen âge*, [Paris], 1961, pp. 168-173.

sick and the wounded, the reception and protection of pilgrims and the defence of the territories conquered from the Turks. They led a monastic life, recited a prescribed number of prayers as their office, observed a rule and took vows to lead a specific type of communal life. The Order of Saint John (Hospitallers of Saint John) originated in Saint John's Hospital, established in Jerusalem by Master Gerard of Amalfi around 1100.[122] After his death in 1120, Raymond du Puy succeeded to the leadership, and joined the by then numerous foundations in the East and in Europe together into a tightly knit group structure. He possibly also wrote the rule.[123] Additional statutes were confirmed in 1184 by Lucius III.[124] The German (Teutonic) Order developed along the same lines, albeit at a slower pace. It became an independent military order only in 1197 in Akko, having begun as a hospitaller society founded around 1128 in Jerusalem to care for German pilgrims.[125] Its area of action subsequently shifted to Europe, especially Prussia, part of Poland and the Baltic states, where its members set up a state of the order in the thirteenth century. The legislation of the order, which was created in several stages, was only completed during the mid-thirteenth century.[126] The Order of

---

122 The origins and development of this order in the twelfth century are treated by J. Delaville Le Roulx, *De prima origine Hospitalariorum Hierosolymitanorum*, Paris, 1885. See also the other works by this author and the other authors in the bibliography attached to the article by A. Waas, *Johanniter-Orden*, in LTK, vol. V, 1960, col. 1107-1110. We were unable to consult C. H. C. Flugi van Aspermont, *De Johanniterorde in het Heilige Land, 1100-1292* (Van Gorcums Historische Bibliotheek, vol. 54), Assen, 1957.

123 Raymond du Puy was the grand master of the order from 1125 to 1153. It is not known when he wrote his rule. Cf. J. Delaville Le Roulx, *Les statuts de l'ordre de l'Hôpital de Saint-Jean de Jérusalem*, in *Bibliothèque de l'École des chartes*, vol. XLVIII, 1887, pp. 343-344; M. Ambraziejutè, *Studien über die Johanniter-Regel*, Fribourg (Switzerland), 1929, pp. 6-8; E. Nasalli Rocca di Corneliano, *Origine et évolution de la règle et des statuts de l'ordre hiérosolymitain des Hospitaliers de St-Jean (aujourd'hui dit de Malte)*, in *Annales de l'O.S.M. de Malte*, vol. XIX, 1961, pp. 41-45, 119-125; vol. XX, 1962, pp. 45-50. Cf. also E. J. King, *Rule, Statutes and Customs of Hospitallers 1099-1310*, London, 1934. The rule was published by J. Delaville Le Roulx, *Cartulaire général de l'ordre des Hospitaliers de Saint-Jean de Jérusalem*, vol. I, no. 70, pp. 62-68.

124 Cf. *Regesta Pontificum Romanorum* (ed. Ph. Jaffé), no. 15136. A series of *statuta* by the general chapter of 1182 was published by J. Delaville Le Roulx, *Cartulaire général*, vol. I, no. 627.

125 Good overviews of the history of this order can be found in H. Prutz, *Die geistlichen Ritterorden*, pp. 62-70, 133-137; J. Delaville Le Roulx, *Les anciens Teutoniques et l'ordre de Saint-Jean de Jérusalem*, in *Mélanges sur l'ordre de Saint-Jean de Jérusalem*, vol. X, Paris, 1910, pp. 1-10; M. Tumler, *Der deutsche Orden im Werden, Wachsen und Wirken bis 1400*, vol. I, Vienna, 1955, pp. 21-42. Literature can be found in M. Tumler, *op. cit.*, pp. 631-677; M. Hellmann, *Neue Arbeiten zur Geschichte des deutschen Ordens*, in *Historisches Jahrbuch*, vol. LXXV, 1956, pp. 201-213; Id., art. *Deutscher Orden*, in LTK, vol. III, 1959, col. 274-277.

126 See the extensive critical study by M. Perlbach, *Die Statuten des deutschen Ordens*, Halle, 1890. The legislation consists of three main parts. The *Regula* (*ibid.*, pp. 27-56) contains the rules on the monastic life that are usually called *consuetudines* in other orders. The *Institutiones* (*Gesetze, ibid.*, pp. 57-89) give supplementary disciplinary ordinances and stipulations on offences and penalties. The *Consuetudines maiores* (*Gewohnheiten, ibid.*, pp. 90-118) discuss the structure of the order and the activity of its members. These three parts were possibly joined together with the prologue (*ibid.*, pp. 23-26) shortly before 1264, but most texts, originally in Latin, predate this year, some even originating in the first quarter of the thirteenth century (*ibid.*, pp. XXIX-LII). Incidentally,

Templars originated from a group of knights who had sworn in 1113-1119 to ensure the protection of Christians.[127] In 1127, their leader Hugues de Payens travelled to France. He was present at the Council of Troyes in 1128, where the issue of a rule for his society was discussed.[128] The legislation of the order was further developed by the general chapters. The text of these statutes was approved by Clement III in 1188.[129]

Following the example of the hospitaller orders, various societies of more modest size were founded in Europe towards the end of the twelfth century. A number of military orders, especially in Spain, had a mainly lay membership that secured the safety of pilgrims.[130] The Order of the Holy Spirit originated in a fraternity that cared for the poor and the sick in Montpellier before 1180. Its membership was originally almost exclusively lay, but it gradually evolved into a clerical order.[131] Innocent III approved its way of life and confirmed its possessions as early as 1198.[132] In 1204, he also placed the hospital of S. Maria

---

Honorius III confirmed the way of life and customs of the German Order according to the *ordo* of Hospitallers of Saint John and of the Templars as early as 1220 (letter of 15 December 1220: see E. Strehlke, *Tabulae Ordinis Theutonici*, Berlin, 1869, p. 277). For the indebtedness to these two orders, see M. Perlbach, *op. cit.*, pp. XXXII, XXXIII, XXXVII, LX, XLVII, L-LI.

127 The studies by H. Prutz, *Entwicklung und Untergang des Templerordens*, Berlin, 1888; Id., *Die geistlichen Ritterorden*, pp. 24-36, 56-61, 317-350; G. Schnürer, art. *Templer*, in LTK, vol. IX, 1937, col. 1045 still belong to the more reliable works on the Templars. Popularising works are M. Melville, *La vie des Templiers*, Paris, 1951[8]; A. Ollivier, *Les Templiers* (Le temps qui court, vol. 10), Paris, [1958].

128 The text of the *Regula pauperum commilitonum Christi Templique Salomonici* was published for instance in Mansi, vol. XXI, col. 359-372 and in PL, vol. 166, col. 857-874. The edition by H. de Curzon, *La règle du Temple*, pp. 11-74 (including the French and Latin versions) is more critical, as is G. Schnürer, *Die ursprüngliche Templerregel*, Freiburg im Breisgau, 1903, pp. 130-153. For the origins and content of the text, see also J. Leclercq, *Un document inédit sur les débuts des Templiers*, in RHE, vol. LII, 1957, pp. 81-91. Many customs were included in this rule that were already observed by the first Templars in Palestine: see G. de Valous, *Quelques observations sur la toute primitive observance des Templiers et la* Regula pauperum commilitonum Christi, in *Mélanges saint Bernard (8e Centenaire de la mort de saint Bernard)*, Dijon, 1953, pp. 32-40. For Saint Bernard's share in the redaction of the rule, see also P. Cousin, *Les débuts de l'ordre des Templiers et saint Bernard, ibid.*, pp. 41-52.

129 Ed. H. de Curzon, *La règle du Temple*, pp. 75-350. These statutes contain several parts that were compiled between 1128-1265, but it has not so far been possible to date them more precisely.

130 The more famous are the Knights of Calatrava and Alcantara, founded in the mid-twelfth century, the Knights of Saint James of the Sword, the Canons of Saint Eligius in Santiago de Compostela, the Orders of Mountjoy, of Evora and of Saint Michael in Portugal. See H. Prutz, *Die geistlichen Ritterorden*, pp. 73-100. See also the study by M. Cocheril, *Essai sur l'origine des ordres militaires dans la Péninsule ibérique*, in *Collectanea Ord. Cist. Ref.*, vol. XX, 1958, pp. 346-361; vol. XXI, 1959, pp. 228-250.

131 See for instance A. F. La Cava, *Liber Regulae S. Spiritus*, pp. 19-29; A. Mens, *Begijnen- en Begardenbeweging*, p. 61; A. Fliche – Chr. Thouzellier – Y. Azais, *La chrétienté romaine (1198-1274)* (Histoire de l'Église depuis les origines jusqu'à nos jours, ed. A. Fliche – V. Martin – E. Jarry, vol. 10), [Paris, 1950], pp. 177-178; A. Fliche, *La vie religieuse à Montpellier sous le pontificat d'Innocent III (1198-1215)*, in *Mélanges d'histoire du moyen âge dédiés à la mémoire de Louis Halphen*, Paris, 1951, pp. 217-224.

132 See the text of his two letters, of 22 and 23 April 1198 respectively, in PL, vol. 214, col. 83-84 and 85-86.

in Sassia in Rome under its authority.[133] The *Regula S. Spiritus*, whose content and structure were original, was drawn up during the first years of the thirteenth century.[134] The Trinitarians occupy a special place in the history of charitable institutions.[135] They took a vow to redeem Christian slaves and prisoners of war from the hands of the Moors. Their founder, John of Matha, obtained papal approval of his rule in 1198.[136]

§ 3. Characteristics and nomenclature

Because of their form and content and their origin, *statuta* belong to a different type of legislation than *consuetudines*. They are immediately recognisable by their more juridical and abstract style and terse formulation, with the verbs usually in the subjunctive mood and in the future tense. Instead of offering a description of life in a community, they set out the norms that are to govern community life in the abbeys and the institutions of an order. Concrete expressions such as *monachi* and *fratres* are eschewed in favour of collective and abstract terms or titles of officers.[137] The characteristic term *statuta*, which is used in scholarly literature for this genre of legal codes, is derived from the formulas *statuimus, statutum est* that occur repeatedly as introduction to the individual stipulations.[138] As far as we can tell from the extant copies, the term was rarely used by medieval legislators

---

133 The bull *Inter opera pietatis*, of 19 June 1204, in PL, vol. 215, col. 376-380.

134 The text was published in PL, vol. 217, col. 1137-1156; also in A. F. La Cava, *Liber Regulae S. Spiritus*, pp. 120-209. A *regula* is already mentioned in the bull of 19 June 1204 (see previous footnote). But according to P. Brune, *L'ordre hospitalier du Saint-Esprit*, Paris, 1894, pp. 200-201, final approval was not granted until 1213.

135 Antonin de l'Assomption, *Les origines de l'ordre de la très Sainte-Trinité d'après les documents*, Rome, 1925; M. Heimbucher, *Die Orden und Kongregationen*, vol. I, pp. 448-450.

136 See the bull, dated 17 December 1198, in PL, vol. 214, col. 444-449. These statutes were compiled under the supervision of the bishop of Paris and the abbot of Saint-Victor (*ibid.*, col. 444).

137 A number of examples from the *Statuta cap. gen. Ord. Cist.*, vol. I: "Si quis monachus vel conversus…" (p. 16); "Intra monasterium nullus vescatur…" (p. 18); "Prohibitum est ne quis abbatum…" (p. 19); "Nemo nostri ordinis…" (p. 30); "Ante orationem nemo aliquem osculetur" (p. 57). Numerous brief ordinances of this type appear on this last page.

138 In addition to the examples quoted from the *Institutiones Praemonstratenses* (*supra*, p. 204, note 119), we could also refer here to many Cistercian texts. The earliest documents (1119-1123) already contain formulas such as: "…inter omnes cisterciensis ordinis abbatias statutum est…" (*Collectanea Ord. Cist. Ref.*, vol. XVI, 1954, p. 99); also: "Ordinatum est…, stabilitum est…" (*ibid.*, p. 101). The *Statuta capitul. general. Ord. Cist* contain the formulas *statuimus* and synonyms in many variations. To limit ourselves to vol. I (up to the year 1220): "statuimus" (pp. 185, 187); "statuitur" (pp. 182, 189, 209); "statutum est in capitulo generali" (pp. 45, 120, 181, 186, 197, 211); "cum statutum sit" (pp. 49, 101); "ordinamus" (p. 46); "prohibetur" (p. 48); "caveatur" (p. 48); "statuimus et praecipimus" (p. 106); "statuitur et firmiter praecipitur" (p. 249); "et ideo constituimus" (p. 30); "constituta sunt" (p. 117); "contra statuta capituli" (p. 20); "decretum est et communi consilio confirmatum" (pp. 65, 84); "capituli decreta" (p. 156); "diffinitum est" (p. 124).

and copyists to designate the legal code as a whole.[139] It occurs frequently for the first time in the hospitaller institutes of the twelfth and thirteenth centuries.[140]

Like *consuetudines*, *statuta* address disciplinary issues, the horarium, monastic asceticism and prayer. But they had less to say about the liturgy. Nor are they a fully homogeneous type of legislation as regards their content. Some collections, like the *Statuta Murbacensia*[141] and the *Statuta congregationis Cluniacensis*,[142] consist of lists of concisely formulated obligations and exhortations that do not stand in any strictly logical relation to each other. The *Instituta generalis capituli*[143] of Cîteaux were clearly compiled in purely chronological order. The *statuta annalia* of the chapters of the Cistercians were organised according to a particular programme,[144] but the decisions of different years were never organised systematically. A number of rules for canons[145] and the statutes of military and charitable societies developed into real legal codes that addressed all aspects of the communal life and are arranged according to a specific order. The legislation of the Knights of Saint John, the Templars and the German Order contain several chapters that are similar to the *consuetudines* of the monks, followed by texts that address the structure of the order.[146] The interpretation of the Trinitarians and the Hospitallers of the Holy Spirit is distinctive. Their legal codes were called

---

139 Some manuscripts of Cistercian legislation from the twelfth century already used *statuta* as a collective name: "Origo, statuta, usus et officia ecclesiastica" (see C. Bock, *Les codifications du droit cistercien*, p. 16, note 41). In this title, *statuta* possibly means the collection of chapter ordinances: cf. *supra*, pp. 202-203.

140 The statutes issued by Raymond du Puy (1125-1153) begin as follows: "In dei nomine, ego Raymundus, … cum consilio totius capituli clericorum et laycorum fratrum, statui hec precepta et statuta in domo Hospitalis Ierosolimitana" (J. Delaville Le Roulx, *Cartulaire générale*, vol. I, p. 62). For the hospital in Paris (c. 1220): *Statuta domus Dei Parisiensis* (L. Le Grand, *Statuts d'hôtels-Dieu et de léproseries*, p. 43).

141 See *supra*, p. 201, note 101.

142 See *supra*, p. 202, note 103.

143 See *supra*, p. 203, with notes 110-111.

144 The subjects treated were arranged as follows: 1) rules relating to the liturgy and monastic discipline; 2) penalties for major faults; 3) *commissiones*, that is, charges to investigate or deal with certain issues; 4) answers to *petitiones*, petitions by secular persons to be permitted a share in the spiritual goods of the order; 5) composition of commissions to adjudicate on disputes between abbeys: see in the *Statuta cap. gen. Ord. Cist.*, passim.

145 The *Institutio canonicorum* of Aachen (see *supra*, p. 202, with footnote 105), in its first part (c. 1-113) contains numerous excerpts from the works of church fathers relating to the functions and moral obligations of the clergy. The second part (c. 114-145) contains the decisions of the council of 816 and primarily addresses the horarium and the common office of the canons.

146 In the legislative texts of the Hospitallers of Saint John from the thirteenth century, the *Regula* by Raymond du Puy is followed by an *Ordinarium* containing the liturgical and monastic customs. This is followed by the statutes from the eleventh and twelfth centuries which deal with the organisation and government of the order (cf. J. Delaville Le Roulx, *Les statuts de l'ordre de l'Hôpital de Saint-Jean de Jérusalem*, in *Bibliothèque de l'École des chartes*, vol. XLVIII, 1887, pp. 348-349; for the text see Id., *Cartulaire général*, vol. I, no. 70). – The rule of the Templars first discusses prayer, the monastic observances and the exercises (chap. 1-28), then military equipment (chap. 29-40), and then provides all manner of rules on discipline, the reception of new members and the care of the sick. Later

regula by their compilers and they were also approved by the pope under that name,[147] even though they never enjoyed the authority and inviolability of the traditional monastic rules. The merging of the two forms of monastic legislation, *consuetudines* and *statuta*, is as striking here as it is for the canons regular.[148]

Whereas *consuetudines* derived their authority from the normative force of a way of life that had been practiced for a long time, *statuta* sprang from the will of leaders who issued measures with a view to the present and the future.[149] Although certain ordinances aimed to promote the observance of already existing laws or of customary law,[150] legislators were well aware that in some cases their instructions contradicted existing customs. They therefore motivated their decisions by appealing to the approval of authoritative counsellors or by pointing to the necessity of abolishing customs that had become injurious or obsolete.[151] In some monastic communities, like the Benedictines, statutes appear to have been rare and they arose through chance, on the occasion of reforms or under the influence of circumstances that were by their nature short-term. But in centralised orders, like Cîteaux and Prémontré, this form of legislation acquired institutional significance. The annual general chapters used *statuta* to deal with current administrative affairs as well as issues of more fundamental importance for the organisation and government of the order.[152]

A number of other expressions also occurs in the legislation of monks and canons: *instituta* and *institutiones*, which are etymologically closely related to

---

statutes address the government of the order (see the texts in H. de Curzon, *La règle du Temple*, pp. 11-74, 75-350). – For the legislative texts of the German Order, see *supra*, p. 205, note 126.

147 For the Trinitarians: "...regulam iuxta quam vivere debeatis..." (bull of 17 December 1198, in PL, vol. 214, col. 444). For the Hospitallers of the Holy Spirit: "...regulam eiusdem hospitalis professi ... secundum eamdem regulam..." (bull of 19 June 1204, in PL, vol. 215, col. 377).

148 See *supra*, pp. 203-204, for the Premonstratensians.

149 A number of texts from canon law focus on this aspect of the *statuta*: "Quoties vero novum quid statuitur, ita solet futuris formam imponere, ..." (c. *Cognoscentes*, 2, X, *de constitutionibus*, I, 2, in *Corpus iuris canonici*, vol. II, col. 8); "...secundum priorem consuetudinem..., vel secundum rationabilem institutionem in posterum observandam, ..." (c. *Quum omnes*, 6, X, *de constitutionibus*, I, 2; *ibid.*, col. 9).

150 *Statuta cap. gen. Ord. Cist.*, *passim*.

151 The authority of the custom was never absolute and there are some explicit references to the possibility that established customs later degenerated into abuses: see *supra*, p. 196, note 73. In other cases, the customs had lost their usefulness. They were similarly changed or abrogated. Peter the Venerable justified the changes that he had introduced to a number of customs of Cluny thus: "...quod ab hominibus, utilitatis cuiuslibet causa, ad tempus, non in perpetuum, imperatur, ... quandoque mutatur, quia quod aliquando utile fiierat, aliquando noxium comprobatur ... Multa enim priores utilitatis causa instituerunt, quae sequentes certa causa utiliter mutaverunt" (*Statuta congregationis Cluniacensis*, in PL, vol. 189, col. 1025).

152 For Cîteaux, see *Statuta cap. gen. Ord. Cist.* For the Premonstratensians, the number of extant chapter ordinances is not very great: see *supra*, pp. 203-204, with notes 119 and 120.

statuta.[153] In the context of the monastic life, *institutio* mainly refers to the act of *instituere*, that is, the foundation or organisation of a community, or indeed the object or result of this act, the entirety of legal stipulations, customs and organs that regulate the communal life. The term *institutio*, in the singular, then refers to the religious state in general, as an organised way of life with its own laws and institutions,[154] or to this state in particular, as instantiated in a specific abbey or order.[155] In many texts, the plural *institutiones* is used as a collective term for the various elements of the religious frame of life[156] or for the written documents in which these norms are recorded.[157] In the canonical communities, in particular, the latter meaning appears to have been widespread, and the legal

---

153 For the meaning of *instituere* and *institutio* in the Middle Ages, see for instance C. Du Cange, *Glossarium*; E. Habbel, *Mittellateinisches Glossar*, Paderborn, 1931; J. F. Niermeyer, *Mediae latinitatis lexicon minus*, under the words in question.

154 In church documents, *regularis institutio* often means the monastic state, monastic statute or way of life: "...quoniam ibi et regularis est institutio et observantia salutaris..." (*Corpus iuris canonici*, vol. II, col. 7); "Quum ... regularis institutio interdicat, ..." (*ibid.*, col. 574). This can be compared with the use of *institutio* in documents relating to the reform of the canonical communities quoted by Ch. Dereine, *Vie commune*, pp. 366-385: "post apostolicam institutionem" (no. 14); "canonica institutio" (no. 66); "institutionem regularium clericorum ... constituit" (no. 113, cf. no. 127); "secundum Patrum institutionem" (no. 131); "iuxta beati Augustini institutionem" (no. 143).

155 *Institutio* appears in this sense in the *privilegium* for Cistercian abbeys: "Imprimis siquidem statuentes, ut ordo monasticus, qui secundum Deum et beati Benedicti regulam atque institutionem Cisterciensium fratrum ... in eodem monasterio institutus esse dinoscitur, perpetuis temporibus inviolabiliter observetur" (M. Tangl, *Die päpstlichen Kanzleiordnungen*, p. 229). This formula was used on a number of occasions for the Cistercians during the pontificate of Innocent III: PL, vol. 214, col. 501, 502, 504, 550; vol. 216, col. 16, 47, 70, 111, 135, 173, 176. For the Premonstratensians, the text was as follows: "...secundum Deum et beati Augustini regulam atque institutionem Praemonstratensium fratrum..." (M. Tangl, *op. cit.*, p. 233). Cf. PL, vol. 214, col. 564, 607.

156 This meaning occurs in the following text, where a distinction is drawn between the office and the other uses or institutions: "...quae ad divinum officium vel ad ceteras quaslibet huius religionis institutiones pertinent" (*Acta primi capituli Ordinis Carthusiensis*, in PL, vol. 153, col. 1127). A letter by Alexander III mentions houses that have transferred from another observance (*institutiones*) to the Order of Cîteaux: "...quae de aliis institutionibus ad vestrum ordinem se transtulerunt" (*Corpus iuris canonici*, vol. II, col. 597).

157 In 1076, the reform was implemented in Toulouse "secundum institutiones beati Augustini, Gregorii, Hieronymi et coeterorum Patrum" (quoted by Ch. Dereine, *Vie commune*, p. 377, no. 82). *Institutiones* here certainly means texts (see *supra*, p. 189, notes 33 and 34). Cf. "sanctorum Patrum institutionibus contraire" (*Corpus iuris canonici*, vol. II, col. 503). For the Carthusians: "Prior autem qui substituendus in domo illa fuerit, secundum praescriptas institutiones de fratribus eius domus ... assumetur" (*Acta primi capituli Ordinis Carthusiensis*, in PL, vol. 153, col. 1126). The *praescriptae institutiones* perhaps refer to the *Consuetudines*, c. 15, *De ordinatione prioris*: "...ex seipsis unum eligunt, ..." (*ibid.*, col. 662).

codes themselves are called *institutiones*.[158] The term *instituta* can be regarded as a synonym with more or less the same nuances.[159]

In the thirteenth century, the name *constitutiones* arose as a designation of a corpus of monastic laws. It appears that the word was previously used more as a plural than as an umbrella term. In Roman law, legal stipulations that issued from the person of the emperor were called *constitutiones*.[160] In the legal language of the church, the term was used mainly for laws issued by the pope *motu proprio*,[161] but additionally also for the decrees of the ecumenical councils.[162] In the texts brought together under the title *De constitutionibus*[163] in the *Decretales* of Gregory IX, the words *constituere* and *constitutio* often serve as synonyms for *statuere* and *statutum*. They refer to ordinances by both ecclesiastical and secular authorities.[164] In the documents relating to the reform of the canonical communities in the eleventh century, the *constitutiones beati Hieronymi et Augustini* stand almost in isolation amid many other expressions such as *instituta, institutiones, statuta*

---

158 "Incipit prologus Institutionum Praemonstratensium" (twelfth-century text, ed. E. Martène, *De antiquis Ecclesiae ritibus*, vol. III, p. 323); "Incipiunt Institutiones patrum Praemonstratensium" (*ibid.*, p. 325). In the thirteenth-century redaction: "Incipiunt Institutiones patrum Premonstratensis Ordinis", ed. Pl. F. Lefèvre, *Les statuis de Prémontré*, p. 1. For this latter redaction, see also *supra*, p. 204, with note 120. For the canons of Arrouaise: "...secundum institutiones canonicorum regularium Arrowasiensium..." (PL, vol. 214, col. 595). For the canons of Reims: "Ille promittat secundum regulam B. Augustini et institutiones bonas et approbatas" (E. Martène, *op. cit.*, vol. III, p. 300).

159 This text appears in a Benedictine profession formula as early as the eighth century: "Promitto ... secundum instituta beati Benedicti..." (quoted by I. Herwegen, *Geschichte der benediktinischen Professformel*, in *Beiträge zur Geschichte des alten Mönchtums und des Benediktinerordens*, vol. III, 2, Münster in W., 1912, p. 9). In the twelfth century, the *instituta Patrum* formed the basis for the legislation of the canons regular: see Ch. Dereine, *Vie commune*, pp. 366-383, nos. 1, 21, 43, 109, 124. The Cistercians called their chapter ordinances *Instituta generalis capituli* (see *supra*, p. 203, with note 110). Cf. also: "Instituta sancti Stephani Muretensis" (Paris, Bibl. Nat., *ms. lat.* 14762, fol. 222ᵛ); "...quae contra ... sanctorum Patrum veniunt instituta" (*Corpus iuris canonici*, vol. II, col. 506); "...iuxta beati Benedicti regulam et apostolica instituta, ... regularia instituta..." (*ibid.*, col. 601).

160 "Quodcumque igitur imperator per epistulam et subscriptionem statuit..., legem esse constat. Haec sunt quas vulgo constitutiones appellamus" (*Digesta*, lib. I, tit. 4, § 1, in *Corpus iuris civilis*, vol. I, p. 35). Cf. *Paulys Real-Encyclopädie der klassischen Altertumswissenschaft*, vol. IV, 1, col. 1106.

161 A. Van Hove, *Prolegomena* (Commentarium Lovaniense in Codicem iuris canonici, vol. I, 1), Mechelen, 1945², pp. 69-70. This meaning appears in *Corpus iuris canonici*: "constitutio apostolicae sedis" (vol. II, col. 16); "Leonis papae constitutione" (*ibid.*, col. 573); "canonica constitutione cavetur" (*ibid.*, col. 910).

162 See for instance the following texts in *Corpus iuris canonici*: "constitutionem nostram" (vol. II, col. 506); "constituimus, ... statuimus" (*ibid.*, col. 652); "generali constitutione sancimus" (*ibid.*, col. 31).

163 *Corpus iuris canonici*, vol. II, col. 7-16.

164 In relation to chapters of canons: "post illam constitutionem..., praedictae constitutiones" (vol. II, col. 9); "contra capituli constitutionem" (*ibid.*, col. 11); "non obstante aliqua constitutione super hoc a canonicis ipsis facta" (*ibid.*, col. 15); "ecclesiae vestrae constitutiones et consuetudines approbatas" (*ibid.*, col. 41). – In relation to other communities: "cives Tervesini ... constituerunt..., constitutionem huiusmodi" (*ibid.*, col. 9); "Licet a vobis [masters of the university of Paris] fide praestita fuerit constitutum..." (*ibid.*, col. 15).

and *decreta sanctorum Patrum*.[165] In the twelfth century, the special regulations of some canons regular were already called *constitutiones*.[166] But the expression only became common in the following century as one of the customary names for monastic legal codes.[167]

Without prejudice to the authority of their customary law, some monastic institutes judged it necessary to supplement their *consuetudines* and, in certain cases, to interpret or amend them through statutes. The occasion for using this special legislative procedure could differ according to the circumstances. In the older orders, it was usually the need to protect existing legislation and ensure its implementation, to introduce certain reforms or to extirpate or prevent certain abuses. New foundations felt obliged to clearly formulate their own views on monastic communal life and to give detailed descriptions of their organisation and aims, and sometimes to adjust these. For the monks, such ordinances usually existed as separate collections alongside the *consuetudines*. For the canons regular, and especially for the military orders and charitable institutes, they were joined together with the monastic customs to form a single legal code. In both cases, the *statuta* formed a separate type of monastic legislation, not just because of their origins and authority, but also because of their structure and style.

Section III. The *propositum* of the apostolic societies

At the same time as the military orders and hospitaller societies, religious associations of an entirely different kind developed during the twelfth century. Their members felt compelled by an inner urge to dedicate themselves to the apostolate and the practice of perfect austerity. In earlier times, the promoters of reform of the canonical institutes had appealed to the *vita apostolica* to restore or introduce strict communal life and certain ascetical practices. But the leaders of the evangelical poverty movement believed that preaching and the renunciation of all property were also required for the perfect imitation of the apostles. The new ideas first emerged towards the end of the eleventh century, and they took more permanent shape in the appearance of itinerant preachers in the first half of the twelfth century.

---

165 Ch. Dereine, *Vie commune*, p. 379, no. 83.
166 See the letter in which Innocent III approved the reform of the chapter of Osma in 1199: "Volentes igitur quod a te videtur pia deliberatione statutum, debita firmitate gaudere, constitutiones ipsas... apostolica autoritate confirmamus" (PL, vol. 214, col. 604). Cf. *Regula S. Spiritus*, c. 71: "Regula et constitutiones tunc ei legantur... Qui si regulam et constitutiones domus et cuncta sibi imperata promiserit observare..." (ed. A. F. La Cava, *Liber Regulae S. Spiritus*, p. 189).
167 In addition to the Dominicans, various other religious orders had *constitutiones* in the thirteenth century. See for instance: *Constitutiones Ordinis Vallis-Scholarium*; *Constitutiones Sororum S. Mariae Magdalenae*; *Constitutiones Ordinis S. Crucis*; *Constitutiones Camaldulensis Ordinis*; *Constitutiones antiquae Fratrum Servorum S. Mariae*.

§ 1. Religious life, poverty and preaching

The first leaders of the new religious movement were the so-called *Wanderprediger*.[168] They came from a monastic environment (Bernard of Thiron, Henry of Lausanne),[169] and from communities of canons (Robert of Arbrissel, Norbert of Xanten).[170] They called themselves *pauperes Christi*, "followers of the naked cross", who gloried in "following in the footsteps of the apostles".[171] They followed to the letter Christ's exhortation to renounce all possessions. Dressed in garments of undyed wool, without money for the journey, living on what they received or found along the way, they travelled across extensive territories as preachers of penance and peace. On their journeys, they were accompanied by a mass of

---

168 The most complete and synthetic work on this movement is still H. Grundmann, *Religiöse Bewegungen im Mittelalter*, Hildesheim, 1961². This edition contains the anastatic reprint of the original work (Historische Studien, vol. 267, Berlin, 1935). It also contains a supplementary study, *Neue Beiträge zur Geschichte der religiösen Bewegungen im Mittelalter* (pp. 485-538), with bibliographical details. On p. 492, the author focuses on the new aspect of the *vita apostolica*: "...weil ein neues religiöses Ideal sich nicht nur 'okkasionell' aus dem Eremiten- oder Kanoniker- oder Mönchs-Leben ergab, sondern es als aktiver Impuls aufrüttelnd umgestaltete: das Ideal der *vita apostolica* in einem neuen Sinn, des apostolischen Wirkens in der Welt und auf die Welt statt nur im Kloster oder im Eremus". Various aspects of the religious movement are also discussed in A. Mens, *Oorsprong en betekenis van de Nederlandse Begijnen- en Begardenbeweging*, especially pp. 16-95; J. Siegwart, *Die Chorherren- und Chorfrauengemeinschaften in der deutschsprachigen Schweiz*, pp. 231-238, 239-249. J. Leclercq – F. Vandenbroucke – L. Bouyer, *Histoire de la spiritualité chrétienne*, vol. II: *La spiritualité du moyen âge*, [Paris], 1961, pp. 315-328. – The term *Wanderprediger* has also frequently been used in Dutch-language literature since the publication of the classic work by J. von Walter, *Die ersten Wanderprediger Frankreichs*, 2 vols., Leipzig, 1903-1906. These preachers are also the subject of thorough studies by H. Grundmann, *op. cit.*, pp. 38-42, 503-513; A. Mens, *op. cit.*, pp. 16-23.
169 Bernard of Thiron (c. 1046-1117) was initially a monk in the Benedictine abbey of Saint Cyprian near Poitiers. Around 1096 he became a hermit and in 1101 he began his life as an itinerant preacher: see J. von Walter, *Wanderprediger*, vol. II, pp. 31-65; J.-B. Mahn, *L'ordre cistercien et son gouvernement*, pp. 29-31; A. Mens, *Begijnen- en Begardenbeweging*, pp. 19-20; St. Hilpisch, art. *Bernhard von Tiron*, in LTK, vol. II, 1958, col. 249. – Henry of Lausanne (died before 1145) had also been a monk, perhaps in a Cluniac abbey. He became a penitential preacher in 1116. On him, see J. von Walter, *op. cit.*, vol. II, pp. 130-140; A. Borst, art. *Heinrich "von Lausanne"*, in LTK, vol. V, 1960, col. 194-195.
170 Robert of Arbrissel (c. 1050 – c. 1115) was initially an archpriest in Rennes. In 1093 he withdrew into solitude near Craon (diocese of Angers). In 1097 he began to preach: see J. von Walter, *Wanderprediger*, vol. I, pp. 105-117; R. Niderst, *Robert d'Arbrissel et les origines de Fontevrault*, Rodez, 1952, p. 23. – Norbert (c. 1082-1134), initially a canon of Saint-Victor in Xanten, felt called around 1115 to become an itinerant preacher. The critical study of his person and work is far from complete. Good overviews and literature can be found for instance in J. von Walter, *op. cit.*, vol. II, pp. 119-129; D. S. Santa, *La spiritualità di S. Norberto*, in Analecta Praem., vol. XXXV, 1959, pp. 15-53; F. Petit, *L'ordre de Prémontré de saint Norbert à Anselme de Havelberg*, in *La vita comune dei clero nei secoli XI e XII*, vol. I, Milan, 1962, pp. 456-479; N. Backmund, art. *Norbert von Xanten*, in LTK, vol. VII, 1962, col. 1030-1031.
171 Characteristic details and texts on the way of life of the *Wanderprediger* and their adherents can be found in H. Grundmann, *Religiöse Bewegungen*, pp. 38-42; A. Mens, *Begijnen- en Begardenbeweging*, pp. 17-19. See also E. Werner, *Pauperes Christi. Studien zu sozial-religiösen Bewegungen im Zeitalter des Reformpapsttums*, Leipzig, 1956, pp. 25-52. This latter author regards the religious movements from a Marxist-materialist point of view and therefore fails to sufficiently explore the religious motives.

enthusiastic men and women, who wished to imitate their life of penance and earn merit by works of charity, especially the care of the sick and indigent.

Soon the actions of these preachers and their followers elicited sharp criticism and opposition in ecclesiastical circles.[172] The accusations they levelled against less exemplary clerics, and their emphasis on the imitation of the apostles as a prerequisite for the exercise of the apostolic ministry lost them favour.[173] From a social perspective, too, their movement could easily be regarded as a cause of disorder. Its utter lack of organisation and its radical idealism prevented it from proving its viability and from acquiring civil rights in medieval society.

When, after a number of years, the itinerant preachers abandoned their original activity, a solution had to be found for the problem of the religious popular movement which they had brought about. In order to safely accommodate their numerous followers, most of them became founders or reformers of monasteries. Vitalis of Savigny yielded to the persistence of his companions.[174] Around 1100 Robert of Arbrissel founded the abbey of Fontevrault, which became the centre of a double order.[175] In 1114, Bernard withdrew as a hermit to the forest of Thiron and subsequently organised several monasteries for men and women.[176] Norbert established himself with some of his followers in Prémontré near Laon in 1119.[177] His order later counted a great number of double monasteries.[178] This return to the monastic life in fact heralded the end of this religious movement. The new foundations adopted the traditional monastic customs. It is true that some founders afterwards resumed their itinerant preaching, but only for brief periods of time.[179]

The ecclesiastical authorities' reservations about these new movements were based on the actions of suspicious groups, whose members called themselves *apostolici*.[180] Externally, their way of life was not much different from that of the

---

172 Saint Bernard (see his *Epist. 242*, in PL, vol. 182, col. 437) and Ivo of Chartres (see his *Epist. 192*, in PL, vol. 162, col. 201) warned against certain *praedicantes*.

173 Cf. A. Mens, *Begijnen- en Begardenbeweging*, p. 21; J. Siegwart, *Die Chorherren- und Chorfrauengemeinschaften in der deutschsprachigen Schweiz*, p. 231.

174 He founded his monastery in Savigny (Normandy) c. 1115, "tandem precibus fratrum coactus" (*Vita*, c. 14, ed. E. P. Sauvage, in *Analecta Bollandiana*, vol. I, 1882, p. 382). Cf. J. Rambaud-Buhot, *L'abbaye de Savigny*, in *Cahiers Leopold Delisle*, vol. II, 1948, pp. 3-15.

175 H. Grundmann, *Religiöse Bewegungen*, pp. 43-44; R. Niderst, *Robert d'Arbrissel et les origines de Fontevrault*, Rodez, 1952, pp. 37-62.

176 J. von Walter, *Wanderprediger*, vol. II, pp. 56-64.

177 Ch. Dereine, *Les origines de Prémontré*, in RHE, vol. XLII, 1947, pp. 352-378.

178 A. Erens, *Les sœurs dans l'ordre de Prémontré*, in *Analecta Praem.*, vol. V, 1929, pp. 1-26. The double monasteries were abolished following an ordinance issued by the general chapter of 1140. The earliest *Consuetudines* still describe monastic discipline for the sisters: see R. Van Waefelghem, *Les premiers statuts de l'ordre de Prémontré*, pp. 63-67.

179 For Robert of Arbrissel, see J. von Walter, *Wanderprediger*, vol. I, p. 136; for Vitalis of Savigny and Norbert of Xanten, see *ibid.*, vol. II, pp. 89, 126-129.

180 On these heterodox groups, see H. Grundmann, *Religiöse Bewegungen*, pp. 18-38, 493-503; A. Mens, *Begijnen- en Begardenbeweging*, pp. 23-30. Of course, the term *apostolicus* as such did not have a pejorative connotation. For its use in expressions such as *vita apostolica, forma apostolica* and others,

preachers discussed above. But they preached doctrines that were labelled heretical by writers of the time.[181] Moreover, they attacked as avaricious clerics who did not live the apostolic life, and turned against the established hierarchical order in the church. Their externally pious lives and their propaganda caused confusion among the simple people. The desire to contain the danger of contamination was perhaps one of the motives that led the ecclesiastical authorities to nudge the followers of the apostolic movement in the direction of the monastic life.

During the last quarter of the twelfth century, the desire to imitate the apostles received a new impetus from laypeople who, at least initially, wished to operate under the guidance of the church. Around 1173-1175, the wealthy merchant Waldo from Lyon gave away his possessions to the poor and began to act publicly as a preacher of penance.[182] After the archbishop banned him from doing this, he went to Rome, where he was authorised by the Third Lateran Council, which recognised his orthodoxy, to dedicate himself to preaching, together with his followers.[183] Contacts with other movements, including the Humiliati in Lombardy, led some of his followers to adopt deviant views, which precipitated their excommunication by Pope Lucius III in 1184.[184] Yet the Waldensians do not appear ever to have fallen into radically anti-Christian doctrine, as their controversies with the Cathars in Southern France amply prove.[185]

---

see H. Grundmann, *op. cit.*, pp. 503-513, including bibliographical details on p. 505, note 31;
L. Spätling, *De apostolicis, pseudoapostolis, apostolinis*, especially pp. 48-110. Some medieval writers repeatedly warned against suspect preachers who called themselves *apostolici*, but who had unlawfully assumed this name. Saint Bernard had the following to say about them: "...iactant se esse successores apostolorum et se apostolicos vocant" (*Sermo 66*, in PL, vol. 183, col. 1098). For this kind of expression, cf. H. Grundmann, *op. cit.*, pp. 19-21; A. Mens, *op. cit.*, p. 25. Many texts there are quoted from a letter by Everwinus of Steinfeld to Saint Bernard (PL, vol. 182, col. 676-680).

181 See various texts quoted by H. Grundmann, *Religiöse Bewegungen*, pp. 21-22, notes 16-17.
182 The traditional views on Waldo and his movement have profoundly changed over the last few decades thanks to new text editions and studies, for instance by A. Dondaine, *Aux origines du valdéisme. Une profession de foi de Valdès?* in *Arch. F.P.*, vol. XVI, 1946, pp. 191-235. An edition of the sources (1179-1218) was published by G. Gönnet, *Enchiridion fontium Valdensium. Recueil critique des sources concernant les Vaudois au moyen âge*, vol. I, Torre Pellice, 1958. See also W. Mohr, *Waldes und das frühe Waldensertum*, in *Zeitschrift für Religions- und Geistesgeschichte*, vol. IX, 1957, pp. 337-363; G. Koch, *Neue Quellen und Forschungen über die Anfänge der Waldenser*, in *Forschungen und Fortschritte*, vol. XXXII, 1958, pp. 141-149.
183 The activities of the Waldensians were described by a contemporary as follows: "Hii certa nusquam habent domicilia, bini et bini circueunt, nudi pedes, laneis induti, nil habentes, omnia sibi communia tanquam apostoli, nudi nudum Christum sequentes" (Walter Map, *Liber de nugis curialium*, dist. I, c. 31, ed. F. Liebermann – R. Pauli, in MGH, *Scriptores*, vol. XXVII, Leipzig, 1925, p. 67). On the influence of the expression "nudum Christum nudus sequi", which appears already in Saint Jerome's work (*Epistula ad Rusticum monachum*, c. 20, in PL, vol. 22, col. 185), see L. Spätling, *De apostolicis*, p. 45.
184 According to W. Mohr, *Waldes und das frühe Waldensertum*, p. 362, Waldo must have died in 1184.
185 On this see Chr. Thouzellier, *Controverses vaudoises-cathares à la fin du XIIᵉ siècle (d'après le livre II du* Liber antiheresis, *ms. Madrid 1114 et les sections correspondantes du ms. B.N. lat. 13446)*, in *Archives d'histoire doctrinale et littéraire du moyen âge*, vol. XXVII, 1960, pp. 137-227. According to A. Dondaine, *Durand de Huesca et la polémique anti-cathare*, in *Arch. F.P.*, vol. XXIX, 1959, especially

§ 2. Evangelical poverty in the mission to the Albigensians

Innocent III launched a large-scale mission to secure the extirpation of heretical sects and the conversion of their adherents.[186] From the start of his pontificate, he deployed the Cistercians as preachers in the south of France, more specifically in the area between Toulouse and Narbonne. He exhorted his legates and missionaries in many letters to strengthen the faithful in their beliefs and to win the heterodox for the church through their edifying example and uplifting words.[187] But the endeavours of these monks, who received little support from the bishops and the clergy, were unavailing in an environment where the Cathar Albigensians and Waldensians, through their externally exemplary and ascetical life, exercised a much more direct influence over the common people, while they could count on the open collaboration or covert sympathy of the aristocracy.[188] After several years of difficult toil, the Cistercians were disappointed by the scant success of their actions. The scandalous behaviour of the clergy was thrown in their faces whenever they preached before the heretical population. Disheartened by this hopeless situation, they desired to be relieved of their mission.[189]

It was under these circumstances that the encounter took place that was to give new impetus to the ailing mission. In the summer of 1206, Diego, bishop of Osma, was travelling through Southern France in the company of Dominic of Caleruega, the subprior of the chapter. Together they had acquitted themselves of an assignment in Denmark on the instructions of King Alfonso VIII of Castile.[190] They had visited Rome in spring, where Diego had tried unsuccessfully to be discharged from his episcopal task so that he could dedicate himself wholly to missionary work among the pagans.[191] On their way back to Spain, in Montpellier,

---

pp. 228-248, the *Liber antihaeresis* was the work of the Waldensian Durand of Huesca. Cf. Chr. Thouzellier, *Le* Liber antiheresis *de Durand de Huesca et le* Contra hereticos *d'Ermengaud de Bézières*, in RHE, vol. LV, 1960, pp. 130-141.

186 For the history of the mission, see for instance H. Thilmann, *Papst Innocenz III* (Bonner historische Forschungen, vol. 3), Bonn, 1954, pp. 186-212; M. H. Vicaire, *Histoire de saint Dominique*, vol. I, pp. 177-188, including sources and literature.

187 In his letter of 21 April 1198 (PL, vol. 214, col. 81-83), Innocent III informed the bishops of the church province of Aix that he had appointed his legates, the Cistercians Rainer and Guido, as preachers to wrest the people from the hold of the heretical sects. In his letter of 12 July 1199 (*ibid.*, col. 675-676), he addressed Rainer directly: "...dum quod in solitudine et claustrali silentio didicisti, iuxta mandatum evangelicum praedicaveris super tecta et talenta tibi credita erogaveris ad usuras". He had already exhorted the archbishop of Arles and his suffragans on 7 July 1199 to support the legates (*ibid.*, col. 676-677).

188 On the attitude of the clergy, the activities of the heretical sects and their influence over the people, see Peter of Vaux-de-Cernay, *Hystoria Albigensis*, nos. 5-19; M. H. Vicaire, *Histoire*, vol. I, pp. 151-163.

189 *Hystoria Albigensis*, no. 20.

190 Jordan of Saxony, *Libellus de principiis Ordinis Predicatorum*, nos. 14-16. Cf. J. Gallén, *La province de Dacie de l'ordre des Frères Prêcheurs*, pp. 196-216.

191 On the Roman visit, see *Hystoria Albigensis*, no. 20; Jordan, *Libellus*, no. 17. Both authors confirm that the bishop's request was declined. According to the *Hystoria Albigensis*, Diego was even told to return to his diocese: "...immo precepit ei ut ad propriam sedem remearet". It is difficult to

they met the Cistercians who had gathered there to consult about one last attempt to make their missionary work fruitful. Having made enquiries, the bishop soon understood the situation and discovered the cause of their modest success. The population of the area could hardly resist the pressure exercised by the Cathars and the Waldensians given their example of evangelical poverty and austerity, whereas they could only be scandalised by the lifestyle of the clergy, and even by the actions of the legates and missionaries, who travelled the land on horseback with their retinue of servants. He considered that these people could only be reached and won by preachers of the faith who themselves would practice the perfect imitation of Christ and the apostles. As preachers, they would have to travel on foot, wearing shabby clothes. The Cistercians were reluctant to embrace the practice of evangelical poverty on their own authority, because this was still associated with the lifestyle of heterodox groups, and Diego therefore set the example himself. He sent the members of his retinue back to his diocese, retaining only a few clerics, among them Dominic.[192]

The bishop's inspiring example convinced the Cistercians. They too sent their retinue back to their abbeys, including horses and travel equipment, and during the following months embarked on intense activity under Diego's leadership. In addition to the latter, only Dominic and the Cistercians Peter of Castelnau and Rudolf of Fontfroide were initially mentioned as his helpers. But after a few months, Arnaud Amaury, the abbot of Cîteaux, and a number of other abbots and monks joined them. In small groups, they travelled the area and began to preach *in forma apostolica*, travelling on foot, like evangelical poor, wearing frugal clothes, without money for the journey, carrying only their books of hours and necessary study books.[193] They had in the meantime secured Innocent III's full approval of their actions and their method of practising the apostolate.[194] Their activity consisted mainly of preaching and holding public disputations on the faith, which were attended by many adherents of the heretical movement.[195] The missionary work apparently produced promising results among the Waldensians, but less so

---

interpret this order as a commission to go and perform missionary activity in Southern France, as M. H. Vicaire has attempted to do (*Innocent III, Diègue et Dominique en 1207*, in P. Mandonnet – M. H. Vicaire, *Saint Dominique*, vol. I, pp. 143-156). This view, which was sharply criticised by H. C. Scheeben (*Dominikaner oder Innozentianer*, in Arch. F.P., vol. IX, 1939, pp. 237-279), was later partially repudiated by the author (M. H. Vicaire, *Histoire*, vol. I, p. 136).

192 "Memoratus autem episcopus … salubre dedit consilium, monens et consulens ut, ceteris omissis, predicationi ardentius insudarent, et ut possent ora obstruere malignorum, in humilitate procedentes, exemplo pii Magistri facerent et docerent, irent pedites, absque auro et argento, per omnia formam apostolicam imitantes" (*Hystoria Albigensis*, no. 21). The evangelical inspiration of this proposal is clear. See also Jordan, *Libellus*, nos. 20-21; Chr. Thouzellier, *La pauvreté, arme contre l'albigéisme, en 1206*, in *Revue de l'histoire des religions*, vol. CLI, 1957, pp. 79-92.

193 "Audito igitur abbates, qui missi fuerant, huiuscemodi consilio et animati exemplo …, pedes, sine expensis, in voluntaria paupertate fidem annuntiare ceperunt" (Jordan, *Libellus*, no. 22).

194 See Innocent III's letter to Rudolf of Fontfroide of 17 November 1206 (PL, vol. 215, col. 1024-1025).

195 For the activities of the missionaries, see *Hystoria Albigensis*, nos. 22-27, 47-54; Jordan, *Libellus*, nos. 22-26.

among the Albigensians, who obstinately clung to their doctrines and form of life. Several women from distinguished families converted and formed a community in Prouille, between Fanjeaux and Montréal.[196] Their house, which is called *sancta praedicatio*[197] in the sources, was a centre of support for the missionary work in the area and later became the first convent of Dominican Sisters.

The departure of Bishop Diego and of most of the Cistercians in 1207 deprived the mission of its leaders.[198] The crusade against the Albigensians which was being prepared from 1208 onwards, after the murder of the papal legate Peter of Castelnau, made any organised apostolate entirely impossible.[199] During the following years, Dominic alone continued to work without respite as *praedicator apostolicus*. From time to time he received the assistance of his countryman Dominic and of William Claret, both of whom would later join the order.[200] The centre of his apostolate was the convent of the sisters in Prouille, which he had come to direct after Diego's death. There is nothing to suggest that he followed the example set by several prelates who took an active part in the crusade.[201] His apostolic attitude and activity are highlighted by Jordan of Saxony and are also evident from the documents that he signed as *Dominicus praedicator*.[202] The later *legenda* literature embellished his time in this heretical region with a series of anecdotes that stress the hostility of the population.[203] It can be deduced from the fact that he issued certificates of reconciliation to converted heretics that he was able to achieve results even in these unfavourable circumstances.[204] On several occasions he was offered an episcopal see.[205] For a few months in 1213, he

---

196 Jordan, *Libellus*, no. 27. See also H. C. Scheeben, *Die Anfänge des zweiten Ordens des hl. Dominikus*, in *Arch. F.P.*, vol. II, 1932, pp. 284-315; O. Decker, *Die Stellung des Predigerordens zu den Dominikanerinnen*, especially pp. 33-40; M. H. Vicaire, *Histoire*, vol. I, pp. 235-274.

197 See for instance the deed of donation by Sancius Gascus of 8 August 1206: "...damus et laudamus nosmetipsos et omnia nostra domino Deo, ... et sancte predicationi et domino Dominico de Oscua..." (Laurent, no. 6).

198 For the circumstances and date of the departure, see *Hystoria Albigensis*, nos. 48-51; Jordan, *Libellus*, nos. 28, 30; Robert of Auxerre, *Chronicon*, ed. O. Holder – Egger, in MGH, *Scriptores*, vol. XXVI, Leipzig, 1925, p. 271.

199 The course of the crusade up to the Battle of Muret (13 September 1213) is described in *Hystoria Albigensis*, nos. 55-484. Cf. A. Luchaire, *Innocent III*, vol. II: *La croisade des Albigeois*, Paris, 1905; P. Belperron, *La croisade contre les Albigeois et l'union du Languedoc à la France*, Paris, 1942.

200 Jordan, *Libellus*, no. 31.

201 Guido, abbot of Vaux-de-Cernay and bishop of Carcassonne since 1211, usually accompanied the army and even took an active part in the battle: "...qui nunquam ab exercitu recedebat" (*Hystoria Albigensis*, no. 317; see also nos. 155, 307, 324, 339-351, 508, 520, 526).

202 Laurent, no. 10 (charter from the year 1211); F. Balme, *Cartulaire de saint Dominique*, vol. I, p. 484 (deed of 1215 or 1216).

203 See Peter Ferrand, *Legenda*, no. 20; Constantinus of Orvieto, *Legenda*, no. 16; Humbert of Romans, *Legenda*, nos. 23-24.

204 See the documents in F. Balme, *Cartulaire de saint Dominique*, pp. 171-173, 468-471, 484. Cf. M. H. Vicaire, *Histoire*, vol. I, pp. 297-299.

205 Dominic was a candidate for the sees of Béziers, Couserans and Comminges: see *Proc. Bon.*, no. 28; *Proc. Tolos.*, nos. 3, 5, 18, 21; F. Balme, *Cartulaire de saint Dominique*, vol. I, p. 479; J. Guiraud,

was *vicarius in spiritualibus* for the bishop of Carcassonne, who was absent on a propaganda journey for the crusade in the north of the country.[206]

§ 3. New religious societies

The mission in Southern France may not have had the success that the pope had hoped for, but it did produce some limited results that became extremely important for religious associational life and for relations between the ecclesiastical authorities and the apostolic movement at the beginning of the thirteenth century. Durand of Huesca and a number of his companions converted after a public doctrinal disputation with Bishop Diego of Osma and Dominic of Caleruega in Pamiers, in Southern France, in 1207.[207] They formed a small society in which they continued to live the evangelical form of life that they had previously lived, but henceforth under the name of the "Catholic Poor".[208] They now focused their activities on their erstwhile friends and spread across the south of France, Lombardy and Aragon. Innocent III confirmed their *propositum conversationis*: not a monastic rule in the strict sense, but a collection of guidelines for their religious life and for their external activities.[209] They were permitted to continue to live in poverty and to fight heresy through preaching. As religious who lived in the world, they observed the evangelical counsels and recited a series of Our Fathers, the Creed and the Psalm *Miserere* by way of the office. They retained the shabby clothes to which they were accustomed, albeit with a number of changes to distinguish them from the Waldensians.[210] A few years later, in 1210, Bernard Primus, the leader of a group of preachers in Southern France who were regarded

---

Cartulaire de Notre-Dame de Prouille, vol. I, p. CCCXII; B. Altaner, *Der hl. Dominikus*, pp. 29-30; H. C. Scheeben, *Der heilige Dominikus*, pp. 103-104.

206 Constantinus of Orvieto, *Legenda*, no. 55. On the journey of bishop Guido of Vaux-de-Cernay, see also *Hystoria Albigensis*, no. 508.

207 *Hystoria Albigensis*, no. 48. New light has been shed on the figure of Durand of Huesca, for instance by A. Dondaine, *Durand de Huesca et la polémique anticathare*, in *Arch. F.P.*, vol. XXIX, 1959, pp. 228-276; Chr. Thouzellier, *Un traité cathare inédit du début du XIIIe siècle d'après le* Liber contra Manicheos *de Durand de Huesca* (Bibliothèque de la Revue d'histoire ecclésiastique, vol. 37), Leuven, 1961, which gives an overview of the literature. Durand's *Liber contra Manicheos*, published by the same author, will appear as vol. 32 of the *Spicilegium sacrum Lovaniense* series.

208 See on this J. B. Pierron, *Die katholischen Armen*, pp. 22-117; H. Grundmann, *Religiöse Bewegungen*, pp. 100-118; M. H. Vicaire, *Histoire*, vol. I, pp. 271-272.

209 See the text in PL, vol. 215, col. 1512-1513.

210 "...calceamentis desuper apertis ita speciali signo compositis et variatis, ut aperte et lucide cognoscamur nos esse, sicut corde, sic et corpore, a Lugdunensibus et nunc et in perpetuum segregatos..." (PL, vol. 215, col. 1513).

as Waldensians, came to Rome and promised reverence to the church and the clergy.[211] He, too, received a *propositum* as the programme of life for his society.[212]

The desire for a religious but not traditionally monastic life also underlay the movement of the Humiliati in Italy.[213] Even before 1180, there were people in Lombardy who, like the *continentes* of the first centuries, attempted to practice the evangelical precepts and counsels of perfection in their own environment, either alone or in groups. They called themselves *humiliati* on account of their shabby garments of undyed cloth.[214] Their leaders similarly demanded official approval from the pope of their way of life and their work against the heretics. Alexander III granted this under certain conditions, but he banned them from public preaching. They flouted this injunction and were excommunicated because of their disobedience in 1184.[215] Some remained obstinate, others were prepared to respond to the conciliatory gestures made by Innocent III. In 1198 or 1199, two of their leaders went to Rome to treat with the pope. It was agreed that the various branches of the movement would be reduced to three groups. A first order would consist of *clerici*, lay brothers and sisters who were to live separately from each other. The second order would consist of men and women who were to form separate regular communities. Both groups were given a rule in 1201, which contained not only their own traditional statutes, but also guidelines from the rules of Benedict and Augustine.[216] The third order, which chronologically speaking was possibly the first, brought together those persons who continued to live the original way of life of the members of the movement in the world. They received a *propositum*, which must be regarded as the first officially approved programme for lay people who wish to live a religious life in the world.[217]

---

211 See on him H. Grundmann, *Religiöse Bewegungen*, pp. 118-128. For Bernard's profession of faith, see PL, vol. 216, col. 289-293.

212 Published in PL, vol. 216, col. 648-650. Various points are similar to Durand of Huesca's *Propositum*. – See also M. Maccarrone, *Riforme e sviluppo della vita religiosa con Innocenzo III*, in *Rivista di storia della Chiesa in Italia*, vol. XVI, 1962, pp. 54-55.

213 See for instance L. Zanoni, *Gli Umiliati nei loro rapporti con l'eresia, l'industria della lana ed i comuni*, pp. 19-93; H. Grundmann, *Religiöse Bewegungen*, pp. 72-91; A. Mens, *Begijnen- en Begardenbeweging*, pp. 45-54, with literature on pp. 45-46, note 1.

214 "Hii se Humiliatos appellaverunt, eo quod tincta indumenta non vestientes, simplici sunt contenti…" (*Chronicon universale anonymi Landunensis*, ed. G. Waitz, in MGH, *Scriptores*, vol. XXVI, Leipzig, 1925, p. 450).

215 "Quibus papa concessit, ut omnia eorum in humilitate fierent et honestate, sed ne conventicula ab eis fierent, signanter interdixit, et ne in publico predicare presumerent, districte inhibuit. Ipsi vero mandatum apostolicum contemnentes, facti inobedientes, se ob id excommunicari permiserunt" (*ibid.*, pp. 449-450).

216 See the text of this communal rule in L. Zanoni, *Gli Umiliati*, pp. 352-370, who also indicates the sources (especially the rule of Saint Benedict, the *Institutio canonicorum* of Aachen and a number of passages from Gregory the Great).

217 The text was published by H. Tiraboschi, *Vetera Humiliatorum monumenta*, vol. II, pp. 128-134. For the content and meaning of this *Propositum*, see L. Zanoni, *Gli Umiliati*, pp. 112-131.

Francis of Assisi arrived in Rome perhaps in the same year as Bernard Primus, 1210.[218] Since his conversion in 1206, he had been trying, together with his companions, to live the gospel according to the letter. His *sensus catholicus* was never in doubt, and submission to the bishops and priests was a principle that always guided and directed his actions. Innocent III permitted him to continue his evangelical way of life and his preaching among the people. In all probability no formal approval of a written *propositum* was given at that time.[219] The definitive confirmation of his rule, in which he formulated the fundamental principles of the apostolic life of his society, was left to Pope Honorius III,[220] who had also approved Dominic's religious community at the beginning of his pontificate.

Perhaps to clearly mark the distinction with the traditional monastic institutes, the rules upon which the religious life in these new societies was based were no longer called *regula* but *propositum*.[221] It is true that this term had already long become customary in the terminology of the monastic life. It referred not to the written regulations, but the *regularis institutio*, the monastic way of life as a whole.[222] But communal life, the profession of vows, and liturgical and ascetical

---

218 On this year (rather than 1209), see the critical comments by H. Grundmann, *Religiöse Bewegungen*, pp. 127-128, note 111. Most sources and studies on the life of Francis and the society he established can be found in H. Boehmer – Fr. Wiegand – C. Andresen, *Analekten zur Geschichte des Franciscus von Assisi*, pp. VII-XI. In addition, we must mention the thorough studies by K. Esser, *Das ministerium generale des hl. Franziskus von Assisi*, in *Franziskanische Studien*, vol. XXXIII, 1951, pp. 329-348; Id., *Ordo Fratrum Minorum. Über seine Anfänge und ursprünglichen Zielsetzungen*, ibid., vol. XLII, 1960, pp. 97-129, 297-355; F. van den Borne, *Voornaamste feiten uit het leven van Franciskus in het licht van de historische kritiek*, in *Sint Franciscus*, vol. LIX, 1957, pp. 163-239, 243-316; L. Hardick – J. Terschlüssen – K. Esser, *La règle des Frères Mineurs. Étude historique et spirituelle*, Paris, 1961.

219 The existence of a written rule c. 1210 is not accepted by A. Quaglia, *Origine e sviluppo della regola francescana*, Naples, 1948, but it is accepted by L. Casutt, *Die älteste franziskanische Lebensform. Untersuchungen zur Regula sine bulla*, Graz-Vienna-Cologne, 1955. According to H. Boehmer, *Analekten*, pp. 60-61, it is possible to identify a number of text fragments from this original *propositum: Regulae antiquissimae fragmenta*.

220 See the *Regula non bullata quae dicitur prima* (1221) in H. Boehmer, *Analekten*, pp. 1-18. According to a number of authors, this rule contains the text of the earliest *Regula* (1210): see V. Kybal, *Die Ordensregeln des heiligen Franz von Assisi und die ursprüngliche Verfassung des Minoritenordens. Ein quellenkritischer Versuch*, Leipzig-Berlin, 1915, pp. 16, 24; H. Boehmer, *op. cit.*, pp. XV-XVI; K. Esser, *Zur Textgeschichte der Regula non bullata des hl. Franziskus*, in *Franziskanische Studien*, vol. XXXIII, 1951, pp. 219-237. The *Regula bullata* was approved by Honorius III on 29 November 1223. See the text in H. Boehmer, *op. cit.*, pp. 20-24.

221 From 1220 onwards, the Franciscans did speak of a *regula*, but the term *propositum* still appears in the *Memoriale propositi* of 1221-1228, the rule for the *penitentes* in the world who were affiliated with the Order of Francis. The text of the *Memoriale*, published by H. Boehmer, *Analekten*, pp. 49-56, was reprinted in G. G. Meersseman, *Dossier de l'ordre de la Pénitence au XIIIᵉ siècle* (Spicilegium Friburgense, vol. 7), Fribourg (Switzerland), 1961, pp. 92-112.

222 The monastic use of *propositum* is in evidence as early as the seventh century, for instance in the *Regula cuiusdam patris ad monachos*, c. 15: "Propositum monachi, quod promisimus, ... quod in tribus renuntiationibus consistit" (PL, vol. 66, col. 990). In the ninth century, *propositum* meant the commitment to lead a communal life and observe the other monastic obligations, and the term was even used as a synonym for *votum* and monastic profession (C. Capelle, *Le vœu d'obéissance des origines au XIIᵉ siècle*, pp. 165-166). Cf. *Decretum Gratiani*: "Propositum monachi ... deseri non

practices were alien to the *propositum* of the Third Order of the Humiliati, the Catholic Poor, the followers of Bernard Primus and the first Franciscans, or at most appeared there only in limited and restricted form.[223] In their place came a number of evangelical precepts on poverty, prayer and the apostolate. The freer and less complicated programme of these new societies thus in many ways approximated the *propositum* of the consecrated people of the Early Christian age, who, without any formal vows and outside the context of any community in the strict sense of the term, committed themselves to persevering in the state of perfection (*propositum sacrum, professio sacra*).[224] By contrast with the original

---

potest absque peccato" (c. *Propositum*, 1, C. XX, q. 3, in *Corpus iuris canonici*, vol. I, col. 848; cf. col. 845, 1045, 1051). Cf. L. Hertling, *Die Professio der Kleriker und die Entstehung der drei Gelübde*, in *Zeitschrift für kath. Theol.*, vol. LVII, 1932, pp. 155-160, which mentions many texts on *propositum*. The approximation between *propositum* and *institutio* is even clearer in the twelfth century, for example in the annals of the first Carthusians: "Hic [Guigo] Carthusiensis propositi institutionem et scripto digessit et exemplo monstravit" (quoted by A. Wilmart, *La chronique des premiers chartreux*, in *Revue Mabillon*, vol. XVI, 1926, p. 126). Perhaps *institutio pro positi* may be translated here as "the organisation of the monastic way of life" or as "the organised monastic life". The same approximation can be found in Guigo's *Consuetudines*: "…ex mensura … qua propositum poscit et institutio" (c. 41, no. 5; PL, vol. 153, col. 723). Cf. *ibid.*, c. 41, no. 2; also *Acta primi capituli Carthusiensis*, in PL, vol. 153, col. 1126. Guigo sent a number of monks from Grande Chartreuse on a mission to introduce the Carthusian observance and customs to Mont-Dieu: "… nostro proposito aedificando et conservando" (letter by Guigo to Archbishop Rainald, in C. Le Couteulx, *Annales Ordinis Carthusiensis*, vol. I, p. 405). Cf. also Peter Abelard, *Epist. 8*: "Restat … aliquam vobis institutionem, quasi quandam propositi vestri regulam, a nobis scribi…" (PL, vol. 178, col. 257); *Regula Humiliatorum*, c. 42: "…iuxta propositum et regulam fratrum vivere…, propositi humilitatem…" (L. Zanoni, *Gli Umiliati*, p. 368). See also the *arenga* of the *privilegium commune* for religious: "…aut eos a proposito revocet, …" (quoted *infra*, p. 227, note 240).

223 C. 1 of Saint Francis' *Regula bullata* does already mention the observance of the evangelical counsels: "…vivendo in obedientia, sine proprio et in castitate" (H. Boehmer, *Analekten*, p. 20). There is not a trace yet, however, of an organised monastic life with the customary regular *institutio* and observances. Care for the formation of the novices was entrusted to the *minister provincialis*, but there is no mention of initiation into monastic customs. Nor is there any reference to a communal liturgical office. It does say that "Clerici faciant divinum officium secundum ordinem sanctae Romanae ecclesiae excepto psalterio, ex quo habere poterunt breviaria" (c. 3, *ibid.*, p. 21). But the *breviarium* was, of course, the book of hours intended for travelling clergy. – The *propositum* of the other religious societies mentioned was even more succinct.

224 For the use and meaning of *propositum* in relation to *professio*, see C. Capelle, *Le vœu d'obéissance*, *passim*. Many details for the period between the third and the tenth centuries can be found in L. Hertling, *Die Professio* (cf. *supra*, note 222), pp. 150-154. Initially, the *propositum* of the *virgines* meant their determined interior decision to persevere in a life of virginity and the practice of pious exercises, as well as the way of life and state of consecrated women and their commitment to this, not through a public vow, but by accepting the veil (C. Capelle, *op. cit.*, pp. 16-49). The decision, once taken, and its public announcement by the external practice of the *professio sacra*, sufficed to give this way of life *stabilitas* and an obligatory character (pp. 83-87). Even after the *propositum* had acquired a monastic meaning (cf. *supra*, note 222), the earlier connotation continued in the institution of the *mulieres religiosae*, who lived a consecrated life outside the monastery. Many texts deal with the *virgines velatae* (sometimes also *non velatae*) and the widows, who practiced their *propositum* at home or at least outside a monastic environment. The Second Council of Rome (826) gave these women a choice: "Mulieres obtentu religionis velatae aut in monasterio regulariter vivant aut in

meaning of the word, *propositum conversationis* in the thirteenth century already referred to the complex of written guidelines which the church authorities had approved. But it could not be regarded as a *regula* in the sense of the term that was current at the time.[225]

Two different kinds of religious communal life developed from the many groups that made up the apostolic movement of the twelfth century. The evangelical enthusiasm that itinerant preachers had aroused among the people through their words and example culminated in foundations of religious houses of the traditional type. However, throughout the twelfth century, the imitation of the apostolic example remained a popular ideal which also inspired laypeople to practice poverty and preaching. Initially, the church refused this offer of assistance and even excommunicated groups that arrogated to themselves the right to preach without authorisation from the ecclesiastical authorities. It was not until the early thirteenth century that Innocent III succeeded in bringing about a rapprochement. He encouraged the members of the papal mission who were attempting to convert the Albigensians in Southern France to persevere in their apostolic form of life. He reconciled adherents or sympathisers of heretical sects with the church, and subsequently set them to work in the apostolate as religious societies that were bound not to a monastic rule and *institutio*, but only to a *propositum conversationis* with evangelical guidelines. His attitude towards the leaders of two small communities that were to grow into the two largest mendicant orders demonstrated that he expected positive results from the apostolic movement.

Section IV. Origins and first legislation of the Dominicans

The Dominicans were perhaps the last of the many religious communities that requested approval for their evangelical form of life and their apostolic mission during the pontificate of Innocent III. In early 1215, Dominic left the region of Prouille and moved the centre of his life and work to Toulouse. Together with a number of clerics, he soon formed a community of preachers recognised by the bishop as diocesan pastoral ministers. After negotiations with Pope Innocent III, they were confirmed by Honorius III as a community of canons regular, and they also received approval of their apostolic mission.

---

domibus susceptum habitum caste observent" (can. 28, ed. A. Werminghoff, in MGH, *Legum sectio III: Concilia*, div. II: *Concilia aevi Karolini*, vol. I, Hanover-Leipzig, 1906, p. 579). The Fourth Council of Toledo (633) banned *viduae sanctimoniales* from abandoning their *propositum castitatis* (Mansi, vol. X, col. 632-633). See also c. *Viduas*, 2, C. XXVII, q. 1: "Viduas a proposito discedentes ..., quae necdum sacro velamine tectae, tamen in proposito virginali semper se simulaverint permanere..." (*Corpus iuris canonici*, vol. I, col. 1047-1048). Cf. *ibid.*, col. 1050 (c. 9); col. 1055 (C. 21).

225 Gregory IX explicitly said as much with regard to the Catholic Poor: see H. Grundmann, *Religiöse Bewegungen*, p. 106, note 70. But the same was true for the other societies.

§ 1. The apostolic community in Toulouse

Perhaps acquiring a base in the urban area of Toulouse meant not just the prospect of a new work area for Dominic, but also the possibility to surround himself with a team of permanent assistants and to live and work in community. During the ten years that he had been in Southern France, he had had little experience of the stable communal life he had known in the chapter of canons regular in Osma. He laid the foundations for a religious community around Easter 1215. Jordan of Saxony described the entry of two members, Peter Seila and Thomas, as an *oblatio*, a typically contractual act, which, according to the medieval legal custom, involved both a commitment on the part of the person in question and the renunciation of all possessions.[226] Peter ceded the property of his spacious house near the southern city wall on the basis of this commitment.[227] From that moment on, they lived there together as *religiosi*.[228] Fulk, the bishop of Toulouse, appointed them as diocesan preachers and entrusted them with the task of combating heresy

226 "Ingruente autem tempore, quo ad Lateranense concilium Romam adire ceperunt episcopi, obtulerunt se fratri Dominico duo probi viri et idonei de Tholosa, quorum unus fuit frater Petrus de Selani, postmodum prior Lemovicensis, alter vero frater Thomas, vir admodum gratiosus et sermone facundus" (Jordan, *Libellus*, no. 38).

227 "Horum primus frater Petrus sublimes et nobiles domos, quas Tholose circa castrum Narbonense possederat, tradidit fratri Dominico et eius sociis" (Jordan, *ibid.*). It can be deduced from a notarial deed of 25 April 1215, in which the division of the estate of the Seila brothers is described, that this transfer of property was also regarded as valid under civil law. While Bernard acted in a personal capacity with respect to the division, Peter's share was received by Dominic, "qui hoc accepit, pro eodem Petro Seilano et pro se et pro omnibus suis successoribus et habitatoribus domus, quam idem dominus Dominicus constituerat" (Laurent, no. 61). For the purport of this deed, see also M. H. Vicaire, *Fondation, approbation, confirmation de l'ordre des Prêcheurs*, in RHE, vol. XLVII, 1952, pp. 127-128. In 1214 (7 April) Peter Seila had still acted in full possession of his goods: see Vl. J. Koudelka, *Notes sur le cartulaire de S. Dominique*, in Arch. F.P., vol. XXVIII, 1958, p. 100, note 1.

228 "A quo tempore ceperunt primum apud Tholosam in eisdem domibus commorari, atque ex tunc omnes, qui cum ipso erant, ceperunt magis ac magis ad humilitatem descendere et religiosorum se moribus conformare" (Jordan, *Libellus*, no. 38). The expressions used by Jordan are strongly reminiscent of the treatise of Bernard of Clairvaux, *De gradibus humilitatis* (ed. in PL, vol. 182, col. 941-958), which itself was inspired by the *Reg. S. Ben.*, c. 7, *De humilitate*, which addresses the twelve *gradus humilitatis*. *Humilitas* was, however, also a typical feature of the externally visible life style of the adherents of the religious movements of the eleventh and twelfth centuries. Ivo of Chartres was suspicious of those who "humilitate vestium et vilitate ciborum merita sua populis ostentant" (*Epist. 193*, in PL, vol. 162, col. 201). On the Humiliati, see *supra*, p. 220, notes 214-215; on the Waldensians: "Humillimo nunc incipiunt modo..." (Walter Map, *Liber de nugis curialium*, dist. I, c. 31, ed. F. Liebermann – R. Pauli, in MGH, *Scriptores*, vol. XXVII, Leipzig, 1925, col. 67). The first Franciscans were required to live a life "in paupertate et humilitate" (*Regula bullata*, c. 6, ed. H. Boehmer, *Analekten*, p. 22). The Franciscan Penitents had to wear a "humilitatis chlamydem" (*Memoriale propositi*, c. 1, ed. *ibid.*, p. 50). Cf. *Regula S. Spiritus*, c. 6: "...et vestitus eorum sit humilis..." (ed. A. F. La Cava, *Liber Regulae S. Spiritus*, p. 126). Peter of Vaux-de-Cernay wrote about the preachers against the Albigensians: "Et hi omnes, ... omnem sectantes humilitatem, ... pedites procedebant" (*Hystoria Albigensis*, no. 47).

and strengthening the Christian spirit among the population.[229] Their field of activity was circumscribed by the boundaries of the diocese, but was not limited to the jurisdiction of any particular church. As they were missionaries, they had the right to live off the gospel, and they were partly supported by ecclesiastical revenue. They received a sixth share in the tithe levied for parish churches and for worship, part of which had to be given to the poor according to the custom of the time.[230]

In their position as licensed preachers, the members of the new community were able to observe all aspects of the way of life that Dominic had adopted during his apostolic work in the previous years. The charter in which Bishop Fulk appointed them as his helpers in pastoral ministry also provided a number of details on their activity and status. During their preaching journeys through the diocese, they would travel on foot as *religiosi*, and practice evangelical poverty in the way they lived.[231] The words *praedicatio, evangelicus* and *paupertas* each appear several times in the text and together indicate the keynote of the programme approved by the bishop.[232] All these characteristic elements mean that Dominic's first foundation was closely related to the new apostolic societies that had gained a foothold in the life of the church at the time. Evangelical poverty, preaching and the religious life were also the main features of the *propositum* of the converted Waldensians and of the followers of Francis which Innocent III had approved.[233] The only new elements in the case of the first Dominicans were their appointment as diocesan preachers and the granting of the tithe.

Neither the bishop's charter, nor Jordan's narrative suggest that the society led by Dominic was organised as a monastic community in the traditional sense. There is no reference to an *institutio regularis*, based on a monastic or canonical rule. The *oblatio* of the first members is similar in many respects to religious

---

229 "Notum sit omnibus presentibus et futuris quod nos, F., Dei gratia tolosane sedis minister humilis, … instituimus predicatores in episcopatu nostro fratrem Dominicum et socios eius…" (Laurent, no. 60). The charter bears the year of 1215 and must therefore have been drafted after 25 March, as the style of the Incarnation or of Easter was in use in Toulouse at the time (A. Giry, *Manuel de diplomatique*, Paris, 1894, pp. 122-123). It perhaps dates from the spring of 1215, as it must be assumed that Dominic must have led his society of preachers for a few more months before he travelled to Rome together with the bishop in September: see p. 227.

230 "…assignamus in perpetuum predictis predicatoribus et aliis, quos zelus Domini et amor salutis animarum eodem modo ad idem predicationis officium accinxerit, medietatem tercie partis decime que assignata est ornamentis et fabrice ecclesiarum omnium parrochialium ecclesiarum…" (Laurent, no. 60). The ecclesiastical rules concerning the tithe in question had been fixed already in *Decretum Gratiani*, c. 26-30, C. XII, q. 2 (*Corpus iuris canonici*, vol. I, col. 696-697). Cf. G. Lepointe, art. *Dîme*, in *Dict. de droit canon.*, vol. IV, 1949, col. 1238-1239.

231 "…qui in paupertate evangelica, pedites, religiose proposuerunt incedere et veritatis evangelice verbum predicare" (Laurent, no. 60).

232 The text is overloaded, as it were, by such expressions: "…instituimus predicatores …, in paupertae evangelica, … veritatis evangelice verbum predicare … qui evangelium predicat, de evangelio debet vivere, … cum predicando incesserint, … predictis predicatoribus …, illis pauperibus …, qui, pro Christo, evangelicam paupertatem eligentes, …".

233 See *supra*, pp. 219-223.

profession.[234] And yet it appears closer to other forms of commitment, forms that also involved the renunciation of property.[235] The commission to preach in itself formed no impediment to a monastic way of life. However, like the members of the contemporaneous apostolic societies, the preachers of Toulouse could hardly be regarded as a *religio approbata*. Instead, they formed a religious society of an original type.[236] Whether they observed any written regulations other than the

234 This is how this act is interpreted by M. H. Vicaire, *Fondation… des Prêcheurs*, pp. 126-127. Cf. Id., *Histoire*, vol. I, p. 333. The formula of profession used by many canons regular in fact does express this *oblatio*: "Ego, frater N., offerens trado meipsum Deo, ecclesiae sancti Ioannis…" (quoted in Ch. Dereine, *Saint-Ruf et ses coutumes*, p. 180). The Premonstratensians used the following formula: "Ego, frater N., offerens trado meipsum ecclesiae…" (quoted in Adam Scotus, *De ordine, habitu et professione canonicorum Praemonstratensium*, in PL, vol. 198, col. 479). See also Pl. F. Lefèvre, *Les statuts de Prémontré*, p. 25.

235 The *oblatio* of children, mentioned in the rule of Saint Benedict in c. 58, *De filiis nobilium aut pauperum qui offeruntur*, is famous. Adults, too, were affiliated to Benedictine abbeys through an *oblatio*: "Tous ces familiers étaient de pieux laïques, qui, par piété, s'offraient à une abbaye, eux, leur travail et leurs biens, en tout ou en partie… Un contrat fixait les devoirs et les droits réciproques. L'acte s'appelait *oblatio* ou *offertio*" (Ph. Schmitz, *Histoire de l'ordre de saint Benoît*, vol. I, Maredsous, 1942, p. 285). For *oblatio* formulas, see G. Schreiber, *Kurie und Kloster*, vol. I, p. 285; E. Martène, *De antiquis Ecclesiae ritibus*, vol. IV, p. 233. In the *Chronica monasterii Casinensis*, lib. I, c. 46 (ed. W. Wattenbach, in MGH, *Scriptores*, vol. VII, Leipzig, 1925, p. 613), the *oblatio* of Walamir and Hermefrid, who offered themselves and their goods to the church and the monastery, certainly did not have the meaning of a ritual profession following a period of probation, as the rule of Saint Benedict, c. 58, describes. The medieval *oblatio*, usually accompanied by the *immixtio manuum*, the typical act of feudal homage (F. L. Ganshof, *Qu'est-ce que la féodalité?*, Brussels, 1957³, especially pp. 43-44, 98-101), was still a frequent form of dedication in the early thirteenth century. Dominic may even have been present at such forms of covenant making, for instance when Arnold of Crampagna, who had abjured heresy in Pamiers in 1206, made a commitment before the bishop of Osma by an *oblatio*: "Ille etiam qui constitutus erat iudex … renuntiavit pravitati heretice et in manus domini Oxomensis episcopi obtulit se et sua" (*Hystoria Albigensis*, no. 48). This certainly did not refer to a monastic profession. Dominic accepted such *oblationes* himself in Prouille: see for example Laurent, nos. 6, 23, 25, 66.

236 In the Middle Ages, *religiosi* did not always mean the inhabitants of a monastery, but in many cases also referred to people who, like in Christian Antiquity, practiced their consecrated life (*vita religiosa* or *professio religiosa*) outside any monastic context. The word retained this meaning until far into the Middle Ages, even when the monastic life had become the standard environment for the pursuit of Christian perfection, and *religiosi* had come to mean primarily monks and later canons regular. In the latter cases, *vita religiosa* was synonymous with *vita regularis*: see for instance the address in the letter of privilege for monks and canons regular: "*Religiosam vitam* eligentibus…" (M. Tangl, *Die päpstlichen Kanzleiordnungen*, pp. 229, 233). For the various meanings of *religiosus*, see the many quotations in L. Hertling, *Die Professio der Kleriker und die Entstehung der drei Gelübde*, in *Zeitschrift für kath. Theol.*, vol. LVII, 1932, pp. 148-174. The original meaning of the term acquired a new currency in the twelfth and thirteenth centuries as the apostolic movements emerged, whose members, both men and women, claimed the titles of *religiosi* and *mulieres religiosae*: see for instance H. Grundmann, *Religiöse Bewegungen, passim*; A. Mens, *Begijnen- en Begardenbeweging*, especially pp. 275-278, 313-322, 361-363. See also the *propositum conversationis* by Durand of Huesca and his followers, which contains the passages "religiose vivere … religiosus et modestus habitus…" (PL, vol. 215, col. 1513).

succinct *propositium* described in the episcopal charter cannot be determined on the basis of the documents.

Like John of Matha, the founder of the Trinitarians, Francis of Assisi and the leaders of the other apostolic societies in their day, Dominic, too, wished to obtain papal approval for his foundation. The opportunity for a visit to Rome presented itself in late 1215, when he was permitted to accompany his bishop Fulk to the Fourth Lateran Council.[237] According to Jordan of Saxony, it was their intention to seek confirmation of the institute for diocesan preachers, as well as of the revenues with which the bishop and Count Simon de Montfort had endowed the apostolic work.[238] Even before the thirteenth century, many religious societies had asked the Holy See to confirm their organisation and legislation and to extend its protection to their possessions. In some cases, such approbations were granted by the chancery in documents drawn up specifically for that case and pertaining only to a particular order or monastery. But during the course of the thirteenth century, the chancery increasingly began to use standardised texts, which required only minor changes and adjustments to serve for a wide range of religious institutes. The form *Religiosam vitam* became the classic type of confirmation document for abbeys of monks and canons regular.[239] It was always issued in the form of a *privilegium*, more specifically a solemn bull, consisting of some twenty formulas. The first two (*arenga* and *notificatio*) contained the papal protection.[240] This was

---

237 The council was opened on 11 November 1215. The last session took place on 30 November. For the history of the council, see for instance F. Vernet, art. *Latran (IVe Concile oecuménique du)*, in *Dict. de théologie cath.*, vol. VIII, 1925, col. 2652-2667. The canons were published in Mansi, vol. XXII, col. 981-1068; Ch.-J. Hefele – H. Leclercq, *Histoire des conciles*, vol. V, Paris, 1912, pp. 1323-1388.

238 "Adiunctus est autem eidem episcopo frater Dominicus, ut simul adirent concilium, et pari voto dominum papam Innocentium precarentur, confirmari fratri Dominico et sociis eius ordinem, qui predicatorum diceretur et esset; confirmaret nihilominus predictos reditus tam a comite quam ab episcopo fratribus assignatos" (Jordan, *Libellus*, no. 40). Count Simon de Montfort's donations are listed in *ibid.*, no. 37.

239 See G. Schreiber, *Kurie und Kloster*, vol. II, pp. 367-378. The text that was included in the formulary of the papal chancery in the early thirteenth century was published in M. Tangl, *Die päpstlichen Kanzleiordnungen*, pp. 229-234. During the pontificate of Innocent III, dozens of religious houses received this *privilegium* (PL, vols. 214-217, mentions 27 cases). Innocent III granted the same privilege on six occasions during the last three months of 1216: *Regesta Honorii Papae III*, ed. P. Pressutti, vol. I, nos. 53, 60, 70, 72, 130, 193. Cf. *Regesta Pontificum Romanorum*, ed. A. Potthast, nos. 5340, 5343, 5403.

240 "Religiosam vitam eligentibus apostolicum convenit adesse presidium, ne forte cuiuslibet temeritatis incursus aut eos a proposito revocet, aut robur, quod absit, sacre religionis infringat. Eapropter, dilecti in Domino filii, vestris iustis postulationibus clementer annuimus et monasterium ... in quo divino mancipati estis obsequio, sub beati Petri et nostra protectione suscipimus et presentis scripti privilegio communimus" (M. Tangl, *Die päpstlichen Kanzleiordnungen*, p. 229). The first sentence was the original text. Such short letters of protection were still used in the twelfth century. But from the thirteenth century onwards, the text was extended and became stable, and it was included in the formulary of the papal chancery as a template. For the history of papal *protectio*, see for instance J. Vincke, art. *Schutz*, in LTK, vol. X, 1938, col. 257-258; G. Schreiber, *Kurie und Kloster*, vol. I, pp. 6-23; A. Scheuermann, *Die Exemtion nach geltendem kirchlichen Recht, mit einem Überblick über die geschichtliche Entwicklung*, Paderborn, 1938, pp. 44-50, 63-65.

followed by the *dispositio* containing the confirmation of the regular way of life, a list of the real estate and the grant or confirmation of a number of privileges to ensure the good conduct of monastic life.[241]

It must be assumed that Fulk and Dominic were sufficiently acquainted with the customs of the papal curia to realise that they would be expected to submit a petition containing at least a brief description of the way of life and activities of the members of the community in question. Just like papal protection of monastic and canonical communities was granted only on the basis of a *regula approbata* and of a clear description of the possessions, so, too, approbation of apostolic societies required a written document that explained the statute, purpose and form of life.[242] The letters of confirmation that Innocent granted to these new societies made no mention of a traditional monastic rule, but of a *propositum* that was possibly identical to the guidelines drawn up by the founders themselves and presented to the pope. We may accept on the authority of Humbert of Romans that the Dominicans hoped as early as 1215 to acquire the approval of a written *propositum*.[243] But it is not certain if they had developed a wholly new programme of life. Perhaps the episcopal charter that described their way of life and apostolic activities was regarded as sufficient guarantee of the orthodoxy of their views and intentions.

§ 2. The community of canons regular at the church of Saint Romanus

The discussions that Bishop Fulk and Dominic had with Innocent III did not immediately produce the desired result. In fact, the time was not opportune for the definitive approbation of new institutes. The Lateran Council had decided to examine two issues with which Dominic's foundation was intimately caught up: the reform of the cure of souls and the foundation of religious associations. The first issue was dealt with in can. 10, *De praedicatoribus instituendis*,[244] in which the bishops were exhorted to seek the assistance of capable helpers who could

---

241 "In primis quidem statuentes ut ordo monasticus (canonicus) … Preterea quascumque possessiones … Sane novalium (laborum) vestrorum … Liceat quoque vobis…".

242 For the circumstances under which these societies received Innocent III's approval, see *supra*, p. 207, note 136; pp. 219-223.

243 "Proinde beatus Dominicus et fratres sui temporis, cum non potuissent obtinere a domino Papa secundum fervorem conceptum novam et arctam regulam, et ab hoc repulsi proposito, elegissent regulam beati Augustini…" (Humbert of Romans, *Expositio super Constitutiones*, p. 3). The view that Dominic sought to have a written programme confirmed is shared by H. C. Scheeben, *Der heilige Dominikus*, p. 16; Id., *Dominikaner oder Innozentianer*, pp. 292-293. For a different view, see M. H. Vicaire, *Fondation… des Prêcheurs*, p. 140, note 1; Id., *Histoire*, vol. II, p. 17.

244 "Unde praecipimus, tam in cathedralibus quam in aliis conventualibus ecclesiis viros idoneos ordinari, quos episcopi possint coadiutores et cooperatores habere, non solum in praedicationis officio, verum etiam in audiendis confessionibus et paenitentiis iniungendis, ac ceteris, quae ad salutem pertinent animarum" (c. *Inter cetera*, 15, X, *de officio iudicis ordinarii*, I, 31, in *Corpus iuris canonici*, vol. II, col. 192; also in Mansi, vol. XXII, col. 998-999).

aid them not only with preaching, but also with the other tasks of the priestly ministry. But these diocesan assistant preachers were required to operate as a clearly distinct group and had to be attached to a cathedral or collegiate church. Dominic also had an interest in can. 13, *De novis religionibus prohibendis*,[245] which prohibited, not the founding of new monasteries or orders, but of new forms of monastic life. Thenceforth no new foundations would be permitted unless they modelled their form of life on already existing institutes and adopted one of the *regulae approbatae* with the corresponding *institutio*.

The texts of the council drew no link between the two canons. The *praedicatores* (can. 10) and the *religiosi* (can. 13) were treated as two separate categories, each with their own statute and task.[246] But the union of the religious life and pastoral ministry through preaching was an urgent matter for Dominic. He and his companions had been engaged as helpers of the bishop of Toulouse, but not as a fellowship attached to any specific church. As itinerant preachers, their activity would extend across the entire diocese. Nor was their religious community life based on any of the traditional monastic rules. This meant that their project failed to meet the requirements of the council in two respects. There can be no doubt that the pope acted in conformity with the decisions of the council and informed Dominic of the conditions which the members of his society would have to meet to qualify for recognition as both *religiosi* and *praedicatores*. According to can. 13 their community life had to be based upon an already existing, approved *regula* and *institutio*. And can. 10 stipulated that their apostolic activity should be carried out from a collegiate church as their base.[247]

After his return to Toulouse, Dominic wasted no time in organising his community according to the directives of the pope and the council. In consultation with his confreres, he expressed a preference for the rule of Saint Augustine, with which he had long been familiar through his profession as a canon regular of Osma.[248] It is not possible to reconstruct precisely and with certainty what

---

245 "Ne nimia religionum diversitas gravem in ecclesiam Dei confusionem inducat, firmiter prohibemus, ne quis de cetero novam religionem inveniat, sed quicunque ad religionem converti voluerit, unam de approbatis assumat. Similiter qui voluerit religiosam domum de novo fundare, regulam et institutionem accipiat de [*religionibus*] approbatis" (c. *Ne nimia*, 9, X, *de religiosis*, III, 26, in *Corpus iuris canonici*, vol. II, col. 607; also in Mansi, vol. XXII, col. 1002).

246 This is sufficiently clear from the sequence of the ordinances. Can. 10-11 belong to the previous series (can. 6-11), which deals with the bishops, their task of government and their helpers. The subject then changes to another estate in the church, the *religiosi* (can. 12-13).

247 "Auditis igitur eis super hac postulatione Romane sedis antistes hortatus est fratrem Dominicum, reverti ad fratres suos et, habita cum eis plena deliberatione, cum unanimi omnium consensu eorum regulam aliquam iam approbatam eligere, *quibus ecclesiam assignaret episcopus*, ac demum, iis exactis, rediret ad papam confirmationem super omnibus accepturus" (Jordan, *Libellus*, no. 41). The italicised words do not belong to the first redaction of the text: see the editor's critical apparatus. But the addition does prove that the corrector (perhaps the author himself) believed even before 1242 that the pope's answer referred to the matter of a church of their own.

248 "Itaque celebrato concilio revertentes, verbo pape fratribus publicato, mox beati Augustini, predicatoris egregii, ipsi futuri predicatores regulam elegerunt" (Jordan, *Libellus*, no. 42). The chapter

text was adopted in 1216, as no manuscript has survived. The earliest Dominican version of the rule was the product of a revision carried out in the middle of the thirteenth century.[249] The text of RA is still preceded there by the first sentence of the *Ordo monasterii*.[250] We may be certain that these words were not added by the revisers but belonged to the text that had been in use in the order from the beginning.[251] It does not follow from this that the Dominicans adopted their *Regula Augustini* directly from the canons, who at the time followed the rules of the OM and belonged to the stricter *ordo novus*. In fact, parts of the Pseudo-Augustinian *ordo* can also be found in Saint-Ruf.[252] The corrected text of the Dominicans otherwise offers no clues as to its provenance. Various textual traditions appear to have been used interchangeably in many places.[253] As it is not

---

of Osma had observed the rule of Saint Augustine since as early as 1136 (M. Alamo, art. *Burgo de Osma*, in DHGE, vol. X, 1938, col. 1267). On the reform of this chapter, see also Jordan, *op. cit.*, nos. 4, 11-13; M. H. Vicaire, *Histoire*, vol. I, pp. 81-112.

249 This correction was made at the behest of the general chapter of 1254: "Committimus magistro ordinis totam ordinationem ecclesiastici officii … et quod corrigat litteram regule" (*Acta capitulorum generalium O.P.*, vol. I, p. 68). It was completed by 1256 (*ibid.*, p. 78). Cf. W. R. Bonniwell, *A History of the Dominican Liturgy*, pp. 83-84. The text of the rule was part of the martyrology: W. R. Bonniwell, *op. cit.*, p. 89. Cf. L. Rousseau, *De ecclesiastico officio Fratrum Praedicatorum secundum ordinationem venerabilis magistri Humberti de Romanis*, in *Anal. O.P.*, vol. XVIII, 1927-1928, pp. 109-110. The text of the rule was published in *Anal. O.P.*, vol. II, 1895-1896, pp. 616-619, preceded by historical elucidations on pp. 610-616. See also A. Walz, *"Magne Pater Augustine". Dominikanisches zur Regel des hl. Augustinus*, in *Angelicum*, vol. XXXI, 1954, pp. 213-231.

250 "Ante omnia, fratres carissimi, diligatur Deus, deinde proximus, quia ista sunt precepta principaliter nobis data". Some manuscripts retained this sentence as an introduction to the *Regula tertia* (RA) even after the stricter rules of the *Regula secunda* (OM) had been abandoned. For the history of the *Ordo monasterii* among the canons of Springiersbach and Prémontré, especially at the beginning of the twelfth century, see *supra*, pp. 192-193.

251 Around the middle of the thirteenth century, the OM had in fact not been in use for a long time. It would not have made sense at that point to insert part of it into the *textus receptus* of the rule of Saint Augustine.

252 The *Consuetudines* of Las Abadesas in Spain still contained excerpts from the *Ordo monasterii* (see *supra*, p. 191), and yet this abbey was affiliated to the Order of Saint-Ruf and did not therefore belong to the communities that observed the OM as rule.

253 The edition by R. Arbesmann – W. Hümpfner, in *Iordani de Saxonia Liber Vitasfratrum* (cf. *supra*, footnote 37), pp. 494-504, diverges in many places from that by D. De Bruyne, in *Revue bénéd.*, vol. XLII, 1930, pp. 318-326. A. Walz, *"Magne Rater Augustine"*, pp. 223-226, gives the variants of the Dominican text alongside those of the two critical editions mentioned. In most cases, the Dominican text is consistent with the manuscripts of the Laon, Vatican, Monte Cassino, Florence, Bamberg group. In some cases, it has the variants of the manuscript of Florence. On the other hand, only the manuscripts of Munich and four Spanish manuscripts contain the sentences "Alia quippe…, ut pereant" and "Quod si aliquis…, condemnetur", which also appear in the Dominican text. There are agreements with only one of the manuscripts indicated in other places. And in more than thirty instances, the diverging version of the Dominican text is unique. Cf. F. Chatillon, *Etiam… (Animadversiones Augustinianae)*, § V: *En marge du Décret de Gratien et des Constitutions de l'ordre des Frères Prêcheurs*, in *Revue du moyen âge latin*, vol. IX, 1953, pp. 307-341. The author draws the following conclusion: "Voilà qui peut inviter, je crois, à prêter désormais plus d'attention au texte dominicain (qui le mérite peut-être encore à d'autres titres)" (p. 341).

clear what criteria were used by the revisers of 1254-1256, it is also impossible to determine how much of the original text they retained.

The obligation imposed upon the new religious foundations by the Lateran Council was not only to adopt a rule, but also the *institutio* of a *religio approbata*. Jordan of Saxony characterised the monastic customs of the first Dominicans as *arctiores consuetudines*.[254] But his text does not indicate whether he meant *consuetudines* in the general sense of monastic customs or in the more technical sense of written rules observed by the monks and canons as additions to the rule.[255] The council of 1215 did not make it obligatory to adopt the legal code of an approved order. Strictly speaking, the *institutio* mentioned in can. 13 required only the monastic order of life, the *vita regularis*, including the exercises and institutions that were part of it by virtue of a centuries-old tradition.[256] But in the *institutio* defined as such, the *consuetudines* were the formal element, the basis and fixed norm upon which the organisation of the community and its members' way of life were founded. Due to can. 13, adopting a series of written *consuetudines* had more or less become a condition for obtaining ecclesiastical approval for any new religious community. There was no better way for such a community to prove that it had truly derived its *institutio* from a *religio approbata* than to adopt the legal code or the written *consuetudines* of an existing monastic community.

The term *arctior* which Jordan uses to further define the *consuetudines* possibly has the same meaning in this context as it had in the ecclesiastical documents concerning the monastic institutions. The expressions *arctior religio* and *arctior vita* became commonplace in the twelfth century during the polemic about the legitimacy of the transfer of religious to another order.[257] In the twelfth century, as a rule, canons regular were not permitted to transfer to an abbey of monks, not even if the abbey in question practiced a stricter observance.[258] But from the

---

254 After mentioning the rule of Augustine, the text continues with: "...quasdam sibi super hec in victu et ieiuniis, in lectis et laneis arctiores consuetudines assumentes" (Jordan, *Libellus*, no. 42).

255 See *supra*, pp. 185-195.

256 The meaning of *institutio* has been correctly defined as follows by M. H. Vicaire: "...l'organisation de la maison religieuse telle qu'elle est garantie pratiquement par le grand Privilège *Religiosam vitam*: noviciat, profession, élection, ordre intérieur, etc. ... (l'*institutio* est fixée communément par la règle: on a l'institution bénédictine ou augustinienne; elle peut être en outre précisée dans telle famille déterminée: on a l'institution de Prémontré ou de Saint-Victor)" (P. Mandonnet – M. H. Vicaire, *Saint Dominique*, vol. I, p. 179, note 58). The following texts could also be mentioned in this context: "pro institutione Ordinis" (*Statuta cap. gen. Ord. Cist.*, vol. I, p. 121); "contra institutionem Ordinis" (p. 186); "possessiones quas institutio vestra non recipit" (*Corpus iuris canonici*, vol. II, col. 597). For the Carthusians, cf. A. De Meyer – J. M. De Smet, *Guigo's Consuetudines van de eerste Kartuizers*, p. 15, note 3.

257 See for instance G. Schreiber, *Kurie und Kloster*, vol. II, pp. 342-346; Ch. Dereine, *L'élaboration du statut canonique des chanoines réguliers, spécialement sous Urbain II*, in RHE, vol. XLVI, 1951, pp. 534-565; M. A. Dimier, *Saint Bernard et le droit en matière de transitus*, in *Revue Mabillon*, vol. XLIII, 1953, pp. 48-82; C. M. Figueras, *De impedimentis admissionis in religionem usque ad Decretum Gratiani* (Scripta et documenta, vol. 9), Montserrat, 1957, pp. 137-162.

258 This view was based upon a bull by Urban II to the canons of Saint-Ruf, issued possibly between 1088 and 1092: "Statuimus etiam ne professionis canonicae quispiam..., vel districtioris religionis obtentu,

second half of the twelfth century onwards, the *transitus* to an officially more observant *institutio* was permitted,[259] even without the express permission of the superiors, and was generally acknowledged as legitimate for monks and canons on the basis of the *privilegium commune*.[260] At the time, certain orders of monks, such as the Cistercians and Carthusians, were regarded as *arctior ordo* or *religio*.[261]

In Jordan's context, the term *arctior* refers not to monastic, but to canonical customs. The stricter practices that were introduced by the Dominicans concerned the sources of revenue of the community, fasting, the dormitory and clothing, that is, the points often used as criteria to distinguish between two categories of communities of canons: the moderate (*ordo antiquus*) and the stricter observance (*ordo novus*).[262] The latter group included the canons of Springiersbach, the Premonstratensians and any institute that had been influenced by them in choosing their regular customs.[263] By adopting the *arctiores consuetudines*, the Dominicans, too, acceded to this stricter movement in the monastic life.

As canons regular of Saint Augustine, the first Dominicans needed to have a church to which, according to their *institutio*, they would be tied by the legal bond of their profession, and in which they would also have to perform the

---

ex eodem claustro audeat, sine abbatis totiusque congregationis permissione, discedere" (quoted by Ch. Dereine, *L'élaboration du statut canonique*, p. 547). This text was disseminated widely and was also included in the *Decretum Gratiani* (c. *Statuimus*, 3, C. XIX, q. 3, in *Corpus iuris canonici*, vol. I, col. 840-841).

259 The transition to the new view is clearly evident in the fact that the traditional formula, "vel arctioris vitae obtentu" was changed into "nisi arctioris vitae obtentu" or something similar. See for instance in letters by Alexander III: "nisi ad arctiorem vitam voluerit transire" (PL, vol. 200, col. 992, 1011); "nisi arctioris vitae obtentu" (*ibid.*, col. 1035, 1104). Cf. PL, vol. 211, col. 369.

260 Under Alexander III's successors, the clause "nisi arctioris vitae obtentu" was similarly inserted frequently into the *privilegia* for monasteries. For Lucius III (1181-1185), see for instance PL, vol. 201, col. 1207, 1212, 1219, 1235, 1258, 1314. The stipulations of canon law at the beginning of the thirteenth century are briefly summarised in c. *Licet quibusdam*, 18, X, *de regularibus*, III, 31 (*Corpus iuris canonici*, vol. II, col. 575-576).

261 G. Schreiber, *Kurie und Kloster*, vol. II, p. 342. In some cases, however, the status of the monks as such already counted as *vita arctior*: "...quod monachis, qui secundum regularem institutionem artiorem ducunt vitam, paenitus inhibitum est, ..." (*Institutio canonicorum* of Aachen (a° 816), c. 115, ed. A. Werminghoff, in MGH, *Legum sectio III: Concilia*, sect. II: *Concilia aevi Karolini*, vol. I, Hanover-Leipzig, 1906, p. 397). The opposition here is between monks and canons. The same identification of *vita arctior* with *ordo monasticus* can be found in Hugh of Rouen, *Dialogorum liber V*, c. 1 (PL, vol. 192, col. 1216). Other authors regarded the eremitical way of life as the *vita arctior* by comparison with the life of the canons regular: "Si qui fratres sub eodem canonico habitu arctiorem vel solitariam vitam ducere optaverint..." (Peter de Honestis, *Regula clericorum*, lib. I, c. 32, in PL, vol. 163, col. 719).

262 See *supra*, pp. 192-194, with footnote 55 on p. 192. The *Consuetudines* of the Premonstratensians, who belonged to the stricter school, prescribed a fast lasting from 14 September until Easter: *Institut. Praem.* of the twelfth century (ed. E. Martène, *De antiquis Ecclesiae ritibus*, vol. III), d. I, c. 6 (p. 326); on food: d. I, c. 13 (p. 327), d. IV, c. 12 (p. 335); on sleep: d. I, c. 14 (p. 327); on clothing (*laneae vestes*): d. IV, c. 14 (p. 335).

263 See *supra*, pp. 194-195.

officium laudis.[264] Moreover, according to can. 10 of the council, having a church of their own was a condition for the exercise of the apostolate to which they had committed themselves the previous year.[265] This church would have to serve as the basis for their activities in the diocese of Toulouse. The cathedral chapter ceded the chapel of Saint Romanus to them in July 1216 with the approval of the bishop.[266] They immediately began to build a house that would be sufficiently large to accommodate ordered communal life.[267] Their installation as Augustinian canons did not impede them from remaining true to their original intention. In their new *institutio*, they attempted, as much as possible, to practice the apostolic poverty which they had included in their 1215 *propositum*. They resolutely rejected the possession of real estate, which was at the time one of the customary ways in which canons regular supported themselves. They retained only the revenues that they had accepted the previous year as *pauperes.*[268]

Having thus made the adjustments necessary to comply with the papal and conciliar requirements, Dominic was ready to go back to Rome. Honorius III, who had in the meantime been elected as Innocent III's successor, gave him three documents, two of which, each with their own focus, contained the approbation of his foundation in Toulouse. The first, *Religiosam vitam*, is dated 22 December 1216.[269] This document bestowed upon the community of Saint Romanus its definitive canonical status, the assurance of the unmolested possession of three churches, the confirmation of a number of fixed sources of revenue, and the customary privileges. As regards the norms for the *vita regularis*, the confirmation limited itself to the minimum. It applied only to the *ordo canonicus*, the canonical

---

264 The *traditio ecclesiae,* the commitment to the monastery church, was a specific element in the way of life of the canons, one expressed in the formula of profession: see *supra*, p. 193, note 234. See also the letter of privilege for the canons regular: "Eapropter… ecclesiam sancti…, in qua divino mancipati estis obsequio, sub beati Petri et nostra protectione suscipimus…" (PL, vol. 176, col. 640). The importance of the church as the centre of the regular life is also highlighted in the documents in which the reform of certain chapters is approved: "…clericorum in Bremensi ecclesia Deo servientium…" (Ch. Dereine, *Vie commune*, p. 368, no. 6); "…coeperunt simul in ecclesiis stare…" (*ibid.*, p. 370, no. 27); "…similiter omnes alii in iam dicta nostra ecclesia adunati fuerint…" (*ibid.*, p. 371, no. 30); "…ut cum fratribus ad ecclesiam communiter vivere posset" (*ibid.*, p. 374, no. 52).

265 See *supra*, pp. 225, 228-229.

266 Laurent, no. 70; Jordan, *Libellus*, no. 44. No community was founded at the other two churches that they were given (Jordan, *op. cit.*, nos. 43-44).

267 "At vero in predicta ecclesia sancti Romani protinus edificatum est claustrum, cellas habens ad studendum et dormiendum satis aptas. Erant autem tunc fratres numero circiter XVI" (Jordan, *Libellus*, no. 44).

268 "Proposuerunt etiam et instituerunt possessiones non habere, ne predicationis impediretur officium sollicitudine terrenorum, sed tantum reditus eis adhuc habere complacuit" (Jordan, *Libellus*, no. 42). *Proponere* and *instituere* obviously are technical terms here to designate the acceptance of a fixed programme of life: see *supra*, pp. 219-223, 228 and 210-211 respectively.

269 The bull was published in facsimile by F. Balme, *Cartulaire de saint Dominique*, vol. II, at p. 78. The text can be found in *Anal. O.P.*, vol. XII, 1915-1916, pp. 262-264. The edition by Laurent, no. 74, contains significant printing errors. For the legal significance of this *privilegium*, see *supra*, pp. 227-228.

way of life, based on the rule of Saint Augustine.[270] The absence of the *institutio*, which in such bulls usually followed immediately after the rule, is remarkable but not entirely exceptional.[271]

The commission to preach, which was not mentioned in this document, was confirmed by the pope in the brief *Gratiarum omnium* of 21 January 1217.[272] As regards its form, this charter belongs to the category of the lesser bulls, more specifically to the *mandamenta*, which were normally used for the administrative correspondence of the Holy See.[273] Its content affirmed the apostolic mission which had been recognised by the bishop of Toulouse the previous year. In the address, Dominic and his companions were officially given the title *praedicatores*,[274] and in the corpus they were entrusted with the preaching of the gospel as their proper task.[275] Compared to other examples of this genre, the *narratio* is extensive, consisting of a series of passages from the Bible that all exhort to perseverance and arduous combat against the enemies of the faith. One has the impression that the papal chancery, which still lacked a fixed repertoire of stylistic forms for such charges, quoted the most appropriate scriptural passages for the occasion. The content of the *mandamentum* only applies to Dominic's and his companions' apostolic activity. There are no details whatsoever concerning their evangelical way of life or the observance of poverty which they had included in their *propositum* in 1215.

---

270 "In primis siquidem statuentes ut ordo canonicus, qui secundum Deum et beati Augustini regulam in eadem ecclesia institutus esse dignoscitur, perpetuis ibidem temporibus inviolabiliter observetur".

271 Bulls for chapters attached to churches often mentioned no *institutio* after the *regula beati Augustini*: PL, vol. 214, col. 959; vol. 215, col. 885, 1430; vol. 216, col. 381. Similarly, for Benedictine abbeys the *regula beati Benedicti* appears without *institutio*: PL, vol. 214, col. 152; vol. 215, col. 194, 590, 1460, 1515; vol. 217, col. 41, 126, 182.

272 Laurent, no. 77.

273 For this type of bull (lesser bulls and *litterae*), see for instance A. Giry, *Manuel de diplomatique*, Paris, 1894, pp. 688-691. The name *mandamentum* derived from the frequently found formula "per apostolica vobis scripta mandamus…" or similar words.

274 The address is: "Honorius…, priori et fratribus sancti Romani, predicatoribus in partibus Tolosanis…". Little credence was long given to Thomas of Cantimpré's story about the circumstances under which Honorius III agreed to substitute *predicatoribus* for the word *predicantibus*, which originally appeared in the document: see Thomas of Cantimpré, *Miraculorum et exemplorum memorabilium sui temporis libri duo*, lib. I, c. 9, ed. G. Colvenerius, Douai, 1605, p. 36; Stephen of Salagnac, *De quatuor in quibus Deus Praedicatorum Ordinem insignivit*, pp. 13-19. A recent palaeographical study of the original of this bull and of its transcript in the registers of the papal chancery confirms the reliability of the medieval story: see Vl. J. Koudelka, *Notes sur le cartulaire de S. Dominique*, pp. 93-100.

275 "…caritatem vestram rogamus et hortamur attente, per apostolica vobis scripta mandantes et in remissionem peccatorum iniungentes, quatenus magis ac magis in Domino confortati, evangelizare verbum Dei studeatis, opportune importune instantes, et opus evangeliste laudabiliter adimplentes" (Laurent, no. 77).

§ 3. The spread of the order and the genesis of its first constitutions

Having received their canonical mission from the bishop of Toulouse and from the pope, the members of the apostolic community attached to Saint Romanus's church in Toulouse were prevented from immediately engaging in intensive and fruitful ministry due to the tense political situation. Count Raymond VI, who had been excommunicated and whose feudal rights had been declared forfeit in 1211 due to his sympathy for the heretics, had used his exile in Aragon to raise an army and prepare for the reconquest of his lands. Thanks to the support of his adherents in the city, he met with little resistance when he entered Toulouse on 13 September 1217. Simon de Montfort, who returned in quick march from the far side of the Rhone, vainly attempted to relieve the city and perished during the siege.[276]

Dominic must have been able to observe the growing resistance against his protector Count Simon de Montfort as soon as he returned from Rome in the spring of 1217. He announced his plan, which he had possibly been considering for months, during the tumultuous weeks that preceded the decisive battle for Toulouse: he decided to disperse the members of his community.[277] He sent four of his religious to Madrid.[278] Two groups, one of four and one of three friars, were told to go to Paris.[279] Before long this resulted in a series of new foundations in different countries. In the four years between 1217 and 1221, the year of Dominic's death, a further ten houses were established in France, two in Spain, eight in Italy, two in the German lands, and one in Hungary.[280]

The transformation of the community of canons in Toulouse into an apostolic order bears the marks of the systematic execution of a premeditated plan rather than of flight before imminent danger, or branching out due to overpopulation.[281]

---

276 Cf. Jordan, *Libellus*, no. 46; M. H. Vicaire, *Histoire*, vol. II, pp. 86-88.

277 "Et invocato sancto Spiritu convocatisque fratribus dixit hoc esse sui cordis propositum, ut omnes licet paucos per mundum transmitteret, nec iam ibi diutius insimul habitarent. Admirati sunt omnes tam subite dispositionis prolatam ab eo sententiam; sed quoniam animabat eos evidens in ipso sanctitatis auctoritas, acquievere facilius ad bonum hec omnia finem proventura sperantes" (Jordan, *Libellus*, no. 47). This text shows that the decision was unexpected. The later hagiographers, after Jordan of Saxony, linked the dispersal of the friars to a vision that Dominic had had during his sojourn in Rome, in the winter of 1216-1217: see Constantinus of Orvieto, *Legenda*, no. 25. A less fanciful explanation of the motives that might have convinced Dominic in Rome to disperse his religious and go to Northern Europe as a missionary himself can be found in M. H. Vicaire, *Histoire*, vol. II, pp. 75-86.

278 Jordan, *Libellus*, no. 49.

279 Jordan, *Libellus*, nos. 51-53.

280 Details on the new foundations can be found in Jordan, *Libellus*, nos. 54-59. More ample overviews, based on critical study of sources and literature on the origins of the various houses, are provided by H. C. Scheeben, *Der heilige Dominikus*, pp. 349-363; M. H. Vicaire, *Histoire*, vol. II, pp. 309-314.

281 The decisiveness with which Dominic carried out his plan is further emphasised by John of Spain, who himself was sent to Paris: "Item dixit, quod cum esset cum dicto fratre Dominico apud Tholosam in conventu ecclesie supradicte, ipse frater Dominicus contra voluntatem comitis Montisfortis et archiepiscopi Narbonensis et episcopi Tholosani et quorumdam aliorum prelatorum misit hunc

The designation of places for foundations was not a matter of chance, but the result of a reasoned choice. The first houses were founded in important population centres, preferably university cities, such as Paris, Bologna and Oxford; cities that were suitable terrain for study and the cure of souls, as well as for the recruitment of new members.[282] It is evident that this plan was executed very purposefully, because the founders were often already in possession of papal letters of recommendation, which facilitated their introduction to the population and the spiritual authorities of the places selected for a new foundation.[283]

Some elements of the canonical community in Toulouse were accentuated more clearly during the expansion of the order while other elements were marginalised. From the start, preaching and poverty were regarded and imposed as essential obligations. In the many letters of recommendation, the full emphasis is on the Dominicans' apostolic charge and their evangelical way of life, but there is scarcely a reference to their status of canons regular. As early as 1218, Dominic's community, with the pope's permission, received its own name of *ordo praedicatorum*,[284] an expression used in the ecclesiastical literature of the preceding centuries to designate a variety of diverse groups and estates that had, since the beginning of the history of salvation, exercised the *officium praedicationis*.[285] In ever more precise terms, preaching and the other forms of priestly pastoral ministry were regarded as the specific mission that the Dominicans had accepted

---

testem, quamvis invitum, Parisius cum quinque fratribus clericis et uno converso, ut studerent et predicarent et conventum ibi facerent..." (*Proc. Bon.,* no. 26).

282 After Paris, in 1217 (see *supra*, p. 235), came Bologna, in the spring of 1218 (Jordan, *Libellus*, no. 55). The first group of friars sent to England by the general chapter of 1221 established itself in Oxford (*ibid.*, no. 88; W. A. Hinnebusch, *The Early English Friars Preachers*, pp. 1-4).

283 The friars sent to Paris were in possession of a letter by the pope: "Ii, inquam, sunt destinati Parisius cum litteris summi Pontificis, ut ordinem publicarent" (Jordan, *Libellus*, no. 51). The first letter whose content has been fully preserved dates from 11 February 1218 (Laurent, no. 84). Over the following three years, a further thirty such letters of recommendation were issued (Laurent, *passim*; M. H. Vicaire, *Histoire*, vol. II, pp. 374-375). The text *Quoniam abundavit iniquitas* was included in the formulary of the papal chancery: M. Tangl, *Die päpstlichen Kanzleiordnungen*, pp. 285-286, no. LXVII.

284 The letter of recommendation of 11 February 1218 (see previous footnote) is the oldest document to contain *ordo praedicatorum* as the name of Dominic's religious community: "...quatinus fratres ordinis Predicatorum, quorum utile ministerium et religionem credimus Deo gratam, ... habeatis pro nostra et apostolice sedis reverentia commendatos...". According to Jordan of Saxony, it was Dominic's intention to have his society of preachers approved as early as 1215 as an *ordo praedicatorum*: see *supra*, p. 227, note 238. It is not certain, however, that this expression was already in use in 1215. Perhaps Jordan simply projected the later technical term, which had long been commonplace at the time that he wrote his *Libellus* in 1233, back onto the society that had just been founded in 1215.

285 On the meaning and usage of *ordo praedicatorum* in the works of the church fathers and in the Middle Ages, especially in Joachim of Fiore, see R. Ladner, L'Ordo Praedicatorum *avant l'ordre des Prêcheurs*, in P. Mandonnet – M. H. Vicaire, *Saint Dominique*, vol. II, especially pp. 49-68. The expression can be found in Gregory the Great, who used it for the various groups of preachers of the faith in the New Testament. In conformity with the medieval mentality, some Dominican authors saw in the *ordo praedicatorum* a prefiguration and even a prophecy of their own order: cf. M. H. Vicaire, *Histoire*, vol. II, pp. 8-13.

by their vocation to and profession in the order.[286] The older annals mention the achievements in the field of the apostolate with satisfaction.[287]

The guidelines issued in 1215 in respect of poverty were not subsequently abandoned. On the occasion of the first departure on mission of his friars, Dominic desired that the precept of begging should be assiduously observed. The friars sent out for a new foundation had to travel like poor people, on foot, without money for the journey and without any excess supplies.[288] Their poverty was the title upon which they must seek the support of the people, according to the papal letters of recommendation.[289] Dominic was vigilant to ensure that the soberness of their external way of life should be visible. He even occasionally intervened personally, for instance in the building of the house in Bologna.[290] Under no circumstances would he accept that the economy of a house should be based upon the possession of real estate.[291] The fixed income that had initially been allowed and the lands that had already been accepted were finally rejected in 1220 and ceded to other religious institutes or exchanged for churches.[292]

---

286 The commission to preach is successively described as an "utile ministerium" (letter of 11 February 1218: Laurent, no. 84), an "officium predicandi ad quod deputati sunt" (letter of 8 December 1219: Laurent, no. 103), an "officium predicandi, ad quod sunt ex professione sui ordinis deputati" (letter of 18 January 1221: Laurent, no. 127). For the evolution of the terminology, see M. H. Vicaire, *Histoire*, vol. II, pp. 372-382.

287 One of the first members of the community in Toulouse, Thomas, later became a talented preacher (Jordan, *Libellus*, no. 38). The bishop of Toulouse looked favourably on the work of the first Dominicans (*ibid.*, no. 39). On Reginald's activity in Bologna and Paris, see *ibid.*, nos. 58, 63, 69. On Henry of Cologne, see *ibid.*, no. 79. Bonivisus testified that Dominic sent him to Piacenza to preach, even though he believed he was not sufficiently prepared: "Et ipse testis obediens ivit Placentiam et predicavit ibi. Et tantam gratiam contulit sibi Deus in predicatione, quod ad predicationem eius tres fratres intraverunt ordinem predicatorum" (*Proc. Bon.*, no. 24).

288 *Proc. Bon.*, no. 26; see also no. 38. It is evident that Dominic issued such guidelines as early as 1217 from his attitude to John of Navarra, whom he gave travel money only after refusing it first for a long time: see Stephen of Salagnac, *De quatuor in quibus Deus Praedicatorum Ordinem insignivit*, p. 155.

289 "…habeatis pro nostra et apostolice sedis reverentia commendatos, in suis eis necessitatibus assistentes, qui verbum Domini gratis et fideliter proponentes, intendentes profectibus animarum, ipsum Dominum solum secuti, paupertatis titulum pretulerunt" (Laurent, no. 84, see also nos. 87, 97); "…in abiectione voluntarie paupertatis eunt" (*ibid.*, no. 103; see also nos. 112, 127). For the practice of mendicant poverty, see for instance the testimony by John of Navarra (*Proc. Bon.*, no. 26), Stephen of Spain (*ibid.*, no. 38), Paul of Venice (*ibid.*, no. 42), Frugerius of Penna (*ibid.*, no. 47).

290 He ordered the works to be stopped because the cells were too spacious: *Proc. Bon.*, no. 38; cf. nos. 17, 32, 42, 47.

291 Dominic refused an important donation in Bologna, and he destroyed the deed (*Proc. Bon.*, no. 32).

292 According to John of Spain, the Dominicans in Paris and in the area around Toulouse and Albi received "multas possessiones et reditus" (*Proc. Bon.*, no. 26; Laurent, no. 92). In Madrid, they were the recipients of an estate (*ibid.*, no. 95). For an explanation of the motives for accepting donations in certain areas, see H. C. Lambermond, *Der Armutsgedanke des hl. Dominikus*, pp. 10-15. The canons regular had been obliged by the synods of 1212 and 1214 to take what they needed on their journey, particularly in the area of Paris and Rouen, where begging by the clergy was regarded as an "opprobrium Domini et ordinis": see Mansi, vol. XXII, col. 828 and 908 respectively. All such possessions were rejected by the general chapter of 1220: "Tunc etiam ordinatum est, ne possessiones vel reditus tenerent fratres nostri, sed et iis renuntiarent, quos habuerant in partibus

Despite their geographical spread, the houses were never independent of each other as autonomous monasteries, but together they formed an organic whole under a centralised government initially consisting of Dominic alone. He personally took the initiative for various foundations by choosing their location and sending suitable people; some owe their origins and continued existence to him.[293] He obtained the required letters of recommendation from the pope for many houses[294] and travelled repeatedly to Rome to defend the interests of his foundations.[295] The last part of his life, from 1217 to 1221, was one uninterrupted visitation journey through France, Spain and Italy.[296] When travelling, he continued to exercise the higher government both of the houses and of the individual members of the order, who had made a commitment to him personally at their profession.[297]

The central place that Dominic occupied is confirmed by the successive titles he held; titles which changed as the order expanded. From 1215 onwards, he acted as the superior of the Toulouse community, and from late 1216 to March 1217 he was called *prior Sancti Romani*.[298] The title *prior ordinis praedicatorum* appears several times in documents from 1219.[299] His role as general superior was eventually expressed clearly in the title *magister ordinis praedicatorum*, which came into use in 1221 and remained the customary title.[300] Dominic's legal position was

---

Tholosanis" (Jordan, *Libellus*, no. 86). This ordinance was also implemented in practice: "Et date fuerunt possessiones de Francia monialibus ordinis Cisterciensium et aliae aliis" (*Proc. Bon.*, no. 26; see also Laurent, no. 111, 114).

293 For the establishment of the houses in Paris and Madrid, see *supra*, p. 235. For Bologna, see Jordan, *Libellus*, nos. 49, 55, 58, 60. For the foundations in Madrid and Segovia, see *ibid.*, no. 59. The establishment of the friars in Rome, first at Saint Sixtus, later at Saint Sabina, similarly occurred under his supervision: H. C. Scheeben, *Der heilige Dominikus*, pp. 278-289; Vl. J. Koudelka, *Le "monasterium Tempuli" et la fondation dominicaine de San Sisto*, in *Arch. F.P.*, vol. XXXI, 1961, pp. 48-53. On Dominic's sense of purpose in choosing friars for the various houses, see Jordan, *Libellus*, no. 62.

294 For Dominic's role, see M. H. Vicaire, *Histoire*, vol. II, p. 272.

295 During Dominic's stay at the papal curia in Viterbo, from the autumn of 1219 to early 1220, Honorius III intervened twice in favour of the Dominicans in Paris: see Laurent, nos. 99, 101. The letter of 29 July 1220 is concerned with the same subject: see *ibid.*, no. 117. Cf. H. C. Scheeben, *Der heilige Dominikus*, pp. 285-289; M. H. Vicaire, *Histoire*, vol. II, pp. 138-141, 177-178.

296 For Dominic's itinerary see A. Walz, *Compendium historiae Ordinis Praedicatorum*, pp. 8-9; M. H. Vicaire, *Saint Dominique de Caleruega d'après les documents du XIIIᵉ siècle*, pp. 309-310.

297 No reference can be found after 1216 to a Dominican profession that includes the commitment to canonical *stabilitas*. Dominic accepted several candidates through a *professio manualis*, a rite that perhaps bore many similarities to the *oblatio* of the first members of the order: see *supra*, p. 224, with footnote 226; pp. 225-226, with footnotes 234-235.

298 Laurent, nos. 71-74, 79-80.

299 Laurent, nos. 103 (letter of 8 December 1219), 105 (17 February 1220), 113 (12 May 1220), 119 (8 December 1220), 132 (29 March 1221), 145 (24 May 1221).

300 "Honorius ... magistro et fratribus ordinis Predicatorum..." (letter by Honorius III, 28 April 1221; Laurent, no. 138); "...vice ac nomine fratris D., magistri totius ordinis..." (letter by Cardinal Hugolin, 13 June 1221: *ibid.*, no. 151). The titles *magister praedicatorum* and *magister praedicationis*, which Dominic held even beforehand (in charters dated July 1216 and 28 April 1221 respectively: *ibid.*, no. 70 and 134 respectively) derived from the title *magister*, which was bestowed on the leaders of

also highlighted by the witnesses at his canonisation process. They testified that the authority of the founder included complete executive power, subject only to the pope's supervision.[301] He used his powers repeatedly to ensure that certain rules were included in the constitutions.[302]

From 1220, the expansion of the legislation was entrusted to the general chapter. It is possible that Dominic personally appointed the participants of the first assembly, held in Bologna.[303] But his position as the highest legislator within the order came to an end at this chapter. He freely abdicated his personal prerogatives and transferred full executive power to a college composed of *diffinitores*, whose decisions were binding for the entire order. These decisions would constitute the first *constitutiones* or collective laws on the organisation and government of the order.[304] Jordan lists a number of these ordinances, but also says that many more were issued.[305] This is how the fundamental principles of Dominican legislation were fixed, although the modalities would be determined later. As early as 1220,

---

the mission to the Albigensians, in which Dominic had participated in 1206-1208: *Hystoria Albigensis*, nos. 51, 101, 155. On the course of this mission, see *supra*, pp. 216-219. In the twelfth century, itinerant preachers such as Robert of Arbrissel (*Vita*, in PL, vol. 162, col. 1052), Norbert of Xanten (*Vita*, c. 8, ed. R. Wilmans, in MGH, *Scriptores*, vol. XII, Leipzig, 1925, p. 678; c. 14, p. 686) and Bernard of Thiron (*Vita*, in PL, vol. 172, col. 1405, 1406) were also called *magister*. The title *magister* had similarly replaced that of *prior* or *abbas* in certain monastic orders: see *Vetera Hyreevallis statuta*, ed. C. L. Hugo, *Sacrae antiquitatis monumenta*, vol. I, p. 136 and also, *passim*; *Regulae Ordinis Sempringensis*, ed. L. Holstenius – M. Brockie, *Codex regularum*, vol. II, pp. 468-469, 471 and also, *passim*; L. Le Grand, *Statuts d'hôtels-Dieu*, pp. 36, 37, 44, 193. *Magister* was also the title of persons who exercised certain functions in the monastery or who were charged with overseeing certain groups of religious: *magister novitiorum, m. puerorum, m. grangiae* (*Usus conversorum*, c. 6, ed. J. A. Lefèvre, in *Collectanea Ord. Cist. Ref.*, vol. XVII, 1955, p. 91; *Statuta cap. gen. Ord. Cist.*, vol. I, pp. 149, 261). The title *magister* that Dominic already held when he was the leader of his group of preachers appears to have gradually replaced his legal title of *prior* (*S. Romani* or *ordinis*), which he had held as the head of his canonical religious community: for references see footnotes 298 and 299). The transition appears to have taken place in early 1221. The title *magister ordinis* was perhaps officially adopted by the general chapter of 1221: cf. P. Mandonnet – M. H. Vicaire, *Saint Dominique*, vol. II, p. 226, note 63; M. H. Vicaire, *Histoire*, vol. II, p. 122, note 90, p. 302, note 5. Given the evolution of the use of the term *magister* as a title for Dominic, it is not likely that the title *magister ordinis* was derived directly from a military order, as was suggested by H. C. Scheeben, *Der heilige Dominikus*, p. 376; Id., *Die Konstitutionen des Prediger Ordens unter Jordan von Sachsen*, p. 37.

301 *Proc. Bon.*, no. 2.

302 *Proc. Bon.*, nos. 37, 38, 41, 42, 47.

303 "Anno domini MCCXX primum capitulum generale huius ordinis Bononie celebratum est, cui ipse ego interfui, missus de Parisius cum tribus fratribus, eo quod magister Dominicus mandasset per literas suas, quatuor fratres de eadem domo Parisiensi ad Bononiense capitulum sibi mitti" (Jordan, *Libellus*, no. 86).

304 "Et tunc placuit ipsi fratri beato Dominico, quod diffinitores constituerentur in capitulo, qui haberent plenam potestatem super totum ordinem et super ipso magistro et ipsis diffinitoribus, scilicet diffiniendi, ordinandi, statuendi et puniendi, salva reverentia magistrali" (*Proc. Bon.*, no. 2).

305 "In eodem capitulo de communi fratrum consensu statutum est, generale capitulum uno anno Bononie, altero vero Parisius celebrari, ... Tunc etiam ordinatum est, ne possessiones vel reditus de cetero tenerent fratres nostri, ... Alia quoque plura ibi constituta sunt, que usque hodie observantur" (Jordan, *Libellus*, no. 87). The use of the three typical terms *statuere, ordinare* and *constituere* is

the general chapter was constituted as the body competent to lead the order, through *statuta* or *constitutiones*. Later, these terms referred not to transitory measures, but to the major stipulations which, together with the *consuetudines*, were to form the order's own legal code.[306]

The Dominican Order originated in a period in which the older religious orders, especially of monks and canons regular, had maintained their position through their numbers and influence, while the desire for new forms of religious associational life had yielded its first results in the form of the approval of several apostolic societies at the beginning of the thirteenth century. Even while working for his new foundation, Dominic was legally still a member of the chapter of Osma, where he had lived the canonical life for five years. And yet there is no indication that he wanted his foundation in Toulouse in 1215 to be a community of canons regular. His society of diocesan preachers had many traits in common with the group of papal missionaries to the Albigensians and with the evangelical fraternities which Innocent III had approved. The reorganisation of the foundation as a society of Augustinian canons according to the wishes of the Fourth Lateran Council never impeded its apostolic orientation. From the very start, the Dominicans had received a canonical mission to preach. Many papal letters of recommendation confirmed the evangelical poverty that they had included in their *propositum* in 1215, and they applied it radically by renouncing all landed property and fixed revenues.

Conclusion

The foregoing overview has discussed various forms of legislation for religious institutes. Among the oldest written texts are the *regulae* attributed to authoritative monastic founders and always upheld and observed as inviolable regulations. The other texts can be divided into three categories, each with their own origin and characteristics. The *consuetudines* are the written record of the ancient customs that supplemented the rule in communities of monks and canons regular. In some cases, they contain nothing more than an account or concrete description of daily life and of the periodically recurring liturgical ceremonies and communal

---

striking. They were normally used for such legal ordinances. See also the previous footnote and *supra*, pp. 207-208 and 211-212.

306 The term *statuere* is relatively infrequent in the *Acta capitulorum generalium O.P.*, as the Dominicans used a specific terminology (*inchoamus, approbamus, confirmamus*) depending on whether the stipulation in question was being approved for the first, second, or third time (see *Acta C.G.*, vol. I, pp. 7-8, 10-11; also, *passim*). Five ordinances by the general chapter of 1239 begin with *statuimus* (*ibid.*, p. 11). The *Acta* used the singular *constitutio* for one specific ordinance, while the plural *constitutiones* also appears as the collective term for the legal code as a whole. See for example in the reports of 1236: "Ubi dicitur in constitutionibus: itinerantes tamen bis possunt refici, addatur..." (*ibid.*, p. 6). "In constitutionibus, ubi dicitur ... Confirmamus hanc constitutionem..." (*ibid.*, p. 7).

exercises. In due course, this customary law itself required supplementation and correction, and *statuta* provided this. They were issued by a single superior, or by various authorities in conjunction with each other, or by a fixed governing body, and sometimes submitted to the pope for approval. Some only contained measures on certain specific points. Others were more extensive and continued to exist as collections in their own right or were inserted into the *consuetudines*. Finally, other *statuta* again developed into separate legal codes. Outside the strictly monastic sphere, brief regulations emerged for societies that sprang from the religious movement of the twelfth century and were confirmed by Pope Innocent III at the beginning of the thirteenth. The *propositum conversationis* of these small societies usually consisted only of a number of rules for the spiritual life and apostolic activities of their members.

It was to be expected that the Dominicans, who were frequently exposed to the way of life, organisation and activity of other monastic and apostolic communities, would benefit from the experience of older and contemporaneous religious institutes when it came to their legislation. The details contained in charters and literary sources are not always extensive or precise, but they are clear enough to justify the conclusion that the various forms of legislation discussed above found their way into the Dominican legislation. As diocesan preachers in the diocese of Toulouse, the first Dominicans observed the evangelical guidelines practiced by the papal missionaries in Southern France, the Waldensian converts and the Franciscans. The charter in which Bishop Fulk described their apostolic mission and activity can be regarded as the original core of their *propositum*. In accordance with the rules of the Fourth Lateran Council, they gave their priestly community at Saint Romanus's church a monastic statute that was based on the rule of Augustine and on *consuetudines* belonging to the stricter tendency within the canonical world. The expansion of the order from 1217 onwards heralded the beginning of the third phase of the legislation, with the development of the order's own constitutions. These consisted initially of the ordinances of the founder, but from 1220 onwards, they were exclusively supplemented and further adapted by the *statuta* of the annual general chapters.

This introductory survey, based on the legal documents and on external literary sources, has already led to a number of preliminary conclusions on the origins, dependence and contents of the earliest Dominican legislation. In the following chapters, the results of this research will be further specified and supplemented by a study of the text of the constitutions itself.

CHAPTER II

The text

Any study of medieval monastic legislation is likely to be confronted at the outset with text-critical problems due to a lack of adequate source material. Immediate witnesses to the original legislation are scarce for most orders. The earliest manuscripts were often corrected and supplemented by new stipulations that were written between the lines or in the margins. The costliness of the materials meant that codices were used for as long as possible. But if the legislation had been adapted very extensively, the codices could no longer be used. Some remained in circulation as palimpsests, others were torn apart to serve as binding for new manuscripts, others again disappeared without a trace. The original written testimonies to the laws and customs of many monastic institutes were lost in this way. In many cases, we have to rely for knowledge of the *consuetudines* on later copies and seventeenth- and eighteenth-century editions, which are not always very safe from a text-critical point of view. In very rare cases, medieval manuscripts were handed down to the present day fully intact, discovered through happenstance or through the persevering sleuth work of researchers.

A similar text-critical problem exists in relation to the earliest constitutions of the Dominicans. The oldest manuscript, which was copied at the beginning of the fourteenth century, does not contain the full text, nor does it have the correct version of the text. The current chapter will contrive to reconstruct the earliest legislation of the order using other documents that contain at least parts of the same text. The first section will address the study of the various legal codes of Dominican origin that can be regarded as witnesses to the earliest text. The second section will attempt to further determine the value and authority of the various witnesses and to formulate the principles that must guide the reconstruction of the earliest text.

Section I. The various witnesses to the text

The Dominicans never ceased to add to and adapt their earliest legislation from the very start. And yet there are many parts that remained unchanged throughout the thirteenth and later centuries. Moreover, the text was partially preserved outside the order, in legal codes based on the Dominican constitutions. An analysis of these will demonstrate the extent to which certain parts of the original text were adapted and changed, whereas other parts escaped all editing. The main witness, the Rodez manuscript, the only one intended to present the legislation of the Dominicans in its earliest form, will be examined first. Later redactions, for instance by Raymond of Peñafort (1241) and Humbert of Romans (1256), will be discussed subsequently. The enquiry will then look at the legislation of the Dominican Sisters as it is contained in the legal codes of the German Penitent Sisters. Testimony derived from the Friars of the Penitence of Jesus Christ will also be considered, as they adopted the text of their constitutions from the Dominicans around 1250. Finally, the reports of the general chapters will be discussed.

§ 1. The earliest constitutions according to the Rodez manuscript

The only known medieval manuscript that contains the text of the earliest Dominican constitutions dates from the early fourteenth century. It is part of a collection of legal documents usually called the *Codex Ruthenensis miscellaneus* in the literature, after its place of origin, the priory of Rodez in the south of France.[1] The text of the constitutions fills some twenty folios in this collection (28^r-47^r), paginated in modern script as pages 55 to 93. It was copied, perhaps by a French copyist, in a semi-italic Gothic script that does not appear again in other parts of the codex.[2] There are normally thirty lines per page (22.3 cm by 16 cm), with an outside margin wider than the inside margin. The heading *Constitutiones antique ordinis fratrum predicatorum* is written out in full on the first page. The first two words of this title appear further down on the left-hand page, the last three on the right-hand page. The chapter titles are written in red ink and the chapters begin with a larger decorated capital letter set partially into the margin.

The text of the constitutions proper is preceded by a brief introduction (pp. 55-56) which lists the main decisions of the general chapter of Paris in 1228.[3] This is followed by a *prologus* (pp. 56-57) containing a number of comments on the usefulness of written legislation, the spirit and general division of the constitutions, and finally a summary table of the contents of the first part. The body of the text consists of two *distinctiones*, subdivided into chapters of lengths ranging between a few lines (e.g., dist. I, ch. 18) and two full pages (e.g., dist. I, ch. 21). The first *distinctio* (pp. 57-74) has twenty-five chapters and deals with the horarium including the office in choir, meals, monastic observances, the admission of novices, the novitiate and profession, and finally faults and penalties. It regulates life within the houses according to the traditional customs. The second *distinctio* (pp. 74-93) in its thirty-seven chapters describes the interconventual

---

1 The codex is currently in the General Archives of the Dominicans in Rome (Cod. XIV A 4). It was analysed and described by D. Planzer, *De codice Ruthenensi miscellaneo in tabulario Ordinis Praedicatorum asservato*, in *Arch. F.P.*, vol. V, 1935, pp. 5-123. The manuscript containing the text of the constitutions will hereinafter be referred to as C (= *Constitutiones antiquae*).

2 D. Planzer, *art. cit.*, p. 10.

3 On this, see also pp. 403-405. Cf. H. C. Scheeben, *Die Konstitutionen des Predigerordens unter Jordan von Sachsen*, pp. 39-46.

organisation, government and activities of the order. The manner in which the rules are formulated presupposes the existence of an extensive community with a considerable number of members and priories that are juridically connected to each other and are geographically organised into provinces. The text contains rules on the powers and tasks of the superiors, on election to various offices, on study and the apostolate. This is ultimately followed by a *Regula conversorum* with specific rules for lay brothers.

In a lengthy title added to the top and bottom of the first page, the copyist further described the *Constitutiones antiquae* as the law that was in force during the generalate of Jordan of Saxony; in the strict sense, this would mean from 1222 to 1237.[4] The absence of a logical sequence in the arrangement of certain sentences and chapters,[5] the presence of a series of *extravagantes* at the end of the second *distinctio*[6] and the arrangement and division of the text allow us to identify the content of the manuscript as the constitutions in their first form, before their revision by Raymond of Peñafort (1238-1241).[7] However, the chronological *termini* indicated must not be taken too precisely. The copyist used vague expressions, perhaps intentionally so. With regard to the *terminus a quo* (1220), he does not say explicitly that the constitutions were only compiled then, but that they existed and were valid in that year. The *terminus ante quem* (1237) must perhaps be taken more strictly, as the history of the old legislation was practically complete by 1236. However, the text continued to be valid until the official approbation of Raymond's redaction in 1241. But as it happens, the constitutions were not subject to any further changes between 1236 and 1251, at least as far as we can tell from the acts of the general chapters. Only in 1241 were six new stipulations approved, one of which was included in the manuscript.[8]

The Rodez manuscript is therefore a key document when studying the primitive legislation of the Dominicans, to which it is currently the earliest direct witness. But it cannot be regarded as a perfect instantiation of the earliest constitutions. It is not, after all, a thirteenth-century original, but a copy that was only completed in the following century. Its value and authority depend on the

---

4 "Iste sunt constitutiones prime ordinis fratrum predicatorum, que erant tempore magistri Iordanis, beati Dominici immediate successoris, ex quibus formavit et ordinavit constitutiones alias, que nunc habentur, frater Raymundus de Pennaforti, magister ordinis tertius" (p. 55). The text can be found in larger and thicker letters in the upper right corner of the page and, in smaller characters, in the lower margin. The expressions used prove that the compiler or copyist was already relatively far removed from the earliest years of the order, as he considered it necessary to identify the masters general mentioned. The vague indication of the period in which the old constitutions were in use also points in the same direction: "que erant tempore magistri Iordanis".

5 See *infra*, pp. 372-373.

6 In the manuscript on pp. 91-92, after the chapter *De edificiis* (dist. II, cap. 35). Cf. H. C. Scheeben, *Die Konstitutionen*, pp. 79-80.

7 On this, see also pp. 246-249.

8 *Acta C.G.*, p. 18: "Fratres nostri laici quingenta *Pater noster* dicant"; in the manuscript: "...laici quingenta *Pater noster*..." (d. II, c. 22, *De anniversariis*, p. 85; cf. H. C. Scheeben, *Die Konstitutionen*, p. 75).

accuracy with which the copyist worked and also on the value of the example he used. Its defects include not just almost inevitable transcription errors,[9] but also other inaccuracies that were perhaps already present in the model used. The additional rules placed at the end of the second *distinctio* as *extravagantes* apparently do not belong there and would be better off transferred to the individual chapters with which they are concerned.[10] Of the many new stipulations approved by the general chapter of 1236, ten were omitted.[11] Such details demonstrate sufficiently that the Rodez manuscript does not in all respects give a faithful and complete picture of the constitutions during the generalate of Jordan of Saxony. If it is to serve as the basis for a critical edition of the text, it will have to be compared with other related documents and, wherever necessary, be corrected and completed. This is why we will now examine the later text of the Dominican constitutions, specifically the redactions by Raymond of Peñafort and Humbert of Romans.

§ 2. The constitutions of Raymond of Peñafort and Humbert of Romans

Medieval and modern historians have unanimously ascribed the new *ordinatio* of the Dominican constitutions approved by the general chapter of 1241[12] to Raymond of Peñafort, the third master general (1238-1240).[13] The many corrections and additions had not only marred the original text of the constitutions, but also rendered it burdensome to use as a legal code. Raymond was perhaps charged with the task of revising the text by the general chapter of 1238, which elected him general. This authoritative canonist, who had been a professor at the university

---

9 I do not mean the variants (see the edition of the text in Appendix I, *passim*), but writing errors or mistakes in the strict sense of the term: see for instance d. I, c. 21, line 19: *in* instead of *unde*; d. I, c. 23, l. 53: *habeatur* instead of *frater*; d. II, c. 17, l. 6: *loca suadentibus* instead of *loca sua tenentibus*.

10 They were probably already placed there in the thirteenth-century copy by the monastic copyist, who found no room for them in the relevant chapters when recording the additions to the constitutions, or who added all the new stipulations at the end for reasons of convenience.

11 The following stipulations are missing: "Magister ... utili" (*Acta C.G.*, p. 6, line 2-3); "Priores ... converso" (*ibid.*, l. 9-11); "Nullus ... provideatur" (*ibid.*, l. 21-23); "Fratres ... comedant" (*ibid.*, l. 24-25); "Extra domum ... et aqua" (*ibid.*, l. 29-31); "Omnes fratres ... relinquendo" (p. 7, l. 3-5); "Quilibet ... debitorum" (*ibid.*, l. 6-8); "Generalissimum capitulum ... necessitas" (p. 7, l. 35 – p. 8, l. 3); "Confirmamus ... preceptum" (p. 8, l. 4-7); "Vestes ... scapulare" (*ibid.*, l. 27-28).

12 "Quod hec correctio et ordinatio et additio constitutionem nostrarum ab omnibus universaliter observetur" (*Acta C.G.*, p. 18).

13 The first explicit witness to Raymond's personal share in the improvement of the text appears in the *Chronica Ordinis* (before 1260): "Per eius etiam diligentiam constitutiones nostre redacte sunt ad formam debitam sub certis distinctionibus et titulis, in qua sunt hodie, que sub multa confusione antea habebantur" (MOPH, vol. I, p. 331). See also the testimony, already quoted, by the copyist of Rodez in the title of the manuscript (*supra*, p. 245, note 4); Bernard Gui, *Tractatus de tribus gradibus praelatorum in Ordine Praedicatorum*, col. 407; also the recent authors mentioned by the editor of the text, R. Creytens, *Les constitutions des Frères Prêcheurs dans la rédaction de saint Raymond de Penafort (1241)*, in *Arch. F.P.*, vol. XVIII, 1948, p. 5, note 1. The manuscript from the Holy Cross monastic library in Coimbra, currently in the city library of Porto (MS. 101), which served as the basis for the edition, was copied in 1241 (R. Creytens, *op. cit.*, pp. 12-14).

of Bologna from 1218 to 1222,[14] had previously distinguished himself by his compilation of the *Decretales* at the request of Gregory IX.[15] The expressions of older writers have deceived some commentators into thinking that his *ordinatio* must be seen simply as a more logical division and arrangement of the constitutions. But the introduction to the recent edition of the Porto manuscript clearly shows that Raymond's personal share involved a great deal more. Not only did he move chapters and sections, he also wholly or partially omitted certain sentences, and occasionally added to the text.[16] The result of his labour met with general acclaim as a model of codification, worthy of its eminent lawyer-author. In fact, his *ordinatio* remained in use, for the most part, up to the early twentieth century.

Raymond's codification (R) cannot, as a whole, be viewed as a parallel copy of the Rodez manuscript, but there are parts where there is extensive literal similarity. More than anything else, the redactor strove to achieve a more logical ordering of the content and greater precision in the formulation of the rules. With this goal in mind, he often felt obliged to tear the previous text apart. Not a single chapter was left unchanged.[17] Wherever possible, he brought texts that dealt with the same subject together, reducing the number of chapters from sixty-two in the old constitutions to thirty-five in his *ordinatio*.[18] On several occasions, he clarified

---

14 For details on the life and work of Raymond, see for example F. Balme – C. Paban – J. Collomb, *Raymundiana seu documenta quae pertinent ad S. Raymundi de Pennaforti vitam et scripta* (MOPH, vol. VII), Rome, 1898-1901; J. Rius Serra, *San Raimundo de Penyaforte. Diplomatario, documentos, vida antigua, crónica, procesos antiguos*, Barcelona, 1954. Raymond joined the Dominican Order on 1 April 1222 (*Raymundiana*, p. 9; R. Naz, art. *Raymond de Pennafort*, in *Dict. de droit canon.*, vol. VII, 1959, col. 461). On his professorship in Bologna, see Kuttner, *Repertorium der Kanonistik (1140-1234) – Prodromus Corporis glossarum*, vol. I (Studi e testi, vol. 71), Vatican City, 1937, pp. 438-440.

15 See for instance the *Chronica Ordinis* quoted *supra*, p. 330: "Qui, mandante domino Gregorio papa IX, compilaverat decretales...". Cf. Stephen of Salagnac, *De quatuor in quibus Deus Praedicatorum Ordinem insignivit*, p. 32; A. Van Hove, *Prolegomena* (Commentarium Lovaniense in Codicem iuris canonici, vol. I, 1), Mechelen, 1945², pp. 358-359. The letter in which Gregory IX announced the completion of the compilation on 5 September 1234 has been published, for instance in *Bull. O.P.*, vol. I, p. 69 and in *Corpus iuris canonici*, vol. II, p. 1-2.

16 See R. Creytens, *Les constitutions ... de s. Raymond de Peñafort*, pp. 18-22. The passages omitted by Raymond can be found on pp. 23-26. But this list is incomplete: thus, the following sentences from dist. I, c. 21 are missing (indicated here with the numbering from the edition by H. C. Scheeben, *Die Konstitutionen*, pp. 60-62): nos. 2, 3, 7, 8, 9, 10, 16, 17, 18, 19, 22, 30, 39. In the Coimbra manuscript, Raymond's text was omitted in various places and replaced by later chapter ordinances. On each occasion the editor restored the text to its previous form on the basis of the earliest constitutions, Humbert's constitutions and possibly of other documents: see R. Creytens, *op. cit.*, pp. 30, 32-33, 37-39, 43, 45-47, 49-51, 54-56, 59-60, 62, 64-65, in the footnotes.

17 He limited himself to minor changes in the following chapters: R, I, 8, *De minutione* = C, I, 12; R, I, 10, *De vestitu* = C, I, 19, *De vestibus*; R, I, 11, *De rasura* = C, I, 20; R, I, 12, *De silentio* = C, I, 17; R, I, 20, *De apostatis* = C, I, 24, *De fratre qui apostataverit*.

18 Raymond has 20 chapters in dist. I and 15 chapters in dist. II; the old version (Rodez) had 25 and 37 chapters respectively. C, I, 5, *De refectione* and I, 6, *De ieiunio* were joined together by Raymond in I, 4, *De ieiuniis*. Similarly, R, I, 5, *De cibo* contains C, I, 7, *De prandio* and I, 8, *De pulmentis*. R, II, 1, *De domibus concedendis* was compiled from fragments that belonged to five separate chapters in the old text: C, II, 23, 25, 26, 27 and I, 3. Elsewhere, Raymond split chapters from the Rodez text: C,

the meaning by making minor corrections and additions[19] and elsewhere he removed superfluous repetitions by omitting a few words.[20] In some cases, he also looked at the style, by giving greater care to the connections between sentences.[21] But he left a great number of shorter passages unchanged. The details of the internal criticism thus confirm the oldest information we have about Raymond's share in the revision of the old constitutions. Even without the explicit testimony of the annals, we are able to see in this redaction the hand of a lawyer who had no hesitations about making incisive changes wherever necessary, but who retained useful elements as far as possible.[22]

I, 9, *De collatione et completorio* was divided over R, I, 6, *De collatione* and I, 1, *De officio ecclesie*. A good overview of Raymond's modus operandi can be found in R. Creytens, *Les constitutions… de s. Raymond de Peñafort*, pp. 16-18: *Analyse des sources.*

19 In dist. I, c. 4, *De ieiuniis* he added: "in vigilia sancti Laurentii et Assumptionis sancte Marie". These words were missing in the Rodez text, incorrectly so, because it spoils the parallelism with the previous chapter. Raymond added these words in conformity with the statutes of Prémontré (*Institut. Praem.*: according to the twelfth-century text, in d. IV, c. 13, ed. E. Martène, *De antiquis Ecclesiae ritibus*, vol. III, p. 335; according to the thirteenth-century text, in d. I, c. 10, ed. Pl. F. Lefèvre, *Les statuts de Prémontré*, p. 20). The election of the monastic superior was described as follows by C, II, 24: "Priores a suis conventibus eligantur". Raymond (II, 2) added to this: "secundum formam canonicam".

20 In the Rodez manuscript, in the same chapter (II, 15, *De electione priorum provincialium*) the electors are indicated twice: "Mortuo igitur priore provinciali vel amoto, duo fratres de unoquolibet (*sic*) conventu illius provincie eligantur, qui cum suo priore conventuali, secundum formam superius positam, electionem prioris provincialis celebrabunt… Item statuimus quod electio prioris provincialis spectet tantum ad priores conventuales cum duobus fratribus de quolibet conventu electis…". This last stipulation was evidently added later. Raymond merged the two sentences into the following one: "Volumus autem quod electio predicta spectet tantum ad priores conventuales et duos fratres de quolibet conventu ad hoc idem electos, omnibus fratribus ad conventum illum pertinentibus, si ccmmode potest fieri, convocatis, qui secundum formam inferius in electione magistri positam, electionem huiusmodi celebrabunt…" (R, II, 3).

21 Raymond has a preference for conjunctions such as *autem* where no or another conjunction appears in the old version: "Matutinas autem et missam" (R, I, 1; cf. C, I, 4: "Matutinas et missam"); – "A festo autem sancte Crucis" (R, I, 4; cf. C, I, 6); – "Servitores autem" (R, I, 5; cf. C, I, 7: "Verumtamen servitores"); – "Quotquot autem remanserint" (R, I, 5; cf. C, I, 7: "et quotquot remanserint"); – "Fratribus autem nostris" (R, I, 5; cf. C, I, 8: "Et fratribus nostris"); – "Poterunt autem quidam" (R, I, 7; cf. C, I, 11: "Poterunt etiam quidam"); –"Prohibemus autem" (R, I, 13; cf. C, II, 27: "Prohibemus etiam"); – "Si quis autem" (R, I, 14; cf. C, I, 18); – "Preter hoc autem" (R, I, 17; cf. C, I, 22: "de cetero"). – In other places, Raymond prefers *vero*: "In inclinationibus vero" (R, I, 2; cf. C, II, 36); – "Quando vero prelatus" (R, I, 2; cf. C, I, 2); – "Infra lectionem vero" (R, I, 6; cf. C, I, 9: "et infra lectionem"); – "Causa vero minutionis" (R, I, 8; cf. C, I, 12: "et causa minutionis"); – "Cappa vero brevior sit" (R, I, 10; cf. C, I, 19); – "Rasura vero fiat" (R, I, 11; cf. C, I, 20); – "Infirmi vero" (R, I, 12; cf. C, I, 17); – "Probationis vero tempus" (R, I, 13; cf. C, I, 15); – "Qui vero semel apostataverit" (R, I, 20; cf. C, I, 24). These conjunctions were required in some cases where phrases were moved to other chapters.

22 This method is reminiscent of that used by Raymond when compiling the *Decretales*; cf. the letter by Gregory IX, 5 September 1234, quoted above (*supra*, note 15); A. Van Hove, *op. ibid. cit.*, pp. 358-359; P. Torquebiau, art. *Corpus iuris canonici. II. Les Décrétales de Grégoire IX*, in *Dict. de droit canon.*, vol. IV, 1949, col. 627-629.

The relationship between the Rodez manuscript and Raymond's redaction already allows us to make a partial and preliminary judgment on the status of the old Dominican constitutions. We can be sure that the fragments where both texts are literally identical represent the earliest accessible official text of the legislation from the first half of the thirteenth century. The regrouping of the chapters, the new formulation of some rules and the stylistic corrections indicated must evidently be ascribed to Raymond and are therefore of a later date. In addition, in the parts that show great literary resemblance, there are a number of variants that differ to a greater or lesser degree. In order to ascertain which of these probably constitute the earliest text, it is not always sufficient to compare the texts of the constitutions that have been discussed so far. The Rodez manuscript cannot always be regarded as such, as it proves on numerous occasions to be an incomplete and not fully reliable witness. And Raymond of Peñafort's redaction contains an edited and evolved text. It can often be ascertained which of the two versions is most reliable as a witness to the earliest constitutions by confronting them with later redactions of the legislation.

A few years after Raymond's redaction, the text of the constitutions was once again revised on the occasion of the correction of the liturgical books.[23] From 1244 onwards, the general chapters of the order had urged uniformity in the liturgical services.[24] The constitutions and the rule of Augustine, from which a chapter was read on certain days as part of the *Pretiosa* prayers, were among the texts used during the office in choir.[25] Humbert of Romans, who was renowned in the order for his attempts to bring unity to liturgical customs in the Roman province,[26] was elected master general in 1254 and was charged with revising the office.[27] His *ordinatio* was approved by the chapter of 1256 and confirmed by Pope Clement IV in 1267.[28] The copy thus corrected was entrusted to the priory of Saint-Jacques in Paris for safekeeping and was to serve as the prototype for the choir books used throughout the order.[29] After many vicissitudes, it ended up in the Central Archives of the Dominicans in Rome in 1841, where it is still kept today.[30] It has

---

23 On this, see L. Rousseau, *De ecclesiastico officio Fratrum Praedicatorum*, in *Anal. O.P.*, vol. XVII, 1925-1926, vol. XVIII, 1927-1928 and esp. vol. XIX, 1929-1930, pp. 813-825.

24 *Acta C.G.*, p. 29 (a° 1244), p. 33 (a° 1245), pp. 35-36 (a° 1246).

25 The constitutions, with the *evangelia* and the *Regula S. Augustini*, therefore followed the text of the martyrology.

26 For Humbert's share in the revision of the liturgy, see F. Heintke, *Humbert von Romans*, pp. 71-73; W. R. Bonniwell, *A History of the Dominican Liturgy*, pp. 79-84; *Litterae encyclicae magistrorum generalium Ordinis Praedicatorum*, p. 42.

27 F. Heintke, *op. cit.*, p. 53. In the *Acta C.G.*, p. 68, the commission is described as follows: "Committimus magistro ordinis totam ordinationem ecclesiastici officii tam diurni quam nocturni et eorum que ad hoc pertinent et correctionem librorum ecclesiasticorum et quod corrigat litteram regule".

28 *Acta C.G.*, p. 78. For the papal bull (7 July 1267), see *Bull. O.P.*, vol. I, p. 486.

29 *Acta C.G.*, p. 88 (a° 1257).

30 L. Rousseau, *op. cit.*, vol. XVII, pp. 822-824.

been described in detail, but there is as yet no full edition.[31] The British Museum in London has a copy.[32] No significant changes were made to the constitutions in Humbert's revision. The text is largely similar to Raymond's redaction, with the addition of stipulations that had since been adopted by the general chapters.[33] But it can be used for the study of the old Dominican legislation in the reconstruction of the texts that were omitted from the manuscript of Raymond's constitutions and replaced by later ordinances.[34]

§ 3. The legislation of the Dominican Sisters

A. Affinity with the constitutions of the Dominican Friars

The legislation of the Dominican Sisters in the first half of the thirteenth century was, naturally, closely related to the constitutions of the male branch of the order. Initially, the female convents were even entirely under the direction of the Dominicans, and they have always regarded this as an inalienable privilege.[35] The pastoral care of so many communities soon impeded the friars' exercise of their ordinary pastoral ministry, so that they asked Gregory IX in 1239 to be discharged of the *cura monialium*.[36] Under Innocent IV, some Dominican nuns succeeded in reclaiming their previous privileges, following the example of the convent of Saint Sixtus in Rome, which was once again incorporated into the order as early as 1244 by a papal letter.[37] The bulls of incorporation usually stipulated that the superiors of the Dominicans were to provide the affiliated female convents with their own statutes.[38] The constitutions of the Dominican Sisters of Montargis, compiled

---

31 L. Rousseau, *op. cit.*, vol. XVIII, pp. 104-120, 142-163, 193-203, 252-273. Only the *ordinarium* has been published, by F. M. Guerrini, *Ordinarium iuxta ritum sacri Ordinis Fratrum Praedicatorum*, Rome, [1921].

32 *Additional manuscr.* 23935; see G. R. Galbraith, *The Constitution of the Dominican Order*, Appendix I, pp. 193-201. According to the same author, *op. cit.*, p. 197, the greater part of the codex (fol. 23-571) was written between 1255 and 1263. W. R. Bonniwell, *op. cit.*, p. 94, believes that this manuscript was the copy that the master general carried on his visitation journeys.

33 For the edition of the text according to Humbert's prototype, see *Anal. O.P.*, vol. III, 1897-1898, pp. 31-60, 98-122, 162-181. The same text can be found in the British Museum manuscript on fol. 74-80 (G. R. Galbraith, *op. cit.*, p. 193).

34 See *supra*, p. 247, note 16.

35 For the history of the Dominican Sisters between 1206 and 1237, see O. Decker, *Die Stellung des Predigerordens zu den Dominikanerinnen*, pp. 28-84. For the attempts by the sisters to remain under the jurisdiction of the order, see R. Creytens, *Les constitutions primitives des sœurs dominicaines de Montargis*, in *Arch. F.P.*, vol. XVII, 1947, pp. 41-43, including literature on p. 41, note 1.

36 *Bull. O.P.*, vol. I, p. 107.

37 For the papal bull for Saint Sixtus, see *Bull. O.P.*, vol. I, p. 131. In 1246, approximately thirty convents of sisters were again subject to the jurisdiction of the order (R. Creytens, *Les constitutions ... de Montargis*, p. 42).

38 In the bull in favour of Montargis (8 April 1245): "... monasterium ipsarum incorporantes Ordini supradicto, duximus statuendum, ut eaedem priorissa et sorores sub magisterio et doctrina magistri et prioris provincialis Franciae... debeant retineri... ipsique magister et prior... animarum ipsarum

between 1249 and 1251 by Humbert of Romans, provincial of France, prove that this instruction was heeded. For the greater part, they are a faithful copy of Raymond's constitutions, adapted for use by a female monastic community.[39] As general, Humbert in 1259 received authority from the pope to impose a uniform text of the constitutions upon all communities of nuns.[40]

The statutes of Montargis are the earliest currently known copy of the constitutions of which we can be certain that they originated from a community of Dominican nuns. We do not have the legislation for the sisters from the first quarter of the thirteenth century in its authentic form. But it has been suggested that this can be found in large part in a number of documents related to the Penitent Sisters of Saint Mary Magdalene in Germany. These sisters were one of the many groups of female penitents which emerged at the end of the twelfth and the beginning of the thirteenth century, and which continued as a community even after the period of first ardour.[41] After the official approval of their monastic status in 1227 by Gregory IX, they lived for several years according to the rule of Benedict and the *consuetudines* of Cîteaux.[42] In October 1232, at their own request, they were given the status of canonesses regular and were granted the *Institutiones ordinis monialium Sancti Sixti de Urbe* as the basis for their monastic customs.[43] On this occasion, their legislation was supplemented by a series of rules for observance, the *Constitutiones Sororum Sanctae Mariae Magdalenae*.[44] Even cursory perusal of these two legal codes unmistakeably reveals their Dominican origins. A closer analysis will reveal their close relationship with the earliest legislation of the Dominicans.

---

sollicitudinem et curam gerentes ac ipsis constitutionibus eiusdem Ordinis, sine difficultate qualibet exhibentes…" (*Bull. O.P.*, vol. I, p. 148). – Similar letters, *ibid.*, pp. 131, 134, 150, 151, 153, 158, 159.

39 It suffices here to compare the list of the chapters and the text of Montargis (ed. R. Creytens, *Les constitutions … de Montargis*, pp. 67-78) with Raymond's first *distinctio* (ed. R. Creytens, *Les constitutions … de s. Raymond de Peñafort*, pp. 30-47).

40 R. Creytens, *Les constitutions … de Montargis*, pp. 55, 59, 61-64. Humbert's text was published in *Anal. O.P.*, vol. III, 1897-1898, pp. 337-348.

41 See A. Simon, *L'ordre des Pénitentes de Ste Marie-Madeleine en Allemagne au XIIIᵉ siècle*, pp. 10-20.

42 See the text of the bull in A. Simon, *op. cit.*, pp. 183-184.

43 A. Simon, *op. cit.*, pp. 33-34. The text of the *Institutiones* can be found on pp. 142-153. It was copied from the bull *Gaudete et exsultate* by Nicholas IV (1 January 1291), the original of which is in the State Archives in Breslau, *Naumburg* 24 (*op. cit.*, pp. 142, note 2; pp. 258-259). This bull repeats the text of Gregory IX's bull *Exsurgentes*, dated 23 October 1232 (*op. cit.*, pp. 202). For other manuscripts and editions, see *op. cit.*, pp. 143. – The text of the *Institutiones S. Sixti* will hereinafter be referred to as *Inst.*

44 A. Simon, *op. cit.*, pp. 34-36. The text of the *Constitutiones* can be found on pp. 155-169. Cf. M. P. Coenegracht, *De kloosterwetgeving van de Brabantse Witte Vrouwen*, in *Ons Geestelijk Erf*, vol. XXXIV, 1960, pp. 337-373.

B. *The* Institutiones S. Sixti

The title of the *Institutiones S. Sixti* refers to the convent of Saint Sixtus in Rome. That is where Dominic gathered together the nuns he had persuaded to lead a stricter monastic life in early 1221. At Honorius III's behest and in cooperation with Cardinal Hugolinus, he had begun to reform a number of female convents in 1219.[45] He found candidates who were willing to observe strict monastic enclosure particularly among the Benedictine Sisters of S. Maria in Tempulo and S. Bibiana. In order to ensure the proper conduct of the regular life, he asked several sisters to come from Prouille in Southern France, where a convent of nuns had been founded in 1206 that had since been under the supervision of the Dominicans.[46] The customs of the new Roman community were thus directly influenced by the traditions of the first Dominican enclosed convent. They subsequently developed into a fixed set of rules for observance that were also introduced in other monastic environments. A slightly adapted version known as the *Institutiones S. Sixti* was adopted by a number of female monasteries as their legal code from 1230 onwards, particularly in Germany, where they were also adopted by the Penitents in 1232.[47] Gradually, they lost their specifically Dominican character and assumed the status of a basic statute, a kind of "rule" in the general sense, that grouped together the various communities into a single community of observance, the *Ordo S. Sixti*, without, however, joining them together into a religious order as such.[48]

The *Institutiones S. Sixti* must not be seen as wholly original legislation, but rather as a new ordering of elements derived from older monastic rules. Analysis of the text preserved by the German Penitents reveals a number of non-Dominican sources. Several rules explicitly refer to Benedictine customs.[49] Perhaps they

---

45   On Hugolinus's and Dominic's reform, see H. C. Scheeben, *Der heilige Dominikus*, pp. 290-293; Id., *Die Anfänge des zweiten Ordens*, pp. 307-311; O. Decker, *Die Stellung des Predigerordens zu den Dominikanerinnen*, pp. 48-50; P. Mandonnet – M. H. Vicaire, *Saint Dominique*, vol. I, pp. 60, 61-65; vol. II, pp. 244, note 6; M. H. Vicaire, *Histoire de saint Dominique*, vol. II, pp. 278-289; esp. VI.
J. Koudelka, *Le "monasterium Tempuli" et la fondation dominicaine de San Sisto*, in *Arch. F.P.*, vol. XXXI, 1961, pp. 5-81, which corrects previous authors' mistakes.

46   On the foundation of Prouille, see Jordan of Saxony, *Libellus de principiis Ordinis Predicatorum*, no. 27. For a more extensive history and bibliography, see O. Decker, *op. cit.*, pp. 33-46; H. C. Scheeben, *Die Anfänge des zweiten Ordens des hl. Dominikus*, pp. 285-289; H. Grundmann, *Religiöse Bewegungen im Mittelalter*, pp. 208-212; P. Mandonnet – M. H. Vicaire, *Saint Dominique*, vol. I, pp. 99-113; M. H. Vicaire, *Histoire*, vol. I, pp. 235-274.

47   On the spread of the *Institutiones*, see A. Simon, *L'ordre des Pénitentes*, pp. 32-33; H. Grundmann, *op. cit.*, pp. 233-235.

48   See H. Grundmann, *op. cit.*, pp. 236-237; R. Creytens, *Les constitutions … de Montargis*, pp. 52-53.

49   "Infirmis autem … indulgeatur cibus carnium, prout regula beati Benedicti permittit" (c. 4). Cf. *Reg. S. Ben.*, c. 36. The passages in question can be easily located in A. Simon, *L'ordre des Pénitentes*, pp. 144-153. – "Post vesperas omnes simul ad collationem veniant, ubi legatur lectio, prout in Cisterciensi ordine fieri consuevit" (c. 5). Cf. *Ecclesiastica officia Ord. Cist.*, c. 81, *De collatione*, ed. Ph. Guignard, *Les monuments primitifs de la règle cistercienne*, Dijon, 1878, pp. 185; *Stat. cap. gen. Ord. Cist.*, vol. I, pp. 109, no. 9. The formula of profession similarly appears to contain echoes of the

already formed part of the rule of the nuns of Saint Sixtus themselves, the great majority of whom came from Benedictine abbeys.[50] But it is also possible that they were added later, in the years before 1232, when the Penitent Sisters still observed the rule of Benedict and were affiliated to the Order of Cîteaux.[51] A number of chapters were added to the second half of the text, mainly on enclosure, the management of temporal goods and manual labour. They are very clearly related to the rule of Sempringham, either literally or in content.[52] In other places, chapters or shorter stipulations were inserted so as to describe the nature and organisation of the institute of the Penitents in greater detail.[53] Otherwise, the Dominican origins are unmistakeable. Many texts are literally identical to the

---

Benedictine *stabilitas*: "Quelibet, cum recipitur in sororem, promittat obedientiam, loci stabilitatem et ordinis…" (c. 1).

50 Specifically from S. Maria in Tempulo and S. Bibiana: see *supra*, p. 252, and M. H. Vicaire, *Histoire*, vol. II, pp. 280-281, 285, 288-289.

51 See *supra*, p. 251.

52 This order, a typically English foundation, emerged from a female monastic community founded by Gilbert of Sempringham (c. 1085-1189) c. 1131. It consisted of double monasteries in which a small group of *canonici* was responsible for the spiritual direction of the *moniales*, who formed a separate community. The sisters followed the rule of Saint Benedict and constitutions that derived much from Cîteaux. The canons observed the rule of Saint Augustine. For further details and literature, see for example M. Heimbucher, *Die Orden und Kongregationen*, vol. I, pp. 417; R. Foreville, *Un procès de canonisation à l'aube du XIIIᵉ siècle (1201-1202). Le Livre de saint Gilbert de Sempringham*, [Paris, 1943], pp. IX-XII; D. Knowles, *The Monastic Order in England*, Cambridge, 1950, pp. 205-207. Innocent III had entrusted the abbey of Saint Sixtus to the Gilbertines with a view to the reform of the cloistered convents of Rome (Vl. J. Koudelka, *Le "monasterium Tempuli" et la fondation dominicaine de San Sisto*, pp. 44-45). But the canons of Sempringham were relieved of this commission at their own request due to lack of numbers (Laurent, no. 88, bull of 3 August 1218; no. 100, bull of 4 September 1219). – The constitutions of the order have been published under the title *Regulae Ordinis Sempringensis sive Gilbertinorum canonicorum*, in L. Holstenius – M. Brockie, *Codex regularum*, vol. II, pp. 467-536. – C. 22, *De preiudicio vitando* of the *Institutiones S. Sixti* was derived literally from Sempringham. The affinity between the following passages is less textual in nature:

Sempr.	Inst., c. 25
"*In singulis domibus* nostris sint *quatuor viri Deum timentes*, ordinis et religionis amatores … quorum curam…"	"*In singulis* huius ordinis *domibus* ordinentur, si haberi poterunt, *quatuor viri* religiosi, *Deum timentes*, qui exteriora procurent".
(*Capitula de quatuor procuratoribus domorum*, ed. cit., p. 476).	

Furthermore, compare *Inst.*, c. 16-22 with *Reg. Ord. Sempr., Institut, monialium*, c. 3-7 (*ed. cit.*, pp. 516-518). Cf. F. Balme, *Cartulaire de saint Dominique*, vol. II, pp. 444-453.

53 *Inst., c. 6, De receptione puellarum* deals with the education of girls who were in danger in the world. The chapters (c. 17-25) contain constant references to the hierarchy of the superiors: the Penitents were an autonomous order under the direction of priors, a *praepositus generalis* and a general chapter. The Dominican cloistered nuns, on the contrary, did not form an *ordo* in the proper sense of the term, but consisted of *monasteria* that stood under the direct authority of the provincial and were affiliated to a province and to the Dominican Order.

corresponding places in the old constitutions of the Dominicans. The similarity is particularly striking in the sections that deal with meals and fasting, the care of the sick, *silentium*, clothing, sleep, tonsure and, especially, the punishment of faults against monastic discipline.[54]

It would be too venturesome to simply identify the *Institutiones S. Sixti* as preserved by the German Penitents with the authentic earliest monastic rule of the Roman nuns. As it exists today, including all that belongs to it according to the bull of Gregory IX,[55] the text cannot be dated with certainty to before 1232. Some elements must, however, be older and may have belonged to the legislation of Saint Sixtus since 1221. This is primarily the case with the chapters that are related to the Dominican tradition.[56] They form a kind of résumé of the primitive constitutions of the order and were possibly adopted directly from Prouille. Similarly, the strict rules on monastic enclosure were most probably inserted at the time of the reform of the Roman cloistered convents in 1221. The campaign launched by Cardinal Hugolinus and Dominic was directed first and foremost against the frequent and unauthorised egress of the nuns.[57] The chapters in question and almost all subsequent chapters were inspired by the rule of the Gilbertines. This similarity in its turn points to the period indicated of 1219-1221, because Dominic was in fact the immediate successor to these religious when he introduced these reforms.[58]

There are good grounds, therefore, to believe that the *Institutiones* of the German Penitents to a large extent represent the original *Regula S. Sixti* of 1221, so that it is possible to arrive at a fairly accurate reconstruction of the legislation of the Roman cloistered convent. The first half consisted of the chapters that describe the Dominican customs; the second of additional prescripts influenced by the rule of Sempringham.[59] Only those passages that are directly relevant to the constitutions of the Dominicans interest us for present purposes. An additional argument for an early dating of these parts can be found in the arrangement and division of the text. Like most other chapters from the first *distinctio* of the

---

54 *Inst.,* c. 2, *De rejectione*: to be compared with C, I, 5; – c. 3, *De pulmentis*: cf. C, I, 7; – c. 4, *De infirmis*: cf. C, I, 11; – c. 7, *De silentio*: cf. C, I, 17; – c. 8, *De vestibus*: cf. C, I, 19; – c. 9, *De lectis*: cf. C, I, 21-25. The similarities and variants are indicated in the edition of the text, see Appendix I.

55 Gregory IX gave the Penitent Sisters the text of the *Institutiones* in his bull of 23 October 1232: see *supra,* p. 251, note 43.

56 See *supra,* note 54.

57 See *supra,* p. 252. Cf. M. H. Vicaire, *Histoire,* vol. II, pp. 280-281, 283-284; Vl. J. Koudelka, *Le "monasterium Tempuli"*, pp. 47-48. How little the Roman nuns observed enclosure can be gleaned from a text by Benedict of Montefiascone, who was prior of Saint Sixtus in 1316 and who wrote a brief history of the origins of this convent: "Innocentius papa III monasterium Sancti Sixti cum devotione animi de bonis Ecclesiae aedificare cepit, ut mulieres Urbis et moniales aliorum monasteriorum Urbis, per diversa vagantes possent ibi sub arcta clausura et diligenti custodia Domino famulari" (quoted by Vl. J. Koudelka, *loco cit.*).

58 See *supra,* p. 253, note 52.

59 This passage itself, as the second half of the text, presupposes the presence, previous or contemporaneous, of the previous chapters.

Dominican constitutions, the rules concerning the faults were similarly derived from the *consuetudines* of Prémontré.[60] Between the *culpae leviores* and the *culpae graves*,[61] the Premonstratensians added another category of grave faults, the *culpae mediae*,[62] which the Dominicans, according to the text of Rodez, classified under the title of *culpae leviores*.[63] But in the *Institutiones S. Sixti*,[64] the *culpae mediae* still form a separate series, like in the Prémontré text. There are a few other, similar cases.[65] They clearly prove that the text of the sisters in many places preserved an older version of the original Dominican legislation, one derived from the statutes of the Premonstratensians.

The clearly Dominican character of the *Institutiones* of the German Penitent Sisters was due to their close affinity with the original *Regula S. Sixti*, which itself was strongly dependent on the Dominican constitutions, possibly through the mediation of Prouille,[66] as the circumstances under which the reform of the Roman abbey took place suggest. The sisters of the Southern French convent themselves mentioned the links between Saint Sixtus and Prouille when they asked Gregory IX in 1236 for permission to be placed permanently under the protection and spiritual direction of the Dominicans, supporting their request with the argument that they had lived in Rome according to the rule of Saint Sixtus since the time of Dominic.[67] If taken literally, this expression appears to

---

60 On this, see *infra*, pp. 138-140.

61 *Institut. Praem.*, d. III, c. 1 and c. 3 respectively (ed. E. Martène, *De antiquis Ecclesiae ritibus*, vol. III, pp. 332; ed. Pl. F. Lefèvre, *Les statuts de Prémontré*, pp. 65-66 and 69).

62 D. III, c. 2.

63 C, d. I, c. 21.

64 For the text see A. Simon, *L'ordre des Pénitentes*, p. 147. The penalty for the *culpae leviores* (c. 11) is followed by: "Media vero culpa est talis…" (c. 12). The next chapter is *De gravi culpa*.

65 See the various cases in the apparatus of the text edition in Appendix I, with the older text alongside the more recent version. For the *Const. S. M. Magd.*, see under c. 1: ad matutinas; ad collectam; – c. 2: de regula; prosternat se, suscipiens; – c. 7: percutiat; incipiat nolam pulsare, qua pulsata. For the *Institutiones S. Sixti*, see under c. 22: habuerit; – c. 23: fuerit; ut est furtum, sacrilegium vel aliud huiusmodi; quousque intraverint et exierint; provolutus omnium pedibus; ecclesiam visitandam.

66 The main historians are in agreement on the general outline of the history of the legislation of Prouille. There is also agreement on when the Dominican constitutions were adapted for the sisters at Prouille (c. 1218). See for example H. C. Scheeben, *Der hl. Dominikus*, pp. 87-89; Id., *Die Anfänge*, p. 311; O. Decker, *Die Stellung des Predigerordens*, p. 45. M. H. Vicaire opts for a date between 1216 and 1220, preferably 1218 (*Histoire*, vol. II, pp. 395-396). One argument for this year is that the bull of protection *Religiosam vitam* was issued for the male community in Prouille on 30 March 1218 (Laurent, no. 86). On this occasion, Dominic purportedly completed the juridical organisation of the female community by compiling a rule derived from that of the Dominicans. But M. H. Vicaire does not exclude the possibility that the rule was older, was inspired by the *consuetudines* of Cîteaux and Prémontré, and was compiled before 1217, probably in 1212-1213 (P. Mandonnet – M. H. Vicaire, *Saint Dominique*, vol. II, p. 227, note 8; M. H. Vicaire, *Histoire*, vol. I, pp. 262-263).

67 The missive written by the sisters of Prouille is quoted in a letter by Gregory IX to the general of the Dominicans, Jordan of Saxony (24 March 1236): "Sane lecta coram nobis earum petitio continebat, quod cum ipsae, quae beati Dominici, Magistri iam dicti Ordinis, inductae sacris monitis et exemplis, relicta pompa saeculi, elegerunt Domino famulari sub regula monialium Sancti Sixti de Urbe…" (*Bull. O.P.*, vol. I, p. 86, no. 149). It is also possible that Saint Sixtus subsequently influenced Prouille.

assign chronological priority to the *Institutiones S. Sixti*. In fact, the relationship of dependence must of course be understood in the opposite sense. The sisters of Prouille evidently used this expression to point to the fundamental similarity between their observances and the customs that had since become known under the name of the Roman cloistered convent reformed by Gregory himself while still a cardinal.[68] On the basis of their connection with the rule of Saint Sixtus proper, the statutes adopted by the German Penitents as *Institutiones S. Sixti* may be regarded as indirect witnesses to the primitive Dominican constitutions. In certain places, they highlight the deep indebtedness of these constitutions to the legislation of the Premonstratensians more vividly than the Rodez manuscript.

C. *The* Constitutiones Sororum S. Mariae Magdalenae

The *Constitutiones Sororum Sanctae Mariae Magdalenae*, the second legal code of the German Penitent Sisters, are in fact a supplement to the *Institutiones*, to which they refer very frequently. The only known manuscript was once in the possession of the library of Saint Dorothea's monastery in Vienna and is currently in the Nationalbibliothek of that city.[69] It dates to the first half of the fourteenth century[70] and was written in clear, graceful Gothic letters with enlarged initials at the beginning of each chapter. The text covers nine folios (320^r-328^v), with twenty-five lines per page. The title was written in the upper right corner of the first page in between the text. The sequence number of each chapter is indicated in the margin with the letters of the alphabet.[71] The text was first published by R. Duellius in 1723.[72] A. Simon used this publication for his new edition of the Vienna manuscript. He then collated the text with the later German translations[73] and with the old Dominican constitutions.[74] On the basis of these documents, he attempted to restore the text to its original form in several places.

For the most part, the *Constitutiones S. Mariae Magdalenae* are simply the earliest constitutions of the Dominicans, adapted to a female community. The first eighteen chapters correspond as regards both sequence and content to the first

---

68 On the role played by Cardinal Hugolinus, later Pope Gregory IX, see M. H. Vicaire, *Histoire*, vol. II, p. 281, including literature.

69 *Lat.* 4724.

70 This chronology was confirmed by Dr F. Unterkircher, curator of the manuscripts.

71 The numbering is regular for the first sixteen chapters (a to p). No letter was assigned to the following chapters (17-21). The letter x appears beside *De domibus concedendis* (c. 22).

72 R. Duellius, *Miscellaneorum liber I*, Vienna-Graz, 1723, pp. 182-198.

73 A. Simon, *L'ordre des Pénitentes*, pp. 154-169. To this the following could be added: F. Discry, *La règle des Pénitentes de Ste Marie-Madeleine, d'après le ms. de St-Quirin de Huy*, in *Bull. de la Comm. royale d'histoire*, vol. CXXI, 1956, pp. 85-145 (ed. of the French text). The monasteries of Lauban (Silesia) and Studenitz (Styria) still have a *Regelbuch* from the eighteenth century, whose rules on the whole reflect the older Latin *Constitutiones* faithfully, even though they are sometimes derived from a more recent source (A. Simon, *op. cit.*, pp. 104, 154, note 1).

74 The affinity between the *Constitutiones S. M. Magdalenae* (hereinafter M) and the old constitutions of the Dominicans (C, dist. I) is clear from a comparison of the chapter titles: see for this Appendix II.

distinctio of the Rodez manuscript.[75] Only the chapter *De clausura claustri*[76] is new; it contains measures that were naturally more numerous and stricter for cloistered nuns than for the members of an active male order. For the chapters that already appeared in the *Institutiones S. Sixti*, the title was given with the reference.[77] The chapters *De infirmis* and *De vestitu* were even copied at length, so that they largely repeat the *Institutiones*.[78] The last series of chapters (19-26), between rules that stipulate the special obligations of the Penitents, contains certain more or less extensive fragments from the second *distinctio* of the Dominicans.[79] The compiler of the *Constitutiones* evidently wished to complement the legislation of the Penitent Sisters as much as possible with authentically Dominican texts.[80]

Judging by their content and purport, the *Constitutiones S. Mariae Magdalenae* were originally not intended for the Penitent Sisters. The terminology used for the various offices is not attuned to the legal structure of the German Penitents as described in the *Institutiones S. Sixti*: an autonomous, centralised order with

---

75 See footnote 74 and Appendix II.

76 In *Const. S. M. Magd.*, c. 3 (A. Simon, *L'ordre des Pénitentes*, pp. 157-158).

77 M, c. 5, *De refectionibus et regularibus ieiuniis, sicut in regula continetur, inviolabiliter observetur*: cf. *Inst.*, c. 2-3. – M, c. 17, *De tonsura*. "Tonsura et ablutio capitis fiat sicut regula continet": cf. *Inst.*, c. 10. – M, c. 18, *De culpis*. "De culpis, sicut in regula continetur, firmiter volumus observari": cf. *Inst.*, c. 11-15. – M, c. 20, *De electione priorisse*. "De electione priorisse, sicut in regula continetur, ita observetur": cf. *Inst.*, c. 24. – M, c. 23, *De festivitatibus*. "Sorores nostre et fratres, sicut regula precipit...": cf. *Inst.*, c. 21. The *regula* referred to here are the *Institutiones S. Sixti*, which indeed discuss all these issues at length and which were accepted by the sisters as an almost immutable rule, like the rules of Benedict and Augustine (R. Creytens, *Les constitutions ... de Montargis*, p. 53).

78 *De infirmis*: M, c. 10; *Inst.*, c. 4. The only significant difference is that the reference to the rule of Benedict in *Inst.* was replaced in M by the formulas of the old Dominican constitutions:

Inst.	M
"... ut citius releventur. Infirmis autem debilibus et senibus tantum in infirmitorio indulgeatur cibus carnium, prout regula beati Benedicti permittit. Si qua..."	"... ut citius releventur. Poterunt etiam vesci carnibus, prout earum gravior requirit infirmitas, secundum quod visum fuerit prelate. Si qua..."

The divergences with regard to the corresponding chapter in *Inst.* (c. 19) are more frequent in the chapter *De vestitu* (M., c. 16).

79 The following is a schema of the texts (derived from *Const. ant. O.P.* = C) in the chapters of M in question. The numbers between brackets refer to the numbering in the edition by H. C. Scheeben, *Die Konstitutionen*, pp. 71-80. – M, c. 19, *De secretis capituli vel domus vel ordinis servandis* = C, II, 14, *De infamia ordinis vitanda*. – M, c. 21, *De labore* = C, II, 26 (2). – M, c. 22, *De domibus* = C, II, 35 (1), 36 (1), 27 (2), 34 (6). – M, c. 24, *Quod sorores nostre ... casibus* = C, II, 31 (2), 34 (1), 34 (3), 34 (4), 36 (5), 34 (2), 36 (7). – M, c. 35, *De recipiendis fratribus et conversis* = C, II, 37 (1, 3, 3), I, 19, II, 37 (3), I, 19, 10, II, 37 (3). – M, c. 26, *De suffragiis mortuorum* = C, II, 22. In fact, everything from the Dominican constitutions that could be used for the sisters was adopted.

80 This desire even caused him to adopt texts that are in fact superfluous. C. 24, *Quod sorores claustrum non egrediantur nisi in quatuor casibus*, says that the sisters may only leave the convent to flee imminent catastrophe. However, the guidelines which the compiler gives for such occasions are derived from the Dominican constitutions' rules for friars who go out to preach (C, II, 31).

several houses and with a *praepositus generalis* as their own highest superior.[81] The *Constitutiones*, by contrast, know only of a single isolated convent of nuns, under the authority of a *priorissa* or *praelata* assisted by a council of *discretae* and *seniores*,[82] dependent on a male order.[83] This administrative arrangement reflects the situation of the Dominican cloistered convents, which together did not constitute an *ordo* of their own, but each of which was individually connected with the Order of the Dominicans, under the leadership of an external superior, the provincial of the province in which the convent was located. The *Constitutiones S. Mariae Magdalenae* were not therefore originally compiled for the use of the Penitent Sisters, but were derived by them from a community of Dominican Sisters who had previously adopted them from the old constitutions of the Dominicans.[84]

It may be presumed on the basis of the organic relationship between the *Constitutiones S. Mariae Magdalenae* and the *Institutiones S. Sixti* that the two texts were adopted by the Penitent Sisters at the same time, in 1232.[85] An examination of the text itself points in the same direction. The *Constitutiones* are evidently derived from a version of the Dominican constitutions whose evolution was completed after 1228 but before 1236. They contain no chapter ordinances from the year 1236,[86] but they do include a rule that most likely dates

---

81 *Inst.*, c. 1, *De recipiendis* and c. 19, *De mutatione personarum* speak of the transfer "ad conventum alium eiusdem ordinis" (A. Simon, *L'ordre des Pénitentes*, pp. 144 and 152 respectively). Cf. c. 23: "in singulis huius ordinis domibus". Various expressions are used for the general superior (never *magister ordinis*, as in the constitutions of the Dominican Sisters): *maior prepositus* (c. 17); *prepositus generalis* (c. 18, c. 19, c. 24); *prepositus* (c. 18, c. 19, c. 22). Elsewhere, the term used is *prior provincialis* (c. 17, c. 19). These terms do not appear in the parts inspired by the Dominican tradition (see *supra*, p. 254, note 54), but they do occur in the second half of the *Institutiones*, the text of which, as has been seen, often derives from the constitutions of Sempringham, which had a comparable organisation. For a detailed description of the structure of the Order of Penitents, see A. Simon, *op. cit.*, pp. 38-46.

82 The expressions *priorissa* and *prelata* appear almost in every chapter; "secundum maturiorum et seniorum sororum consilium" (c. 3); "secundum quod discretio priorisse et discretarum sororum providerit" (c. 13).

83 The affinity with the Dominicans is mentioned in a number of expressions; "infamatio ordinis" (c. 3); "unde noster ordo vel domus posset turbari vel infamari … destructrix nostri ordinis et conventus" (c. 19). These refer to the Dominican Order as a whole and they were, incidentally, adopted from the Dominican constitutions (C, II, 14). Also: "nulla soror vel frater ordinis nostri" (c. 19). The sisters were obliged to observe the *suffragia* "pro anniversario omnium fratrum et sororum … pro fratre defuncto vel sorore alterius conventus nostri ordinis" (c. 26). All this is derived almost literally from *Const. O.P.* (C, II, 22).

84 The text itself contains sufficient indications to support the conclusion that the constitutions were already in use by the Dominican cloistered nuns before they were adopted by the Penitent Sisters. It stands to reason that Dominican Sisters would have spared no effort to observe the constitutions of the Dominicans as literally and fully as possible, and even to adopt them rather slavishly (see *supra*, footnotes 79-80). If the Penitent Sisters had adopted the text of their *Constitutiones S.M.M.* directly from the Dominicans, they would not have had any motive to take anything that was even remotely useful from the second *distinctio* too.

85 See A. Simon, *L'ordre des Pénitentes*, pp. 35, 37; M. H. Vicaire, *Histoire*, vol. II, pp. 387, 390.

86 Most chapter ordinances of 1236 dealt with the government of the Dominican Order. But even the rules that were applicable to the sisters are missing in M. In the chapter *De silentio* (C, I, 17) the

from 1228.[87] Viewed as a whole, the text appears to be somewhat older than the constitutions of the Rodez manuscript. This conclusion is confirmed in c. 16, *De vestitu*.[88] Like most chapters in the first *distinctio*, the Dominicans derived this chapter from the Premonstratensians.[89] But the literary affinity is no longer as clear in the *Constitutiones antiquae O.P.* The text was obviously redacted and changed. However, the *Constitutiones S. Mariae Magdalenae* are considerably closer to the statutes of Prémontré. The chapter in question is still introduced by a quotation from the gospel and reflections on the modesty of monastic dress.[90]

---

sentence "Prior ad mensam loqui poterit" was changed as follows by the chapter of 1236: "Ubi agitur de silentio et dicitur: Prior ad mensam loqui poterit, illud removeatur et dicatur sic: In mensa autem ubique omnes fratres ... infirmi decumbentes" (*Acta C.G.*, pp. 6-7). This correction does not appear in the *Constitutiones S. Mariae Magdalenae*, which still has the old text: "Priorissa ad mensam loqui poterit..." (M, c. 15). See also *infra*, in the text edition, Appendix I, dist. I, c. 17. Nor does the addition "Item in domibus ... domo hospitum" (*Acta C.G.*, p. 6) appear in M; for the Dominicans C, I, 11; in the constitutions of Montargis: c. 7, *De infirmis* (R. Creytens, *Les constitutions ... de Montargis*, p. 71). Nor was the short addition to the chapter *De vestibus* included: "Item ubi dicitur: Fratres non utantur lineis ad carnem, addatur: nec etiam infirmi. Linteamina omnino removeantur de infirmitoriis nostris" (*Acta C.G.*, p. 6). This correction was made in C, I, 19 and in the constitutions of Montargis (c. 10, *ed. cit.*, p. 72) but not in M, c. 16.

87 M, c. 19, *De secretis capituli vel domus vel ordinis servandis* (p. 164) was very clearly derived from *Const. ant. O.P.*, d. II, c. 14, to which it was added in 1228, see *infra*, p. 405, note 208.

88 *Const. ant. O.P.*, d. I, c. 19, *De vestibus*.

89 Cf. *Institut. Praem.*, d. IV, c. 14 (ed. E. Martène, *De antiquis Ecclesiae ritibus*, vol. III, p. 335); d. II, c. 13 (ed. Pl. F. Lefèvre, *Les statuts de Prémontré*, pp. 56-58).

90 For the quotation at the beginning of the text: cf. Matthew 11:8. The following shows the texts of the Dominicans (C, I, 19) and the Penitent Sisters (M, c. 16) alongside that of Prémontré (ed. E. Martène, *loco cit.*). The thirteenth-century text (ed. Pl. F. Lefèvre, *loco cit.*) only has a number of variants.

Prém.	Magd.	O.P.
"*Qui in domibus regum sunt, mollibus vestiuntur.* Clericos autem, qui seculo abrenuntiant, decet asper vestitus et humilis.	"*Que in domibus regum sunt, mollibus* induuntur. Mulieres, que seculo abrenuntiarunt, decet asper vestitus et humilis.	
Eapropter proposuimus lineis non uti nisi femoralibus.	Eapropter proposuimus ut grossis camisiis utantur sorores.	"Vestes laneas non attonsas, ubi hoc servari poterit, deferant fratres nostri. Ubi vero non poterit, utantur vilibus... Et lineis non utantur ad carnem, nec etiam infirmi".
Lanee autem vestes, quibus utimur, non sint nimis subtiles nec nimis splendide, nec de foris attonse, ut adimpleatur illud in regula: *Non sit notabilis habitus vester, nec affectetis vestibus placere, sed moribus*".	Lanee autem vestes, quibus utimur, non sint nimis subtiles nec tonse deforis, ut impleatur illud in regula: *Non sit notabilis habitus vester, nec affectetis vestibus placere, sed moribus*".	

The German Penitents thus preserved an original version of the Dominican constitutions that would otherwise have been lost.

Although the titles contain nothing to suggest it, the legislative documents of the German Penitent Sisters thus encompass texts that are of the utmost importance for the history of the primitive Dominican constitutions. In two different but closely related versions, they have preserved the *consuetudines* of the Dominican cloistered nuns from the earliest period, for which other witnesses are lacking. Analysis and comparative study of their content generally confirm the data from the other historical sources on the origins and evolution of the legislation. In some cases, they even make it possible to correct or enhance certain conclusions. The *Institutiones S. Sixti* and the *Constitutiones S. Mariae Magdalenae* not only contain a great number of authentically Dominican customs, but in certain places offer very interesting variants and can even lead to the discovery of an older and more original version, one subsequently replaced and not included in the Rodez manuscript. The two documents therefore have sufficient authority from the perspective of textual criticism to serve as guides in the study and reconstruction of the text of the primitive Dominican constitutions.

§ 4. The constitutions of the Friars of the Penitence of Jesus Christ

The statutes of the *Fratres de Paenitentia Iesu Christi* are also useful for the textual criticism of the earliest Dominican constitutions. This order was one of the smaller mendicant societies of the first half of the thirteenth century, and it was abolished as early as 1274 by the Council of Lyon.[91] It has only belatedly attracted the attention of historians, possibly due to its short lifespan and the minor role it played in the history of religious life. Founded in Provence even before 1250, it was confirmed by Pope Innocent IV in 1251.[92] It expanded remarkably rapidly. At its suppression, the order counted dozens of houses spread across seven provinces.[93] Its members were also called *saccati*, Friars of the Sack, after the

---

The texts "non attonsas... lineis non utantur" prove that there was still a literal correspondence between Prémontré and the Dominicans. The Penitent Sisters dropped these words when they adapted the text for their own use. But otherwise, the agreement between Prémontré and the Penitent Sisters is much more striking and significant.

91 See for instance P. Mandonnet – M. H. Vicaire, *Saint Dominique*, vol. II, pp. 250-251, including literature; R. W. Emery, *The Friars of the Sack*, in *Speculum*, vol. XVIII, 1943, pp. 323-334; G. M. Giacomozzi, *L'Ordine della Penitenza di Gesù Cristo*, in *Studi storici dell'Ordine dei Servi di Maria*, vol. VIII, 1957-1958, pp. 3-60.

92 It is difficult to date the foundation accurately. According to R. W. Emery (*art. cit.*, p. 325), the order was founded before 1251; G. M. Giacomozzi (*art. cit.*, p. 12), believes in 1248. The testimonies of Thomas of Eccleston and Salimbene (see *infra*, p. 261, note 101) indicate that the Friars of the Sack already existed as a society around 1245. According to M. H. Vicaire (see *infra*, p. 263, note 106) they were founded as early as 1240 or 1241.

93 G. M. Giacomozzi, *art. cit.*, pp. 21-22. R. W. Emery, *A Note on the Friars of the Sack*, in *Speculum*, vol. XXXV, 1960, pp. 591-595, lists a hundred and eleven houses.

rough material of the clothes they wore, like so many other groups of penitents at the time. Like the Dominicans and the Franciscans, they dedicated themselves to the cure of souls through preaching and hearing confessions.[94] The backlash of the secular clergy against the activities and privileges of the *mendicantes* proved to be the undoing of the Friars of the Sack. At the Council of Lyon (1274), which in principle abolished all mendicant orders, they were unable to defend their *evidens utilitas* as successfully as the Dominicans and the Franciscans, who were left untouched, or the Augustinians and the Carmelites, who were provisionally tolerated.[95] In fact, their society was not immediately disbanded, but the ban on receiving new novices meant that their houses were doomed to die out.[96]

The most important document that the Friars of the Sack have left and that testifies to their existence and way of life are their constitutions, which have been preserved in a single manuscript currently in the British Museum in London.[97] It was copied in a generally readable English Gothic minuscule, possibly in the first half of the fourteenth century. The text runs to twenty folios.[98] The identification poses no serious problems. In the heading and the *explicit*, the first words after *constitutiones fratrum* have been deleted, but the chapter *De forma decreti*[99] still clearly reads: *ordinis fratrum de penitentia Iesu Christi*. Further confirmation can be found in the chapter *De studio et magistro studentium*, which situates the origins of the order in Provence.[100] This is consistent with the data from the old sources about the origins of the Friars of the Sack.[101]

---

94 G. M. Giacomozzi, *art. cit.*, pp. 14-16.

95 P. Mandonnet – M. H. Vicaire, *Saint Dominique*, vol. II, pp. 250-251, footnote 19. For the constitution *Religionum diversitatem* (17 July 1274), see Mansi, vol. XXIV, col. 97.

96 G. M. Giacomozzi, *art. cit.*, pp. 57-59.

97 *Cottonian Collection*, Cod. Nero A XII, 13. The *Catalogue of the Manuscripts in the Cottonian Library, deposited in the British Museum* (London, 1802, p. 204), describes the text as follows: "Constitutiones fratrum, ubi plurima de vita et regimine monachorum". The various parts were first joined together and bound in the seventeenth century and rebound in the nineteenth century (according to information received from Mrs Antonia Gransden, Assistant Keeper of the Department of Manuscripts of the British Museum). After the current study was completed, the text of the *Constitutiones Fratrum de Paenitentia* was published by G. M. Giacomozzi, as the second part of his article, quoted above, in *Studi storici dei Servi di Maria*, vol. X, 1960 (published in 1961), pp. 52-92. The two parts were published together in the series *Scrinium historiale*, vol. II, Rome, 1962. The text of the *Constitutiones* appears there on pp. 73-113. References here are to this latter publication.

98 Fol. 155^r-174^v. For further details on the manuscript, cf. G. M. Giacomozzi, *op. cit.*, pp. 63-65.

99 Dist. II, c. 12, fol. 165^v; G. M. Giacomozzi, *ed. cit.*, pp. 96-97.

100 Whereas the other provinces were permitted to send two students each to a *studium generale*, only the province of Provence could send four "quia ipsa est mater et principium aliarum" (dist. II, c. 27, fol. 171^r; G. M. Giacomozzi, *ed. cit.*, p. 106).

101 Thomas of Eccleston: "Frater Petrus recepit primo fratres de Paenitentia Iesu Christi…, qui in Provincia tempore concilii Lugdunensis ortum habuerunt…" (*Fratris Thomae vulgo dicti de Eccleston Tractatus de adventu Fratrum Minorum in Angliam*, ed. A. G. Little, Manchester, [1951], p. 103). Salimbene de Adam: "Anno 1248, cum essem cum fratre Hugone in provincia Provinciae apud castrum Arearum, ubi Saccati sumpserunt initium …" (*Chronica*, ed. O. Holder – Egger, in MGH, *Scriptores*, vol. XXXII, Hanover-Leipzig, 1905-1913, p. 294).

The constitutions of the Friars of the Penitence of Jesus Christ are closely related to those of the Dominicans both as regards content and structure.[102] The general introduction with prologue and two *distinctiones* is identical in both cases. There are a number of minor deviations as regards the number and sequence of the chapters.[103] In the first *distinctio*, a number of folios are absent from the manuscript; the text of six entire chapters and that of most of two other chapters has gone missing. This lacuna cannot be blamed on the copyist's negligence, but was possibly due to carelessness in the binding process or to deliberate damaging of the codex. It was not noticed by the person who later assigned sequence numbers to the folios.[104] In the second *distinctio*, four chapters of the Dominicans were not adopted, a few others were placed in a different order, and two new chapters were added.[105] This first cursory examination already shows that the model was not

---

102 The similarity was previously pointed out by E. Little, *The Friars of the Sack*, in *English Historical Review*, vol. IX, 1894, pp. 121-127.

103 The following overview includes only the titles that are not in full correspondence with each other. The chapters are not numbered in either codex. The words between brackets appear before each chapter in the titles, but do not appear in the list of chapters before *Distinctio prima* (fol. 155ʳ, ed. G. M. Giacomozzi, p. 74).

O.P.	Friars of the Sack
3. *De mulieribus non intromittendis.*	3. *De (matutinis et) horis et modo dicendi.*
4. *De horis et de modo dicendi.*	4. *De mulieribus (et muneribus et collocutionibus earum).*
5. *De refectione.*	5. *De refectione (fratrum).*
8. *De pulmentis.*	8. *De pulmentis (fratrum in conventibus).*
10. *De lectis.*	10. *De lectis (fratrum).*
16. *De modo faciendi professionem.*	16. *De modo faciendi professionem et benedictione vestium novitiorum.*
	21. *De confessione et confessoribus et communionibus.*
21. *De levioribus culpis.*	22.
22. *De gravi culpa.*	23.
23. *De graviori culpa.*	24.
24. *De fratre qui apostataverit.*	25. *De apostatis.*
25. *De gravissima culpa.*	26.

The list of the chapters before dist. I ends with c. 21.

104 According to the pagination in modern script, fol. 161 normally follows fol. 160, but the text ends on fol. 160ᵛ with the words: "... incipiat prelatus subscriptos versiculos" (dist. I, c. 14, *De recipiendis*) and begins on fol. 161ʳ with the words: "statuto tempore non previderit..." (that is, in the middle of c. 22, *De levioribus culpis*). – According to Mrs Antonia Gransden, Assistant Keeper, there is no hope that the missing folia will ever be found.

105 In the Dominican text, the four chapters are called (C): *De morte magistri* (c. 13); *De conventu mittendo* (c. 23); *De doctore* (c. 30); *De edificiis* (c. 35). – *De anniversariis* (c. 22 in C of the Dominicans), appears as c. 33 in the text of the Friars of the Sack. – The *Regula fratrum* (c. 37 of the Dominicans), became c. 35 in the text of the Friars of the Sack. – The following were added by the

Raymond of Peñafort's codification, but Jordan of Saxony's constitutions, which at the time of adoption had already been obsolete some ten years.[106]

The Friars' text in many places is a faithful reproduction of the constitutions of the Dominicans. Some chapters were copied almost literally.[107] Others were changed in more or less significant ways, especially in relation to expressions and the order of words and sentences.[108] At the end of several chapters, one or more sentences were added to clarify the text or adapt it to the particular views of the Friars of the Sack on the way monastic customs should be observed.[109] The chapters on meals, fasting and sleep were redacted in certain places and supplemented by rules that usually mitigate the rigour of the monastic observances.[110] Here

---

Friars of the Sack: c. 12, *De forma decreti* and c. 25, *De paupertate*. See the list of chapters of the second *distinctio* in Appendix III.

106 The fact that the Friars of the Sack copied the earliest version of the Dominican constitutions led M. H. Vicaire (*Saint Dominique*, vol. II, p. 250, note 19) to conclude, wrongly, that the Friars of the Sack adopted their text before 1241, and that the date of the foundation of their society must therefore be moved back (cf. *supra*, p. 260, note 92). It is not impossible that the Friars of the Sack copied their constitutions later, even after 1250, from a copy of the earliest *Constitutiones O.P.* that was still in use in one or other of the houses. This hypothesis can explain why their text contains a number of ordinances that appear in the *Acta cap. gen. O.P.* from the 1242-1258 period. The chapters of 1254-1256 added the following text to the constitutions: "Caveat autem quilibet frater ne proclamet aliquem in capitulo de crimine, nisi posset probare. Quod si accusatus negaverit et accusans in probatione defecerit, secundum exigentiam culpe gravius puniatur. Ne autem vitia occultentur, prelato suo nuntiet quod vidit vel audivit" (*Acta C.G.*, pp. 69, 74, 78). This same ordinance, barring a number of insignificant variants, appears literally in the constitutions of the Friars of the Sack (I, 23; ed. G. M. Giacomozzi, p. 86). Less textual similarities with texts from the chapter reports can be found in I, 7: "Et sciendum quod omnes fratres in Parasceve debent ieiunare per totum diem in pane et aqua..." (ed. G. M. Giacomozzi, p. 80; cf. *Acta C.G.*, pp. 80, 85, 90, years 1256-1258). In II, 28: "Libri etiam fratrum omnium, post mortem eorum, redeant ad conventum domus, unde et quocumque modo fuerint adquisiti" (ed. G. M. Giacomozzi, p. 107; cf. *Acta C.G.*, pp. 14, 19, 22, years 1240-1242). Perhaps this must be taken as an indication that the Friars of the Sack only derived their constitutions from the Dominicans after 1258. Real proof of an earlier date of this adoption is lacking. G. M. Giacomozzi, *L'Ordine della Penitenza*, p. 67, has the year 1252 as *terminus post quem*.

107 See dist. I, c. 13 and 21; dist. II, c. 3, 13, 24, 31.

108 Minor changes can be found in the following chapters: dist. I, c. 2, 5, 12, 22, 23, 24, 25; dist. II, c. 4, 7, 8, 9, 10, 11, 19, 20, 21, 26, 28.

109 Additions can be found at the end of the following chapters: dist. I, c. 2, 6, 7, 8, 9, 11, 12, 22, 23, 24, 25; dist. II, c. 6, 14, 15, 22, 23, 27, 28, 29, 30, 32, 33, 35.

110 The Friars of the Sack (whose text will hereinafter be called S = *Saccati*) had a shorter and less onerous fast than the Dominicans.

C, I, 6	S, I, 6
	"Ieiunium vero inchoatum a festo Omnium Sanctorum terminabitur in Pascha.
"A festo sancte Crucis usque ad Pascha continuum tenebimus ieiunium et nona dicta comedemus, exceptis dominicis diebus ...	A festo autem Omnium Sanctorum usque ad Adventum intus et extra liceat fratribus nostris comedere lacticinia atque ova. Quo tempore cum itinerantibus priores poterunt dispensare

and there, rubrics and liturgical texts were added; according to the Dominican tradition, these belong not in the constitutions but in the *Ordinarium*.[111] Perhaps the Friars of the Sack attempted to bring everything together into a single legal code.[112]

---

	ut bis reficiantur, si tamen hoc exigat laboris vel itineris difficultas…
Itinerantes tamen bis refici possunt, nisi in Adventu et Quadragesima, exceptis ieiuniis principalibus ab Ecclesia institutis".	Itinerantes autem bis refici possunt, nisi in predicto Adventu vel Quadragesima et ieiuniis principalibus ab Ecclesia constitutis. Si autem a festo Pasche usque ad festum sancti Michaelis in sexta feria duplex festum advenerit, ob solemnitatis reverentiam possunt fratres bis refici illo die".

I, 8	I, 8
"Pulmenta nostra sint ubique sine carnibus in nostris conventibus.	"Pulmenta nostra sint ubique sine carnibus in nostris conventibus. Cum pinguedine tamen carnium possunt nostra cibaria preparari, nisi in diebus sabbatis.
Et fratribus nostris, ne sint hominibus onerosi, …"	Et fratres nostri, ne sint hominibus onerosi, extra claustrum…".

111 On the content and evolution of the *Ordinarium* of the Dominicans before the middle of the thirteenth century, see R. Creytens, *L'ordinaire des Frères Prêcheurs au moyen âge*, in *Arch. F.P.*, vol. XIV, 1954, pp. 115-119. Neither the Premonstratensians, nor the Dominicans and the Dominican Sisters have the *versiculi* before and after meals in the text of the constitutions.

112 The texts of the prayers before meals, which appear in the Dominican *Ordinarium* (ed. F. M. Guerrini, Rome, [1921], pp. 132-133, nos. 509-510), were inserted in the chapter *De prandio* (d. I, c. 7) by the Friars of the Sack:

C, I, 7	S, I, 7
"Quibus ingressis, dicat *Benedicite*, qui dicit versiculos	"Quibus ingressis, dicat *Benedicite*, qui dicit versiculos, et immediate cantor incipiat *Oculi omnium* vel *Edant pauperes* pro tempore
et conventus prosequatur benedictionem et comedant".	et conventus prosequatur benedictionem".

Ordinarium O.P., loco cit.

"Dicto vero *Benedicte*, tempore quo bis reficiuntur fratres, cantor vel succentor, secundum quod fuerit hebdomada, ad prandium incipiat vers. *Oculi omnium*, et conventus ipsum et sequentem communiter prosequatur… ante comestionem dicitur vers. *Edent* pauperes… Quando autem ieiunatur, ante comestionem dicitur vers. *Edent pauperes*…".

On the office:

Ordin. O.P., p. 120	S, I, 9
"… cantetur post completorium antiphona *Salve, Regina*…".	"… dicto completorio, det benedictionem… et cantent fratres antiphonam *Salve, Regina*".

Many changes were made to the ceremonial of the general chapter[113] and to the stipulations on the choice of the *diffinitores* in the second *distinctio*.[114] The chapter on the *suffragia* for the dead was almost completely reworked and was, moreover, assigned a different place.[115] The chapter *De paupertate* is original and contains the detailed list of the measures that the Friars of the Sack took to preserve the spirit and practice of poverty.[116] Similarly, the rules concerning legislation were gathered together in a separate chapter.[117] The general superior was not called *magister ordinis*, as in the Dominican Order, but consistently *rector ordinis*.[118] He did not enter into office immediately upon his election, but only after confirmation by the pope. A new special chapter, *De forma decreti*, was therefore added to the constitutions.[119] This is in fact a form, a judicial certificate of the election, followed by a request to the pope for approval of the new general.

Despite the frequent changes, the constitutions of the Friars of the Sack in some senses reproduce the earliest legislation of the Dominicans more faithfully than the Rodez manuscript. Thus, a number of chapter ordinances from 1236 are more accurately rendered, as comparison with the Dominican *Acta capitulorum*

Ordin. O.P., p. 115

"A festo Purificationis usque ad Ramos Palmarum… in Laudibus antiphona *Ave, Stella*".	In sabbatis ad Laudes… cantetur pro commemoratione *Ave, Stella matutina*".

At the taking of the habit:

Ordin. O.P., p. 123   S, I, 14

"… Cantor incipiat cantando hymnum *Veni, Creator*. Et… egrediatur conventus processionaliter ad ecclesiam…".	"Post hoc cantor incipiat hymnum *Veni, Creator* et intrent processionaliter ecclesiam".

113 *De capitulo generali* (d. II, c. 17), *De questionibus* (d. II, c. 21) and *De solutione et terminatione questionum, de correctione fratrum et modo penitentiarum* (d. II, c. 22).

At the end of the chapter, the formulas for the *absolutio* of the members of the chapter were added in full whereas the Dominicans only had a resumé:

O.P.   Friars of the Sack

"In fine communis fiat confessio et absolutio, perseverantibus benedictio, apostatis et profugis anathematis maledictio".	"In fine capituli communis fiat confessio in hunc modum… *Confiteor Deo*…" (this is followed by the formulas, which cover one page in the manuscript) (169ʳ).

114 D. II, c. 5 and c. 7: see the list of chapter titles in Appendix III.
115 D. II, c. 33, *De anniversariis*.
116 The chapter of the Friars of the Sack (d. II, c. 25) only has a few lines in common with d. II, c. 26 of the Dominicans.
117 D. II, c. 34, *Qualiter fieri debeant constitutiones et qualiter roborari*.
118 "Poterit autem eum rector ordinis confirmare" (d. II, c. 4) and *passim*.
119 This chapter follows immediately after d. II, c. 11, *De forma electionis*.

and the later text of the constitutions shows.[120] In other cases, too, they preserved the original version more precisely.[121] Generally speaking, later additions were inserted in the place in the body of the text best suited content-wise, rather than added as *extravagantes* at the end, as in the Rodez manuscript.[122] But neither text contains the *Constitutiones antiquae* in full. At the chapter of 1236, the Dominicans adopted twenty-eight corrections to the constitutions.[123] All of them can be found in Raymond of Peñafort's redaction. Only eighteen of them appear in the Rodez manuscript.[124] Four of the other ten were included in the constitutions

---

120 A number of cases is given below in which both Raymond of Peñafort's text (R) and that of the Friars of the Sack (S) literally follow the text of the *Acta capitulorum*, while the Rodez manuscript (C) has a different version:

R, I, 7; S, I, 11	C, I, 7
"Item in domibus nostris *non sint* nisi duo loca…".	"Item in domibus nostris *ubique non habeant* nisi duo loca…".
(= *Acta C.G.*, p. 6).	
R, II, 3; S, II, 15	C, II, 15
"… cum duobus fratribus de quolibet conventu *ad hoc* electis…"	"… cum duobus fratribus de quolibet conventu electis…".
(= *Acta C.G.*, p. 7).	

For such cases, see the critical apparatus of the text edition, including d. II, c. 11: scrutinium *voluntatum*; d. II, c. 15: *poterit … confirmare*.

121 S on several occasions corresponds literally with R where C has a different version, see the critical apparatus, *passim*.

122 In C, most stipulations that were added later appear together after d. II, c. 35. They were not arranged under one title, but the first rule of the series begins with a large decorated capital, like the *initium capitis* of the other chapters. H. C. Scheeben (*Die Konstitutionen*, pp. 79-80) regards these *extravagantes* together as a new chapter: d. II, c. 36. He has also numbered the individual stipulations in the list. The following table compares the place of the various ordinances in C (according to H.C. Scheeben's numbering) with that in the constitutions of the Friars of the Sack (S).

C	S
d. II, c. 36, no. 1	d. II, c. 24
3	31
5	31
6	31
7	d. I, c. 4
8	8
11	1
12.	1.

123 *Acta C.G.*, pp. 6-8.

124 The stipulations that are missing in C are listed *supra*, p. 246, note 11. – See also the comparative table in Appendix IV.

of the Friars of the Sack,[125] although others are missing there.[126] The conclusion must be that the Friars of the Sack and the copyist of Rodez, independently of each other, based their work on older copies of the constitutions that were redacted somewhat carelessly by the respective monastic copyists.

§ 5. The reports of the general chapters

Finally, the *Acta capitulorum generalium O.P.* can also count as witnesses to the text of the Dominican constitutions. A number of old authors and the witness statements for Dominic's canonisation process contain valuable details on the general chapters, which were held annually from 1220 onwards.[127] But the activities of the chapters are most clearly visible in the reports that have been preserved.[128] These reports always began with the legislative decisions taken. A fixed procedure was followed even before 1239. The constitutions could only be adapted or supplemented with the approval of three consecutive chapters.[129] In the first year, the new text appeared in the *Acta* as *inchoatio*. If the proposal was again adopted the following year, it was included as *approbatio*. *Confirmatio* followed in the third year, making the new ordinance part of the constitutions *de iure*.[130]

The *Acta capitulorum generalium* thus in a certain sense contain the texts of the constitutions in their original and authentic form. The legal stipulations had to be inserted into the constitutions in the formulation in which they appeared in the *Acta*.[131] However, only the chapter reports for 1236 apply for the period during which the *Constitutiones antiquae* were in force, as only *admonitiones*

---

125 They appear in the table as nos. 1, 8, 11, 24.

126 Apart from those missing in both manuscripts (nos. 4, 9, 13, 14, 23, 28) there are also ten others that do appear in the Rodez manuscript (nos. 2, 5, 6, 12, 15, 16, 17, 18, 19, 22). This means that sixteen chapter ordinances of 1236 are missing from the constitutions of the Friars of the Sack. It does not follow that the manuscript (or the sample used by the copyist) was less meticulously updated than the Rodez manuscript (or its model). Two of the missing ordinances (nos. 6, 12) belonged to the part that disappeared in the constitutions of the Friars of the Sack (see *supra*, p. 262, including footnote 104). – Three other ones (nos. 2, 5, 15) appeared in the Dominican constitutions in chapters that were not used at all by the Friars of the Sack (see *supra*, p. 262, including footnote 105). – Nor was there any reason to insert no. 16, because the general chapter of the Friars of the Sack was organised differently: it met, not each year, like that of the Dominicans (C, II, 11), but only once every three years: "...ut solum de tribus in tribus annis fiat nostrum capitulum generale" (S, II, 5).

127 See for instance Jordan of Saxony, *Libellus*, nos. 86-88; Humbert of Romans, *Instructiones de officiis Ordinis*, pp. 182-183, 339-345; Bernard Gui, *Tractatus de tribus gradibus praelatorum in Ordine Praedicatorum*, col. 403, 417; *Proc. Bon.*, no. 2.

128 The edition of the *Acta capitulorum generalium O.P.*, vol. I (MOPH, vol. III), pp. 1-5, also includes the information that Bernard Gui collected concerning the chapters of 1220-1236 (cf. *supra*, p. 161).

129 See *Const. ant. O.P.*, vol. II, c. 6. This stipulation was probably inserted into the constitutions in 1228, see also pp. 403-404, with notes 196 and 205.

130 The technical term *confirmamus* was used as early as 1236: *Acta C.G.*, pp. 7-8. The *inchoationes* and *approbationes* appeared in 1239: *ibid.*, p. 11.

131 The new stipulations were inserted *in locis suis* as early as 1228: see the preamble (*praeambulum*) to the *Const. ant. O.P.*, in Appendix I.

were preserved for the preceding years.[132] Another difficulty arises from the fact that the texts that are known are not derived directly from the official documents drawn up during the assembly, but from transcripts that were made by participants to communicate the new ordinances to the monasteries of their own provinces.[133] It may be presumed that these transcripts were not always made with due care and that they do not provide a fully accurate version of the text proposed by the presidium and adopted by the assembly. This can perhaps explain why the version of some ordinances in the chapter reports does not fully correspond to the text found in the constitutions.[134] Yet, in any case, the value and authority of the *Acta capitulorum* are sufficiently assured to include them as witnesses in the reconstruction of the text of the constitutions.

The analysis of the various manuscripts and texts already permits us to draw a number of preliminary conclusions. Only the Rodez manuscript can count as a direct witness to the Dominican constitutions as they were before Raymond of Peñafort's *ordinatio*. But it is an imperfect rendering of them. In some cases, the other legal codes have preserved the original text more fully and more faithfully, but also, like the constitutions of the sisters, in a more archaic form, closer to the statutes of the Premonstratensians.

Section II. Reconstructing the text

To determine to what extent the legal codes discussed above can help to discover the original text of the Dominican constitutions, it is necessary to conduct a prior enquiry into their mutual relationships. A first section attempts to establish whether the manuscripts in which the text has been handed down can truly count as independent witnesses. Their respective value and authority are then examined more closely. It will become clear in the course of this investigation that the Rodez manuscript must be used as the basis for the reconstruction of the earliest text. To what extent it can be supplemented or corrected with the help of the other legal codes will be determined in a second section. Finally, it will be demonstrated to what extent some stipulations that appear to be of a later date in fact already belonged to the earliest legislation.

§ 1. The mutual relationships between the various texts

It is clear from the above that Raymond's text is not based upon the other legal codes that have been discussed. This is so because his manuscript was written in

---

132 *Acta C.G.*, pp. 3-5.

133 See *supra*, p. 161. See also Humbert of Romans, *Instructiones de officiis Ordinis*, pp. 343 and 345, where the task of the *diffinitor* and his *socius* is described.

134 See *supra*, pp. 265-266, with note 120; *infra*, p. 271, with note 147.

1241,[135] that is, before all the others. However, it cannot have served as a model for C or S, or indeed for *Inst.-M*, as it does not reflect the Dominican constitutions in the older version, but in the form these had acquired only in 1241.[136] Whatever Raymond retained from the earliest constitutions he must have reproduced from the copy he used for his revision of the text. Nor are there any relationships of dependence between the legislation of the German Penitents and the Rodez manuscript. The *Institutiones S. Sixti* were preserved in a document dating from 1291, which is therefore older than C.[137] It is true that the *Constitutiones S. Mariae Magdalenae* were copied at approximately the same time as C, that is, the first half of the fourteenth century,[138] but their immediate source were the *consuetudines* of the Dominican cloistered nuns from the period before 1236.[139] Their connection with the earliest constitutions of the Dominicans therefore followed a different path.

The Rodez manuscript and that of the Friars of the Sack are similarly independent of each other. C was copied in the fourteenth century from a document dating from the first half of the thirteenth century which contained the text of the constitutions in the period before 1238-1240. S is an even later copy of the legislation of the Friars of the Sack, drawn up in the second half of the thirteenth century, more precisely between 1251 and 1274,[140] and was dependent on the earliest redaction of the Dominican constitutions. Both C and S therefore ultimately derive from the same legislation, but not from a single prototype or form of it. A great number of the variants discussed cannot possibly be ascribed to the copyists and must therefore already have been present in the copies that served as models for each separately. The same conclusion imposes itself from the fact that the missing chapter ordinances of 1236 are not identical in both sources.[141] The different location of the later text corrections points in the same direction.[142] The texts of Rodez, Raymond, the Friars of the Sack and the Penitents of Mary Magdalene must therefore be regarded as separate, mutually independent witnesses to the constitutions of the Dominicans in the thirteenth century.[143]

When viewed separately, the documents examined are each defective witnesses of the earliest constitutions, because they hand down the text either partially, or indirectly, or inaccurately. None of them gives an adequate picture of the Dominican legislation, neither in its historical growth after 1216, nor at the

---

135 See *supra*, p. 246, note 13.
136 See *supra*, pp. 246-249.
137 See *supra*, p. 251, note 43.
138 See *supra*, p. 256.
139 See *supra*, p. 258.
140 See *supra*, p. 260, with footnote 92, p. 263, with footnote 106.
141 See *supra*, pp. 266-267.
142 See *supra*, p. 266, with note 122.
143 For the relationship between the various texts, see the schema at the end of the text of the constitutions in Appendix V.

end of its development around 1237. This observation applies not only to the Penitent Sisters and the Friars of the Sack, who only adopted and handed down what corresponded to their spirit and ideals, but also to Raymond, who primarily – and thoroughly – changed the structure and division, and who, moreover, in various places expanded or abridged the text. And even the Rodez manuscript does not always transmit the old constitutions fully and entirely faithfully.

A number of general conclusions can be drawn from this. Any passages that are identical in the four legal texts are, without a doubt, the authentic Dominican textual tradition. Whenever these texts diverge, the original version can only be reconstructed by comparing the manuscripts.

Complete concordance between all manuscripts occurs only in several relatively rare cases. This is so because not all the legal texts in question contained the Dominican constitutions in their entirety. First, the Penitent Sisters omitted almost the entire second *distinctio*, because the internal organisation of a male order, containing guidelines for the apostolate and for studies, did not apply to them. They adopted only four chapters.[144] The first *distinctio*, containing the rules on the regular life, the observances and the *culpae*, can be found for the most part both in the *Institutiones S. Sixti* and in the *Constitutiones S. Mariae Magdalenae*. Not so for the Friars of the Sack, because their manuscript lacks seven chapters from the *distinctio prima*.[145] A confrontation between the four legal texts is only possible, therefore – apart from the chapters from the second *distinctio* already mentioned – for the chapters in the first *distinctio* that deal with the office in choir (c. 1-4), meals and fasting (c. 5-9), sleep and the care of the sick (c. 10-12), the novitiate (c. 13) and part of c. 14 (to the extent that the text has been preserved in the case of the Friars of the Sack) and the penalties for faults (c. 21 partially, where the text of the Friars of the Sack begins again, up to and including c. 25). And there are numerous variants even in the parts that are present in all four manuscripts, so that complete concordance occurs only very sporadically.

§ 2. The Rodez manuscript as the basis for the reconstruction of the old text of the constitutions

In most cases, if we wish to discover the original text, we must have recourse to a comparison of four, three or two manuscripts. The Rodez manuscript must be used as much as possible as the basis for this, as it is the only one that was intended to preserve the Dominican constitutions in their primitive form. Unless there is reason to prefer one or more others, C must be considered the best version. This methodological principle can be applied without hesitation whenever C can be compared with only one other manuscript. This is so because

---

144 M, c. 26, *De suffragiis mortuorum* (cf. C, II, 22, *De anniversariis*); c. 24, *Quod sorores claustrum non egrediantur…* (cf. C, II, 31, *De predicatoribus*); c. 22, *De domibus* (cf. C, II, 35, *De edificiis*); c. 25, *De recipiendis conversis* (cf. C, II, 37, *Regula conversorum*).

145 See *supra*, p. 262, with note 104.

the potential competitor, R, *Inst.*-M or S, may in each case have had reasons of its own to deviate in some detail from the *Constitutiones antiquae O.P.*, so that it must always be presumed that C has preserved the authentic text, except if there are clear orthographic errors, lacunae or other inaccuracies. The version of the other manuscript is noted in each occasion as a variant, or is taken as the original text in place of the corrupt text in C.

The reconstruction of the text becomes more complex when C must be confronted with two or more manuscripts. If C concurs either with R, or with S, M-*Inst.* or Prémontré, the text may be regarded as wholly reliable.[146] The version contained in the other manuscripts can in this case be ignored, unless their mutual correspondence forms an indication for the existence of a double textual tradition.[147] But if C is the only source with a version that differs from two or more of the other manuscripts, the chances are that it no longer represents the original constitutions in their correct version.[148] To put it differently, correspondence between R and M-*Inst.* or S – or between it and both of these – against C must usually be explained by assuming that the Rodez copyist, on his own initiative or on account of his prototype, deviated from the authentic text

---

146 Instances in which C agrees only with R are frequent. First of all, there are parts of the text that appear only in C and R, especially in dist. II: that is, c. 13, *De morte magistri* (in d. II, c. 4, *De electione magistri* in R); c. 23, *De conventu mittendo* (in d. II, c. 1, *De domibus concedendis* in R); c. 30, *De doctore* (the last part of d. II, c. 14, *De studentibus* in R); c. 35, *De edificiis* (in d. II, c. 1, *De domibus concedendis* in R). But in shorter passages, too, C and R often agree only with each other; at the end of d. I, c. 1, both have an explanation on why the morning chapter was omitted: "aliquando etiam intermittitur, ne studium impediatur" (*om.* M and S).

    In other cases, C and S concur. These instances clearly show where R deviated from the older version.

147 Compare the following cases (A = *Acta cap. gen. O.P.*):

	C – S		R – M
intrante	C, I, 2	ingresso	R, II, 6
	S, I, 2		M, c. 2
De anniversariis	C, II, 22	*De suffragiis*	R, I, 3
	S, II, 32	*mortuorum*	M, c. 26
	C – A		R – S
commode	C, II, 15	*om.*	R, II, 3
	A, p. 8, l. 8		S, II, 15
commissas	C, II, 16	*om.*	R, II, 3
	A, p. 6, l. 8		S, II, 16

148 No fewer than 76 of such cases were found:
    C vs. R-M-S: 16 cases;
    C vs. R-S: 52 cases (including A in six cases);
    C vs. R-M: 7 cases;
    C vs. R-A: 1 case.

of the constitutions, while the other manuscripts, independently of each other, transmitted the original text intact.[149] The version of C has in such cases been included in the critical apparatus, either as a variant or possibly as a reflection of a second textual tradition.

Special attention must also be given to the relation between R and S. In dozens of places, they go against the other manuscripts together. In more than fifty of the cases in which the C version is unique, R and S are in correspondence with each other.[150] In other cases, they stand together against other texts, C, *Inst.*-M, A and Prémontré, which either differ among or correspond with each other. It would be unwarranted to regard the correspondences between this pair as simply a matter of chance. It is more likely that R and S often derive from a single, old textual tradition, while the other groups have either each individually diverged from this, or have jointly used a different text of the Dominican constitutions. In the latter case, however, the methodological principle formulated above dictates that preference must be given to the group to which C belongs, but the possibility always remains that R and S represent a second textual tradition.[151]

---

149 The place of a number of chapters in C is also called into question by the comparison with the other manuscripts. C has *De anniversariis* as d. II, c. 22. But this arrangement is not very logical, as the chapter appears between rules on the organisation of the order. The place which this chapter occupies in S and M is more appropriate: at the end of dist. II, as d. II, c. 32 (the antepenultimate chapter) in S, as c. 26 (last chapter) in M. In R, it appears as d. I, c. 3, in conjunction with the liturgical rules contained in d. I, c. 1-2. Perhaps the copyist of C positioned this chapter as d. II, c. 22 because he found available space in his copy after the chapters that regulate the government of the order (d. II, c. 1-21) and before the rules on the internal organisation of the monasteries. – The chapter *De edificiis*, by contrast, is best kept as d. II, c. 35, as C indicates. In M, too, this rule occurs among the later additions (c. 22). S does not have any separate chapter on buildings, but places all rules on poverty together in a new chapter, d. II, c. 24, *De paupertate*, which is an extended version of the corresponding chapter in C, d. II, c. 26, *De possessionibus*.

150 See *supra*, footnote 148.

151 The following are a number of characteristic examples (but see also the critical apparatus with the edition of the text in Appendix I):

		R – S	
I,	1 (l. 8)	profunde pro tempore	profunde C
			pro tempore M
	10 (l. 6-7)	iacere poterunt, sicut fuerit eis stratum	sicut eis stratum fuerit, iacere poterunt C, A
	22 (l. 21)	preter hoc autem	de cetero C, Prém.
II,	15 (l. 13)	mortuo priore provinciali vel amoto	item provinciali priore mortuo vel amoto C
			item provinciali mortuo vel amoto A
	16 (l. 6)	*om.*	commissas sibi C, A

In the third case it is unlikely that accidental carelessness on the part of the copyist can explain the use of two different expressions, particularly as the texts of Prémontré also testify to one of the two parties. Only a double textual tradition can sufficiently explain this.

The hypothesis of diverging traditions in the earliest constitutions is supported by something else: the clear affinity between R and the legislation of the
sisters. The field covered by the current study is of course limited and the cases
observed are not always such that they permit drawing well-founded conclusions.
Often it is merely a matter of style or of minor additions or omissions.[152] But in
a number of cases, there are more important similarities that permit us to draw a
clear dividing line between R-M (*Inst.*) and the group of the other manuscripts,
including occasionally also Prémontré. Thus, only R and M-*Inst.* contain the vow
of renunciation of the world made by novices when they are admitted.[153] The two
texts have the same title for certain chapters, while C and S together appear to
represent a different tradition.[154] The structure of the *Regula fratrum conversorum*
chapter points in the same direction.[155]

The frequent correspondence between R and Prémontré vis-à-vis C and S
does not permit definite conclusions as to the existence of a double textual
tradition. It is not impossible, of course, that Raymond, in revising the old text,
consulted the statutes of the Premonstratensians to correct certain details in his
sample that appeared unclear or mistaken on the basis of these statutes, which

---

152 See also the following cases in which R and M correspond:

		R – M		C – S
D, I, c.	2 (l, 2)	ingresso		intrante
	13	ubique		*om.*
	(l. 14)	*om.*		in claustro C
	(l. 21)			ubique S
	14 (l. 6)	austeritatem.		asperitatem.

153 See the texts in R, I, 13 (ed. R. Creytens, *Les constitutions … de s. Raymond de Peñafort*, p. 39) and M,
c. 13 (ed. A. Simon, *L'ordre des Pénitentes*, p. 162).

154 By way of comparison see:

	R – M			C – S
De officio ecclesie	R, I, 1	*De horis et modo dicendi*	C, I, 4
	M, c. 4			S, I, 4
De suffragiis mortuorum	R, I, 3	*De anniversariis*	C, II, 22
	M, c. 26			S, II, 32
De vestitu	R, I, 10	*De vestibus*	C, I, 19
	M, c. 16			(S in the list before dist. I).

155 C, II, 37; R, II, 15; M, c. 25; S, II, 35 respectively.
   The fragment "in aliis autem horis septem *Pater noster* dicent et in vesperis quatuordecim" (C)
appears as follows in R and M: "in vesperis (vero: R) quatuordecim, in aliis autem horis septem *Pater
noster* dicant"; and is missing in S. – The sentence "Et hoc totum…" appears immediately after the
sentence "Loco Pretiosa" in C and S, but immediately before this sentence in R and M.

were the primary source for the Dominican constitutions.[156] No double textual tradition probably yet existed in the original constitutions, from 1216 to 1220.[157] It appears to have come into being as a result of the revisions of the text by the general chapters starting in 1220.[158] Perhaps the new texts were not recorded fully accurately and completely in every detail by the representatives of the provinces, so that the copies of the constitutions in the houses in certain areas were amended in a way that deviated from the official version approved by the chapter.[159]

§ 3. Certain text-critical problems

In order to properly define the content of the earliest constitutions it is necessary to examine certain text-critical issues in detail. The *terminus ad quem* of the pre-Raymundian legislation corresponds with the definitive approval of the new redaction in 1241. Theoretically, the textual evolution of the *Constitutiones antiquae* therefore ended with the chapter of the previous year, 1240;[160] in fact, it ended in 1236, the year in which the last changes were made.[161] However, both the Rodez manuscript and that of the Friars of the Sack and the Penitent Sisters contain a number of corrections that appear to date from 1241 or even later. Logically these should therefore be omitted from the earliest constitutions in order to restore the text to its earlier state. But closer inspection reveals that various texts assumed to be the work of later chapters in fact were part already of the earliest constitutions.

---

156 The following are a few typical cases in which R corresponds more closely with the text of Prémontré than with the other manuscripts:

	R – Prém.	C – S
Prol. (l. 11)	si	sed
I, 6 (l. 5-6)	in vigilia Laurentii et Assumptionis sancte Marie	*om.*
I, 14 (l. 7-8)	*om.*	et seculo abrenuntiare
I, 23 (l. 58-59)	*om.*	proclamatione
I, 25 (l. 5-6)	*om.*	primam et secundam.

157 For the evolution of this legislation, see *infra*, chapter IV.
158 The hypothesis of a double textual tradition on the basis of the relationship R-S (p. 272) is indeed supported by texts that appear in the chapter reports of 1236 (see *supra*, p. 266, note 120) and in the chapters of the constitutions that were apparently edited subsequently by the Dominicans. For the dating of the texts listed on p. 272, footnote 151, see the apparatus of the edition of the text (only variant I, 22 (l. 21) appears to have been part of the earliest text). – As regards the relationship R-M (p. 273), the grouping of the manuscripts into various families appears to date from an earlier period: some variants already appear in the texts derived from Prémontré (see footnote 151). This presupposes that there were diverging versions as early as 1216-1220.
159 See *supra*, pp. 267-268.
160 Only the general chapter had the authority to change the constitutions: *Const. ant.*, d. II, c. 6-7.
161 See *supra*, p. 245.

The chapter *De levioribus culpis* mentions a penalty to be imposed upon those who show excessive animosity in proclaiming the faults of others during the daily chapter.[162] Judging from the text of the *Acta*, this rule was originally placed somewhere else and was positioned here only in 1241.[163] But the sentence was already included in the chapter in question, not only in the Rodez manuscript and in that of the Friars of the Sack,[164] which both derived, independently of each other, from the earliest constitutions, but also in the statutes of Prémontré,[165] which were adopted remarkably faithfully by the Dominicans in these sections. It is certain, therefore, that both manuscripts represent the original arrangement of the Dominican constitutions. Very probably, Raymond also found this fault listed among the *culpae leviores* in his copy, but decided to move it to *De gravi culpa* on his own initiative.[166] However, this change was rejected by the chapters that had to judge his revision of the text. The ordinance found in the *Acta capitulorum* of 1239-1241 is therefore merely a correction of Raymond's *ordinatio*, as the context of the *Acta* in fact also suggests to a certain extent.[167]

Something similar applies to a different fragment that ended up among the *culpae graves* in Raymond's manuscript and was moved to the lighter faults by the chapters of 1240-1242.[168] Both the Rodez manuscript and the constitutions of the Friars of the Sack and the German Penitents already include the sentence in question in the chapter *De levioribus culpis*, albeit not in the place determined

162 "Si quis clamans in clamatione sua iudicium fecerit" (d. I, c. 21, ed. H. C. Scheeben, *Die Konstitutionen*, p. 61, no. 34).
163 "Item illud: Si quis in proclamatione sua iurgium fecerit, ponatur in levi culpa, post illud verbum: vindicando clamare presumpserit" (*Acta C.G.*, vol. I, p. 13 (1240); p. 19 (1241). The *inchoatio*, which must have taken place in 1239, does not appear in that year's *Acta*). – This text differs in two minor details from that of the constitutions: "proclamatione … iurgium" (in 1241 the *Acta* also have "iudicium", perhaps due to a transcription error).
164 In C, d. I, c. 21, p. 69 (ed. H. C. Scheeben, *Die Konstitutionen*, p. 61); in S, d. I, c. 22 (ed. G. M. Giacomozzi, *L'Ordine della Penitenza*, p. 85).
165 *Institut. Praem.*, d. III, c. 2.
166 R, d. I, c. 17: "Si quis clamans in clamatione sua iurgium fecerit" (ed. R. Creytens, *Les constitutions… de s. Raymond de Peñafort*, p. 43). It must be noted that this text also has "iurgium", like the *Acta*.
167 "Hec ordinatio et correctio et additio [of Raymond] universaliter observetur… Et hec habet duo capitula. Hoc tamen addimus… Item si quis in proclamatione sua iurgium fecerit, ponatur in levi culpa…" (*Acta C.G.*, p. 13). The correction was not made in the copy containing Raymond's constitutions, where the sentence still appears in *De gravi culpa*: see previous footnote and R. Creytens, *ed. cit.*, p. 43, with comment on p. 42 (footnote 66) and pp. 13-14 (footnote 31, no. 6). The sentence in question occurs twice, once in *De gravi culpa* and a second time in *De levi culpa*, in the following copies: constitutions of Montargis, c. 16, *De levi culpa* and c. 17, *De gravi culpa* (R. Creytens, *Les constitutions… de Montargis*, pp. 76 and 77 respectively); constitutions of Humbert, d. I, c. 16 and c. 17 (in *Anal. O.P.*, vol. III, 1897-1898, p. 57); constitutions of the Dominican Sisters (1259), c. 18 and c. 19 (in *Anal. O.P.*, tomo cit., p. 344).
168 "Quod dicitur in gravi culpa: Si indumenta vel alia data fratri vel concessa sine ipsius licentia alius acceperit etc., ponatur in titulo de levi culpa post illud: negligenter tractaverit" (*Acta C.G.*, pp. 14, 19, 21).

by the *Acta*.[169] This is yet another indication that all three had found this rule in the old text of the constitutions, as a special admonition to ensure that the right to use articles of clothing be respected. Included among the *culpae graves* by Raymond,[170] it was moved back to its previous chapter by the chapters of 1240-1242, although not to the same place it had originally occupied, but this time to the rules on the use and treatment of material goods; a more suitable place.[171] In the later constitutions, the correction was made according to the text of the chapter reports.[172]

The general chapters of 1252-1255 added a text to clarify the concept of *praedicator generalis*.[173] According to some, this late stipulation was included in the manuscripts C and S at the beginning of the second *distinctio*.[174] However, the formulation is not identical in the two cases, neither as regards form nor content. According to the *Acta*, the appointment of *praedicatores generales* was entrusted to the provincial chapter. But according to the relevant text in the constitutions, appointment to this function was first and foremost the business of the general chapter, and only subsequently of the provincial chapter. This disposition is a logical consequence of the process of decentralisation in the government of the order. Initially, issues related to preaching were the exclusive preserve of the general chapter.[175] The provincial chapter gradually acquired limited powers, until it was given the full and exclusive right to appoint *praedicatores generales* in 1255.

---

169 In C, I, 21: p. 69 (ed. H. C. Scheeben, *Die Konstitutionen*, p. 62, no. 39). In S, I, 22 (ed. G. M. Giacomozzi, *L'Ordine della Penitenza*, p. 85). This sentence appears at the end of the chapter in both cases, as the penultimate in a series of *culpae*. It does not appear in the rest of this chapter. In *Inst.*, the sentence in question appears in c. 12, *De culpis mediis* (ed. A. Simon, *L'ordre des Pénitentes*, p. 147), the chapter that corresponds to *De levioribus culpis* with the Dominicans (see *supra*, p. 255 and in the edition of the text, Appendix I).

170 R, d. I, c. 17 (ed. R. Creytens, *Les constitutions... de s. Raymond de Peñafort*, p. 43).

171 The correction was made only partially in R: the sentence was not omitted from *De gravi culpa* (see R. Creytens, *ed. cit.*, p. 43, note 70), but was added in the margin of the chapter *De levi culpa* (*ibid.*, p. 42, note 65).

172 In the constitutions of Montargis: c. 16 (R. Creytens, *Les constitutions... de Montargis*, p. 76). In Humbert's constitutions: d. I, c. 16 (*Anal. O.P.*, vol. III, 1897-1898, p. 57). The sentence no longer appears in the constitutions of the Dominican Sisters (1259), because the whole chapter was thoroughly reworked compared to the earlier constitutions of the sisters (represented by *Inst.* and Montargis): *Anal. O.P., tomo cit.*, p. 344 (c 17).

173 "In capitulo de capitulo provinciali, ubi dicitur: et predicatores generales, addatur: Predicatores autem generales dicimus, qui per priorem provincialem et diffinitores provincialis capituli fuerint instituti" (*Acta C.G.*, pp. 61, 67, 72).

174 "Predicatores autem generales sunt, qui per capitulum generale vel priorem provincialem et diffinitores capituli provincialis fuerunt approbati" (*Const. ant. O.P.*, vol. II, c. 1).

175 One of the main points in the general chapter's programme was precisely enquiry into the suitability of the preachers. *Const. ant. O.P.*, d. II, c. 20, draws a clear distinction between preachers who had been mandated only by their prior, and those approved by the general chapter: "Post hec qui idonei ad predicandum ab aliquibus estimantur, presententur et illi, qui de licentia et mandato sui prioris, necdum licentia maioris prelati vel capituli predicationis officium receperunt... et hiis de eis testimonium perhibentibus, consensu et consilio maioris prelati approbabunt...". These texts are very old, see *infra*, pp. 384-385, including note 88; p. 389, and note 122. On this issue, see H. C. Scheeben,

The earlier procedure can still be found in C and S, which represent the earliest constitutions. Raymond omitted this stipulation together with many others, for reasons that we can no longer ascertain.[176] Some years later it was included again in a new form that reflected the evolution that had occurred in the governmental organisation of the order.

The chapters of 1245-1247 inserted an ordinance in the constitutions that banned asking favours for relatives.[177] This rule can already be found, in more or less identical terms, in the Rodez manuscript, but also in the constitutions of the Friars of the Sack and of the Penitents of Mary Magdalene.[178] The fact that it appears in the three representatives of the *Constitutiones antiquae* appears to indicate that the text in question belonged to the pre-Raymundian legislation. Otherwise, it would have to be assumed that the three manuscripts C, S, and M, which were created independently of each other, would together have adopted only this text from among the dozens of ordinances that were added to the constitutions by the chapters after 1240.[179] Of course, it is not absolutely impossible that we are dealing here with an ecclesiastical ordinance that applied to all religious. But there is no trace of it in the constitutions of other orders. The most likely explanation, therefore, is that Raymond also omitted this rule, whether intentionally or unintentionally. Later general chapters, wishing to remind the friars of this issue, reintroduced it into the constitutions.

The investigation described above warrants a number of conclusions on the mutual relationships and value of the legal codes that have been discussed. First, it is clear that none of these manuscripts are directly dependent on each other. Not only were they copied at different times, they also each render the Dominican legislation in a different form. Wherever they correspond with each other, there is no doubt that the passage in question reflects the earliest constitutions in their authentic form. In most cases, however, the original text can only be approximated after studying the similarities and divergences that are present in the manuscripts. The Rodez manuscript must naturally serve as the basis for this comparison, but it requires correction in many places, especially if two or more of the other legal codes together represent the oldest version more accurately. The correspondence that can be observed between pairs of texts leads us to hypothesise that diverging

---

Prediger und Generalprediger im Dominikanerorden des 13. Jahrhunderts, in *Arch. F.P.*, vol. XXXI, 1961, esp. pp. 112-122.
176 See R. Creytens, *Les constitutions... de s. Raymond de Peñafort*, p. 9, note 17.
177 "Nullus frater instare audeat vel rogare pro beneficiis suis consanguineis obtinendis" (*Acta C.G.*, pp. 31, 34, 38).
178 In C, II, 26 (ed. H. C. Scheeben, *Die Konstitutionen*, p. 76); in S, II, 30 (ed. G. M. Giacomozzi, *L'Ordine della Penitenza*, p. 109); in M, c. 21 (ed. A. Simon, *L'ordre des Pénitentes*, p. 165).
179 From 1242 to 1247, the general chapters made no fewer than 28 textual emendations to the constitutions, see: *Acta C.G.*, pp. 21-34. It is striking that the Friars of the Sack adopted only this chapter ordinance from the 1242-1247 period. The other rules of a later date which they adopted were from 1240-1242 and 1254-1258 (see *supra*, p. 263, note 106).

traditions must have emerged at an early stage with regard to certain details. In such cases it is not always possible, on the basis of the documents currently at our disposal, to restore the text of the Dominican constitutions to its original form.

Conclusion

Textual study of the earliest constitutions of the Dominicans has so far always been based on the Rodez manuscript, the text of which has been presented as faithfully as possible by the editors upon correction of clear writing errors. Our investigation of a number of related documents has brought to light certain facts which show that this manuscript possesses only limited value and that it is possible to achieve a better edition of the text. Use can be made here of the legislation of the Dominican Sisters, which has in large part been preserved in the *Institutiones S. Sixti* and in the *Constitutiones S. Mariae Magdalenae*. In various places, these two legal codes accurately reflect the original rule of the Dominican cloistered nuns, which itself derived from the *Constitutiones antiquae O.P.* The statutes of the Friars of the Sack are similarly useful for the reconstruction of the text, as they were copied from the first *consuetudines* of the Dominicans. And Raymond of Peñafort's redaction also preserved a great part of the old text.

Despite its many imperfections, the Rodez manuscript must still be the basis for a new edition of the text, as it is the only one we currently have that was intended to represent the primitive constitutions of the Dominicans. However, it must be compared with Raymond of Peñafort's *ordinatio* and with the legal codes of the Penitent Sisters of Mary Magdalene and the Friars of the Penitence of Jesus Christ. In some cases, the *Acta* of the general chapters can also be consulted, either to supplement the text or to clarify the mutual relationships between the various manuscripts. The *consuetudines* of Prémontré, the main source for the first *distinctio* of the Dominicans, are occasionally also of service. Often, these texts can help to approximate the authentic version whenever the other manuscripts fail to offer sufficient criteria, and they can also help to recognise the oldest text in a number of fragments that have been preserved only in the legislation of the sisters.

It is evident from this preliminary enquiry that the study of the sources can help solve certain problems that arise in relation to the text of the earliest Dominican constitutions. We will shed further light on the issue of the origins and dependencies of this legislation by systematic research of the Premonstratensian *consuetudines*, as well as of the other documents that influenced the constitutions of the Dominicans or that are somehow related to it.

CHAPTER III

The sources

Serious study of the sources is indispensable if we are to gain deeper insight into the origins and development of the medieval monastic statutes, and penetrate to the correct meaning of their content. It was a generally applied and accepted method in the Middle Ages to quote texts from other works. Explicit or implicit quotations were used to illustrate, but also as material for scholarly treatises. The name of acknowledged *auctoritates* was always a good reference and a guarantee of the reliability and soundness of the doctrines proposed. Modern editors of scholastic treatises and ascetical writings must often spend many hours to identify the passages in Holy Scripture and the works of the church fathers and other Christian writers that served as source material for medieval authors. Chroniclers and annalists eagerly copied what they found in previous works. Similarly, legal writing often quoted traditional legal texts as arguments from authority. Ecclesiastical legislators and canonists preferred to base their solutions for new problems and situations upon the regulations and rulings of previous popes and councils, which had been included in private and official compilations and made the subject of standard glosses in the *summae* by decretists and decretalists. In their interpretation of the legal texts, the commentators tried to draw as much as possible upon the works of authoritative authors who had preceded them. The legislation of communities such as cities, guilds and confraternities consists largely of codified customary law, or of rules derived from the statutes of neighbouring or influential municipalities.

The link with tradition was seen as a secure guarantee, particularly in the field of monastic customs. *Novatores* were regularly treated with suspicion.[1] As research of the sources advances, it is becoming ever clearer that even the most brilliant monuments of monastic legislation were inspired by previous examples. Benedict's *Regula monasteriorum* contains undeniably original opinions and guidelines, but also many elements derived from other writings.[2] The *consuetudines* of the

---

1 The *opusculum* by an anonymous author, *Quidam contra singularitatem quorumdam*, perhaps contains an echo of Saint Bernard's warnings against unmotivated innovations in the field of monastic customs. "Est enim disciplina correctio morum iuxta exempla maiorum et pacem sociorum et regulam praeceptorum ... Novitas offendit antiquitatem, singularitas universitatem, ..." (ed. J. Leclercq, *Études sur saint Bernard et le texte de ses écrits*, in *Analecta S. Ord. Cist.*, vol. IX, 1953, p. 201).

2 See Ph. Schmitz, *Histoire de l'ordre de saint Benoît*, vol. I, Maredsous, 1942, pp. 27-30, with bibliography. For sources and parallel texts, see *Sancti Benedicti Regula monachorum*, ed. C. Butler, Freiburg im Breisgau, 1935; see also the ed. by B. Linderbauer (Florii. Patrist., vol. 17), Bonn,

various Benedictine families are largely variations on a single basic theme of laws and customs.[3] The Carthusians looked to other monks and authoritative ecclesiastical authors for the organisation of their eremitical life.[4] The traditions of the Benedictines shaped the legislation of canonical institutions, mainly through the influence of Cîteaux.[5] The mutual affinities between the various congregations of canons regular are also unmistakable.[6] They can be explained by accidental circumstances, such as geographical proximity, or by the spiritual dominance of a certain *ordo*, the contribution of a member of another monastery in the redaction or revision of the statutes, or by the fact that the popes issued certain guidelines simultaneously for several orders at once. Sometimes the sources are explicitly referenced, either in the text itself or in related documents. In other cases, the mutual dependence of the texts is evident even at cursory comparison, but in others again it can only be discovered through thorough textual analysis.

As regards the Dominican constitutions, some research of the sources has already taken place. In an incomplete work, Humbert of Romans a few times pointed out the reliance of the Dominicans on the Premonstratensians, although he did not explore the issue further.[7] He also consulted the statutes of the Cistercians, Carthusians, Victorines, Franciscans, Templars and other orders, not so much to establish their literary influence upon the Dominican legislation, but to acquire a better understanding of the essence and obligations of the monastic life.[8] H. Denifle was the first to give a more precise impression of the manner in which

---

1928. For the relationship between the *Regula S. Benedicti* and the *Regula Magistri*, see *supra*, p. 184, footnote 4, with the work by G. Penco quoted there, who defends the chronological priority of the *Reg. Mag.*, in contrast to Th. Payr, *Der Magistertext in der Überlieferungsgeschichte der Benediktinerregel*, in *Regula Magistri – Regula S. Benedicti* (Studia Anselmiana, vol. 44), Rome, 1959, pp. 1-84.

3 For the origins and history of the *consuetudines* of the Benedictines, see *supra*, pp. 185-186.

4 A. De Meyer – J. M. De Smet, *Guigo's* Consuetudines *van de eerste Kartuizers*, pp. 65-76.

5 For the origins of the Cistercian customs, see *supra*, p. 188, note 27. For the dependence of Prémontré on Cîteaux, Cluny and Hirsau, see *supra*, p. 193, footnote 61. Objections have been raised to certain ideas in H. Heijman's work quoted there, for example by Pl. Lefèvre, *Prémontré, ses origines, sa première liturgie, les relations de son code législatif avec Cîteaux et les chanoines du Saint-Sépulcre de Jérusalem*, in *Analecta Praem.*, vol. XXV, 1949, pp. 96-103. See also P. Vermeer, *De invloed van de* Carta caritatis *van Cîteaux op de statuten van Prémontré*, in *Studia catholica*, vol. XXVI, 1951, pp. 65-77. For the influence of Cîteaux on other orders, see *supra*, p. 195, footnote 66.

6 For the dependence of Marbach on Saint-Ruf, see *supra*, p. 192; of the Holy Sepulchre and Arrouise on Prémontré, see *supra*, pp. 194-195; of Hérival on Prémontré, see H. Heijman, *Untersuchungen über die Praemonstratenser-Gewohnheiten*, in *Analecta Praem.*, vol. IV, 1928, pp. 225-241; of Val-des-Écoliers on Saint-Victor, see *supra*, p. 195.

7 "Notandum est quod constitutiones Praemonstratensium omnino eodem modo incipiunt, et ex hoc elicitur, quod verum est, quod constitutiones nostrae extractae sunt ab illorum constitutionibus, cum ipsi nos praecesserint: et hoc iustum fuit" (Humbert of Romans, *Expositio super Constitutiones*, pp. 2).

8 "Sciendum autem quod compilator huius opusculi diligenter respexit statuta religionum diversarum et approbatarum in Ecclesia Dei, videlicet Cisterciensium, Carthusianorum, Sancti Victoris, Fratrum Minorum, Templariorum et aliorum multorum..." (*ibid.*).

the Dominicans had used their main source.[9] He referred to the corresponding places in the Prémontré text in the footnotes to the first *distinctio* in his edition of the Rodez manuscript. In a number of places he gave the full texts, explaining the technical details of the derivation. The same method was used by H. C. Scheeben, who supplemented or corrected his predecessor's work in several places.[10] He also showed the necessity of taking a broader approach to the study of the sources, one which also includes the *consuetudines* of the other monastic institutions.[11]

For these reasons, our analysis of the sources of the Dominican constitutions must be as wide-ranging as possible, and may not a priori exclude any relevant documents. As the affinity and dependencies of the first *distinctio* are wholly different from those of the second, the analysis will be done separately for these two parts. This provides an obvious structure for this chapter, in two sections. Each section begins with a comparison of the constitutions of the Dominicans with those of other monastic institutes, which makes it possible to draw up an inventory of the various influences and related texts. This is followed by an attempt, through more systematic analysis, to identify the source texts and determine the nature and extent of the similarities and dependence more precisely. Whenever appropriate, the technical details of the derivation will be addressed and solutions to certain issues will be proposed. Texts that cannot be identified with certainty as sources despite striking literary similarity, but that are perhaps merely parallels or indirect derivations, have also been noted.[12] Further study or future chance discoveries will perhaps one day confirm and explain their deeper affinity with the Dominican constitutions.

---

9 H. Denifle, *Die Constitutionen ... vom Jahre 1228.*

10 H. C. Scheeben, *Die Konstitutionen*, pp. 49-66.

11 H. C. Scheeben, *op. cit.*, pp. 17, 34-38.

12 As is the case today, many terms and expressions were commonplace in the Middle Ages. Remote textual affinity is rarely the result of accidental use of identical or related texts by two authors. Usually, it can be explained by unconscious quoting of terms and sayings that had wide currency, or by the purposeful editing of derived texts with the intention of adapting them to the deriver's own insights. In both cases, attempts to identify the source would take too much time and might ultimately not produce any satisfactory results. On the other hand, highlighting textual affinity, as has been done for example in the edition of the *Regula S. Ben.* by C. Butler and B. Linderbauer (see *supra*, p. 279, note 2), can help to point other researchers in the right direction. Cf. also *Expositio quatuor magistrorum super Regulam Fratrum Minorum (1241-1242). Accedit eiusdem Regulae textus cum fontibus et locis parallelis* (Storia e letteratura. Raccolta di studi e testi, vol. 30), ed. L. Oliger, Rome, 1950. In the Appendix (pp. 173-193), the editor gives the text of the *Regula bullata*, with sources and parallel texts, which he happened to have noted over the course of forty years. His references are to three kinds of texts: sources proper ("...veram fontis habent rationem..."); parallel texts ("...loci paralleli, qui easdem saepe continent ideas..."); accidentally similar texts ("...velut fortuito verbis eisdem expressi...") (pp. 171-172).

Section I. The sources of the first *distinctio*

The first part of the Dominican constitutions consists mainly of a description of daily life in a religious community and of rules for specific categories or individual members. Their content and form clearly mark the texts as belonging to the genre of the *consuetudines*, which most medieval communities of monks and canons regular had. The Dominicans stayed well within the boundaries of tradition by deriving the rules for their community life primarily from existing monastic legislation. By far the largest part of this first *distinctio* coincides with texts from the statutes of the Premonstratensian canons. A first subsection will address the relationship between the two orders. Other texts, though significantly fewer in number, have no literary or substantive similarity with Prémontré, but with other institutions, especially of monks, canons and other monastic communities. A second subsection explores these various influences and textual similarities, and investigates the traces of certain ecclesiastical ordinances for the monastic life.

§ 1. The consuetudines *of Prémontré as the principal source*

Even without Humbert of Romans's testimony, a superficial encounter with the first *distinctio* of the Dominicans suffices to show that it is strongly dependent on Prémontré. However, no precise picture has so far been drawn of the extent of the material derived, because the constitutional history of the two orders was insufficiently known. Not all problems have now been resolved, but recent critical studies and text editions make it possible to complement previous results.

The study of the text conducted above has shown that certain parts of the earliest constitutions of the Dominicans have been preserved more faithfully in the *Institutiones S. Sixti* and the *Constitutiones Sororum S. Mariae Magdalenae* than in the Rodez manuscript, and that these parts resemble the legislation of Prémontré even more closely than had hitherto been realised.[13] As regards the *Consuetudines* of the Premonstratensians, previously scholars had to make do with a text from the second half of the twelfth century.[14] Only in 1946 was a later codification, dating from approximately 1236-1238, made available.[15] The editor of this text used two manuscripts copied in the fourteenth and sixteenth century respectively.[16] A manuscript in the Bibliothèque Nationale in Paris has

---

13 See *supra*, esp. pp. 255 and 258-260.

14 *Institutiones Patrum Praemonstratensium*, ed. E. Martène, *De antiquis Ecclesiae ritibus*, vol. III, pp. 323-336. These statutes give the legislation as it was perhaps around 1174 (cf. Pl. F. Lefèvre, *op. infra cit.*, pp. X-XIII and XXXII, note 1). This text will henceforth be referred to as Pa.

15 *Institutiones patrum Premonstratensis Ordinis*, ed. Pl. F. Lefèvre, *Les statuts de Prémontré réformés sur les ordres de Grégoire IX et d'Innocent IV au XIIIe siècle*, pp. 1-143. This text will henceforth be referred to as Pb.

16 Pl. F. Lefèvre, *op. cit.*, pp. XXVI-XXVIII.

the same text in an older transcription.[17] It once belonged to the abbey of the Premonstratensians in Wedinghausen-Arnsberg in Westphalia, as the top margin of fol. 1ᵛ notes in modern script: *monasterii Wedinghausani*.[18] It was copied in a regular, decorous hand that appears older than it actually is. The copyist cannot have completed his work before 1256, as he copied a number of papal bulls (*privilegia*) in the same hand, the last of which was issued by Alexander IV.[19] The text of the constitutions in this manuscript has relatively many variants, but it is generally not better than the text in Pl. F. Lefèvre's edition, and is less complete. The lists of the chapters before each *distinctio* already contain the titles as they appear in the edition mentioned, but some chapters have been wholly or partially omitted in the body of the text.[20]

It is thanks to these two publications that we now have both the *terminus a quo* and the *terminus ad quem* of the development that the statutes of Prémontré experienced for over half a century. For our purposes – a study of the sources – we would like to have the specific text that the Dominicans used as a model, probably around 1215-1220. But as long as the full reports of the general chapters of Prémontré from the late twelfth and the early thirteenth century are lost, it will not be possible to reconstruct the text of the legislation of this order with certainty for the years in question.[21] For the time being, we will have to content ourselves with the two known codifications.

---

17 *Ms. lat.* 9752, fol. 1ᵛ-25ᵛ. Cf. L. Delisle, *Inventaire des manuscrits latins*, Paris, 1863, p. 48.

18 On this abbey, see N. Backmund, *Monasticon Praemonstratense*, vol. I, Straubing, 1949, pp. 149-151.

19 Bull *Apostolicae auctoritatis* of 21 August 1256. Cf. *Regesta Pontificum Romanorum*, ed. A. Potthast, no. 16525.

20 Dist. III, c. 10, *De crimine effornicationis* (cf. Pl. F. Lefèvre, *ed. cit.*, p. 80) was omitted. The copyist copied only a third of dist. IV, c. 1, *De annuo capitulo*, up to and including "et conversi *Miserere mei* et *Pater noster*" (cf. Pl. F. Lefèvre, *ed. cit.*, p. 86). The following chapters (c. 2-8) were omitted. The text continues with c. 9, *De hiis que non licet habere* (cf. Pl. F. Lefèvre, *ed. cit.*, p. 108). The following chapters appear on fol. 25ʳ: d. IV, c. 12, *De non recipiendis sororibus* (cf. Pl. F. Lefèvre, *ed. cit.*, pp. 114-115), immediately followed by c. 19, *De custodia sigilli et pecunie aliene* (cf. Pl. F. Lefèvre, *ed. cit.*, p. 122: *De custodia sigilli conventus, pecunie proprie et aliene*). This is followed by c. 23, *De culpis incertis et penis earum* (cf. Pl. F. Lefèvre, *ed. cit.*, p. 125). It is no longer possible to identify a specific motive for these omissions. – We will refer continually to the edition by Pl. F. Lefèvre for the comparative study of the Premonstratensian and Dominican statutes. The variants of the Paris manuscript are of little importance, except at the end of d. I, c. 20, *De rasura*, where the text is as follows: "…sextadecima in festo Omnium Sanctorum, septimadecima in Adventu" (cf. *infra*, p. 296).

21 Twelfth- and thirteenth-century decisions of the chapters that have been preserved are rare and almost never dated. The statutes of the twelfth century were followed by twelve further statutes (see *supra*, p. 204, note 119). Pa, IV, 12-16 perhaps also contains ordinances of a general chapter. For chapter texts from the twelfth and thirteenth centuries, see *supra*, p. 204, note 120. For other additions to the legislation of the twelfth and early thirteenth centuries, for instance on the basis of papal bulls, see Pl. F. Lefèvre, *Les statuts de Prémontré, passim*, in the footnotes.

A. Textual affinity

1. The external arrangement of the chapters

The first *distinctio* of the Dominicans was compiled using material spread across four *distinctiones* in the Prémontré text.[22] Of the twenty chapters from the first *distinctio* in the Prémontré text, nine were omitted.[23] From the second *distinctio*, which deals with the monastic offices, only the ninth chapter (*De magistro novitiorum*) was adopted, and this only partially.[24] The third *distinctio* (on faults and penalties) was copied almost in its entirety.[25] Only a few chapters were used from the fourth *distinctio* (on interconventual organisation): chapters that had been added later in the Prémontré text and that in fact belonged to the first *distinctio* as regards their content.[26]

Generally speaking, the order of the chapters was respected, except for the regulations on the care of the sick, which the Dominicans placed before the chapters on admission and the novitiate.[27] The chapter *De vestibus*, from the second *distinctio* in the Prémontré text, was inserted before c. 20, *De rasura*.[28] The third and fourth chapters of the first *distinctio* in the Prémontré text lack any parallel and interrupt the natural progression of the text.[29] It is clear from the list of chapters at the end of the *prologus* of the constitutions, *De capitulo et prima, missa et horis aliis*, that the Dominicans originally had the same order as Prémontré. Whereas all the other titles correspond with at least one separate chapter, the titles *De prima* and *De missa* no longer have any matching content in the Rodez manuscript. The place

---

22 See the list with the concordance of the chapters in Pl. F. Lefèvre, *Les statuts de Prémontré*, Annexe III, pp. 146-151. For an overview of the relationship between the Dominican constitutions and both redactions of Prémontré, see the list printed *infra*, in Appendix VI. For affinity with other statutes, see Appendix VII.

23 In Pa (as the basis for the comparison): d. I, c. 2-3, 7-9, 11-12, 15, 18. For Pb, see the concordance in Pl. F. Lefèvre, *loco cit.*

24 Dist. II has seventeen (Pa) and nineteen (Pb) chapters respectively in the Prémontré text.

25 With the exception of c. 5, *Quid faciendum sit si quid de Sacramento Dominici Corporis alicubi ceciderit*, which interrupts the logical sequence of chapters in Pa and was moved to the end of dist. III in Pb.

26 The schema below indicates the location of the chapters in question in both the constitutions of the Dominicans and in the Prémontré text:

O.P.		Pa		Pb	
D. I, c. 8,	*De pulmentis*	D. IV, c. 12-13,	*De victu*	D. I, c. 10,	*De victu*
19,	*De vestibus*	14,	*De vestitu*	II, 13,	*De vestitu*
20,	*De rasura.*	15,	*De rasura.*	I, 20,	*De rasura.*

As can be seen, these chapters were moved to the first *distinctio* in the later redaction of the Prémontré text, except for the chapter *De vestitu*.

27 D. I, c. 11, *De infirmis*; c. 12, *De minutione*. See the list of chapters in Appendix VI.

28 See *supra*, footnote 26.

29 The Prémontré text does indeed follow the sequence of the liturgical ceremonies in the morning: c. 1, *De matutinis*; c. 2, *De prima et Missis post primam*; c. 3, *De privatis confessionibus*; c. 4, *De capitulo.*

occupied in the Prémontré text by the second and third chapters is occupied in the Dominican text by two newly inserted chapters (c. 3-4). But as the section *De capitulo* logically followed the office, it was placed immediately after *De matutinis*, the last words of which were changed to accommodate the connection.[30] The rules on the cloister and the office in choir thus occupied the third and fourth place respectively.

The Dominicans did not always copy the titles of the chapters faithfully. Chapters 5-8 deal with meals and fasting. C. 5, *De refectione*, and c. 6, *De ieiunio*, correspond with the chapters in the Prémontré text that give the detailed horarium for the summer and winter months.[31] By far the largest part of the text, the part that stipulates the time of work, reading, rest and prayer, was omitted, except for the first sentences. The chapters *De refectione* and *De victu* in the Prémontré text were renamed *De prandio* and *De pulmentis* respectively in the Dominican text.[32] C. 10, *De lectis,* was composed by bringing together three sentences from two different chapters in the Prémontré text.[33] Finally, it is not clear why c. 18, *De scandalo fratrum*, should form a separate chapter. In the statutes of the Penitents of Mary Magdalene, it appears as the last sentence of the preceding chapter.[34] It is derived from the Prémontré text, where it appears in the chapter *Quomodo se habeant fratres tempore lectionis*.[35]

The Dominicans list all lighter faults against regular discipline under a single title, *De levioribus culpis*, whereas Prémontré divides them into *culpae leviores* and *culpae mediae*.[36] A number of stipulations have been inserted between the two series, and three of these insertions correspond with Pa.[37] Five other insertions are related to studies and preaching and are clearly of Dominican origin.[38] The disappearance of the title *De mediis culpis* is perhaps not due to carelessness on the

---

30 "Finitis matutinis tenetur capitulum, vel aliquando post primam, aliquando etiam intermittitur, ne studium impediatur, secundum quod videbitur prelato" (d. I, c. 1).

31 In Pa and Pb: c. 5, *Quomodo se habeant fratres in estate* and c. 6, *Quomodo se habeant fratres in hieme*.

32 Pa, I, 10 and IV, 12; Pb, I, 9 and I, 10 respectively.

33 "Super ... possint" is from Pa, I, 17, *De dirigendis in via*. This sentence does not occur in Pb. The rest, "Cum tunica ... licebit" was taken from the chapter *Quomodo se habeant fratres post completorium* (Pa, I, 14; Pb, I, 12).

34 C. 15, *De silentio* (ed. A. Simon, *L'ordre des Pénitentes*, p. 164). The text of the Friars of the Sack is proof that this sentence constituted a chapter of its own in the original constitutions of the Dominicans, because it is announced there separately in the list of chapters at the beginning (ed. G. M. Giacomozzi, *L'Ordine della Penitenza*, p. 74). The text is missing in the corpus of the constitutions, as it was one of the chapters that disappeared from the manuscript of the Friars of the Sack (see *supra*, p. 262, footnote 104). – Raymond of Peñafort moved it to c. 14, *De novitiis et eorum instructione* (see R. Creytens, *Les constitutions ... de s. Raymond de Peñafort*, p. 40).

35 Pa, I, 9. This sentence no longer appears in Pb.

36 D. I, c. 21 in the Dominican text; d. III, c. 1-2 in the Premonstratensian one.

37 "Si quis potum ... sumpserit" = Pa, III, 2; – "si quis parentibus ... presumpserit" = Pa, III, 3; – "si ad *Gloria* primi ... non satisfecerit"; cf. Pa and Pb, I, 2: "Qui ad primum psalmum non occurrerit, satisfaciat stans ante gradum presbiterii...".

38 D. I, c. 21: "si in studio ... intenderit". Even a slight omission in these matters was considered a fault by the Dominicans because these obligations were closely linked to the apostolic mission of the order.

part of the copyist. It is more likely that it was omitted purposefully, because the last sentence of the previous chapter and the first of the following in fact deal with the same subject: failure to be on time during the office. In the *Institutiones S. Sixti*, the two chapters were still separate.[39] But a few short sentences had already been added to the end of c. 11, *De levioribus culpis*, concluding with the penalty for the faults: the recitation of a Psalm. A more substantial punishment was prescribed at the end of the following chapter, *De culpis mediis*: a *disciplina* and a number of Psalms. The Dominicans added both kinds of punishment together at the end of the single chapter *De levioribus culpis*. The following schema gives a clearer picture.

Pa, III, 1	Pb, III, 1	Magd., c. 11	O.P., I, 21
De his omnibus veniam petentibus iniungatur psalmus unus.	De hiis omnibus veniam petentibus iniungatur psalmus unus, et unius correctionis fiat eis disciplina.	Pro singulis harum culparum iniungatur pro pena petenti veniam unus psalmus.	

III, 2	III, 2	c. 12	
Clamatis de supradictis et veniam petentibus fiat unius correptionis disciplina, cum tot psalmis quot placuerit illi, qui capitulum tenebit.	Clamatis de supradictis et veniam petentibus fiat unius correctionis disciplina, cum tot psalmis quot placuerit illi, qui capitulum tenebit.	Clamata in capitulo pro aliqua predictarum culparum petat veniam et unam recipiat disciplinam modestam, cum tot psalmis quot ei placuerit, que capitulum tunc tenebit.	Clamatis de supradictis et veniam petentibus iniungitur unus psalmus vel duo, vel cum psalmo disciplina vel amplius, secundum quod quod prelato videbitur expedire.

2. The internal structure of the chapters

a. The prologue

The *prologus* was clearly drafted on the basis of the Prémontré text. The first part, with its striking reflections on the purpose of written laws and on the necessity of external uniformity as a condition and sign of spiritual unity, was copied literally.[40] The following section on the superior's broad powers of dispensation

---

39 See *supra*, p. 255; A. Simon, *L'ordre des Pénitentes*, p. 147.
40 "Quoniam … defluamus".

presents somewhat of a contrast from a literary perspective. It was not derived from Prémontré,[41] but was interpolated by the Dominicans themselves, with the clear intention of giving priority to the free pursuit of study and the apostolate as their basic principle. The statement on the penal character of the legislation was added in 1236[42] and also appears in the statutes of the Premonstratensians at that time.[43] The division of the constitutions is succinctly indicated at the end of

---

41 The thirteenth-century statutes of Prémontré (Pb) do not assign any general power of dispensation to the abbot. The canons of Saint-Pierremont described the competencies of the abbot as follows at the end of their constitutions: "Sciendum est quod de omnibus supradictis abbas cum suis canonicis ex causa rationabili poterit dispensare" (*Antiquae constitutiones … S. Petri-Montis*, p. 438).

42 "Confirmamus hanc constitutionem quod in constitutionibus, ubi dicitur: 'Eapropter unitati et paci', etc. volumus et declaramus ut constitutiones nostre non obligent nos ad culpam, sed ad penam, nisi propter contemptum vel preceptum" (*Acta C. G.*, p. 8). Previously, this sentence ran as follows, as in Prémontré: "Eapropter, ut unitati et paci totius ordinis provideamus, librum istum, quem librum consuetudinum appellamus, diligenter conscripsimus, in quo duas distinctiones notavimus" (thus in C, which lacks the interpolation of 1236: see H. C. Scheeben, *Die Konstitutionen*, p. 49).

43 "Institutiones vero, quas in presenti libro conscripsimus, non ad culpam obligare intelligimus transgressores, sed ad penam, nisi aliquis eas transgredi presumpserit ex contemptu" (Pb, prol.). According to Humbert of Romans, *Expositio super Constitutiones*, p. 47, the Premonstratensians depended in this on the Dominicans: "Item nota, quod non solum nos habemus huiusmodi constitutionem, sed etiam Praemonstratenses, et dicuntur eam accepisse a nobis, et non habuisse ab initio". Most authors who have dealt with the question assume almost as a matter of course that the Dominicans were the first to include the penal character of their monastic laws in their constitutions (see for example G. Renard, *La théorie des leges mere poenales*, Paris, 1929, p. 20; I. M. Tonneau, *L'obligation ad poenam des constitutions dominicaines*, in *Revue des sciences philos. et théol.*, vol. XXIV, 1935, p. 107; Fidel de Pamplona, *Obligatoriedad de las reglas en los siglos XII y XIII*, in *Revista española de derecho canonico*, vol. VIII, 1953, p. 780. See however the comments by V. Vangheluwe, *De lege mere poenali*, in *Ephem. theol. Lovan.*, vol. XVI, 1939, pp. 384-388). And yet Humbert's statement can hardly be regarded as sufficient evidence. He acknowledges that the issue had been dealt with previously by the Dominicans and that Dominic had personally decided the matter in the way indicated (Humbert, *op. cit.*, p. 46). But it is not impossible that the Premonstratensians, too, had adopted their ordinance in the prologue of their statutes before 1236, as was the case for many stipulations that were adopted by the Dominicans (see *infra* in this chapter, particularly pp. 304-306). Furthermore, it is not certain that the two orders were immediately dependent on each other in respect of the rule in question, because both the place and the formulation is different (it appears after "Librum istum…" in the Dominican text, and at the end of the *prologus* in the Premonstratensian text). Perhaps the two orders decided this issue – which was then at the forefront of attention and had caused all kinds of difficulties for the Franciscans – independently of each other (see Fidel de Pamplona, *art. cit.*, pp. 772-775; Id., *La obligatoriedad de la regla franciscana*, in *Estudios franciscanos*, vol. LVI, 1955, pp. 347-364). The problem also arose with regard to the obligatory nature of the rules of non-monastic communities, such as the various secular penitential fraternities. The statutes of cities often similarly contained only fines as punishments for infractions. G. Meersseman, *La loi purement pénale d'après les statuts de confréries médiévales*, in *Mélanges J. de Ghellinck* (Museum Lessianum. Section historique, vol. 14), vol. II, Gembloux, 1951, pp. 975-1002, esp. pp. 983-985 made an attempt to seek the origins of the *obligatio ad poenam tantum* in the history of the cities and spiritual sodalities. The penal obligation appeared even before 1236 in the *Memoriale propositi* for Franciscan penitents (see *supra*, p. 221, footnote 221): "In supradictis omnibus nemo obligetur ad culpam, sed ad penam, …" (c. 9, ed. H. Boehmer, *Analekten*, p. 54). According to G. Meersseman, *art. cit.*, p. 985, this text was added to the existing regulations in or before 1228. It does not appear

the prologue. But instead of the four *distinctiones* in the Prémontré text, only two are announced. This is followed, finally, by a summary of the chapters of the first *distinctio*.

b. *Liturgical customs*

Among the passages that were adopted most literally in this first part are the chapters on the office in choir and the daily chapter. C. 1, *De matutinis*, is a faithful copy of Prémontré, except for the last third, which was wholly omitted.[44] There are striking divergences in a passage where Pa and Pb themselves also differ significantly. The Dominicans have certain phrases in common with the first redaction, others with the second. It gives the impression that the text they used represented a middle way between the two. The relations with the various texts have been outlined in the following schema, in which the Dominican text has been placed between the earlier and later redaction of the Prémontré text.

Pa I, 1	O.P., I, 1	Pb, I, 1
Hora itaque devote incepta,	Hora itaque devote incepta, versi ad altare, muniant se signo crucis. Et	Hora itaque devote incepta,
ad *Gloria Patri* inclinent chorus contra chorum profunde	ad *Gloria Patri* inclinet chorus contra chorum profunde vel prosternant se pro tempore	ad *Gloria Patri* inclinent chorus contra chorum, modo predicto iuxta quod tempus exigerit,
usque ad *Sicut erat,* quod faciendum est	usque ad *Sicut erat.* Et hoc faciendum est	usque ad *Sicut erat*; quod faciendum est ad omnes horas diei et noctis, excepto quod inter duo signa inclinandi et surgendi a priore danda, antequam hora incipiatur, non dicitur nisi *Pater noster* tantum.
quotiens *Gloria Patri* dicitur vel *Pater noster* nisi in missa, et *Credo in Deum*	quotiens *Pater noster* et *Credo in Deum* dicuntur, nisi in missa, et ante lectiones et in gratiarum actione. Idem etiam faciendum est	Sed et quotiens dicitur *Gloria Patri* post psalmos, post versiculum introitus misse, post *Venite*,

---

to reflect a Franciscan view, but it cannot be proven with certainty that it must be attributed to Dominican influence, as the author does.

44 "Hoc ... ad signum prime pausent" (approximately twenty lines in Pb, I, 1).

et prima collecta ad missam	ad primam collectam in missa et ad postcommunionem et	ad primam collectam misse et ad primam collectam post communionem numquam super formas sed super genua inclinatur, preterquam cum pro pace et tribulatione Ecclesie et huiusmodi celebratur.
	similiter ad orationem pro Ecclesia	
et ad horas canonicas.	et in singulis horis ad collectam et ad *Gloria Patri*…	

It must be noted that the Dominican text contains a number of passages that occur in neither of the two Premonstratensian codifications. Pa is the shortest text, and all its parts appear both in the Dominican text and in Pb. Pb has several fragments that appear neither in Pa nor in the Dominican text. The latter and Pb have several passages that do not occur in Pa.

The following chapter, *de capitulo*,[45] has only three passages in common with Prémontré: the reading of the martyrology and the reciting of the *Pretiosa*, self-accusation and the imposition of punishment, and the rules for accusing others and accepting commands. In between, diverging rules were inserted concerning the course of the daily chapter. The Dominican text is considerably less detailed, especially towards the end. It appears to be based on the statutes of Prémontré, which it severely condensed.

Pa, I, 4	O.P., I, 2
Cum conventus capitulum ingreditur, singuli suo ordine versus maiestatem inclinent. Et cum omnes ad sedes suas pervenerint, omnibus stantibus, dicat lector: *Iube, domne*, et hebdomadarius vel abbas, si duplex festum fuerit, dicat hanc benedictionem: *Divinum auxilium.*	Intrante conventu capitulum
Deinde lector pronuntiet lunam et que de calendario pronuntianda sunt, et sacerdos prosequatur: *Pretiosa*, etc. Et residentibus fratribus, lector subiungat lectionem de regula. Postea pronuntiet in tabula fratres qui notati sunt ad aliquid legendum vel cantandum; et qui… resideant.	lector pronuntiet lunam et que de kalendario pronuntianda sunt. Et sacerdos prosequatur: *Pretiosa*, etc. Et residentibus fratribus, lector pronuntiet lectionem de institutionibus vel de evangelio pro tempore, premisso *Iube, domne*. Et hebdomadarius subiungat benedictionem: *Regularibus disciplinis* vel *Divinum auxilium* pro tempore.

---

45 D. I, c. 2 in the Dominican text; d. I, c. 4 in the Premonstratensian one.

Cum ille qui capitulum tenet, *Benedicite* dixerit, humilient se omnes, respondentes: *Dominus.*

Et facta absolutione pro defunctis, dicat qui tenet capitulum: *Benedicite* et, responso *Dominus*, inclinent omnes. Deinde, recitatis … *qui se reos estimant.*

Continuo, qui se reos intellexerint, prostrati veniam petant.

Continuo, qui se reos intellexerint, prostrati veniam petant. Deinde surgentes humiliter confiteantur culpas suas.

Et quorum culpa talis est, … quam correptionem prior vel supprior, vel alius cui iniunctum fuerit, faciat.

Et quorum culpa talis est, … Quam correctionem faciat prior vel ille, cui ipse iniunxerit.

c. *Faults and penalties*

The lists of faults against regular discipline,[46] which were the fullest and most literal derivation, confirm our supposition that an evolved version of the Prémontré text served as the source. In the first part of c. 21, only a few sentences from the corresponding chapters in Pa and Pb were omitted.[47] The second half closely followed the chapter *De mediis culpis* in Prémontré.[48] The only adaptations were that certain stipulations were assigned a different place,[49] others were omitted,[50] and some were abridged.[51] A number of additions in the Dominican constitutions relate to the duty of study, the demeanour to be adopted outside the monastery, and the observance of poverty.[52] A comparison can once again clarify the relationships between the various texts.

---

46 D. I, c. 21-25 in the Dominican text; d. III, c. 1-10 in the Prémontré text.

47 "Si cereum (maiorem) fregerit" (Pa and Pb, III, 1); "si corrigiam rasoriorum inciderit" (*ibid.*); "si quid vestimenti sui peioraverit vel perdiderit" (*ibid.*).

48 On the difference between *culpae leviores* and *culpae mediae*, see *supra*, p. 255.

49 "Si commune mandatum dimiserit" in the Prémontré text appears after the words "ad collationem non venerit"; – "si quis de via … exierit": in the Prémontré text after "iudicium fecerit"; – "si quis potum … sumpserit": in the Prémontré text after "non interfuerit".

50 Pa, III, 2: "Si ad opus manuum non occurrerit; si dormientibus fratribus per negligentiam defuerit; si quis hore canonice vel communi refectioni non interfuerit". In addition, three lines after "cantores in officiis" have been omitted; as have three lines after "infirmorum custos in infirmis…".

51 After "cantores in officiis suis", Prémontré has: "quibus annotati sunt, exequendis".

52 After "priores in conventu custodiendo", the Dominican text has: "magistri in docendo, studentes in studendo, scriptores in scribendo." Another new addition is: "si oculos … direxerint; si indumenta … acceperit".

Pa, III, 1	O.P., I, 21	Pb, III, 1
He sunt leviores culpe: si quis, mox ut signum datum fuerit, non relictis omnibus … si in conventu venire distulerit;	Hec sunt leviores culpe: si quis, mox ut signum datum fuerit, non relictis omnibus… si in conventu, hora qua debet, venire dis- tulerit; …	He sunt leviores culpe: si quis, mox ut signum datum fuerit, non relictis omnibus
	si ad mensam cum ceteris non venerit; …	si ad mensam cum ceteris non venerit;
si corporale … stolam vel fanonem negligenter ad terram deiecerit, …	si corporale … stolam vel phanonem negligenter deiecerit …	si corporale … stola vel manipulus per eius negligentiam ad terram ceciderint; ….

On the other hand, there are differences between the two redactions of the Prémontré text. Pb is much more extensive and adds rules on silence.[53] The Dominican text most closely resembles Pb in the chapter *De gravi culpa* (c. 22).[54] Two-thirds of c. 23, *De graviori culpa,* is literally derived from the Prémontré text.[55] The last part was omitted[56] and replaced by three sentences that together nearly fill the space left by the omission.

Pa, III, 6	O.P., I, 23	Pb, III, 4
	…vel si in peccatum carnis quis lapsus fuerit, quod gravius ceteris puniri censemus.	Porro si in peccatum carnis extra monasterium quis lapsus fuerit, vel de eo gravi- ter infamatus,
Si quis etiam in alio monasterio tale quid commiserit,	Si quis tale quid extra monasterium commiserit, frater qui cum eo est, studeat excessum eius quam citius corrigendum prelato intimare.	magister vel frater qui cum eo est, excessum huiusmodi quam citius poterit, abbati vel ei qui loco eius fuerit, studeat intimare corrigendum.
	Correctus autem, ad locum, in quo tale quid commiserit,	Punitus vero modo predicto, ad locum in quo tale quid commiserit,

---

53 Pb, III, 2: "Qui autem silentium … ieiunent".

54 And yet three little sentences that are present in Pa and in the Dominican text are missing in Pb: "Si quis silentium …; si quis inter fratres …; si quis mala …".

55 Pa, III, 6; Pb, III, 4.

56 Pa, III, 6: "Quod si quis domno abbate, … ceteris parcitur". In Pb, III, 4, this section was substantially abridged.

ulterius non redeat, etiamsi per omnia correptus inventus fuerit.

ulterius non redeat, nisi ita religiose fuerit conversatus, quod generale vel provinciale capitulum ipsum illuc censeat reversurum.

ulterius non redeat, nisi religiose fuerit conversatus et sine scandalo possit illuc remitti. ...

Si quis autem pro huiusmodi suspectus est, re veniente in dubium, differatur interim ... probata,

Si vero huiusmodi peccatum occultum fuerit,

Quando autem abbas venerit, si peccatum occultum fuerit et res in dubium venerit,

districtione tamen secreta, secundum personam et tempus, condignam agat penitentiam, in qua non sibi, sed ceteris parcitur.

disquisitione secreta, secundum tempus et personam, condignam agat penitentiam.

facta super hoc inquisitione secreta, secundum tempus et personam, si reus inventus fuerit, puniatur.

d. *Monastic customs and obligations*

The chapters on meals and fasting (c. 5-8), which already deviated from the order in the Prémontré statutes by their position in the text,[57] are also less similar to their model as regards content. C. 7, *De prandio*, is a strongly abridged copy of the corresponding chapter in the Prémontré text.[58] As it turns out, the second part ("Verumtamen ... contenti") was inspired by a monastic tradition,[59] but the prohibition on passing on items of food is indebted to the customs of the canons.

Pa, I, 10	Pb, I, 9	O.P., I, 7
De cibo communi nemo dividat alicui; quod si cui aliquid superadditum fuerit, ...	Quod si cui aliquid preter communem cibum vel potum speraddendum fuerit, ... ille cui missum fuerit,	
poterit dare iuxta se sedenti ad dexteram vel ad sinistram, ille vero ultra nulli dare debent.	sedenti ad dexteram, si voluerit, et ad sinistram; nullus tamen mittat pitantiam alicui preter illum qui tenet mensam maiorem.	Frater non mittat fratri pictantiam, excepto priore, sed sibi datam potest dare a dextris et a sinistris.

---

57 See *supra*, p. 285.
58 *De refectione*: Pa, I, 10; Pb, I, 9.
59 See *infra*, pp. 308-310.

The text of the Dominicans is closely linked to the later legislation of the Premonstratensians, which itself appears to have been influenced by the *consuetudines* of the monks.[60]

The following chapter, c. 8, *De pulmentis*, derived only a few sentences from the corresponding place in the Prémontré text.[61] The last part was adopted from other chapters.[62] The evolution of the texts is illustrated in the following schema.

Pa, I, 10	O.P., I, 8	Pb, I, 9
Si quis vero de comedentibus vel servitoribus	Si quis de servitoribus vel comedentibus serviendo vel comedendo	Si quis vero de comedentibus
aliquid offenderit aliquo modo,	in aliquo offenderit, surgentibus fratribus,	in aliquo offenderit, surgentibus fratribus post cibum, in medio refectorii prostratus,
veniam petat	veniam petat	veniam petat, nola dimissa;
et, facto sonitu ab abbate vel priore, surgat et redeat ad locum suum.	et, facto signo a prelato, redeat ad locum suum.	et, facto sonitu a prelato, surgat, revertens in suo ordine inter fratres. Et servitores quotienscunque offenderint, veniam petent prostrati.[63]

Only the first two sentences of the chapter *De magistro novitiorum* (c. 13) are reminiscent of Prémontré.[64] There is a very close affinity with the old text of Prémontré with regard to the external ceremony for the acceptance of new members (c. 14),[65] but one important rite was omitted. According to the customs of certain medieval monastic institutes, novices had to renounce their possessions

---

60 The rule concerning the *pitantia* can be found in Cistercian sources as early as circa 1137: "Abbas ... in conventum pitantiam non mittat, praeter abbatem loci" (*Statuta cap. gen. Ord. Cist.*, vol. I, p. 27. See also J.-B. Van Damme, *Genèse des* Instituta generalis capituli, in *Cîteaux*, vol. XII, 1961, p. 57). There is no doubt that there is a connection between the statutes of Prémontré and those of Cîteaux. In the latter, the text continues as follows at the indicated place: "Nullusque abbatum ... faciat pitantiam nisi ille qui sedet ad nolam, nisi forte iuxta se sedenti".

61 The first sentence ("Pulmenta ... conventibus") and the fourth sentence ("Singulis ... permiserit") were taken from the chapter *De victu* (Pa, IV, 12; Pb, I, 10).

62 "Si quis ... ad locum suum" was almost literally adopted from *De refectione* (Pa, I, 10; Pb, I, 9).

63 The rule of the *venia* was a classical feature even of older monastic customs: *Memoriale qualiter* (eighth century), c. 4, ed. C. Morgand, in *Initia consuetudinis Benedictinae*, Siegburg, 1963, p. 245; *Antiquae consuetudines ... S. Victoris*, c. 41; *Antiquae consuetudines ... de Monteforti*, c. 14. One of the last rules in this chapter in the Dominican text, "Quicumque ... accipiat", appeared in Pa as a separate chapter (d. I, c. 12), but had already been moved to the end of *De refectione* in Pb (d. I, c. 9).

64 "Prior novitiis ... potest dare" = Prém., d. II, c. 9.

65 The text of Pa, I, 16, *De novitiis probandis*, and that of the Dominicans begin with the ceremonial of the admission itself, while Pb, I, 14, *De novitiis recipiendis*, starts with the conditions for admission.

and the world when they entered.[66] Pa does not quote the formula itself, but there is a clear reference to its substance, "abrenuntiantes seculo et proprietatibus communem vitam promittant". The Dominicans retained the same terms, but placed them in the context of a slightly adapted sentence, thus lifting the obligation of immediate *abrenuntiatio*. Pb similarly no longer demanded the renouncing of possessions that Pa prescribed.[67] A comparison clearly reveals the redaction of the text.

Pa, I, 16	O.P., I, 14
Quod si responderint se velle cuncta servare,	Qui si respondeant se velle cuncta servare et seculo abrenuntiare,
dicat post cetera: *Deus … perficiat.* Et respondeat conventus: *Amen.* Postea abrenuntiantes seculo et proprietatibus,	dicat post cetera: *Dominus … perficiat.* Et conventus respondeat: *Amen.* Et tunc, depositis vestibus secularibus et religiosis indutis, in nostram societatem in capitulo recipiantur. Sed tamen adhuc, antequam stabilitatem et
communem vitam promittant	communitatem promittant et obedientiam
et ab hinc incipient tempus probationis.	prelato et successoribus suis faciant, tempus probationis assignetur.

A large part of the chapter *De silentio* is indebted in substance, though less so in form, to the statutes of Prémontré. The Premonstratensians in the thirteenth century had relatively few explicit rules on silence. Pa even lacked a specific chapter on the subject. A few brief admonitions in other chapters and the penalties for infractions were all this text had on the obligations of recollection and silence.[68] In the later redaction Pb, the number of rules was considerably extended, especially in the chapter on demeanour outside the cloister, whose title was expanded to

---

66 The rule of Benedict (c. 58), upon which Prémontré is evidently based, twice mentions a *promissio* before the professing of vows proper: "Si promiserit de stabilitate sua perseverantiam, … Et si habita secum deliberatione promiserit se omnia custodire et cuncta sibi imperata servare…". – The canons of Reims (*Constitutiones … S. Dionysii Remensis*, c. [10], *De modo recipiendi canonicum*) and Hérival (C. L. Hugo, *Sacrae antiquitatis monumenta*, vol. I, p. 138) also had such a promise. – The text of a formula of this promise can be found in the statutes of Mary Magdalene: "Ego N. voveo et promitto Deo et beate Virgini et beate Marie Magdalene me de cetero in religione victuram et numquam ad seculum reversuram, et in huius rei testimonium subscribo" (A. Simon, *L'ordre des Pénitentes*, p. 162). It disappeared from the earliest constitutions of the Dominicans, but was reinstated in Raymond of Peñafort's text (d. I, c. 13, *De recipiendis*): R. Creytens, *Les constitutions … de s. Raymond de Peñafort*, p. 39. This was, however, a promise *ad libitum* of the candidate.

67 "… et respondeat conventus: *Amen.* Qui tunc non cogantur abrenunciare seculo vel proprietati, sed a die receptionis erunt in probatione per annum" (Pb, I, 14).

68 Pa, I, 14, *Quomodo se habeant fratres post completorium*; I, 17, *De dirigendis in via*; I, 19, *De infirmis qui sunt in infirmitorio*; III, 2, *De mediis culpis* (in the last sentence, which was evidently added later).

De dirigendis in via et silentio observando.[69] This meticulously listed the conditions under which religious were permitted to speak during meals taken outside the monastery. *Silentium* within the cloister was only discussed under the grave faults.[70] The second part of this chapter consists of an extensive addition to the short statute of Pa and it lists the penalties that are to be imposed according to the gravity of the faults. The substance of a number of these stipulations appears in the Dominican text in c. 17, which was adapted and supplemented in 1236.[71]

Pa, I, 17	O.P., I, 17	Pb, I, 16
Egredientes fratres ad mensam silentium tenebunt, nisi necessitate cogente.	In mensa autem omnes fratres ubique intus et extra silentium teneant, tam priores quam alii,	Fratres egredientes, tam abbates quam subditi, … ubique intus et foris, in mensa comedentes silentium observabunt,
Si plures fuerint, prior pro eis loquatur. Similiter abbates si plures fuerint, unus loquatur, ceteri taceant.	excepto uno, qui maior fuerit inter ipsos, vel alio, cui pro se loqui commiserit, et tunc ipse taceat.	Absente vero abbate, prior … vel … maior ordine loqui potest, et uni tantum de sociis suis … licentiam, si voluerit, det loquendi …
III, 2		III, 2
Qui autem silentium fregerit, sicut in generali capitulo statutum est,	Si quis vero silentium illud fregerit ex proposito, vel licentiam loquendi dederit,	Qui autem silentium scienter fregerit [I,16: Qui si multum facilis vel pronus fuerit ad dandam licentiam loquendi, …] unam correctionem accipiat et
unam diem in pane et aqua ieiunabit.	in uno prandio aquam tantum bibat absque dispensatione, et similiter unam disciplinam coram omnibus recipiat in capitulo.	unam diem in pane et aqua sine remissione ieiunet. Qui autem … veniam … postulaverit … sine dispensatione ieiunabit … una die non bibat nisi aquam tantum, …

The conclusion of the section and the following sentences again closely resemble the rules that relate to the care of the sick in the Prémontré text.[72] The laws were not as strict for the sick.

---

69 Pb, I, 16.
70 Pb, III, 2, *De mediis culpis.*
71 "In mensa autem … infirmi decumbentes" (*Acta C. G.*, p. 6-7).
72 Pb, I, 18.

Pb, I, 18	O.P., I, 17
… de silentio … observando, illi qui graviter infirmantes decumbunt in lectis non ligantur…	Ab hiis autem excipiuntur infirmi decumbentes.
Infirmi qui sunt in infirmitorio sedentes in mensa non loquantur; … Infirmi autem … dicto completorio suo … silentium observabunt.	Infirmi non decumbentes a prandio usque ad vesperas silentium teneant, similiter et post signum quod fit post completorium.

In c. 20, *De rasura*, the old text of Prémontré was supplemented on two separate occasions by a general chapter.[73] In the thirteenth-century codification and in the Dominican text, this chapter obtained its normal place, as the last of the stipulations on monastic observance.[74] The first part is fully identical in the three texts.[75] In the second part, which gives the *termini rasurae*, the Dominican text much more closely resembles Pb than Pa.[76] The *termini* are much more numerous compared to the latter text.

Pa, IV, 13	O.P., I, 20	Pb, I, 20
Rasura fiat hiis terminis:	Que rasura et tonsura fiant hiis terminis:	Que rasura et tonsura fiant hiis terminis:
prima in Nativitate Domini,	prima in Nativitate, secunda inter Nativitatem et Purificationem, partito tempore,	prima in Nativitate Domini, secunda inter Nativitatem et Purificationem, partito tempore,
secunda in Purificatione, tertia partito tempore inter Purificationem et Pascha,	tertia in Purificatione, quarta inter Purificationem et Pascha,	tertia in Purificatione, quarta inter Purificationem et Pascha, partito tempore,
quarta in Pascha, … septima in festo apostolorum Petri et Pauli, octava ad festum S. Petri ad Vincula, …	quinta in Cena Domini, … nona in festivitate eorundem, decima in festivitate sancte Marie Magdalene, …	quinta in Pascha, … nona in festo beati Iohannis, decima … undecima in festo beate Marie Magdalene
decima ante festum S. Dionysii,	tertiadecima in festo sancti Dionysii, quartadecima in festo Omnium Sanctorum,	quinta decima in festo beati Dionysii, [B.N. 9752: sextadecima in festo Omnium Sanctorum]

---

73 Pa, IV, 13.
74 In Pb and O.P., as d. I, c. 20.
75 "Rasura superius … desuper aures".
76 Pa has eleven *termini*, the Dominican text fifteen, Pb sixteen. The Dominican text is closer to Pb as regards the expressions, too. For the variant in Pb (B.N. 9752), see *supra*, p. 283, note 20.

| undecima ad festum | quintadecima in festo beati | sexta decima in Adventu. |
| S. Martini. | Andree. | |

e. *Profession*

The Dominicans' formula of profession[77] shows traces of its original affinity with that of the Premonstratensians, although the precise form of the two texts is not particularly similar. The formulas that were used in Prémontré in the twelfth and thirteenth centuries show only slight variations.[78] They all follow the same pattern and belong to the classical type of the canonical profession, in which the *traditio*,[79] the commitment to serve a particular church, is followed by the three obligations of *conversio morum, stabilitas* and *obedientia,* which already appear in the rule of Saint Benedict[80] and which have since been the traditional constituents of monastic profession.[81]

Due to its simple text, which mentions only *obedientia* explicitly, the Dominican formula is reminiscent more of certain eleventh-century Benedictine

---

77 CA, I, 16.

78 The oldest known formula, from the twelfth century, can be found not in the constitutions of Prémontré, but in the treatise by Adam Scotus, *De ordine, habitu et professione canonicorum Praemonstratensium,* sermo V, no. 1 (PL, vol. 198, col. 479). The thirteenth-century formula can be found in the constitutions in d. I, c. 14 (Pl. F. Lefèvre, *Les statuts de Prémontré,* pp. 25-26). For the texts, see *infra,* pp. 301-302.

79 The *traditio* already occurs in the oldest profession formulas of the canons regular, starting with Saint-Ruf (see *infra,* footnote 83). For Marbach and Saint-Pierremont, see *ibid.*

80 *Reg. S. Ben.,* c. 58: "Suscipiendus autem in oratorio coram omnibus promittat de stabilitate sua et conversatione morum et oboedientiam coram Deo et sanctis eius …". For the meaning of the various expressions in this formula, see for example M. Rothenhäussler, *Zur Aufnahmeordnung der Regula S. Benedicti,* in *Beiträge zur Geschichte des alten Mönchtums und des Benedektinerordens,* vol. III, 1, Münster, 1912, pp. 1-96; Ph. Schmitz, *Bénédictine (Règle),* art. in *Dict. de droit canon.,* vol. II, 1937, col. 300-301.

81 For the history of the Benedictine profession, see for instance I. Herwegen, *Geschichte der benediktinischen Professformel,* in *Beiträge zur Geschichte des alten Mönchtums und des Benediktinerordens,* vol. III, 2, Münster, 1912, pp. 1-72. In Monte Cassino, the threefold formula from the *Regula* was replaced after the restoration (717) by a twofold one, with *stabilitas* and *obedienta* (*ibid.,* pp. 9-35). At the beginning of the ninth century, the original triad was reinstated, but *conversatio* was replaced by *conversio* (*ibid.,* pp. 39, 47-57). This became the traditional form for Cluny (*Antiquiores consuetudines Cluniacenses,* lib. II, c. 27), the Carthusians (*Consuetudines domini Guigonis,* c. 23), and the Cistercians (MS. Dijon 114, fol. 149ʳ, as L. Hilkens, O.C.R. assures us).

profession formulas[82] and of those of Saint-Ruf, Marbach and Saint-Pierremont,[83] which refers only to *obedientia* after the *traditio ecclesiae*. They even more closely resemble the partially new type of profession that emerged towards the end of the twelfth and the early thirteenth century, which omitted the *stabilitas in loco* of the monks and canons regular. The *traditio* to a specific church or abbey was replaced by a formula of commitment that expressed a more personal relationship. This kind of *traditio* to God can already be found in earlier texts, such as in Saint-Ruf,[84] Montfort,[85] the canons of Peter de Honestis,[86] but it was accompanied there by the vow of stability. In the new formulas, the commitment to a particular place was replaced by dedication to the Divine Persons or the Blessed Virgin. A typical example is the profession formula of the Order of the Holy Spirit,[87] which included a promise of service to the sick who were in the care of the order. This expression, which perhaps originally had an ascetical sense, obtained the force of a legal obligation in the profession formula. The formula of Val-des-Écoliers dates from the same period, and similarly suppressed the *oblatio* to the monastery church.[88]

The short Dominican formula was therefore certainly not unique, although there are no corresponding prior models. As regards its substance, it deviates most clearly from the profession formulas of monastic institutes that had adopted the threefold scheme (*stabilitas, conversio morum, obedientia*)[89] or that of the

---

82 See for instance the formula of Reichenau: "Ego ille, domne abba ille, obedientiam vobis secundum regulam sancti Benedicti … Deo et vobis promitto custodire …" (MGH, *Legum sectio V: Formulae Merovingici et Karolingici aevi*, ed. K. Zeumer, Hanover, 1886, p. 569). See also the formulas of Sankt Gallen (I. Herwegen, *Geschichte der benediktinischen Professformel*, p. 24, footnote 2) and Albi (E. Martène, *De antiquis Ecclesiae ritibus*, vol. IV, p. 224, no. XII). For the origins of this formula and its link with the Frankish oath of fealty, see I. Herwegen, *op. cit.*, pp. 25-30. The Cistercians made a promise of *obedientia* immediately after the novitiate, before the profession proper (C. Bock, *La promesse d'obéissance ou la* professio regularis, Westmalle, 1955, p. 3). See also *Usus conversorum*, c. 12: "… promittat ei obedientiam de bono usque ad mortem…" (quoted by J. A. Lefèvre, *L'évolution des Usus conversorum de Cîteaux*, in *Collectanea Ord. Cist. Ref.*, vol. XVII, 1955, p. 94).

83 "Ego, frater ille, offerens trado me ipsum Deo, ecclesiae sancti Ioannis et promitto obedientiam secundum canonicam regulam S. Augustini domno N., praefatae ecclesiae abbati, et successoribus eius quos sanior pars congregationis canonice elegerit" (quoted by Ch. Dereine, *Saint-Ruf et ses coutumes*, p. 180, according to MS. 149 (fol. 11ᵛ) in the Museo Episcopal in Vich. The same text also appears in *ms. lat.* 1233 (fol. 27ʳ) in the Bibl. Nat. in Paris). Cf. *Consuetudines Marbacenses*, c. 55; *Antiquae constitutiones … S. Petri-Montis*, p. 426.

84 See previous footnote.

85 "Ego, frater ill., offerens trado me ipsum Deo et ecclesiae sancti ill. …." (*Antiquae consuetudines … de Monteforti*, c. 29).

86 "Ego, frater S., meipsum omnipotenti Deo offero, et servitium et stabilitatem meam his Sanctorum pignoribus" (*Regula clericorum*, c. 9).

87 "Ego N., offero et trado me ipsum Deo et beate Marie, et sancto Spiritui et dominis nostris infirmis, …" (*Regula S. Spiritus*, c. 2).

88 "Ego, frater N., offero me Deo et beate Marie in ordine Vallis-Scholarium …" (Paris, Bibl. Ste-Genev., MS. 2972, fol. 68ᵛ).

89 Most monks and some canons regular, like Prémontré (see *infra*, pp. 301-302) and Saint-Victor (see next footnote), as well as the Templars (bull *Omne datum optimum* by Alexander III (18 June

three evangelical counsels (*obedientia, castitas, paupertas* or *communitas*).[90] It much more closely resembles Saint-Ruf and related institutes,[91] whose members, after professing the *traditio* to God or to the collegiate church, promised only *obedientia*. Certain details, however, are similar to the profession formulas of other canons, such as the reference to the *consuetudines* as a norm alongside the *regula*[92] and the direct address of the superior who received the vows.[93] This custom has distinctly non-monastic origins. The Benedictines and most other monastic orders made their vows *in praesentia abbatis*,[94] not directly to the abbot, but only in his presence. By contrast, in the new formula of Prémontré, and also in Arrouaise and Val-des-Écoliers, the superior was addressed in the second person.[95] The custom of vowing obedience to future prelates in advance[96] and the addition of the words *usque ad mortem* after *obedientia*,[97] betray a similar affinity.

1163), ed. M. Tangl, *Die päpstlichen Kanzleiordnungen*, p. 243; F. Wilcke, *Geschichte des Ordens der Tempelherren*, vol. I, Halle, 1860², p. 361, footnote 22, which also gives the formula of profession).

90 "Ego ... stabilitatem corporis mei ecclesiae B. Victoris promitto ... emendationem morum meorum, praecipue in castitate, in communione, in obedientia…" (*Antiquae consuetudines ... S. Victoris*, c. 81). This is possibly one of the oldest profession formulas to expressly mention the three evangelical counsels. For the formula of Regny (diocese of Amiens, twelfth century), see Ch. Dereine, *Les coutumiers de Saint-Quentin de Beauvais et de Springiersbach*, p. 436, footnote 5. The formula of Beauvais contained the same elements (*ibid.*, p. 436) as did that of Arrouaise: "Ego, frater N., iam abrenuntiatis omnibus proprietatibus, tibi, reverendo Patri et Domino, huius monasterii abbati, et tuis successoribus promitto obedientiam, castimoniam et huius loci stabilitatem vitamque canonicam secundum regulam B. Augustini et eiusdem loci statuta, usque ad mortem" (F. Gosse, *Histoire de l'abbaye… d'Arrouaise*, p. 89). See also the formula of Val-des-Écoliers: "…promittens emendationem morum meorum, praecipue in castitate et proprii abrenuntiatione. Promitto etiam obedientiam…" (Paris, Bibl. Ste-Genev. MS. 2972, fol. 68ᵛ). The *Regula non bullata* of Saint Francis says: "… vivere in obedientia, in castitate et sine proprio…" (c. 1, ed. H. Boehmer, *Analekten*, p. 1). For the origins of the *obedientia, castitas, paupertas* triad, see L. Hertling, *Die Professio der Kleriker und die Entstehung der drei Gelübde*, in *Zeitschrift für kath. Theol.*, vol. LVII, 1932, pp. 170-172.

91 See *supra*, p. 298, note 83.

92 For the Dominicans: "… secundum regulam B. Augustini et institutiones fratrum ordinis Predicatorum…" (CA, I, 16). For the canons of Arrouaise, see *supra*, footnote 90. The canons of Reims promised obedience "secundum regulam B. Augustini et institutiones bonas et approbatas ecclesiae et dictae regulae consonas" (*Constitutiones ... S. Dionysii Remensis*, c. [10], *De modo recipiendi canonicum*). For the formulas of Prémontré in the twelfth and thirteenth centuries respectively, see *infra*, pp. 301-302. For the connection between the *consuetudines* and *institutiones* on the one hand and the *regula S. Augustini* on the other, see *supra*, pp. 188-195.

93 For the Dominicans: "…promitto obedientiam Deo et beate Marie et tibi, N., magistro ordinis Predicatorum…" (*loco. cit.*).

94 The formula of Cluny (PL, vol. 149, col. 713) and most Benedictine professions concluded with the words: "…in praesentia domini N. abbatis".

95 For Prémontré, see *infra*, pp. 301-302. For Arrouaise, see *supra*, footnote 90. For Val-des-Écoliers: "Promitto etiam obedientiam tibi, frater N., huius ecclesiae prior, et successoribus tuis canonice institutis" (Paris, Bibl. Ste-Genev., MS. 2972, fol. 68ᵛ).

96 For Prémontré, Arrouaise and Val-des-Écoliers, see previous footnote.

97 These words appear in the old formulas of Prémontré (see *infra*, pp. 301-302) and Arrouaise (see *supra*, footnote 90).

Only the introduction *facio professionem* did not previously appear in profession formulas. The term *professio* has retained its wider meaning, which rests on the etymology of the verb *pro-fateri*. In Antiquity and far into the Middle Ages, it referred to the public profession of a conviction, a resolution or, connected to this, a promise, as well as the announcement of an occupation or state of life, or indeed the occupation or state itself, as is still the case in various modern languages.[98] In the context of the monastic state, up until the sixth and seventh centuries, *professio* first and foremost meant the public exercise of the monastic way of life, to which one usually acceded by taking the habit and not by any specific rite of initiation.[99] The word *professio* only acquired its full technical-legal meaning in the seventh and eighth centuries, when it began to mean the express and definitive commitment to the monastic state, not just as a prior declaration of intent, but as the formal confirmation *scripto aut verbo* of the *propositum*, the fixed and binding decision to accept and live the monastic life with all its obligations.[100] The expression *facere professionem*, which can be found in ecclesiastical documents even before the seventh century in relation to the formal promise that priests, deacons, widows and the subjects of clerical institutes were required to make,[101] increasingly acquired[102] the meaning of a particular visible act and an explicit commitment in certain conciliar ordinances and in monastic *ritualia*.[103] The introduction to the Dominican profession formula, *Ego facio professionem*, is therefore original only in the sense that an expression that had been part of the monastic ritual of profession was now incorporated into the text of the formula itself.

The Dominican formula of profession was thus compiled from elements that existed already, either separately or together. Although its simple structure is most

---

98 For the meaning in Roman law, the works of the church fathers, monastic writings and canon law, see C. Capelle, *Le vœu d'obéissance*, pp. 16-87.

99 For the meaning of the expressions *professio monastica, professio sancta, professio monachi*, see C. Capelle, *op. cit.*, pp. 59, 139-140; L. Hertling, *Die Professio der Kleriker* (cf. note 90), pp. 154-156.

100 The connection between *propositum* and *professio* has been studied by C. Capelle, *op. cit.*, whose conclusion is: "Il semble qu'ainsi le sens va passer de l'une à l'autre expression et *professio* tendra de plus en plus à désigner la déclaration solennelle de l'engagement monastique" (p. 168). *Professio* acquired the meaning of "la déclaration ou manifestation extérieure du *propositum*" (p. 196). Cf. P. Séjourné, art. *Vœux de religion*, in *Dict. de théol. cath.*, vol. XV, 1950, esp. col. 3250-3271.

101 For priests and deacons, see canon 27 of the Fourth Council of Toledo (633), in Mansi, vol. X, col. 627. On widows, see canon 4 of the Tenth Council of Toledo (656), in Mansi, vol. XI, col. 35. On *liberti*, see canon 9 of the Sixth Council of Toledo (638), in Mansi, vol. X, col. 666.

102 The expression was already used by the synod held in 828 or 830 in the Abbey of Saint-Denis (MGH, *Legum sectio III: Concilia*, sect. II: *Concilia aevi Karolini*, vol. I, Hanover-Leipzig, 1906, p. 685). See also the *rituale* of the Abbey of Le Bec: "…dicto psalmo, surgentes faciant professionem…" (E. Martène, *De antiquis Ecclesiae ritibus*, vol. IV, p. 227, no. XXIX).

103 In the twelfth century, *professio* was also taken to mean the formula that expressed an action: "…ut de verbis professionis vestrae aliquid tractemus…" (Adam Scotus, *De ordine, habitu et professione canonicorum Praemonstratensium*, sermo V, in PL, vol. 198, col. 479; see also col. 442, 484). For the various meanings of *professio*, see C. Bock, *La promesse d'obéissance ou la* professio *regularis*, Westmalle, 1955, p. 12.

closely associated with the Frankish-Benedictine type[104] and with Saint-Ruf and related institutes,[105] in fact it was based on the example of Prémontré. It is very likely that the formula as it appeared in the earliest constitutions was not the original one.[106] According to the stipulations of the bull *Religiosam vitam*, the first Dominicans, as canons regular, were legally bound by their profession to the church of Saint Romanus in Toulouse.[107] Like the other canonical institutes, their profession formula similarly served to express the promise of *stabilitas*. Traces of the earliest version were preserved in the chapter on admission, which alludes to the essential duties of the monastic life. The terms used are clearly reminiscent of the monastic-canonical scheme of profession (*stabilitas, communitas, obedientia*), while the reference to future superiors was also derived from the customs of the canons regular.[108]

The new Dominican formula of profession can best be explained as a simplification and adaptation of the text of Prémontré. An overview of the three formulas can show this more clearly.[109]

Prém. I	O.P.	Prém. II
Ego, frater N., offerens trado meipsum ecclesie sancti illius et promitto conversionem morum meorum et stabilitatem in loco	Ego N. facio professionem	Ego, frater N., offerens, trado meipsum ecclesie tali, et promitto conversionem morum meorum, emendationem vite et stabilitatem in loco.
	et promitto obedientiam Deo et beate Marie et tibi	Promitto etiam obedientiam perfectam in Christo
(domno N., prefate)	N., magistro ordinis	(tibi, Pater N.,)
(ecclesie preposito,)	Predicatorum, et successoribus tuis,	

---

104 See *supra*, p. 298, note 82.

105 See *supra*, p. 298.

106 The use of the current formula cannot have been adopted before 1220-1221: see *infra*, p. 388, footnote 118.

107 See the letter of privilege *Religiosam vitam* of 22 December 1216: "... et ecclesiam sancti Romani Tolosani, in qua divino mancipati estis obsequio, ... post factam in ecclesia vestra professionem ..." (Laurent, no. 74). See also *supra*, p. 233, footnote 264.

108 "Sed tamen adhuc, antequam stabilitatem et communitatem promittant et obedientiam prelato et successoribus suis faciant, tempus probationis assignetur" (CA, I, 14). According to Gerard of Frachet, *Vitae fratrum*, p. 153, there was mention of *promissio stabilitatis* even in 1219, but it is not clear from the context that this was the formula of profession.

109 In the schema below, the profession formula of the Dominicans (d. I, c. 16) has been placed between the old formula of Prémontré (twelfth century, in Adam Scotus, *De ordine, habitu et professione canonicorum Praemonstratensium* in PL, vol. 198. col. 479) and the new (thirteenth century, in Pl. F. Lefèvre, *Les statuts de Prémontré*, pp. 25-26). The words between brackets are located in the quoted texts at the place indicated by empty brackets.

(et successoribus eius,)	successoribus tuis,	(et successoribus tuis,)
(quos pars sanior)		(quos sanior pars)
(huius congregationis)		(huius congregationis)
(canonice elegerit.)		(canonice elegerit.)
secundum evangelium Christi et secundum apostolicam institutionem et secundum canonicam regulam beati Augustini. Promitto etiam obedientiam usque ad mortem in Christo Domino	secundum regulam beati Augustini et institutiones fratrum ordinis Predicatorum, quod ero obediens tibi tuisque successoribus usque ad mortem.	secundum evangelium Christi et regulam beati Augustini et regularia Premonstratensis ordinis instituta,
( )		( )

In reconstructing their profession formula, the Dominicans first of all omitted the monastic elements of *conversio morum* and *stabilitas*. Instead of the specifically canonical *traditio ecclesiae*, they used a more general introductory formula, *facio professionem*, which in earlier texts had come to mean a definitive commitment to the monastic state.[110] The term *praepositus* or *pater*, used for the prelate of a particular abbey, was replaced by a reference to the general superior, *magister ordinis*, as the recipient of the vow. The words *institutiones fratrum ordinis Praedicatorum* perhaps are a rephrasing of the more abstract formula of Prémontré, *secundum apostolicam institutionem* or an adaptation of the expression *secundum regularia Praemonstratensis ordinis instituta*, which appeared in the first half of the thirteenth century. The addition *usque ad mortem* was deleted from the profession of the Premonstratensians during the course of the same century,[111] but was still part of the older text, which perhaps served as an example for the Dominicans.[112] The comparison with the first formula of Prémontré can also explain to a certain extent the double reference to *obedientia* in the Dominican profession.[113]

---

110 See *supra*, p. 300, footnote 102.

111 These words no longer appeared in the formula in the manuscript of Schäftlarn, currently *Clm* 17174 (Pl. Lefèvre, *Les cérémonies de la vêture et de la profession dans l'ordre de Prémontré*, in Analecta Praem., vol. XIII, 1932, p. 7; G. Van den Broeck, *De professione solemni in Ordine Praemonstratensi*, Rome, 1938, p. 92) nor in that of Grimbergen, which dates from approximately 1228-1236 (E. Martène, *De antiquis Ecclesiae ritibus*, vol. II, p. 180; Pl. Lefèvre, *art. cit.*, pp. 13-14).

112 See table above.

113 According to H. C. Scheeben, *Die Konstitutionen*, pp. 36-37, the Dominicans derived their profession formula from the German Order. The two texts are indeed almost literally identical (cf. M. Perlbach, *Die Statuten des deutschen Ordens*, p. 128). H. C. Scheeben bases his contention primarily on the expression *institutiones*, which also occurs elsewhere in texts of the German Knights. But it can be argued against this that *institutiones* had long been a typically canonical term (see *supra*, p. 189, 210-211) and was used particularly in Prémontré (see *supra*, pp. 193, 204, 210-211). Nor is there any proof that the profession formula in question was used in the Teutonic Order before the mid-thirteenth century. The oldest known manuscript of their statutes was completed in 1264 (M. Perlbach, *op. cit.*, p. XVI), although certain rules supposedly predate this. The profession ritual

B. *The Premonstratensian* Consuetudines *of the early thirteenth century as a direct source*

1. *The material derived from the* Consuetudines

The above survey of the textual affinity has demonstrated that the first *distinctio* of the Dominicans was constructed largely with material derived from elsewhere. The passages copied from the Prémontré statutes constitute approximately one third of the Dominican text, while conversely, approximately one tenth of the Premonstratensian *Consuetudines* can be found in the Dominican constitutions. The legislation of Prémontré can therefore be regarded with good reason as the primary source for the first part of the Dominican constitutions.

The nature and extent of the material adopted also provide insight into the spirit and intent with which the Dominicans used their main source. Prémontré offered them the framework for daily monastic life, the *observantiae canonicae*: the horarium with its recurring elements such as the liturgical office, meals, chapter, rules on admission, investiture, the care of the sick, and finally the penal code as a guideline for behaviour in a wide range of circumstances. They made no use of anything relating to the organisation, either internal (the second *distinctio* with the *officiales* of the monastery[114]) or external (the fourth *distinctio* with the relationship between the abbeys).[115] Of the laws of Prémontré, they adopted the

---

usually appears in the *Gesetze* (*Leges*) or as the conclusion of the *veniae*, that is, in those parts that were composed around 1251 (*op. cit.*, pp. XLVIII, LII). Various chapters in the *Veniae* were adopted from the Dominican constitutions (*op. cit.*, pp. 120-121), but possibly shortly after 1231. The closer ties between the Dominicans and the German Knights date from this time, as a result of the collaboration between the two orders in the Christianisation and colonisation of Prussia (*op. cit.*, p. L). Finally, it is positively certain that the Teutonic Knights derived their breviary and the ritual of their monastic customs from the Dominicans in 1244, as a letter from Innocent IV of 13 February 1244 states: "… caeterum, quia divinum officium secundum ordinem sancti Sepulchri, pro eo quod a pluribus ex iisdem fratribus clericis ignoretur, vix absque scandalo, sicut accepimus, in vestro potest ordine observari, quod illud secundum ordinem fratrum Praedicatorum (amodo) in vestris ubique domibus celebretur, vobis concedimus facultatem" (E. Strehlke, *Tabulae Ordinis Theutonici*, Berlin, 1869, p. 357, no. 471; cf. *Regesta Pontificum Romanorum*, ed. A. Potthast, no. 11257). They probably also adopted the profession ceremony on this occasion, which was described for the Dominicans in a separate *directorium* (see R. Creytens, Le *"Directoire" du* Codex Ruthenensis *conservé aux Archives générales des Frères Prêcheurs*, in *Arch. F. P.*, vol. XXVI, 1956, pp. 117-119). This conjecture appears to be confirmed by the fact that the ritual of the German Knights continues as follows after the formula of profession: "Hiis vero expletis vestiendus est, sicut in regula in capitulo de recepcione continetur". But this chapter appears nowhere in their statutes. Perhaps they adopted this reference from the Dominicans, who *could* refer to their constitutions, which did in fact describe the ceremonies for the investiture, in d. I, c. 13, *De recipiendis* (ed. R. Creytens, *Les constitutions … de s. Raymond de Peñafort*, p. 38).

114 This does not mean that there were no *officiales* in the monasteries of the Dominicans (see Humbert of Romans, *Instructiones de officiis Ordinis*, c. 6-37, pp. 233-338). But the stipulations governing them were not included in the constitutions.

115 See *supra*, p. 284.

consuetudines, but not the constitutional rules proper.[116] Interesting conclusions can moreover be drawn from the passages the Dominicans omitted from the chapters they did adopt: detailed regulations on liturgy[117] and the horarium,[118] extensive regulations on meals[119] and the care of the sick,[120] the obligation to perform manual labour[121] and the *lectio*,[122] or study according to the older monastic view. Their practice of deriving texts was not slavish but calculated, and they did not hesitate to make the adaptations required to render the texts suitable for their own community. Humbert of Romans very accurately characterised this method when he wrote that the Dominicans made a selection by using only the most valuable and suitable elements from the statutes of Prémontré.[123]

2. Further identification of the Premonstratensian text used

If we place the related passages in the Dominican and the Premonstratensian texts side by side, it becomes clear that the text of Prémontré that served as an example does not correspond exactly with the twelfth-century codification (Pa), nor with that of 1236-1238 (Pb). The direct source must have been an evolved text of the statutes of Prémontré that stands somewhere between these two redactions. Only this hypothesis can explain why the Dominican constitutions correspond in some places only with Pa or only with Pb. Thus, the results of our study of the sources can also offer useful clues for research of the constitutional history of Prémontré. Given the absence of the chapter reports of this order, it has hitherto not been possible to date the transition from Pa to Pb. But we can now indicate, at least for some ordinances, either the *terminus post quem* or the *terminus ante quem*. The

---

116 For the distinction between *consuetudines* and *constitutiones*, see *supra*, pp. 195-198, 207-212 (especially pp. 210-212).

117 The first chapter (*De matutinis*) from the first *distinctio* of Prémontré was substantially shortened. The second and third were omitted entirely (see *supra*, pp. 288-289; see also Appendix VI, with a concordance of the chapters in the texts of Prémontré and of the Dominicans).

118 The horarium was meticulously set out according to the seasons in the Prémontré text, particularly in d. I, c. 5-6. The Dominicans in each case just adopted the first sentence: see *supra*, p. 285.

119 Only a few sentences were used from the chapter *De refectione* (Pa, I, 10; Pb, I, 9): see *supra*, p. 293.

120 Two extensive chapters in the Prémontré text (Pa, I, 18-19; Pb, I, 17-18), of which the Dominicans adopted only one sentence, see *infra*, p. 314, footnote 175.

121 The chapter *De labore* (Pa, I, 8; Pb, I, 9) was omitted in the Dominican text. The punishment prescribed in the Prémontré text for persons late for manual labour ("si ad opus manuum non occurrerit": d. III, c. 2) was dropped by the Dominicans from the corresponding chapter in their constitutions (d. I, c. 22).

122 In Prémontré: *Quomodo se habeant fratres tempore lectionis* (Pa, I, 9; Pb, I, 8). Study was an essential obligation in the Dominican text: d. II, c. 28-30. The failings were regarded and punished as an infraction against the observance of the rule: d. I, c. 22. See also p. 285, footnote 38.

123 "Proinde beatus Dominicus et fratres sui temporis ... assumpserunt quod arduum, quod decorum, quod discretum invenerunt in illis, si competens reputarunt" (Humbert of Romans, *Expositio super Constitutiones*, p. 3). Of course, we must take into account the possibility and likelihood that the original constitutions of the Dominicans were even more closely related to the statutes of Prémontré in some places than the text preserved in the manuscript of Rodez (see *supra*, pp. 254-255, 258-260).

passages which the Dominican constitutions share only with Pa were still part of the statutes of Prémontré at the moment of adoption. Conversely, the texts which the Dominicans have in common only with Pb, must already have been part of the legislation of Prémontré at that time.

A contrary hypothesis could be that the statutes of Prémontré were themselves influenced by the Dominicans. The testimony of Humbert of Romans can be used as proof for this view in one specific case,[124] and more generally there is the fact that some monastic statutes were drafted or revised under Dominican influence during the thirteenth century.[125] We believe nonetheless that our conclusion holds up, and this because of the following considerations, which may not constitute proof in the strict sense but do all point in the same direction. It would have been contrary to the customs of the time for a monastic order, a century after its foundation, to have looked for the revision of its legislation to an order whose own constitutions had been influenced to a large extent by the former order. Such a conclusion would require clear textual proof or other compelling indications. It is difficult to imagine a great canonical order like Prémontré, with an established tradition of its own, consulting the Dominicans, whose existence as an order extended no further back than twenty years at most and who, as an apostolically oriented community, could not aspire to the same prestige with regard to canonical and monastic customs.

Nor does the hypothesis of Dominican influence make much sense in the context of the constitutional history of Prémontré. When writing its own legislation in the twelfth century, this order had looked to the *Consuetudines* of Cîteaux, and in the thirteenth it found guidelines in the decrees of Gregory IX and Innocent IV.[126] Moreover, as it turns out, the codification of 1236-1238 was carried out by its own legislative organs. The general chapters revised the text and adapted it to the needs of the time. Sentences or phrases were added, moved or omitted in almost all chapters. It may be assumed that the revision of the twelfth-century redaction happened gradually and that the annual chapters only made those corrections which were necessary at certain specific instances.[127] As the *prologus* of the statutes required, the new stipulations were inserted in the fourth *distinctio*, but minor textual changes were undoubtedly made wherever they seemed necessary.[128] It must be emphasised, therefore, that the Premonstratensians had their own legislative tradition. Only in certain cases, when there are positive

---

124 In the section on the *obligatio ad poenam* of the constitutions. However, see *supra*, p. 287, footnote 43.
125 See *supra*, in the Introduction, pp. 158-159.
126 See *supra*, pp. 282-283, Pl. F. Lefèvre, *Les statuts de Prémontré*, pp. XV-XX.
127 See *supra*, pp. 203-204; p. 283, footnote 21.
128 "In hac quarta distinctione quedam que in generali capitulo communi consilio pro conservatione ordinis sunt posita, possunt reperiri. Et si qua pro diversitate emergentium actionum postmodum fuerint ordinanda, hic competenter poterunt inseri" (Pa, prol.; cf. Pb, *ibid.*). – For the chapter ordinances that were inserted in the body of the *Consuetudines*, see *supra*, p. 204, footnotes 119 and 120.

indications, may we regard dependence on the constitutions of other orders as certain or probable.

The study of a number of specific passages confirms our hypothesis that the Premonstratensians were not dependent on the Dominicans, but that on the contrary, the Dominicans were dependent on the Premonstratensians. In c. 1, *De matutinis*, both orders added a considerable amount of text.[129] But only Pb has interpolated a number of lines after the words "quod faciendum est", which cannot therefore have been derived from the Dominicans.[130] The same is true for the chapter *De pulmentis* (c. 8), in the passage on the *venia* for those who had committed some fault during meals, where Pb changed the ending of the sentence "ad locum suum" so that it speaks only of the *servitores*.[131] In Pa and in the Dominican text, by contrast, the *comedentes* and *servitores* are discussed together. In the chapter *De infirmis* (c. 11), the Dominican text most closely resembles Pa, while Pb twice omitted a sentence and added another one.

Pa, I, 19	O.P., I, 11	Pb, I, 18
Si quis talem habet infirmitatem…	Si quis autem talem infirmitatem habeat, …	Si quis talem habuerit infirmitatem…
hic talis nec super culcitram iaceat, nec ieiunia consuetudinaria solvat, nec cibos refectorii mutet:	talis nec super culcitram iaceat, nec ieiunia consuetudinaria frangat, nec cibos refectorii mutet.	hic talis nec ieiunia consuetudinaria frangat, nec cibos refectorii mutet, nisi quandoque fiat pro magna debilitate ipsius ex caritativa dispensatione abbatis, sive prioris absente abbate.
legat et operetur non ad suum arbitrium, sed horis quibus ei constituetur.	Legat autem vel operetur, secundum quod ei a suo prelato iniungetur.	

The other cases in which Pb and the Dominican constitutions both diverge from Pa can similarly all be explained by dependence of the Dominicans on the evolved text of Prémontré, while the converse hypothesis runs into insoluble difficulties.

§ 2. Subsidiary sources

The chapters of the Dominican constitutions that were partially derived from the legislation of the Premonstratensians not infrequently contain passages that are reminiscent of the customs of other monastic orders. In some cases, these usually

---

129 See *supra*, pp. 288-289.

130 The fact that the Dominicans declined to adopt this passage can be explained by their endeavour to cut back on liturgical ceremony.

131 See *supra*, p. 293.

brief texts show a direct affinity with the *consuetudines* of monks and canons regular. In other cases, they appear to have originated in ecclesiastical ordinances issued for various monastic institutions collectively. The following pages contain a study of these text fragments.

A. Textual affinity

1. Canonical and monastic customs

a. Liturgical customs

As regards the reciting of the office in choir, the Dominicans generally followed the customs of Prémontré.[132] But the rules for the alternating of sitting and standing appear to have been influenced by a different tradition. The *consuetudines* of Cluny[133] and of the Victorines[134] permitted sitting during long Psalms, not one half of the choir in turn, but each monk in turn on the same side of the choir. The canons of Saint-Denis in Reims[135] and of Saint-Pierremont[136] changed this rubric, so that the choirs facing each other would stand or sit alternately, rather than individual persons separately. The substance of this arrangement was adopted by the Dominicans. The change is evident when the text of the Dominicans is compared with that of Prémontré.

Prém., I, 1	O.P., I, 1
Et postquam solito more inclinaverint, stet chorus contra chorum usque ad *Gloria* post hymnum, et tunc vertant se ad altare, quod ad omnes hymnos faciendum est.	… postquam ad *Gloria* post *Venite* inclinaverint, stet chorus contra chorum.
Deinde ad primum psalmum simul sedeant, et ad secundum simul stent, etiamsi sub uno *Gloria* dicuntur. Et ita alternent usque ad finem.	Deinde ad primum psalmum sedeat unus chorus, ad secundum stet et similiter sedeat alter chorus. Et sic alternent usque ad *Laudate Dominum…*

---

132 In both the Dominican and Prémontré texts: d. I, c. 1, *De matutinis.* For the dependence of the one text on the other, see *supra*, pp. 288-289.

133 "Quod si sedere voluerit inter psalmodiam, observat ne sedeat iuxta alium sedentem, sed ita, ut unus stet et sedeat alter, et invicem exhibere debent occasionem sedendi…" (*Antiquiores consuetudines Cluniacenses*, lib. II, c. 7).

134 "In omnibus horis regularibus alternatim sedeant fratres, ita ut in primo psalmo ex parte septimanae primus, et in altera secundus, et ab eis semper uno praetermisso, alter stans, et alter sedens a summo deorsum inveniatur" (*Antiquae consuetudines, … S. Victoris*, c. 62). For Marbach: "…fratres sibi invicem sedendi copiam praebeant, uno stante inter duos sedentes…" (*Consuetudines Marbacenses*, c. 11).

135 "…et sedeat pars quae chorum habet ad primum psalmum, altera stante; deinde altera sedeat, alia stante" (*Constitutiones … S. Dionysii Remensis*, c. [2], *De nocturnis vigiliis*).

136 "Chorus qui per psalmi decantationem sederit, ad standum surgat, et qui steterit, sedendo imbecillitatem suam refoveat" (*Antiquae constitutiones. … S. Petri-Montis*, p. 428).

In c. 2, *De capitulo*, derived for the most part from Prémontré,[137] the Dominicans supplemented their text by rules from other *consuetudines*. The benediction formula *Regularibus disciplinis* was unknown to the Premonstratensians at the time, but it does appear in the customs of Saint-Ruf.[138] The concluding prayers, too, can be found almost literally in the constitutions of these canons. The differences with Prémontré and the similarities with Saint-Ruf are particularly clear in the following schema.[139]

Prém., I, 4	St-Ruf, c. 13	O.P., I, 2
Tractatis igitur hiis que tractanda sunt, surgentibus omnibus, dicatur psalmus *De profundis* pro episcopis …	… cum psalmo *Laudate Dominum, omnes gentes* a capitulo surgimus. Quo finito, dicit hebdomadarius:	Auditis culpis, dicitur psalmus *Laudate Dominum, omnes gentes*
	Ostende nobis, Domine; Domine, exaudi;	cum versu *Ostende nobis, Domine*
	Dominus vobiscum. Oratio *Actiones nostras, quesumus, Domine* …	et *Dominus vobiscum* et collecta *Actiones nostras* etc.

b. *Monastic customs*

A number of stipulations inserted by the Dominicans into c. 7, *De prandio*, are clearly reminiscent of monastic customs for meals. There were no specific rules for the serving of victuals in Prémontré,[140] but most Benedictine abbeys followed an elaborate ceremonial. Depending on the nature of the food and the class of the feast, the dishes had to be brought first to the superior or to the youngest members of the community.[141] The Cistercians and the Benedictines of Subiaco

---

137 See *supra*, p. 289-290.

138 A. Carrier de Belleuse, *Coutumier du XIᵉ siècle de l'ordre de Saint-Ruf*, p. 62.

139 For Prémontré: d. I, c. 4; for Saint-Ruf: *Consuetudines*, c. 13 (*ed. cit.*, p. 63); for the Dominicans: d. I, c. 2.

140 No sequence is indicated in Pa, I, 10. According to later codification, meals had to be served first "maiorem mensam tenenti" (Pb, I, 9).

141 See *Consuetudines Farfenses*, lib. II, c. 18. The *Consuetudines* of Dijon stipulated: "Omne generale a novissimis incipit, pitantia vero a primo" (L. Chomton, *Histoire de l'église Saint-Bénigne de Dijon*, p. 375). Cf. also *Memoriale qualiter*, c. 5, in *Initia consuetudinis Benedictinae*, pp. 255-257; *Consuetudines Hirsaug.*, lib. I, c. 57. *Generale* was understood to mean the ordinary food served to all: "Ubi communia dantur conditionibus personarum" (C. Du Cange, *Glossarium*, vol. IV, p. 53). "Generale appellamus, quod in singulis scutellis datur" (*Cons. Hirsaug., loco cit.*). *Pictantia* meant an additional allowance consisting of more substantial food (or drink), such as fish etc. (C. Du Cange, *Glossarium*, vol. VI, p. 313). "Pictantiam, quod in una scutella duobus verbi gratia" (*Cons. Hirsaug., loco cit.*).

always started with the abbot.[142] The Dominicans appear to have joined the Benedictine tradition.[143]

Ben.	O.P., I, 7
… qui ministrant, a novissimis incipiant et usque ad domnum abbatem ministrando perveniant.	Verumtamen servitores incipiant ab inferioribus, usque ad mensam prioris ascendentes.

But they simplified the customs considerably by deciding that the youngest religious would always be served first and the prior last.[144]

The obligation for the superiors to take their meals in the common refectory appears in various monastic statutes and was emphasised by papal ordinances.[145] The Dominican formula for this obligation bears greater resemblance to the letter from Innocent III to the Abbey of Val-des-Choux than to the Prémontré text.[146]

Val-d.-Choux, *loco cit.*	O.P., I, 7
Prior vobiscum in eodem refectorio comedet, simili cibo et veste contentus…	Priores comedant in refectorio et cibariis conventus sint contenti.

---

142 For Cîteaux: "…hoc feratur ordine, scilicet ut due scutelle prius deferantur, una scilicet priori vel abbati, si affuerit … et sic due hinc et due inde usque ad ultimum" (*Ecclesiastica officia, c.* 76, ed. Ph. Guignard).

143 *Memoriale qualiter, ed. cit.,* pp. 255-256.

144 The *Const. S. M. Magdalenae,* c. 6, stipulated the exact opposite: "Servitrices incipiant a priorissa, et sic usque ad iuniores" (A. Simon, *L'ordre des Pénitentes,* p. 159). In this case, it would be wrong to deduce from the presence of this rule in the constitutions of the sisters that the original constitutions of the Dominicans also contained this text. The Penitent Sisters of Mary Magdalene belonged at the time to the Cistercian Order, where the abbot was always served first (see *supra,* pp. 251, 253 and 257, footnote 78). – In the later constitutions of the sisters, the text is identical to that in the Dominican constitutions: "Servitrices autem incipiant ab inferioribus, usque ad mensam priorisse ascendentes" (*Constitutiones sororum Ord. Pred.,* 5, in *Anal O.P.,* vol. III, 1897-1898, p. 340).

145 *Statuta Murbacensia:* "Quarto, ut abbates communes esse debeant suis monachis in manducando, in bibendo, … Vigesimotertio capitulo, … abbas vero contentus sit cibo fratrum, …" (ed. B. Albers, *Consuetudines monasticae,* vol. III, p. 83). For Prémontré: "Abbas debet … in refectorio comedere…" (Pb, II, 1). – See also the letter from Innocent III to the Abbey of Val-des-Choux (following footnote) and from Gregory IX to Prémontré, on 22 June 1232: "…omnesque in refectorio eodem pane, pulmentis eisdem et eodem potu vescantur … Abbates quoque, secundum instituta prefati Ordinis, in communi refectorio comedant…" (Pl. F. Lefèvre, *Les statuts de Prémontré,* pp. 130-131).

146 The Abbey of Val-des-Choux (diocese of Langres) was founded c. 1193-1195 and was a *caput ordinis* as early as the beginning of the thirteenth century. Its first *institutio* was approved by Innocent III on 10 February 1205. The greater part of its *Consuetudines,* compiled between 1224 and 1238 (ed. W. de Gray Birch, *Ordinale conventus Vallis-Caulium,* London, 1900), was adopted by the Cistercians (cf. P. Vermeer, *Cîteaux en Val-des-Choux,* in *Collectanea Ord. Cist. Ref.,* vol. XVI, 1954, pp. 35-44; R. Folz, *Le monastère du Val-des-Choux au premier siècle de son histoire,* in *Bulletin philologique et historique du Comité des travaux historiques et scientifiques,* 1959, pp. 91-115). The text included below is from the letter from Innocent III (PL, vol. 215, col. 531).

It is also clear from the place of this rule on the common table in the text that there is no direct dependence on Prémontré. In the Premonstratensian text, it appeared in the chapter *De abbate*[147] and not in *De prandio*, as is the case in the Dominican text.

c. *The collation*

The ninth chapter, *De collatione et completorio*, again offers a striking illustration of the way Benedictine customs were interpolated in texts derived from Prémontré. Up to the thirteenth century, the *collatio*, in its original meaning of spiritual reading or conference, was regarded as a separate ritual in the monastic life.[148] It was introduced by oriental coenobites, and in the West it became known primarily through the works of Cassian,[149] whose *Collationes* were very highly regarded reading until late in the Middle Ages. It was allocated a fixed place in the monastic horarium in the rule of Benedict.[150] On days of fasting, the monks were required to assemble sometime after vespers, and on other days immediately after the evening meal, to attend a reading from the *Collationes* or the *Vitae Patrum*.[151] In the following centuries, the custom became almost universal and certain details were elaborated. Previously, the reading was held in the church, as the rule of Benedict stipulated.[152] Some Benedictines and Cistercians moved it to the *claustrum*,[153] but most monks and canons regular held it in the chapter.[154]

---

147 See footnote 145.
148 For a history of the *collatio*, see E. Martène, *De antiquis Ecclesiae ritibus*, vol. IV, pp. 35-37; M. H. Lavocat, *Les observances monastiques*, I. *La collation*, in *L'année dominicaine*, vol. LX, 1924, pp. 62-70.
149 After a stay in the East, John Cassian became abbot of Saint-Victor in Marseille. Between 419 and 426 he wrote his *De institutis coenobiorum et de octo principalium vitiorum remediis libri XII* (ed. M. Petschenig, in *Iohannis Cassiani opera*, vol. I (Corpus Script, eccles. lat., vol. 17), Prague-Vienna-Leipzig, 1888, pp. 3-231). His *Conlationes XXIII* (ed. M. Petschenig, in *Iohannis Cassiani opera*, vol. II (Corpus ..., vol. 13), Vienna, 1888) date from the years 420-428 (B. Altaner, *Patrologie*, Freiburg im Breisgau, 1958⁵, pp. 416-417).
150 *Reg. s. Ben.*, c. 42.
151 Biographies by various authors, originally in Greek, but later (in the sixth century) translated into Latin (B. Altaner, *op. cit.*, p. 201). The text was published in PL, vols. 73-74. Humbert of Romans, *Expositio super Constitutiones*, pp. 112-113 mentions both works.
152 The *collatio* appears to have been held in the same place where compline was said: "...omnes ergo in unum positi conpleant, et exeuntes a conpletoriis..." (*Reg. S. Ben.*, c. 42); "...facto signo, in ecclesiam initietur collatio..." (*Regularis concordia*, in PL, vol. 137, col. 484).
153 According to Nicolaus de Fractura, *Explicatio Regulae S. Benedicti*, c. 42: "Sedeant omnes in unum, idest conveniant omnes in claustro, si habent..." (quoted by E. Martène, *De antiquis Ecclesiae ritibus*, vol. IV, p. 30). The *Ecclesiastica officia* of Cîteaux (c. 81, ed. Ph. Guignard) do not indicate any specific place. According to B. Van Haeften, *Disquisitionum libri XII*, Antwerp, 1744, p. 871, the *collatio* was held in the *claustrum*.
154 *Consuetudines Farfenses*, lib. I, c. 68: "Omnes qui remanent de capitulo, finita collatione, egressi de capitulo...". In addition to Prémontré (Pa, I, 13; Pb, I, 11) this was also the case in Saint-Victor (*Antiquae consuetudines ... S. Victoris*, c. 42, *De collatione et completorio*). In Saint-Denis in Reims, the *collatio* appears to have taken place in the claustrum in summer and in the chapter room in winter (*Constitutiones ... S. Dionysii Remensis*, c. [8], *De vesperis, coena, collatione et completorio*). The

The evening meal and the *collatio* were therefore originally separate things, although they were associated in the sense that the *collatio* immediately followed the meal outside times of fasting. In some abbeys, the reading was interrupted on certain days by what the *consuetudines* called the *caritas*.[155] Instead of going immediately from the chapter or the *claustrum* to the church for compline, the monks went in procession to the refectory where they were offered wine.[156] After the ritual benediction, the reading was continued by the *lector collationis*, who was then served himself.[157] This custom was originally limited to the days of fasting but was subsequently extended to the other days.[158] From the eighth century onwards, it can be found with most Benedictines[159] and later with canons regular like those of Saint-Victor.[160] In the abbey of Saint-Germain-des-Prés, the monks were even permitted a *potus* twice in the afternoon on certain days: one before the *mandatum* (washing of feet), and another after or rather during the *collatio*.[161] The Benedictines of Monte Cassino even took a small amount of food with the wine.[162] Thus, in certain monastic environments, the link between spiritual reading and the evening meal became ever stronger, and in some cases, this led to the merging of the two practices. In Cîteaux and Prémontré, however, there was no custom yet of interrupting the *collatio* for the *potus*.[163]

---

text of Val-des-Écoliers briefly gives the sequence of Prémontré: "Tempore vero … omnes fratres…" (*Constitutiones Ordinis Vallis-Scholarium*, c. 24).

155 The *caritas* is perhaps closely associated with the custom of taking a refreshment in the refectory on Holy Thursday after the reading of the first half of the *Sermo dominicus* (John 13-17): "Tunc vadant in refectorium … sequentia evangelii cepti usque ad *et ego in ipsis* legatur. Post hec miscentibus abbate et priore bibant fratres cum caritate" (*Consuetudines Vallymbrosanae*, c. 24). On occasion it was also held without any connection with the *collatio* (*Consuetudines Fructuarienses*, lib. I, c. 35; lib. II, c. 11).

156 A lengthy description of the ceremony can be found in the *consuetudines* of Saint-Germain-des-Prés: "Tunc hebdomadarius lectionis de collatione accipiet benedictionem… Cum autem dicti de lectione duo versus vel circiter fuerint … tunc surgent omnes, ibunt ordinatim in refectorium… Et tunc debet legere lector lectionis … tunc surgent quatuor, aut quinque, vel plures, et accipient modellos vitreos aut argenteos, et implebunt eos vino … Finito potu, prior … tunc surgens dicet: Adiutorium nostrum etc…" (quoted by E. Martène, *De antiquis Ecclesiae ritibus*, vol. IV, pp. 36-37).

157 *Consuetudines* of Saint-Germain-des-Prés, *loco cit.*

158 "Verum non solum diebus ieiunii, sed aliis insuper diebus propinatam fuisse huiusmodi caritatem, docent nos ms. consuetudines S. Germani a Pratis, in quibus etiam dominicis diebus caritatem vini ad collationem praeberi praecipitur" (*loco cit.*).

159 See E. Martène (*loco cit.*), who refers to other *consuetudines* of the Benedictines. See also *Consuetudines Floriacenses*, in B. Albers, *Consuetudines monasticae*, vol. V, p. 147; *Consuetudines Fructuarienses*, lib. I, c. 11; *Regularis concordia*: "…quotiescumque fratribus caritas, interim dum collatio legitur, praebetur…" (PL, vol. 137, col. 484).

160 *Antiquae consuetudines … S. Victoris*, c. 42; *Constitutiones … S. Dionysii Remensis*, c. [8], *De vesperis, coena, collatione et completorio.*

161 *Consuetudines*, quoted by E. Martène, *op. cit.*, p. 37.

162 "Cum autem liberi a vindemia fuerint, statim ad Nonam horam refecerint, et post Vesperas gustum manducant, et bibunt iterum, quod in Regula non est scriptum" (quoted by E. Martène, *ibid.*).

163 The moments of *potus* mentioned in Prémontré ("bibere post nonam": d. I, c. 5; "bibere extra horam": Pa, I, 12; Pb, I, 9) are clearly distinguished from the subsequent *collatio*, which is held entirely in the chapter (Pa, I, 13; Pb, I, 11).

All one has to do is compare the text of the Dominicans with that of Prémontré to see that the succession of the practices in the two orders was quite different.[164]

Pb, I, 11	O.P., I, 9
Diebus ieiuniorum[165]	A. Tempore ieiunii
I. 1. fratres sedeant in conventu intrent REFECTORIUM.	I, 1. fratribus venientibus in conventum [REFECTORIUM],[166] legat lector, premisso *Iube, domne.* Et sequatur benedictio *Noctem quietam.*
2. Et dicto *Benedicite*, det hebdomadarius benedictionem et fratres ingrediantur mensas et bibant.	2. Et infra lectionem poterunt fratres bibere, dicto *Benedicite* et data benedictione *Largitor* …
II. 1. Post hec intrent CAPITULUM.	
2. dicat lector: *Iube, domne*, et data hac benedictione *Noctem quietam*, sedeant.	
3. Lectione finita, qui preest dicat: *Adiutorium nostrum*	3. Finita lectione, dicat qui preest: *Adiutorium nostrum*
III. 1. et eant ad ECCLESIAM.	III. 1. et intrent ECCLESIAM.
2. [Completorium: cf, c. 14: Dicto completorio…]	2. [Completorium: cf. title *De collatione et completorio*].
	B. Alio vero tempore
	ante completorium legatur lectio in ecclesia: *Fratres, sobrii estote.* Et facta confessione et dicto completorio…

Although the *collatio* in Prémontré appeared under the same title as the evening meal in times of fasting, in reality it remained a separate ritual, both as regards time and place. It was held in the chapter, after the *potus* in the refectory. The Dominicans lifted this twofold distinction by moving the reading and its

---

164 For Prémontré, there is very little difference between Pa (I, 13) and Pb (I, 11), the text of which appears schematically below.

165 Pb (I, 11) is the only Premonstratensian text to distinguish between days of fasting and other days in this respect: "…quod est diebus ieiuniorum tantummodo faciendum…". These words appear after "ingrediantur mensas et bibant".

166 It is clear that everything that appears in the Dominican text under A.I. took place in the refectory, even though the earliest text of the constitutions quoted above says: "fratribus venientibus in conventum". Raymond of Peñafort clarified the text: "fratribus venientibus in refectorium" (d. I, c. 6, ed. R. Creytens, *Les constitutions … de s. Raymond de Peñafort*, p. 35).

customary ceremonies and benedictions to the refectory. On days of fasting, they went to the church immediately afterwards for compline. On other days, the brief *lectio* at the beginning of compline was considered to constitute the *collatio*, although it involved only a few sentences from the first epistle of Saint Peter.[167] They evidently wished to preserve an ancient custom, following the entire monastic tradition and the statutes of Prémontré. But as their apostolic vocation already obliged them to spend much time on the study of Sacred Scripture and of the theological books, and they had time for this due to the exclusion of manual labour, the *collatio*, in the sense of a communal spiritual reading, no longer held the same importance for them as it did in the monastic tradition. It was perhaps for this reason that they merged it with the evening meal. There were precedents for the combining of these two monastic rituals, but these had had a different meaning and had been for a different reason. The Benedictines consumed some food or drink during the *collatio* (reading), while the Dominicans listened to a reading during the *collatio* (evening meal).[168]

d. Novitiate and the care of the sick

There are further traces of the Benedictine tradition in other chapters. In c. 13, *De magistro novitiorum*, only the first two sentences were derived from Prémontré.[169] The rest is a kind of *speculum novitiorum*, a complex of guidelines on the spiritual formation of young religious. The exhortations to humility and obedience show affinity with the rule of Saint Benedict.[170] The exhortation to hold the cup with both hands while drinking is a classic feature of medieval monastic statutes, although it usually appears in a different context: in the chapters on meals, which applied to all monks.[171] Only in the *consuetudines* of Cluny is it given

---

167 1 Peter 5:8-9. Incidentally, these verses are still read before compline today.
168 Around the mid-thirteenth century, the meal on days of fasting was itself called *collatio*: "In collatione vero et coena debet providere quod legantur libri aliqui bonae aedificationis, … ut sunt *Vitae Patrum*, libri *Collationum* et similes. In prandio vero…" (Humbert of Romans, *Instructiones de officiis Ordinis*, p. 300). In this text, *collatio* is evidently equivalent to *prandium* and *coena*.
169 See *supra*, p. 293, footnote 64.
170 Saint Benedict regarded the *humilitas corporis* as one of the *gradus humilitatis*: "Duodecimus humilitatis gradus est, si non solum corde monachus, sed etiam ipso corpore humilitatem videntibus se semper indicet, …" (*Reg.*, c. 7). Cf. the Dominican text: "Humilitatem cordis et corporis doceat habere …" (d. I, c. 13). – Benedict had the follow to say on obedience: "…et voluntatem propriam deserentes…" (*Reg.*, c. 5). For the Dominicans: "…et voluntatem propriam deserere" (*loco cit.*).
171 See for instance for the Cistercians: "Qui bibit, duabus manibus teneat scyphum" (*Ecclesiastica officia*, c. 76, *De refectione*, ed. Ph. Guignard). The Premonstratensians had the same text (Pa, I, 10; Pb, I, 9).

as a specific stipulation for novices.[172] The chapter *De infirmis*[173] similarly testifies to the influence of a double tradition. It begins with an exhortation reminiscent of the rule of Benedict.[174] The second half of this chapter was adopted almost literally from the Premonstratensians.[175]

2. Monastic statutes and ecclesiastical regulations

a. *Entry into the monastery*

The Dominican constitutions have various regulations relating to entry that they share with other monastic statutes from the early thirteenth century. According to the existing law, no one could be admitted below the age of eighteen.[176] This rule had been in force even in the older monastic orders and was adopted by the canons regular.[177] Superiors were required to conduct an enquiry into the suitability and canonical freedom of the candidate. The list of questions that the candidate had to answer shows some similarities with the statutes of Prémontré, Saint-Pierremont, Val-des-Écoliers and the Order of the Holy Spirit.[178] The following schema illustrates how similar the two texts are.

---

172 The text in question appears in the second part of the *Antiquiores consuetudines Cluniacenses*, which is wholly dedicated to the education of the novices: "Minime quoque bibit aliquando, nisi pateram cum ambabus manibus tenendo, et numquam nisi sedendo" (lib. II, c. 23). In the Dominican text: "…quod duabus manibus sit bibendum et sedendo…" (d. I, c. 13). The last words "et sedendo" in particular, which do not appear anywhere else, are an indication of mutual affinity. – The *Consuetudines Hirsaugienses*, lib. I, c. 64, have the same text as Cluny, from which they are in fact derived (see *supra*, p. 186, with notes 12-13).

173 CA, I, 11.

174 The correspondence here is more substantive than textual. Benedict's *Regula* has: "Ergo cura maxima sit abbati, ne aliquam neglegentiam patiantur … Sed et carnium esus infirmis omnino debilibus … concedatur" (c. 36). The Dominican text: "Circa infirmos caveat ne sit negligens prelatus … Poterunt etiam quidam vesci carnibus, prout eorum gravior requirit infirmitas, secundum quod prelato visum fuerit" (d. I, c. 11). The constitutions of the Humiliati, which are literally identical to Benedict's Rule as regards the first sentence, have the following second sentence: "Carnium esus infirmis omnino et debilibus … concedatur quandiu prelato melius visum fuerit" (*Regula Humiliatorum*, c. 28).

175 "Si quis autem … iniungetur". Cf. Pa, I, 19; Pb, I, 18 (see *supra*, p. 306). The Dominicans did not adopt the rest of this chapter nor the entire previous chapter in the statutes of Prémontré.

176 The Council of Paris of 1212 forbade the admission of young candidates: "Iuxta aetatem recipiendorum ad religionem, cuiuscumque fuerint ordinis, districte prohibemus ne aliquis recipiatur infra decimum octavum annum" (can. 2, in Mansi, vol. XXII, col. 826). This ban was repeated in Rouen in 1214 (can. 2, in Mansi, vol. XXII, col. 906).

177 For the monastic statutes, see for example *Statuta cap. gen. Ord. Cist.*, vol. I, p. 62 (aº 1157) and furthermore pp. 190, 209, 264, 275, 278, 422; *Constitutiones Ordinis Vallis-Scholarium*, c. 13; *Antiquae constitutiones … S. Petri-Montis*, p. 431. – In the Dominican text: "Nemo recipiatur infra octodecim annos" (d. I, c. 14).

178 For the Dominicans: d. I, c. 14; for Prémontré: Pb, I, 14. Also: *Constitutiones Ordinis Vallis-Scholarium*, c. 13; *Regula S. Spiritus*, c. 70; *Antiquae constitutiones … S. Petri-Montis*, p. 438. For the Templars: F. Wilcke, *Geschichte des Ordens der Tempelherren*, vol. I, Halle, 1860, p. 357.

Pb, I, 14	O.P., I, 14
Tunc abbas requirat ab eis utrum sint coniugati, an servi, an debitis obligati, vel alterius professionis vel aliquam habeant infirmitatem occultam.	Nullus recipiatur nisi requisitus an sit coniugatus, an servus, an ratiociniis obligatus, vel alterius professionis, vel occultam habeat infirmitatem.

The legislation of Val-des-Écoliers and the *Regula S. Spiritus* also contain rules for cases in which a candidate had already taken vows before.[179] Postulants who had professed vows before were only accepted by the Dominicans if the provincial chapter or general chapter authorised it. In Val-des-Écoliers, the decision was left to a commission consisting of two priors and several members of the order. The *Regula S. Spiritus* required the approval of the bishop and of the previous monastic superior. The terminology used suggests that the three texts derive from a common source.[180]

Val-des-Écol., c. 13	O.P., I, 14	*Reg. S. Spir.*, c. 70
Si vero in alio ordine fuerit, non recipiatur nisi per consilium duorum priorum nostri ordinis, et per consilium fratrum...	Quod si alterius religionis fuerit, non recipiatur in ordine nostro, nisi a capitulo provinciali vel generali fuerit approbatus.	Si vero ... alterius religionis fuerit, ... non recipiatur, nisi litteras ab episcopo, seu a monasterio suo habuerit...

Professed Cistercians were accepted by the Dominicans only if they had express permission from the pope.[181] This rule was first introduced by Honorius III, as a letter from Gregory IX of 19 May 1235 shows.[182]

---

179 The ban on accepting professed members of other orders followed from the binding force of the monastic profession. See the text of the Council of Paris, *infra*, p. 326, footnote 239. For the *transitus* to another order or monastery, see *supra*, pp. 231-232. Specific papal rulings furthermore prohibited defection from certain orders. For the Benedictines, see Ph. Schmitz, *Histoire de l'ordre de saint Benoît*, vol. II, Maredsous, 1942, p. 41. For the Cistercians, there were prohibitions by Alexander III (*Regesta Pontificum Romanorum*, ed. Ph. Jaffé, no. 8916) and Callixtus II (PL, vol. 163, col. 1147). For the Dominicans, such bans were issued twice during Dominic's life: on 7 February 1217 (Laurent, no. 71) and on 23 January 1221 (*ibid.*, no. 128).

180 For the places in the legislation of the Dominicans, Val-des-Écoliers and the Order of the Holy Spirit, see *supra*, footnote 178.

181 "Cistercienses non admittantur nisi de speciali licentia domini pape" (d. I, c. 14).

182 "Sane mirantes accepimus quod, cum a bonae memoriae Honorio Papa, praedecessore nostro, fuerit demandatum ut nullus de ordine fratrum Praedicatorum in vestrum, aut ex vobis aliquis in eorum collegium, sine speciali mandato Summi Pontificis admittatur ..." (*Bull. O.P.*, vol. I, p. 77, which erroneously mentions 21 June as the date; cf. L. Auvray, *Les registres de Grégoire IX*, nos. 2566-2568). We were unable to find the text of Honorius III's letter itself, either in *Honorii III opera omnia*, vols. II-V (ed. C. A. Horoy), or in *Regesta Honorii Papae III* (ed. P. Pressutti), or in *Regesta Pontificum Romanorum* (ed. A. Potthast), or in the Cistercian *bullaria*. The ordinance in question was not the same as the *titulus* of 7 February 1217 (Laurent, no. 79). The issue must have been raised later. In

The superior had no authority to grant definitive admission himself. First the candidate had to appear before a commission of three members which had to ascertain his moral integrity and intellectual ability. The results were to be presented to the prior and the chapter, who then decided together.[183] This rule possibly originated in papal reform decrees on the organisation of the monastic life. The older statutes of Prémontré show no trace yet of these regulations. However, in 1232 Gregory IX instructed a number of abbots of the order to ensure that the community was consulted on admissions.[184] An ordinance on this subject was added to the statutes of 1236-1238,[185] and the canons of Saint-Pierremont and Val-des-Écoliers contained an identical stipulation.[186] A section in the Dominican constitutions closely matches the Prémontré text, but even more closely resembles the letter by Gregory IX just mentioned.

Greg. IX, *loco cit.*	O.P, I, 14
Sed nec abbates aliquos recipiant in canonicos et in fratres sine prioris et supprioris et aliquorum maiorum de domo requisito consilio et assensu.	Conventualis prior nullum in conversum recipiat, in canonicum vero neminem, nisi requisito consensu totius vel maioris partis capituli et obtento.

According to the rule of Benedict, the candidate had to be prepared for his *promissio* in the *cella novitiorum* for the duration of twelve months.[187] Towards the end of the twelfth century, Innocent III wrote that this probationary year was to be regarded as one of the established customs of the monastic life.[188] In the same letter, he recognised the validity of professions that had been made after a

---

1223, the general chapter of Cîteaux prohibited "Monachi vel conversi qui ad ordinem Praedicatorum vel Fratrum Minorum transierint, habeantur pro fugitivis" (*Statuta cap. gen. Ord. Cist.*, vol. II, p. 24, no. 12). The ban by Honorius III mentioned above must probably have been issued during or close to the year 1223. – The Dominicans removed the stipulation on the entry of Cistercians from their constitutions at the behest of the general chapters of 1240-1242 (*Acta C. G.*, pp. 14, 19, 22).

183 "In quolibet autem conventu eligantur tres idonei fratres de communi consensu capituli, qui recipiendos in moribus et scientia diligenter examinent et examinationem priori et capitulo referant, eorum iudicio, an recipi debeant, relinquentes" (d. I, c. 14).

184 The text of the papal bull can be found in Pl. F. Lefèvre, *Les statuts de Prémontré*, p. 133.

185 "Novitii canonici sive conversi, cum fuerint recipiendi, non recipiantur nisi prioris, supprioris et aliquorum maiorum de domo requisito consilio et assensu" (Pb, I, 14).

186 For Saint-Pierremont: "Cum canonicus ad ordinem fuerit promovendus, habeat super hoc abbas consilium cum saniori parte capituli" (*Antiquae constitutiones ... S. Petri-Montis*, p. 431). For Val-des-Écoliers: "Si prior illum qui recipi postulaverit, receptione perceperit esse dignum, referat fratribus in capitulo quid super hoc videatur, atque eorum assensum et voluntatem pro illius susceptione exquirat, et secundum consilium sanioris partis faciat quod fuerit faciendum" (*Constitutiones Ordinis Vallis-Scholarium*, c. 13).

187 *Reg. S. Ben., c. 58.* The entire probationary period consisted of three periods, which lasted two, six and four months respectively.

188 "Quum monachum fieri ante unius anni probationem regularis institutio interdicat..." (letter of 23 November 1198, in *Corpus iuris canonici*, vol. II, col. 574; also in PL, vol. 214, col. 430).

shorter period. He motivated this by pointing out that the novitiate, according to the spirit of the tradition, was a probationary period, both for the monastic community and for the novice, and that it was admissible in certain cases for the two parties to shorten this period.[189] The pope implied that no objection would be made as long as the superiors operated with suitable circumspection.[190] The Dominicans' decision to insert stipulations in their constitutions that may seem surprising at first sight was perhaps based on this text, or on a more relaxed practice. Whereas other institutes usually prescribed a full year's novitiate,[191] they required only six months or more, depending on the prior's judgment.[192] In certain cases, when the candidate was of a certain age and demonstrated sufficient spiritual maturity, he could even be admitted to profession immediately. This shortening of the probationary period was also permitted in the Order of Sempringham and by the Canons of Saint Andrew in Beneventum.[193]

---

189 "…licet tempus probationis a sanctis Patribus sit indultum non solum in favorem conversi, sed etiam monasterii, ut et ille asperitates istius, et istud mores illius valeat experiri,… si tamen ante tempus probationis regulariter praefinitum is, qui converti desiderat, habitum recipit et professionem emittit, abbate per se vel per alium professionem recipiente monasticam, et monachalem habitum concedente: uterque renunciare videtur ei, quod pro se noscitur introductum. Ideoque obligatur quidem per professionem emissam pariter et acceptam ad observantiam regularem, et vere monachus est censendus…" (*Corpus iuris canonici*, vol. II, col. 575).

190 The text continues as follows: "Prohibendum est tamen abbatibus, ne *passim* ante tempus probationis *quoslibet* ad professionem recipiant, et, si contra formam praescriptam quoslibet indiscrete receperint, animadversione sunt debita corrigendi…". (Italics ours.)

191 For Prémontré: Pb, I, 14 (Pa does not yet stipulate any specific duration); for Cîteaux: *Statuta cap. gen. Ord. Cist.*, vol. I, p. 487 (a° 1220); for Val-des-Choux: letter from Innocent III, 10 February 1205, in PL, vol. 215, col. 532; for the Order of the Holy Spirit: bull *Inter opera pietatis* of Innocent III, 18 June 1204, in PL, vol. 215, col. 379.

192 "Probationis tempus statuimus sex mensium vel eo amplius, prout prelato videbitur, ut et ipse austeritates ordinis et fratres mores experiantur ipsius, …" (d. I, c. 15). Cf. the text of the *Regula Petri de Honestis*: "Probationis autem modum et tempus non statuimus, sed in prudentia et arbitrio prioris vel pariter fratrum semper statuendum dimittimus" (lib. I, c. 9). For the Cistercians, the pre-probationary period for the *conversi* similarly lasted six months: "…sex mensibus serviat in habitu saeculari…" (*Statuta cap. gen. Ord. Cist.*, vol. I, p. 516, a° 1220). – The last part of the Dominican text quoted above is linked to the letter from Innocent III (see *supra*, footnote 189): "…ut et ille asperitates istius, et istud mores illius valeat experiri".

193 *Regulae Ordinis Sempringensis, Capitula de canonicis et novitiis*, c. 2. For the Canons of Saint Andrew in Beneventum, see P. Kehr, *Papst Gregor VIII als Ordensgründer*, in *Miscellanea Fr. Ehrle*, vol. II (Studi e testi, vol. 38), Rome, 1924, p. 268.

Sempr., c. 2	O.P., I, 15	Benev., *loco cit.*
Si triginta annos etatis vel amplius habentes ad conversionem venerint, ad omnia premissa non cogantur nisi habilioris et subtilioris ingenii fuerint.	Probationis tempus statuimus sex mensium … nisi forte aliquis maturus et discretus probationi predicte renuntiare voluerit et instanter se offerat professioni faciende.	Receptio alicuius sine unius ad minus anni probatione non fiat, nisi forte persona fuerit, que annum quadragesimum iam transierit, circa quam professionis tempus poterit breviari.

In 1236, Gregory IX insisted on the obligatory character of the probationary period, including for the Dominicans, but he did not expressly demand a full year.[194] The former rule that mentioned a novitiate lasting a mere six months continued to be part of the constitutions until 1257.[195]

During the probationary period, the novices formed a separate group under the leadership of their master. As they had not yet been definitively incorporated into the community, they did not enjoy all the rights of the professed. In order to test their suitability and educate them to become fully fledged religious, they were subjected to an adapted rule of life. The emphasis was on the acquisition of Christian and monastic virtues, dignified participation in the divine office, and fruitful reception of the sacraments. Some institutes had a more or less extensive manual, a *speculum novitiorum*, which described the special obligations and exercises of the novitiate.[196] The constitutions of the Dominicans are rather sober in this respect; they have only three chapters that contain such regulations.[197] Most medieval statutes prescribed that the novices should have their own *capitulum culparum* and must not be present in the chapter while the older religious confessed their faults.[198] During the novitiate, they were not permitted to stay outside the

---

194 Letter of 11 July 1236 (*Bull. O.P.*, vol. I, p. 90).
195 The redaction by Raymond of Peñafort (1238-1240) also has the older text (see R. Creytens, *Les constitutions … de s. Raymond de Peñafort*, pp. 38-39). This stipulation was suppressed at the command of the chapters of 1255-1257 (*Acta C.G.*, pp. 75, 79, 84), after Innocent IV had already prescribed a full probationary year on 17 June 1244 (*Bull. O.P.*, vol. I, p. 144).
196 These manuals constituted a special section in the *Consuetudines*, as was the case for Cluny (*Antiquiores consuetudines Cluniacenses*, lib. II), or a separate legal code alongside the *Consuetudines*, as in the Order of Grandmont (*Liber de doctrina novitiorum Ordinis Grandimontensis*, in E. Martène – U. Durand, *Thesaurus novus*, vol. V, col. 1823-1844). Hugh of Saint-Victor's work *De institutione novitiorum* (ed. in PL, vol. 176, col. 926-952) is well known. See also E. Mikkers, *Un Speculum novitii inédit d'Étienne de Salley*, in *Collectanea Ord. Cist. Ref.*, vol. VIII, 1946, pp. 17-68; J. Leclercq, *Deux opuscules sur la formation des jeunes moines*, in *Revue d'ascétique et de mystique*, vol. XXXIII, 1957, p. 399.
197 CA, I, 13-15.
198 For the Dominicans: "Novitii non intersint capitulo…" (d. I, c. 15), that is, they had to leave before the accusations: "Post egrediantur novitii. Quibus egressis, dicat, qui preest: *Faciant venias* …" (d. I, c. 2). – The same in the Prémontré text: "Pendente vero tempore probationis,

monastery except in cases of necessity.[199] The ban on receiving ordinations before making profession also appears in the Prémontré text.[200]

b. *Monastic discipline*

The regulations on *silentium*,[201] too, appear to originate in rules issued by the church authorities for monastic institutes. Silence is repeatedly emphasised in the rule of Benedict and a *Regula canonicorum* of the second half of the eleventh century,[202] and it was consistently regarded as a serious obligation. The Council of Rouen in 1214 felt it necessary to underline this obligation again and to mention the places where particular care should be taken to observe it.[203] This ordinance appears to have found its way into the legislation of various French monastic orders. A special stipulation was inserted in several *consuetudines*, evidently inspired by the council. The message everywhere was that *silentium* should be more rigorously observed in the church, the choir, the cloister, the refectory and the dormitory,[204] and the Dominicans similarly adopted this rule in their

---

ubique conventum teneant cum professis, hoc solo excepto quod in capitulo non remanebunt ad emendationem culparum, sed tabula lecta, inde exibunt" (Pb, I, 14). – Val-des-Écoliers: "Novitii intersint lectioni regulae in capitulo. Postquam vero pronuntiati fuerint qui ponuntur in brevi, recedant" (*Constitutiones Ordinis Vallis-Scholarium*, c. 13). – The Dijon Benedictines: "Et ex illa hora sequentur per omnia conventum, excepto quod, donec in albis sunt, exeunt capitulum facto sermone" (*Consuetudines*, c. 30, quoted by E. Martène, *De antiquis Ecclesiae ritibus*, vol. IV, p. 224).

199 In the Dominican text: "Novitii, tam clerici quam laici, infra annum, ad longinquas partes nisi ob causam necessariam non mittantur ..." (d. I, c. 15). Cf. *Constitutiones ... S. Dionysii Remensis*: "...et infra annum non mittantur ad commorandum" (c. [10], *De modo recipiendi canonicum*).

200 In the Dominican text: "...nec ipsi ante professionem ordinentur" (d. I, c. 15). In the Premonstratensian text: "Nullus donec fecerit professionem acolitus, subdiaconus, dyaconus sive presbyter ordinetur" (Pb, I, 15).

201 "Silentium ... poterunt" (CA, I, 17).

202 *Reg. S. Ben.*, c. 38, 42, 52. For the origins and authorship of this *Regula canonicorum*, see *supra*, p. 202, footnote 106. The rules in relation to the *silentium* can be found in the edition by Ch.-J. Hefele – H. Leclercq, *Histoire des conciles*, vol. V, Paris, 1912, p. 97.

203 Can. 11: "In monasterio quoque, claustro, dormitorio et refectorio et in aliis locis, secundum statutum ordinis, silentium districte praecipimus observari" (Mansi, vol. XXII, col. 907).

204 In the Prémontré statutes, the obligation of silence was addressed in the chapter *De dirigendis in via* (Pa, I, 17; Pb, I, 16). The list of "dangerous" places can be found in Pb, III, 2: "Qui autem silentium scienter fregerit in ecclesia, dormitorio, refectorio sive claustro, si clamatus inde fuerit, unam correctionem accipiat..." For the Norman Benedictines: "Omni tempore silentium monachi studeant observari, praecipue in ecclesia, in choro, in claustro, in refectorio, in dormitorio..." (J. Laporte, *Un règlement pour les monastères bénédictins de Normandie*, in *Revue bénéd.*, vol. LVIII, 1948, p. 131). For similar texts in other orders, see for instance *Vetera Hyreevallis statuta*, p. 137; *Antiquae constitutiones ... S. Petri Montis*, p. 437; *Regula Humiliatorum*, c. 26; A. Carrier de Belleuse, *Coutumier ... de l'ordre de Saint-Ruf*, p. 76; for the canons of Beauvais: Ch. Dereine, *Les coutumiers de Saint-Quentin de Beauvais et de Springiersbach*, p. 436; for the Cistercians, see *Usus conversorum*, c. 6: "Insuper in suo dormitorio et refectorio omnino silentium teneant ... Alibi possunt loqui..." (ed. J. A. Lefèvre, pp. 90-91).

constitutions.[205] Their text most closely approximates a number of ordinances of Gregory IX.[206]

Following the example of the Premonstratensians and of the stricter strands of monastic life, the Dominicans had accepted the obligation to abstain from meat, except for the sick.[207] But to avoid discommoding their hosts, they were permitted to eat any meat prepared for them on their journeys.[208] This relaxation of the law perhaps occasioned some to accept unnecessary invitations outside the monastery. The constitutions took aim at this practice by reminding the religious of their duty to take their meals in the houses of their own order and only rarely elsewhere, not even at the invitation of high-ranking clerics or religious institutes.[209] A similar rule can be found in the statutes of the Trinitarians and the Order of the Holy Spirit.[210] It appears there in the same context, and we may therefore assume that it was derived from a common source. The chapter on the cloister is similar to a text in the constitutions of Prémontré that was copied almost literally from a bull of Gregory IX.[211]

---

205 "Silentium fratres nostri teneant in claustro, in dormitorio, in cellis, in refectorio, in oratorio fratrum…" (d. I, c. 17). The *cella* was not mentioned in other constitutions, as monks at the time did not have separate quarters. The Dominicans had the right to a separate cell due to their obligation to study (see *Const.*, d. II, c. 29). Whereas the Dominican texts and the other statutes that were consulted express the obligation to silence in the form of a prescript, the Premonstratensians formulated the exhortation of the council in the form of a penal law (see footnote 204).

206 In almost all monastic *consuetudines*, the church, *ecclesia*, is listed among the dangerous places. Only the Dominican text has the word *oratorium*. This term also occurs in two letters by Gregory IX, which in other respects also closely approximate the text of the Dominicans. The first letter, *Cum felicis memoriae*, of 7 June 1227, promulgates the rule of the Humiliati of the first and second order: "In ecclesia vel in oratorio et in dormitorio, in refectorio … omnino teneant silentium …" (L. Zanoni, *Gli Umiliati*, p. 363). The second, *Cum pro reformatione*, of 1 July 1228, is addressed to all the abbots of the ecclesiastical province of Narbonne: "Item statuimus, ut silentium teneatur semper in oratorio monasterii, refectorio et dormitorio et in claustro …" (*Bullarium Romanum*, vol. III, p. 435).

207 "Pulmenta nostra sint ubique sine carnibus in nostris conventibus" (d. I, c. 8); for the sick, see d. I, c. 11, and *supra*, p. 314, footnote 174. For Prémontré, see Pa, IV, 12; Pb. I, 10.

208 "Et fratribus nostris, ne sint hominibus onerosi, pulmenta cocta cum carnibus liceat comedere extra claustrum" (d. I, c. 8).

209 "Fratres nostri, tam priores quam alii, in locis ubi conventum habuerimus, nisi cum episcopis vel in domibus religiosorum, et hoc raro, extra claustrum comedere non presumant" (*ibid.*).

210 "In civitatibus, in villis sive castellis, in quibus proprias domos habuerint, nihil omnino extra domos illas, nisi forte in domo religionis [*Reg. mitig.*: et cum archiepiscopis et episcopis] … comedant vel bibant" (*Regula SS. Trinitatis*, in PL, vol. 214, col. 446). The *Regula mitigata* was approved by Clement IV in 1267, but supposedly contained the changes that had been introduced since Honorius III, from 1217 onwards (P. Deslandres, *L'ordre des Trinitaires pour le rachat des captifs*, vol. I, Paris, 1903, pp. 27-28). The *Regula S. Spiritus*, c. 15, has the same text bar a number of minor changes.

211 For the Dominicans: "Mulieres claustrum, officinas nostras et oratorium numquam ingrediantur, nisi in consecratione ecclesie" (vol. I, c. 3). For the Premonstratensians: "Claustrum quoque et refectorium, dormitorium etiam et infirmitorium canonicorum nulla mulier omnino permittatur intrare, … exceptis ecclesiarum consecrationibus et indulgentiis…" (Pb, IV, 13). This text was copied from the bull *Audivimus et audientes* of 23 June 1232 (Pl. F. Lefèvre, *Les statuts de Prémontré*, p. 134).

B. *Probable sources*

The affinity between the Dominican constitutions and those of monastic institutes other than Prémontré is evident only in several scattered places, and in frequent but always brief passages. But the origins and deepest grounds for this textual or substantive similarity create a new problem. We must ask whether the Dominicans consulted a range of different monastic statutes, or found all or some of these passages together in one or more sources that have yet to be identified. The hypothesis of an eclectic method of derivation is unlikely. It is difficult to imagine that the Dominicans would have consulted such a variegated range of *consuetudines* over a period of at most twenty years, and yet have taken only one or two sentences or phrases from each. An attempt will be made in the following pages to group the related material from the various statutes together, and to establish to what extent they can be traced back to one or more basic texts that may have been a direct source for the Dominican constitutions.

1. *The* consuetudines *of Osma*

The affinity of the Dominican constitutions with the *consuetudines* of the Benedictines and the canons regular is limited to a small number of chapters. The rules on meals and the collation, the novitiate and the care of the sick appear to be of Benedictine origin.[212] The chapter on the monastic chapter contains a number of rubrics that can today only be found in Saint-Ruf.[213] Some customs during the office are similar to those of other canons.[214] It is difficult to avoid the impression that the Dominican legislators strove to replace certain details of the regulations on life in the monastery and on the liturgy derived mostly from Prémontré by monastic and canonical customs. The weaker textual affinity can perhaps be explained by the hypothesis that the fragments in question were not derived directly from specific constitutions, but are instead the written record of customs initially adopted only in practice.

As the intersecting point of monastic and canonical traditions, and as one of the probable subsidiary sources of the first *distinctio*, the statutes of the cathedral chapter of Osma are a prime candidate. The history of this chapter, of which Dominic was a member before he went to Southern France,[215] is known, at least in broad outline. Originally the canonries were filled by the Benedictines of Saint

---

212 See *supra*, pp. 308-314.
213 See *supra*, p. 308.
214 See *supra*, pp. 307-308.
215 Jordan, *Libellus*, nos. 11-13. In the papal letters and in the donation charters, Dominic is called "dominus Dominicus Oxomensis", "Oxomensis canonicus" from 1206 to 1216: see Laurent, no. 17 (17 April 1207) ff., *passim*, up to no. 68 (21 April 1216). See also M. H. Vicaire, *Histoire*, vol. I, pp. 81-112. The following title could be added to the literature used there: J. F. Rivera, *Cabildos regulares en la provincia eclesiástica de Toledo durante el siglo XII*, in *La vita comune del clero nei secoli XI e XII*, vol. I, Milan, 1962, which gives a number of details on the chapter of Osma on p. 233.

Michael's abbey. But by the end of the eleventh or the early twelfth century, certainly before 1136, the rule of Saint Augustine was adopted and, according to some, the *consuetudines* of Saint-Ruf, which were being introduced in large parts of France and Northern Spain at the time.[216] Perhaps the new statutes were not observed very strictly, or some noticeable relaxation of observance occurred after a period of time. In any case, by the end of the twelfth century regular life was in need of reform. This reform happened at the bishop's initiative, with the approval of the archbishop of Toledo and of the community as a whole. Innocent III sanctioned it in the bull *Ordinem religionis* of 11 May 1199, in which he also approved the statutes that had been submitted to him.[217]

The text of the statutes of Osma has not so far been found.[218] But it can be concluded from what Innocent III writes in his bull of confirmation that the rules approved in 1199 largely corresponded to the earlier regulations, which had perhaps fallen into desuetude during the course of the twelfth century.[219] According to the pope, the draft that had been submitted to him for confirmation by the bishop of Osma, with the full approval of the chapter, provided for the

---

216 The charter that mentions this fact is dated 5 June 1136: "…ego Adefonsus [VII] B. Mariae de Oxoma et canonicis sub regula b. Augustini viventibus decimas … dono" (M. Alamo, art. *Burgo de Osma*, in DHGE, vol. X, 1938, col. 1267). The author of this article also believes that the customs of Saint-Ruf were observed in Osma: "Ils continuèrent la vie régulière d'après les observances de Saint-Ruf jusqu'en 1536" (*ibid.*). But he does not provide documentary evidence. We suspect that he found the name of Saint-Ruf in an unpublished work by G. Argaiz, *Memorias ilustres de la S.I. y obispado de Osma* (1661) in the archives of Osma cathedral. But this author, who is generally regarded as less reliable (see A. Lambert, art. *Argaiz*, in DHGE, vol. IV, 1930, col. 1-4) does not say that the *consuetudines* of Saint-Ruf were introduced in Osma: "Y como la (regla) de S. Agustin fuese más acomodada pues el Santo Doctor la hizo también para los sacerdotes y el clero de las catedrales de Africa. Y ahora, pocos años antes la hubiesen resucitado en Francia por diligencia de San Rufo, más de la Iglesia de Tolosa y se viviese con grande ejemplo en todas las Iglesias catedrales que la habían abrazado en aquellas partes y en Pamplona habían hecho lo mismo los canónigos, dejando la regla de S. Benito que guardaron antes" (G. Argaiz, *op. cit.*, p. 180). – On the canons of Saint-Ruf and the spread of their *consuetudines*, see *supra*, pp. 191-192.

217 "Volentes igitur quod a te videtur pia deliberatione statutum debita firmitate gaudere, constitutiones ipsas (quas possemus restitutiones potius nominare, cum a longis retro temporibus hoc ipsum de Oxomensi ecclesia fuerit, sicut asseris, a Romanis pontificibus ordinatum) auctoritate apostolica confirmamus…" (Laurent, no. 1; also in PL, vol. 214, col. 604).

218 A manuscript of the Biblioteca Capitular in Osma (MS. 96, fol. 1^r-41^r) contains the statutes issued by Bishop Peter of Montoya (1454-1475) in 1475 (cf. A. Rojo Arcajo, *Catálogo de los codices que se conservan en la Santa Iglesia catedral de Burgo de Osma*, Madrid, 1929, p. 51). Most ordinances deal with the presence of canons at the office, the distribution of prebends and ecclesiastical ceremonies. They do not give the impression that the members of the chapter still formed a closed regular community, even though they still contain the words *regularis* and *regulariter*. The term *canonici* in the text is sometimes modified by the addition of *portionarii* or *portionarii et capellani* in the margin. On a number of occasions there is reference to previous statutes and customs: "antiquum prefate ecclesie nostre statutum" (fol. 1^r); "ut predicte nostre ecclesie antiqua est consuetudo" (*ibid.*). Fol. 4^r-5^r give the text of an "ordo qui hactenus in prefata nostra ecclesia observatus extitit in quadam tabula super hoc facta" *in extenso*. But this only deals with the canons' turns to officiate on the various feast days.

219 See *supra*, footnote 217.

replacement of the statute of *canonici saeculares* by that of *canonici regulares*. The stricter norms that were reimposed related primarily to a more radical observance of the *vita communis* by excluding any right to dispose of the revenues of the canonical prebend.[220] This clearly resembled the objectives of the founders of Saint-Ruf. It is evident from the way they organised the *vita canonica* that they had not yet adopted the *ordo novus* with its eremitical tendencies. But their radical rejection of the relaxation with regard to property rights that the Aachen rule had accepted also demonstrates that they were part of the stricter wing of the *ordo antiquus*.[221]

It must be doubted, however, that the statutes introduced by the canons of Osma around 1136, and to which they returned in 1199, were a fully homogeneous legal code. Even if they were compiled in immediate dependence on Saint-Ruf, it would still be impossible to reconstruct all its particulars with certainty. As far as we currently know, the legislation of this great congregation of canons already encompassed several traditions as early as the twelfth century, depending on the regions and churches where the *consuetudines* were adopted, adapted and supplemented.[222] Nor were all monasteries associated with Saint-Ruf incorporated into the *ordo*. Some communities, especially cathedral chapters, only adopted its liturgical and monastic customs, but otherwise retained their independence under the authority of the bishop.[223] In the case of the chapter of Osma, there is no indication that it was ever legally incorporated into the Order of Saint-Ruf. This is all the more unlikely as the chapter was not a separate abbey, but a community of clerics bound to the service of a cathedral church. More probably, the dependence on Saint-Ruf was limited to the adoption of a number of rules from the legal code of a canonical congregation that was prominent at the time, also in Spain. On the other hand, it cannot be ruled out that the earliest customs of Benedictine origins were retained in the statutes of Osma, at least in part, particularly those that governed aspects of life in the monastery, for which the canons regular lacked detailed rules.[224]

---

220 "…deliberatione provida statuistis ut, secundum preceptum felicis recordationis Alexandri et Lucii Romanorum pontificum, in Oxomensi ecclesia sint de cetero canonici regulares, nec aliquis in portionarium vel secularem canonicum recipiatur deinceps in eadem" (Laurent, no. 1).

221 See Ch. Dereine, *Saint-Ruf et ses coutumes*, p. 182; Id., art. *Chanoines*, col. 389.

222 The *consuetudines* of Saint-Ruf became predominant in France and in Northern Spain, both in abbeys that were incorporated into this *ordo* and in some monasteries and churches that were not legally dependent on it. See the list in Ch. Dereine, *Saint-Ruf et ses coutumes*, pp. 162-163.

223 See for instance A. Carrier de Belleuse, *Coutumier de XIᵉ siècle de l'ordre de Saint-Ruf en usage à la cathédrale de Maguelone*.

224 It was not uncommon for abbeys to switch from one legal statute to another. Ch. Dereine, art. *Chanoines*, col. 367, gives a number of examples of monks being replaced by *clerici* in the tenth and eleventh centuries. The Abbey of Goldbach in Alsace, founded around 1135 as a *cella* of the Benedictine Abbey of Murbach, wished to become independent and acquire the statute of canons regular according to the rule of Augustine. Celestine III gave his approval in 1192 (H. Dubled, *Bénédictins et augustins. Note sur les chanoines réguliers de St-Augustin de Goldbach en Haute-Alsace*, in *Revue du moyen âge latin*, vol. VIII, 1952, pp. 305-322).

We may perhaps suppose that the chapter statutes of Osma, which combined Benedictine traditions with canonical customs, exercised some limited influence on the first *distinctio* of the Dominicans. One has the impression that the compiler of the constitutions had a specific reason to supplement the legislation of Prémontré, which was certainly not lacking in detail in the chapters in question, with rules from another source. To put it more precisely, it appears that Dominic wished to ensure that the members of his order would observe a number of customs in relation to the office, the chapter and meals with which he himself had become acquainted as a canon of Osma. This hypothesis also provides a partial solution for the problem of the structure of the Dominican profession formula. If we may assume that the canons of Osma followed the customs of Saint-Ruf with regard to the profession, and thus after the *traditio ecclesiae* only made an express vow of *obedientia*,[225] then it is easier to understand why Dominic replaced the threefold Premonstratensian profession formula (*conversio, stabilitas, obedientia*), which the Dominicans had perhaps initially used, by this simple alternative.[226] But the explanations suggested here will remain hypothetical until the text of the statutes of Osma is found.

2. Ecclesiastical legislation for monasteries

The affinity of the Dominican constitutions with a number of early-thirteenth-century monastic statutes perhaps finds its ultimate origins in the general ecclesiastical legislation for regulars. Since the end of the twelfth century, the popes repeatedly had to attend to new problems in relation to the monastic life. At the very start of his pontificate, Innocent III approved the erection of charitable institutes, and he closely supervised the drafting of their constitutions.[227] He also preserved the evangelical poverty movement for the church by recognising the Humiliati, the first Franciscans, and the converted Waldensians as religious societies and by granting them an adapted rule.[228] Honorius III approved the two great mendicant orders, the Dominicans and the Franciscans, and actively supported their expansion and work.[229] Gregory IX, who even as a cardinal had been a devoted protector of and counsellor to Dominic and Francis,[230] as pope proved to be a promoter and reformer of monastic discipline. At his instigation, the statutes of Prémontré were thoroughly revised.[231] During the same period, many councils adopted the papal regulations and supplemented them. The Fourth

---

225 See *supra*, p. 298, note 83.
226 See *supra*, pp. 300-302.
227 See *supra*, p. 206.
228 See *supra*, pp. 219-221.
229 See *supra*, pp. 221, 233-234.
230 See M. H. Vicaire, *Histoire*, vol. II, pp. 77, 103-104, 112. For the Franciscans: L. Zarncke, *Der Anteil des Kardinals Ugolino an der Ausbildung der drei Orden des hl. Franz* (Beiträge zur Kulturgeschichte des Mittelalters und der Renaissance, vol. 42), Leipzig-Berlin, 1930.
231 For Gregory IX's initiative, see Pl. F. Lefèvre, *Les statuts de Prémontré*, pp. XV-XVIII.

Lateran Council (1215) issued two canons that were of fundamental importance to monastic discipline and the government of monastic institutes.[232] Regional synods, especially in Southern and Northern France, similarly dealt with this subject in numerous ordinances.[233]

Before the thirteenth century, the highest authority of the church rarely involved itself in the internal organisation of the monastic life, such as the fixing of the horarium with its various exercises and special obligations, which had in any case been sufficiently defined by authoritative founders and centuries-old traditions. The popes gave more attention to relations between abbeys and between abbeys and third parties. Papal involvement was motivated by the need to maintain or restore social order in the church.[234] As religious formed their own estate alongside the laity and the *clerici*, it was important to determine the rules for transition from one estate to another. This is why canon law took an early interest in the requirements for admission, the novitiate and profession. Candidates were expected to have reached the age of eighteen,[235] and have *libertas status*, the freedom of all bonds under canon or civil law that might impede their definitive admission to the monastic state.[236] Married and non-emancipated persons (*servi*) were obviously unfit to enter.[237] Similarly, the clerical state, obligations in the

---

232 Can. 12, *De communibus capitulis monachorum* and can. 13, *De novis religionibus prohibitis*, in Mansi, vol. XXII, col. 999-1003. Cf. *supra*, p. 229.

233 The second and third series of canons of the Council of Paris, in 1212, deal with religious (Mansi, vol. XXII, col. 825-839). There were three synods in Rouen: in 1214 (Mansi, *tomo cit.*, col. 904-916); in 1223 (*ibid.*, col. 1197-1200); in 1231 (Mansi, vol. XXIII, col. 213-218). A council was held in Southern France in 1215, in Montpellier (Mansi, vol. XXII, col. 943-946).

234 A great many papal documents on monastic institutes deal with issues of an economic nature: confirmations of possessions, disputes concerning tithes, oblation rights etc., see for example *Regesta Pontificum Romanorum*, ed. Ph. Jaffé and ed. A. Potthast; G. Schreiber, *Kurie und Kloster, passim;* Id., *Gemeinschaften des Mittelalters*, Regensburg-Münster, 1948, especially pp. 81-138, 151-282. The *privilegium commune* for monks and canons already contains the customary formulas describing the rights of the monasteries. See the text, for instance in M. Tangl, *Die päpstlichen Kanzleiordnungen*, p. 228; K. Brandi, *Urkunden und Akten*, Berlin-Leipzig, 1932³, pp. 83-84.

235 The ordinances of the synods of Paris (1212) and Rouen (1214) (see *supra*, p. 314, note 176) were repeated at the Council of Rouen in 1231 (see Mansi, vol. XXIII, col. 219).

236 The conditions were succinctly summarised in a formula of the *privilegium commune*: "Liceat quoque vobis clericos vel laicos liberos et absolutos e seculo fugientes ad conversionem recipere et eos absque contradictione aliqua retinere" (M. Tangl, *Die päpstlichen Kanzleiordnungen*, p. 230; K. Brandi, *op. cit.*, p. 84). For the history of the impediments, see C. M. Figueras, *De impedimentis admissionis in religionem usque ad Decretum Gratiani* (Scripta et documenta, vol. 9), Montserrat, 1957. For the dispositions in force for the Benedictines, see Ph. Schmitz, *Histoire de l'ordre de saint Benoît*, vol. I, Maredsous, 1942, pp. 267-268.

237 For marriage as an impediment, see C. M. Figueras, *op. cit.*, pp. 89-112 (tenth century to the *Decretum Gratiani*). A married person could, however, enter a monastery if the other spouse did so too. These cases were treated in the *Decretales Gregorii IX*, lib. III, tit. 32, *De conversione coniugatorum* (*Corpus iuris canonici*, vol. II, col. 579-587). – For the status of a *servitus* as an impediment, see C. M. Figueras, *op. cit.*, pp. 24-27 (eleventh century up to Gratian).

world and poor health were regarded as impediments.[238] Although professed
religious could be admitted to another order or abbey, this was subject to special
rules and it could not happen without the permission of the current superior,
unless the transition was to a *maior religio* or stricter observance.[239]

There is no doubt that such rules on admission were binding and were applied
in practice. But they first make their appearance in monastic constitutions from
the early thirteenth century onwards, particularly in the Dominican texts and in
those of a number of other orders.[240] In addition to the three traditional impediments of marriage, servitude or prior vows, certain obligations to third parties and
serious illness were also mentioned as grounds for unfitness. Candidates had to
be expressly questioned about the possible presence of one or more of the five
impediments.[241] The striking similarity and almost simultaneous insertion of a
questionnaire into the legislation of various orders is probably no coincidence, but
was the result of an ecclesiastical ordinance at the time.[242] One has the impression
that the popes' main concern was to call for greater circumspection in accepting
new members. This is also why they prohibited superiors from admitting persons
to the novitiate on their own authority without the advice of the community.[243]

It is striking that the texts of the Dominican constitutions on the conditions
for admitting new members show many substantive similarities with other monastic statutes, without there being any clear literal affinity with a specific order. There
are only a few parallel texts for the regulations in question in the *Consuetudines*
of Prémontré, which in so many other chapters were adopted almost in their
entirety and literally, and these are similarly present in other statutes. These
stipulations probably had a common source in ecclesiastical ordinances issued
for all monasteries collectively, or addressed to a specific order or community
and subsequently accepted by others. This source in question would have been

---

238 For the clerical state as an impediment, see C. M. Figueras, *op. cit.*, pp. 123-136 (eighth century up
to Gratian). On the Cistercians, see V. Hermans, *De novitiatu in ordine Benedictino-Cisterciensi et in
iure communi usque ad annum 1335*, in *Analecta S. Ord. Cist.*, vol. III, 1947, pp. 20-22. For secular
commitments (public duties, military service) as impediments, see C. M. Figueras, *op. cit.*, pp. 35-44
(eighth century up to Gratian). For the requirement of physical health, see V. Hermans, *art. cit.*,
pp. 33-34.

239 For the meaning of the expressions *arctior religio, maior religio*, and for the history of ecclesiastical
legislation on the *transitus* of religious, see *supra*, pp. 231-232. In the beginning of the thirteenth
century, regional synods also dealt with the issue, such as the Council of Paris, in 1212: "...
praecipimus ut nullus, ex quo alicui loco religioso vinculo professionis fuerit obligatus, recipiatur in
aliud coenobium religiosum, nisi vehementius praesumatur quod sincera devotione illud requirat, vel
hoc ipsum fiat cum licentia abbatis" (Mansi, vol. XXII, col. 827-828). This ordinance was repeated by
the Council of Rouen, in 1214 (*ibid.*, col. 907). See also a stipulation issued by the Council of Rouen,
in 1231 (*ibid.*, vol. XXIII, col. 218).

240 See *supra*, pp. 314-315.

241 See *supra*, p. 314.

242 We were unable to discover any document in the correspondence of the popes, from Innocent III up
to and including Gregory IX (1198-1241), that explicitly prescribes this manner of enquiry.

243 See *supra*, p. 316.

a compendium of regulations that were in fact almost universally applied even before the promulgation of Gregory IX's *Decretales* in 1234. This can explain why some Dominican texts have greater affinity with certain monastic statutes,[244] while other texts appear to be more similar to conciliar decrees or papal documents from which they were perhaps directly copied.[245]

In addition to the organisation and government of the monasteries, the ecclesiastical authorities also concerned themselves in the first half of the thirteenth century with the maintenance or restoration of regular discipline. Innocent III charged special visitors with the reform of certain abbeys.[246] He stimulated the holding of regular general chapters by the Benedictines.[247] In the French territories, he was assisted by the provincial councils of Paris and Rouen.[248] The Fourth Lateran Council (1215) was the culminating point of his pontificate, also with regard to the monastic life. His endeavours were continued by Gregory IX, who, a year after his election, issued the bull *Cum pro reformatione*, which listed the most conspicuous abuses and severely admonished religious to observe the fundamental monastic duties more strictly.[249] Almost all ordinances from his bull *Audivimus et audientes* of 23 June 1232 can be found in the new statutes of Prémontré.[250] From 1230 onwards, he regularly sent legates to the church provinces of Reims and Rouen to implement the reform.[251] In order to pre-empt direct intervention by the pope, the Benedictines of Normandy drafted regulations themselves.[252] The sixty-five *capitula* that these encompassed were copied largely from Innocent III's letter (1202) to the monks of Subiaco, from the ordinances of the Lateran Council and of the three synods of Rouen, held in 1214, 1223 and 1231 respectively.[253] None of this prevented the publication of the bull *In medio Ecclesiae* in 1233, which was worded so strictly that the pope

---

244 See for example *supra*, p. 314 (the enquiry before entry); p. 315 (admission of the professed); p. 317-318 (shortening of the probationary period); p. 318-319 (statute of the novices); p. 320 (ban on consuming meat outside the monastery).

245 See for example *supra*, p. 314 (eighteen years of age); p. 315 (ban on accepting Cistercians); p. 316 (advice of the community required for the admission of novices); p. 317 (purpose of the probationary period); p. 319 (*silentium* in certain places).

246 He instructed the bishop of Poitiers to visit and reform the monasteries in his diocese: "...corrigas et emendes et reformationi eorum taliter procures insistere..." (letter of 21 December 1198, in PL, vol. 214, col. 449). See similar instructions in *ibid.*, col. 5, 67, 128, 365-367.

247 See the bull *Ordinem religionis*, of 25 August 1210 (PL, vol. 216, col. 312).

248 See *supra*, p. 325, footnote 233.

249 See the bull *Cum pro reformatione*, of 1 July 1228, in *Bullarium Romanum*, vol. III, pp. 434-438.

250 See the text in Pl. F. Lefèvre, *Les statuts de Prémontré*, Annexe I, pp. 127-138. The footnotes indicate on each occasion where the various passages of the bull can be found.

251 For more details and bibliographical details, see A. Dimier, *Les statuts de l'abbé Matthieu de Foigny pour la réforme de l'abbaye de Saint-Vaast (1232)*, in *Revue bénéd.*, vol. LXV, 1955, pp. 110-125.

252 J. Laporte, *Un règlement pour les monastères bénédictins de Normandie*, in *Revue bénéd.*, vol. LVIII, 1948, pp. 125-142; the text of the *capitula* can be found on pp. 131-142.

253 J. Laporte, *art. cit.*, p. 128. The letter by Innocent III in question was included in the *Corpus iuris canonici*, vol. I, col. 599-600. The text can also be found in PL, vol. 214, col. 1064-1065.

subsequently felt compelled to grant the request of the abbots to allow certain mitigations.[254]

Although newer monastic orders were not directly subjected to reformist interventions by the highest authority, it is no surprise that they did experience indirect influence. The constitutions of the Dominicans thus contain the traces of several ecclesiastical ordinances. The special emphasis placed on silence,[255] the cloister,[256] and communal life[257] is related to the regulations that popes and councils had issued for religious in general or for specific orders during the first half of the thirteenth century. Various Dominicans were charged by Gregory IX with the visitation and reform of abbeys.[258] Perhaps their performance of these tasks also was an occasion for them to underline the importance of certain points of regular discipline in the constitutions of their own order.[259]

Three layers can be clearly distinguished in the source material of the first *distinctio*, the part that presents the norms for life within the monastery. The passages that were derived from Prémontré are by far the most numerous and were adopted the most literally. They make up approximately a third of the Dominican text. Some chapters were adopted almost in their entirety, in other cases only one or several sentences or just a few words were taken. The sections that are related, either as regards form or content, to the Benedictine *consuetudines* and to monastic statutes of the early thirteenth century are much less numerous.

---

254 The original text (A) and the mitigated form (B) (of 13 January 1237) appear alongside each other in L. Auvray, *Les registres de Grégoire IX*, vol. II, col. 319-332.

255 See *supra*, p. 319. The enumeration of the various places is clearly reminiscent of the ordinances of the Councils of Paris and Rouen and the *statuta* for the Norman Benedictines.

256 See *supra*, p. 320, footnote 211.

257 See *supra*, p. 310.

258 On 7 May 1230, the prior of the Dominicans in Rouen was charged with visiting the Abbey of Saint-Ouen (*Bull. O.P.*, vol. I, p. 31). See also the letters dated 24 and 31 October 1234 and 16 May 1235 in connection with the settling of certain issues in the same abbey (*Anal. O.P.*, vol. IV, 1899-1900, pp. 380-381 and 500). On 28 March 1235, the prior of Reims was instructed to visit a number of monasteries (M. D. Chapotin, *Histoire des dominicains de la province de France*, p. 235). In early 1237, Gregory IX asked John of Montmirail, O.P. to take part in the reform of the Benedictine abbeys in the provinces of Reims and Sens (*ibid.*, p. 228).

259 Perhaps the similarity between the ordinance of the Dominicans and of the Norman Benedictines on absence from the monastery was more than accidental. The Dominicans have the following at the end of their d. 22: "Eadem pena digni sunt, qui postquam missi fuerint, sine licentia prioris reverti presumpserint, vel ultra terminum sibi assignatum moram fecerint". The place of this sentence (at the end of the chapter) and the first words indicate that this is a later addition. The sentence is absent in the Prémontré text, from which the rest of this chapter was derived quite literally (see *supra*, p. 291, footnote 54). In the Benedictine text, the rule is as follows: "Quotiens vero per licentiam abbatis vel prioris alicubi egrediuntur, certus terminus assignetur, infra quem reverti debeant" (J. Laporte, *Un règlement pour les monastères bénédictins de Normandie*, p. 138). The prohibition on sleeping on matrasses, which was not derived from Prémontré, appears as follows in the Dominican text: "Super culcitras non dormiant fratres nostri" (d. I, c. 10). Cf. the Benedictine statutes: "Culcitrae pluminae … in dormitorio penitus auferantur" (J. Laporte, *art. cit.*, p. 131).

They were often interpolated as brief fragments in the chapters derived from the Premonstratensians. Their origins cannot be determined with certainty. Their literary affinity is not such as to warrant the conclusion that they are direct quotations from a certain source. On the other hand, the similarities are so clear that there are good grounds for accepting a substantive affinity. Many of these texts were perhaps derived from the statutes of the chapter of Osma and from ecclesiastical ordinances for monks in general. A diligent estimation shows that the texts and parallel passages thus adopted together make up almost four tenths of the first *distinctio* of the Dominican constitutions.

Section II. The sources of the second *distinctio*

The impact of medieval monastic legislation on the second *distinctio* of the Dominicans was not as strong. This part of the constitutions governs the administrative organisation of the order and the apostolic task of its members. It deals successively with the provincial and general chapters, the functions of the various superiors, study and preaching. It is clear that no recourse could be had to older examples for most of these issues. In the twelfth century, the monastic and canonical orders emphasised the general evangelical values and the specifically ascetical-contemplative aspects of the monastic life, and they adapted their social organisation accordingly. Neither the Cistercians, nor the Premonstratensians had provinces as administrative units between the level of the abbeys and that of the order as a whole. Because they did not regard the cure of souls as their primary task, they had no need to give a particularly prominent place to study, although they contributed outstandingly to the flourishing of intellectual life in the church. At the beginning of the thirteenth century, the organisation of their life and legislation proved to be stable and they were not easily susceptible to effective and rapid adjustment to changing circumstances. The newly founded apostolic orders such as the Dominicans therefore had to develop the blueprint for their own organisation largely by themselves. When it came to institutions that did already exist elsewhere, such as the general chapter, they put the experience of their predecessors to their own advantage.

§ 1. Main sources

A. The statutes of the Cistercians

1. The general chapter

In 1215, the Fourth Lateran Council decided that all religious orders must have a general chapter.[260] It held up the Cistercians as the example due to their long experience with this practice.[261] Their influence can be clearly identified in various monastic statutes from the beginning of the thirteenth century. The annual chapter in Cîteaux was the highest legislative and judicial body in the order.[262] Its organisation, powers and rules of procedure were set out concisely in the *Carta caritatis* and in the *Capitula* that accompanied the *Summa cartae caritatis*, and they were further elaborated in the later *Instituta*.[263] Its decisions were usually arranged in identical order in the *Statuta capitulorum*.[264] But no clear schema of their programme can be found in the official legislative texts of the twelfth century. The oldest known manuscript in which the agenda and ceremonial for the various days of the chapter are described in detail dates from the mid-thirteenth century, although it reflects customs that had mostly become part of tradition before that time.[265] The *Consuetudines* of Prémontré from the twelfth century contain only a few sections on the general chapter.[266] In the thirteenth-century codification, the chapter *De annuo capitulo* was expanded to several pages.[267] The Premonstratensian ritual was much indebted to that of the

---

260 Can. 12, *De communibus capitulis monachorum*: "In singulis regnis sive provinciis fiat de triennio in triennium, salvo iure dioecesanorum pontificum, commune capitulum abbatum atque priorum, abbates proprios non habentes, qui non consueverunt tale capitulum celebrare…" (c. *In singulis*, 7, X, *de religiosis*, III, 35, in *Corpus iuris canonici*, vol. II, col. 600; also in Mansi, vol. XXII, col. 999-1000). See also J. Hourlier, *Le chapitre général jusqu'au moment du Grand Schisme*, pp. 87-93.

261 "Advocent autem [*caritative*] in huiusmodi novitatis primordiis duos Cisterciensis ordinis vicinos abbates ad praestandum sibi consilium et auxilium opportunum, quum sint in huiusmodi capitulis celebrandis ex longa consuetudine plenius informati…" (*locis cit.*).

262 See for example the series of articles by G. Müller, *Studien über das Generalkapitel*, in *Cistercienzer-Chronik*, vols. XII-XX, 1900-1908; J. Hourlier, *op. cit.*, pp. 55-67; J.-B. Mahn, *L'ordre cistercien et son gouvernement*, pp. 197-216.

263 For the origins and history of these texts, see *supra*, pp. 202-204.

264 For the content and redaction of these *Statuta*, see *supra*, p. 208, footnote 144.

265 See the text in G. Müller, *Studien*, in *Cist.-Chronik*, vols. XIII, 1901, pp. 213-214; XV, 1903, pp. 51-52, 153. According to this author, the manuscript was created between 1244 and 1265 (*op. cit.*, vol. XIII, 1901, p. 209, footnote 1). It still contains the stipulation on singing the *Veni Creator* at the beginning of the chapter (cf. *Statuta cap. gen. Ord. Cist.*, vol. II, p. 274, a° 1244). G. Müller did not personally examine this MS. He derived his information and the text from J. Pelletier de Foucarmont, *Sommaire des remarques chronologiques…*, pp. 127-134. Nor do any of the other works which he references indicate the whereabouts of this MS.

266 Pa, IV, 1, *De annuo colloquio*. Cf. *De annuo abbatum capitulo* (*Summa cartae caritatis*, c. 4, ed. J.-B. Van Damme, *Documenta pro Cisterciensis Ordinis historiae ac iuris studio*, p. 24).

267 Pb, IV, 1, *De annuo capitulo* (in Pl. F. Lefèvre, *Les statuts de Prémontré*, pp. 84-91).

Cistercians,[268] and it transpires that the constitutions of Val-des-Écoliers were similarly influenced by Cîteaux.[269]

The liturgical ceremonies celebrated at the general chapters of the medieval orders ensured that they always retained their character of an extended conventual chapter.[270] The sessions began with the usual *Benedicite*, the reading of the martyrology or of a chapter from the rule or the statutes,[271] whereupon one of the abbots sometimes gave a speech. Prayers for the living and the dead, self-accusation and *proclamationes* were also held. Other ceremonies, like the procession at the arrival of the abbots,[272] the mass in the abbey church, the invocation of the Holy Spirit at the start of the first or indeed also of the following sessions, solemn absolution at the end of the final session, together made up a fitting frame for the annual meeting of the superiors. The business of the chapter of course took up most of the time and attention and was usually dealt with according to a fixed agenda. On the first day, the decisions of the previous year and *litterae* received were usually read out.[273] The following days were spent discussing visitation reports, enquiring into complaints received, and fixing measures against abuses that had come to light. In the meantime, the *diffinitores* worked to solve the various issues placed before them.[274] The final session was used to read out the new ordinances (*diffinitiones*).

---

268 The ceremonies are described by Emo of Werum, *Chronicon*, ed. G. H. Pertz, in MGH, *Scriptores*, vol. XXIII, Leipzig, 1925, pp. 477-478. See also Pl. F. Lefèvre, *ed. cit.*, pp. 144-145, which mistakenly gives the year 1227 instead of 1217.

269 Compare *Constitutiones Ordinis Vallis-Scholarium*, c. 40, with *Ecclesiastica officia*, c. 48 (ed. Ph. Guignard, *Les monuments primitifs de la règle cistercienne*, p. 263):

Cist.	Val-d.-Écol.
"... post absolutionem defunctorum	"Post absolutionem defunctorum, dicto psalmo *Laudate* vel psalmo *Verba mea*,
dicatur *Adiutorium nostrum*, et exeant omnes monachi..."	dicatur *Adiutorium nostrum*, et exeant omnes fratres."

270 For Cîteaux and Prémontré, see the passages indicated *supra*, in footnotes 265 and 266-268 respectively.

271 The texts referenced *supra* in footnote 269 presuppose the normal programme of the daily *capitulum culparum*.

272 The procession is described in great detail only in the Prémontré texts: Pb, IV, 1 (pp. 84-85).

273 All kinds of letters were sent to the general chapter by persons both from within and outside the order, including letters requesting a share in the spiritual benefits of the religious (J.-B. Mahn, *L'ordre cistercien*, p. 242); letters from popes (for example from Innocent III in 1198: *Statuta cap. gen. Ord. Cist.*, vol. I, pp. 221-224); from secular princes (for example from the Emperor Frederick I in 1177: *ibid.*, pp. 85-86; from Frederick II in 1215: *ibid.*, pp. 431-433, with the chapter's reply, *ibid.*, pp. 433-434); from Saint Bernard in 1137 (PL, vol. 182, col. 302). – For Prémontré: *litterae excusationis* from the abbots who could not attend the chapter (Pl. F. Lefèvre, *Les statuts de Prémontré*, pp. 88, 144); *litterae variae* (p. 144); *litterae pro absolutione defunctorum* (*ibid.*); *litterae fraternitatis* (*ibid.*).

274 From the second day onwards in Cîteaux and Prémontré. For the origins and significance of the *diffinitores*, see *infra*, pp. 334-335.

Naturally, the Dominicans also built on the experience of other orders. Their general chapter, held for the first time in 1220,[275] has many features in common with the daily conventual chapter. The ceremonial that is described in the earliest constitutions is reminiscent in many ways of that of Cîteaux and Prémontré. Furthermore, the entire chapter *De capitulo generali*[276] is composed in the traditional *consuetudines* style. The agenda of the chapter for these three orders is remarkably similar, and this cannot easily be explained without mutual dependence. Common features are the solemn invocation of the Holy Spirit, a speech, prayers for the deceased, the reading of letters received, proclamations and self-accusation, the promulgation of the new statutes and the closing ceremony, including absolution and benediction.[277] There is clear substantial affinity, even though it is not always obvious in the formulation. In some cases, the text of Cîteaux was preserved more faithfully by Prémontré, in other cases by the Dominicans.

Cist., *loco cit.*	Pb, IV, 1	O.P., II, 17
Prima die … postquam decantatus fuerit hymnus *Veni, Creator* etc. cantore ipsum incipiente, cum versu *Emitte* etc. et collecta *Actiones* etc., dicatur …	Secunda die, cantato *Veni, Creator Spiritus* cum versiculo *Emitte Spiritum* et collecta *Deus, qui corda fidelium*…	… primo omnium devote invocetur Spiritus sanctus, a quo filii Dei aguntur. Et dicatur versus *Emitte Spiritum tuum et creabuntur* cum collecta de Spiritu sancto.
	Emo, *loco cit.*	
Deinde si littere legende fuerint, interim legi possunt	… procurantur littere varie pro causis quibuscumque …	Et si littere dande sunt, dentur et recipiantur
Quo facto … statim omnes exeant monachi … Egressis monachis …	Hiis ita peractis, prior capituli … publice pronunciat ut exeant capellani …	Et sic omnes qui non sunt de capitulo, egrediantur. Quibus egressis, …

However, the text of the Dominicans is much shorter. There is no mass in the monastery church, nor any procession to the meeting hall. Nor does the text include an agenda for the various days.[278] On some points, such as the *suffragia* for the dead, the affinity with the Cistercians is greater, whereas the ritual of the final

---

275 Jordan, *Libellus*, no. 86: "Anno Domini M°CC°XX° primum capitulum generale huius ordinis Bononie celebratum est, …".
276 CA, II, 17.
277 For Cîteaux: G. Müller, *Studien*, in *Cist.-Chronik*, vol. XIII, 1901, p. 213; for Prémontré, Pb, IV, 1, pp. 88-90 and Emo of Werum, *Chronicon* (see *supra*, footnote 268) respectively; for the Dominicans: CA, II, 17.
278 The chapter took five days for the Cistercians and three for the Premonstratensians.

session is more similar to the customs of Prémontré.[279] The texts that describe the two ceremonies are given below.

Cist., loco cit.	Emo, loco cit.	O.P., II, 17
Finito illo sermone, fiat generalis absolutio defunctorum nostrorum … hoc modo:	Item pro absolutione defunctorum, … subiungit abbas:	Finito sermone, fiat eis communis absolutio
Anime fratrum … et dicto *Amen,* incipiat cantor *De profundis* …	*Anima eius et anime omnium fratrum defunctorum,* etc. …	et dicatur pro eis psalmus *De profundis.*

Cist.	Emo	O.P., II, 21
Quibus lectis et facta solemni absolutione et dispensatione … et accepta benedictione ab episcopo, si affuerit, omnes recedant.	Postea dicatur *Confiteor,* … et subiuncta absolutione … det benedictionem, nisi episcopus fuerit ibi presens.	In fine communis fiat confessio et absolutio, perseverantibus benedictio, apostatis et profugis anathematis maledictio.

The parallels are less striking when it comes to how the chapter's activities were regulated. Usually, one of the first sessions was spent reviewing the reasons for the absence of members given in *litterae excusationis* or orally by the *socius* of the absent member in question.[280]

Cist., *loco cit.*	Prém., IV, 1	O.P., II, 17
Tunc littere excusationis absentium legantur in audientia, et cause excusationis eorundem a presidente capituli querantur et diligenter examinentur.	… qui habuerint litteras excusationis, … si presentes fuerint, eas prima die presentent, et dum legentur littere, ea que notanda fuerint, notentur.	Quibus egressis, qui missi sunt ad excusandos eos qui non assunt, ad quid venerint, loquantur.
Deinde emendande sunt culpe et proclamationes faciende.		Deinde culpe audiantur.

---

279 Two versions of the closing ceremony in Prémontré have been handed down, one in the *Institutiones* (Pb, IV, 1, pp. 89-90) and a second one in Emo of Werum's chronicle (see *supra*, note 268). The first is more similar to that of Cîteaux, whereas the second has greater affinity with the text of the Dominicans.

280 For Cîteaux, see G. Müller, *Studien,* in *Cist.-Chronik,* vol. XV, 1903, p. 51. For Prémontré, see Pb, IV, 1 (p. 88). For the Dominicans, see CA, II, 17.

The reading of the visitation reports on the second day of the chapter was intended to give a clear overview of the state of regular life in the various abbeys.[281]

Cist., *loco cit.*	Prém., *loco cit.*	O.P., II, 18
Deinde inquirat si que abbatia in hoc anno a patre suo, a quo domus illa exivit, non fuerit visitata.	... surgunt circatores secundum ordinem cum schedulis duo, in quibus recitatur quomodo se habeat domus illa et illa, quam visitarunt, in spiritualibus et temporalibus.	Post hec visitatores, presentes verbo, absentes scripto, referre debent de hiis, quos visitaverint, fratribus: si in pace continui, in studio assidui, in predicatione ferventes, que de eis fama, quis fructus, si in victu ... secundum tenorem institutionum ordo servetur.

The subsequent deliberations focused on the measures that had to be taken to correct any abuses. The Dominican chapter attended primarily to the apostolic activities of the members of the order and to their relations with people in the world. The agenda of their chapter was the only one to feature an enquiry into the suitability of preachers.[282]

The great number of participants was an impediment for fruitful exchange at the chapters in Cîteaux. Discussions were often noisy and confused.[283] The most complicated and important issues were therefore removed from the competency of the plenary assembly and entrusted to a group of *definitores*.[284] This role is first described in the legislative documents of the Cistercians under this name in 1197,[285] but the institution itself is much older. The *Carta caritatis* and the *Statuta* of c. 1125 already urged that controversial matters that could not be settled unanimously should be decided by the abbot of Cîteaux and a number of competent arbiters.[286] Even outside the context of the chapter, small commissions of

---

281 For Cîteaux, see G. Müller, *loco cit.* For Prémontré, see Pl. F. Lefèvre, *Les statuts de Prémontré*, pp. 144-145. For the Dominicans, see CA, II,18.

282 CA, II, 20, *De idoneis ad predicandum.* The *litterae praedicationum* mentioned in the Prémontré text (Pb, IV, 1, p. 90) perhaps refer to the licences to preach mendicant sermons: Cf. Pb, 11,1, p. 43: "Preterea nullus abbas aliquem de canonicis suis mittat ad scholas vel ad predicandum pro questu, nisi de licentia capituli generalis".

283 G. Müller, *Studien*, in *Cist.-Chronik*, vol. XIII, 1901, pp. 179-185.

284 G. Müller, *ibid.*, pp. 365-369; vol. XIV, 1902, pp. 22-27.

285 "Cum dominus abbas Cisterciensis voluerit definitores eligere, ..." (*Statuta cap. gen. Ord. Cist.*, vol. I, p. 221).

286 "...illud inde irrefragabiliter teneatur, quod abbas Cisterciensis et hi qui sanioris consilii et magis idonei apparuerint, iudicabunt, ..." (*Carta caritatis post.*, c. 19, in *Statuta cap. gen. Ord. Cist.*, vol. I, p. XXIX). "Si autem ... inter se dissenserint, pater Cisterciensis monasterii quatuor abbatibus ad hoc idoneis hanc diffinire praecipiat, ..." (*Instituta gen. cap.*, c. 31, ed. J.-B. Van Damme, *Genèse des Instituta generalis capituli*, in *Cîteaux*, vol. XII, 1961, pp. 47-48; cf. Id., *La constitution cistercienne de 1165*, in *Analecta S. Ord. Cist.*, vol. XIX, 1963, pp. 85-86.

abbots were formed from time to time to resolve disputes.[287] As a fixed institution in the legislation of the order, specifically as the body that, according to the statutes, exercised the highest decision-making authority during the chapter, the *definitorium* was perhaps in existence by the mid-twelfth century.[288] Its members were appointed on the second day by the abbot of Cîteaux, on the advice of the four *primi abbates*.[289] Their task was not yet well-defined, and this remained the case during the following years. In 1222 they were the highest judicial authority in the order, but no precise information is available concerning their election and number.[290] In 1234 they were charged with reviewing the legislation.[291] At the general chapter in Cîteaux they had the right to take definitive decisions on issues submitted to them. Their decisions, *diffinitiones*, were read out during the last session and had to be accepted by all without dissent.[292]

Originally, the function of the *diffinitores* at the general chapter of the Dominicans must have been very similar to that of the Cistercians, both as regards their appointment and their task. Traces of this can be found in the chapter *De quaestionibus*, which stipulates that certain affairs must be entrusted to a small number of persons, whose decisions were to count as decisions of the chapter as a whole.[293] The title *diffinitor* does not appear there, but the role is the same as in the Cistercian order. It was known from the very start of the order, at the first chapter, held in 1220 in Bologna, as Dominic himself transferred his authority to *diffinitores* elected from among the members present, who thus received full governing authority and legislative power.[294] The role of the *diffinitorium* at the general chapter later changed fundamentally. According to the revised text of the constitutions, the diffinitors no longer constituted a limited group at the chapter, but the chapter itself as a whole as a legislative assembly, made up of the representatives of the provinces, either the provincials or the *diffinitores generalis*

---

287 "Ad negotia Ordinis ad plenum tractanda nominati sunt abbates isti…" (*Statuta cap. gen. Ord. Cist.*, vol. I, p. 132, a° 1190). One such commission met between Pentecost and the start of the general chapter in 1209 (*ibid.*, p. 368).

288 According to the *Auctarium Savignense, diffinitores* had been appointed regularly since 1147 (J.-B. Mahn, *L'ordre cistercien*, p. 190).

289 "Secunda die capituli nominentur definitores ante tertiam" (*Statuta cap. gen. Ord. Cist.*, vol. I, p. 320, a° 1206). "Ante sextam pronuntiet abbas Cistercii vel alius cui iniunxerit, definitores, quos ipse ad hoc elegerit" (G. Müller, *Studien*, in *Cist.-Chronik*, vol. XV, 1903, p. 51). Cf. *Nomasticon Cisterciense*, p. 315. For Prémontré: "Secunda die … postea seorsum diffinitores capituli assumantur…" (Pb, IV,1).

290 *Statuta cap. gen. Ord. Cist.*, vol. II, p. 15. The decisions of the visitors were also called *diffinitiones* (*ibid.*). See also *Statuta…*, vol. I, p. 495 (a° 1218).

291 *Statuta…*, vol. II, pp. 131-132.

292 "Quinta die … postea recitentur diffinitiones ab abbatibus ad hoc assignatis, quibus nullus debet contradicere…" (G. Müller, *Studien*, in *Cist.-Chronik*, vol. XV, 1903, p. 153).

293 "De solutione et terminatione questionum, … prelatus maior cum aliis, qui ad hoc instituti sunt, tractabit. Et quicquid inde, … ordinaverint, capitulum universaliter et unanimiter et devote suscipiat" (CA, II, 21).

294 Jordan, *Libellus*, no. 86; *Proc. Bon.*, no. 2. See the texts *supra*, p. 239, footnotes 303-304.

capituli appointed by the provincial chapter.[295] Their election therefore no longer took place at the general chapter itself. By contrast, the previous arrangement remained in force for the provincial chapters, and its activities and decisions were entrusted to a limited college of four *diffinitores*,[296] elected on the spot. The number four perhaps is linked to the *quatuor primi abbates* of the Cistercians, who played an important role in the government of the order, especially at the general chapters.[297] The election of the *diffinitores* at the provincial chapter of the Dominicans similarly echoes the customs of the Cistercians.[298]

Cist., *loco cit.*	O.P., II, 1
Cum dominus abbas Cisterciensis voluerit definitores eligere, … inquirat a quatuor primis abbatibus simul vel singillatim, … quos singuli eorum de derivatione sua magis idoneos perspexerint ad hoc opus … Ipse quoque quatuor primos abbates et de aliis filiis suis quos magis discretos et emulatores ordinis cognoverit, assumat.	Statuimus quod singulis annis … quatuor fratres de discretioribus et magis idoneis a provinciali capitulo per disquisitionem … hoc modo eligantur. Predicti siquidem tres vel duo … voluntates singulorum singillatim et seorsum disquirant et conscribant fideliter … (II, 2: Predicti igitur diffinitores …)

A number of precautions that the Cistercians took to ensure that the chapter would be able to perform its functions properly were also adopted by the Dominicans. The statutes strongly insisted that the sessions should be conducted in an orderly fashion. Everyone had to await his turn to stand and speak.[299] The members of the chapter were required to formulate their propositions and make

---

295 "Statuimus etiam ut per duos annos in dictarum provinciarum capitulis aliquis de magis idoneis a capitulo eligatur, qui sit generalis capituli diffinitor … Tertio autem anno priores provinciales dictarum provinciarum generale capitulum celebrabunt" (CA, II, 5).

296 CA, II, 1. See the text below.

297 The abbots in question were the abbots of the first *filiae* of Cîteaux: La Ferté, Pontigny, Clairvaux and Morimond. The first three were already mentioned in the *Carta caritatis prior* (c. 8) of 1119 (ed. J.-B. Van Damme, *Documenta*, p. 19). The four are mentioned in the *Carta caritatis post.* (c. 29-30, ed. *Statuta cap. gen. Ord. Cist.*, vol. I, pp. XXX-XXXI). Further details concerning the *quatuor primi abbates* can be found in J.-B. Mahn, *L'ordre cistercien*, p. 63. For their role at the general chapter, see *ibid.*, p. 189. See also the text below.

298 For the Cistercians: *Statuta cap. gen. Ord. Cist.*, vol. I, p. 221 (a° 1197).

299 For the Cistercians: *Libellus definitionum* of 1202, d. V, c. 16 (MS. Mons 31/192, fol. 80ᵛ). The text already appeared in the *Instituta generalis capituli*, c. 45 (ed. Ph. Guignard, p. 262). For the Dominicans: CA, II, 21.

Cist.	O.P.
"Nulli abbatum preter Cisterciensem liceat clamare vel in audientia omnium loqui, nisi stando, omnibus aliis sedendo auscultantibus."	"… Sed uno stante et loquente, alius non loquatur."

By way of comparison see: "In capitulo unus tantum loquatur et stando" (*Const. Ord. Vallis-Scholarium*, c. 40).

their views known clearly and succinctly. They were not permitted to interrupt or contradict each other. They could only leave the hall during sessions for necessary reasons.[300] When the *definitiones* or general decisions and ordinances were read out, no one was permitted to express dissent, either under his breath or out loud.[301]

Cist. (A)	Cist. (B)	O.P., II, 21
Si forte aliqua controversia inter quoslibet abbates emerserit, …	Si autem … inter se dissenserint, pater Cisterciensis monasterii quatuor abbatibus ad hoc idoneis hanc definire praecipiat, et quod illi utilius iudicaverint, omnis sanctae multitudinis conventus sine retractione teneat.	Si qua vero dissensio inter fratres nostri ordinis, quod absit, emerserit, … prelatus maior cum aliis, qui ad hoc instituti sunt, tractabit.
quicquid inde a capitulo fuerit definitum, sine retractatione observetur.		Et quicquid inde … ordinaverint, capitulum universaliter et unanimiter et devote suscipiat.

Cist. (C)	O.P.
Quibus nullus debet contradicere, nullus etiam loqui, dum recitantur.	Nullus murmuret, nullus reclamet, nullus contradicat.

Like the Cistercians and several other orders, the Dominicans also strove to ensure that nothing discussed at the general chapter would be revealed to outsiders. The presence of strangers was strongly prohibited; under no circumstances were they to be admitted to the deliberations.[302] The text of the Dominican

---

300 For the Cistercians: *Libellus definitionum* (1202), d. V, c. 15 (MS. Mons 31/192, fol. 80ᵛ). The same text also appears in *Nomasticon Cisterciense*, p. 313. For the Dominicans: CA, II, 21.

Cist.	O.P.
"… ad arbitrium presidentis, sine cuius licentia, nutu manus petita, … nullus exeat."	"Et ut in eundo modus sevetur, nullus exeat sine licentia et necessitate."

Cf. for Prémontré: "… nullus abbas, canonicus vel conversus exeat extra portam sine licentia domini Premonstratensis" (Pb, IV, 1, p. 87).

301 There are several Cistercian texts that emphasise the importance of accepting the rulings of the special commissions and of the *definitores* without contradiction. The text of the Dominicans (CA, II, 21) is compared below with the *Carta caritatis posterior*, c. 18 (*Statuta cap. gen. Ord. Cist.*, vol. I, pp. XXVIII-XXіX) (= A); *Instituta generalis capituli*, c. 31 (J.-B. Van Damme, *Genèse des Instituta generalis capituli*, in *Cîteaux*, vol. XII, 1961, pp. 47-48) (= B); chapter ceremonial, fifth day (G. Müller, *Studien*, in *Cist.-Chronik*, vol. XV, 1903, p. 153 (= C).

302 CA, II, 16.

constitutions here appears to reflect the rules that were only formulated by the Cistercians in the thirteenth century.[303]

Cist., *Nom.*	O.P., II, 16	Val-d.-École.
Nullus aliquis saecularis seu persona alterius ordinis duobus diebus ante festum S. Crucis Cistercium ingredi permittatur.	Nullus religiosus alterius ordinis vel professionis nullusque secularis cuiuscumque ordinis vel dignitatis vel professionis vel vite secretis vel tractatibus capituli aliquo modo admittatur.	Ea quae tractantur in capitulo secreta sunt, ita quod nulli alterius ordinis vel saecularibus revelentur.

Cist., *Stat.*, II

… nullusque saecularis … ante festum …

2. *Constitutional regulations*

A number of measures taken by the Cistercians to stimulate the proper conduct of the regular life also appear to have found their way into the Dominican constitutions. The legislation of both orders demands that new foundations must comprise twelve religious from the start.[304] The regulation was adapted to the customs of the monastic life, but less so to the needs and possibilities of an apostolic order, whose goal was to spread quickly to as many places as possible. It was not strictly enforced by the Dominicans. As the sources show, new houses always had fewer than twelve founders, both before and after 1220.[305] They possibly adopted this rule from some external source, either directly from Cîteaux

---

303 *Nomasticon Cisterciense*, p. 312. A slightly different text in *Stat. cap. gen. Ord. Cist.*, vol. II, p. 113 (a° 1233). Cf. *Constitutiones Ord. Vallis-Schol.*, c. 18.

304 This was a traditional custom from the time of Saint Benedict which was adopted by the Cistercians as a legal rule at the foundation of the Abbey of Cîteaux, with a view to preserving the integrity of regular observance. See *Exordium parvum*, c. 14 (ed. J.-B. Van Damme, *Documenta*, p. 14). Echoes of the *Capitula* that follow the *Summa cartae caritatis* of 1123-1124 (*ibid.*, p. 26) can be seen in the relevant statute in the Dominican text (CA, II, 23):

Cist.	O.P.
"Non mittendum esse abbatem novum in locum novellum sine monachis ad minus duodecim nec sine libris istis, psalterio…"	"Conventus citra numerum duodenarium et sine licentia generalis capituli et sine priore et doctore non mittatur."

This law was still in force for the Cistercians in the twelfth century, but in a formula that had been slightly modified in c. 1151: "Duodecim monachi una cum abbate tertiodecimo ad cenobia nova transmittantur" (*Instituta generalis capituli*, c. 12, ed. C. Noschitzka, p. 25). The same text can be found in the codification of 1202 (*Libellus definitionum*, d. I, c. 7, MS. Mons 31/192, fol. 74ʳ), which was immediately available to the Dominicans.

305 See for instance Jordan, *Libellus*, nos. 49, 51-52, 54-55; M. H. Vicaire, *Histoire*, vol. II, pp. 311-315.

or from Prémontré, which has it in the same wording.[306] The stipulation on the *translatio* of monasteries also appears to be connected with the legislation of the Cistercians. In this case, the approval or *maius consilium* of the general chapter of Cîteaux was required since 1152.[307] A much more recent text in the *Institutiones capituli generalis* of c. 1240 seems more like the Dominican version.[308]

To preserve the spirit of poverty and frugality according to their original *institutio*, the Cistercians had from an early stage restricted the possession and use of temporal goods.[309] At the beginning of the thirteenth century, for example in 1206 and 1215,[310] their general chapters confirmed earlier regulations and reiterated the prohibition on acquiring sources of income and land. The Dominicans adopted the same stipulations, although inspired by other motives.[311] The relevant text which they added to their constitutions in 1220 appears to be related to the chapter ordinance of Cîteaux.[312]

In their pursuit of seclusion, frugality and as pure a practice of monastic poverty as possible, the Cistercians from the start declined to accept parish ministry.[313] This measure was perhaps also intended to prevent dissensions and conflict between the secular and the regular clergy.[314] Nonetheless, the order from

---

306 *Institut. Praem.*, d. IV, c. 2. Both the twelfth-century codification (Pa) and the thirteenth-century one (Pb) preserved the Cîteaux text (*clericis* instead of *monachis*).

307 J.-B. Van Damme, *La constitution cistercienne de 1165*, in *Analecta S. Ord. Cist.*, vol. XIX, 1963, p. 65, footnote 5. Cf. *Statuta cap. gen. Ord. Cist.*, vol. I, p. 45: "… consilio et assensu patris abbatis…".

308 *Nomasticon Cisterciense*, p. 288. This text is compared with that of the Dominicans (CA, II, 23) below. The *Statuta cap. gen. Ord. Cist.*, vol. I, p. 429 (a° 1214) and p. 448 (a° 1215) have slightly varying texts.

Cist.	O.P.
"Nulli liceat abbatiam ordinis nostri fundare nec fundatam alias transferre … nisi de licentia capituli generalis."	"Nulla domus nostri ordinis transferatur de provincia ad provinciam nisi per tria capitula fuerit approbatum."

309 See *Exordium parvum*, c. 14 (ed. J.-B. Van Damme, *Documenta*, pp. 13-14); *Carta caritatis prior*, c. 1 (*ibid.*, p. 16); *Capitula* of 1123-1124, no. 23, *Quod redditus non habeamus* (*ibid.*, p. 28).

310 *Statuta cap. gen. Ord. Cist.*, vol. I, pp. 321 and 448 respectively.

311 See *supra*, p. 237.

312 For the Cistercians: *Statuta cap. gen. Ord. Cist.*, vol. I, p. 321; for the Dominicans: CA, II, 26.

Cist.	O.P.
"Sententia de non emendo et non acquirendis possessionibus et redditibus, … firmiter teneatur."	"Possessiones seu redditus nullo modo recipiantur."

313 The following statute was in place as early as 1123-1124: "Ecclesias, altaria, sepulturas, decimas alieni laboris, vel nutrimenti, villas, villanos, terrarum census, furnorum vel molendinorum redditus et cetera his similia monastice puritati adversantia, nostri et nominis et ordinis excludit institutio" (*Capitula*, no. 23, ed. J.-B. Van Damme, *Documenta*, p. 28).

314 It is perhaps no coincidence that these ordinances were issued by the Cistercians in 1123-1124, that is, around the same time as the First Lateran Council (1123), which discussed the issue of parish churches and the cure of souls by regulars. (A. Fliche, *La réforme grégorienne et la reconquête*

time to time made certain concessions during the twelfth century, and exceptionally permitted its monks to exercise priestly ministry in certain churches.[315] But the official legislation on the subject was never changed. The general chapters of the early thirteenth century insisted on observing the full rigour of this rule, even in relation to abbeys that were subsequently incorporated into the order.[316] The Dominicans similarly refused to possess and minister to parish churches, to free themselves for their ordinary apostolate.[317] Like the Cistercians, they also tried to be exempted from the pastoral care of nuns.[318] The legislation of both orders similarly contains prohibitions on attending legal suits[319] or on going to the papal curia without authorisation.[320] Thus, there is similarity in substance between certain parts of the statutes of the Cistercians and those of the Dominicans; a similarity which is sometimes also reflected in the wording of the stipulations.

---

chrétienne (1057-1123) (Histoire de l'Église depuis les origines jusqu'à nos jours, vol. 8), Paris, 1940, pp. 393-394).

315 Cf. Cîteaux, vol. XIV, 1963, pp. 247-248 (reservations with respect to the work of J. Kloczowski, Le problème du ministère paroissial au moyen âge dans l'ordre de Cîteaux, Poznan, 1959).

316 The general chapters of 1234, 1235 and 1236 demanded the immediate recall of monks from all churches and chapels entrusted to the order (Statuta cap. gen. Ord. Cist., vol. II, pp. 126, 139 and 153 respectively). The legislation had been clearly formulated as early as 1214: "Nullus ecclesias parochiales recipiat" (ibid., vol. I, p. 428; cf. p. 448, a° 1215).

317 "Item ecclesias, quibus annexa sit cura animarum, non recipiant" (CA, II, 27).

318 For Cîteaux: "Inhibetur ... ne aliqua abbatia monialium de cetero ordini incorporetur" (Statuta cap. gen. Ord. Cist., vol. I, p. 517, a° 1220; cf. vol. II, p. 68, a° 1228). For the Dominicans: "... districte prohibemus ne aliquis fratrum nostrorum de cetero laboret vel procuret, ut cura vel custodia monialium ... nostris fratribus committatur" (CA, II, 27).

319 For the Cistercians: Nomasticon Cist., p. 335. For the Dominicans: CA, II, 31.

Cist.	O.P.
"Nec intersint personae ordinis placitis nisi suis aut aliorum de ordine."	"Placitis et causis nisi pro fidei negotiis non intersint."

The Instituta of the mid and late twelfth century contain a text that deviates even more than that of the Dominicans (see the ed. by C. Noschitzka, p. 34, c. 23; in the ed. by Ph. Guignard, p. 271, c. 74).

320 For Cîteaux: Statuta cap. gen. Ord. Cist., vol. I, p. 65 (a° 1157); cf. ibid., p. 263 (a° 1201). For the Dominicans: CA, II, 36.

Cist.	O.P.
"Nullus eat ad curiam domini papae ... sine consilio capituli generalis. Quod si ... fiat hoc cum consilio domini Cisterciensis et quatuor primorum abbatum."	"Nullus frater vadat ad curiam nisi de licentia magistri vel capituli generalis."

B. *The Fourth Lateran Council*

1. *Rules for the general chapter*

In addition to regulations related to the customs of Cîteaux, the Dominican constitutions contain a number of texts that betray the more immediate influence of the Fourth Lateran Council. One of the most important canons on the monastic life contained the obligation on all superiors of monks and canons to assemble regularly in a *capitulum commune*.[321] Canon 12 formulated the purpose and organisation of this governing body in a few straightforward ordinances.[322] The council did not concern itself with the details of the ceremonies, but simply referred to the customs of the Cistercians.[323] From this perspective, the Dominicans followed the rules very strictly by fashioning their own legislation on the general chapter to closely resemble that of Cîteaux. In one respect their imitation of their model went even further than the council required. Instead of assembling every three years, they have held a general chapter every year since 1220.[324]

The decrees of the Lateran Council left further traces in the Dominican constitutions in the chapters dealing with the general chapter. The repeated injunction to accept the decisions of the *diffinitores* without dissent is clearly indebted to the regulations of Cîteaux.[325] But in at least one instance, the Dominican text appears to be directly and literally dependent on canon 12 quoted above: it demands the strict application of the ordinances and condemns any recourse against this.[326]

Cist., *loco cit.*	Conc. Lat., *loco cit.*	O.P., II, 8
… causa … ad nutum Cisterciensis capituli terminetur neque inde ad aliam audientiam appellare liceat.	Et quod statutum fuerit, inviolabiliter observetur, omni excusatione et contradictione et appellatione remotis.	Et ipsorum sententia… inviolabiliter observetur, ita quod ab ipsorum sententia a nemine liceat appellari…

---

321 See *supra*, p. 330, footnote 260.

322 The reform and upholding of discipline are described as the chapter's main task: "…in quo diligens habeatur tractatus de reformatione ordinis et observatione regulari" (c. *In singulis*, 7, X, *de religiosis*, III, 35, in *Corpus iuris canonici*, vol. II, col. 600; also in Mansi, vol. XXII, col. 999).

323 "Huiusmodi vero capitulum aliquot certis diebus continue iuxta morem Cisterciensis ordinis celebretur" (*ibid.*). See also *supra*, p. 330, footnote 261.

324 Jordan, *Libellus*, no. 87; CA, II, 5 and 7.

325 See *supra*, p. 337.

326 The text of the Lateran Council mentions a ban on appeals which the Cistercians had had since c. 1145 (*Statuta, cap. gen. Ord. Cist.*, vol. I, p. 30, no. 70; see also J.-B. Van Damme, *Genèse des* Instituta generalis capituli, in *Cîteaux*, vol. XII, 1961, p. 58). This prohibition was repeated in 1196 and 1199 (*Statuta…*, pp. 209 and 249). The substance of the Dominican text (CA, II, 8), too, is derived from this, but the form is more clearly indebted to canon 12 of the council.

Similarly, the decision to convene alternately in Paris and Bologna is an application of the requirement that the place of the next chapter must each time be fixed.[327]

2. Organisation of the provinces

Other traces of the legislation of the Fourth Lateran Council in the Dominican constitutions can be found in the chapter *De capitulo provinciali*. The *commune capitulum* introduced by canon 12 was really more a provincial or regional chapter than a general chapter. It was intended as an assembly of all the abbots and priors of a certain *provincia* or *regnum*.[328] Supervision of the activities and the drafting of decisions at Dominican provincial chapters was entrusted to four *diffinitores*.[329] This term is certainly linked to the customs of the Cistercians.[330] But the appointment of the *diffinitores*, as well as the number four also point to the canon of the Lateran Council.[331] In fact, the structure of this section in the Dominican constitutions cannot be explained except by looking at another canon of the same council.[332]

Lat. coun., *loco cit.*	O.P., II, 1
… statuimus, ut, quum electio fuerit celebranda, praesentibus omnibus, qui debent, et volunt et possunt commode interesse, assumantur tres de collegio fide digni, qui secrete et sigillatim vota cunctorum diligenter exquirant, et in scriptis redacta mox publicent in communi, nullo prorsus appellationis obstaculo interiecto, ut is collatione habita eligatur, in quem omnes, vel maior et sanior pars capituli consentit.	Statuimus quod singulis annis … quatuor fratres de discretioribus et magis idonei a provinciali capitulo per disquisitionem … hoc modo eligantur. Predicti siquidem tres vel duo, … voluntates singulorum singillatim et seorsum, … disquirant et conscribant fideliter. Et … scripturam publicent in medium. Et in quibus maior pars capituli provincialis numero concordaverit, illi pro diffinitoribus habeantur.

---

327 "Capitulum generale uno anno Parisius, alio anno Bononie celebretur" (CA, II, 13). For the council, see *infra*, p. 343.

328 Can. 12 begins as follows: "In singulis regnis sive provinciis…" (see *supra*, p. 330, note 260).

329 "Statuimus quod … quatuor fratres de discretioribus et magis idonei … eligantur" (CA, II, 1). "Predicti igitur diffinitores tractabunt omnia et diffinient cum priore provinciali" (CA, II, 2).

330 See *supra*, pp. 334-335.

331 According to can. 12, four abbots took the chair at the *commune capitulum*: "Advocent autem … duos Cisterciensis ordinis vicinos abbates …; qui absque contradictione duos sibi de ipsis associent, quos viderint expedire, ac ipsi quatuor praesint capitulo universo…" (c. *In singulis*, 7, X, *de religiosis*, III, 35, in *Corpus iuris canonici*, vol. II, col. 600; also in Mansi, vol. XXII, col. 999).

332 Viz. can. 24 (c. *Quia propter*, 42, X, *de electione*, 1,6, in *Corpus iuris canonici*, vol. II, col. 88-89; also in Mansi, vol. XXII, col. 1011).

The rule that the place of the next chapter must be fixed every year also points to this source.[333]

Lat. coun., *loco cit.*	O.P., II, 4
… proviso nihilominus, ubi sequenti termino debeat capitulum celebrari.	Prior provincialis etiam cum suis diffinitoribus … semper locum determinet, ubi sequens capitulum celebretur.

Not just the organisation of the provincial chapter, but also the erection of provinces appears to have been due to the influence of the Fourth Lateran Council. It is true that the decree *In singulis* did not impose fixed administrative units as these existed in the Dominican Order upon monks and canons regular. For the latter, the *provincia* was simply the area within which a number of abbeys or priories would hold their three-yearly *commune capitulum*.[334] But the manner in which the earliest stipulations on provinces are formulated in the Dominican constitutions strongly suggests that the compilers were cognisant of the council's decree. In both cases, the areas were not determined very precisely and the option of using political borders (*regna*) as a basis for the division was kept open.[335]

Province-based territorial divisions played a very minor role in monastic and canonical institutes before the thirteenth century. Most abbeys upheld their autonomy under their own abbot or joined groupings that were not limited to any specific territory.[336] In some military orders, geographical descriptions had always been an important factor in the organisation of their government. To manage their many possessions in East and West, the Knights of Saint John formed a hierarchy of regional superiors who governed more or less extensive territories.[337] Since the second half of the twelfth century, Europe was divided into a number of lieutenancies, which were more or less coterminous with countries such as France, Spain, Italy, England and Germany, but which in some cases were further subdivided into priories and local lieutenancies.[338] The Order of Templars was organised along the same pattern, but its lieutenancies functioned merely as a link

---

333 Can. 12 (see footnote 331); for the Dominicans: CA, II, 4.

334 "In singulis regnis sive provinciis…" (see the text *supra*, p. 330, footnote 260).

335 CA, II, 15: "provinciarum priores vel regnorum"; II, 16: "in sua provincia vel regno; prior provincialis vel regnorum".

336 For the organisation of the Benedictine abbeys and the trend towards association, see Ph. Schmitz, *Histoire de l'ordre de saint Benoît*, vol. I, Maredsous, 1942, pp. 251-305. A good overview of the organisation of the *ordo* of Cluny can be found in G. de Valous, art. *Cluny*, in DHGE, vol. XIII, 1952, col. 137-140. In most orders, the relationship between mother and daughter abbeys also played a role. For Cîteaux, see J.-B. Mahn, *L'ordre cistercien*, pp. 217-228. For the non-territorially organised congregations of canons regular, see Ch. Dereine, art. *Chanoines*, col. 400-401.

337 See J. Delaville Le Roulx, *Les Hospitaliers en Terre Sainte et à Chypre*, Paris, 1904, pp. 355-404.

338 For the lists and titles of the superiors in the various countries, see J. Delaville Le Roulx, *op. cit.*, pp. 414-434. For the local lieutenancies, see *ibid.*, pp. 302-303.

between the individual houses and the general government.[339] Provinces do not appear in the statutes of either order.[340]

The first Dominican provinces were erected during Dominic's lifetime. Jordan of Saxony recounts that he was appointed provincial of Lombardy by the 1221 general chapter.[341] Dominican historians long believed that the eight provinces had been established as early as 1221. This view was based on the words of Bernard Gui, an early fourteenth-century author rightly regarded as a conscientious and reliable historian.[342] Yet his testimony on this matter cannot claim undisputed authority. In fact, his language was less confident in other writings, where he suggested 1220 and even 1219 as possible dates for the establishment of the first provinces, as well as 1221.[343] He gave no written sources, but referred to an oral tradition, whose deficiencies in certain respects he acknowledged.[344]

There are reliable documents that suggest that other provinces were also established in 1221. According to the *Chronica Ordinis*, Bertrand of Garriga was appointed provincial of Provence by Dominic himself, that is, in 1221.[345] This statement corresponds with information from a charter dated October of the same year, which refers to a provincial of the Dominicans.[346] A letter of recommendation by King Ferdinand of Castile mentions Suerius Gomez as provincial of Spain in January 1222,[347] which means that this province must have been erected in 1221. Northern France (*Francia*) and Central Italy (*provincia Romana*) similarly had their own regional superior in the same year or shortly afterwards.[348]

---

339 The *Statuts hiérarchiques* (ed. H. de Curzon, *La règle du Temple*, p. 80, no. 87) lists twelve lieutenancies.

340 The Knights of Saint John had a *prior* or *praeceptor* of each country: "prior Hospitalis in Anglia et eiusdem praeceptor in Francia" (J. Delaville Le Roulx, *Cartulaire*, vol. I, no. 868); "prior in tota Hispania" (no. 416); "prior in Alemannia" (no. 825). – For the Templars: "comandeur de la terre" (in the French *Statuts*, no. 102, ed. H. de Curzon, p. 89); "la terre de Triple ou d'Antyoche" (no. 104, p. 90); "le grant comandor de cele meisme terre" (no. 529, p. 278).

341 "Anno Domini M°CC°XXI°, in Bononiensi generali capitulo visum est eis, mihi officium prioratus super provinciam Lombardie primum imponere" (Jordan, *Libellus*, no. 88).

342 He wrote the following about the general chapter of 1221: "...in quo, fundatis per orbem sexaginta circiter conventibus, dicti conventus per octo provincias sunt distributi, scilicet Hispaniam, Provinciam, Lombardiam, Romanam provinciam, Teutoniam, Hungariam, Angliam" (*Acta C.G.*, p. 2); about the general chapter of 1228: "...in quo capitulo octo prefatis provinciis, per b. Dominicum institutis..." (*ibid.*, p. 3).

343 "...in quo capitulo [1221] vel in praecedenti, quod magis aestimo, ... dicti conventus per octo provincias sunt distincti..." (*Tractatus de tribus gradibus praelatorum*, col. 403). "Anno Domini 1219 vel 1220 coepit ordo Praedicatorum habere provinciales" (*ibid.*, col. 417).

344 "... certitudinem plenariam non inveni..." (*ibid.*, col. 403). "... de quorum aliquibus nondum potui plene, sicut volui, invenire certitudinem veritatis" (*ibid.*, col. 417).

345 "... fuerunt priores provinciales in Provincia frater Bertrandus, positus a beato Dominico..." (MOPH, vol. I, p. 338). This *Chronica* is perhaps the work of Gerard of Frachet (see *ed. cit.*, p. XV).

346 "Nos ... donamus ... omnia iura quae habemus et habere debemus in ecclesia et hospitali s. Laurentii ... R. magistro provinciali ordinis Praedicatorum..." (J. J. Percin, *Monumenta conventus Tolosani*, p. 23, no. 58). The initial R. is perhaps an orthographic or reading error.

347 See the text of the letter in L. G. Alonso Getino, *Capitulos provinciales*, p. 94.

348 See M. H. Vicaire, *Histoire*, vol. II, pp. 307, 310-311.

The foundation of the provinces of Germany (*Teutonia*) and Hungary must perhaps be dated to 1223 or 1224.[349] The English province was in existence before 1230, the year in which the first provincial chapter was held.[350]

The Friars Minor set up their provincial organisation at approximately the same time as the Dominicans. According to the prevailing view, based primarily on L. Wadding, the origin of the Franciscan provinces coincided with the appointment of *ministri* for Italy and the sending out of friars to various other countries in Europe. Wadding himself dated these events to 1216.[351] But his version appears to be contradicted by the silence of one of the earliest witnesses to the history and life of the first Franciscans, James of Vitry, who in a letter written in October 1216 makes no mention of any mission outside Italy and appears to be unaware of the existence of provinces in the technical sense.[352] Most authors therefore assume that the decision to systematically spread the order throughout Europe was taken by the chapter of 1217, at the instigation of Francis, who was planning to go to France and who appointed superiors for the other territories before his departure.[353] No fewer than eleven provinces must then have been erected, although they were not all immediately populated by members of the new order.[354]

However, the earliest sources know of no particular connection between the year 1217 and the establishment of provinces in the Franciscan Order. The *regulae* of Francis, chronologically perhaps the first documents that must be considered, only show that the appointment of *ministri* and *ministri provinciales* had occurred before 1221 and 1223 respectively.[355] Thomas of Celano, who wrote his *vita* of Francis in 1228, mentions two *ministri*, appointed by Francis himself, but does not date the appointments.[356] Thomas of Eccleston, who wrote a few decades or so

---

349 See M. H. Vicaire, *op. cit.*, pp. 312-313.

350 W. A. Hinnebusch, *The Early English Friars Preachers*, p. 1.

351 L. Wadding, *Annales Minorum*, vol. I, Quaracchi, 1931, pp. 273-277.

352 "Homines autem illius religionis semel in anno cum multiplici lucro ad locum determinatum conveniunt, … post hoc vero per totum annum disperguntur per Lombardiam et Thusciam et Apuliam et Siciliam" (*Epist. 1*, ed. R. B. C. Huygens, *Lettres de Jacques de Vitry. Édition critique*, Leiden, 1960, p. 76). In his *Historia occidentalis*, he writes: "Post capitulum iterum ad diversas regiones, provincias et civitates duo vel plures pariter a superiori suo mittuntur" (c. 32, ed. Fr. Moschi, Douai, 1597, p. 351). *Provincias* here appears to have been used in a general sense, like *regiones*.

353 See H. Golubovich, *Series provinciarum Ordinis FF. Minorum saec. XIII-XIV*, in *Arch. Franc. hist.*, vol. I, 1908, pp. 1-22; M. Plasschaert, *De origine officii superioris provincialis*, in *Ephem. theol. Lovan.*, vol. XXXIV, 1958, p. 336.

354 See H. Golubovich, *art. cit.*, pp. 2-4.

355 The *Regula prima* (1221) already speaks of *ministri* in areas outside Italy and even overseas: "Omnes autem ministri, qui sunt in ultramarinis et ultramontanis partibus, semel in tribus annis et alii ministri semel in anno veniant ad capitulum…" (c. 18, ed. H. Boehmer, *Analekten*, p. 12). In the *Regula bullata* (1223): "Quo decedente electio successoris fiat a ministris provincialibus et custodibus in capitulo Pentecostes, in quo provinciales ministri teneantur semper insimul convenire, …" (c. 8, *ed. cit.*, p. 22).

356 "Cum tempore quodam frater Ioannes de Florentia esset a sancto Francisco minister fratrum in Provincia constitutus et capitulum fratrum in eadem provincia celebrasset…" (Thomas of Celano, *Vita prima S. Francisci*, c. 28, in *Analecta Franciscana*, vol. X, 1941, p. 38). The chapter in question was

later, recounts that Agnellus of Pisa was sent to England as *minister provincialis* in 1223 and that he arrived there in 1224.[357] The *Legenda trium sociorum* positively gives the year 1219 as the founding date of the first provinces.[358] The same date appears in the chronicle written by Jordan of Giano, whose main focus is the history of the Franciscans in Germany, but whose work in general is regarded as a reliable source.[359] Later historians have therefore adopted this view and dated the origin of the first Franciscan provinces to 1219.[360]

The foundation of the first Dominican provinces happened shortly after the dispersal of the Franciscans (1217 or 1219), but there is nothing in the documents to prove that there was any direct influence. Francis's first deputies in Italy were not known by the title of provincial but simply as *minister*. And the title *minister provincialis* does not appear in Franciscan texts before 1223.[361] The term *provincia* did not yet mean a province of the order, but referred more generally to the region or country where the Franciscans were already present or to the mission territory where they went.[362] The term appears to have had a more technical meaning from the start for the Dominicans. The title *prior provincialis* is used in charters from 1221 onwards to designate the Dominican superiors in specific areas.[363] In the oldest constitutional texts on provinces, this title alternates with the formulas *prior provinciarum vel regnorum* and *prior provincialis vel regnorum*, which echo the terminology of the Fourth Lateran Council.[364]

---

held in 1224 (see footnote 1 there and E. Grau, *Thomas von Celano. Leben und Wunder des heiligen Franz von Assisi*, Werl, 1955, p. 121, footnote 189). – Paul had been appointed *minister* for the *Marchia Anconita*: "…quem Franciscus ministrum constituerat omnium fratrum in eadem provincia" (Thomas of Celano, *op. cit.*, c. 28, p. 58).

357 Thomas of Eccleston, *Tractatus de adventu Fratrum Minorum in Angliam*, c. 1, ed. A. G. Little, Manchester, [1951], p. 3.

358 "Expletus ergo undecim annis ab inceptione religionis, … electi fuerunt ministri et missi cum aliquot fratribus quasi per universas mundi provincias, in quibus fides catholica celebratur" (*Legenda S. Francisci Assisiensis, tribus ipsius sociis hucusque adscripta*, ed. G. Abate, in *Miscellanea Francescana*, vol. XXXIX, 1939, p. 246).

359 "Anno vero Domini 1219 et anno conversionis eius decimo frater Franciscus in capitulo habito apud sanctam Mariam de Portiuncula misit fratres in Franciam, in Theutoniam, in Hungariam, in Hispaniam et ad alias provincias Italiae, ad quas fratres non pervenerant" (*Chronicon fratris Iordani a Iano*, c. 3, in *Analecta Franciscana*, vol. I, 1885, p. 2).

360 See the *Commentarius praevius* of the Bollandists in *Acta Sanctorum*, Oct., vol. II, pp. 608-609; M. Heimbucher, *Die Orden und Kongregationen*, vol. I, pp. 674, 690-691.

361 See *supra*, footnote 355.

362 See *supra*, footnotes 358 and 359: "Territorium missionis, quod singulis fratrum manipulis obtigerat, mox nomen accepit administrationis vel provinciae, sed non in stricto sensu iuridico moderno, quia significabat tantummodo regionem assignatam pro missionibus praeside ministro provinciali" (H. Holzapfel, *Manuale historiae Ordinis Fratrum Minorum*, Freiburg im Breisgau, 1909, p. 139).

363 See *supra*, p. 344, footnote 346. A charter of 10 October 1221 mentions a sale "magistro Iordano, priori provinciae Lombardiae" (Th. M. Mamachi, *Annalium Ordinis Praedicatorum vol. I*, Appendix, col. 376).

364 See *supra*, p. 343, with footnotes 334-335.

The two mendicant orders also appear to have developed their own separate systems in respect of the nomenclature and circumscription of their provinces. Various names that occur from the beginning, such as *Hispania, Francia, Teutonia*, simply refer to the great regions of Europe. But their names for other areas diverged. Instead of *Lombardia*, one of the first Dominican provinces, the early Franciscan sources called Northern Italy *Marchia Anconita*.[365] The provinces of Rome and Hungary, mentioned before 1224 for the Dominicans,[366] were only erected by the Friars Minor during the generalate of Elias (1232-1239).[367] Before that, the area of Central Italy encompassed only *Tuscia* (Tuscany) and *Terra Laboris* (Campagna). England first saw the arrival of Dominicans in 1221, that is, at least two years before the Franciscans.[368] In the *provincia Provinciae* (Provence), the two orders each had a regional superior before 1224, but the Dominican superior had been there since 1221.[369] The distinction between the two systems is even more apparent in the list of 1263.[370] Of the thirty-two Franciscan provinces that are mentioned there, only five names correspond with those of the twelve Dominican provinces.[371]

3. Rules for elections

The rules of the Fourth Lateran Council are also reflected in part in the Domini-can chapters that describe the election of superiors and of some officers. In order to avoid any occasion for abuse and dispute, the council had ruled that only three *formae electionis* could thenceforth be used for the election of bishops.[372] The council's clearly preferred form was a secret roll call vote (*scrutinium*), which it described first and rather extensively in canon 24.[373] Also valid was the *electio per compromissum*, in which the voters delegated their powers to a small committee of electors who would appoint the suitable candidate in the name of the entire

---

365 See *supra*, p. 345, note 356.

366 See *supra*, pp. 344-345.

367 H. Golubovich, *Series provinciarum* (cf. *supra*, note 353), p. 9.

368 Jordan, *Libellus*, no. 88. For the history of the origins of the English monasteries and province, see W. A. Hinnebusch, *The Early English Friars Preachers*.

369 See *supra*, p. 344.

370 For the importance of this list, attached to Urban IV's register, see H. Golubovich, *art. cit.*, p. 17.

371 The two orders had the following names in common: *provincia Romana, Francia, Hungaria, Anglia, Provincia*.

372 Can. 24 (c. *Quia propter*, 42, X, *de electione*, I, 6, in *Corpus iuris canonici*, vol. II, col. 88-89; also in Mansi, vol. XXII, col. 1011).

373 "...statuimus, ut, ... assumantur tres de collegio fide digni, qui secrete et sigillatim vota cunctorum diligenter exquirant, et in scriptis redacta mox publicent in communi, ..." (*ibid*). Secret ballots already existed in the twelfth century (A. von Wretschko, *Die electio communis bei den kirchlichen Wahlen im Mittelalter*, in *Deutsche Zeitschrift für Kirchenrecht*, vol. XI, 1902, p. 327, note 3). Municipalities apparently only introduced the *scrutinium* after 1215 (L. Moulin, *Sanior et maior pars. Note sur l'évolution des techniques électorales dans les ordres religieux du VIe au XIIIe siècle*, in *Revue historique de droit français et étranger*, vol. XXXVI, 1958, p. 501, note 64).

electorate.[374] Finally, the council in passing also mentioned election *per inspira-tionem,* where the voters, instead of casting their ballots individually and in secret, unanimously and vociferously affirmed their mutual agreement on a particular candidate by acclamation.[375] This latter procedure was still used frequently in ecclesiastical and monastic communities in the Middle Ages.[376]

Of the three procedures proposed, the Dominicans adopted only the first, *elec-tio per disquisitionem vel scrutinium.* The constitutions mention it for the election of the *diffinitores* at the provincial chapter[377] and for the election of the master general.[378] The rules for recording and publishing the votes by three *scrutatores* are similar to those in the canon of the council.[379]

Lat. coun., can. 24	O.P., II, 11
… statuimus, ut, quum electio fuerit celebranda, … assumantur tres de collegio fide digni,	… cum per disquisitionem vel scrutinium voluntatum procedet electio, tres de prioribus provincialibus, qui inter alios provinciales priores primitus habitum nostre religionis susceperunt, voluntates
qui secrete et sigillatim vota cunctorum diligenter exquirant, et in scriptis redacta mox publicent in communi, …	singulorum singillatim et seorsum aliquantulum, tamen in eadem domo, coram oculis omnium disquirant et conscribant.

---

374 "Vel saltem eligendi potestas aliquibus viris idoneis committatur, qui vice omnium ecclesiae viduatae provideant de pastore" (can. 24, *ed. cit.*). For examples of such elections in the twelfth century, see for instance *Historiae Farfenses, Gregorii Catinensis opera,* c. 32 (ed. G. H. Pertz, in MGH, *Scriptores,* vol. XI, Hanover, 1884, p. 578); letter from Innocent II, in 1130 (PL, vol. 179, col 40); election of the bishop of Genua in 1163 (A. von Wretschko, *art. cit.,* p. 328, note 1); letters from Innocent III (PL, vol. 214, col. 65, 257; vol. 215, col. 206, 605).

375 "Aliter electio facta non valet, nisi forte communiter esset ab omnibus, quasi per inspirationem absque vitio celebrata" (can. 24, *ed. cit.*). The expression already appears in a letter from Pope Leo I on the election of the archbishop of Arles (449): "Quia electionem pacificam et concordem … postulationis quidem humanae, sed inspirationis credimus esse divinae" (*Gallia christiana,* vol. I, col. 531). For further details and texts, see for example A. Esmein, *Unanimité et majorité dans les élections canoniques,* in *Mélanges H. Fitting,* Montpellier, 1907, pp. 364-371; A. von Wretschko, *art. cit.,* pp. 328-330.

376 See for example the letter of the monks of Saint Anianus to the archbishop of Narbonne (c. 1120): "…et quasi alter alteri subauriculasset, cum antea mentio ipsius nulla facta fuisset, unum de nostris confratribus nomine Guillelmum conclamantes in Domini nomine pastorem nobis et dominum elegimus…" (*Gallia christ.,* vol. VI, Instrumenta, col. 84). It is clearly pointed out here that this was an *electio informis* (without a roll call). This form of election *quasi per inspirationem* was regarded as the ideal expression of unanimity in ecclesiastical elections (A. von Wretschko, *art. cit.,* pp. 329-330). It was regarded as valid by the Dominicans since 1240-1242 (*Acta C.G.,* pp. 14, 19, 21). For the Premonstratensians, see Pb, IV,6 (p. 99).

377 See *supra,* p. 342.

378 CA, II, 11.

379 This Dominican text contains fewer details than the electoral procedure of the *diffinitores* at the provincial chapter. But the constitutions of the Friars of the Sack still had the expression "facta collatione" in this place (d. II, c. 11, ed. G. M. Giacomozzi, p. 95), a formula that is similar to the canon of the council and that perhaps had previously been part of the Dominican constitutions.

Aliter electio non valeat, nisi forte communiter esset ab omnibus, quasi per inspirationem absque vitio celebrata.

Quod si, gratia Dei inspirante, in unum aliquem omnes unanimiter concordaverint, ille verus magister ordinis habeatur.

… ut is collatione habita eligatur, in quem omnes, vel maior et sanior pars capituli consentit.

Si vero in partes inequales se diviserint, ille in quem plures medietate omnium qui debent eligere, consenserint, …
(*Fr. Paen.*: facta collatione) sit magister.

The *compromissum* in the ordinary sense of the word had disappeared, although the term continued to be used in relation to the appointment of the electors by the provincial chapter.[380] The third mode (*per inspirationem*), similarly, left only a trace in the formula *gratia inspirante*.[381] As the context shows, the *unanimitas* resulting from this inspiration refers not to the unanimity expressed in the *electio informis* without a prior roll call, but to the unanimity of votes that is achieved through the *scrutinium* (first *modus*) and that is also ascribed to the working of grace.[382]

By contrast with the ecclesiastical regulations and most monastic statutes, which always assigned greater importance to the quality than the number of electors,[383] the Dominicans stipulated that if unanimity was lacking, elections should be decided by the numerical majority of votes. Nowhere do their constitutions mention the rights of the *sanior pars* that are expressly acknowledged in canon 24 of the Lateran Council.[384] They did initially use the formula *maior et sanior pars*, and they perhaps also applied it at the election of their first superior, according to the stipulations of the papal letter of privilege *Religiosam vitam* for the first religious community in Toulouse.[385] But when they drafted their constitutions,

---

380 According to the Dominican constitutions, the master general was elected by the provincials and two electors from each province: "…cum duobus fratribus, in capitulo provinciali electis, in quos ceteri ad electionem magistri faciendam compromittant" (CA, II, 10). This last word is misleading, as it could suggest that this is a description of the *compromissio* (cf. Ph. Hofmeister, *Die Kompromiswahl bei den Ordensleuten*, in *Theol. Quartalschrift*, vol. CXL, 1960, pp. 77-78). But a real election *per compromissum* involved the appointment of the *compromissarii* by the electors during the electoral session: see the references on p. 348, note 374. Cf. L. Moulin, *Sanior et maior pars*, p. 495. The Dominicans accepted this procedure in 1240-1242 (*Acta C.G.*, pp. 14, 19, 21).

381 "Quod si gratia inspirante in unum aliquem omnes unanimiter concordaverint, ille verus magister ordinis habeatur".

382 In the Dominican text, the passage "Quod si … habeatur" immediately follows the description of the procedure for the *scrutinium* that concludes with the words "…coram oculis omnium disquirant". The possibility of *unanimitas* is followed by the hypothesis of the division of the votes: "Si vero in partes inequales se diviserint…". For unanimity as an electoral ideal, see *supra*, p. 348, note 375.

383 A. Esmein, *Unanimité et majorité* (cf. *supra*, note 375), p. 355.

384 See table above.

385 "Obeunte vero te, nunc eiusdem loci priore, vel tuorum quolibet successorum, nullus ibi … preponatur, nisi quem fratres communi consensu, vel fratrum pars maioris et sanioris consilii … providerint eligendum" (Laurent, no. 74). For the election of the first superior (Matthew) in 1217, see Jordan, *Libellus*, no. 48; M. H. Vicaire, *Histoire*, vol. II, pp. 90-91.

they retained only the formula *maior pars*, or equivalents such as *maior numerus* or *plures*.[386]

The custom of determining the outcome of elections by the majority of the votes goes back to Greek and Roman Antiquity[387] and traces of it can be found in the canons of the first general councils.[388] It appears to have fallen into desuetude since the beginning of the Middle Ages, perhaps due to the belief that full unanimity must be the goal and that divisions at elections were unseemly for church communities.[389] But if unanimity proved elusive, the decision was not left to a purely mathematical majority. In such cases, the votes had to be weighted rather than counted[390] and in case of disputes, the most worthy and suitable candidate was to prevail.[391] Saint Benedict stipulated in his rule that a new abbot had to be elected either unanimously or by the part of the community *saniore consilio*.[392] This rule was widely disseminated and applied in many abbeys and was also approved by councils.[393] Since the pontificate of Urban II (1088-1099), letters of privilege for monasteries often contained a clause stipulating that the superior was to be elected by the *fratres communi consensu, vel fratrum pars sanioris consilii*.[394] The idea that the *sanior pars* should have the decisive vote even if it

---

386 CA, I, 14; II, 1, II, 2, II, 7, II, 9, II, 19.

387 See for instance E. Ruffini Avondo, *Il principio maggioritario nella storia del diritto canonico*, in *Archivio giuridico*, vol. XVIII, 1925, pp. 16-22 (Greeks), 22-33 (Romans); E. Barker, *Les élections dans le monde antique*, in *Diogène*, (s.a.), no. 8, 1954, pp. 3-17; R. Stark, *Das Majoritätsprinzip bei den Römern*, in *La nouvelle Clio*, vol. VII-IX, 1955-1957, pp. 387-395. These authors quote a number of passages from the *Digesta*: "Quod maior pars curiae effecit, pro eo habetur ac si omnes egerint" (lib. L, tit. 1, § 19, in *Corpus iuris civilis*, vol. I, p. 894); "Refertur ad universos quod publice fit per maiorem partem" (lib. L, tit. 17, § 160, ed. cit., p. 925). They are not certain, however, that these principles were always applied in elections.

388 The Council of Nicaea (325) stipulated in can. 6 that "vincant plurium suffragia" in the *ordinatio* of a bishop (Mansi, vol. II, col. 671). The *Corpus iuris canonici* gives the following version of this: "...obtineat plurimorum sententia sacerdotum" (vol. I, col. 250).

389 For *unanimitas* among the Germanic peoples and in ecclesiastical elections, see for example E. Ruffini Avondo, *Il principio maggioritario*, pp. 33-44. Expressions such as "electio concorditer, unanimiter facta; unanimes conclamaverunt; pari voto unanimique consensu" occur frequently. See A. Esmein, *Unanimité et majorité* (cf. *supra*, note 375), pp. 359-363.

390 The adage "Vota non sunt numeranda, sed ponderanda", which dominated medieval elections, possibly originated from a passage in Pliny: "Numerantur enim sententiae, non ponderantur..." (Plinius Caecilius Secundus, *Epistularum libri novem*, lib. II, ep. 12, ed. M. Schuster – R. Hanslik (Bibliotheca Scriptorum Graecorum et Romanorum Teubneriana), Leipzig, 1958³, p. 55).

391 "Is ... alteri praeferatur, qui maioribus iuvatur studiis et meritis..." (letter from Leo I, in PL, vol. 54, col. 673).

392 *Reg. S. Ben.*, c. 64. See also E. Ruffini Avondo, *art. cit.*, pp. 53-55; Ph. Hofmeister, *Pars sanioris consilii* (Regula, c. 64), in *Studien und Mitteilungen zur Geschichte des Benediktinerordens und seiner Zweige*, vol. LXX, 1959, pp. 12-34.

393 Ph. Hofmeister, *art. cit.*, pp. 13-14.

394 See PL, vol. 151, col. 338, 403, 405, 455, 502, 542; E. Ruffini Avondo, *art. cit.*, p. 55, footnote 1.

constituted a numerical minority remained predominant into the twelfth and the thirteenth centuries.[395]

Perhaps the difficulty of determining in practice which electors belonged to the *saniores* was the reason that the *maior pars* also began to be considered.[396] The formula *maioris et sanioris partis consilio* or a variant, such as *maior et melior pars*,[397] can be found sporadically until it was prescribed as a general principle for canonical elections by the Third Lateran Council.[398] From then on, it appeared regularly in letters of privilege for monasteries. Since the beginning of the twelfth century, it was included in the formulary of the papal chancellery together with the other customary formulas of the *privilegium commune* for monks and canons regular.[399] The Lateran Council of 1215 repeated and further specified the stipulations of 1179 in its definition of the three valid *formae electionis* for the election of bishops.[400]

The diverging interpretations given to the relationship between the *maior pars* and the *sanior pars*[401] lead us to suspect that the combined formula was not a

---

395 In the *Index verborum* to the three volumes of *Acta Pont. Rom.* (ed. J. von Pflugk-Harttung) the entries *pars sanioris consilii* and *electio* contain dozens of references to papal charters from 1100-1200. – The formula "quos sanior pars congregationis canonicae elegerit" appeared in the profession vows of most canons (for Prémontré, see *supra*, p. 302; for Marbach: E. Martène, *De antiquis Ecclesiae ritibus*, vol. III, p. 313; for Saint-Ruf, *ibid.*, vol. II, p. 180). For the Cistercians, see *Carta caritatis (post.)*, c. 19 (*Statuta cap. gen. Ord. Cist.*, vol. I, p. XXIX); for the Carthusians, see *Consuetudines*, c. 15 (PL, vol. 153, col. 661-662). For the use of the formula *pars minor sed sanior* in the twelfth century, see G. Schreiber, *Kurie und Kloster*, vol. I, p. 116. For the thirteenth century, see for example c. *Dudum ad audientiam*, 22, X, de electione, I, 6 (*Corpus iuris canonici*, vol. II, col. 64-66); c. *Congregato*, 53, X, de electione, I, 6 (*ed. cit.*, col. 93).

396 For the interpretation of *pars sanior*, see Richard of Saint Victor, *De questionibus Regule sancti Augustini*, c. 7, ed. M. L. Colker, in *Traditio*, vol. XVIII, 1962, pp. 209-210; Adam Scotus, *De ordine, habitu et professione canonicorum Praemonstratensium*, in PL, vol. 198, col. 597-601.

397 *Decreta Lanfranci*, c. 2: "Abbas cum eligitur, omnes fratres, vel maior et melior pars in eius electionem consentire debent" (ed. D. Knowles, *The Monastic Constitutions of Lanfranc*, London, 1951, p. 72). See also the letter from Innocent II to the Abbey of Prémontré, 21 December 1138 (PL, vol. 179, col. 387), although this does not mention an election, but the removal of abbots.

398 C. *Quum in cunctis*, 1, X, de his, quae fiunt, III, 11 (*Corpus iuris canonici*, vol. II, col. 506). Cf. c. *Licet*, 6, X, de electione, I, 6 (*ibid.*, col. 51). This extensive formula appeared in papal letters after the council: see for example *Acta Pont. Rom.* (ed. J. von Pflugk-Harttung), vol. I, pp. 279 (aº 1180), 318 (aº 1184), 330 (aº 1186), 340 (aº 1188); vol. III, p. 318 (aº 1191). For the election of abbots, the formula appears for the first time only in 1186 (*ibid.*, vol. II, p. 393).

399 "Obeunte vero te, … nullus ibi … preponatur, nisi quem fratres communi consensu vel fratrum maior pars consilii sanioris … providerint eligendum" (*Privilegium speciale Premonstratensis ordinis, sancti Benedicti et sancti Augustini*, no. 15, ed. M. Tangl, *Die päpstlichen Kanzleiordnungen*, p. 234). For the history of this formula, see G. Schreiber, *Kurie und Kloster*, vol. I, pp. 115-126.

400 See *supra*, pp. 347-349.

401 According to some, *maioritas* did not mean numerical majority, but the higher authority or value of the group which might also be the *pars minor* (O. von Gierke, *Das deutsche Genossenschaftsrecht*, vol. III, Berlin, 1881, p. 325, note 247). Others have presumed that the *maior pars respectu numeri* was also *maior respectu sanioris consilii* (E. Ruffini Avondo, *Il principio maggioritario* (cf. *supra*, note 387), pp. 50, 60-61). Or the expressions *maior pars* and *sanior pars* were used as synonyms (L. Moulin, *Sanior et maior pars*, pp. 384-385). For the view of the canonists of the thirteenth

suitable criterion for all cases. First, it could not be applied to elections where no confirmation by a higher authority was required. This is why the Lateran Council of 1179 decided that a qualified majority of two thirds of the votes was required and sufficient for papal elections.[402] But the same canon expressly stated that the normal rule of the *maior et sanior pars* continued to apply to all other canonical elections. To the extent that it can be deduced from reliable documents, the decision of an ordinary majority rarely sufficed to determine the outcome of an election in the twelfth century.[403] Several texts do confirm that the consent of the *maior pars* was required for the validity of certain decisions on questions of common interest or of the management of secular goods.[404] But this stipulation was often lacking when it came to the election of bishops or abbots. Papal letters of privilege issued after 1179, emphasised the *maior pars* in the formula on the election of abbots, but never separated it from the traditional *sanius consilium*.[405] Huguccio and Bernard of Pavia appear to have been the first canonists to argue that the principle of a majority of votes applied generally to all elections.[406]

The expression *maior pars* can be found frequently in ecclesiastical documents since the early thirteenth century. Innocent III ruled that decisions on the government of cathedral chapters required the consent of all or of the majority of the canons.[407] The same rule was issued by the Council of Paris in 1212.[408] Innocent III also approved the rule, for certain elections of bishops, that the wishes of the *maior pars* of the *compromisarii* must be regarded as binding.[409]

---

and fourteenth centuries, see P. Gillet, *La personnalité juridique en droit ecclésiastique* (Universitas Catholica Lovaniensis. Dissertationes ad gradum magistri in Facultate theologica consequendum conscriptae, 2nd series, vol. 18), Mechelen, 1927, pp. 137-140; L. Moulin, *art. cit.*, pp. 381-382.

402 C. *Licet de vitanda*, 6, X, *de electione*, I, 6 (*Corpus iuris canonici*, vol. II, col. 51). Cf. A. Petrani, *Genèse de la majorité qualifiée*, in *Apollinaris*, vol. XXX, 1957, pp. 430-436.

403 Innocent II asked the inhabitants of Pisa on 20 March 1133 to affirm their pact with Genua "omnes simul aut maior pars eorum" (*Acta Pont. Rom.*, ed. J. von Pflugk-Harttung, vol. II, p. 273). The cities of the Lombard League agreed never to enter into any pact with the emperor without the consent of the other cities ("maioris partis civitatum consilio") and of the majority of the city council ("sine … consensu communis meae civitatis vel maioris partis") (L. A. Muratori, *Antiquitates Italicae medii aevi*, vol. IV, Milan, 1741, col. 264, 268, a° 1168 and a° 1170-1171 respectively).

404 *Maioritas* was required for guarantees (*Acta Pont. Rom.*, ed. cit., vol. I, p. 330); for the approval of chapter statutes and the giving of alms (7 March 1198), see PL, vol. 214, col. 41 and 43.

405 For the election of abbots, see for instance *Acta Pont. Rom.*, ed. cit., vol. I, p. 302 (a° 1182); vol. II, p. 393 (a° 1186); vol. III, p. 381 (a° 1191). For the election of the bishop of Perugia (a° 1198), see PL, vol. 214, col. 42.

406 According to Huguccio, *Apparatus in Decretum* (c. 1188), dist. 63, c. 1, v. *canonicam*, the election of bishops must occur "ab omnibus vel a maiori parte" (quoted by P. Gillet, *La personnalité juridique* (cf. *supra*, note 401), p. 96). For the election of abbots: "…illum eligant, quem omnium vel maioris partis arbitrio viderint praeelectum" (Bernard of Pavia, *Summa de electione*, c. 2, ed. E. A. Th. Laspeyres, *Bernardi Papiensis Faventini episcopi Summa decretalium*, Regensburg, 1860, Appendix II, p. 317). This work dates from 1191-1198.

407 Letter from Innocent III to the chapter of Zamora, on 28 October 1210 (PL, vol. 216, col. 334).

408 Mansi, vol. XXII, col. 837.

409 See for example c. *In causis*, 30, X, *de electione*, I, 6 (*Corpus iuris canonici*, vol. II, col. 75); c. *Quum in iure*, 33, X, *de electione*, I, 6 (ed. cit., col. 79).

But the letters of privilege for monasteries issued during his pontificate retained the traditional formula *maior et sanior pars*.[410] The Lateran Council included this formula in canon 12.[411] Honorius III and Gregory IX certainly took the *maior pars* into account in their arbitration rulings, but only to mention its absence as one of multiple grounds for quashing an election.[412] After 1215, some canonists argued for the strict application of the principle of the majority of votes.[413]

At the beginning of the thirteenth century, there had thus been incidental and limited attempts to consider the views of the *maior pars* in elections and other decisions. But this did not detract in any way from the authority of the traditional formula of *maior et sanior pars*, which remained the general rule in many ecclesiastical documents and monastic statutes. The Dominicans apparently systematically excluded the expression *sanior pars*, which still appeared in their first monastic privilege, from their own constitutions and instead recognised the decision of the *maior pars* as binding. They applied this principle to the election of the master general and provincials,[414] to the appointment of the *diffinitores* at the provincial chapter,[415] to the final vote on the ordinances of provincial and general chapters,[416] to the votes of the provincials during vacancies of the generalate,[417] to the decisions of the conventual chapters on the admission of candidates to the novitiate[418] and to the report of the visitors to the general chapter.[419] This radical application of an old, but by then obsolete principle must be regarded as an innovation at the beginning of the thirteenth century. Other monastic communities adopted it only hesitantly.[420]

---

410 PL, vol. 214, *passim*.

411 The edition of this text in Mansi, vol. XXII, col. 1011, has "in quem omnes, *vel* maior, *vel* sanior pars capituli convenerit", as does the Greek version: "εἰς ὅν τὸ πᾶν, ἤ τὸ μεῖζον, ἤ τὸ ὑγιέσερον μέρος συναινέσῃ" (col. 1012). The *Corpus iuris canonici* (see *supra*, p. 348) and the works of the canonists preserved the traditional formula *vel maior* ET *sanior pars*. See on this issue L. Moulin, *Sanior et maior pars*, pp. 396-397.

412 For Honorius III, see a letter from the year 1222 (c. *Ecclesia vestra*, 8, X, *de electione*, I, 6, in *Corpus iuris canonici*, vol. II, col. 91). For Gregory IX, see the letter of 21 March 1228 (c. *Cumana ecclesia*, 50, X, *de electione*, I, 6, *loco cit.*).

413 This principle can be found in the *Glossa ordinaria in Decretum* (c. 1215), in dist. 63, dictum Gratiani post c. 35, v. *Nunc ergo quaeritur*: "...licet ex una parte sit auctoritas et melior zelus, ex altera parte numerus, statur pro numero..." (cf. P. Gillet, *La personnalité juridique*, p. 97, footnote 3); Tancred, *Apparatus in III Compilationem* (c. 1220), I, 1, c. 1, v. *Constitutum*: "(In his quae) facienda sunt ex necessitate ... sufficit quod facit maior pars..." (quoted by P. Gillet, *op. cit.*, p. 157). The same text, with variants, appears in the *Quaestiones Andegavenses* (1226-1234), q. 1: cf. G. Fransen, *Utrumque ius dans les Questiones Andegavenses*, p. 7 (this article will appear in *Études Le Bras*).

414 CA, II, 11 and 15 respectively: "plures medietate omnium qui debent eligere".

415 CA, II, 1: "maior pars numero; maior numerus".

416 CA, II, 2: "sententia plurium prevalebit"; and II, 7: "obtineat sententia plurium" respectively.

417 CA, II, 9: "obtineat sententia plurium; maior numerus".

418 CA, I, 14: "consensu totius vel maioris partis capituli".

419 CA, II, 19: "cum testimonio maioris partis capituli".

420 L. Moulin, *Sanior et maior pars*, pp. 512-515.

§ 2. Subsidiary sources

In many cases, the Dominicans used the decrees of the Fourth Lateran Council to supplement or correct texts derived from the Cistercian tradition. But they often changed the phrasing of quoted conciliar decrees, at least to the extent that they can still be identified in the extant texts of the Dominican constitutions. These frequently contain expressions that refer instead to other documents and customs from ecclesiastical or civil law. The following section examines to what extent such texts and institutions influenced the Dominican constitutions.

A. Ecclesiastical decrees and the works of canonists

1. Election procedures

Instead of the customary *maior et sanior pars*, the Dominican texts contained a formula on elections which mentioned only the majority of votes. These texts were based in part on canon 24 of the Lateran Council.[421] But some expressions appear to be connected with the ordinances of the earliest ecumenical councils. To stipulate what issues required the advice of the majority of the electors, the Dominican constitutions used the formula *obtineat sententia pluri(mor)um* or a variant in several places.[422] This expression does not occur in the *acta* of the Fourth Lateran Council, but it does in the canons of councils of the fourth to sixth centuries[423] and also once in a letter by Innocent III.[424] Perhaps this was a phrase that was often used in these cases and had thus become a technical expression. Its occurrence in the Dominican constitutions does not necessarily imply textual dependence on the old documents, but it does indicate that the drafters of the constitutions were familiar with the terminology of canon law.

The Dominican constitutions required *electio per scrutinium* for the election of the master general and of the *diffinitores* at the provincial chapter. This procedure

---

421 See *supra*, pp. 348-349.

422 See *supra*, p. 353, footnotes 416-417.

423 The formula *obtineat sententia plurimorum* is used in some fifth- and sixth-century translations of the *Acta* of the Council of Nicaea (325), can. 6. See *Ecclesiae occidentalis monumenta iuris antiquissima* vol. I, 1, ed. C. H. Turner, Oxford, 1899, pp. 122-123 (Caecilianus, Atticus and *Prisca*); p. 261 (the two translations ascribed to Dionysius Exiguus). Cf. Mansi, vol. II, col. 680, 687, 895-896, vol. IV, col. 407; PL, vol. 56, col. 761 and 827; *Corpus iuris canonici*, vol. I, col. 250 (c. 1). For the same formula in the *Acta* of the Council of Antioch (341), can. 19, see C. H. Turner, *ed. cit.*, vol. II, 2, Oxford, 1913, pp. 288-289 (translation by Dionysius and *Hispanica*). Cf. Mansi, vol. II, col. 1326 and 1334; *Corpus iuris canonici*, vol. I, col. 250 (c. 3). – Variants such as *vincat sententia plurimorum* (Council of Rome (501), can. 4, in Mansi, vol. VIII, col. 232) appear to have left traces in other formulas in Dominican texts: "*sententia plurium prevalebit*" (CA, II, 2 and 7). These texts of the councils are all translations of the Greek "κρατείτω ἡ τῶν πλειόνων ψῆφος" (Mansi, vol. II, col. 671; vol. VII, col. 444 and 445) or "κρατεῖν τὴν τῶν πλειόνων ψῆφον" (vol. II, col. 1316).

424 Letter of 9 June 1198, in *Corpus iuris canonici*, vol. II, col. 509 (c. 4).

also bears affinity with canon 24 of the Fourth Lateran Council.[425] Here once
again, the Dominican constitutions use expressions that cannot be found in the
canon in question, but that do appear in earlier documents. A number of texts
that discuss the election of Pope Alexander III[426] and a letter by Innocent III[427]
mention not an *inquisitio votorum*, as does the conciliar canon, but an *inquisitio
voluntatum*. The Dominicans similarly used this expression in the rules for the
election of the master general and of the *diffinitores*.[428] These texts, too, give
the impression that they were written by people with detailed knowledge of
canon law. The following schema shows the various texts that are eligible for
comparison:[429]

Card.	Gerhoh	Inn. III
… segregentur aliquae personae de eisdem fratribus, qui audiant voluntatem singulorum et diligenter inquirant et fideliter describant…	… cum … singulorum voluntates secreto ab his, quibus iniunctum fuerat, requisitae fuissent…	… qui, exquisita seorsum et per scripturam fratrum omnium voluntate, illum eligent … in quem maioris et sanioris partis vota concurrent.

O.P., II, 1	Lat. IV
… voluntates singulorum singillatimet seorsum … coram oculis omnium disquirant et conscribant fideliter.	… qui secrete et sigillatim vota cunctorum diligenter exquirant et in scriptis redacta mox publicent in communi…

The Dominicans accepted *maioritas* rather than *sanioritas* as the determining factor in elections. This decision cannot have been inspired by ecclesiastical rules or
monastic customs, where the combined formula of *maior et sanior pars* continued

---

425 See *supra*, p. 348.
426 The first document is a letter from the cardinals of the imperial party, written on the occasion
of the papal election of 1159 (according to I. M. Watterich, *Pontificum Romanorum qui fuerunt ab
exeunte saeculo IX. usque ad finem saeculi XII. vitae*, vol. II, Leipzig, 1862, p. 462). The second text is
a message by Gerhoh of Reichersberg concerning the same election, quoted by A. von Wretschko,
Electio communis (cf. *supra*, note 373), p. 327, footnote 3. We were unable to find Gerhoh's text,
either in the letters (PL, vol. 193, col. 489-618) or in the edition by D. and O. van den Eynde
and A. Rijmersdael, *Gerhohi praepositi Reichersbergensis opera inedita* (Spicilegium Pontificii Athenaei
Antoniani, vols. 8-10), 3 vols., Rome, 1955-1956.
427 Letter to the chapter of Perugia, 7 March 1198 (PL, vol. 214, col. 42).
428 CA, II, 11 and 1.
429 The comparison is between the texts referred to *supra*, in footnote 426, the letter from
Innocent III (*supra*, note 427) and the Dominicans (CA, II, 1). – These four texts must be placed
alongside can. 24 of the Lateran Council (c. *Quia propter*, 6, X, *de electione*, I, 6, in *Corpus iuris
canonici*, vol. II, col. 88-89).

to hold sway.[430] Only canonists from 1215 onwards expressed a clear preference for the *maior pars*.[431] The Dominicans allowed themselves to be persuaded by such statements to adopt the clear principle of the majority of votes in their constitutions.

2. Elections in conclave

For the election of the master general – according to a procedure partially derived from canon 24 of the Fourth Lateran Council – the Dominican constitutions stipulated that the electors must be sequestered and kept under lock and key until the election was decided.[432] This passage is perhaps the earliest text to prescribe a conclave for elections in ecclesiastical and monastic communities. The same regulation was first made for papal elections by Gregory X at the Council of Lyon in 1274,[433] although some authors contend that the cardinals had already been locked up by the Roman senators in 1241 after Gregory IX's death to expedite the choice of a successor.[434] The notion that Honorius III's electors were forced into conclave is based on a mistaken interpretation of a text from the chronicle of Martin of Troppau which discusses these events.[435]

And yet there are indications that the custom of sequestering electors in a particular place existed even before the foundation of the Dominicans. Authors have pointed to the election of the podestà in certain Lombard cities since the beginning of the thirteenth century, perhaps even in the second half of the twelfth century.[436] The earliest known example is Piacenza, where the podestà was chosen in 1223 by electors who remained in the same room for various days and observed a strict fast.[437] But there is no mention in this case of sequestration in the strict

---

430 See *supra*, pp. 351-353.

431 See *supra*, p. 353, footnote 413.

432 CA, II, 10.

433 A. Molien, art. *Conclave*, in *Dict. de droit canon.*, vol. III, 1942, col. 1323; W. M. Plöchl, art. *Papstwahl*, in LTK, vol. VIII, 1963, col. 61; F. Spoorenberg, *De pauskeuze*, Roermond-Maaseik, 1948, pp. 64-67.

434 A. Wenck, *Das erste Konklave der Papstgeschichte, Rom August bis Oktober 1241*, in *Quellen und Forschungen aus italienischen Archiven und Bibliotheken*, vol. XVIII, 1926, pp. 101-170; O. Joelson, *Die Papstwahlen des XIII. Jahrhunderts bis zur Einführung der Conclaveordnung Gregors X* (Historische Studien, vol. 178), Berlin, 1928, p. 27; F. Spoorenberg, *op. cit.*, p. 62.

435 The oldest version is: "...et cessavit papatus per unum diem, Perusinis causa electionis papae cardinales strictissime artantibus" (*Martini Oppaviensis chronicon*, ed. G. H. Pertz, in MGH, *Scriptores*, vol. XXII, Hanover, 1872, p. 438). An addition was later made to the text, possibly by the author himself, after the election of Clement IV in 1265: "...Perusinis cardinales pro electione papae cicius facienda ipsos recludentibus et strictissime artantibus. Similiter fecerunt in creatione Clementis IV". For a critical analysis of this passage, see A. Wenck, *art. cit.*, pp. 109-110.

436 See O. Joelson, *op. cit.*, p. 28; U. Stutz, *Neue Forschungen über den Ursprung des Konklaves*, in *Zeitschrift der Savigny-Stiftung für Rechtsgeschichte, Kanonist. Abt.*, vol. XLVIII, 1928, pp. 555, 558; A. Wenck, *art. cit.*, pp. 107-108.

437 "...qui steterunt in camera comunis pro potestate eligenda usque ad diem sabbati proximum, non comedentes neque bibentes" (*Annales Placentini Guelfi*, ed. G. H. Pertz, in MGH, *Scriptores*, vol. XVIII, Hanover, 1863, p. 438).

sense of the term. There is explicit reference to a conclave for the election of the doge in Venice in 1229, although this appears only in Andrea Dandolo's chronicle, which was written around 1340, more than a century later, and does not appear to be based on older documents.[438] The material collected by older and more recent historians in connection to conclaves in elections in the cities of Northern Italy is therefore rather limited.

There are more positive and reliable indications that conclaves were a topical issue in the writings of a number of canonists from the early thirteenth century. Alanus Anglicus discussed papal elections in his *Apparatus* (1208-1210). If no candidate received the required two-thirds majority, he wrote, the secular power should intervene and lock the cardinals up to expedite a decision.[439] Tancred confirmed this in his *Glossa ordinaria*, compiled c. 1210-1215.[440] It is evident from this that the canonists at this time did not regard the conclave as a fixed institution, a custom to which the cardinals submitted voluntarily, but as a measure they might be compelled to accept. Strikingly, the Dominicans formulated their rule on a conclave at the election of the master general in terms that are very similar to Alanus Anglicus's.[441] Perhaps this is an indication that this stipulation was included by persons who were acquainted with the canonical literature and who adopted a procedure originally intended for papal elections as a precaution in the election of their own major superior.

B. Civil law

1. The participation of subjects in government

The external organisation and ceremonial of the Dominican general chapter were influenced extensively by the example of the Cistercians and the guidelines of the Fourth Lateran Council.[442] But even the earliest constitutions contain stipulations on the composition and activities of this governing body that deviate in many respects from previous customs. The local or provincial superiors did not attend every chapter, but the *diffinitores* or elected representatives of the various

---

438 "Quia XLᵃ electores, ex nobilibus et antiquis popularibus, in conclavi reclusi, vota sua in hunc, et Martinum Dandulo diviserunt..." (*Andreae Danduli chronica*, lib. X, c. 5, ed. L. A. Muratori, *Rerum Italicarum scriptores*, vol. XII, 1, new ed., Bologna, s.a., p. 291).

439 "Quid ergo fiet, si nullo modo due partes possunt consentire? Respondeo: recurratur ad brachium seculare; ... hoc modo, quod veniant Romani et includant cardinales in conclavi et compellant eos consentire" (Alanus Anglicus, *Apparatus*, in c. *Licet de vitanda* (*Compil. I*, I, 4, 15), v. *superiorem*, quoted by A. Wenck, *Das erste Konklave* (cf. *supra*, note 434), p. 106, footnote 8). Details on Alanus and his work can be found in A. M. Stickler, *Alanus Anglicus als Verteidiger des monarchischen Papsttums*, in *Salesianum*, vol. XXI, 1959, especially pp. 346-380.

440 In c. *Licet de vitanda* (*Compil. I*, I, 4, 15), v. *superiorem*, according to A. Wenck, *art. cit.*, p. 111.

441 CA, II, 10: "... in uno conclavi firmiter includantur...". Cf. Alanus: "...et includant cardinales in conclavi" (see *supra*, note 439).

442 See *supra*, pp. 330-338, 341-342.

provinces attended twice within a cycle of three years, and the provincials once.[443] In both Cîteaux and Prémontré, where the chapter had become a stable institution since the first quarter of the twelfth century, and in other orders that followed their example, only the abbots attended.[444] And the decree of the Lateran Council of 1215 similarly only spoke of *commune capitulum abbatum atque priorum*.[445] It is true that even in the twelfth century the presence of monks who were not superiors is sometimes attested, but they were there as assistants to the abbots.[446] They only attended the ceremonial part of the meetings and did not participate in the discussions or votes.[447] Only in rare cases, for example in the Carthusian order,[448] do ordinary religious – even *conversi* in the Order of Grandmont – appear to have acted together with the abbots as *diffinitores*.[449] But there is no indication anywhere that they could have constituted the entire chapter on their own, without the superiors.

Perhaps the Dominicans were motivated by the circumstances and needs of their own order when they entrusted the government of the order not only to the provincials, as natural governors of the provinces, but also to elected representatives at the general chapter. The obligation to attend the general chapter in person would have required the provincials not only to undertake a tiring journey every year, but also to absent themselves from the government of their province for a considerable period of time. Similar difficulties were perhaps the reason that a number of Cistercian abbots absented themselves from the chapter at Cîteaux every year.[450] But the Dominicans could have solved this problem by holding a chapter every third year, as the Fourth Lateran Council required and as was the custom in other orders at the time.[451] We may therefore presume that there were other reasons to entrust such an important task to the chosen representatives of the provinces at the general chapter. Perhaps the lawmakers who adopted this regulation around 1225 thought it would most accurately reflect the spirit and the wishes of their founder. The first chapter, held in 1220, was comprised not only of priors, but also in large part of ordinary religious invited by Dominic himself from the various monasteries.[452]

---

443 CA, II, 6.
444 In the Order of Cîteaux, the chapter was an *annuum capitulum abbatum* from the start (cf. *Summa cartae caritatis*, c. 4, ed. J.-B. Van Damme, *Documenta*, p. 24). – For Prémontré, see Pb, IV, 1.
445 See *supra*, p. 330, footnote 260.
446 The number of abbots' *socii* was limited: see *Instituta generalis capituli, c* 42, *Quot sociis abbas veniens ad capitulum contentus esse debeat* (ed. J.-B. Van Damme, *Genèse des* Instituta generalis capituli, in *Cîteaux*, vol. XII, 1961, p. 35). Severe punishment was reserved for those who attended the chapter without permission (J.-B. Mahn, *L'ordre cistercien*, p. 177). – For Prémontré, see Pb, IV, 1 (p. 86).
447 See *supra*, p. 331, footnote 269.
448 J. Hourlier, *Le chapitre général*, p. 109.
449 J. Hourlier, *op. cit.*, pp. 113-114.
450 J.-B. Mahn, *L'ordre cistercien*, pp. 178-183.
451 See *supra*, p. 330, footnote 260. According to the *Regula bullata*, c. 8, the Franciscans held the chapter "semel in tribus annis" (ed. H. Boehmer, *Analekten*, p. 22).
452 Jordan, *Libellus*, no. 86. See also M. H. Vicaire, *Histoire*, vol. II, pp. 203-205.

The stipulations of the Dominican constitutions on the presence of representatives of ordinary religious at the general chapter can be understood more easily if they are viewed in the context of similar tendencies in contemporary secular communities. Particularly in the northern half of Italy, in the area around Bologna, many cities had wrested themselves from the control of the emperor and had organised themselves into autonomous communities.[453] The right to live according to their ancient customs (*consuetudines*) and to compose *statuta* of their own was explicitly mentioned in the charters, or tacitly permitted by the emperor.[454] Initially, the *ius statuendi* was exercised by the members or representatives of the old Lombard aristocracy, imperial officials and the new bourgeoisie.[455] But since the end of the twelfth century, the lower classes (*populares*) took a stand vis-à-vis the higher classes to demand a voice in the government and in legislation.[456] This opposition regularly led to sharp conflicts. In Bologna, since the recognition of the *commune* in the early twelfth century, the life and government of the city were dominated to a large extent by the various parties and corporations.[457] The rivalry between the conservative *pars imperii* (the Ghibellines) and the progressive *pars populi* (Guelfs), called the *Lambertazzi* and the *Geremei* after the names of two major families, led to the democratic revolution of 1228, which resulted in the leaders of the guilds and the *societates armorum* being admitted to the great

---

453 See for instance E. Besta, *Fonti: legislazione e scienza giuridica dalla caduta dell'impero romano al secolo decimosesto* (Storia del diritto italiano pubblicata sotto la direzione di P. del Giudice, vol. 1), vol. II, Milan, 1925, pp. 455-556; P. S. Leicht, *Storia del diritto italiano. Le fonti*, Milan, 1956⁴, pp. 170-225; F. Valsecchi, *Comune e corporazione nel medio evo italiano*, Milan-Venice, (1949); E. Sestan, *La città comunale italiana dei secoli XI-XIII nelle sue note caratteristiche rispetto al movimenta comunale europeo* (XIᵉ Congrès international des sciences historiques, Stockholm, 1960, Rapports, vol. I), Göteborg-Stockholm-Uppsala, 1960, pp. 75-95.

454 This customary law developed particularly in the south (Sicily). For the north, we know of collections of *consuetudines* from the twelfth century, including from Pisa (1156) and Alessandria (1179). The customs of Milan were recorded and newly edited since 1162 in the *Liber consuetudinum civitatis Mediolanensis* (1215-1216). On this, see for example E. Besta, *Fonti: legislazione e scienza giuridica*, vol. II, pp. 458-473; Id., *Fonti del diritto italiano dalla caduta dei impero romano ai tempi nostri*, Milan, 1944, pp. 139-141; P. S. Leicht, *op. cit.*, pp. 188-190.

455 Most *libri statutorum* that have been preserved date from the thirteenth century, but they often contain older elements (*brevia consulum, brevia populi, conventiones* with the emperor etc.). For the origins, content and redaction of the *statuta* of cities, see E. Besta, *Fonti: legislazione e scienza giuridica*, vol. II, pp. 455-556 (including an overview of the extant statutes of various cities, on pp. 557-679); Id., *Fonti del diritto italiano*, pp. 126-134; P. S. Leicht, *op. cit.*, pp. 188-205. For the *statuta* of corporations and universities, see E. Besta, *Fonti: legislazione e scienza giuridica*, vol. II, pp. 680-721. There is a list of the known *statuta* with extensive commentary in *Catalogo della raccolta di statuti, consuetudini, leggi, decreti, ordini e privilegi dei comuni, degli associazoni e degli enti locali italiani dal medio evo alla fine del sec. XVIII*, 6 vols. Rome-Florence, 1943-1963.

456 For the power struggle of the lower citizenry and the artisans (*artigiani*) against the *magnati*, and sometimes also against the clergy, see for instance F. C. von Savigny, *Geschichte des römischen Rechts im Mittelalter*, vol. III, Heidelberg, 1834, pp. 103-136; P. S. Leicht, *op. cit.*, p. 199; F. Valsecchi, *op. cit.*, pp. 13-17.

457 For the history and organisation of Bologna, see for instance F. C. von Savigny, *op. cit.*, pp. 137-151.

and the minor council, as well as a number of elected members (*anziani*) as representatives of the people.[458]

It is possible that several participants at the first chapters of the Dominicans, held in Bologna, had witnessed the struggle for power in various cities at close quarters. Clergy and religious were frequently involved as observers in agreements between rival parties. In the spring of 1221, Cardinal Hugolinus, who was in Lombardy as papal legate, repeatedly acted as a mediator.[459] In Piacenza, he was able to convince the leaders of the popular party that had come to power to vow loyalty to him and agree to a reconciliation with the nobility. Six Dominicans were present when the pact was made.[460] In Bologna in July, just after the conclusion of the second general chapter of the order, a peace accord was reached and the parties of the aristocracy (*milites*) and of the people (*pedites*) agreed to conditions drafted by the cardinal himself.[461] Events such as these confirm that government and authority were highly topical issues in the environment in which the Dominican constitutions were drafted. This may have induced the first legislators to seek a satisfactory solution to this problem for their own religious community.

The idea that all interested parties should have a voice also gained ground in another field. Since the mid-twelfth century, it had become customary to invite representatives of subordinate communities, such as cities, counties and religious communities to the councils of princes, parliaments, assemblies of the estates, and councils.[462] The Justinian principle of *Quod omnes similiter tangit...* had often been commented on by jurists and canonists,[463] but for various reasons it now began to be applied in practice and representatives of the various groups were allowed to participate in the discussions. In the second half of the twelfth century, the Spanish cities were represented by *cives electi* in the *cortes* on certain occa-

---

458 F. C. von Savigny, *op. cit.*, pp. 148-149; F. Valsecchi, *op. cit.*, pp. 80-81.

459 Chr. Thouzellier, *La légation en Lombardie du cardinal Hugolin (1221). Un épisode de la cinquième croisade*, in RHE, vol. XLV, 1950, pp. 508-542.

460 *Ibid.*, pp. 534-535.

461 *Ibid.*, pp. 535-536.

462 The most complete synthetic overview of the history of these institutions, also outside Italy, is A. Marongiu, *Il parlamento in Italia nel medio evo e nell'età moderna* (Études présentées à la Commission internationale pour l'histoire des assemblées d'états, vol. 25), Milan, 1962. Similarly well documented is G. Post, *Roman Law and Early Representation in Spain and Italy, 1150-1250*, in *Speculum*, vol. XVIII, 1943, pp. 211-232. See also H. M. Cam – A. Marongiu – G. Stökl, *Recent Work and Present Views on the Origins and Development of Representative Assemblies* (X° Congresso internazionale di scienze storiche, Roma, 1955, Relazioni, vol. I), Florence, 1955, pp. 1-101 (including an overview of the terminology, such as *curia, cortes, parlamentum, concilium, consilium, colloquium*, on p. 7).

463 "...ut, quod omnes similiter tangit, ab omnibus comprobetur" (C. V, 59, 5, § 2; in *Corpus iuris civilis*, vol. II, p. 231). For the origins and use of this principle for representatives of private persons and communities, see Y. M.-J. Congar, *Quod omnes tangit, ab omnibus tractari et approbari debet*, in *Revue hist. de droit français et étranger*, 4th series, vol. XXXVIII, 1958, pp. 210-259; A. Marongiu, *op. cit.*, pp. 34-46.

sions.[464] In England, *discreti milites* from every county were invited to attend the royal council in 1213.[465] In Italy especially, representatives of the cities repeatedly attended the imperial council. In 1158, Frederick I invited *consules* and *iudices* to participate in the diet of Roncaglia together with the imperial princes.[466] As head of the Papal States, Innocent III admitted plenipotentiary *procuratores* from six cities in the March of Ancona to his *curia* in 1200.[467] The custom of representing corporations through chosen deputies appears to have become widespread in ecclesiastical life before it was in secular society. Representatives of churches, chapters, dioceses, monasteries and universities are mentioned at certain events such as court suits, the papal curia or provincial synods, particularly in Italy, from the mid-twelfth century onwards.[468]

Needless to say, conditions in the Italian cities and the appearance of plenipotentiary representatives of subordinate communities in secular and ecclesiastical governing bodies bear only remote similarity to the presence of chosen representatives at the general chapters of the Dominicans. The analogy masks certain very important differences. First, there is no example of representatives of the cities and other communities meeting as a separate group, without the presence of the established bodies (*cortes*, royal councils, church councils), that is, as a homogenous group, constituting the highest legislative body on its own, as was the case with the Dominicans. Nor do we know for certain what role the representatives of the civic corporations actually fulfilled in the great councils. Specifically, it is unclear whether they were active representatives who had a real share in the discussions and decisions, or passive representatives who had to serve the prince's interests and whose only task was to communicate the decisions to their own community.[469] These facts can, however, to a certain extent clarify the social and political climate in which the constitutions of the Dominicans were composed.

---

464 Representatives of the cities attended the *Cortes* of Aragon (1163), Castile (1169), León (1188, 1203), Lerida (1214). See G. Post, *Roman Law*, pp. 217-224; Y. M.-J. Congar, *art. cit.*, pp. 231-232; A. Marongiu, *op. cit.*, pp. 103-118.

465 King John I's letter of 7 November 1213, stated the following: "Praecipimus tibi quod … quatuor milites discretos de comitatu tuo illuc venire facias ad nos…" (ed. W. Stubbs, *Selected Charters … to the Reign of Edward the First*, new ed. by H. W. C. Davis, Oxford, 1942, p. 282). – See also A. Marongiu, *op. cit.*, pp. 125-132.

466 "Confluunt ex omnibus regni partibus cum magna frequentia archiepiscopi, … comites et proceres, consules et civitatum iudices" (*Ottonis et Rahewini Gesta Frederici I Imperatoris*, lib. IV, c. 1, ed. G. Waitz, in MGH, *Scriptores rerum Germanicarum in usum scholarum*, Hanover-Leipzig, 1912³, p. 234). For Italy, see also A. Marongiu, *op. cit.*, pp. 175-199.

467 PL, vol. 214, col. 910. See the text *infra*, in footnote 482.

468 G. Post, *Roman Law*, pp. 212-217. In his letter *Vineam Domini*, of 18 April 1213, Innocent III invited not only the bishops, but also the representatives of the chapters to attend the Fourth Lateran Council: "…ut praepositum vel decanum, vel alios viros idoneos ad concilium pro se mittant, cum nonnulla sint in ipso tractanda, quae specialiter ad ecclesiarum capitula pertinebunt" (PL, vol. 216, col. 823). There are clear echoes here of the influence of the principle of "Quod omnes tangit…".

469 G. Post, *Roman Law*, pp. 224, 228.

2. Plenipotentiary representatives

There are several passages in the Dominican constitutions that appear to have a more intimate connection with the terminology of representatives in the civil sphere. The chapter of 1228, the first *generalissimum*, was attended not only by the provincials, but also by two *diffinitores* of each province, that is, by the three groups that would normally separately and successively constitute the annual chapter.[470] The two *diffinitores* were presented as the representatives of the provincial chapters.[471] And the entire assembly was regarded as a body that held full powers from all the members of the order to issue laws that would be binding for the order, including in the future. What interests us here is the way in which this mandate was given. The term *potestas plenaria*, which also appears in a number of other passages in the constitutions,[472] is in fact a variant of the expression *plena potestas*, which was often used at the time for the powers given to representatives of ecclesiastical and secular corporations.

The question of mandated full powers (*plena potestas*) attracted attention from the second half of the twelfth century onwards, in connection with the involvement of *procuratores* in legal cases, trade and government affairs.[473] Their authority was initially not well defined, so that it was unclear whether they could act in the place of and with the authority of their principal. To prevent dispute, jurists and canonists attempted to define as precisely as possible under what conditions the *mandans* (*dominus*) was bound by the actions of his representatives. They did this on the basis of a passage on the powers of the *procurator* in Justinian's *Codex*. If a representative had received only a limited mandate and exceeded his authority, his actions were invalid. But if he had *plena potestas agendi*, then his principal was obliged to accept the agreement reached or the judicial ruling given.[474] This theory was applied to the government of states and to diplomatic representation as early as the second half of the twelfth century. Governors of

---

470 "Anno ab incarnatione Domini MCCXXVIII convenerunt Parisius ... priores provinciales una cum Iordano, magistro ordinis nostri, singuli cum duobus diffinitoribus sibi a provincialibus capitulis deputatis..." (CA, praeamb.). "Statuimus ut per duos annos in dictarum octo provinciarum capitulis aliquis de magis idoneis a capitulo eligatur, qui sit generalis capituli diffinitor" (CA, II, 5). "Tertio autem anno priores provinciales duodecim provinciarum generale capitulum celebrabunt" (CA, II, 5). Cf. CA, II, 7.

471 "...ubi omnes fratres vota sua unanimiter transtulerunt, eisdem potestatem plenariam concedentes, ut quicquid ab ipsis fieret, ... de cetero firmum et stabile permaneret, ..." (CA, praeamb.).

472 "Isti autem diffinitores plenariam habeant potestatem super excessum magistri ordinis corrigendum vel de eo penitus removendo" (CA, II, 8). "Mortuo autem magistro vel a magisterio remoto, priores dictarum provinciarum in omnibus, quousque magister fuerit electus, plenariam ipsius obtineant potestatem..." (CA, II, 9).

473 G. Post, Plena Potestas *and Consent in Mediaeval Assemblies. A Study in Romano-Canonical Procedure and the Rise of Representation*, in *Traditio*, vol. I, 1943, esp. pp. 355-383.

474 "Si procurator ad unam speciem constitutus officium mandati egressus est, id quod gessit nullum domino praeiudicium facere possit. Quod si plenam potestatem agendi habuit, rem iudicatam rescindi non oportet, ..." (C. II, 12,10, in *Corpus iuris civilis*, vol. II, p. 104).

territorial circumscriptions, emissaries of princes, popes and cities were promoted on certain occasions to the status of plenipotentiary representatives.[475] Initially, the term *plena potestas* was rarely used for the concept of full powers, and formulas such as *libera et generalis administratio* were more common.[476] But from the beginning of the thirteenth century, *plena potestas* became a customary expression in commentaries on Roman and church law and in the mandates of the representatives.[477]

The formula *plena potestas* does not occur in the Dominican constitutions, but *plenaria potestas* does, a variant which appeared from the last quarter of the twelfth century onwards.[478] In the *Ordo iudiciarius Bambergensis* (1182-1185) it is still used for representatives acting for private persons.[479] In a 1195 letter, the Emperor Henry VI asked Pope Celestine III to send three cardinals with the required full powers to deal with a number of ecclesiastical issues.[480] In the statutes of the Cistercians, the expression *plenaria potestas* was used to describe the mandate which the general chapter gave to the visitors.[481] Plenipotentiary representatives of city communities made their first appearance in a letter from Innocent III dated 12 November 1200, which mentions the *responsales idonei* which the city of Fermo had sent to him to treat about the rights of the Holy See and about peace in the March of Ancona.[482] In December 1220, three canons of the chapter of Notre Dame in Paris were given full powers to arbitrate in a dispute between the parish church of Saint-Benoît and the Dominicans of Saint-Jacques.[483] *Plenaria*

---

475   See the examples given by G. Post, *Plena Potestas*, pp. 364-370.

476   G. Post, *art. cit.*, p. 357.

477   G. Post, *art. cit.*, pp. 358-364.

478   Examples of commissions with *plena potestas* from the time of the Dominican constitutions can be found in a letter from Gregory IX to the podestà and people of Pisa, of 6 April 1227: "...et super hiis in quibus Ecclesiam offendistis, procuratorem idoneum ... ad nostram presentiam transmittatis, qui ad agendum ... plenam habeat potestatem" (L. Auvray, *Les registres de Grégoire IX*, no. 17). See also the letter to the king of France of 21 March 1228, in which the pope writes that he was sending his legate "cum libera potestate" (*ibid.*, no. 229).

479   "Procurator super his, quae ad ipsam procurationem spectare noscuntur, plenariam recipit potestatem" (ed. J. F. von Schulte, in *Sitzungsberichte der kaiserlichen Akademie der Wissenschaften zu Wien, Philos.-hist. Cl.*, vol. LXX, 1872, p. 300).

480   "Ad hec discretionis vestre plenitudinem exoratam esse cupimus, quatinus dilectos vestros et nostros cardinales, ... ad nostre serenitatis presentiam transmittatis, plenariam eis dantes potestatem, ut ipsi ad decidendas causas ecclesiasticas vel spirituales, ... ordine iudiciario vicem vestram adimplere possint et debeant" (ed. L. Weiland, in MGH, *Legum sectio IV*, vol. I, Hanover, 1893, p. 514).

481   "Abbates visitatores habeant plenariam potestatem deponendi officiales quos invenerint inordinatos" (*Statuta cap. gen. Ord. Cist.*, vol. I, p. 111, a° 1189; see also p. 188, a° 1195). Cf. Innocent III's letter of privilege to the German Order, 27 June 1209: "...ut eligendi magistrum, qui vobis et domui vestre presit, habeatis plenariam potestatem..." (ed. E. Strehlke, *Tabulae Ordinis Theutonici*, Berlin, 1869, p. 267).

482   "...ut usque ad festum sancti Lucae responsales idoneos ad nostram praesentiam mitteretis, deliberantes communiter et firmiter statuentes, certumque dantes mandatum eisdem et plenariam potestatem, ..." (PL, vol. 214, col. 910).

483   "Notum facimus quod, ... decanus et capitulum nobis tribus commiserunt plenariam potestatem disponendi et componendi..." (Laurent, no. 120).

potestas was used, therefore, both for the full powers given to representatives sent to foreign bodies and for administrative tasks within a certain community, and both for a charge imposed from above and for powers granted through a vote by the representatives' peers.

In the Dominican constitutions, too, *plenaria potestas* has several meanings. In the chapter *De potestate diffinitorum*, it does not mean the authority given to representatives sent to someone else, but refers exclusively to the full powers given to the diffinitors to judge the policies of the master general.[484] In the following chapter, *plenaria potestas* appears to be a synonym for the highest governing authority in the order, which automatically devolves on the provincials if the general dies or is relieved of his functions.[485] But in the text that preceded the *prologus* of the constitutions in 1228, the formula appears to refer to representation. The provincials and the *diffinitores* of the general chapter are regarded there as representatives of the provinces, who had received full powers from the provincial chapters to constitute the central legislative body and the highest governing body of the order.[486]

C. The influence of the university environment in Bologna

1. The natones at the university

Neither ecclesiastical nor political factors played a decisive role in the creation and naming of the first eight provinces of the Dominicans.[487] None of the provinces had borders that were coterminous with those of a diocese or church province.[488] Neither were their borders based exclusively on civil circumscriptions (*regna*).[489] The grouping together of the monasteries of a specific linguistic area can explain the distinction between the provinces of Spain, Italy, Germany, Hungary and

---

484 "Isti autem diffinitores habeant plenariam potestatem super excessum magistri ordinis corrigendum…" (CA, II, 8).

485 "Mortuo autem magistro vel a magisterio remoto, priores dictarum provinciarum in omnibus, quousque magister fuerit electus, plenariam ipsius obtineant potestatem…" (CA, II, 9).

486 See *supra*, p. 362, footnote 471.

487 See CA, II, 1 and *supra*, pp. 344-345.

488 For the division of countries such as Spain, France, Germany etc. into church provinces, see the so-called *Provinciale*, the first official list of dioceses, compiled in the late twelfth or early thirteenth century (ed. M. Tangl, *Die päpstlichen Kanzleiordnungen*, pp. 1-32. Cf. H. Bresslau, *Urkundenlehre*, vol. I, Leipzig, 1889, p. 253).

489 The province of *Hispania* extended across the entire Iberian peninsula, which was home to five kingdoms in the early thirteenth century. – The province of *Francia* consisted of the northern half of contemporary France (M. Lugge, *"Gallia" und "Francia" im Mittelalter. Untersuchungen über den Zusammenhang zwischen geografisch-historischer Terminologie und politischen Denken vom 6.-15. Jahrhundert* (Bonner historische Forschungen, vol. 15), Bonn, 1960, pp. 160-180, especially p. 173). Some older monasteries, such as Limoges and Poitiers, which belonged to the province of *Francia*, were situated in Aquitaine, which was then under English rule. – Lombardy and the *provincia Romana* partly belonged to the German empire, partly to the Papal States.

England. Even for France, the division into a southern and a northern half reflected the distinction between the territory of the *langue d'oc* and of the *langue d'oïl*.[490] Only the division of Italy into a Lombard and a Roman province cannot have been based on language, and the fact that these two areas are separated by a natural border, the Apennines, must perhaps be considered. There is, however, one criterion of division that accurately reflects the delimitation and title of all Dominican provinces: the distinctions between the various *nationes* at the medieval universities.

The academic *nationes* were not a pure reflection of the nations as these existed at the general European level, but were a more flexible form of mutual association in the student environment.[491] The country of origin played an important role in the emergence and development of the *nationes*.[492] A spontaneous sense of belonging and the need to defend common interests caused students from the same region to unite. According to James of Vitry, the *scholares* in Paris were grouped into twelve *nationes* shortly after 1200.[493] Around 1250, this number had fallen to four, but the new division was artificial and no longer accurately reflected the many nationalities represented.[494] Bologna, too, initially had many corporations, which were reduced around the middle of the thirteenth century to two large groups, the *Ultamontani* and the *Citramontani*, although they retained the name of their own nation afterwards.[495] Most associations of foreign students, English, French, Germans, Provençals, were mentioned in Bologna and also in Vicenza in the first years of the thirteenth century, but they perhaps dated from the end of the previous century.[496] The Italians appear to have felt the necessity of

---

490 In the Middle Ages, the boundary between the two linguistic areas ran along a line from La Rochelle to Limoges, Clermont-Ferrand, Lyon and Grenoble (cf. B. E. Vidos, *Handboek tot de Romaanse taalkunde*, 's Hertogenbosch, 1956, pp. 221-223, 323-325; A. Bernelle, *Le malentendu provençal*, in *Vie et langage*, vol. II, 1953, pp. 81-84, with map on p. 83).

491 For the concept of *natio*, see for instance P. Kibre, *The Nations in the Mediaeval Universities*, Cambridge, Mass., 1948, pp. 188-189; F. Hertz, *Nationality in History and Politics*, New York, 1944, p. 6, which contains an overview of the use of the term *natio* in the older Latin sources and in certain medieval works. See also F. Chabod, *L'idea di nazione*, Bari, 1961.

492 See on this F. Kibre, *op. cit.*, who mainly based his argument on the sources already used in the classic works: H. Denifle, *Die Entstehung der Universitäten des Mittelalters bis 1400*, Berlin, 1885; H. Rashdall, *The Universities of Europe in the Middle Ages*, new edition by F. M. Powicke and A. B. Emden, Oxford, 1936.

493 James of Vitry, *Historia occidentalis*, c. 7, ed. Fr. Moschi, Douai, 1597, p. 279. The first official mention of the *nationes* appears in a charter of 31 May 1222 (ed. H. Denifle – E. Chatelain, *Chartularium Universitatis Parisiensis*, vol. I, Paris, 1889, no. 45, p. 103).

494 The oldest document to mention the four *nationes* (French, English, Picards, Normans) is dated October 1249 (H. Denifle, *Chartularium*, vol. I, no. 187, p. 215).

495 On the *nationes* in Bologna, see for example P. Kibre, *The Nations*, pp. 5-14; H. Denifle, *Die Entstehung der Universitäten*, pp. 135-160; H. Rashdall, *The Universities*, vol. I, pp. 154-161, 182-183. This merging occurred before 1250, the year in which separate rectors were appointed for the *Ultramontani* and the *Citramontani*.

496 The existence of these various *nationes* in Bologna can be deduced from the fact that they were present in Vicenza, and this university originated in a group of students that took refuge there from

association the least and the latest. They reportedly formed two corporations just before 1217, the Lombard and the Roman, which united the students from Rome, Tuscany and the Campagna.[497] Some countries which previously may have had an association of their own subsequently joined another *natio* because they lacked the numbers to act independently.[498]

The first eight provinces of the Dominicans were named after the regions whose names also occurred among the *nationes* at the university of Bologna at the beginning of the thirteenth century. Nowhere do the sources draw any explicit connection between the two institutions. And yet the importance that the Dominicans gave to the region of Provence does point to an external influence. None of the monasteries that belonged to this province was actually located in the territory of Provence.[499] It is not unlikely, therefore, that the choice of name for the Southern French province was determined by the traditions of the oldest Italian universities, especially Bologna, where there were many Provençal students who also formed their own *natio*.[500] The erection of separate provinces in Lombardy and in the Romagna, which belonged to the same linguistic area,[501] can similarly be explained by dependence of the provincial organisation of the Dominicans on the university system.

2. *Bolognese canonists*

The first general chapters of the Dominicans were held in Bologna, in 1220 and 1221 respectively.[502] As the seat of a university that developed into a flourishing centre for the study of law since the first half of the twelfth century, this city

---

Bologna in 1204 (H. Rashdall, *op. cit.*, vol. II, pp. 6-7). A charter dated 1209 mentions eight *nationes* in Vicenza (J. B. Mittarelli – A. Costadoni, *Annales Camaldulenses*, vol. IV, Venice, 1759, p. 213).

497 See H. Denifle, *Die Entstehung der Universitäten*, pp. 136-137, footnote 321. The letter from Honorius III which refers to these corporations was published in H. Rashdall, *op. cit.*, vol. I, p. 585. A Lombard and a Tuscan *natio* were first mentioned towards the end of the twelfth century (H. Denifle, *op. cit.*, p. 137, note 321).

498 The English and Norman students in Padua were counted among the French in 1228 and the Spanish and Catalan among the Provençal (H. Denifle, *op. cit.*, p. 139; H. Rashdall, *op. cit.*, vol. II, p. 13).

499 The province consisted of the following monasteries: Toulouse (founded in 1215), Lyon (1219), Montpellier (1219), Limoges (1219), Bayonne (1221), Le Puy (1221). Cf. M. H. Vicaire, *Histoire*, vol. II, pp. 131, 219, 310. Medieval Provence as such was limited to the south-eastern part of France, with a line that roughly followed the course of the Rhône as its western boundary (cf. G. de Manteyer, *La Provence du premier au douzième siècle* (Mémoires et documents publiés par la Société de l'École des chartes, vol. 8), Paris, 1908, pp. 163-191). *The Cambridge Mediaeval History, Volume of Maps*, Cambridge, 1936, map no. 58 gives the division of the territory of France around the mid-thirteenth century (1260). See also M. Lugge, *"Gallia" und "Francia"* (cf. *supra*, note 489), p. 161.

500 See *supra*, footnotes 496 and 498. Fourteen *nationes*, including Provence, were mentioned as existing in Bologna in 1265 (H. Rashdall, *op. cit.*, vol. I, p. 156, footnote 1).

501 See *supra*, footnote 497.

502 Jordan, *Libellus*, nos. 86 and 88.

attracted countless students from the countries of Europe.[503] After the dispersal of the first Dominican community of Toulouse and the foundation of new monasteries, Bologna, which was located on the route from Italy to the other parts of Europe, became the administrative centre of the order. It was the place where Dominic lived from September 1219 onwards, after his return from Spain and France.[504] He made several voyages to the papal curia in Rome or Viterbo from there and undertook his last preaching mission in Lombardy. In Bologna, he sought contact with the students of the university.[505] And it was there that he died a few months after the second general chapter of his order.[506] His successor Jordan of Saxony displayed the same preference for Bologna in one of his letters.[507]

There were close contacts between the Dominicans and the university of Bologna even before 1220. Reginald of Orleans, previously professor of canon law in Paris, was accepted into the order in the spring of 1218.[508] Under his influence, several students as well as certain professors joined the Dominicans. Clarus de Sesto, professor of canon law, was one of the first to enter the new order.[509] His example was followed by Moneta and Roland of Cremona, professors in the faculty of the *artes*, who joined in August 1218 and the summer of 1219 respectively.[510] Paul of Hungary, prior of the monastery in Bologna, compiled a *Summa de poenitentia* for the benefit of his confreres[511] and continued to teach

---

503 See for instance H. Denifle, *Die Entstehung der Universitäten*, pp. 132-218; H. Rashdall, *The Universities*, vol. I, pp. 87-268; A. Sorbelli, *Storia della Università di Bologna*, vol. I: *Il medio evo*, Bologna, 1940; G. de Vergottini, *Lo studio di Bologna. L'impero. Il papato* (Studi e memori per la storia dell'Università di Bologna, N.S., vol. 1), Bologna, 1954; H. Grundmann, *Vom Ursprung der Universität im Mittelalter* (Berichte über die Verhandlungen der Sächsischen Akademie der Wissenschaften zu Leipzig, Philologisch-historische Klasse, Band 103, Heft 2), Berlin, 1957, esp. pp. 39-48.

504 According to Jordan, *Libellus*, no. 60, Dominic lived there ("mansionem faciens") after his journey to Spain and France in 1219. "Et a dicto tempore, ex quo venit Bononiam, usque ad finem vite sue stetit in dicta civitate Bononie, nisi quando ivit ad curiam Romanam, et visitavit quasdam terras Lombardie, et etiam civitatem Venetiarum" (*Proc. Bon.*, no. 30). For Dominic's itinerary in 1219-1221, see M. H. Vicaire, *Saint Dominique de Caleruega*, p. 310. For the mission in Northern Italy, see Id., *Histoire*, vol. II, pp. 239-263.

505 *Proc. Bon.*, no. 36; M. H. Vicaire, *Histoire*, vol. II, p. 162.

506 Jordan, *Libellus*, nos. 92-94.

507 "Bononia inter omnes civitates Lombardiae, Thusciae, Franciae, Angliae, Provinciae, et fere etiam Alemaniae, est quoddam singulare peculium cordis mei" (*Epist. 5*, ed. A. Walz, *Iordani de Saxonia epistulae*, p. 8).

508 Jordan, *Libellus*, nos. 56-60; M. H. Vicaire, *Histoire*, vol. II, pp. 113-115, 150-159.

509 Gerard of Frachet, *Vitae fratrum*, p. 26. – For Moneta's entry, see Gerard of Frachet, *op. cit.*, pp. 169-170; M. H. Vicaire, *Histoire*, vol. II, pp. 152-153.

510 Roland entered in May or July. See Gerard of Frachet, *op. cit.*, pp. 25-27; E. Filthaut, *Roland von Cremona O.P. und die Anfänge der Scholastik im Predigerorden*, Vechta, 1936, pp. 11-19.

511 Gerard of Frachet, *op. cit.*, Appendix, p. 305; St. Kuttner, *Repertorium der Kanonistik (1140-1234)*, *Prodromus Corporis glossarum*, vol. I (Studi e testi, vol. 71), Vatican City, 1937, pp. 414-415. Cf. P. Mandonnet – M. H. Vicaire, *Saint Dominique*, vol. I, pp. 249-269. On his *Summa*, see P. Mandonnet, *La Summa de poenitentia magistri Pauli, presbyteri S. Nicolai (Magister Paulus Hungarus O.P., 1210-1221)*, in *Aus der Geisteswelt des Mittelalters. Festschrift für Martin Grabmann. Beiträge zur Geschichte der Philosophie und Theologie*, Supplementband, III, Münster,

canon law at the university until the general chapter sent him and other friars to his home country in 1221.[512] Finally, the Spanish canonist Raymond of Peñafort, who had been a professor in Bologna since 1218, will also have had frequent contact with the Dominicans until he joined the order himself in 1222.[513]

Various professors and former students of the university were among the attendees at the general chapters of Bologna in 1220 and 1221, which expanded the structure of the order. It is very likely that the canonists among them in particular, such as Paul of Hungary and Clarus de Sesto, placed their authority and legal knowledge at the disposal of the drafters of the first constitutional regulations, which, Jordan of Saxony writes, were numerous and continued to be in force subsequently.[514] Raymond of Peñafort was there at the chapters of 1222 and subsequent years to give active assistance. Perhaps the intervention of jurists familiar with the theories and documents of both canon and Roman law can explain the use of technical terms and passages in the Dominican constitutions.[515] The legal style is also evident in the meticulousness of certain stipulations[516] and in the bold application of theories defended by canonists at the time.[517] Some expressions and formulas would make a somewhat exaggerated and contrived impression if we did not realise that they were possibly drafted by people used to dealing with normative texts, who knew that strong wording is necessary to enjoin the observance of certain rules.[518]

The second *distinctio* was influenced by other monastic statutes to a much lesser degree than the first. Hardly a trace of affinity with Prémontré can be found there, and references to the statutes of other societies are too few and vague to warrant any definite conclusions. Only the legislation of Cîteaux was used as an example in this part, particularly in the chapters on the general chapter and in various

---

1935, pp. 525-548; P. Michaud – Quantin, *Sommes de casuistique et manuels de confession au moyen âge (XIIᵉ-XVIᵉ siècles)* (Analecta mediaevalia Namurcensia, vol. 13), Leuven-Lille-Montréal, 1962, pp. 24-26.

512 B. Altaner, *Die Dominikanermissionen des 13. Jahrhunderts*, pp. 206-207.

513 See *supra*, p. 247, note 14.

514 Jordan, *Libellus*, no. 87.

515 On the terminology of the electoral procedure, see *supra*, pp. 348, 352-355, footnotes 414-419 and 423. Certain electors in elections of the master general and of the provincial were appointed by an *electio ad hoc* (CA, II, 11 and 15). For the use and meaning of *plenaria potestas*, see *supra*, pp. 362-364.

516 Thus there is a sharp distinction between the chapters on the general chapter (CA, II, 17-21), which partly derive from Cîteaux (see *supra*, pp. 332-337), and the chapters at the beginning of the second *distinctio*, which address the tasks of the provincial and the general chapter (CA, II, 2-9). – In CA, II, 11 the legislators were at pains to stipulate that the required majority is an absolute majority: "in quem plures medietate omnium, qui debent eligere, consenserint".

517 On the *maior pars*, see *supra*, p. 353, footnote 413. On the conclave, see *supra*, p. 357, with footnotes 439-441.

518 Severe penalties were formulated in the chapters that address the election of the master general (CA, II, 10-11), the activities of the diffinitors at the general chapter (II, 6 and 8), respect for the institutions and the unity of the order (II, 9 and 14).

regulations on the government and organisation of the monasteries and the order as a whole. The direct influence of the Fourth Lateran Council appears more likely in a number of other stipulations, on the general chapter, the organisation of provinces and the procedure for the election of superiors and other officers. Our comparison of the texts and examination of the circumstances under which the Dominican constitutions were written has shown that other church documents and works of canonists were also used. Finally, we may assume that the customs of civil law, the emancipation movements in secular societies and the climate of the university environment in Bologna exerted some influence over certain rules on the participation of ordinary members and the representation of the provinces at the general chapter. Perhaps the second *distinctio*'s unique character can best be appreciated by considering that this part of the Dominican constitutions was largely composed in Bologna with the assistance of canonists.

Conclusion

Our study of the sources has shown that the earliest constitutions of the Dominicans were much more indebted to tradition than scholarship had previously demonstrated. Particularly in the first *distinctio*, the collection of norms for the monastic life, many things were derived from other institutes. About four tenths of it consists of textual quotations or *loci paralleli*, which at least confirms the substantive influence of the old monastic legislation. According to the medieval custom, the sources were not mentioned explicitly, except for a few references to the rule of Augustine. The various pieces were put together to form a colourful mosaic, in which three main layers can be identified. The foundation was derived from the early thirteenth-century *consuetudines* of Prémontré. Here and there shorter fragments of monastic derivation were interpolated, perhaps from the capitular statutes of Osma in Spain. The third layer consists of a number of more general rules, which must be regarded as the *ius commune religiosorum* of the time. Despite the heterogeneity of these influences, the first part of the constitutions appears as a legal code with a predominantly canonical slant. By taking the monastic observances of Prémontré as their norm, the Dominicans associated themselves with the *ordo* of the canons regular, whose way of life in turn was determined largely by the monastic customs of Benedictine monachism.

Their respect for tradition did not stop the Dominicans from forging new paths whenever they believed it necessary. Analysis of their method of derivation has shown that they did not adopt the legislation of Prémontré slavishly and wholesale, but critically and selectively. They omitted several traditional monastic exercises such as manual labour, the *mandatum* or washing of feet on days of fasting, the *collatio* or reading of edifying texts. They attached little or no importance to regulations on the various offices within the monastery. Liturgical customs, such as the divine office and the daily chapter, were retained, but less time was set aside for them and an explicit stipulation added that superiors could dispense communities and individuals from them if they required more time for study. Other obligations such as fasting and abstinence were adopted in all their rigour, but were formulated more succinctly. Their formula of profession no longer mentioned the *traditio ecclesiae*, a promise of stability and commitment to the service of the monastery church. This meant giving up one of the essential elements of the canonical *institutio*, which effectively put them in a different category of religious.

In the second *distinctio*, good use was again made of material from tradition, while the regulations of ecclesiastical authority and the example of other institutes were also taken into account. The capitular customs of the Cistercians had set the tone for various monastic communities even in the twelfth century, and they had been held up for emulation to monastic and canonical orders by the Fourth Lateran Council as recently as 1215. The dependence of the Dominican constitutions on Cîteaux is evident not so much from any striking similarity between the texts, but from a close correspondence in substance between the customs described. It must not be concluded from this that the Dominicans used only an oral tradition. The few cases of unmistakeable textual affinity show that written sources were also used. Moreover, it must be borne in mind that the capitular ceremonies of Cîteaux were still evolving in the first half of the thirteenth century and that they have only been handed down in a non-official version in a manuscript dating from the middle of this century.

On the other hand, early monastic legislation had little to offer that was directly suitable for the organisation and life of an apostolic order. In this respect, the Dominicans had to build their own institutions and communal structures. Their second *distinctio* gave ample attention to study and preaching, and the *prologus* defined the mutual relationship between them as that of means to an end. Such guidelines existed only in rudimentary form or were wholly lacking in most previous monastic statutes. The rules in the Dominican constitutions on the election and task of the superiors of monasteries, provinces and the order as a whole, and on the authority and activity of the provincial and general chapters are almost entirely original. Nor was there any sufficient model for Dominican interconventual organisation, based as it was on provinces with their own superior and chapter. The fact that the Dominicans drew inspiration for this from ecclesiastical regulations and, partly, from customs and trends in civil society, proves once again that they wished to benefit from all that was happening around them. This purposeful adaptation of useful elements from tradition to the needs of their own time and their own mission may well be regarded as one of the most striking features of the earliest Dominican constitutions.

The fact that the legislation of the Dominicans contains texts from such a wide range of sources shows that the material derived was not all adopted and included at the same time. Instead, we may suspect that several years passed before the constitutions assumed the form in which they were preserved in the Rodez manuscript. The following pages address the origins and development of the text of the constitutions.

Origins and development

The legislation of most medieval religious orders was subject to more or less incisive changes during the first decades of their existence. The succinct guidelines of a founder and his immediate successors, sometimes approved or supplemented by episcopal or papal decrees, initially sufficed as a rule of life for a limited group of highly motivated followers. Several years of practical experience then demonstrated the inadequacy of the existing rules, particularly when the entry of less idealistically minded members seemed to endanger the integrity of the original inspiration. New conditions and ideas similarly necessitated the review and adaptation of the old regulations, either to mitigate their rigour, or to formulate the authentic spirit and mission of the institute more clearly for the benefit of a younger generation. Some orders, like Cîteaux and Prémontré, honoured the principle of making as few changes as possible to the text of the *consuetudines*. Any additions were made separately, in the form of capitular statutes gathered in a new legal code or added to the constitutions as a distinct part. They undertook new codification only after a longer period, and often after consultation with the papal curia. By contrast, in other monastic institutes, constant revision and correction of the legislation was regarded as normal and new ordinances issued by yearly or three-yearly general chapters were immediately inscribed in the copies of the constitutions. The Dominicans belonged to this latter category.

The primitive constitutions of the Dominicans had undergone many developments even before they were revised by Raymond of Peñafort. In 1216-1217, the life of the community in Toulouse was based on the *arctiores consuetudines* that Jordan of Saxony mentions. But new problems arose regarding the organisation and government of the community after the expansion of the order. The issue of the relationship between superiors and subjects and between the various monasteries had to be settled. Most institutions that appear in the second *distinctio* must have been added at a later date. Certain organs of government, like the general and provincial chapter, first appeared or came to their full development only after 1220-1221. The sources contain only very summary information about the evolution of the legislation between 1221 and 1236. In the first period, before 1228, the chapter had the authority to add to or change the constitutions every year.[1] The year 1228 marked a new important date in the development of the

_____

1 "Ab initio enim quodlibet capitulum generale poterat statuere … et quod uno anno statuebatur ab aliquibus diffinitoribus, in sequenti capitulo frequenter destruebatur" (Humbert of Romans, *Expositio super Constitutiones*, p. 58). This custom was perhaps related to views on the validity of

legislation.[2] The ordinances of the chapter of 1236, the last that has any bearing on the history of the *Constitutiones antiquae*, have been fully preserved in the chapter reports.[3]

The internal criticism, too, shows that the text of the constitutions, taken as a whole, cannot possibly have been the work of one person or group. Stylistic contrasts between the two *distinctiones* must not be emphasised too strongly, as the first *distinctio* consists largely of derived material and was not, therefore, the original work of Dominicans. But even within the two large parts it is possible to recognise the influence of various redactions. In the first *distinctio*, the traditional style of the *consuetudines* predominates in the description of the daily rituals and obligations of the monastic community and its members. But in certain places the earliest parts, derived from Prémontré, were interrupted and supplemented by short fragments taken from other sources, or that expressed the Dominican legislators' own views.[4] The second *distinctio* is characterised primarily by the dense and abstract style of the *constitutiones*, with rules for the organisation and government of the order. But in this part, the chapters on the general chapter and on study and preaching are strikingly different.[5] Their concrete style is more reminiscent of the first *distinctio*. They appear to be the oldest core around which the additional regulations were subsequently arranged.

In both *distinctiones*, a number of additions are clearly recognisable as such due to their introductory formula *statuimus* or *item*.[6] Some can even be dated precisely

---

the statutes in certain Italian cities, which stipulated that the legislation had to be reviewed and approved annually. See for instance for Ferrara (1208): "Adiicientes, quod de anno in annum hoc Statutum firmetur, et cetera supradicta, et scribantur annuatim in corpore Statutorum ..." (quoted in C. Chelazzi, *Catalogo della raccolta di statuti, consuetudini, leggi, decreti, ordini e privilegi dei comuni, delle associazioni e degli enti locali italiani dal medioevo alla fine dei secolo XVIII*, vol. III, Rome, 1955, p. 51). For Cannobio (1211): "... et quae statuta confirmata, laudata, et approbata sunt singulis annis per homines dictae Iurisditionis in publica concione ... et quae statuta confirmata sunt per consilium generale dicti Communis anno 1211 de mense Februarii..." (*Catalogo...*, vol. II, Rome, 1950, p. 45). According to the *Liber consuetudinum* of Milan (c. 1215), all *consuetudines* had to be confirmed each year (E. Besta, *Fonti: legislazione e scienza giuridica dalla caduta dell'impero romano al secolo decimosesto*, vol. II, Milan, 1925, p. 686). The same was true for Modena and Vicenza (*ibid.*). The legislation of Pistoia stipulated in 1296 that the *statuta* would be in force "per annum et non plus" (E. Besta, *op. cit.*, p. 503; for Padua, see *ibid.*, p. 533).

2 "Priores igitur iam prefati cum suis diffinitoribus ... quasdam constitutiones ad utilitatem et honestatem et conservationem ordinis, premissa diligenti examinatione, unanimiter et concorditer ediderunt, quas in locis suis inter constitutiones alias inserere procurarunt" (CA, praeamb.).

3 *Acta C.G.*, pp. 6-10.

4 See *supra*, pp. 307-320; in the text of CA, d. I, c. 1 (l. 36-38), c. 2 (l. 34-36), c. 7 (l. 11-12, 18-19), c. 8 (l. 5-7), c. 11 (l. 2-6), c. 13 (l. 8-11, 30-31), c. 14 (l. 16-23), c. 15 (l. 2-6, 25-27), c. 17 (l. 2-5). See also the places where the constitutions of the Dominican Sisters preserved the old text of Prémontré, while the Dominicans subsequently changed their text: CA, d. I, c. 1 (l. 2-3, 15), c. 2 (l. 5, 32), c. 7 (l. 6, 8-9), c. 19 (l. 1-18, 21-22, 25), c. 21 (l. 30-34, 63-67), c. 22 (l. 5), c. 23 (l. 4, 7-8, 22, 25, 33, 65-68).

5 CA, II, 17-21, 28-29, 31.

6 The chapter reports usually began with *item*, sometimes followed by *statuimus* (see for instance five ordinances of 1239: *Acta C.G.*, p. 11). See also *supra*, p. 240, with footnote 306.

on the basis of the chapter reports.[7] Others were interpolated between the older parts, or, as in the Rodez manuscript, simply added at the end as *extravagantes*.[8] The constant revisions and additions left traces in the arrangement of the text, particularly in the second *distinctio*. The interpolation of parentheses separated sections and sentences that originally belonged together and dealt with the same content.[9] When additional rules were inserted, the editors did not always adapt the context to the new stipulations, so that some phrases acquired a new meaning in their new context.[10] In certain places, there are ordinances that either wholly or partially repeat previous ordinances.[11] Such editing errors must not be ascribed to the copyist of Rodez, as they also occurred in the copy on which the constitutions of the Friars of the Sack were based. Instead, they are proof that various editors were involved successively in drafting the legislation.

There are thus sufficient indications, both within the text of the constitutions and outside it, that allow us to sketch the outline of its evolution. In this chapter, an attempt will be made to establish the origins of the various parts and to order them chronologically. We may assume a priori that the redaction of the texts happened in tandem with the development of the order itself and with the expansion of its institutions. This means that it is practically certain that the *consuetudines*,

---

7 The dated ordinances (of 1236) have been marked in the apparatus of the edition of the text (Appendix I).

8 In the edition in H. C. Scheeben, *Die Konstitutionen*, pp. 79-80, the *extravagantes* appear in the place where they were entered in the Rodez manuscript.

9 CA, II, 1 has a series of later ordinances on the provincial chapter in the second half ("Nullus prior ... nisi a provinciali"). The old text continues with the first words of d. II, c. 2, which were edited to clarify the relationship with the preceding "Predicti igitur diffinitores...". – A similar case can be found in d. II, c. 7, where the first words ("Isti autem…") were changed to establish a link with d. II, c. 5, from which c. 7 was separated by the interpolation of c. 6. – The first sentence of d. II, c. 9 refers to the beginning of c. 8, because the continuation of c. 8 is an interpolation ("Et ipsorum ... delicta corrigere"). – The second half of d. II, c. 16 ("Capitulum provinciale ... inchoari") does not match the title of the chapter, *De potestate prioris provincialis*, and must also be an interpolation. – D. II, c. 19 interrupts a series of chapters that all deal with the agenda of the general chapter (d. II, c. 17-21). – Presumably, the titles of certain chapters in the second *distinctio* were also inserted later, for instance for c. 1-4 (originally *De capitulo provinciali*). See *infra*, p. 395, with footnote 155. Cf. also P. Mandonnet – M. H. Vicaire, *Saint Dominique*, vol. II, pp. 284-292.

10 The second sentence of d. II, c. 4 ("Quod si ipsum abesse contigerit nec vicem suam alii commiserit, idem prior cum diffinitoribus capituli provincialis in celebratione procedat eiusdem") apparently belongs to d. II, c. 3 and concerns the provincial's absence, as the parallelism with the master general's absence at the general chapter also shows (d. II, c. 7). This is why the phrase *idem prior* originally meant the "prior loci, ubi capitulum provinciale celebratur" (d. II, c. 3). After the interpolation of the first sentence of d. II, c. 4 ("Statuimus ... confirmatus"), *idem prior* in its new context refers grammatically to the "prior conventualis illius loci, in quo provinciale capitulum in sequenti anno fuerit celebrandum". The expression was interpreted in this sense in Raymond of Peñafort's new codification: "... prior illius loci ubi capitulum fuerit celebrandum" (d. II, c. 7; see R. Creytens, *Les constitutions de ... s. Raymond de Peñafort*, p. 56).

11 D. II, c. 1: "Item conventus ... nisi dicat a quo audierit. Sed utique caveat ... nisi dicat a quo audiverit". – D. II, c. 15: "Mortuo igitur priore provinciali ... Item provinciali priore mortuo ...". – D. II, c. 16: "Capitulum provinciale ... celebretur". Cf. c. 4: "Prior provincialis ... celebretur".

which are described in the first *distinctio* and were largely copied from other institutes, were drafted before the constitutional stipulations of the second *distinctio*. Given that both parts were repeatedly edited and supplemented by the general chapters of the order since 1220, it would be mistaken, when discussing the textual evolution, to treat the two *distinctiones* separately and successively; it is better to use an approach that reflects the chronology. The first section describes the origins and early development of the legislation under the leadership of Dominic (1216-1221). A second section examines the further expansion of the constitutions during the generalate of Jordan of Saxony (1222-1237).

Section I. The legislation under Dominic's rule

Between 1215 and 1221, the first Dominican community in Toulouse developed into a widely ramified society. During this period, the order recorded its laws of observance in writing, as well as part of the legislation concerning its organisation and government. From 1216 onwards, life in its monasteries was ruled by the *arctiores consuetudines* that Jordan of Saxony mentioned. The nature and substance of these monastic customs will be examined in a first part. Then we will address the general chapters of 1220 and 1221, which, under Dominic's leadership, issued many of the constitutional rules on study and the apostolic life of the members, as well as the stipulations on the organisation and the government of the order.

§ 1. The legislation in 1216

A. Further identification of the first **Consuetudines**

The oldest tradition of the Dominican legislation agrees unanimously with Jordan of Saxony that the laws of observance go back to the founder of the order.[12] The *legendae* from the thirteenth century limit themselves to almost literal repetition of the succinct statement in the *Libellus*.[13] Humbert of Romans discussed the issue more extensively, declaring that Dominic and his first followers adopted the constitutions of Prémontré as the foundation for the communal life.[14] This view was shared by eighteenth-century historians, such as Th. Mamachi, J. Quétif and J. Échard.[15] However, since the end of the previous century, some scholars have

---

12 "Itaque celebrato concilio revertentes, verbo domini pape fratribus publicato, mox beati Augustini, predicatoris egregii, ipsi futuri predicatores regulam elegerunt, quasdam sibi super hec in victu et ieiuniis, in lectis et laneis arctiores consuetudines assumentes" (Jordan, *Libellus*, no. 42).

13 See the *legendae* of Peter Ferrand (no. 28, p. 230); of Constantinus of Orvieto (no. 22, p. 302); of Humbert of Romans (no. 31, p. 391).

14 Humbert of Romans, *Expositio super Constitutiones*, p. 3.

15 Th. M. Mamachi, *Annalium Ordinis Praedicatorum vol. I*, pp. 376-378; J. Quétif – J. Échard, *Scriptores Ordinis Praedicatorum*, vol. I, pp. 12-13, footnote E, p. 20, footnote S.

dismissed this idea. Misled by the title H. Denifle gave to his edition of the Rodez manuscript in 1885, they came to believe this text was the work of the general chapter of 1228.[16] This opinion has since often been repeated uncritically on the authority of this deserving medievalist, even by specialists in the history of the order.[17] More recently, some who have researched the sources thoroughly have concluded that the constitutions were in large part drafted considerably before 1228, and that they were even written down during Dominic's lifetime.[18]

The criticism made short work of H. Denifle's theory, or rather of what others believed this to be. All it took to gain a proper understanding of the significance of the 1228 general chapter for the history of the Dominican constitutions was to consult the text of the *praeambulum*. The *editio constitutionum* which this mentions must indeed not be taken as referring to the drafting of a wholly new legal text, but instead to an addition to the existing book of constitutions.[19] Positive and explicit proof of the existence of written legislation during Dominic's life comes from the reports of the canonisation process held in Bologna in 1233. A number of witnesses were heard there according to a method that is entirely sound from a critical perspective. Several among them had known the founder of the order personally and gave testimony about facts that they had witnessed themselves.[20] They stated that Dominic had had certain rules added to the constitutions.[21] And the expressions they used suggest they were referring to a written legal code.

---

16 H. Denifle, *Die Contitutionen des Predigerordens vom Jahre 1228.* At the beginning of his article, the author nuances his argument as follows: "Die Constitutionen vom J. 1228 sind nicht in dem Sinne die ältesten des Ordens, als habe es vor ihnen keine gegeben … Allein die Constitutionen hatten vor 1228 noch keine bestimmte Ordnung, waren ausserdem sehr mangelhaft und, waren sie niedergeschrieben, schwerlich in mehreren Exemplaren verbreitet" (p. 165).

17 In his edition of the *Acta capitulorum generalium*, vol. I, p. 3, footnote 2, C B. Reichert says: "Hoc anno [1228] promulgatae sunt primae constitutiones ordinis, ed. Denifle in *Archiv…*". – The editor of the text of the constitutions in *Analecta S. Ord. Fr. Praed.*, vol. II, 1895-1896, writes on p. 619: "Quonam anno sit conscriptus [*Liber consuetudinum*] non praecise constat; sed, ut verisimiliter, immediate post primum Capitulum Generalissimum Parisiis anno 1228 habitum inceptum fuisse facilius crederem".

18 P. Mandonnet, *La crise scolaire au début du XIIIe siècle*, in RHE, vol. XV, 1914, p. 44, footnote 5; Id., *Saint Dominique*, pp. 52, 70; P. Mandonnet – M. H. Vicaire, *Saint Dominique*, vol. II, pp. 204-221; H. C. Scheeben, who argued in his *Der heilige Dominikus* (1927) that the constitutions were compiled in 1222 at the earliest (p. 133, footnote 57; pp. 316-317, 372-373, 376), assumed in his later work (*Die Konstitutionen*, 1939) that at least the first *distinctio* was drafted by the general chapter in 1220 (pp. 12-13, 18-21).

19 See the text *supra*, p. 372, footnote 2. See also P. Mandonnet – M. H. Vicaire, *Saint Dominique*, vol. II, p. 208; H. C. Scheeben, *Die Konstitutionen*, p. 13.

20 They were repeatedly asked how they had acquired their information: "Interrogatus, quomodo scit hoc, respondit quia sepissime invenit eum in ecclesia orantem et plorantem…" (*Proc. Bon.*, no. 6: testimony of Ventura of Verona; see also no. 10). They also distinguished between things they knew with certainty and things they only remembered vaguely: "Et in infirmitatibus in quibus eum vidit eodem modo se habebat. Interrogatus ubi vidit eum infirmum alias, respondit apud Viterbium, sed non recordatur quam infirmitatem patiebatur" (no. 12: testimony of William of Monferrato; see also nos. 14, 18, 20, 22, 26-28, 39, 41, 46, 48).

21 "Et ad hoc idem hortabatur fratres, et etiam in constitutionibus suis posuit" (*Proc. Bon.*, no. 37). "Et hoc fecit in regula sua scribi" (no. 38). "… et in regula fratrum predicatorum hoc scribi fecit"

Very few of the old sources considered the problem of the origins and de-velopment of the constitutions. Neither the witnesses during the canonisation process, nor the first historiographers of the order made any attempt to chronolo-gically describe Dominic's legislative activity. It is true that Jordan of Saxony in passing indicated the times, roughly, at which the founder of the order had been compelled to address the development of the legislation. According to his *Libellus*, the first laws of observance were recorded as early as 1216, to serve together with the rule of Augustine as the guideline for the community in Toulouse.[22] The second legislative phase coincided with the first general chapter in Bologna (1220), which dealt primarily with constitutional issues. Jordan underlined the importance of this meeting for the organisation and government of the order. He listed only a few of the many decisions that were taken at that time.[23] Of the later thirteenth-century authors, Humbert of Romans was the only one to address the content of the primitive *consuetudines* at some length. When interpreted ob-jectively, his commentary provides evidence for the theory that the Dominicans used the texts of the Premonstratensians as early as 1216 for that part of their constitutions that is called the *distinctio prima* in the Rodez manuscript.[24]

Very few historiographers have themselves examined the content of the consti-tutions of the Dominicans during the first few years after the foundation of the order. The eighteenth-century historians who addressed the issue believed that the legislation of Prémontré already formed the basis for the *arctiores consuetudines* adopted in 1216. J. Quétif, who accepted this view on Humbert's authority, nonetheless also thought it likely that elements of the first customs were derived from other orders.[25] Moreover, Th. Mamachi presented extensive arguments to explain the influence of the legislation of the Premonstratensians on that of the

---

(no. 41). "Et posuit in constitutionibus suis, ne possessiones reciperentur in ordine" (no. 42). "Et hoc in fratrum regula fecit scribi" (no. 47).

22 See the text *supra*, p. 374, footnote 12.

23 "In eodem capitulo de communi fratrum consensu statutum est, generale capitulum uno anno Bononie, altero vero Parisius celebrari, ita tamen ut proxime futuro anno apud Bononiam ageretur. Tunc etiam ordinatum est, ne possessiones vel reditus de cetero tenerent fratres nostri, sed et iis renuntiarent, quos habuerant in partibus Tholosanis. Alia quoque plura ibi constituta sunt, que usque hodie observantur" (Jordan, *Libellus*, no. 87).

24 "Praemonstratenses enim reformaverunt et auxerunt religionem beati Augustini ... Proinde beatus Dominicus et fratres sui temporis, cum ... elegissent regulam beati Augustini, non immerito cum illa regula de constitutionibus illorum qui alios illius ordinis excedebant, assumpserunt quod arduum..." (Humbert of Romans, *Expositio super Constitutiones*, pp. 2-3).

25 "... statim a reditu Dominicum anno MCCXVI ac proinde circa pascha, quod eo anno X aprilis accidit, socios in monasterio Pruliano coegisse, unaque omnes ut pontifici morem gererent, regulam S. Augustini et instituta quaedam in victu arctiora e Pr[ae]monstratensibus, inquit Humbertus, sed quae apud quasdam alias canonicorum regularium congregationes tum florentes et severiores, et forte in ipsa Oxomensi reformatione in usu erant adoptasse sibique imposuisse, ut non tam novus ordo, quam nova canonicorum regularium praedicationi speciatim addictorum congregatio videretur ..." (J. Quétif – J. Échard, *Scriptores Ord. Praed.*, vol. I, p. 13, footnote E). We have already shown to what extent the currently available sources allow us to regard the statutes of Osma as a source, *supra* pp. 321-324.

Dominicans.[26] But both authors limited themselves to general reflections without direct reference to the sources. Nor did they have access to the Rodez manuscript, which was not published by H. Denifle until a century later. Two recent researchers who have studied the origins of the Dominican constitutions have in many respects reached diverging conclusions. Fresh examination of the oldest historical documents and of the text of the constitutions itself led M. H. Vicaire to conclude that the *consuetudines* of 1216-1217 were in fact derived from Prémontré and can be found in the first *distinctio* of the text of Rodez. In 1220, the general chapter added the *constitutiones* proper as the second *distinctio*.[27] By contrast, H. C. Scheeben pointed to the literary affinity between the *distinctio prima* and the prologue and certain chapters of the *distinctio secunda*, which he believes date from Dominic's lifetime, albeit not 1216. According to him, these oldest parts were drafted at the same time, specifically at the general chapter of 1220.[28]

The problems that the nature and content of the *consuetudines* adopted by the Dominicans in 1216 pose for us find their origin in the vagueness of Jordan of Saxony's account of the events of those years, as this is the main source for this issue. He describes the first customs in general terms as *quasdam arctiores consuetudines*, without explicitly linking them to Prémontré.[29] In the earlier legislation of monastic orders, *consuetudines* meant both written rules and unwritten customs that guided the communal life, sometimes for a considerable period of time.[30] But more recently founded institutions possessed their own adapted rule of life from the start, usually called *regula* or *propositum*.[31] Innocent III was at pains to grant approval only if there was a well-defined programme of life.[32] By the beginning of the thirteenth century, a written legal code was therefore regarded as a necessary condition for ecclesiastical recognition of a new monastic community. The Fourth Lateran Council gave this requirement the force of law by stipulating that any new foundation could be recognised only on the basis of an acknowledged *regula et institutio*.[33] Dominic and his first companions were well aware that the conciliar legislation also applied to them. Their first concern, therefore, after the choice

---

26 "Secundum haec a Praemonstratensibus, quorum est imprimis austerum vivendi genus, multa decreta de ratione vitae, de diuturnis ieiuniis, de silentio, deque aliis rebus eiusmodi sumpserunt, eaque in unum corpus collecta, aliisque praeterea legibus, decretisque aucta *Ordinis Constitutiones* appellaverunt" (Th. M. Mamachi, *Annalium Ord. Praed. vol. I*, p. 376).

27 P. Mandonnet – M. H. Vicaire, *Saint Dominique*, vol. II, pp. 210-230.

28 H. C. Scheeben, *Die Konstitutionen*, pp. 18-21 and 24-25.

29 See the text *supra*, p. 374, footnote 12.

30 See *supra*, pp. 183-199, especially pp. 195-199.

31 See *supra*, pp. 219-223.

32 See *supra*, pp. 206 and 208-209, note 147 (Order of the Holy Spirit and the Trinitarians), p. 219 (Catholic Poor), pp. 219-220 (fraternity of Bernard Primus), p. 220 (Humiliati).

33 See *supra*, p. 229.

of the rule, was to define the *institutio* of their community, which under the circumstances could best be based on written legislation.[34]

They looked mainly to the statutes of Prémontré as a source and example for the *consuetudines* of the Dominicans. The Premonstratensians were one of the most widely spread and influential congregations of canons regular. Their Abbey of La Vid was located not twenty kilometres from Caleruega and must have been known to Dominic from his youth.[35] They had many houses in Southern France, including the Abbey of La Capelle about ten kilometres from Toulouse.[36] Situated as it was in the territory of the Albigensians, it underwent the effects of the confusion caused by the religious disputes.[37] During his missionary activity in this area, Dominic remained in touch constantly with the religious of this abbey.[38] He was a close friend of the abbot, John I, whom he visited regularly. Obviously, he would have been able to find the documentation required to draft his own constitutions there.[39]

Moreover, despite their vagueness, the expressions that Jordan used were very suitable as a reference to the legislation of Prémontré.[40] The term *consuetudines*, which as such could mean several things, could be applied very easily even in 1216 to the first part of the Dominican legislation, which was still called the *Liber consuetudinum* in the Rodez manuscript.[41] Similarly, the fact that Jordan characterised these *consuetudines* as *arctiores* points to the stricter canonical *institutio* to which the Premonstratensians belonged.[42] Finally, it is striking that the summary table of contents of the first *consuetudines* according to Jordan is very similar to the

34 See *supra*, p. 231.

35 On this abbey, see N. Backmund, *Monasticon Praemonstratense*, vol. III, Straubing, 1956, pp. 305-311. There is no reason to assume that Dominic joined the Abbey of La Vid, as E. de Noriega, *Dissertatio historica de Sto. Dominico de Guzman, Ordinis Praedicatorum Patriarcha, canonico regulari Augustino-Praemonstratensi, in observantis simo monasterio Stae. Mariae de La Vid*, Salamanca, 1723, contends. See the refutation of this hypothesis in Th. M. Mamachi, *Annalium Ord. Praed. vol. I*, pp. 378-381.

36 See M.-A. Erens, *Capelle (La)*, art. in DHGE, vol. XI, 1949, col. 850-852; N. Backmund, *Monasticon Praem., tomo cit.*, pp. 168-169. The abbey was destroyed twice, in the thirteenth century and in 1570. The archives were lost on this occasion.

37 The abbey was excommunicated at the beginning of the thirteenth century as its members were accused of maintaining close relations with the Albigensians. See the letter that Gervase, abbot general of Prémontré, addressed to Pope Honorius III to ask for absolution, in C. L. Hugo, *Sacrae antiquitatis monumenta*, vol. I, p. 13.

38 C. L. Hugo, *Sacri et canonici Ordinis Praemonstratensis annales*, vol. I, Nancy, 1734, col. 465 (erroneously col. 433 in this work).

39 J. J. Percin, *Monumenta conventus Tolosani Ordinis FF. Praedicatorum primi*, p. 18, no. 39, which appears to be based on old documents.

40 "...quasdam sibi super hec in victu et ieiuniis, in lectis et laneis arctiores consuetudines assumentes" (Jordan, *Libellus*, no. 42).

41 Cf. CA, prol.: "...librum istum, quem librum consuetudinum appellamus...".

42 See *supra*, pp. 231-232.

sequence in which the same issues are treated in the statutes of Prémontré and in the earliest constitutions of the Dominicans.[43]

The vagueness of Jordan's expressions cannot be used as an argument against the existence of written legislation based on the customs of the Premonstratensians in 1216. His circumspection may have been inspired by the desire to be strictly objective and avoid explicitly claiming anything of which he was not entirely sure, either through personal experience as a witness or through confirmation by a reliable source.[44] Moreover, in speaking of *quasdam consuetudines*, he may have been conforming to the medieval custom of not specifically identifying persons or issues even if the author was quite certain whom he was talking about.[45] Nor can it be ruled out that Jordan was purposely vague because the issue of the origins of the first constitutions was no longer a matter of current interest in 1233. At that time, the Dominican Order had long been approved and established and was widely disseminated. Its original statutes had been expanded by the general chapters in later years to form a well-ordered legal code. In a work intended as a historical document on the life of Dominic, as well as a homage to him on the occasion of his canonisation,[46] it was perhaps safer not to emphasise too much that the founder of the order had made ample use of the texts of other institutes when drafting his legislation.

The authors who reject the early origins of the constitutions do not deny that the community of Toulouse had its own written legislation as early as 1216. But they believe the content of this text cannot be equated with the texts of the earliest constitutions preserved in the Rodez manuscript. Thus H. C. Scheeben contended that the customs of Prémontré were not used as a source before 1220, because the Dominicans wore the *superpellicium* between 1215 and 1220, whereas this had been abolished by the Premonstratensians.[47] But he failed to

---

43 It could also be mentioned here that the rule of Augustine as used by the Dominicans begins with the first sentence of the *Ordo monasterii*, as it does in the Premonstratensian text: "Ante omnia ... nobis data" (cf. *supra*, p. 230, note 250). It has been pointed out that other canons, like those of Saint-Ruf, had similarly included excerpts from the OM in their *Consuetudines* (cf. *supra*, pp. 191 and 230). But the *Regula S. Augustini* of Las Abadesas, which was mentioned as an example (*ibid.*) immediately begins with the customary first sentence of the RA: "Hec igitur sunt..." (MS. Vich 149, p. l). The excerpts from the OM only appear after the RA, on pp. 11-12 (cf. *supra*, p. 191, with note 47). These canons therefore did not have the first sentence of OM, which does appear in the Premonstratensian and Dominican texts.

44 Jordan says at the beginning of his work that he will only write "ea que vidi personaliter et audivi, et primitivorum fratrum relatione cognovi..." (*Libellus*, no. 3).

45 This manner of quoting was common in the works of the medieval theologians and philosophers. The *quidam* always referred to certain *auctoritates* or opponents.

46 B. Altaner, *Der hl. Dominikus*, p. 213.

47 John of Spain says of the first Dominicans: "... cum ordo Praedicatorum ... equitarent et superpellicia deferrent..." (*Proc. Bon.*, no. 26). H. C. Scheeben says on the wearing of the *superpellicium* by the Premonstratensians: "...die Prämonstratenser dagegen hatten es abgelehnt" (*Die Konstitutionen*, p. 23, with a reference to *Institut. Praem.*, d. IV, c. 14). – However, it is clear from the text in question that the *superpellicium* was in fact worn on certain occasions: "Pellicium non portetur nisi opertum tunica, nisi frater *superpellicio* et alba induitur. Si vero solo *superpellicio*

consider that the wearing of this specifically canonical garment had been made obligatory for all canons regular in the church province of Narbonne by the Council of Montpellier as recently as 1214, less than two years beforehand.[48] The Dominicans therefore had a compelling reason to deviate from their model in this respect.

Scheeben points to other possible sources to give a positive characterisation of the content of the primitive *Consuetudines*, such as the statutes of the chapter of Osma or of an unidentified congregation of Augustinian canons.[49] Study of the sources does indeed show that fragments of monastic and canonical origins were interpolated between the Prémontré texts,[50] but there is nothing to stop us from accepting that this redaction had already taken place in 1216. As a whole, the statutes of Osma were not suitable for the apostolic community of Toulouse. As the legal code of a chapter that had adopted a regular life but that probably did not belong to the *arctior ordo*, they were less suited to serve as a norm for the stricter observance of the *vita religiosa* which the Dominicans had embraced. Moreover, it is unlikely that Dominic had the text of these statutes at hand, as he had been living outside Spain for fifteen years. It was possibly for these reasons that he limited himself to deriving a number of ordinances of minor importance which he still recalled from his earlier years in the monastery.[51]

There is admittedly no single element in the earliest sources which, as such, proves that the original constitutions of the Dominicans were derived from the *Consuetudines* of Prémontré as early as 1216 and that they can be found in the first *distinctio* of the Rodez manuscript. But taken together, the various indications make up a sufficiently robust argument. It is possible, of course, to continue to ask why Jordan of Saxony and the other witnesses were so unspecific in their statements on this issue. But the difficulties are multiplied if we build a counterargument on their silence. If we deny that the *Consuetudines* were derived from Prémontré in 1216, we would have to acknowledge that that order's constitutions

---

induitur, tunicam exuat" (Pa, IV, 14). See also the constitutions from the first half of the thirteenth century (Pb, II, 13). The use of the *superpellicium* is further described in the *Ordinarium* of the order, in the chapter *Quando superpelliciis utendum sit* (c. 2): "Et quia plerique causantur quod, ceterorum more canonicorum, passim superpelliciis non utimur, nec nos utique eorum usum, cum opus fuerit, abdicamus; quin potius ea non ubicumque circumferenda, sed tantum divino cultui deputanda et reservanda credimus..." (ed. Pl. Lefèvre, *L'ordinaire de Prémontré d'après des manuscrits du XIIᵉ et du XIIIᵉ siècle* (Bibliothèque de la Revue d'histoire ecclésiastique, vol. 22), Leuven, 1941, p. 6).

48 Can. 26: "Item districte praecipimus, ut canonici regulares superpelliceis semper utantur, nisi propter infirmitatem vel aliam necessitatem, de permissione suae regulae quando quoque eis id intermittatur" (Mansi, vol. XXII, col. 945).

49 "Meiner Auffassung nach hat der Orden wohl Satzungen gehabt, aber keine eigenen. Man denke nur an die Consuetudines der zahlreichen Kongregationen von Regularkanonikern, die alle zur Verfügung standen ... Reste dieser unbekannten Satzungen sind wahrscheinlich noch in den Teilen enthalten, die als ursprünglich anzusehen sind und mit den Consuetudines der Prämonstratenser nicht übereinstimmen" (*Die Konstitutionen*, pp. 21-22).

50 See *supra*, pp. 321-324, where the possible influence of the statutes of Osma is discussed.

51 See *supra*, p. 324.

replaced the hypothetical primitive laws of observance by 1220 at the latest. But it is impossible that such a major change in the Dominican legislation would have escaped the notice of contemporaries. And yet Jordan says nothing about any such supposed fundamental reorientation. It is easier to understand that he would have spoken tersely and vaguely about the first legislative assembly of 1216, at which he was not present, than that he would have remained silent about the main decision of the general chapter of 1220, which he did attend.[52]

B. *The content of the first legislation*

We must now look more closely at the content of the primitive *Consuetudines*. The *prologus* was already part of the text in 1216; it was in fact organically linked to the text in the statutes of Prémontré as well. But it would be an exaggeration to claim that this introduction must therefore have been written down integrally at once.[53] Like the rest of the constitutions, it bears the traces of changes and additions. The section on the superior's powers of dispensation is a later addition.[54] The statement on the penal obligation of the code dates from 1236.[55] The division into two *distinctiones* is original, as it reflects a distinction that is also present in the subject matter itself.[56] In the list of chapters, the series of titles of the first *distinctio* was initially more complete and it mirrored the sequence in the body of the text more clearly, as was the case in the Premonstratensian text.[57] By contrast, the content of the second *distinctio* was indicated very summarily, without reference to the general and provincial chapters, two institutions that did not yet exist in 1216 and whose emergence could not be predicted with any certainty at the time.[58]

---

52 Jordan, *Libellus*, no. 87. See the text quoted *supra*, p. 239, note 305. Jordan would hardly have failed to mention that the so-called older *Consuetudines* were at the same time replaced by new legislation on the basis of the customs of Prémontré, if that is what actually happened in 1220.

53 H. C. Scheeben, *Die Konstitutionen*, p. 21, who for this reason dates the *prologus* to 1220, like the first *distinctio*.

54 It appears to be a later summary of the partial dispensation faculties that appear in other chapters, including in d. I, c. 1: "aliquando etiam intermittitur … secundum quod videbitur prelato"; c. 4: "…nisi cum aliquibus prelatus aliter dispensare voluerit"; c. 6: "…nisi cum aliquo propter laborem dispensetur"; c. 7: "…nisi cum aliquibus dispensaverit prior"; c. 11: "…secundum quod prelato visum fuerit". The editor of the section in the *prologus* appears to be writing at some remove from the foundation of the order: "*ab initio* noscatur institutus fuisse." On the other hand, the general dispensation faculty is still assigned only to the *praelatus*, the prior. The interpolation must therefore have happened at the time that there were no other superiors yet, that is, in 1220 at the latest.

55 See *supra*, p. 287, with footnote 42.

56 See *infra*, p. 383.

57 See *supra*, pp. 284-285. The constitutions of the Friars of the Sack similarly contain a detailed list of all the chapters (ed. G. M. Giacomozzi, *L'Ordine della Penitenza*, p. 74).

58 For H. C. Scheeben, *Die Konstitutionen*, p. 21, this is further proof that the prologue cannot have been composed before 1220. With regard to the constitutions of the Premonstratensians, it must be noted that their prologue stipulated that the ordinances of the general chapters should be added in the fourth part of the statutes: "In hac quarta distinctione quaedam quae in generali

In addition to the texts derived from Prémontré, which formed the basis of the Dominican *consuetudines* since 1216, the first *distinctio* contains a number of rules that were either grouped together or woven into the various chapters separately and fragmentarily.[59] The textual corrections of 1236 can be identified on the basis of the chapter reports.[60] Other corrections can similarly be recognised as chapter ordinances because of their introductory formula or the place they occupy; they were inserted in 1220 at the earliest.[61] The rules that are related to other canonical traditions or that are based on ecclesiastical ordinances were possibly added after 1216.[62] Only the fragments that appear to be derived from the statutes of the chapter of Osma are probably older and may have been included in the *Consuetudines* as early as 1216.[63] They include a number of liturgical rules on the office in choir and the daily chapter,[64] guidelines on meals and on the *collatio*,[65] care of the sick,[66] and perhaps the *speculum novitiorum*.[67] It is difficult to imagine that Dominic would have waited until 1220 or later to incorporate these few specific customs, which he remembered from his previous communal life, into the legislation of his new order.

The *speculum praedicatorum* at the end of the second *distinctio* is among the oldest parts of the constitutions.[68] It is written in the same concrete style as the *consuetudines* of the first *distinctio*. It paints the ideal image of the itinerant preacher in a few broad strokes. Like the apostles, the friars were to go out two by two and behave everywhere as *viri evangelici* and followers of Christ, in constant contact with God, without money for the journey and without concern for their

capitulo communi consilio pro conservatione ordinis sunt posita, possunt reperiri. Et si quae pro diversitate emergentium actionum postmodum fuerint ordinata, hic competenter poterunt inseri" (Pa, prol.; cf. Pb, *ibid.*). This text cannot be seen as evidence that the Dominicans similarly anticipated the provincial and general chapters in the prologue of their constitutions in 1216, before these two institutions actually existed, as M. H. Vicaire does (P. Mandonnet – M. H. Vicaire, *Saint Dominique*, vol. II, pp. 228-229, footnote 72). The Premonstratensians could speak of the task of the general chapter in their *prologus* because it actually existed and was fully functioning, whereas the Dominicans in 1216 could not be certain yet that their society would ever grow into a "religious order" with a general chapter as its governing body.

59 See *supra*, pp. 307-320.
60 See *infra*, p. 406, with footnote 213.
61 For the first general chapter, see *infra*, pp. 384-385. Regulations issued by the chapters between 1220 and 1236 often begin with *item*: d. I, c. 1 (l. 32), c. 4 (l. 11), c. 15 (l. 7, 9, 15, 20, 25), c. 24 (l. 22); d. II, c. 5 (l. 14), c. 17 (l. 14), c. 27 (l. 10), c. 35 (l. 8, 12, 14), c. 36 (l. 14), c. 37 (l. 28). – Other ordinances begin with *statuimus*: d. II, c. 1 (l. 2), c. 4 (l. 2), c. 6 (l. 2), c. 12 (l. 2), c. 15 (l. 2, 6), c. 19 (l. 2), c. 28 (l. 12), c. 31 (l. 2), c. 33 (l. 8).
62 See *supra*, pp. 314-320, 324-328; *infra*, p. 410, with note 241, p. 408, with note 226, pp. 405-407, with notes 216-217.
63 See *supra*, pp. 321-324.
64 See *supra*, pp. 307-308.
65 See *supra*, pp. 308-313.
66 See *supra*, pp. 313-314.
67 See *supra*, pp. 313-314.
68 CA, II, 31: "…cum in predicationem exire debuerint, … nec accipient nec portabunt".

sustenance. These guidelines form the core of the original *propositum* that was presented to Innocent III for confirmation in 1215.[69] They are a concise summary of the programme of life that Dominic had observed since 1216[70] and that his first companions had practiced as preachers of the diocese of Toulouse, with the approval of the bishop.[71] After adopting the new *institutio* on the basis of the *Consuetudines* of Prémontré, the apostolic regulations were perhaps added to the laws of observance as a second *distinctio*. They are a résumé of a statute for diocesan preachers according to the decrees of the Lateran Council,[72] and they vouchsafed the name and role of *praedicatores* that Honorius III granted to the first Dominicans.[73]

§ 2. The constitutions from 1216 to 1221

A. Dominic's guidelines

The order did not possess a fixed legal system before 1220. Dominic had consulted his confreres in 1216 on the choice of rule and the first *consuetudines*.[74] But he insisted occasionally on his own view, even if this went against the wishes of others, as he did at the sending out of the community of Toulouse.[75] In subsequent years, too, he exercised a strongly personal authority over his order.[76] Under his influence, a number of guidelines were adopted that fell outside the range of traditional monastic customs and that were directly linked to the apostolic mission of the Dominicans. In addition to stipulations on the necessity of modesty[77] and the prohibition on taking money for the journey,[78] the witnesses at the canonisation process mentioned the strict observance of poverty and the

---

69 See *supra*, p. 228, with Humbert of Romans's text in footnote 243. Cf. Jordan, *Libellus*, no. 45: "… et iuxta propositum ordinationemque conceptam confirmationem ordinis … impetravit". For the *proposita* of the other religious communities, see *supra*, pp. 219-223.

70 See *supra*, pp. 217-218.

71 See *supra*, p. 225.

72 Can. 10, *De praedicatoribus instituendis* (see *supra*, pp. 228-229).

73 The bull *Gratiarum omnium* of 21 January 1217 (see *supra*, p. 234).

74 Jordan, *Libellus*, nos. 41-42. Cf. *supra*, p. 229.

75 Jordan, *Libellus*, no. 47. Cf. *supra*, pp. 235-236.

76 Testimony of Ventura of Verona: "Et tunc temporis ipse beatus frater Dominicus habebat plenam potestatem et dispositionem et ordinationem et correctionem totius ordinis fratrum Predicatorum post dominum papam" (*Proc. Bon.*, no. 2).

77 "Item dixit, quod consuetudo sua erat, ut de Deo vel cum Deo semper in domo et extra domum et in via loqueretur. Et ad hoc idem hortabatur fratres, et etiam in constitutionibus suis posuit" (*Proc. Bon.*, no. 37; see also nos. 38 and 47). Cf. CA, II, 31: "…cum Deo vel de Deo secum vel proximis loquendo…".

78 "Unde iniunxit eis, ut vilibus vestibus uterentur et in via pecuniam numquam portarent, sed ubique de elemosinis viverent. Et hoc fecit in regula sua scribi" (*Proc. Bon.*, no. 38). Cf. CA, II, 31: "…aurum, argentum, pecuniam … nec accipient nec portabunt".

renunciation of all immovable property,[79] simplicity of dress,[80] the desire to relieve the preachers and professors of as many administrative duties as possible[81] and the exhortation that monastic buildings should be frugal.[82] These guidelines were possibly added to the existing constitutions at Dominic's behest either in 1216, or in 1220.[83]

B. *The general chapter of 1220*

A new phase in the history of Dominican legislation began in 1220, when the first general chapter was held and was upgraded to the position of central governing body.[84] Jordan of Saxony only mentions a few of the ordinances that were issued in 1220, including the decision to meet every year from then on, alternatively in Bologna and Paris.[85] But the *alia plura constituta* probably include other stipulations on the organisation and functioning of the chapter.[86] As our study of the sources has shown, most monastic orders modelled their chapter on the example of Cîteaux, according to the guidelines of the Fourth Lateran Council.[87] This influence is also visible in the Dominican constitutions. The chapters on the ceremonial and order of business at the general chapter clearly bear the imprint of the customs of the Cistercians. They were composed in the style of the *consuetudines* and form a sharp contrast with the rest of the second *distinctio*. This,

---

79 "Et posuit in constitutionibus suis, ne possessiones reciperentur in ordine" (*Proc. Bon.*, no. 42). Cf. CA, II, 26: "Possessiones seu redditus nullo modo recipiantur". See also *supra*, p. 376, with note 23.

80 See *supra*, note 78. Cf. CA, I, 19: "Ubi vero servari non poterit, utantur vilibus. Et potius vilitas in cappis observetur".

81 "Et ut fratres fortius intenderent studio et predicationibus, voluit dictus frater Dominicus, quod conversi eius ordinis illiterati preessent fratribus literatis in administratione et exhibitione rerum temporalium..." (*Proc. Bon.*, no. 26; see also no. 32). Cf. CA, II, 31: "Omnes qui ad officium predicationis vel studium sunt deputati, nullam habeant curam seu administrationem temporalium...".

82 "Et volebat quod haberent parvas domos et viles vestes" (*Proc. Bon.*, no. 32). Cf. CA, II, 35: "Mediocres domos et humiles habeant fratres nostri...".

83 The rules in d. II, c. 31, mentioned in footnotes 77 and 78, were part of the constitutions of 1216. Cf. *supra*, p. 382, footnote 68. The other rules, listed in footnotes 79-82, were perhaps added by the general chapter of 1220. There is explicit confirmation of this for one of these stipulations, on the obligation of collective poverty (cf. note 79), in Jordan, *Libellus*, no. 87. For the rule on buildings, see *infra*, p. 387, footnote 104; on dress, see *infra*, pp. 388-389, with footnotes 119-121.

84 Jordan, *Libellus*, no. 86.

85 Jordan, *Libellus*, no. 87: "In eodem capitulo de communi fratrum consensu statutum est, generale capitulum uno anno Bononie, altero vero Parisius celebrari...". It may be deduced from the fact that the decisions were taken "de communi fratrum consensu" that the chapter was already functioning as a collective governing body. The ordinance was interpolated in the constitutions in d. II, c. 13: "Capitulum generale uno anno Parisius, alio anno Bononie celebretur".

86 "Alia quoque plura ibi constituta sunt, que usque hodie observantur" (Jordan, *Libellus*, no. 87).

87 See *supra*, pp. 330-331; the text of can. 12 of the council, p. 187, footnotes 260-261.

too, may be regarded as an indication of their early origins. Perhaps they were adopted ready-made from Cîteaux as early as 1220.[88]

According to the *acta* of the canonisation process, the appointment of the *diffinitores* also took place at the first general chapter in 1220. Two eye witnesses recount that Dominic wished to resign as superior, but that he agreed to remain in his post at the request of his confreres, on condition that responsibility for the government of the order would be transferred to a group of representatives of the community.[89] This initiative of the founder, interpreted by the attendees as a gesture of deep humility, was in fact proof of administrative wisdom, as well as simply a matter of implementing ecclesiastical rules. According to the Fourth Lateran Council, the leadership of the *commune capitulum* was to be entrusted to a group of four *praesidentes*, a decision possibly inspired by the example of the *diffinitores* of Cîteaux.[90] The second *distinctio* of the constitutions, in the chapters that describe the powers of the diffinitors, gave Dominic's proposal concerning the collective government of the order the force of law.[91] The ordinance on their power over the master general is similarly a clear echo of the founder's desire to be relieved of his post, although the members of the chapter added a proviso, carefully describing the conditions under which a resignation would be accepted.[92] But these texts were not necessarily drafted when the issues in question were discussed.[93]

The procedure for the election of the *diffinitores* of the general chapter cannot have been part of the constitutions as early as 1220, as it presupposes the existence of provinces.[94] Similarly, the introductory formula *statuimus* betrays its character as an interpolation. The original rules for the election of the diffinitors are very probably those that can currently be found in the part on the provincial chapter.[95] Judging by its style, this section is of early provenance. It still shows dependence on Cîteaux, while the capping of the number of *diffinitores* at four

---

88 The chapters in question are: d. II, c. 17-18, c. 19 (partial) and c. 20-21. For the affinity with Cîteaux, see *supra*, pp. 332-337.

89 Rudolf of Faventia testified: "Tempore quo primum capitulum fratrum predicatorum fuit celebratum in civitate Bononiensi, dictus frater Dominicus dixit inter fratres: *Ego sum dignus depositione, quia ego sum inutilis et remissus*. Et humiliavit se multum in omnibus. Et cum fratres nollent eum deponere, placuit ipsi fratri Dominico, quod constituerentur diffinitores qui haberent potestatem, tam super ipsum quam super alios et super totum capitulum, statuendi, diffiniendi et ordinandi, donec duraret capitulum" (*Proc. Bon.*, no. 33; see also the testimony of Ventura of Verona, *ibid.*, no. 2).

90 See *supra*, pp. 335-336 and 342.

91 The *potestas statuendi, diffiniendi et ordinandi* is granted to the diffinitors in CA, II, 7.

92 CA, II, 8-9 discusses the authority of the *diffinitores* to review the policies of the master general. The ninth chapter discusses the possibility of removal from office and even literally repeats Dominic's pretext: "inutilis et remissus". But the members of the chapter replied to this by defining in the text of the constitutions that only cases of grave negligence and unfitness would be grounds for removal.

93 See *infra*, pp. 390-391.

94 CA, II, 5: "Statuimus etiam ut per duos annos in dictarum octo provinciarum capitulis aliquis de magis idoneis a capitulo eligatur, qui sit generalis capituli diffinitor".

95 CA, II, 1.

echoes the Lateran Council's guidelines for the *commune capitulum* of autonomous abbeys and monasteries in the various church provinces.[96] We may assume
that the Dominicans wished to incorporate this canon in 1220, when they drafted
the first legislative texts for their own chapter. Later, when the decision had been
made that the *diffinitores capituli generalis* would no longer be appointed by the general chapter itself, but by the provincial chapter,[97] the existing election procedure
was no longer required. But instead of being deleted from the constitutions, it
was later used for the election of the four *diffinitores capituli provincialis*, who were
chosen by the members of the provincial chapter itself.

The lawmakers of 1220 had to give some thought to the internal organisation of the monasteries. There were already some twenty houses spread across
various countries, either established or in the process of being founded, but as
yet no legal provisions for the conditions of their foundation or government.[98]
Hitherto, the initiative for the sending out of the members of new communities
and the appointment of the superiors rested with Dominic himself.[99] It may be
assumed that he also transferred his powers in this field to the first legislative
assembly of the order. The chapters in the constitutions on the general chapter are
immediately followed by various brief rules on the foundation and organisation
of the monasteries.[100] The requirements that apply to new foundations are a
paraphrase of an old statute of Cîteaux.[101] The chapter on the election of the
prior originally consisted only of the first sentence, which guarantees the rights of
the monastic community.[102] The regulations on the appointment and task of the
subprior logically followed suit, as they did in the *consuetudines* of the Cistercians
and the Premonstratensians.[103] The exhortation to make the monastery buildings

---

96 For the relationship with the capitular customs of Cîteaux, see *supra*, pp. 335-336. For the influence of
    the guidelines of the Lateran Council, see *supra*, p. 342.

97 According to CA, II, 5. For the dating of this ordinance (1225), see *infra*, pp. 395-396.

98 The first *distinctio* does describe the various duties of the superiors in the performance of the
    monastic exercises, but not their canonical appointment and powers.

99 For the sending out of the religious in 1217 and the foundation of the first monasteries, see *supra*,
    pp. 235-238.

100 The parts on the general chapter are followed in the Rodez manuscript by the chapter *De anniversariis*
    (d. II, c. 22), which is clearly not in its proper place and has been moved to d. II, c. 36 in the critical
    edition of the text (Appendix I).

101 D. II, c. 23, *De conventu mittendo*. Cf. *supra*, pp. 338-339, with notes 304-306.

102 D. II, c. 24: "Priores a suis conventibus eligantur". The word *conventuales* was possibly only added after
    the erection of the provinces, whose superiors were called *prior provincialis*.

103 For Cîteaux: *Officia ecclesiastica*, c. 110, *De abbate*; c. 111, *De priore*; c. 112, *De suppriore* (ed. Ph.
    Guignard, pp. 229-232). The same sequence appears in the Premonstratensian text (Pa and Pb, d. II,
    c. 1-3).

modest in form was perhaps also added in 1220.[104] At any rate it clearly articulates Dominic's views.[105]

Most of the rules on study and preaching at the end of the constitutions[106] were similarly drafted by the first general chapter. They were announced in the *prologus* and still show the literary features of the first *distinctio* and of the parts drafted in 1220. From the foundation of the order onwards, study was regarded as a strict obligation and it was included as an integral part in the monastic *horarium*.[107] The organisation of this aspect of life is still inchoate and reflects the period before the erection of the provinces. There is no mention yet of the authority of the provincial and of the provincial chapter, and the care of the students is entrusted exclusively to the *praelatus* and the *magister studentium*.[108] Most of the stipulations in the following chapters are elaborations of the original *speculum praedicatorum*.[109] The exhortations and instructions that they contain already presuppose a certain experience of the dangers and difficulties that beset the office of preacher. Initially they were perhaps part of a single body of guidelines for preachers.[110] These were subsequently interrupted by a number of interpolations on the authority to preach, and supplemented by several rules relating to travel.[111]

---

104 D. II, c. 35, *De edificiis*. Perhaps the first sentence originally was "Mediocres domos et humiles habeant fratres nostri, ita quod nec ipsi expensis graventur nec seculares vel religiosi in nostris sumptuosis edificiis scandalizentur" (cf. *Const. Sororum S. Mariae Magdalenae*, c. 22, ed. A. Simon, *L'ordre des Pénitentes*, p. 166).

105 *Proc. Bon.*, nos. 17, 32, 38. Cf. *supra*, p. 237 and p. 384, note 82.

106 D. II, c. 28-29, 31-34.

107 The duty of study was even imposed on novices: "Qualiter intenti esse debeant in studio, ut de die, de nocte, in domo, in itinere legant aliquid vel meditentur, et quidquid poterunt, retinere cordetenus nitantur" (CA, I, 13). This emphasis on studies was largely due to Dominic personally: "Item dixit, quod dictus frater Dominicus sepe monebat et hortabatur fratres dicti ordinis verbis et litteris suis, quod semper studerent in novo et veteri testamento. Et hoc scit, quia audivit eum illa dicentem, et litteras eius vidit" (*Proc. Bon.*, no. 29). Cf. P. Mandonnet – M. H. Vicaire, *Saint Dominique*, vol. II, p. 66, with footnotes 259 and 260.

108 Study in the *cellae* (CA, II, 29) is an echo of how studies were organised in the first monastery in Toulouse: "At vero in predicta ecclesia sancti Romani protinus edificatum est claustrum, cellas habens ad studendum et dormiendum desuper satis aptas" (Jordan, *Libellus*, no. 44).

109 See *supra*, pp. 382-383, where the oldest core of d. II, c. 31 was dated to 1216. The first sentence ("Statuimus … annos") has a more technical character, particularly because of the introductory formula *statuimus*. It was perhaps composed by a later general chapter. Possibly in 1220, the following sentence ("Ad exercitium…" up to and including "qui apti sunt") was placed before the ordinances that already existed in 1216. The conclusion of the chapter ("Omnes qui … aliquando occupari") also contains rules that presuppose specific experience and that must therefore have been part of the sections added in 1220. Cf. *supra*, p. 384, note 81.

110 From c. 31 up to and including the first half of c. 34 ("…in omnibus obediat"). The later additions or *extravagantes* begin at this point in the Rodez manuscript, introduced by *statuimus* (see H. C. Scheeben, *Die Konstitutionen*, p. 78), while the Friars of the Sack have a passage that does not appear in the Dominican text: "Honestatem … requirant" (ed. G. M. Giacomozzi, *L'Ordine della Penitenza*, p. 110).

111 The first sentence of c. 32 ("Predicare…summi pontificis") is formulated in a more technical manner ("non audeat aliquis", versus the repeated "fratres nostri" in the following sections). The same

The *Regula conversorum* at the end of the constitutions was probably also drafted by the general chapter of 1220.[112] These special regulations for the lay brothers cannot have been part of the earliest *consuetudines*.[113] Nor is it certain that the Dominicans could at that early stage have used the legislation of Prémontré for this purpose, as they did for the rest of their monastic customs.[114] Moreover, the first monastery in Toulouse was a community of canons regular, that is, clerics. The sources first mention lay members of the order in 1217 on the occasion of the sending out of the religious to the various countries.[115] The following year, a *conversus* was one of the founders of the monastery of Bologna.[116] From that point on, lay brothers were possibly admitted regularly, so that it became necessary to include a special chapter on them in the constitutions. Before long, their number had risen so markedly that Dominic considered entrusting the responsibility for worldly goods to them.[117] The general chapter of 1220 was consequently the right opportunity to define their position further.

The aspects of the legislation of 1220 discussed so far concern the organisation and external activity of the order. The ordinances issued were new compared to the *consuetudines* of 1216 and were therefore included in a separate part, the second *distinctio*. And yet a number of important changes were also made to the first *distinctio*. The profession was stripped of its essentially canonical elements and adapted to suit the centralised and apostolic character of the order.[118] The chapter on dress was also edited.[119] The introduction, including a quotation from

---

ordinance appears in Francis's *Regula prima* (1221) and the *Regula bullata* (1223) (ed. H. Boehmer, *Analekten*, pp. 11 and 23 respectively). It was perhaps interpolated in the Dominican constitutions around the same time. – Similarly, the second sentence of c. 33 ("Nullus assumatur … infra viginti quinque annos") is of a later date (cf. *infra*, p. 410, note 241).

112 CA, II, 37.

113 A different view is defended by P. Mandonnet – M. H. Vicaire, *Saint Dominique*, vol. II, p. 230.

114 There was no specific chapter on the *conversi* in the twelfth-century Premonstratensian text (Pa). See also Pl. F. Lefèvre, *Les statuts de Prémontré*, pp. 110-111, with footnote 1 on p. 110.

115 A lay friar joined the priest friars who were sent to Paris: "…habentes secum conversum Normannum, cui nomen Oderius" (Jordan, *Libellus*, no. 51; cf. *Proc. Bon.*, no. 26). A charter of July 1216 on Saint Romanus's church does state: "…et quod ibi habere et facere possint cimeterium ad opus fratrum suorum canonicorum et conversorum professorum" (Laurent, no. 70), but this legal stipulation does not necessarily mean that *conversi* had then already joined the order.

116 See Jordan, *Libellus*, no. 55.

117 See the testimony of John of Spain (*Proc. Bon.*, no. 26), quoted on p. 384, footnote 81. The same witness stated that Dominic abandoned this plan due to the opposition of the priest friars (*ibid.*). We may presume that this happened on the occasion of the general chapter of 1220, all the more so because the passage referred to in *Proc. Bon.* immediately follows the same chapter's ordinance to relinquish all landed possessions (compare Jordan, *op. cit.*, no. 87, with *Proc. Bon.*, no. 26, and CA, II, 26).

118 The sources do not give any date for this change in the formula of profession. But in its current form, the formula in the constitutions (CA, I, 16; cf. *supra*, pp. 297-302) cannot have been in use before 1220, because it mentions the *magister ordinis* (cf. *supra*, p. 238, with note 300). On the other hand, it does not appear to be aware yet of any *prior provincialis*, so that we may presume that it was drawn up before 1221.

119 CA, I, 19.

the gospel, derived from the statutes of Prémontré, was replaced by an exhortation to keep monastic dress as frugal as possible.[120] Contemporaries ascribed the initiative for these ordinances to Dominic himself.[121]

After the general chapter of 1220, the legal code consisted of the first *distinctio*, which contained the *consuetudines* or regular customs, and a substantial part of the second *distinctio*, encompassing the *constitutiones* proper, specifically the first stipulations on the organisation and remit of the general chapter,[122] the government of the monasteries,[123] studies,[124] preaching,[125] and finally, as a kind of appendix, a succinct *regula conversorum*.[126] By contrast with the first *distinctio*, where the text was divided into many chapters each with their own title, and following the example of the statutes of Prémontré, the second *distinctio* was not initially arranged into the sometimes very short chapters that appear in the Rodez manuscript. The entire series of new stipulations originally perhaps consisted of a small number of rather long sections, under four or five titles, that corresponded with the subjects mentioned above and with the summary of the contents of this part at the end of the *prologus*.[127]

C. The general chapter of 1221

Ever since 1220, the annual general chapters had regularly added stipulations to the constitutions as the expansion of the order and the evolution of its institutions required. No substantial changes were made to the first *distinctio* before the new redaction by Raymond of Peñafort. The second *distinctio* was further enlarged by the addition of laws on the organisation and governance of the provinces,

---

120 Cf. *supra*, p. 384, with footnote 80.

121 Testimony of John of Spain: "…quia in vilibus vestibus gloriabatur" (*Proc. Bon.*, no. 27); testimony of Rudolf: "Et volebat quod haberent parvas domos et viles vestes" (*ibid.*, no. 32); testimony of Stephen: "Unde iniunxit eis, ut vilibus vestibus uterentur … Et hoc fecit in regula sua scribi" (*ibid.*, no. 38; see also no. 42). Due to its close connection with the stricter observance of collective poverty, which was also enacted in 1220 (see *supra*, p. 376, note 23), this ordinance on dress is best ascribed to the first general chapter.

122 Including not only the parts that still refer to the general chapter in the Rodez manuscript (d. II, c. 13, last sentence: "Capitulum … celebretur"; c. 17-18, c. 19 (partially) and c. 20-21), but also the regulations on the *diffinitores* (d. II, c. 1), which were originally intended for the general chapter, but later applied to the provincial chapter (see *supra*, pp. 385-386).

123 Viz. d. II, c. 23: "Conventus … non mittatur"; c. 24: "Priores conventuales a suis conventibus eligantur"; c. 25, *De suppriore*; c. 26: "Possessiones seu redditus nullo modo recipiantur"; c. 35: "Mediocres domos et humiles habeant fratres nostri".

124 D. II, c. 28-29.

125 D. II, c. 31, c. 32: "Cum fratres … obedientes erunt"; c. 33: "Caveant fratres … emendare procurent"; c. 34: "Predicatores … aliquando conversantur".

126 D. II, c. 37.

127 Without the reference to the *capitulum provinciale*, which was added after 1221, this part of the *prologus* would have read as follows in 1220: "De capitulo generali et studio et predicatione". The rules on the monastery and the *conversi* were therefore not announced, neither in the Rodez manuscript nor in that of the Friars of the Sack (cf. G. M. Giacomozzi, *L'Ordine della Penitenza*, p. 74).

the election of the diffinitors for the general chapter, the master general and the provincials. These new chapters were not placed at the end, but were collated to form the first part of the second *distinctio*[128] and were more or less logically arranged alongside the ordinances of 1220 that defined the tasks of the *diffinitores* at the general chapter. Various sections and fragments can be dated with the aid of the *Acta capitulorum* of 1236. The lack of the earlier chapter reports makes it impossible to reconstruct the growth of the legislation from year to year from 1221 to 1236. Only the *praeambulum* that precedes the text of the constitutions in the Rodez manuscript mentions a number of ordinances issued in or before 1228.

The appointment of *diffinitores* in 1220 gave the subjects a say in the government of the order.[129] We may assume that the general chapter of that year also addressed their powers and role. In accordance with Dominic's wishes, they were given full and supreme legislative power, the task to decide issues raised during the sessions and the task to judge the policies of the master general. All this is the subject of three chapters (7-9) in the second *distinctio*,[130] which were, however, probably not included in the constitutions until after 1220, as they would otherwise have been inserted after c. 17, *De capitulo generali*, which introduces the earliest text on the general chapter of the Dominicans.[131] Their actual place, under separate titles, among stipulations on issues discussed only after 1220, is an indication that they cannot have been composed before 1221.[132]

---

128 Chapters 1-16.

129 See *supra*, pp. 385-386.

130 C. 7, *De diffinitoribus generalis capituli*; c. 8, *De potestate diffinitorum*; c. 9, *De excessu magistri corrigendo*.

131 For the same reason we may assume that the last sentence of c. 16 ("Et ea que dicta sunt de generali capitulo, in secunda feria post Pentecosten debent inchoari") was similarly added after 1220, together with c. 7-9. It was intended as a further clarification of the date on which the general chapter was to begin. But it cannot have been composed in 1220 together with c. 17-21, because then it would have been integrated into those chapters. Nor does it occur, incidentally, in the texts of the Friars of the Sack, which is a further indication that it is a later addition (see previous footnote). The striking conflict between the clarification ("in secunda feria") in question and the first sentence of c. 17 ("in quarta feria") is due to the fact that the latter words (which do not occur in the text of the Friars of the Sack) are an interpolation, probably made after the chapters on the election of the master general had been composed. These stipulated that the electors must gather "in secunda feria post Pentecosten" (c. 10), so that the master general would have been elected on the Wednesday after Pentecost at the latest, whereupon the chapter could begin its work: "... ut semper in quarta feria Pentecostes magistrum habeat capitulum, ... quia tunc incipit solemniter celebrari, ..." (c. 11). When the words "in quarta feria" were inserted in c. 17, the editors possibly forgot to make the required adjustment in the immediately preceding sentence of c. 16, which thus mistakenly retained "in secunda feria post Pentecosten".

132 Certain texts of a later date can be identified in these chapters: in c. 7 the words "duodecim diffinitores duobus annis et duodecim priores provinciales tertio anno", which are not just an application of the ordinance adopted in 1225 on the task of the diffinitors and the provincials at the general chapter (see *infra*, p. 396), but also presuppose the existence of twelve provinces. C. 8 originally consisted only of the first part, up to and including "appellatio habeatur". The rest, in the first person plural, is of a later date (see *infra*, p. 404, footnote 207). The second section of c. 9 ("Mortuo autem magistro...") contains parts that were added after 1221 (see *infra*, p. 398, footnote 169).

The laws on the organisation and government of the provinces make up a considerable part of the constitutions issued after 1220.[133] Their *terminus a quo* is the second general chapter of 1221, which erected the first provinces of the order.[134] The chapters in the second *distinctio* that address this issue must have existed in essence before 1228. This *terminus ante quem* is implicitly indicated in the *praeambulum* added to the text of the constitutions by the *capitulum generalissimum* of that year.[135] It presupposes the existence of the provinces, each with their own superior and chapter, which had the authority to appoint delegates to the general chapter.[136] The legislation evolved quite strongly during this period, and traces of this can still be found in the arrangement of the text.

The organisation of the provincial chapter and the role of the provincial are addressed in various places in the constitutions: the beginning (c. 1-4) and middle (c. 15-16) of the second *distinctio*. This order does not reflect the chronological sequence in which these parts were drafted, but resulted from an attempt to come to a logical arrangement of the texts. The chapters on the provincial chapter were placed at the beginning, immediately before the rules on the general chapter, because of the organic connection between the two institutions – the composition of the general chapter was determined to a large extent by the provincial chapter.[137] By contrast, everything on the appointment and authority of the provincial was placed at the back, as c. 15-16, after the rules on the election of the master general. These two chapters only gradually acquired their final form. Their oldest cores can be easily recognised by the archaism of the expressions *provincia vel regnum* and *prior provincialis vel regnorum*, which still contain echoes of canon 12 of the Fourth Lateran Council.[138] These parts possibly date from 1221, when the first provincials were appointed.[139] The stipulation on the date and place of the provincial chapter, which was retained somewhat incongruously in c. 16, similarly still contains the older terminology and may therefore be regarded as the earliest constitutional regulation on the provincial chapter.[140] It partly contains the same

---

133 CA, II, 1-4, 15-16; to a certain extent also II, 5 (see *infra*, p. 396).

134 See *supra*, pp. 344-345.

135 On the meaning of this *praeambulum*, see *infra*, pp. 403-404.

136 "Anno ab incarnatione Domini 1228 convenerunt Parisius in domo sancti Iacobi [octo] priores provinciales … singuli cum duobus diffinitoribus sibi a provincialibus capitulis deputatis…" See also M. H. Vicaire, *Histoire*, vol. II, p. 315, note 57.

137 According to CA, II, 5. See the text quoted on p. 396, footnote 162.

138 See *supra*, pp. 343 and 346.

139 See *supra*, p. 344.

140 D. II, c. 16: "Capitulum provinciale in festo sancti Michaelis in loco statuto in provincia vel regno, ubi prior provinciarum vel regnorum cum consilio diffinitorum elegerit, celebretur". For the dating (1224), see *infra*, p. 396, note 160. The rule appears to be out of place here and should normally have been moved to the first part of dist. II, which addresses the provincial chapter (c. 1-4). However, it did occupy this place originally in the Dominican constitutions, not only in the Rodez manuscript, but also in that of the Friars of the Sack, although the words "in festo sancti Michaelis" and "vel regno(rum)" were omitted in the latter (ed. G. M. Giacomozzi, *L'Ordine della Penitenza*, p. 99).

content as the ordinance that was later inserted at the beginning of the second *distinctio*.[141]

Chapters 15-16 contain the first laws on the organisation of the provinces. In their original redaction, which perhaps dates from 1221, they consisted only of a brief indication of the manner in which the provincial was to be appointed and of a rather vague description of his authority.[142] The first provincials were not elected but appointed by the general chapter.[143] This appointment procedure was set out at the time in the first section of c. 15, which was later changed and expanded to entrust the election to the provincial chapter, while assigning the right of confirmation to the general chapter.[144] The election procedure that immediately follows was also defined on this occasion.[145] The ordinance stipulating that the master general may also personally confirm the election was added later.[146] Finally, three further stipulations were added in 1236.[147] The title *De potestate prioris provincialis* (c. 16) only applies to the first part of this chapter. The second part

---

141 "Prior provincialis etiam cum suis diffinitoribus in capitulo provinciali semper locum determinet ubi sequens capitulum celebretur" (d. II, c. 4). It cannot be deduced from the fact that the Fourth Lateran Council, upon which the Dominicans depended in certain respects, did not order the erection of provinces but only the organisation of regular chapters, that the Dominicans introduced the provincial chapter at the same time as, or even before, the provinces (1221), as M. H. Vicaire, *Histoire*, vol. II, p. 305, note 14, appears to do.

142 This primitive legislation perhaps consisted only of one continuous text, introduced by *statuimus*: "Statuimus ut provinciarum priores ... vel amoveantur" (c. 15, beginning); "Provincialis autem prior ... extiterit" (c. 16, beginning); "Curet prior provincialis ... revocati" (c. 16, middle).

143 The earliest testimony for this comes from Jordan of Saxony, who says that he was appointed provincial of Lombardy by the chapter of 1221 (*Libellus*, no. 88). This manner of appointment was the only one possible at the time. On the origin of the provinces, see *supra*, pp. 344-345.

144 C. 15, end of the first section: "Nam eorum electio ad provinciale capitulum pertinebit". Because this stipulation mentions the provincial chapter, it may have been added around 1225 (cf. *infra*, pp. 395-396). The interpolation is clearly recognisable. The future tense "pertinebit" means something like: the election will henceforth be made by the provincial chapter. Incidentally, this sentence appears in a different place in the constitutions of the Friars of the Sack, which indicates that it was an additional correction (cf. Appendix I, in the critical apparatus of the edition of the text). This adaptation of the text perhaps even took place in 1225, that is, from the establishment of the provincial chapters, which, as representative assemblies, could also appoint the superiors of the provinces, just like the monasteries could elect their own superior according to the constitutions (d. II, c. 24). Cf. M. H. Vicaire, *Saint Dominique de Caleruega*, p. 121, footnote 39. – Previously, this first section of c. 15 perhaps read as follows: "Statuimus ut priores provinciales ... instituantur et amoveantur". *Institutio* referred to appointment by a higher authority, as in d. II, c. 25: "Prior ... instituat suppriorem...". When the change was made as per the interpolation, the previous sentence was possibly also adapted to assume its current form.

145 "Mortuo igitur ... non oporteat" (c. 15).

146 "Statuimus ut magister solus possit confirmare priorem provincialem" (c. 15). This ordinance corrects the first section, which presumes that the master general and the *diffinitores* would be together at the general chapter. The new text gives the general the authority to confirm the elections of provincials in between two chapters. This stipulation was issued between 1225 and 1235.

147 In c. 15: "Item provinciali priore ... transferatur" (*Acta C.G.*, p. 8); "Item volumus ... convocatis" (*ibid.*, p. 7). – In c. 16: "Item priores provinciales ... vices suas" (*ibid.*, p. 6).

contains two ordinances on the provincial chapter and ends with a rule intended as an introduction to the laws on the general chapter.[148]

The Dominicans composed the greater part of their earliest constitutions during the rather short period that elapsed between the foundation of the order and Dominic's death. They organised communal life within their monasteries on the basis of the Premonstratensian *consuetudines*, which were adopted in 1216, possibly together with a number of additional customs of the canons of Osma, and which form the entire first *distinctio*. In addition, the chapters of 1220 and 1221 laid the foundations for the legislation on the structure and administration of the order, the provinces and the houses. Also, rules were formulated for study and for the apostolate. Together with the *regula conversorum* and a number of regulations that bear Dominic's personal imprint, these *constitutiones* encompassed more than half of the second *distinctio* and formed the core of the legal code of the Dominican Order.

Section II. The constitutions during Jordan of Saxony's generalate

When Jordan of Saxony was elected Dominic's successor by the general chapter of Paris in 1221, he accepted the task to guide the order in its further development and adapt its structure and legislation to the new requirements. Apart from the normal additions to the constitutions, two issues in particular appear to have attracted his attention from the beginning of his tenure. The first concerned the proper task and significance of the provinces that had been founded since 1221. A solution was sought over the following years by issuing rules on the government of the provinces and on the participation of their representatives in the government of the order as a whole at the general chapter. The constitutional regulations for this were for the most part drafted before 1228. The second issue was to do with the system of legislation itself. Initially, the constitutions could be supplemented and revised every year by the general chapter. The advantages of flexibility and of being able to adapt quickly that this system had perhaps did not outweigh the inconveniences it also entailed. The general chapter of 1228 addressed this problem and issued a number of guidelines to ensure the regularity

---

148 "Capitulum provinciale … celebretur" (cf. *infra*, p. 396, note 160); "Nullus religiosus … aliquo modo admittatur"; "Et ea que dicta sunt … debent inchoari" (for the connection between this stipulation and legislation on the general chapter, see *supra*, p. 390, note 131). Given the similarity between the second ordinance ("Nullus religiosus …") and the capitular customs of the Cistercians (see *supra*, p. 338) one might be inclined to apply it to the general chapter of the Dominicans and therefore also see it as an introduction to the following chapter (c. 17). But in his codification, Raymond of Peñafort placed this rule in the chapter *De capitulo provinciali* (d. II, c. 6) (see R. Creytens, *Les constitutions … de s. Raymond de Peñafort*, pp. 56-57). Perhaps he was preserving the sequence of the earliest legislation.

and continuity of the legislation. This chapter thus marked the start of a second phase in Jordan's policy. As these two periods each have their own significance for the development of the legislation, they will be discussed in two separate sections.

§ 1. The legislation from 1222 to 1228

A. The provincial chapter

Just like the general chapter was instituted a few years after the foundation of the order, the organisation of the provincial chapter must perhaps be situated chronologically after the erection of the provinces. The year 1221 must therefore be viewed more as the *terminus post quem* than as the year in which the provincial chapter was founded. Early sources other than the constitutions are extremely vague and give little information.[149] According to a catalogue from the fourteenth century, whose compiler appears to have had access to documents containing specific details, the first chapter of the German province was held in Magdeburg in 1226.[150] But the *Teutonia* may not have been founded before 1223. It may be assumed, therefore, that the older provinces, which had been in existence since 1221 and had several monasteries even before that year, also held their provincial chapter before 1226.[151]

The laws on the provincial chapter, in the first four chapters of the second *distinctio*, initially consisted of a single section, introduced by a *statuimus*. They comprised a brief guide for the discussion of the most important points on the agenda. The whole text was simply an extensive adaptation of the earlier rules on the general chapter, including a number of interpolated passages.[152] There

---

149 The *acta* of the earliest provincial chapters have been handed down only fragmentarily. For the province of Provence (since 1239), see C. Douais, *Acta capitulorum provincialium Ordinis Fratrum Praedicatorum*, Toulouse, 1894. For the Roman province: *Acta capitulorum provincialium provinciae Romanae (1243-1344)*, ed. Th. Kaeppeli – A. Dondaine, Rome, 1941. There are references to earlier provincial chapters, for instance for Lombardy (1227): cf. G. Odetto, *La Cronaca maggiore dell'Ordine domenicano di Galvano Fiamma*, in *Arch. F.P.*, vol. X, 1940, p. 325. For England (1230): cf. W. A. Hinnebusch, *The Early English Friars Preachers*, p. 1.

150 "Beatus Conradus eligitur MCCXXI. Primum capitulum celebravit in Madenburg MCCXXVI, tantum novem fratribus extraneis supervenientibus" (P. von Loë, *Statistisches über die Ordensprovinz Teutonia*, Anhang I, p. 23). For the catalogue in question, see *ibid.*, p. 11. The author also quotes the *acta* of the provincial chapter of Trier of the year 1236 (*ibid.*, p. 23). For France, M. D. Chapotin, *Histoire des dominicains de la province de France*, pp. 47-48, mentions a provincial chapter in Paris in 1222, together with the general chapter, but without referencing any sources.

151 See *supra*, pp. 344-345.

152 The second half of c. 1 ("Nullus prior conventualis … nisi a provinciali"), which even contains ordinances from 1236 (see *infra*, p. 409, footnote 234), is of a later date. The first sentence of c. 4 deals with another issue and interrupts the train of thought: "Statuimus etiam … et confirmatus". See also *supra*, p. 373, footnote 10.

is a striking parallelism between the two series of texts.[153] The election of the *diffinitores* is discussed first, then their remit and work methods, and finally their powers vis-à-vis the provincial and the general respectively. These two groups of stipulations were very clearly drafted in coherence with each other, but the texts on the general chapter, which were derived to a certain extent from the customs of the Cistercians, came first chronologically.[154] The titles were added later and do not always match the content of the chapters.[155]

The following two chapters (c. 5-6) offer clues for a more precise dating of the laws on the provincial chapter. C. 6 exhorts the provincials and elected diffinitors to avoid all partisanship in their decisions at the general chapter.[156] According to

---

153 The title of d. II, c. 1 (*De capitulo provinciali*) does not fully match the content of this chapter; the title in the constitutions of the Friars of the Sack is more apt: *De electione diffinitorum capituli provincialis* (ed. G. M. Giacomozzi, *L'Ordine della Penitenza*, p. 91). –The following is a schematic overview of the two series of chapters in the Dominican text.

Prov. chapt.	Gen. chapt.
C. 1. *De electione diffinitorum capituli provincialis*	C. 5. *De electione capituli generalis diffinitoris*
"… quatuor fratres de discretioribus … hoc modo eligantur … donec in parte altera maior possit numerus inveniri."	(Originally the same text as for the provincial chapter. Later replaced by the current text: cf. *supra*, pp. 385-386)
C. 2. *De diffinitoribus capituli provincialis*	C. 7. *De diffinitoribus generalis capituli*
"Predicti igitur diffinitores tractabunt omnia et diffinient cum priore provinciali. Quod si in suis diffinitionibus in partes equales se diviserint, illorum sententia prevalebit, in quorum partem prior provincialis concordaverit. Alias autem sententia plurium prevalebit."	"Isti autem … diffinitores … cum magistro ordinis omnia diffinient et constituent et tractabunt. Quod si in partes equales se diviserint, illorum sententia prevalebit, in quorum partem magister ordinis declinaverit. Si vero in partes inequales, obtineat sententia plurium."
C. 3. *De potestate horum diffinitorum*	C. 8. *De potestate diffinitorum*
"Isti autem quatuor diffinitores	"Isti autem diffinitores …
	C. 9. *De excessu magistri corrigendo*
excessum prioris provincialis … emendent … Si autem, quod absit, incorrigibilis extiterit…"	Diffinitores predicti excessum magistri … corrigant et emendent. Si autem in tantum excesserit, quod removeri debeat…

154 See *supra*, p. 336.

155 The title *De diffinitoribus capituli provincialis* (c. 2) also includes the material of c. 3 and c. 4 and might more accurately have been replaced by the title of c. 3, *De potestate (horum) diffinitorum*. The title of c. 4, *Quis obtineat*, only covers the first half of the chapter. It was apparently added together with this first sentence ("Statuimus … et confirmatus") and is more fitting for c. 15-16. It separates c. 3 and the second half of c. 4, which originally belonged together, as the parallelism with the chapters on the general chapter shows.

156 D. II, c. 6, *De preiudicio vitando*: "Statuimus autem … ne priores provinciales fratribus diffinitoribus aut fratres diffinitores prioribus provincialibus per suas diffinitiones preiudicium aliquod audeant generare. Quod si facere attentaverint, eadem districtione prohibemus ne in hoc eis aliquis presumat obedire".

the *praeambulum*, this ordinance was already part of the constitutions in 1228.[157] The severe penalty that accompanied this warning leads us to assume that the actions of the two groups who alternately constituted the general chapter, as c. 5 describes,[158] had given rise to certain difficulties. This means the system must already have been functioning for at least two years, in 1226 and 1227, and must therefore have been given force of law at the latest in 1225.[159] The fifth chapter in turn presupposes the existence and organisation of the provincial chapter, to which the election of *diffinitores* for the general chapter had been entrusted. The first redaction of the legislation on the provincial chapter, described in c. 1-4, must therefore also have been part of the constitutions already in 1225. But these stipulations are more technical in nature and therefore possibly came later than the ordinances in c. 16, which still preserve the terminology of the Fourth Lateran Council.[160]

The fifth chapter of the second *distinctio* in a certain sense still belongs to the legislation on the provinces, as its main subject are the *diffinitores generales*, who were elected by the provincial chapter. At the same time, it serves as an introduction to the new section, which had previously already described the composition and activities of the general chapter.[161] In 1225, c. 5 perhaps contained no more than a brief outline of how the provinces were represented at the general chapter, alternately through their *diffinitor* and their provincial. This oldest core consists, in somewhat altered form, of the first and third sentences.[162] The stipulations on the

---

157 "Inter constitutiones autem ... et quod non possit per fratres diffinitores prioribus provincialibus neque per priores fratribus in suis diffinitionibus in aliquo preiudicium generari".

158 See the quoted text *infra*, footnote 162.

159 The importance of these texts was pointed out by M. H. Vicaire, *Histoire*, vol. II, p. 315, note 57.

160 "Capitulum provinciale in festo sancti Michaelis in loco statuto in provincia vel regno, ubi prior provinciarum vel regnorum cum consilio diffinitorum elegerit, celebretur". This stipulation was drafted before 1225, possibly in 1224. It appears to be older than d. II, c. 4 ("Prior provincialis ... celebretur"), which addresses the same issue, but no longer uses the term *regnum* (cf. *supra*, pp. 391-392, with footnotes 140-141). Moreover, the provincial chapter in d. II, c. 4 looks more like an established institution consisting of the provincial and the *diffinitores* who take decisions together, while d. II, c. 16 still portrays the *diffinitores* as the counsellors of the provincial ("cum consilio diffinitorum"). The fixing of the date upon which the provincial chapter must begin, "in festo sancti Michaelis" (29 September), is perhaps connected to the custom of the Franciscans of meeting in the various regions on the same date, as the *Regula prima*, c. 18, stipulated: "Quolibet anno unusquisque minister cum fratribus suis potest convenire, ubicumque placuerit eis, in festo S. Michaelis archangeli de hiis, quae ad Deum pertinent, tractaturi" (ed. H. Boehmer, *Analekten*, p. 12). But it is clear that this did not refer to a governing body of a limited number of representatives, but a kind of public meeting for the purposes of fraternisation between all the friars. As the *Regula bullata* (1223), c. 8, shows, however, such assemblies were not obligatory and were left to the initiative of the *ministri et custodes* "si voluerint et eis expedire videbitur" (*ed. cit.*, p. 23).

161 This section contained a number of stipulations, mostly dating from 1221 (cf. *supra*, p. 390, with footnotes 130-132), spread across chapters 7-9.

162 "Statuimus etiam ut per duos annos in dictarum *octo* provinciarum capitulis aliquis de magis idoneis a capitulo eligatur, qui sit generalis capituli diffinitor ... Tertio autem anno priores *duodecim* provinciarum generale capitulum celebrabunt". The words in italics are not original.

socius appear to have been added later to provide for situations, which had perhaps actually occurred, in which the representative of a province at the general chapter was suddenly unable to attend.[163] The section which acknowledges the right of the four *provinciae superadditae* to be represented must also be an interpolation, as these provinces did not yet exist or were not yet sufficiently developed in 1225 to hold a chapter of their own to delegate a representative to the general chapter.[164] If it is stripped of later additions, c. 5 is very much like the beginning of the first part of the second *distinctio*.[165]

B. Stipulations on the government of the order

The rules on the government of the order during a vacancy of the generalate are consistent with the legislation on the general chapter. The diffinitors have the power to judge the general's policies and, if needs be, to remove him from office.[166] In the interval, the central authority is not exercised by any one single person, but by a group: the college of provincials. It is clear from the manner in which their powers are described that they were to meet in person from time to time. They had to be able to exchange ideas, take decisions and, if necessary, appeal to other members of the order to reach agreement in case of disputes.[167]

---

163 "Cui socius competens … diffinitor habeatur". The interpolation is especially clear in the stipulation on the *socius* of the provincial: "Item statuimus…".

164 "Statuimus quod quatuor provincie … in singulis capitulis generalibus". For the origins of the four new provinces, see *infra*, pp. 401-402.

165 The parallelism between the two texts is clear.

C. 1	C. 5
"Statuimus quod singulis annis in singulis capitulis provincialibus … quatuor fratres de discretioribus et magis idoneis a capitulo provinciali … eligantur."	"Statuimus etiam ut per duos annos in dictarum provinciarum capitulis aliquis de magis idoneis a capitulo eligatur."

Moreover, the texts should be compared with the beginning of the decree of the Fourth Lateran Council: "In singulis regnis sive provinciis fiat de triennio in triennium … commune capitulum" (see *supra*, p. 329, footnote 260).

166 D. II, c. 9: "Diffinitores predicti … honeste conversari".

167 D. II, c. 9: "Mortuo autem magistro vel a magisterio remoto, priores dictarum provinciarum in omnibus, quousque magister fuerit electus, plenariam ipsius obtineant potestatem, et eis omnes tamquam magistro teneantur obedire. Si autem inter se medio tempore super aliquo discordaverint, obtineat sententia plurium. Quod si partes fuerint pares, assumant unum de fratribus illis qui vocem habent in electione magistri, et cui parti ille concordaverit, vigorem obtineat firmitatis. Quod si adhuc discordaverint, iterum alius eligatur, et sic deinceps, donec in parte altera maior possit numerus inveniri". This arrangement is somewhat reminiscent of the customs of the Cistercians, particularly the meetings during which the abbot of Cîteaux, the *quatuor primi abbates* and other abbots dealt with particular business (see *supra*, p. 335, footnote 287). But this intermediate collegial form of government entailed certain difficulties for the Dominicans once provinces became numerous, given their geographical distance from each other. The chapters of 1274-1276 adopted a different arrangement, in which the government of the order during an intermediate period was entrusted

This section as it is cannot have been drafted in its entirety in 1221, as the associated chapters were.[168] Certain expressions give rise to the suspicion that additions were made to the original text in 1222 and later.[169]

The election of the master general is discussed in chapters 10-11. The inclusion of a definitive, detailed procedure proved urgent when Dominic died in 1221. The chapter of Pentecost 1222 appointed Jordan of Saxony as his successor.[170] The ceremonial used on the occasion of his election cannot have been identical in its particulars to the guidelines in the constitutions, as there were not yet twelve provinces in 1222 each with their own chapter that could have appointed one or two electors in addition to the provincial.[171] Nevertheless, the chapters in question, at least their oldest parts, do appear to have been part of the legislation before 1228.[172] The chapter *De forma electionis* (c. 11) even contains material from 1220-1221. It quotes passages verbatim from preceding parts which describe the election of the diffinitors and the procedure to be followed for consultations

---

to a single individual: the provincial of the province where the next general chapter was to be held (*Acta C.G.*, pp. 172, 178, 182). – The Friars of the Sack, who derived their text from the Dominicans after 1252, worked around the difficulty by granting the provincials full authority for their own province: "Mortuo autem ... priores provinciales in suis provinciis in omnibus ... plenariam habeant potestatem..." (ed. G. M. Giacomozzi, *L'Ordine delle Penitenza*, p. 94).

168 See *supra*, p. 390, with footnote 130.

169 As the first part of d. II, c. 9 ("Diffinitores predicti ... honeste conversari") only discusses the case of the removal from office of the master general, one would expect the second section to begin with the words "Magistro a magisterio remoto...". The two words "Mortuo autem", with which this section currently begins, may have been added by the chapter of 1222, after Dominic's death. Nor did the expression "priores dictarum provinciarum" (eight provinces) reflect reality as it was in 1221 (cf. *supra*, pp. 344-345). Furthermore, the section mentions the electors who choose the general: "qui vocem habent in electione magistri". But these *electores* were to be appointed by the provincial chapter (d. II, c. 10). Again, this is a rule that was not issued before 1225 (cf. *supra*, p. 396, and *infra*, footnote 171).

170 *Acta C.G.*, p. 2.

171 D. II, c. 10: "Predicti ergo priores provinciales ... singuli cum duobus fratribus in capitulo provinciali electis, ... et quatuor priores provinciales de superadditis provinciis, ... singuli cum singulis ad hoc idem electis...".

172 The last part of c. 10 ("Et hoc tam ab electoribus ... sustinebit") and the third section of c. 11 ("Et hec omnia ... subiaceat") date from 1228 (see *infra*, p. 405, note 208). These sanctions presuppose the preceding regulations (except the parts that were added later: cf. *infra*, note 174).

during the provincial and general chapters.[173] The first section was altered in 1236, but it retains certain elements of the original version.[174]

A similar development must have taken place in respect of the chapter *De morte magistri*,[175] which is comprised of two parts in the Rodez manuscript. A first section deals with the prompt announcement of the death of the general.[176] The second section consists exclusively of the ordinance of 1220 that the general chapter was to be held alternately in Paris and Bologna.[177] The connection between

---

173 The votes at the election of the master general (d. II, c. 11) are taken in the same way as at the provincial chapter (c. 1):

C. 11	C. 1
"… tres de prioribus provincialibus … voluntates singulorum singillatim et seorsum aliquantulum, tamen in eadem domo, coram oculis omnium disquirant et conscribant."	"Predicti siquidem tres … voluntates singulorum singillatim et seorsum aliquantulum, coram oculis omnium disquirant et conscribant fideliter."

For the connection between this passage and canon 42 of the Lateran Council, see *supra*, p. 342. The parallelism between the guidelines for the election of the master general (c. 11) and the texts on the provincial (c. 4) and the general chapter (c. 7) is also evident from the way in which the various possible cases are listed and organised:
a) "Si vero in partes inequales se diviserint…" (c. 11);
    cf. "Si vero in partes inequales …" (c. 7);
b) "Quod si aliquem vel aliquos … contigerit non venire…" (c. 11);
    cf. "Quod si ipsum abesse contigerit …" (c. 4);
    "Quod si … non omnes venerint…" (c. 7);
    "Quod si magistrum abesse … contigerit …" (*Ibid.*).
Only the possibility of a tied vote, which was mentioned so often in the previous chapters (see in c. 1: "Si autem partes fuerint pares…"; in c. 2: "Quod si … in partes equales se diviserint…"; in c. 7: "Quod si in partes equales se diviserint…"; "Si autem … partes fiant equales…"; in c. 9: "Quod si partes fuerint pares…"), is not mentioned in relation to the election of the master general. Instead, there is a reference to unanimity of the vote: "Quod si, gratia Dei inspirante, in unum aliquem omnes unanimiter concordaverint…". See on this *supra*, p. 349.
174 The chapter reports of 1236 (*Acta C.G.*, p. 8) do not clearly show what the text used to be. Nor are they a good source for the new text, as they partially deviate from the *Constitutiones antiquae*, which are identical to the later redaction of the legislation: constitutions of Raymond (d. II, 4: R. Creytens, *Les constitutions … de s. Raymond de Peñafort*, p. 53); constitutions of Humbert (d. II, c. 4: *Anal. O.P.*, vol. V-VI (1897-1898), pp. 108-109); fourteenth-century constitutions (d. II, c. 4: G. R. Galbraith, *The Constitution*, p. 233). According to the *Acta*, the correction of 1236 deleted an older text which at the time immediately preceded the words "Quod si aliquem…": "…et huius constitutionis sit magister, cetera radantur usque: Quod si aliquem etc." (*Acta C.G.*, p. 8). What was this lost text about? It was possibly an ordinance for the case of a tied vote. If this hypothesis is correct, the original parallelism with the previous chapters would have been complete (see the end of the previous footnote). – It is possible that it originally described the third mode of election that canon 24 of the Fourth Lateran Council indicates: *per compromissum* (cf. *supra*, p. 349, footnote 380, which says that this procedure was subsequently dropped by the Dominicans, but reintroduced in 1240-1242).
175 CA, II, 13.
176 "Si ante festum … ubi prius debuerat celebrari".
177 "Capitulum generale uno anno Parisius, alio anno Bononie celebretur". Cf. Jordan, *Libellus*, no. 87.

the two parts is loose and artificial.[178] The first part, certainly if it is taken as a whole, is a few years younger than the second, as it already mentions eight provinces. On the other hand, it is remarkable that the four *provinciae minores* are not yet mentioned, so that the final redaction of the text must be dated to shortly after 1225. The list of provinces, which overloads and unnaturally extends the text, has all the characteristics of an interpolation.[179] But this means the original parts of the text must be a few years older and may perhaps date to the period during which the first core of the chapters *De electione magistri* was drafted: circa 1222. This rather early dating is not exceptional if we realise that there were models for the Dominicans in the form of similar regulations in the legislation of the Templars, the Gilbertines and the Hospitallers of the Holy Spirit.[180] They probably used written monastic statutes in the first redaction and then a few years later revised this section and adapted it to the situation created by the rapid expansion of the order across various provinces.

The original Dominican version possibly more closely resembled Innocent III's bull for the Order of the Holy Spirit, where the alternative concerned not the time, but the place of the general's death: "citra montes ... ultra montes". It is interesting that the Dominicans, like the Hospitallers, in fact also had two centres that are both mentioned in the text: Paris (*ultra montes*) and Bologna (*citra montes*). One of these, depending on the place of death, had to transmit the announcement to the rest. This alternative was retained in the Dominican text, but was given lower importance. The emphasis lies primarily on the time of death in the way the regulation is formulated. This shift can be explained as an adaptation of the legislation to the altered organisation of the order, as the provincial chapters around 1225 acquired the authority to appoint the *electores* of the master general (d. II, c. 10). But as the date of the provincial chapter was fixed for Michaelmas (29 September) (d. II, c. 16), the provinces would not have been able to legally elect their representatives if the master general died after that date. That is why in that case, the general chapter had to be postponed, so that the

---

178   It is not clear who was responsible for this title and the joining together of the two texts: the Rodez copyist or the drafters of the constitution. There are no points of comparison. The two texts are separated in Raymond's edition: the first section ("Statuimus ut, si ante festum ...") there appears in d. II, c. 4, *De electione magistri*, but without the last sentence "Sequenti vero ... celebrari", which was omitted (cf. R. Creytens, *Les constitutions ... de s. Raymond de Peñafort*, pp. 51-52; p. 25 with footnote 63). The second part is in d. II, c. 8, *De capitulo generali* (cf. ed. cit., p. 57). The chapter is missing entirely in the text of the Friars of the Sack.

179   The formula with which the first sentence ends naturally ("...teneatur similiter reliquis nuntiare") is repeated after the list of provinces: "...teneatur quam citius intimare". The list does not entirely deliver on the announcement in the first sentence: the transmission of the announcement of a death from monastery to monastery: "Et alteruter istorum conventuum ... teneatur similiter reliquis nuntiare". Immediately afterwards, the text speaks instead about communicating the announcement to the superiors of the provinces.

180   See H. de Curzon, *La règle du Temple*, p. 143 (nos. 200-201); *Regulae Ord. Sempringensis*, c. 3, in L. Holstenius – M. Brockie, *Codex regularum*, vol. II, p. 468; the bull *Inter opera pietatis* by Innocent III for the hospital of Montpellier, 18 June 1204, in PL, vol. 215, col. 378, respectively.

provinces could appoint their representatives for the general chapter of the next year (Pentecost) on the following 29th of September. This is perhaps why the text of the chapter was edited to shift the focus from the place to the time of death, as this was what determined the date of the following general chapter.[181]

C. Erection of four new provinces

In addition to the first eight provinces, the constitutions mention four additional provinces: Palestine, Greece, Poland and *Dacia* (Scandinavia), which always appear as a group.[182] Bernard Gui, who based his work on written notes and on an oral tradition, writes that these *provinciae superadditae* were erected by the chapter of 1228.[183] But it is difficult to dispel the impression that he, or his source – perhaps Stephen of Salagnac[184] –, was overly schematic in ascribing the erection of this group of provinces to a specific chapter. The author of the *Brevis historia Ordinis Praedicatorum* dated their origins a few years earlier.[185] The sequence and names of the provinces are the same in this work as they are in Bernard's, but the difference in foundation dates excludes the possibility of mutual dependence. Perhaps the order of the four provinces in the two texts reflects the chronological sequence of the foundations as it was believed to be in the thirteenth century.[186]

---

181 The original text can possibly be reconstructed as follows, in accordance with the bull for the Hospitallers (the words between angle brackets, except *Bononiam* and *Parisios*): "Si <apud [Bononiam] vel ubilibet citra montes> magistrum mori contigerit, prior conventualis qui propinquior illi loco extiterit, ubi magister decesserit, Bononiensi conventui <eius obitum> cum festinatione denuntiet. Si autem <apud [Parisios] vel ubilibet ultra montes> magister decesserit, Parisiensi conventui obitus magistri denuntietur. Et alteruter istorum conventuum, cui primo denuntiatum fuerit, teneatur similiter reliquis nuntiare".

182 "… quatuor provincie, scilicet Ierosolimitana, Grecia, Polonia, Dacia…" (CA, II, 5); "… quatuor priores provinciales de superadditis provinciis, scilicet Ierosolimitana, Grecia, Polonia, Dacia…" (CA, II, 10).

183 "Tempore quoque ipsius [Iordani] anno Domini MCCXXVIII, in primo capitulo generalissimo ordinis, quod fuit Parisius celebratum, primis octo provinciis per B. Dominicum institutis fuerunt quatuor superadditae scilicet Polonia, Dacia, Graecia, Terra Sancta, sicut notatum inveni, scilicet in notulis cuiusdam antiqui fratris, qui fuit circa huiusmodi studiosus, et ab eius ore ipse audivi" (Bernard Gui, *Tractatus de tribus gradibus praelatorum*, col. 406). Bernard gives the same year and the same order in his collection of reports of the general chapters (*Acta C.G.*, p. 3).

184 In fact, Bernard completed Stephen of Salagnac's historical work. See the introduction by the editor Th. Kaeppeli, to the work of both writers *De quatuor in quibus Deus Praedicatorum Ordinem insignivit*, p. V, XXIV-XXV.

185 "In eodem anno in generali capitulo tertio Parisius celebrato sub magistro Iordane erant superaddit[ae] provinciis supradictis aliae quatuor provinciae, scilicet Polonia, Dacia, Graecia, et Terra-Sancta" (col. 352). The author appears to have confused the years here. In this part of his work, he recounts events that happened in the year 1227: "…mortuo D. Honorio papa … D. Gregorius nonus…". But the third general chapter held in Paris took place not in 1227 but in 1226 (*Acta C.G.*, p. 2).

186 Cf. J. Quétif – J. Échard, *Scriptores O.P.*, vol. I, p. 1, which gives the sequence of the representatives of the provinces at the general chapter of Bordeaux of 1279.

Neither 1228, nor 1227 can be accepted as the foundation year for all four provinces together. According to a thirteenth-century chronicle which must be regarded as a reliable source, a provincial was appointed for Poland as early as 1225.[187] The foundation of the province of *Dacia*, which encompassed the northern parts of Europe, presumably took place a year later. The first provincial, Rano, was perhaps admitted into the order in 1225 and then returned to Scandinavia.[188] As regards Greece, there are no additional documents from the first half of the thirteenth century, which means that the constitutions and reports of the general chapters contain the oldest information for an approximative dating of the origins of this province.[189] Only the province of the Holy Land is likely to have been founded in the year 1228. According to Thomas of Cantimpré, the German Henry of Marsberg,[190] the first provincial, was sent to Palestine by a chapter attended by the master general together with the *diffinitores* and the provincials.[191] This can only have been the *capitulum generalissimum* of 1228, which was indeed made up of a wider range of delegates than the previous general chapters.[192] The stipulations in the constitutions relating to the four *provinciae superadditae* were therefore perhaps not inserted before 1228.[193]

---

187 "Frater Gerardus, natione Wratislaviensis, studens Parisiensis, primus provincialis Polonie, per Iordanem magistrum generalem ordinis Predicatorum preficitur, anno Domini millesimo ducentesimo vigesimo quinto, absque omni fratrum electione" (quoted by R.-J. Loenertz, *Une ancienne chronique des provinciaux dominicains de Pologne*, in *Arch. F.P.*, vol. XXI, 1951, p. 7). For the importance of this source, see *ibid.*, pp. 6, 11-14.

188 J. Gallén, *La province de Dacie de l'ordre des Frères Prêcheurs*, pp. 12-14.

189 On the earliest history of the province of *Graecia*, in the Latin kingdom of Constantinople, see R. Loenertz, *Documents pour servir à l'histoire de la province dominicaine de Grèce*, in *Arch. F.P.*, vol. XIV, 1944, pp. 72-74. The traditional date of foundation (1228) is accepted without comment by B. Altaner, *Die Dominikanermissionen des 13. Jahrhunderts*, pp. 9-10.

190 Jordan of Saxony also called Henry of Marsberg *Ultramarinus*: "Interim frater Henricus, prior provincialis Ultramarinus, consolabitur te ..." (*Epist. 26*, ed. A. Walz, *Iordani de Saxonia epistulae*, p. 39). See also *Epist. 4* and *Epist. 7* (*ed cit.*, pp. 7 and 9 respectively). These three letters were written in the summer of 1233 (cf. *ed. cit.*, p. X).

191 He undertook his second journey to the Holy Land "a magistro ordinis et diffinitoribus ac provincialibus fratrum in Terram Sanctam transmissus" (Thomas of Cantimpré, *Miraculorum ... libri duo*, lib. II, c. 43, no. 4, ed. G. Colvenerius, Douai, 1605, p. 417), clearly with a specific charge which was perhaps related to the foundation of a province of the order overseas. Thomas's statement is consistent with Jordan's, as we may assume that Henry of Marsberg spent at least a few years in Palestine before returning to Italy, where he met Jordan (*Epist. 26*). Another text by Thomas gives no further chronological clarifications: "Eo existente priore provinciali fratrum Praedicatorum in partibus transmarinis..." (*op. cit.*, lib. II, c. 57, no. 29, p. 562). On Henry of Marsberg, cf. also J. Quétif – J. Échard, *Scriptores O.P.*, vol. I, p. 148.

192 The ordinary general chapters were attended either by *diffinitores*, or by the provincials separately (CA, II, 5). For the composition of the chapter of 1228, see CA, praeamb., and *infra*.

193 These four provinces are mentioned in d. II, c. 5 (l. 9-11): "Statuimus quod quatuor provincie ... in singulis capitulis generalibus"; in c. 10 (l. 5-7): "...et quatuor priores provinciales de superadditis provinciis ... cum singulis ad hoc electis..."; also in the phrase "priores provinciales duodecim provinciarum" (c. 5, l. 12-13) and the "duodecim diffinitores ... et duodecim priores provinciales" (c. 7, l. 2-3).

§ 2. The legislation from 1228 to 1236

A. The general chapter of 1228

The chapter of 1228 marked the beginning of a new period in the constitutional history of the order. Its extraordinary significance is sufficiently highlighted by the introduction to the text of the constitutions in the Rodez manuscript. Its composition alone made this chapter the most extensive representation of the order as a whole. As the first *capitulum generalissimum*, it was made up not just of a single delegate per province, like previous chapters, but of two *diffinitores* who had been appointed by the chapter of each province, in addition to the provincials.[194] Vested with special powers, the *capitulares* did not limit their activities to issuing new ordinances, but they also took a number of measures which they believed would be inviolable for ever.[195] They radically changed the legislative procedure by stipulating that the text of the constitutions could no longer be changed by any general chapter on its own, but only with the approval of three consecutive chapters.[196] This decision was made to ensure the continuity of the legislation and to end a situation that had, before 1228, led to confusion and inconsistency.

The *praeambulum* itself was not initially part of the constitutions, although Raymond of Peñafort later included it in the body of the text.[197] According to the Rodez copyist, it was an accompanying or preliminary instruction written on the first page of the manuscript. Both its solemn style and the legal force that was assigned to it mean that it must be regarded as a text drafted by the chapter of 1228, and which continued to be closely associated with the *acta* and even with the constitutions.[198] Its original purpose may have been to account for the extraordinary power wielded by the chapter members of 1228. In order to justify

---

194 "Anno ab incarnatione Domini MCCXXVIII convenerunt Parisius in domo sancti Iacobi octo priores provinciales una cum Iordano, magistro ordinis nostri, singuli cum duobus diffinitoribus sibi a provincialibus capitulis deputatis..." (CA, praeamb.). – The expression *capitulum generalissimum* first occurs in the reports of the chapter of 1236 (*Acta C.G.*, p. 7).

195 "Priores igitur iam prefati cum suis diffinitoribus ... quasdam constitutiones ... unanimiter et concorditer ediderunt, quas in locis suis inter constitutiones alias inserere procurarunt. Inter constitutiones autem quasdam voluerunt inviolabiliter et immutabiliter in perpetuum observari, ... Quasdam vero sic voluerunt immutabiles permanere, ut nonnisi a consimili capitulo, ... de ipsis possit aliquid pro tempore immutari..." (*ibid.*).

196 The text of the *praeambulum* mentions this decision under the *immutabilia* of the second series, but without stating explicitly that it was only made in 1228. Humbert of Romans regards it as the work of 1228: "Ab initio enim quodlibet capitulum generale poterat statuere; sed tempore generalissimi capituli primi fuit facta ista constitutio" (*Expositio super Constitutiones*, p. 58).

197 In d. II, c. 10, *De capitulo generalissimo* (R. Creytens, *Les constitutions ... de s. Raymond de Peñafort*, pp. 61-62).

198 The preamble is: "Anno ab incarnatione Domini...". Other details similarly prove that the redaction was carried out by the 1228 chapter: there is a list of those present; the various decisions are enumerated in an orderly way. The solemn character of the text is also evident from a number of expressions, such as "gratia Spiritus sancti invocata, ... premissa diligenti examinatione, unanimiter et concorditer ediderunt...".

the profound changes they made to constitutional law, they referred to the source of their power: the special commission (*potestas plenaria*) given to them for this occasion by the provincial chapters.[199] It could therefore be interpreted as a kind of protocollary memorandum, an introduction to the activities of the *capitulum generalissimum*. According to this hypothesis, it was addressed exclusively to the Dominicans themselves. But its purpose was possibly even wider. According to Jordan of Saxony, the *capitulares* of 1228 intended to submit their most important decisions to the pope for ratification.[200] The way in which this statement is formulated suggests that this ratification never took place, either because the Dominicans changed their minds and did not request it, or because Gregory IX declined to grant it. Perhaps the *praeambulum* must be seen as part of a draft request.[201]

None of the articles in the constitution referenced in the *praeambulum* is explicitly ascribed to the chapter of 1228. Some clearly belong to an earlier stage of the legislation and even go back to Dominic, such as the obligation of collective poverty,[202] of not carrying money for the journey,[203] the ban on travelling on horseback and on the consumption of meat.[204] But the content and formulation of various other articles are entirely consistent with the spirit and intent of the *capitulum generalissimum*, which set out to revise the legislative procedure and establish it for the future. The exhortation addressed to the provincials and the *diffinitores* not to be guided by partisanship in taking decisions, appears almost literally in the constitutions.[205] The ban on appealing against chapter ordinances already appeared in earlier legislation on the general chapter.[206] But the sanction at the end of the section clearly resulted from later redaction.[207] It was repeated in a less severe form in other chapters to reiterate the strict observance of certain

---

199 For the meaning of the terminology (*potestas plenaria*), see *supra*, pp. 362-364. The chapter reports of Cîteaux similarly added a solemn preamble to important decisions, as in 1214: "Anno ab Incarnatione Domini MCCXIV, statutum est in generali capitulo..." (*Statuta cap. gen. Ord. Cist.*, vol. I, p. 427, no. 54). Cf. also *Exordium parvum* (1119), c. 1 (ed. J.-B. van Damme, *Documenta*, p. 6); J.-B. Mahn, *L'ordre cistercien*, p. 199.

200 "Nihil siquidem tam grave in constitutionibus continetur cuius mihi dispensatio credita non exsistat ... tribus illis articulis dumtaxat exceptis, qui in praeterito Parisiensi capitulo fuerant adeo firmiter stabiliti, ut nec revocari possint nec dispensationem admittere, quos etiam volebamus tunc vobis per curiam confirmari" (*Epist. 19*, ed. A. Walz, *Iordani de Saxonia epistulae*, p. 56).

201 An example of such a petition can be found in the *Constitutiones Fratrum de Paenitentia*, d. II, c. 12, *De forma decreti*, which includes a form for the requesting of papal approval for the election of the *rector ordinis* (ed. G. M. Giacomozzi, *L'Ordine della Penitenza*, pp. 96-97).

202 See *supra*, p. 376, with footnote 23, p. 384, with footnote 79.

203 See *supra*, p. 237, with footnote 288, p. 383, with footnote 78.

204 Both can already be found in d. I, c. 22 and therefore perhaps were part of the rules on observance of 1216 (cf. *supra*, p. 381).

205 D. II, c. 6.

206 D. II, c. 8: "Isti autem ... appellatio habeatur" (see *supra*, p. 390, footnote 132).

207 The second part of this c. 8 ("Appellationem ... corrigere") suddenly shifts from the third person to the first person plural, which points to the existence of other editors.

rules.[208] The legislators of 1228 apparently wished to bolster solidarity in the order by emphasising the necessity of obedience to the central authority and by nipping all attempts at opposition in the bud. These measures date from before 1236, as they are no longer mentioned in the *acta* of that year. And none of the chapters held before that year could speak with the same authority as the chapter of 1228. According to Jordan of Saxony, the Dominicans also decided in 1228 no longer to accept the pastoral care of nuns or religious women. The stipulations to this effect can be found in the text of the constitutions.[209] It is likely that the ban on accepting parish churches, which appears in the same chapter, was adopted on the same occasion.[210]

B. *The legislation after 1228*

Little can be said with certainty about the evolution of the legislation between 1228 and 1236. General chapters were held annually, but the reports for this period were either not preserved at all or only fragmentarily.[211] In any case, as per the decision taken in 1228, the first corrections of the text could only be implemented after approval by three general chapters, that is, in 1231 at the earliest. We do have a number of *admonitiones* from this year and from subsequent years before 1236, but no ordinances that were intended to be inserted in the constitutions. Perhaps the last part of d. II, c. 28, is identical to the *ordinatio de studiis*, which the *acta* of 1234 say was issued by the general chapter of Paris.[212]

---

208 In d. II, c. 9: "Precipimus autem ... immutare"; in c. 10: "Et hoc tam ... sustinebit"; in c. 11: "Et hec omnia ... subiaceat"; in c. 14: "In virtute Spiritus sancti ... supradicte"; in c. 35: "Si quis de cetero ... subiacebit".

209 "In virtute Spiritus sancti ... ad professionem recipiat" (CA, II, 27). Cf. Jordan, *Epist. 48-49* (ed. A. Walz, pp. 54-56). According to the editors, both letters date from 1229 (ed. A. Walz, p. X; ed. B. Altaner, p. 95). Jordan speaks there of the "praeteritum capitulum Parisiense" as the source of the ordinances on the *moniales* and the *mulieres* (*Epist. 49*, p. 56). But this cannot have been the chapter of 1229, as that was held in Bologna (*Acta C.G.*, p. 3). In his interpretation of these ordinances, Jordan uses expressions that also occur in the constitutions: "Alia fuit causa, quare illud statuimus, non propter sorores nostras quidem, sed propter personas extraneas mulierum, quas fratres nostri in diversis provinciis, dum converti vellent, tondere, induere, vel ad professionem continentiae recipere facile consueverunt" (*Epist. 48*, p. 54). Cf. CA, II, 27: "Prohibemus etiam ne aliquis de cetero aliquam tondeat vel induat vel ad professionem recipiat". In 1228, the Cistercians similarly repeated the ban relating to nuns that had been issued in 1220 (*Statuta cap. gen. Ord. Cist.*, vol. I, p. 517, vol. II, p. 68 respectively).

210 "Item ecclesias, quibus annexa sit cura animarum, non recipiant". In the Rodez manuscript, this stipulation in fact appears immediately before a text that can also be found in the constitutions of the Penitent Sisters, which was therefore added before 1232: "Numerum quoque missarum non admittant" (M, c. 22, ed. A. Simon, *L'ordre des Pénitentes*, p. 166). For the dating of the legislation of the Penitent Sisters, see *supra*, pp. 258-259, and *infra*, p. 406, footnote 217.

211 *Acta C.G.*, pp. 3-5.

212 This text, introduced by a *Statuimus*, imposes the obligation to provide students with the necessary study books: "ad minus in tribus libris theologie, videlicet biblia, sententiis et historiis". This *ordinatio* is confirmed in the *acta* of 1236, with a proviso: "Approbamus ordinationem studii factam

The *capitulum generalissimum* of 1236, the last to be held during the generalate of Jordan of Saxony, to all intents and purposes marks the end of the textual history of the primitive constitutions. Its numerous ordinances are well known, as they have been handed down *in extenso* in the reports of that year.[213]

When drawing up their *consuetudines* in 1216, the Dominicans used the monastic customs of Prémontré as their primary foundation. But some texts in the first *distinctio* were later replaced or supplemented by rules derived from other canonical traditions, ecclesiastical guidelines or ordinances that further outlined the order's own spirit and purpose.[214] Chapters 3-4 were inserted to replace the two chapters that hitherto defined liturgical customs for the morning on the basis of the Premonstratensian horarium.[215] This revision may well have been carried out in the years 1220-1221, together with the many other changes commanded by the first general chapters. In any case, the two chapters in their new form were part of the constitutions before 1232, because they also appear in the *Constitutiones S. Mariae Magdalenae*, where they are in the same place as in the Dominican text.[216] For the same reason, c. 12, *De minutione* and c. 17, *De silentio,* must have been compiled largely between 1220 and 1232.[217]

The many ordinances that were added at the end of the constitutions in the Rodez manuscript[218] also mostly date from before 1232. They should in fact have been inserted in the chapters where they belonged on the basis of their content, like the other interpolations,[219] and as was actually done in most cases in the manuscripts of the Friars of the Sack and the Penitent Sisters of Mary

in penultimo capitulo Parisius celebrato, excepto quod fratres bibliam perlegere non teneantur" (*Acta C.G.,* p. 8).

213 *Acta C.G.,* pp. 6-10. For the presence or absence of these ordinances in the various redactions of the Dominican constitutions (Rodez manuscript, Friars of the Sack, Raymond of Peñafort), see *supra,* p. 246, note 11, p. 266, with note 120, pp. 266-267, with notes 123-126; *infra,* Appendix IV.

214 See *supra,* pp. 307-320.

215 See *supra,* pp. 284-285.

216 C. 3, *De clausura claustri* (ed. A. Simon, *L'ordre des Pénitentes,* pp. 157-158); c. 4, *De officio ecclesie* (*ed. cit.,* pp. 158-159).

217 C. 12, *De minutis* (*ed. cit.,* p. 161). This chapter also occurs in the Premonstratensian text (Pa, I, 20; Pb, I, 19), but literal similarity is limited to a few words. The text of the Penitent Sisters is similar to that of the Dominicans. – C. 17, *De silentio,* similarly occurs almost word for word in the text of the Penitent Sisters (c. 15, *ed. cit.,* pp. 163-164). Only the additional ordinance of the chapter of 1236: "In mensa autem ... infirmi decumbentes" (*Acta C.G.,* pp. 6-7) is missing. In its place there is still the older text: "Priorissa ad mensam loqui poterit ...". The evolution of the text clearly did not go beyond 1232. On the other hand, this chapter is not as closely connected with the text of Prémontré as the other texts of the first *distinctio* are (see *supra,* pp. 294-295). It was therefore possibly not composed in 1216, but at the earliest in 1220, together with the first *Consuetudines.*

218 The full list appears in H. C. Scheeben, *Die Konstitutionen,* pp. 78-79 (dist. II, c. 34, nos. 5-12; c. 36, nos. 1-14).

219 See *supra,* p. 266, footnote 122.

Magdalene.[220] But the monastic copyist of Rodez simply wrote them down after the second *distinctio* as *extravagantes*, in two lists that were clearly not arranged systematically but most probably chronologically.[221] The first begins with a *statuimus* after c. 34, *De itinerantibus fratribus*, and encompasses eight stipulations, the first four of which were issued between 1220 and 1232, and the others between 1225 and 1236.[222] The second list, after c. 35, *De edificiis*, consists of fourteen

---

220 The following shows the place that the *extravagantes* in the Rodez manuscript (C) were given in the texts of the Friars of the Sack (S), the Penitent Sisters (M), and our critical edition (CA). The missing ordinances are marked by a hyphen.

C		S		M	CA	
d. II, c. 23 no.	5	–		–	d. II, c.	33
	6	d. II, c.	24	c. 22		35
	7		26	–		28
	8	–		c. 23		35
	9	–		–		1
	10		17	–		17
	11	–		–		1
	12		31	–		34
c. 36, no.	1		24	–		35
	2	–		–	prol.	
	3		31	–		34
	4	–		–	d. I, c.	19
	5		31	c. 24	d. II, c.	34
	6		31	–		34
	7	d. I, c.	4	c. 24		34
	8		8	–	d. I, c.	8
	9	–		–	d. II, c.	28
	10	–		–		28
	11		1	c. 1	d. I, c.	1
	12		1	1		1
	13	–		–		1
	14	–		–		4

221 The *Instituta generalis capituli* of Cîteaux were also organised chronologically (cf. J.-B. van Damme, *Genèse des* Instituta generalis capituli, in *Cîteaux*, vol. XII, 1961, pp. 28-60).

222 The first group contains the following stipulations: "Statuimus ne fratres … persona speciali" (CA, II, 33); "Item nullus … communem utilitatem" (CA, II, 35); "In diebus dominicis … se abstineant" (CA, II, 28); "Item in diebus dominicis … prohibemus" (CA, II, 35). The substance of the last stipulation of this group (C, II, 34, no. 8) also occurs in the text of the Penitent Sisters of Mary Magdalene (cf. *supra*, note 220) and must therefore, together with the previous one, date from 1232 at the latest (cf. *supra*, note 210). – None of the four stipulations from the second group (C, II,

ordinances in the Rodez manuscript.[223] The last of the series are a number of liturgical rules that can also be found in the constitutions of the German Penitent Sisters, and must therefore have been written before 1232.[224] That year may therefore be regarded as the *terminus ante quem* for all the preceding texts.[225] For this same reason, the other texts that were not derived from the Premonstratensians, but do appear in the text of the Penitent Sisters, must have been part of the Dominican constitutions before 1232.[226]

In the second *distinctio*, various additional stipulations in c. 1, *De provinciali capitulo*, were inserted after 1228. The first part, containing the procedure for

---

34, nos. 9-12) occur in the text of the Penitent Sisters. The first stipulation (II, 34, no. 9) is itself a supplement to legislation on the provincial chapter: "Nullus prior conventualis secum plures fratres ducat ad capitulum generale vel provinciale …" It cannot therefore have been added before 1225 (cf. *supra*, p. 396). In CA, this sentence has been placed in d. II, c. 1. The second stipulation "Item nullus de cetero … non fuerint approbate" (C, II, 34, no. 10; CA, II, 17) does not appear in the *Acta* of 1236 and must therefore have been added beforehand. The following ordinance "Item nulla petitio … nisi a provinciali" (C, II, 34, no. 11; CA, II, 1) dates from 1236 (*Acta C.G.*, p. 7). The last rule, "Fratres minores … honeste procurentur" (C, II, 34, no. 12; CA, II, 34) was also added before 1236, as it does not occur in the *Acta*. Its original place was perhaps immediately after no. 10, and it was separated from this when the ordinance "Item nullo petitio…" was inserted there in 1236, as it dealt with the same issue as no. 10, that is, *petitiones* addressed to the chapter.

223 D. II, c. 36 (ed. H. C. Scheeben, *Die Konstitutionen*, pp. 79-80). This text has no title, but is rightly regarded as a separate chapter (cf. *supra*, p. 266, footnote 122).

224 C, II, 36, nos. 11-12: "In ferialibus diebus … flectimus genua" (ed. H. C. Scheeben, *Die Konstitutionen*, pp. 79-80). These stipulations also appear in d. I, c. 1 in the texts of the Friars of the Sack and of the Penitent Sisters of Saint Mary Magdalene. They were also placed in the same location in CA. For the dating of the constitutions of the sisters, see *supra*, pp. 258-259, p. 406, footnote 217.

225 Viz. the following stipulations, which appear in the Rodez manuscript in d. II, c. 34 (according to H. C. Scheeben's numbering):

1. Fratres non sint … Depositarii esse possunt	(CA, II, 35).
2. Priores utantur … alii fratres	(CA, prol.).
3. Prior priorem … moram faciat	(CA, II, 34).
4. Bote extra … non portentur	(CA, I, 19).
5. Inclinationibus conformemur … quos declinamus	(CA, II, 34).
6. Nullus fratrum … videatur facere	(CA, II, 34).
7. Fratres non recipiant … maxime confessores	(CA, II, 34).
8. Si quid petitum … ad minorem	(CA, I, 8).
9. Cum frater … quos habuerit, pertinebunt	(CA, II, 28).
10. Tres fratres … de provincia	(CA, II, 28).

226 D. I, c. 7: "Nullus fratrum presentium… cum aliis fratribus procurentur" (for the Penitent Sisters: M, c. 6, ed. A. Simon, *L'ordre des Pénitentes*, pp. 159-160); c. 8: "Et fratribus nostris … comedere non presumant" (cf. M, 7 *ed. cit.*, p. 160); c. 14: "Nullus recipiatur … fuerit approbatus" (cf. M, c. 13 *ed. cit.*, p. 163). – D. II, c. 26: "Nullus fratrum nostrorum … obtinendis" (cf. M, c. 21, *ed. cit.*, p. 165); c. 36, *De anniversariis* (cf. M, c. 26, *De suffragiis mortuorum, ed. cit.*, pp. 168-169).

the election of the *diffinitores*, is followed by a series of regulations of various dates, which relate mainly to the composition of the provincial chapter.[227] As with the Cistercians and the Premonstratensians, unauthorised Dominicans were sometimes present in the place where the chapter was held.[228] In order to exclude the curious but unwanted, it proved necessary to define very precisely who was permitted to attend the assembly. Initially, the provincial chapter consisted of the representatives of the monasteries: the prior and his *socius*.[229] The *praedicatores generales*, too, were admitted as full members due to their prominent position in the life of this apostolic order.[230] Other religious were not entirely excluded, but their presence was wholly passive and was limited to the preparatory ceremonies. Before 1236, attendance at the *capitulum culparum* was limited to friars who had been professed at least a year.[231] This last stipulation was partly changed in 1236,[232] after having previously been separated from the rules on the presence of the *praedicatores generales* by an ordinance on the *socius*.[233] The last part of this chapter consists of stipulations added in 1236.[234]

---

227 CA, II, 1: "Capitulum autem provinciale ... poterunt interesse".
228 For Cîteaux, see J.-B. Mahn, *L'ordre cistercien*, p. 177. For Prémontré, see *Institut. Praem.* (Pb), d. IV, c. 1 (pp. 86-87). For the Dominicans, see G. R. Galbraith, *The Constitution of the Dominican Order*, pp. 120-121. Cf. *Acta C.G.*, p. 17, which addresses the penalties for faults.
229 The stipulation on the presence of the *socius* ("Capitulum autem provinciale appellamus priores conventuales cum singulis sociis a capitulo suo electis et predicatores generales") occurs in the Rodez manuscript and in the text of the Friars of the Sack (ed. G. M. Giacomozzi, *L'Ordine della Penitenza*, p. 91, with an interesting variant: "*Ad* capitulum autem provinciale appellamus, ...") in this place and perhaps belonged to the earliest legislation on the provincial chapter (1225). It was later clarified in an ordinance ("Nullus prior conventualis ... secundum electionem capituli sui") added before 1236, as it no longer appears in the chapter reports of that year.
230 Little can be said with certainty about the origin of this title and position. The chapter reports first mention the *praedicatores generales* only in 1235 (*Acta C.G.*, p. 5). But the texts in the constitutions, d. II, c. 1, c. 12, c. 31 and, as far as the substance is concerned, also c. 20 (cf. *supra*, p. 276, footnote 175), are older. The first stipulation in d. II, c. 1 ("Capitulum autem provinciale ... et predicatores generales", see previous footnote) was later supplemented by a further clarification: "Predicatores autem generales sunt, qui per capitulum generale vel priorem provincialem et diffinitores capituli provincialis fuerint approbati". For the presence of this stipulation in the earliest constitutions, see *supra*, pp. 276-277, with notes 173-176. The attempt to determine the number of attendees of the provincial chapter very precisely and to define the concept of *praedicator generalis* is consistent with the intentions of the *capitulum generalissimum* of 1228.
231 "Accusationi vero et correctioni post annum sue professionis poterunt interesse".
232 Since 1236, the text read: "...post triennium ab ingressu ordinis..." (*Acta C.G.*, p. 7).
233 "Nullus prior ... et assumat quilibet prior socium sibi secundum electionem capituli sui" (cf. *supra*, footnote 229). This stipulation appears in d. II, c. 34 in the Rodez manuscript, but is more appropriately placed here. The Friars of the Sack also have a rule on the presence of a *socius* in this place: "Et si commode fieri potest, ad illud capitulum veniat unus frater discretus cum socio, de voluntate prioris" (G. M. Giacomozzi, *L'Ordine della Penitenza*, p. 91).
234 "Item conventus qui mittit accusationes ... nisi dicat a quo audierit" (*Acta C.G., ibid.*). The following words of d. II, c. 1 ("Sed utique caveat ne malum quod audierit de alio fratre, referat aliquatenus, nisi dicat a quo audiverit") do not appear in the *Acta* and may therefore be older. For the stipulations in d. II, c. 1 ("Item quilibet prior ... causas debitorum" and "Item nulla petitio ... nisi a provinciali") see *Acta C.G.*, p. 7.

Between 1228 and 1236, it was necessary to add new stipulations to the regulations on the composition of the general chapter. According to the original arrangement of 1225, this central governing body consisted alternately of the provincials and the *diffinitores*, that is, the elected delegates of the provinces, but never of both groups together.[235] Provision was made for the wider representation of the entire order on the occasion of the election of the master general, where both the provincials and the two *electores* had a vote.[236] According to the letter of the law, one of the two groups would have no further role to play once the election was done, and was to be excluded from the activities (*diffinitio*) of the chapter proper, which commenced immediately afterwards. Perhaps objections were raised to this system which led to a change of the text of the constitutions. First, the provincials were authorised to participate in the consultations of the chapter, even if the election of the general fell in a year in which it was not their turn to act as *diffinitores* under the normal arrangement.[237] In 1236, this privilege was also granted to the *electores*.[238] The rule on the appointment of the visitors was added between 1225 and 1235.[239] Another additional ordinance from 1231-1235 was inspired by practical considerations. It stipulated that the provincial chapter should meet in the same place as the general chapter whenever this was held in the province in question.[240]

Neither the constitutions nor other sources offer firm criteria for the precise dating of several texts in the first and second *distinctio*. A number of additional regulations that were not derived from Prémontré and that do not appear in the text of the Penitent Sisters were added between 1220 and 1235.[241] For other

---

235 D. II, c. 5.

236 D. II, C. 10.

237 D. II, c. 11: "Si vero in anno ... diffinitio sit communis". For the *terminus a quo* (1231), cf. *supra*, pp. 402-403, with note 196. On the other hand, this stipulation must have been inserted before 1236, as it does not appear in the *acta* of that year.

238 "Statuimus autem ... cum eis pariter admittatur" (*Acta C.G.*, p. 7). In the constitutions (Rodez manuscript), this sentence was placed before the older text (cf. previous footnote), the first words of which were altered to highlight the connection: "Si *vero* in anno...". The Friars of the Sack did not have this stipulation as they organised their general chapter differently (cf. G. M. Giacomozzi, *L'Ordine della Penitenza*, p. 92).

239 D. II, c. 19. The provincial chapter is already mentioned (1225: cf. *supra*, p. 396). On the other hand, this stipulation no longer occurs in the *Acta C.G.* of 1236.

240 D. II, c. 12: "Statuimus insuper ... teneatur". The introductory formula appears to indicate that this stipulation was added together with the previous one (c. 11, cf. footnote 237).

241 D. I, c. 1: "Item si in ferialibus diebus ... de Spiritu sancto non"; c. 4: "Item numquam terminamus missam cum *Alleluia*. Totum officium ... aliquid innovare". For this last stipulation, see R. Creytens, *L'ordinaire des Frères Prêcheurs*, pp. 123-126, who gives 1228 as a possible date for the addition of this statute. There is also d. I, c. 14: "Conventualis prior ... capituli et obtento. Nullus recipiatur infra octodecim annos. In quolibet autem conventu ... an recipi debeant, relinquentes". The first of these three stipulations is partially identical to the bull issued by Gregory IX on 23 June 1232 for Prémontré, and was possibly adopted shortly afterwards by the Dominicans (cf. *supra*, p. 316). The following two ordinances could then have been added between 1232 and 1235. The following also date from the 1220-1235 period: c. 15, *De tempore probationis*, as a whole; c. 22 (l. 23-25): "Eadem

stipulations, which already mention the provincial chapter, the year 1225 must be regarded as *terminus a quo*.[242] The fact that these ordinances no longer appear in the chapter reports of 1236 indicates that they were issued before this year.

Under Jordan of Saxony's leadership, the general chapters of 1222 to 1236 frequently exercised their legislative powers in addition to their ordinary activities. The ordinances that were inserted in the constitutions during these fifteen years were modest in length. They consisted primarily of additions to the existing legislation. And yet their importance must not be underestimated. Some introduced significant adjustments and changes. Four new provinces were erected and the provincial chapter was organised as a permanent institution during this period. Also, the work method and composition of the general chapter were partially changed by new stipulations on the representation of the provinces in the order's central governing body. The decisions issued by the general chapter of 1228 testify to the wish to ensure the stability of the legislation and the existing institutions for the future.

Conclusion

The old constitutions of the Dominicans clearly show the traces of a lengthy evolution. In the first two decades during which they served as legal code, they underwent many changes and additions, especially the second *distinctio* and certain chapters of the first *distinctio*. The general chapters that met regularly since 1220 in fact exercised the authority of a constituent assembly, because they revised the legislation every year and immediately gave their decisions the force of law. During these frequent revisions, certain older parts of the text were irrevocably lost or were altered to such an extent that they can only be reconstructed adventitiously, through comparison with other documents. The pace of the evolution slowed from 1228 onwards, as every correction of the text from that point on required the approval of three consecutive chapters. The absence of logical order that is repeatedly in evidence in the Rodez manuscript, the only direct witness to the constitutions in their earliest stage, was not due to carelessness on the part of the monastic copyist. The text has the same form in the manuscripts of the Friars of the Sack and of the Penitent Sisters of Mary Magdalene. Such editorial imperfections must therefore have been "objective",

---

pena digni sunt ... moram fecerint". – D. II, c. 17: "Item nullus de cetero ... non fuerint approbate"; c. 30: "Nullus fiat publicus doctor ... theologiam audierit"; c. 31: "Statuimus ut nullus fiat predicator ... per tres annos"; "Placitis et causis ... non intersint"; c. 33: "Nullus assumatur ... infra viginti quinque annos"; c. 35: "Item in quolibet conventu ... edificia non fiant"; c. 37: "Item nullas conversus ... se audeat occupare".

242 D. I, c. 24 (l. 22-25): "Item qui semel apostataverit ... fuerit restitutus". – D. II, c. 5: "Item statuimus ... a diffinitoribus capituli provincialis"; c. 16: "Nullus religiosus ... aliquo modo admittatur".

inherent in the official text itself, as a result of repeated redactions by changing groups of legislators. It was not without good reason that Raymond of Peñafort set to work on a new *ordinatio* in 1238.

The evolution of the text is dominated by a number of dates and events, the significance of which for the constitutional history of the Dominicans had already been underlined by other sources, but which can now be seen more clearly. Five legislative assemblies, spread across some twenty years, produced the broad outlines of the legislation. The foundation was laid by Dominic and his first companions in 1216. The *consuetudines* of Prémontré served as a model for the regular customs of the Toulouse community, while the apostolic life was based on a small number of terse instructions on the observance of evangelical poverty and on preaching. This oldest core comprised almost all the first *distinctio* and several sections that were later brought together in the second *distinctio*. A second important contribution to the formation of the legislation of the order was made by the first general chapter, held in Bologna in 1220 under Dominic's leadership. This laid the basis for the interconventual organisation of the community that had, in the space of a few years, grown into a religious order.

The second chapter, in 1221, which began the expansion of the provincial organisation, had a more modest impact on the legislation. The influence of the 1228 chapter was greater; its composition made this the first *capitulum generalissimum*. It partially revised the legislative procedure as it had existed for a number of years and it adopted the principles that would be followed from then on. The second *capitulum generalissimum*, in 1236, during Jordan of Saxony's generalate, forms the last phase. Although this chapter did not introduce any radical structural reforms, it was important because of the large number of ordinances it added to the constitutions.

To the extent that we can reach a motivated judgment on the basis of the documentary evidence, we must conclude that the periods in between these phases left little mark on the legislation. The general chapters mentioned were highpoints in the legislative history. They thoroughly studied the urgent issues and found the solution that seemed the most suitable for that time. The immediately following years were a time of relaxation and legal stagnation, until the circumstances created new problems. It is true that a relatively great number of additional stipulations was created by intermediate chapters. But these do not appear to have been of great importance, and they are difficult to date precisely as the text itself rarely provides reliable clues, and other sources only sporadically contain useful information. For a number of ordinances and textual changes, any attempt to obtain a more precise date can for the time being only lead to limited and hypothetical results.

General conclusion

The Dominican Order originated in Dominic's desire to meet the urgent pastoral needs of the diocese of Toulouse together with a group of collaborators. But its inception and the specific shape it assumed were also due to factors outside this limited geographical and historical context. They were part of wider attempts since the eleventh century to put ecclesiastical and monastic life in order and to find suitable organisational forms for the religious movements of the twelfth century. In Benedictine monasticism, a yearning for the original ardour in the observance of monastic obligations gave rise to partial reforms, inspired by the desire to achieve literal observance of the rule and by the example of oriental eremitism. The same concern for a return to the apostolic and early Christian norms was also present in communities of canons. Many chapters foreswore their customary, mitigated rules and adopted the strict *vita communis* according to the *Regula Augustini* and the guidelines of other church fathers, often supplemented by ecclesiastical customs derived from the life of the monks.

The urge to lead a life according to authentically Christian norms was not limited to the monasteries and to communities of clerics. From these monastic and canonical environments came forth the first leaders of the religious movements of the twelfth century, who counted many laypeople among their followers. Animated by the desire to live the *vita apostolica* in its entirety and to have a fruitful influence on their own era, they felt compelled to unite their experience of radical evangelical poverty as *pauperes Christi* with apostolic preaching. Their actual or alleged contacts with heterodox sects, their presumptuous attitude towards the clergy and the hierarchy, and certainly also their lack of sound organisation made the groups that formed around itinerant preachers a cause of growing concern and suspicion for popes and bishops. Attempts to shape the ideals of the movement in adapted forms of communal life ran aground. Most of the new foundations had an ephemeral existence. Others transformed themselves into monastic or canonical communities, thus becoming part of traditional religious life. The end of the twelfth century marked a moment of crisis in the relationship between the hierarchy of the church and the religious movement, which was at the time led mainly by laypeople. On several occasions, the latter's claim that they had the right to preach without ecclesiastical sanction was punished by excommunication.

The pontificate of Innocent III, which is usually regarded as significant particularly in the ecclesiastical-political field, was also of crucial importance for the development of religious and monastic societies. This pope's open and positive attitude to the new aspirations allowed him to bring a number of separated groups back to orthodoxy and to ecclesiastical unity. He also harnessed their fresh vigour for pastoral ministry so as to neutralise the attraction that continued to emit from certain heretical sects. This gave both charitable societies and groups that had previously been excluded due to their pretensions to an apostolic life and to preaching the opportunity to develop freely within the church and to enshrine their ideals in enduring communities. Several of these foundations broke through the traditional pattern of the monastic life and adapted their organisation to their own needs. Among the religious communities that arose from the evangelical movement of the early thirteenth century were the Dominicans, with the double proviso that they were, from the start, *clerici* and, like the Franciscans, never broke off contact with the ecclesiastical leadership in their activities and development.

Until recently, the foundation of the Dominicans was regarded as almost exclusively the result of certain needs and circumstances in the south of France at the beginning of the thirteenth century, without sufficient regard for the historical background. Chroniclers of the thirteenth century and historians of later years saw the order as an instrument for the suppression of heretical sects, particularly the Albigensians. Of course, all were aware of its canonical nature, given Dominic's links with the chapter of Osma. And authors such as H. Denifle had already pointed out the affinity between its laws and those of the Premonstratensians. But it was not until the second quarter of this century that serious and successful attempts were made to study more closely the dependence of the order upon, and its similarity to, earlier and contemporary religious societies, and thus simultaneously to highlight its originality. Just as Dominic was himself formed by traditional monastic life and yet remained very intimately in touch with the needs and aspirations of his time, so his foundation had its deepest roots in the past, while developing into a new form of monastic community with a structure adapted to contemporary needs. These views of the life and work of the founder have been presented compellingly in scholarly biographies by authors such as P. Mandonnet, H. C. Scheeben and M. H. Vicaire, and they can now be regarded as the generally accepted perspective. Our intention here has been to examine to what extent these ideas were realised in one specific aspect of the order: its legislation.

Any serious study of the nature, history and significance of the earliest Dominican constitutions presupposes as full a reconstruction of their content as possible. It was necessary therefore to critically study and piece together the text as it was before 1240. This goal could largely be realised by comparing the Rodez manuscript with Raymond of Peñafort's codification, and with the legislation of the Penitent Sisters and that of the Friars of the Penitence of Jesus Christ, which partially reflect the earliest constitutions of the Dominicans. This made it possible not only to remediate and complement the inaccuracies and lacunae of the various manuscripts, but also to acquire better insight into the manner in which the text was preserved and, for some parts of it, the diversity of traditions that existed from the start. Moreover, the study of a number of fragments preserved in the constitutions of the sisters revealed that the earliest text was even more closely related to the *consuetudines* of the Premonstratensians. On the basis of this information, it has proven possible to reconstruct the text of the Dominican constitutions more accurately in its original form. Furthermore, it was possible to propose a satisfactory explanation for several problems that had not been observed or solved by previous editors.

When expanding their legislation, the Dominicans as a matter of principle adopted as much as they could from what was available to them in the form of existing laws of religious orders; this was the medieval custom and it also reflected an attitude of caution. Almost every chapter of the first part of their constitutions, which describes the monastic customs, contains either a literal quotation from or the substance of the *consuetudines* of the Premonstratensians. Here and there, these derived texts were supplemented or corrected by regulations related to the customs of other canons, monks and monastic institutions in the twelfth or early thirteenth century. A number of rules on the admission of new members, the novitiate and silence must be regarded more as canonical precepts that held general validity for religious. In the second *distinctio*, the affinity is less obvious. The Cistercians rather than Prémontré served as the model for this part, particularly with regard to the organisation of the general chapter, as the Fourth Lateran Council required. But the similarities are limited to the external ceremonies and the agenda. The Dominicans went their own way in respect of the composition of the chapter and its proper task. They were inspired by the canons of the Lateran Council in the formulation of several stipulations, but also made certain corrections and inserted additions that point to the influence of other ecclesiastical documents and the writings of canonists. Other dispositions again, particularly in relation to the election of superiors and the government of the order, appear to be related more to texts and customs from secular law.

It took a long time before the earliest constitutions assumed the form in which they were handed down in the Rodez manuscript. In fact, during the two decades that they were in force, they evolved almost without interruption, and the traces of this are still clearly visible in the various parts of the text. Using external criteria, like the *Acta* of the general chapters and information from other sources, it is possible to situate certain parts very precisely in time, whereas other stipulations can be dated at least approximately through comparison and by viewing them in the context of the history of the order and the expansion of its governing bodies. By far the largest part of the text – the entire first *distinctio* and several chapters from the second – were drafted during Dominic's lifetime and under his personal influence. The legislation of the order is not therefore the work of the chapter of 1228, as has usually been argued on the basis of erroneous interpretations. Among the oldest parts are the monastic customs described in the first *distinctio*; these can be equated with the *arctiores consuetudines* upon which Dominic and his first companions founded their canonical communal life. The general chapters of 1220 and 1221 primarily dealt with the expansion of the structure and administration of the order, and composed a number of chapters of the second *distinctio*. Under the leadership of Jordan of Saxony, the annual chapters from 1222 to 1235 made the required additions and adaptations and completed the organisation of the order. The external arrangement of the primitive constitutions was thoroughly revised by Raymond of Peñafort, but there were no further important changes as regards their substance.

The positive results of our study are reflected and summarised to a certain extent in the text edition of the earliest constitutions in Appendix I. Thanks to meticulous comparison of the various manuscripts, it has proven possible to form a more accurate picture of the content and state of the *Constitutiones antiquae* and to publish a critical edition of them that approximates the original form of the Dominican laws more closely than earlier publications have done. In the presentation of the text, we have endeavoured to highlight dependence on or affinity with other monastic statutes and documents, to show more clearly how the Dominicans went about incorporating the derived texts into their own legal code. The comparative tables in the third chapter and in the Appendices show the relationship with the earlier and later statutes of the Premonstratensians. They demonstrate that the immediate source of the first *distinctio* must be sought neither in the twelfth-century codification, nor in that of 1236-1238, but in an intermediate, previously unknown redaction which reflects the state of the *Institutiones Praemonstratenses* at the beginning of the thirteenth century. For each case, the critical apparatus indicates which stipulations from Prémontré belonged to the earliest text, but no longer appear in the Rodez manuscript, nor in the following redactions of the Dominican constitutions. The footnotes accompanying the text edition also indicate, as far as possible, when the various chapters and sections were added. They do so on the basis of the results of the fourth chapter, which described the development of the text.

The clearly dyadic character of the Dominican constitutions reflects the two aspects of the order's way of life and its work. Its affinity with Prémontré and other institutes makes the first *distinctio* a typically canonical legal code, a succinct summary of the most characteristic customs that tradition had forged into a guideline for the communal life of canons regular. It mainly contains rules on the liturgical office, the monastic horarium and its various exercises and penitential stipulations. On the basis of these observances, the Dominicans must be classified as representatives of the stricter tendency (*ordo novus*). Most communities that were founded or reformed in the twelfth century remained faithful to the moderately observant way of life of the *ordo antiquus*, which was based on the rule of Aachen and on the *Instituta Patrum*, the writings of Augustine and other church fathers. But the Premonstratensians and other canons, true to the guidelines that they believed were part of the authentic *Regula Augustini*, were more exacting when it came to the observance of collective poverty and monastic asceticism. The Dominicans preserved these *arctiores consuetudines* in the prescripts on the extended fast, absolute abstinence from meat, continuous silence and the wearing of coarse woollen habits. In this respect, they followed the purest canonical tradition, more so than many other institutes from the twelfth and early thirteenth century.

And yet, the structure and content of the first *distinctio* already reflect a concern that the regular life must be an aid and not a hindrance to the apostolate. The monastic horarium differs in many respects from the canonical and monastic *consuetudines* that served as source material. Daily life is less heavily burdened with liturgical ceremonies and ascetical obligations. The elimination of manual labour created space in the horarium that could be filled by study within the monastery and by apostolate outside it. The possibility of dispensation, which is mentioned explicitly in various places, further underlined the flexible character of the legislation. The formula of profession no longer contained the usual commitment of the canons regular to their monastery church, but only a promise of obedience to the master general and the prior as his substitute. This direct incorporation into the community of the order was a guarantee of the mobility and availability of the members for the apostolate.

The unique character of the Dominican constitutions is even more clearly to the fore in the second *distinctio*, which addresses the social structure, the administration of the order and its members' activities. The *ordo* is a geographically dispersed community in which the smallest cells, local houses or monasteries, are grouped into larger corporations, the provinces, which in certain respects lead an autonomous life and have a task of their own, but which are subject in their turn to a central authority. Each of these communities stands under the personal authority of a superior, either the prior, the provincial or the master general, whereas the provinces and the order are also governed collegially, by the provincial and the general chapter respectively. One important element that the Dominicans introduced is a high degree of participation of the members in the government of the order. Similarly, the stipulations on study and the guidelines for preachers are features that distinguish the Dominican constitutions from monastic and canonical legislation, and that are an original contribution to the medieval legislation of religious orders.

Perhaps both the Dominicans' connections with the monastic tradition and their openness to the new needs helped to secure for these constitutions the regard in which they were held in ecclesiastical circles. It is remarkable that most religious communities that emerged in the early thirteenth century in large part adopted the heritage of the preceding centuries in their spirituality and legislation, as they were occasionally exhorted to do by the leadership of the church. The guidelines of Innocent III and the decrees of the Fourth Lateran Council sprang primarily from the concern not to discard lightly what had been built up in a monastic tradition spanning centuries. At first sight, these ordinances appear to have had a stifling rather than a stimulating effect on the desire for renewal and adaptation. And yet the religious leaders who saw their endeavours come to fruition and their foundations develop into robust monastic communities, were precisely those who heeded the instructions of the pope and the bishops. The ecclesiastical authorities' favourable attitude, in its turn, was not unrelated to the allure and influence of the Dominican constitutions. Several religious institutes adopted this legal code almost in its entirety or made ample use of it. The central and provincial organisation and the participation of subjects in government, first set down in law by the Dominicans, have since become commonplace and have remained essential elements of the structure and administration of monastic communities to this day. In this way, the legislation of the Dominicans has left its mark on the religious life of the thirteenth century and thereafter.

Their activities and organisation helped the Dominicans to develop their own solution to two problems that had arisen even before the thirteenth century and that had been the subject of constant concern on the part of the ecclesiastical authorities: the search for new forms of religious community life and the renewal of pastoral care through preaching. The newly founded institutes that emerged from the religious movement had been unsuccessful in translating their ideals of the imitation of Christ and evangelical poverty into stable communities. Only under Innocent III were the reconciled Humiliati and Waldensians granted ecclesiastical approval. But the Fourth Lateran Council in 1215 sought to prevent repetition of such experiments by ruling that new societies had to adopt the rule and *institutio* of a *religio approbata*, and thus had to integrate into the existing monastic life. The groups mentioned above never became widespread and soon ceased to exist. Only the Franciscans succeeded in maintaining themselves and developing. But to do so, they had to relinquish certain aspects of their original way of life by moving into *conventus* after 1220 and embracing the regular monastic life.

The needs of religious life within and outside the monasteries, among rural populations and in the growing cities, demanded an adapted form of pastoral care and catechesis. The bishops could rarely count on effective assistance from the clergy to meet these needs, as it mostly lacked the required intellectual and moral qualities. Individual preachers, both secular clerics and religious, had a limited geographical radius of action and did not have continuity in the form of an institute or a group that could carry on the work. Monks and canons occasionally assisted in the ordinary cure of souls in parishes, but only on a local basis and to the extent that bishops and their own superiors permitted. The communities that were founded by itinerant preachers in the twelfth century gradually adopted the ascetical-contemplative way of life of the monks, and their horariums did not allow for much apostolic work. The laypeople who, at the end of the twelfth century, claimed the right to preach soon clashed with the church authorities, who regarded the office of preacher as a privilege of the bishops and of clerics mandated by them.

The ecclesiastical authorities apparently did not intend to turn to monks and to the members of religious societies to effect the renewal of preaching. The repeated exhortations and ordinances of the councils at the end of the twelfth century and the beginning of the thirteenth all insisted that bishops should have the assistance of educated preachers, to be recruited preferably from the cathedral and collegiate chapters, of which they were to remain members. Innocent III did approve and encourage the Cistercian initiative in Southern France, and on other occasions also asked for the assistance of monks, especially for missionary work in pagan or heretical parts. But evangelical poverty and monastic communal life were not viewed as preconditions for apostolic activity. Significantly, the Lateran Council issued its decrees on preaching and on the monastic institutes in separate canons.

The solution that Dominic proposed and developed, consisted precisely of the joining together of apostolic preaching and religious life in a single institute. Formed as he had been in the canonical community of the chapter of Osma, he encountered religious movements and heretical sects during his mission among the Albigensians in Southern France. After he joined the group of Cistercian preachers under the guidance of his bishop, he became alive to the necessity of the sustained practice of evangelical poverty as a first requirement for fruitful work in that context. His community of preachers in Toulouse was built on this insight. It also constituted a college of priests at the service of the bishop, in anticipation of what the Lateran Council would prescribe as a general rule some months later. By basing his foundation on the rule of Augustine and the customs of the Premonstratensians in 1216, Dominic also complied with the conciliar decree on the legal status of the religious communities. All conditions had thus been met for canonical approval of a religious society of preachers with an *institutio apostolica* in the most comprehensive sense in which that term had been used in previous centuries. The Dominicans attempted to unite, on the one hand, the *vita communis* and the monastic customs that monks and canons regular regarded as requirements for the imitation of the apostles, and, on the other, the evangelical poverty and apostolic preaching that the adherents of the religious movements had proposed as elements of the full *vita apostolica*. The somewhat contrived, but tersely accurate words of an antiphon from the office of the feast of Dominic, where they refer to Dominic himself, may therefore also appropriately be applied to the order and its legislation:

Sub Augustini regula mente profecit sedula.
Tandem virum canonicum auget in apostolicum.

Appendices

Text Edition — the earliest constitutions O.P.

Notes to the Reader

a. The text

1. Fonts used:

   a) large roman type:
   texts for which no sources or parallel places were found;

   b) small roman type:
   texts derived from Prémontré;

   c) l e t t e r – s p a c e d   s m a l l   r o m a n   t y p e:
   texts derived from sources other than Prémontré;
   parallel texts;

   d) *large italics*:
   texts derived from Holy Scripture, the rule of Augustine and the liturgy;
   fixed expressions;

   e) *small italics*:
   derived texts and formulas (see d) which already occur as such in the
   Prémontré text;

   f) *l e t t e r – s p a c e d   s m a l l   i t a l i c s*:
   derived texts and formulas (see d) which occur as such in sources other
   than the Prémontré texts.

2. Punctuation has been modernised and spelling standardised.

3. The sequential numbers of the chapters do not appear in the manuscripts, but
were added by us for reasons of clarity.

4. Whenever two different variants of the text of the constitutions are placed side
by side, the older version appears in the first column and the later version in the
second.

b. The critical apparatus

1. In the positive apparatus, the manuscripts that have preserved the presumptive
original text of the constitutions appear before the colon (:). Manuscripts that
have a different variant appear after the colon.
In the negative apparatus, only manuscripts that deviate from the original text
appear after the square bracket ( ]).

2. If a word included in the critical apparatus appears twice in the line that is referenced, a number in superscript ([1] or [2]) indicates to which of the two it applies.

3. As the arrangement of the texts in certain manuscripts deviates slightly from that in the *Constitutiones antiquae O.P.*, the place has been indicated where the passage in question is to be found in the text of the constitutions that was used, whenever necessary. In such cases, the siglum of the manuscripts is followed by the correct reference between brackets.

E.g., *R (1,5)* = *Constitutiones O.P.* (1241), dist. I, cap. 5;
   I (c.7) = *Institutiones S. Sixti*, cap. 7;
   A (p. 6) = *Acta cap. gen. O.P.*, vol. I, p. 6.

These references between brackets also apply to the subsequent sigla (up to the end of the chapter in question) that have no specific reference.

c. Critical signs

[ ]   words that do not appear in the manuscripts but that probably belonged to the earliest text of the constitutions appear between square brackets;

< >   parts of the text that were later added to a particular chapter appear between angle quotation marks;

…   an ellipsis means that the omitted words are also eligible;

—   a dash means that only the two words indicated are also eligible.

Abbreviations

add.	addidit; addiderunt
adscr.	adscripsit
cet.	ceteri
codd.	codices
corr.	correxit; correxerunt
eras.	erasit
om.	omisit; omiserunt
praem.	praemisit; praemiserunt
transt.	transtulit.

Sigla

A   *Acta capitulorum generalium O.P.*, I.
C   *Constitutiones antique O.P.*, ms. Rodez.
I   *Institutiones sororum S. Sixti de Urbe.*
M   *Constitutiones Sororum S. Marie Magdalene.*
Pa *Institutiones Patrum Praemonstratensium*, ed. E. Martène.
Pb *Institutiones patrum Premonstratensis Ordinis*, ed. Pl. F. Lefèvre.
R   *Constitutiones O.P.* (1241), ed. R. Creytens.
S   *Constitutiones Fratrum de Penitentia.*

CONSTITUTIONES ANTIQUE
ORDINIS FRATRUM PREDICATORUM

PREAMBULUM

Anno ab incarnatione Domini MCCXXVIII convenerunt Parisius in domo sancti Iacobi [octo] priores provinciales una cum Iordano, magistro ordinis nostri, singuli cum duobus diffinitoribus sibi a provincialibus capitulis deputatis, ubi fratres omnes vota sua unanimiter transtulerunt, eisdem p o t e s t a t e m p l e n a r i a m   5 concedentes, ut quicquid ab ipsis fieret, sive in constituendo sive in destituendo, mutando, addendo vel diminuendo, de cetero firmum ac stabile permaneret, nec liceret alicui quantecumque auctoritatis capitulo eorum aliquid immutare, quod ipsi statuerunt perpetuis temporibus permansurum. Priores igitur iam prefati cum suis diffinitoribus, gratia Spiritus sancti invocata, quasdam constitutiones ad utili-   10 tatem et honestatem et conservationem ordinis, premissa diligenti examinatione, unanimiter et concorditer ediderunt, quas in locis suis inter constitutiones alias inserere procurarunt. Inter constitutiones autem quasdam voluerunt inviolabiliter et immutabiliter in perpetuum observari, videlicet de possessionibus et redditibus nullatenus recipiendis, de appellationibus removendis, et quod non possit per   15 fratres diffinitores prioribus provincialibus neque per priores fratribus in suis diffi-nitionibus in aliquo preiudicium generari. Quasdam vero sic voluerunt immutabi-les permanere, ut nonnisi a consimili capitulo, novis emergentibus causis, articulis, casibus et negotiis, de ipsis possit aliquid pro tempore immutari, videlicet de con-stitutionibus non faciendis nisi per tria generalia capitula fuerint approbate, de non   20 equitando, de expensis non portandis, de carnibus nisi causa infirmitatis non comedendis, ita tamen ut in hiis pro loco et tempore prelato liceat dispensare.

Rubr. Iste sunt constitutiones prime ordinis fratrum Predicatorum que erant tempore magistri Iordanis, beati Dominici immediate successoris, ex quibus formavit et ordinavit constitutiones alias, que nunc habentur, frater Raymundus de Pennaforti, magister ordinis tertius *in marg. dextr. et infer. adscr.* C
Preamb., 1 Preambulum] *om. codd.*   **3** octo *textum correxi* : duodecim C, *om.* R *(2,10)*   Iordane R
4 ubi C : in quos R   **7** nec R : non C   **8** quantecumque R : quantumcumque C   eorum aliquid C : aliquid eorum R   **13** constitutiones C : illas R   **20** approbata CR

Preamb., 2/22 for the meaning and dating (1228), see *supra,* pp. 403-404   **3** octo] for the number of provinces in 1228, see pp. 344-345, 401-402   **5** potestatem plenariam] for the meaning and use of this expression, see pp. 363-364

INCIPIUNT CONSUETUDINES
FRATRUM PREDICATORUM

INCIPIT PROLOGUS

Quoniam ex precepto regule iubemur habere *cor unum et anima*m unam *in* Domino, iustum est, ut qui sub una regula et unius professionis voto vivimus, uniformes in observantia canonice religionis inveniamur, quatinus *unitatem,* que interius *serva*nda est in cordibus,
5   foveat et representet uniformitas exterius servata in moribus. Quod profecto eo competentius et plenius poterit observari et memoriter retineri, si ea que agenda sunt, scripto fuerint commendata, si omnibus qualiter sit vivendum, scriptura teste innotescat, sed mutare vel addere vel minuere nulli quicquam propria voluntate liceat, ne, si minima negligimus, paulatim defluamus.
10 ⟨Ad hec tamen in conventu suo prelatus dispensandi cum fratribus habeat potestatem, cum sibi aliquando videbitur expedire, in hiis precipue, que studium vel predicationem vel animarum fructum videbuntur impedire, cum ordo noster specialiter ob predicationem et animarum salutem ab initio noscatur institutus fuisse, et studium nostrum ad hoc principaliter ardenterque summo opere debeat
15 intendere, ut proximorum animabus possimus utiles esse.
Priores utantur dispensationibus sicut et alii fratres.⟩
Eapropter, ut unitati et paci totius ordinis provideamus,

| | volumus et declaramus ut constitutio- |
| | nes nostre non obligent nos ad culpam, |
20 | sed ad penam, nisi propter contemp- |
| | tum vel preceptum. |
librum istum, | Librum autem istum,

quem librum consuetudinum appellamus, diligenter conscripsimus, in quo duas distinctiones notavimus.
25 Prima distinctio continet qualiter se habeant fratres in suo monasterio in die, qualiter in nocte, qualiter novitii, qualiter infirmi, qualiter minuti, et de silentio et de culpis.

Prol., **7** sed *CS* : si *R cum PaPb*   **14/15** ad ... intendere] ad hoc debeat principaliter intendere *R*
16 Priores ... fratres *hic R* : *in extrav.(2,36) C*   sicut] *om. R*

Prol., **1/Prol., 32** cf. *PaPb,* prol.; see *supra,* pp. 286-288; — for the dating (1216), see pp. 381-382
2 cor ... Domino] cf. *Reg. s. Aug.,* c.1: "... et sit vobis anima una et cor unum in Deo"; cf. *Act.,* IV,31
4 unitatem ... servanda] cf. *Eph.,* IV,3: "... solliciti servare unitatem spiritus..."   **10/15** for the dating (1220), see *supra,* p. 381, note 54   **16** for the dating (1220-1231), see p. 407, note 225

Text. rec., **Prol., 18/21** volumus ... preceptum *R cum A(p.8)* : *om. CS*   **20/21** contemptum vel preceptum *scripsi cum A* : preceptum vel contemptum *R*   **22** autem *add. R*

Text. rec., **Prol., 18/21** added in 1236 (*Acta C.G.,* p. 8)

Secunda distinctio, de ⟨provinciali capitulo et generali et⟩ studio et predicatione.

Unicuique autem harum distinctionum propria capitula assignavimus et assignata scripsimus, ut, cum aliquid a lectore queritur, sine difficultate inveniatur.

De matutinis. De capitulo et prima, missa et horis aliis. De refectione et cibo. De collatione et completorio. De infirmis et minutis. De novitiis et silentio. De vestitu. De rasura. De culpis.   30

---

29 scripsimus *C* : conscripsimus *S, om. R., cf.* subscripsimus *PaPb*

---

27 provinciali capitulo et generali et] for the dating (c. 1224), see *supra*, p. 389, note 127   **30** De² ... aliis] for the significance with respect to the original text of the constitutions, see pp. 284-285

[INCIPIT PRIMA DISTINCTIO]

1. DE MATUTINIS

Audito primo signo, ad matutinas | Audito primo signo,
surgant fratres, | surgant fratres,

dicendo matutinas de beata Virgine pro tempore. Quibus finitis, cum fratres in chorum venerint, inclinent ante altare profunde. Et cum ad sedes suas venerint, facto signo
5 a prelato, flexis genibus vel inclinati profunde pro tempore, dicant *Pater noster* et *Credo in Deum*. Et iterum facto signo a priore, surgant. Hora itaque devote incepta, versi ad altare, muniant se signo crucis. Et ad *Gloria Patri* inclinet chorus contra chorum profunde vel prosternant se pro tempore usque ad *Sicut erat*. Et hoc faciendum est quotiens
10 *Pater noster* et *Credo in Deum* dicuntur, nisi in missa, et ante lectiones et in gratiarum actione. Idem etiam faciendum est ad primam collectam in missa et ad

collectam post communionem | postcommunionem

et similiter ad orationem pro Ecclesia et in singulis horis ad collectam et ad *Gloria Patri*, quotiens in inchoatione hore dicitur. Ad omnia autem alia *Gloria Patri* et ad
15 extremos versus hymnorum et ad penultimum versum cantici *Benedicite* inclinamus usque ad genua, et quando cantatur *Gloria in excelsis Deo*, ad *Suscipe deprecationem nostram*, et in *Credo* in missa ad *Homo factus est*, et iterum in benedictione lectionis, item in capitulo ad orationem *Sancta Maria*, et in omni oratione, quando nomen beate Virginis nominatur.
20 ⟨Ad *Salve sancta Parens* et ad *Veni sancte Spiritus* flectimus genua.

In ferialibus diebus iacemus prostrati a *Sanctus* usque ad *Agnus*. In festis vero trium vel novem lectionum iacemus ab elevatione corporis Christi usque ad *Pater noster*. In prostrationibus idem servamus in festo trium vel novem lectionum.

Item, si in ferialibus diebus dicimus missam de Cruce, cadimus ad terram, ad
25 missam de beata Virgine vel de Spiritu sancto non.⟩

Rubr. incipit prima distinctio *om. codd.*
Cap. 1, 2 ad matutinas] *textum antiquiorem habet* M *cum* PaPb : *om.* CSR **6** profunde pro tempore SR(1,2) : pro tempore C, profunde M **6/7** et Credo *in textum antiquiorem habet* M *cum* Pb **20/ 23** Ad ... lectionum *hic* SR(1,2)M : *in extrav.(2,36)* C flectimus R : flectamus CM **21** iacemus MR : *om.* C, prostrati *add.* S **24/25** Item ... non *huc transtuli* : *in extrav.(2,36)* C *om. cet.*

Cap. 1, 1/29 de ... matutinis] cf. PaPb, I,1; see *supra*, pp. 288-289, 306; — for the dating (1216), see p. 381 **2** ad matutinas] oldest text, preserved in *Const. S. M. Magd.* (cf. *supra*, p. 255, with note 65) **12** collectam post communionem] oldest text, preserved in *Const. S. M. Magd.* (cf. *loco cit.*) **20/ 23** for the dating (1220-1231), see *supra*, p. 408, with note 224 **24/25** for the dating (1220-1235), see p. 410, with note 241

Text. rec., **Cap. 1, 12** postcommunionem *textum recentiorem habent* CSR

Hora itaque predicto more incepta, postquam ad *Gloria* post *Venite* inclinaverint, stet chorus contra chorum. Deinde ad primum psalmum sedeat unus chorus, ad secundum stet et similiter sedeat alter chorus. Et sic alternent usque ad *Laudate Dominum de celis*. Et sic faciant ad omnes horas. Finitis matutinis, tenetur capitulum vel aliquando post primam, aliquando etiam intermittitur, ne studium impediatur, secundum   30
quod videbitur prelato.

2. DE CAPITULO

Intrante conventu capitulum, lector pronuntiet lunam et que de kalendario pronuntianda sunt. Et sacerdos prosequatur: *Pretiosa*, etc. Et residentibus fratribus, lector pronuntiet lectionem de
regula vel de institutionibus | institutionibus vel de evangelio   5
pro tempore, premisso *Iube domne*. Et hebdomadarius subiungat benedictionem: R e g u l a r i b u s   d i s c i p l i n i s vel *Divinum auxilium* pro tempore. Et facta absolutione pro defunctis, dicat qui tenet capitulum: *Benedicite* et, responso *Dominus*, inclinent omnes. Deinde, recitatis beneficiis et dicto a priore *Retribuere dignare* etc., dictis etiam a conventu psalmis *Ad te levavi* et *De profundis*, *Kyrie eleison* cum *Pater*   10
noster, subsecutis etiam hiis tribus versiculis, scilicet *Oremus pro domino papa*, *Salvos fac servos tuos*, *Requiescant in pace*, ab hebdomadario dicendis, cum hiis tribus collectis *Omnipotens sempiterne Deus qui facis*, *Pretende*, *Fidelium Deus*, resident fratres. Tunc prelatus poterit dicere breviter, si quid ad honestatem vel correctionem fratrum viderit expedire. Post egrediantur novitii. Quibus egressis,   15
dicat qui preest: *Faciant venias, qui se reos estimant*. Continuo, qui se reos intellexerint,

26 ad] *om.* C   inclinaverint] audiverint C   **27/28** ad[2] ... chorus C : et ad secundum similiter alter chorus S, ad secundum stet et sedeat alter M, et ad secundum similiter stet et sedeat alter chorus R   **28** alternent C *cum* PaPb : alternant S, alternet M, alternetur R   **31** videbitur prelato C : prelato videbitur SR, videbitur prelate M
Cap. 2, 1 de capitulo] *tit.* De capitulo quotidiano *in marg. sin. manu recentiore adscr.* C   **2** CS : Ingresso M R(2,6)   **4/5** de regula vel de institutionibus M : *cf.* de regula Pa(1,4)Pb(1,4)   **11** hiis CS : *om.* MR   **15** fratrum CS : earum M, *om.* R   Post C : post hoc R, deinde S   egrediantur R : egredientur C, recedant S

27/28 Deinde ... chorus] for the origins, see pp. 307-308; — for the dating (1216), see p. 382, with note 64
Cap. 2, 1/30 for the dating (1216) of the oldest parts, see *supra*, p. 381   **1/9** cf. PaPb, I,4; see *supra*, pp. 289-290   **5** regula] oldest text, preserved in *Const. S.M. Magd.* (cf. *supra*, p. 255, with note 65)   **7** Regularibus disciplinis] for the affinity with Saint-Ruf, see *supra*, p. 308; — for the dating (1216), see p. 382, with note 64   **9/16** possibly adopted in 1216 from the chapter of Osma (cf. *supra*, pp. 308 and 382)   **13** Omnipotens ... Deus[2]] for the use of these three orations in the Roman liturgy of the mass, especially since the eighth century, see P. Bruylants, *Les oraisons du missel romain*, vol. II, Leuven, 1952, nos. 779, 880, 567 respectively   **15** Post egrediantur novitii] for a similar regulation in the Prémontré and Val-des-Écoliers texts, see *supra*, p. 318, with note 198

Text. rec., **Cap. 2, 5** institutionibus vel de evangelio CR : de institutionibus vel de regula vel de epistola S

prostrati veniam petant. Deinde surgentes humiliter confiteantur culpas suas. Et quorum culpa talis est, que digna est correctione, preparent se ad correctionem. Quam correctionem faciat prior vel ille, cui ipse iniunxerit. In capitulo fratres nisi duabus de causis non
20   loquantur, scilicet culpas suas vel aliorum simpliciter dicendo et prelatis suis tantum ad interrogata respondendo. Nullus faciat proclamationem super aliquem ex sola suspicione.

Quando prelatus iniunxerit aliquam communem orationem, inclinent omnes. Similiter omnes faciant, quibus aliquid facere vel dicere iniunxerit. Si vero aliquam obedientiam vel officium vel ministerium aliquod cuivis iniunxerit, humiliter
25   prosternat se, suscipiens quod iniunctum | prosternens se, suscipiat quod iniunctum fuerit ei. | fuerit ei.

Auditis culpis, dicitur p s a l m u s   *L a u d a t e   D o m i n u m   o m n e s   g e n t e s* cum versu *O s t e n d e   n o b i s   D o m i n e* et *D o m i n u s   v o b i s c u m* et collecta *A c t i o n e s   n o s t r a s* etc. In fine dicat prior: *Adiutorium nostrum* etc. Et sic solvitur
30   capitulum.

3. DE MULIERIBUS NON INTROMITTENDIS

Mulieres claustrum, officinas nostras et oratorium numquam ingrediantur, nisi in consecratione ecclesie. In Parasceve vero chorum poterunt intrare usque ad officium. Sed in ecclesia laicorum vel extra in loco determinato prior eis de Deo et de spiri-
5   tualibus loquatur.

4. DE HORIS ET DE MODO DICENDI

Matutinas et missam et omnes horas canonicas simul audiant fratres nostri et simul comedant, nisi cum aliquibus prelatus aliter dispensare voluerit. Hore omnes in ecclesia breviter et succincte taliter dicantur, ne fratres devotionem amittant et
5   eorum studium minime impediatur. Quod ita dicimus esse faciendum, ut in medio versus metrum cum pausa servetur, non protrahendo vocem in pausa vel in fine

---

19 ille *CS* : *om. R*   ipse *SR* : prior *C, om. M*   **19/20** fratres ... loquantur *C* : non loquantur fratres nisi duabus de causis *R, aliter SPaPb*   **23** aliquid facere *MSR(1,2)* : facere aliquid *C*   iniunxerit *MSR* : iniunxit *C*   **25** prosternat se suscipiens *textum antiquiorem habet M cum PaPb*   **29** nostras *CM* : *om. SR(2,6)*
Cap. 3, 3 vero *C* : tantum *R(2,1)*   **4/5** Sed ... loquatur *C* : *om. S(1,4)R*
Cap. 4, 1 de¹ ... dicendi *C* : De matutinis et horis et modo dicendis *S(1,3)*, De officio ecclesie *MR(1,1)*

25 prosternat se suscipiens] oldest text, preserved in *Const. S. M. Magd.* (cf. *supra*, p. 255, with note 65)
27/29 psalmus ... nostras] for the affinity with Saint-Ruf, see *supra*, p. 308; — for the dating (1216), see p. 382, with note 64
Cap. 3, 1/5 for the dating (1220-1231), see *supra*, p. 406, with notes 215-216   **2/3** Mulieres ... ecclesie] cf. Pb, IV, 13; see *supra*, p. 320, note 211
Cap. 4, 1/8 de¹ ... observetur for the dating (1220-1231), see *supra*, p. 406, with notes 215-216

Text. rec., **Cap. 2, 25** prosternens se suscipiat *textus recentiorem habent CR* : se prosternens, suscipiat *S*

versus, sed, sicut dictum est, breviter et succincte terminetur. Hoc tamen magis et minus pro tempore observetur.

⟨Item, numquam terminamus missam cum *Alleluia*.

Totum officium, tam nocturnum quam diurnum, confirmamus et volumus ab   10 omnibus uniformiter observari, ita quod nulli liceat de cetero aliquid innovare.⟩

5. DE REFECTIONE

A Pascha usque ad festum sancte Crucis reficiantur bis fratres, exceptis diebus Rogatio-num et sextis feriis et vigilia Pentecostes et ieiuniis Quatuor Temporum, vigilia Iohannis Baptiste, Petri et Pauli, Iacobi et Laurentii, Assumptionis sancte Marie et Bartholomei.

6. DE IEIUNIO

A festo sancte Crucis usque ad Pascha continuum tenebimus ieiunium et nona dicta comedemus, exceptis dominicis diebus. In toto autem Adventu et Quadragesima et ieiuniis Quatuor Temporum, in vigilia Ascensionis et Pentecostes et sancti Iohannis, Petri et Pauli et Matthei, Simonis et Iude et Omnium Sanctorum, Andree apostoli et omnibus   5 sextis feriis, nisi dies Natalis Domini ea die venerit, quadragesimali utimur cibo, nisi cum aliquo propter laborem dispensetur, vel in locis in quibus aliter comederetur, vel nisi precipuum festum fuerit. Itinerantes tamen bis refici possunt,
nisi in Adventu, exceptis   nisi in Adventu et Quadragesima et
ieiuniis principalibus ab Ecclesia institutis.   10

---

9 Item ... Alleluia *huc transtuli* : *in extrav.(2,36)* C, *om. cet.*   **10/11** Totum ... innovare *hic R(1,1)* : *post 2,37C, om. SM*   tam nocturnum quam diurnum C : tam diurnum quam nocturnum R   **4** et sancti Iohannis **4** C : Iohannis S, sancti Iohannis Baptiste *R(1,4)*
Cap. 6, 5 Pauli et Matthei CS : Pauli, in vigilia sancti Laurentii et Assumptionis sancte Marie et Matthei R, *cf.* Pauli, Iacobi, Laurentii, Assumptionis sancte Marie, Bartholomei, Matthei *Pa(4,13)Pb(1,10)*   **7** in²] *om.* C   **9** in Adventu exceptis C, in Adventu et R, in Adventu Domini et Quadragesima *A(p.6)*, in predicto Adventu vel Quadragesima et S

9/11 for the dating (1221-1235), see p. 410, with note 241
Cap. 5, 1/4 cf. PaPb, I, 5; see *supra*, p. 285; — for the dating (1216), see p. 381
Cap. 6, 2/6 A ... cibo] for the dating (1216), see *supra*, p. 381   **2/3** A ... diebus] cf. PaPb, I, 6; see *supra*, p. 285   **3/6** In ... cibo] cf. Pa, IV, 13, Pb, I, 10

Text. rec., **Cap. 6, 1** nisi in Adventu et Quadragesima] added in 1236 (*Acta C.G.*, p. 6)

7. DE PRANDIO

Hora competenti ante prandium vel cenam a sacrista paucis ictibus campana pulsetur, ut fratres ad refectionem venire non tardent. Tunc pulsetur cymbalum, si cibus est paratus, alioquin non pulsetur donec paratus sit. Ablutis vero manibus, prior nolam refec-
5   torii

percutiat   pulset

et tunc fratres ingrediantur. Quibus ingressis,

incipiat nolam pulsare. Qua pulsata,

dicat *Benedicite*, qui dicit versiculos. Et conventus prosequatur benedictionem, et
10   comedant. Verumtamen servitores i n c i p i a n t ab inferioribus, u s q u e   a d mensam prioris ascendentes.

⟨Nullus fratrum presentium a prima mensa remaneat preter servitores et custodes, nisi de licentia. Et quotquot remanserint, comedant in secunda mensa, ita quod tertiam mensam facere non oporteat.

15   Nulla fiat pictantia servitoribus vel ministris, que non fit conventui, nisi sint infirmi vel minuti. P r i o r e s   c o m e d a n t   i n   r e f e c t o r i o et cibariis conventus sint c o n t e n t i . Similiter infirmarii et receptores hospitum et ministri et alii fratres, nisi cum aliquibus prior dispensaverit ob aliquam causam, ut extra conventum aliquando comedant. Si autem priores infirmari contigerit, in infirmaria cum
20   aliis fratribus procurentur.⟩

Frater non mittat fratri pictantiam, excepto priore, sed sibi datam potest dare a dextris et a sinistris.

8. DE PULMENTIS

Pulmenta nostra sint ubique sine carnibus in nostris conventibus.

Cap. 7, 1 de prandio CS : De modo eundi ad prandium *M(c.6)*, De cibo *R(1,5)*   **6** percutiat *textum antiquiorem habet M cum Pa(1,10)Pb(1,9)*   **8** incipiat ... pulsata *textum antiquiorem habet M* : *cf.* priore interim nolam pulsante, qua sufficienter pulsata *PaPb, om. CSR*   **9/10** et comedant *CM* : *om. SR,* Verumtamen servitores *CS* : servitores autem *R,* servitrices *M*   **12** a prima mensa remaneat *SRM* : remaneat a prima mensa *C*   **14** tertiam mensam *SRM* : mensam tertiam *C*   **18** prior dispensaverit *SR* : priorissa ... dispensaverit *M,* dispensaverit prior *C*

Cap. 7, 2/9 Hora ... Benedicite] cf. Pa, I, 10, Pb, I, 9; see *supra,* p. 285, with note 32; — for the dating (1216), see *supra,* p. 381   **6** percutiat] oldest text, preserved in *Const. S. M. Magd.* (cf. *supra,* p. 255, with note 65)   **8** oldest text, preserved in *Const. S. M. Magd.* (cf. *loco cit.*)   **10/11** Verumtamen ... ascendentes] for the affinity with Benedictine customs, see *supra,* pp. 308-309; — for the dating (1216), see p. 382, with note 65   **12/20** for the dating (1220-1231), see p. 408, note 226   **16/17** Priores ... contenti] cf. Innocent III to Val-des-Choux (1205); see *supra,* p. 309   **21/22** cf. Pa, I, 10, Pb, I, 9; see *supra,* p. 292
Cap. 8, 2/12 for the dating (1216) of the parts derived from Prémontré, see *supra,* p. 381   cf. Pa, IV, 12, Pb, I, 10; see *supra,* p. 293, with note 61

Text. rec., **Cap. 7, 1** pulset] *textum recentiorem habent CSR*

⟨Et fratribus nostris, ne sint hominibus onerosi, pulmenta cocta cum carnibus comedere liceat extra claustrum. Fratres nostri, tam priores quam alii, in locis ubi conventum h a b u e r i m u s , n i s i cum episcopis vel i n d o m i b u s r e l i g i o - 5 s orum et hoc raro, e x t r a claustrum c o m e d e r e non presumant.⟩ Singulis diebus, si fieri potest, duo cocta pulmenta habeant. Poterit autem prior superaddere, prout opus esse iudicaverit et facultas permiserit. Si quis iuxta se sedenti viderit aliquid deesse de communi, requirat a cellario vel a ministro. Si quis de servitoribus vel comedentibus serviendo vel comedendo in aliquo offenderit, surgentibus fratribus, veniam petat et, facto signo a 10 prelato, redeat ad locum suum. Quicumque voluerit bibere extra horam, licentiam petat a prelato et unum socium accipiat.

⟨Si quid petitum fuerit ab uno priore, non petatur ab alio, nisi causa exposita. Sed nec, si a maiore petitum fuerit, vadat ad minorem.⟩

9. DE COLLATIONE ET COMPLETORIO

Tempore ieiunii, hora competenti sacrista ad collationem pulset signum. Et fratribus venientibus in conventum, ad signum prioris legat lector, premisso *Iube domne*. Et sequatur benedictio *Noctem quietam* etc. Et infra lectionem poterunt fratres bibere, facto signo a priore et dicto *Benedicite* a lectore et data benedictione ab hebdomadario: 5 *Largitor omnium bonorum* etc. Finita lectione, dicat qui preest: *Adiutorium nostrum* etc. Et tunc cum silentio intrent fratres ecclesiam. Alio vero tempore, ante completorium legatur lectio in ecclesia: *Fratres, sobrii estote*. Et facta confessione et dicto completorio, det benedictionem qui preest. Et hebdomadarius aspergat aquam benedictam. Et postea dicatur *Pater noster* et *Credo in Deum*. Quod etiam fieri debet ante primam 10 et ante matutinas.

Cap. 8, 4 comedere liceat *M(c.7)R(1,5)* : liceat comedere *C*   **5** episcopis *SR* : episcopo *C*   **8** esse] *om. C*   **9** cellario *C* : celleraria *corr. M., cf.* cellerario *Pa(1,10)Pb(1,9), om. S,* servitore *R*   a² *CS : om. MR cum PaPb*   **13/14** Si ... minorem *hic S : in extrav.(2,36) C, in 1,14 R*   **14** Sed *CS : om. R*   petitum fuerit *R :* postulatum fuerit *S,* petierit *C*
Cap. 9, 1 et completorio *CS : om. M(c.8)R(1,6) cum Pa(1,13)Pb(1,11)*   **4** Noctem quietam etc *CS cum Pa :* Noctem quietam et vitam perpetuam tribuat nobis omnipotens et misericors Dominus *M,* Noctem quietam et finem perfectum tribuat nobis omnipotens et misericors Dominus *R, cf.* Noctem quietam et vitam beatam etc. *Pb*

3/6 Et ... presumant] for the dating (1220-1231), see p. 408, note 226   **4/6** Fratres ... presumant] cf. *Reg. S. Trin.* and *Reg. S. Spir.*; see *supra*, p. 320, with notes 209-210   **6/8** Singulis ... permiserit] cf. Pa, IV, 12, Pb, I, 10; see *supra*, p. 293, with note 61   **8/11** Si ... suum] cf. Pa, I, 10, Pb, I, 9; see *supra*, p. 293, with note 62, p. 306, with note 131   **11** Quicumque ... petat] cf. Pa, I, 12, Pb, I, 9   **13/14** for the dating (1220-1231), see *supra*, p. 408, with note 225
Cap. 9, 1/11 for the dating (1216), see *supra*, p. 382, with note 65   **1/9** de ... benedictam] for the influence of Prémontré (Pa, I, 13, Pb, I, 11) and monastic customs, see *supra*, pp. 310-313   **6** Largitor omnium bonorum] cf. *Eccles. officia Cist.*, c. 121 (ed. Ph. Guignard, p. 245)

10. DE LECTIS

Super culcitras non dormiant fratres nostri, nisi forte stramen vel aliquid tale, super quod dormiant, habere non possint. Cum tunica et caligis cincti dormiant. Super stramina et laneos et saccones dormire licebit.

5   ⟨Extra domum autem iacere poterunt sicut fuerit eis stratum, ne hospites molestentur. Qui autem culcitram petierit, ieiunet unam diem in pane et aqua.

Nullus, excepto magistro ordinis, qui in communi tolerari potest, habeat specialem locum ad iacendum, nisi propter rerum custodiam. Lectoribus tamen secundum discretionem priorum provideatur.⟩

11. DE INFIRMIS

Circa infirmos caveat ne sit n e g l i g e n s prelatus. *Sic* enim procurandi *sunt, ut citius* releventur, sicut dicit pater noster Augustinus. Poterunt etiam quidam vesci c a r n i b u s, prout eorum gravior requirit infirmitas, secundum quod p r e l a t o

5   v i s u m   f u e r i t.

Si quis autem talem infirmitatem habeat, que nec eum multum debilitet nec comedendi turbet appetitum, ut inflatura vel incisio membrorum vel aliquid huiusmodi, talis nec super culcitram iaceat, nec ieiunia consuetudinaria frangat, nec cibos refectorii mutet. Legat autem vel operetur, secundum quod ei a suo prelato iniungetur.

10   ⟨Item, in domibus nostris non sint nisi duo loca in quibus comedant debiles vel infirmi, unus carnium et alius ciborum aliorum, nisi sit evidens necessitas vel urgens infirmitas. Similiter nec alii fratres comedant nisi in communi refectorio vel in domo hospitum.

Fratres nostri infirmi in locis, ubi conventum habemus, carnes extra domos

15   non comedant.⟩

Cap. 10, 5 Extra ... molestentur *SR(1,9) cum A(p.6)* : *om.* C   iacere ... stratum *SR* : sicut eis stratum fuerit, iacere poterunt *A*   **6** Qui ... aqua *R cum A* : *om.* CS   unam diem *scripsi cum A* : una die *R*   **7 / 9** Nullus ... provideatur *R cum A* : *om.* CS   Nullus ... ordinis *scripsi cum A* : Excepto magistro ordinis, nullus *R*   **7/8** specialem locum *scripsi cum A* : locum specialem *R*
Cap. 11, 6 habeat CS : habet *M(c.10) cum Pa(1,19)Pb(1,18)*   **7** vel² CS : aut *M cum PaPb*   **10 / 13** Item ... hospitum *SR(1,8) cum A(p.6)* : *ad 1,7 marg. dextr. transt.* C   non sint *SR cum A* : ubique non habeant C   **11** et] *om.* C   **13** in domo hospitum *SR* : domo hospitum *A*, hospitum domo C   **14 / 15** Fratres ... comedant *scripsi cum A(p.6)* : In locis vero, ubi conventum habemus, extra domum carnes non comedant *R(1,7), om.* CS   habemus *R* : non *praem.* A

Cap. 10, 2/4 cf. Pa, I, 17, Pb, I, 14, Pb, I, 12; see *supra*, p. 285, note 33; — for the dating (1216), see p. 381   **5/9** added in 1236 (*Acta C.G.*, p. 6)
Cap. 11, 1 cf. Pa, I, 19, Pb, I, 18; see *supra*, p. 306   **2/5** cf. *Reg. S. Ben.*, c.36, and *Reg. Humiliatorum*, c. 28; see *supra*, p. 314, with note 174; — for the dating (1216), see *supra*, p. 382, with note 66   **2/3** Sic ... releventur] cf. *Reg. S. Aug.*, c.5: "... sic tractandi sunt, ut citius recreentur"   **6/9** Si ... operetur] cf. Pa, I, 19, Pb, I, 18); see *supra*, p. 306; — for the dating (1216), see *supra*, p. 381   **10/15** added in 1236 (*Acta C.G.*, p. 6)

12. DE MINUTIONE

Minutio quater in anno fiat: prima in mense septembri, secunda post Natale, tertia post Pascha, quarta circa festum Iohannis Baptiste. Preter has minutiones nullus audeat sibi minuere, nisi discretio prioris propter aliquam causam iudicaverit aliter esse faciendum.   5

Minuti extra refectorium cum silentio comedant, ubi commode poterit observari. Et secundum quod facultas domus permiserit, commodius procurentur, sed causa minutionis carnes non comedant.

13. DE MAGISTRO NOVITIORUM

Prior novitiis magistrum diligentem in instructione eorum preponat, qui eos de ordine doceat, in ecclesia excitet et, ubicumque negligenter se habuerint, verbo vel signo, quantum poterit, eos studeat emendare. Et necessaria, quantum potest, debet eis procurare. De apertis negligentiis, cum ante eum veniam petierint, penitentiam potest dare   5
vel eos in suo capitulo proclamare.

H u m i l i t a t e m   c o r d is et c o r p o r is doceat habere et studeat ad hoc ipsum instruere, iuxta illud: *Discite a me, quia mitis sum et humilis corde*; frequenter, pure et discrete confiteri, sine proprio vivere e t   p r o p r i a m   v o l u n t a t e m   d e s e -
r e r e   pro voluntate prelati sui, obedientiam in omnibus voluntariam observare,   10
quomodo ubique et in omnibus sese habere debeant, instruere; quod locum, ubi positi fuerint, ubique teneant; quomodo inclinationes sint faciende danti sibi aliquid vel auferenti, male vel bene dicenti; qualiter se contineant ad cameras; ut non habeant *oculos sublimes*; quomodo vel quid orent et quam silenter, ut aliis rugi-
tum non faciant; et ubicumque reprehensi fuerint a prelato, statim veniam petant;   15

Cap. 13, 2 instructione $SR(1,14)$: instructionem C   3 negligenter se CR : se negligenter $M(c.12)S$ *cum*
$Pa(2,9)Pb(2,9)$ 6 eos ... capitulo C : eos in capitulo S, in suo capitulo eos R, in capitulo ... eas M
8 instruere S : novitium *add*.C, *cf*. eas informare M, *om*. R   9 et² CS : *om*. MR   diserere C
11 instruere CS : decenter instruat M, ipsos decenter instruere R   12 ubique MR : *om*. C   12/
13 quomodo ... dicenti C : quomodo inclinationes sint faciende, danti sibi aliquid vel auferenti, male
vel bene dicenti, qualiter sit respondendum S, quomodo sibi danti aliquid vel auferenti, male vel bene
dicenti, inclinare debent R, quomodo inclinent M   15 statim MS : *om*. C

Cap. 12, 1/5 for the dating (1216, 1220-1231), see *supra*, pp. 381 and 406, with note 217   cf. Pa, I, 20, Pb,
I, 19; see p. 406, note 217   3 quarta ... Baptiste] cf. Pb, I, 19: "... secunda post festum Iohannis Baptiste"
4 discretio prioris] cf. Pa, I, 20: "Minutio in discretione abbatis vel prioris sit"
Cap. 13, 1/28 for the dating (1216), see *supra*, p. 406   1/5 de ... dare] cf. PaPb, II, 9; see *supra*, p. 293,
with note 64   7/28 for the dating (1216), see supra, p. 382, with note 67   7/9 Humilitatem ...
deserere] cf. *Reg. S. Ben.*, c. 7 and c. 5; see *supra*, pp. 313-314, with note 170   8 Discite ... corde] *Matth.*,
XI,29   14 oculos sublimes] cf. Goswin of Anchin, *De novitiis instruendis*: "Studeat habere ... oculos
stabiles et non sublimes" (according to MS. Douai 827, quoted by J. Leclercq, *Deux opuscules sur la
formation des jeunes moines*, in *Revue d'ascétique et de mystique*, vol. XXXIII, 1957, p. 390); cf. also *Prov.*,
VI,16-17: "Sex sunt, quae odit Dominus, et septimum detestatur anima eius: oculos sublimes..."; cf. *Is.*,
II,11

ut cum nemine contendere presumant, sed in omnibus magistro suo obediant; in claustro ad processionem socium sibi collateralem attendant; et non loquantur locis et temporibus interdictis; quando etiam quippiam vestimenti tribuitur, profunde inclinantes *Benedictus Deus in donis suis* dicant; ut neminem penitus iudi-

20 cent, sed si que ab ullo fieri viderint, licet mala videantur, bona suspicentur vel bona intentione facta, sepe enim humanum fallitur iudicium; quomodo venia in capitulo vel ubicumque reprehensi fuerint, sit facienda; qualiter disciplinas frequenter suscipiant; et non loquantur de absente nisi que bona sunt; quod dua- bus m a n i b u s sit bibendum e t s e d e n d o ; quod diligenter debeant custodire

25 libros et vestes et etiam res alias monasterii; qualiter intenti esse debeant in studio, ut de die, de nocte, in domo, in itinere legant aliquid vel meditentur, et quicquid poterunt, retinere cordetenus nitantur; quam ferventes esse debeant in predicatio- ne tempore opportuno.

14. DE RECIPIENDIS

Recipiendi ad nos venientes, secundum tempus quod discretio prelati vel quorum- dam seniorum providerit, ducantur in capitulum. Qui cum adducti fuerint, prosternant se in medio capituli. Et interrogati a prelato quid querant, respondeant: *Misericordiam Dei et*

5 *vestram.* Quibus ad iussum prelati erectis, exponat asperitatem ordinis, voluntatem eorum requirens. Qui si respondeant se velle cuncta servare et seculo abrenuntiare, dicat post cetera: *Dominus qui cepit, ipse perficiat.* Et conventus respondeat: *Amen.* Et tunc, deposi- tis vestibus secularibus et religiosis indutis, in nostram societatem in capitulo reci- piantur. Sed tamen adhuc, antequam stabilitatem et communitatem promittant et

10 obedientiam prelato et successoribus suis faciant, tempus probationis assignetur.
⟨Nullus recipiatur nisi requisitus an sit coniugatus, an servus, an ratiociniis obliga- tus, vel alterius professionis, vel occultam habeat infirmitatem. Quod s i a l t e r i u s

---

16/17 in claustro C : ubique S, *om.* MR   **17** sibi collateralem SR : collateralem sibi C, collateralem M
20 sed si SR : si C, et si M   vident C   suspicuntur C   **24** sit bibendum MS : bibendum sit C, bibant
R   **25** et etiam res alias C : et res etiam alias R, et res alias M, aliasque res S   **27** quam ... predicatione
S : quam ferventes esse debeant in oratione M, qualiter ferventes in predicatione esse debeant C
Cap. 14, 4/5 Misericordiam ... vestram M(c.13)R(1,13) cum Pa(1,16)Pb(1,14) : Dei et vestram
misericordiam C, Dei misericordiam et vestram S   **5** asperitatem CS cum PaPb : austeritatem MR
6 velle cuncta CS cum Pa : cuncta velle MR cum Pa   et seculo abrenuntiare CMS : *om.* R cum PaPb
7 Dominus qui cepit CR : Dominus qui incepit S, Deus qui incepit in vobis M, *cf.* Deus qui cepit in
vobis PaPb   conventus respondeat CSR : respondeat conventus M cum PaPb   **8** indutis C : induti SR
recipiantur] *abhinc deficit textus in S usque ad 1,21 (post* 39 *lectionem)*   **9** communitatem C :
communem vitam R cum Pa   **12** vel¹ ... vel² C cum Pb : an -- vel R, an -- an M

23/24 duabus ... sedendo] cf. *Cons. Clun.,* lib. II, c. 23; see *supra,* p. 314, with note 172
Cap. 14, 1/10 cf. Pa, I, 16, Pb, I, 14; see *supra,* pp. 293-394; — for the dating (1216), see p. 381
7 Dominus ... perficiat] cf. II *Cor.,* VIII,7: "... ut quemadmodum coepit, ita et perficiat in vobis etiam
gratiam hanc"   **11/14** Nullus ... approbatus] for the dating (1225-1231), see *supra,* p. 408, note 226   **11/
12** Nullus ... infirmitatem] for the origins, see pp. 314-315   **12/14** Quod ... approbatus] cf. Const.
Vallis-Scholarium and *Reg. S. Spir.;* see *supra,* p. 315

religionis fuerit, non recipiatur in ordine nostro, nisi a capitulo provinciali vel generali fuerit approbatus. Cistercienses non admittantur nisi de speciali licentia domini pape.   15

Conventualis prior nullum in conversum recipiat, in canonicum vero neminem, nisi requisito consensu totius vel maioris partis capituli et obtento.

Nullus recipiatur infra octodecim annos.

In quolibet autem conventu eligantur tres idonei fratres de communi consilio capituli, qui recipiendos in moribus et scientia diligenter examinent et examinatio-   20 nem priori et capitulo referant, eorum iudicio, an recipi debeant, relinquentes.⟩

15. DE TEMPORE PROBATIONIS

Probationis tempus statuimus sex mensium vel eo amplius, prout prela-to videbitur, ut et ipse austeritates ordinis et fratres mores experian-tur ipsius, nisi forte aliquis maturus et discretus probationi predicte renuntia-re voluerit et instanter se offerat professioni faciende.   5

⟨Item, novitii ante professionem de debitis se expediant et omnia alia ad pedes prioris ponant, ut se ex toto absolvant.

Item, nulli certus usus librorum concedatur, nec indignetur a quocumque aufe-rantur vel in cuiuscumque custodia dimittantur.

Item, omnes fratres nostri singulis annis semel omnia sibi commissa prioribus   10 suis exponant et exhibeant, eorum dispositioni omnia relinquendo.

Item, novitii infra tempus probationis sue in psalmodia et officio divino studeant diligenter.

Item, confessiones novitiorum ante professionem recipiantur, et diligenter de modo confessionis et in aliis instruantur.   15

Item, novitii non intersint capitulo nec in dormitorio cum aliis fratribus iaceant, ubi hoc commode poterit observari. Sed magister eorum extra capitulum culpas eorum audiat et ipsos diligenter, quantum potest, in moribus instruat et caritative corripiat.

---

13 religionis] professus *add. R*   14 provinciali vel generali *C* : generali vel provinciali *R*   17 obtentu *C*   18 octodecim *C* : decem et octo *R*   19 autem *C* : *om. R*   eligantur tres idonei fratres *C* : tres idoneis fratres eligantur *R*   de *C* : *om. R*
Cap. 15, 3 austeritates *C* : asperitates *R(1,13)*   6 Item *R(1,14)* : *om. C*   8/9 Item ... dimittantur *hic C* : *in 2,14 R*   Item nulli *C* : *Nulli etiam R*   10/11 Item ... relinquendo *R(1,14) cum A(p.7)* : *om. CS*   Item ... nostri *scripsi cum A* : Similiter omnes fratres *R*   11 omnia *A* : *om. R*   12/22 Item ... ordinentur *hic R* : *in 1,16 C*   Item *R* : *om. C*   14 Item *R* : *om. C*   16 Item *R* : *om. C*

14/15 Cistercienses ... pape] for the origins, see p. 315; — or the dating (c. 1223), see p. 315, note 182   16/17 cf. bull of Gregory IX (1232); see *supra*, pp. 315-316   18/21 for the dating (1232-1235), see pp. 410-411, note 241   for parallel texts, see p. 314, with notes 176-177
Cap. 15, 1/9 for the dating (1220-1235), see *supra*, p. 410, note 241   2/5 for the connection with other texts, see pp. 316-318   10/11 added in 1236 (*Acta C.G.*, p. 7)   12/22 for the dating (1220-1235), see *supra*, p. 410, note 241   16 Item ... capitulo] cf. Pb, I, 14, *Const. Vallis-Schol.* and *Cons. S. Benigni Divion.*; see *supra*, pp. 318-319, note 198

20   Item, novitii, tam clerici quam laici, i n f r a   a n n u m   a d longinquas partes
nisi ob causam necessariam n o n   m i tt a n t u r , nec in aliquo officio occupentur,
et vestes eorum ante professionem non alienentur, nec ipsi ante professionem ordinentur.⟩

16. DE MODO FACIENDI PROFESSIONEM

Modus faciendi professionem talis est: *Ego N. facio professionem et promitto*
obedientiam Deo et beate Marie et tibi N., magistro ordinis Predicatorum, et successoribus
tuis, secundum regulam beati Augustini et institutiones fratrum ordinis Predicatorum, quod
5   *ero obediens tibi tuisque successoribus usque ad mortem.* Cum autem fit alii priori
cuicumque, sic facienda est: *Ego N. facio professionem et promitto obedientiam Deo et*
beate Marie et tibi N., priori talis loci, vice N., magistri ordinis Predicatorum et successo-
rum eius, secundum regulam beati Augustini et institutiones fratrum ordinis Predicatorum,
quod ero obediens tibi tuisque successoribus usque ad mortem.
10   ⟨Vestes novitiorum, quando professionem faciunt, benedicantur, ad minus
scapulare.⟩

17. DE SILENTIO

Silentium fratres nostri t e n e a n t   i n   c l a u s t r o , in d o r m i t o r i o , in
cellis, in r e f e c t o r i o   e t   o r a t o r i o fratrum, n i s i   f o r t e silenter aliquid
l o q u a n t u r , non tamen oratione perfecta. Alibi vero l o q u i   p o teru n t de licen-
5   tia speciali.

---

20 Item *R* : *om. C*   **22** et ... non *C* : nec *R*
Cap. 16, 1 de modo faciendi professionem *C* : De modo professionis *M(c.14)*, De professione *R(1,15)*
4 fratrum ordinis *C* : ordinis fratrum *R*   **5** fit *R* : sit *C*   **6** est *R* : sit *C*   **10/11** Vestes ... scapulare
scripsi cum A(p.8) : *orationem pro benedictione vestium add. R, cf. tit.* De modo faciendi professionem et
benedictione vestium novitiorum *S ante dist. I.*
Cap. 17, 2 fratres nostri teneant *R(1,12)* : sorores nostre teneant *M(c.15)*, teneant fratres nostri *C*

20/21 infra ... mittantur] cf. *Const. S. Dion. Remensis*, see *supra*, p. 319, note 199   **22** nec ... ordinentur]
cf. Pb. I, 15; see *supra*, p. 319, note 200
Cap. 16, 2/5 Ego ... mortem] for the history and affinity of the formula, see *supra*, pp. 297-302;
— for the dating (1216 and 1220), see p. 388, note 118   **10/11** added in 1236 (*Acta C.G.*, p. 8)
Cap. 17, 1/29 for the dating (1220-1231), see *supra*, p. 406, note 217   **2/5** for the sources, see pp. 319-
320

Prior ad mensam loqui poterit.

In mensa autem omnes fratres ubique intus et extra silentium teneant, tam priores quam alii, excepto uno, qui maior fuerit inter ipsos, vel alio, cui pro se loqui commiserit, et tunc ipse taceat. Si quis vero illud silentium fregerit ex proposito, vel licentiam loquendi dederit, in uno prandio aquam tantum bibat absque dispensatione, et similiter unam disciplinam coram omnibus recipiat in capitulo. Ab hiis autem excipiuntur infirmi decumbentes.   10   15

Infirmi non decumbentes a prandio usque ad vesperas silentium teneant, similiter et post signum quod fit post completorium. A minutis etiam post primam diem sue minutionis idem similiter observetur.   20

Pena pro fractione silentii hec est: pro prima vice *Miserere mei* et *Pater noster*; hoc etiam dicitur pro secunda; pro tertia recipiatur disciplina; hoc etiam similiter pro quarta, pro quinta, similiter pro sexta; pro septima vero una die abstineant in pane et aqua in terra sedendo, et hoc in prandio et non in cena. Ultra vero septem vices non computent, sed iterum a principio computare incipiant. Et hoc, quod   25 dictum est, inter duo capitula intelligitur, ita quod ab uno capitulo usque ad aliud incipiant fractiones computare. Disciplinas autem has per se recipere poterunt vel cum aliis fratribus post completorium. Si vero aliqua supersit, cum tenetur capitulum, ibidem recipiatur.

6/18 Prior ... non *textum antiquiorem habet M, cf. A(p.6)*   **19** etiam *CM* : quoque *R*   **21** silentio *C* Miserere] dicatur *praem. M*   **25** hoc] totum *add. R*   **26** ita *MR* : scilicet *add. C*   **27** has *MR* : *om. C* poterunt *MR* : possunt *C*   **28** aliis fratribus *C* : sororibus aliis *M*, aliis *R*   supersit *CM* : sit *R*

23/19, 8 abstineant ... impleatur]

Text. rec., **Cap. 17, 6/17** In ... decumbentes *textum recentiorem habent CR cum A(p.6-7)*   **6/7** In ... teneant *scripsi cum A* : In mensa autem fratres ubique intus et extra teneant silentium *C*, Omnes fratres ubique intus et extra in mensa silentium teneant *R*   **9** ipsos *C cum A* : eos *R*   **11** vero *C cum A* : autem *R*   illud silentium *scripsi cum A* : hoc silentium *R*, silentium istud *C*   **12** licentiam loquendi *CR* : loquendi licentiam *A*   **13** aquam tantum *CR* : tantum aquam *A*   **14/16** et ... capitulo *A* : coram omnibus similiter unam disciplinam recipiat in capitulo *C*, et unam disciplinam coram fratribus omnibus in capitulo accipiat *R*   **16** Ab *C* : de *A*

Text. rec., **Cap. 17, 6/17** In ... decumbentes] added in 1236 (*Acta C.G.*, p. 6-7)   **6/14** In ... dispensatione] for the affinity with Prémontré, see pp. 294-295
16/19 infirmi ... completorium] for the affinity with Prémontré, see p. 295

18. DE SCANDALO FRATRUM

Si quis aliquo modo fratrem suum scandalizaverit, tamdiu ante pedes eius prostratus iaceat, quousque placatus erigat eum.

<table>
<tr><td>19. DE VESTITU</td><td>19. DE VESTIBUS</td></tr>
</table>

Qui in domibus regum sunt, mollibus induuntur. [Clericos] qui seculo abrenuntiarunt, decet asper vestitus et humilis.
5 Eapropter proposuimus lineis non uti, nisi femoralibus. Lanee autem vestes, quibus utimur, non sint nimis subtiles nec deforis attonse, ut impleatur illud in regula: *Non sit notabilis habitus vester, nec affectetis vestibus*
10 *placere, sed moribus.* Sufficit autem [fratri] habere duas tunicas cum pellicio. Pellicium numquam portetur nisi opertum tunica, nisi frater superpellicio et alba induitur. Pellicium sit tunica brevius, ut non appa-
15 reat.

Vestes laneas non attonsas, ubi hoc servari poterit, deferant fratres nostri. Ubi vero servari non poterit, utantur v i l i b u s . Et potius vilitas in cappis observetur. Et lineis non utantur ad carnem, nec etiam infirmi. Et linteamina omnino removeantur de infirmitoriis nostris. Et non plures tunicas [habere liceat] quam tres cum pellicio in hieme vel quatuor sine pellicio, quod semper tunica cooperatum deferatur.

Cap. 18, 2 quis C *cum* Pa(*1,9*) : qua vero M(*c.15*), quis autem R(*1,14*)   aliquo ... suum C *cum* Pa : aliquo modo sororem M, fratrem suum aliquo modo R   **2/3** prostratus iaceat C *cum* Pa : iaceat prostratus MR
Cap. 19, 1 de vestitu M(*c.6*)R(*1,10*) *cum* Pa(*4,14*)Pb(*2,13*)   **3** induuntur M : *cf.* vestiuntur PaPb   Clericos *scripsi cum* Pa : illos Pb, mulieres M   abrenuntiarunt M : *cf.* abrenuntiant PaPb   **5/6** lineis ... femoralibus *scripsi cum* PaPb : ut grossis camisiis utantur sorores M   **7/8** deforis attonse *scripsi cum* PaPb : tonse deforis M   **8** impleatur M : *cf.* adimpleatur PaPb   **10** fratri *textum supplevi* : *cf.* sorori M, canonico PaPb   **12** numquam M *cum* Pb : non Pa   **13** nisi ... induitur *scripsi cum* PaPb : similiter et pellis operta mantello M

Cap. 18, 2/3 cf. Pa, I, 9; see *supra*, p. 285, with note 35; — for the dating (1216), see *supra*, p. 381
Cap. 19, 1/23 for the oldest text, preserved in *Const. S.M. Magd.*, see *supra*, pp. 258-260   **1/14** for the dating (1216), see *supra*, p. 381   **1/10** de ... moribus] cf. Pa, IV, 14, Pb, II, 13; see *supra*, pp. 258-260   **2/3** Qui ... induuntur] cf. *Matth.*, XI,8: "Ecce qui mollibus vestiuntur, in domibus regum sunt"   **8/10** Non ... moribus] *Reg. S. Aug.*, c. 6   **10/11** Sufficit ... pellicio] cf. Pa, IV, 14   **11/14** Pellicium ... appareat] cf. Pa, IV, 14, Pb, II, 13

Text. rec., **Cap. 19, 1** de vestibus CS(*ante dist. I*)   **3** differant C   **6** Et *om.* R(*1,10*)   **7** Et C : sed et R, *om.* A(*p.6*)   **7/9** linteamina ... nostris C *cum* A : sed et linteamina in infirmitoriis nostris non habeantur penitus R   **9/10** habere liceat *scripsi cum* Pb : *om.* C, aliter R   **10** pellicio R   **11** pelliceo R

Text. rec., **Cap. 19, 2/3** Vestes ... nostri] for the dating (1216), see *supra*, p. 381   **4/6** Ubi ... observetur] for the dating (1216-1220), see pp. 383-384, with notes 78, 80, 83   **4/5** utantur vilibus] cf. *Reg. bullata S. Franc.*, c.2: "Et fratres omnes vestimentis vilibus induantur..."   **5/12** for the dating (1216), see *supra*, p. 381   **6** Et lineis non utantur] cf. Pa, IV, 14, Pb, II, 13   **7/8** Et ... infirmitoriis] cf. Pb, II, 13   **9/10** Et ... tres] cf. Pb, II, 13   **10/11** cum ... pellicio] cf. Pa, IV, 14

Pelliciis silvestribus et coopertoriis quarumcumque pellium fratres nostri non utantur.

Tunica non descendat ultra cavillam pedis.	Tunice circa cavillam pedis sufficit ut descendant.

Quibus cappa brevior sit et etiam pellicium. Scapularia nostra circa cooperturam   20
genuum sufficit ut descendant. Caligas et soccos

habeant,	habebimus,

ut necesse fuerit et facultas permiserit. Ocreas non habebimus nec chirothecas.
⟨Bote extra septa monasterii non portentur.⟩

20. DE RASURA

Rasura sit superius non modica, ut religiosos decet, sic ut inter ipsam et aures non sint plus quam tres digiti. Tonsura fiat desuper aures. Que rasura et tonsura fiant hiis terminis: prima in Nativitate, secunda inter Nativitatem et Purificationem, partito tempore, tertia in Purificatione, quarta inter Purificationem et Pascha, quinta in Cena Domini, sexta inter   5
Pascha et Pentecosten, septima in Pentecoste, octava inter Pentecosten et festum Petri et Pauli, nona in festivitate eorundem, decima in festivitate sancte Marie Magdalene, undecima in Assumptione sancte Marie, duodecima in Nativitate eiusdem, tertiadecima in festo sancti Dionysii, quartadecima in festo Omnium Sanctorum, quintadecima in festo beati Andree.   10

21. DE LEVIORIBUS CULPIS

Hec sunt leviores culpe: si quis, mox ut signum datum fuerit, non relictis omnibus cum matura festinatione, differat se preparare, ut secundum regulam ad ecclesiam ordinate et

---

18 Tunica ... pedis *textum antiquiorem scripsi cum Pa* : *cf.* tunica non descendat ultra calcaneum *I(c.8)*
20 Quibus cappa brevior sit *C* : Cappa vero brevior sit tunicis *R*, *cf.* quibus cappa brevior esse debet *Pb*, cappa sit aliquantulum brevior tunica *Pa*   nostra *C* : *om. R*   22 habeant *textum antiquiorem habet M cum PaPb*   24 Bote ... portentur *hic R(1,10)* : *in extrav.(2,36) C*
Cap. 20, 3 Que rasura et tonsura *C cum Pb(1,20)* : Rasura *Pa post dist. 4*, Rasura vero *R(1,11)*   fiant *Pb* : fiat *C*   8 sancte Marie *C* : beate Virginis *R*
Cap. 21, 3/4 ad ... composite *R(1,16)* : *cf.* ad ecclesiam ordinate cum processione et composite *Pa(3,2)Pb(3,2)*, ordinate et composite ad ecclesiam *C*

16/23 for the dating (1216), see *supra*, p. 381   **16/17** cf. Pb, II, 13   **18** Tunica ... pedis] cf. Pa, IV, 14
20 Quibus cappa brevior sit] cf. Pb, II, 13   **21/23** Caligas ... chirothecas] cf. Pa, IV, 14, Pb, II, 13
24 for the dating (1220-1231), see *supra*, p. 408, note 225
Cap. 20, 1/9 cf. Pa, IV, 13, Pb, I, 20; see *supra*, p. 296; — for the dating (1216), see *supra*, p. 381
Cap. 21, 1/25 cf. PaPb, III, 1; see *supra*, p. 291; — for the dating (1216), see p. 381

Text. rec., **Cap. 19, 18/19** Tunice ... descendant *textum recentiorem habent CR cum Pb*   22 habebimus *textum recentiorem habent CR*

Text. rec., **Cap. 19, 18/19** Tunice ... descendant] cf. Pb, II, 13

composite, quando debuerit, veniat, intra septa monasterii vel extra in vicino manens; si
5   quis designatum sibi legendi vel cantandi officium non attente compleverit; si responso-
rium vel antiphonam incepturus, chorum turbaverit; si in choro male legendo vel cantando
offendens, non statim se coram omnibus humiliaverit; si in conventu hora qua debet,
venire distulerit; si aliquid ibi tumultus vel inquietudinis fecerit; si ad mensam cum ceteris
non venerit; si ad communem rasuram presens non fuerit; si in dormitorio aliquam inquie-
10   tudinem fecerit; si per licentiam de claustro egressus, moram fecerit; si corporale vel linteos
ad portandum calicem vel patenam involvendam aptos, stolam vel phanonem negligenter
deiecerit; si vestes suas et libros loco statuto honeste et ordinate non disposuerit vel
negligenter tractaverit; si aliquid utensilium fregerit vel perdiderit; si quid potus effude-
rit; si liber in quo ad refectionem vel capitulum vel ad collationem legendum est, suo
15   neglectu defuerit; si lector mense denotatus benedictionem neglexerit et dixerit aliquid,
unde scandalizentur fratres, vel egerit; si in aliquo gestu reprehensibilis fuerit vel in aliquo
notabilis apparuerit; si quis potum vel cibum absque benedictione sumpserit; si quis parentibus vel nuntiis supervenientibus loqui, ut ab eis rumores audiat, absque testimonio et
licentia prelati sui presumpserit; si in studio ad lectiones dormierit; si libros interdic-
20   tos legerit; si legentes vel audientes inquietaverit; si in predicationem vadens otio-
sa locutus fuerit vel egerit; si dissolute ridens, cacchinnis vel ludis, dictis vel factis,
alios ad ridendum concitare intenderit; si ad *Gloria* primi psalmi non affuerit et ad
gradus altaris non satisfecerit.
Pro singulis harum culparum iniungatur
25   pro pena petenti veniam unus psalmus.

21 bis. DE MEDIIS CULPIS

Media culpa est, si quis in vigilia   Si quis in vigilia
Annuntiationis et Nativitatis Domini in principio capituli per negligentiam non affuerit, ut,
pronuntiatis redemptionis nostre exordiis, corde et corpore gratias agat Deo redemptori; si
30   quis in choro positus, non divino officio intentus, vagis oculis et motu irreligioso minus
que competenti levitatem mentis ostenderit; si lectionem statuto tempore non previderit;
si commune mandatum dimiserit et si aliquid cantare vel legere presumpserit, quam quod

---

5 designatum sibi *I(c.11) cum PaPb* : diligenter *C*   **8/9** si² ... venerit *CI cum Pb* : *om. R cum Pa*
12 disposuerit *C* : reposuerit *R*   **14** ad¹ ... collationem] *om. R*   **16** unde scandalizentur] in
scandelizentur *C*   legerit *cum* l *expuncta C*   **19** studio] quis *add. R*   **20** si¹ ... inquietaverit] *om. R*
predicationem *R* : predicatione *C*   **22** concitare intenderit *C* : concitaverit *R*   si] quis *add. R*   **24/**
27 Pro ... est *textum antiquiorem habet I*   **24/25** Pro ... psalmus *scripsi cum I* : *cf.* De his omnibus
veniam petentibus iniungatur psalmus unus *Pa*   **26** de mediis culpis *scripsi cum Pa(3,2)Pb(3,2)* : De
culpis mediis *I(c.12)*   **27/28** in ... Domini *C* : in vigilia Nativitatis Domini et Annuntiationis *R(1,16), cf.*
in Annuntiatione Domini et Nativitate eius *PaPb*   **31** si] quis *add. R*   lectionem] *abhinc iterum
habetur textus in S(1,22) deficiens inde a c. 14, lin. 8 recipiantur*

17/19 si¹ ... presumpserit] for the place of these stipulations in the Prémontré text, see *supra*, p. 285,
with note 37   **22/23** si ... satisfecerit] cf. PaPb, I, 2   **24/27** for the division into two chapters in the
Prémontré text and in *Inst. S. Sixti*, see *supra*, pp. 254-255, 285-286   **27/52** cf. PaPb, III, 2   **28/**
42 Nativitatis ... studentes]

communis consensus probat; si in choro riserit vel alios ridere fecerit; si ad capitulum vel
collationem non venerit vel communi refectioni non interfuerit; si quis de via veniens,
eadem hora, si fieri potest, benedictionem accipere neglexerit vel absque ea, nisi ad vicina   35
loca vadens, de monasterio plus una nocte moraturus exierit; si quis eum, a quo clamatus
fuerit, eadem die quasi vindicando clamare presumpserit; si quis clamans in clamatione
sua iudicium fecerit; si quis cum iuramento, ut in loquendo fieri solet, aliquid negaverit vel
affirmaverit; si quis turpem sermonem vel vaniloquium dixerit vel, quod gravius est, in
usu habuerit; si quis eorum, qui officiis suis deputati sunt, in aliquo circa officium suum   40
negligens repertus fuerit, ut sunt priores in conventu custodiendo, magistri in docendo,
studentes in studendo, scriptores in scribendo, cantores in officiis suis, procuratores
in exterioribus procurandis, vestiarius in vestibus providendis et custodiendis et
reficiendis, infirmorum custos in infirmis custodiendis et procurandis et mortuis
necessariis ministrandis, et ceteri in officiis suis, ut iniunctum est eis; si oculos   45
vagos per plateas vel villas eundo ad vanitates frequenter direxerit; si indumenta
vel alia fratri data vel concessa, sine ipsius fratris licentia per se alius acceperit; si
temporibus statutis non cum aliis lectiones auditurus affuerit. Clamatis de supradictis et veniam petentibus

[fiat unius correptionis disciplina]   iniungitur unus psalmus vel duo, vel   50
cum tot psalmis, quot placuerit illi, qui   cum psalmo disciplina vel amplius,
capitulum tenebit.   secundum quod prelato videbitur expe-
    dire.

22. DE GRAVI CULPA

Gravis culpa est, si quis inhoneste in audientia secularium cum aliquo contenderit; si
frater cum fratre intus vel foris lites habuerit; vel si quis procedens ubi femine sunt, oculum
fixerit, si tamen hoc in usu
habuerit;   habere voluerit,   5
si quis mendacium de industria dixisse deprehensus fuerit; si quis silentium non tenere in
consuetudinem duxerit; si quis culpam suam vel aliorum defenderit; si quis inter fratres

---

37/38 si ... fecerit *hic CS : in 1,17 (De gravi culpa)* R   38 cum] *om.* C   40 suis *CS : om. I cum* PaPb
41 fuerit repertus C   44 in R *cum* Pa : *om.* CS   et' *SR :* in C   46/47 si ... acceperit *hic CS : in 1,17*
(De gravi culpa) R   si *CS :* quis *add.* R   48/49 Clamatis ... petentibus *CSR cum* PaPb : Clamata in
capitulo pro aliqua predictarum culparum petat veniam I   50/52 fiat ... tenebit *textum antiquiorem*
habet I cum PaPb   fiat ... disciplina *scripsi cum* PaPb : et unam recipiat disciplinam modestam I
51 placuerit illi *scripsi cum* PaPb : ei placuerit I   52 tenebit] tunc *praem.* I
Cap. 22, 4 in usu hoc C   5 habuerit *textum antiquiorem habent* I(c.13)S(1,23) *cum* Pa(3,3)Pb(3,3)

37/38 si ... fecerit] for the place of this rule in the oldest constitutions, see *supra*, pp. 274-275   46/
47 si ... acceperit] for the place of this rule in the oldest constitutions, see *supra*, pp. 275-276   48/
49 Clamatis ... petentibus] for the conclusion of this chapter in the various texts, see *supra*, p. 286
Cap. 22, 1/24 cf. PaPb, III, 3; see also *supra*, p. 291, with note 54   5 habuerit] oldest text, preserved in
Inst. S. Sixti (cf. *supra*, p. 255, with note 65)

Text. rec., **Cap. 21, 50/52** iniungitur ... expedire *textum recentiorem habent CSR*
Cap. 22, 5 habere voluerit] *textum recentiorem habent CR(1,17)*

discordiam seminaverit; si in illum, a quo clamatus est, vel in quemlibet alium minas vel
maledicta seuverba inordinata et irreligiosa malitiose invexisse deprehensus fuerit; si quis
10 alicui fratrum opprobrium dixerit; si quis fratri culpam preteritam, pro qua satisfecerit,
improperaverit; si quis sussurro vel detractor inventus fuerit; si quis mala de patribus vel
fratribus vel domibus suis malitiose evomuerit, que testimonio fratrum suorum probare
nequiverit; si absque licentia et magna necessitate equitaverit, vel carnes comederit,
vel cum femina solus non de confessione aut utilibus vel honestis locutus fuerit,
15 vel ieiunia consuetudinaria sine causa vel licentia fregerit. Pro huiusmodi culpis et his
similibus veniam petentibus et non clamatis tres correctiones in capitulo dentur et tres dies
in pane et aqua ieiunent. Clamatis vero una correctio et una dies superaddatur, de cetero
psalmi et venie, secundum quod discretioni rectoris visum fuerit, pro qualitate culparum
iniungantur.
20 ⟨Eadem pena digni sunt qui, postquam missi fuerint, sine licentia prioris reverti presumpserint vel ultra terminum sibi assignatum moram fecerint.⟩
Si quis autem pro victu vel vestitu vel qualibet alia re murmuraverit, predictam penam
sustineat et quadraginta diebus ab illo genere cibi vel potus vel indumenti, pro quo murmuraverit, abstineat.

23. DE GRAVIORI CULPA

Gravior culpa est, si quis per contumaciam vel manifestam rebellionem inobediens
prelato suo
fuerit,   │ extiterit,
5 vel cum prelato suo intus vel foris proterve contendere ausus fuerit; si quis percussor
fuerit; si quis crimen capitale commiserit,
ut furtum, sacrilegium vel aliud huiusmodi.   │
Si quis proclamatus convictus fuerit, sponte surgat et veniam petens sceleris sui
immanitatem lamentabiliter proferat et denudatus, ut dignam suis meritis accipiat senten-
10 tiam, vapulet, quantum placuerit prelato. Et ut permaneat in pena gravioribus culpis debita,
preceptum accipiat, videlicet ut sit omnium novissimus in conventu, ubi fratres sunt; ut qui,
culpam suam perpetrando, non erubuit membrum diaboli fieri, ad tempus, ut resipiscat,

---

10 culpam preteritam *CS cum Pa* : preteritam culpam *IR cum Pb*   **17** de cetero *C cum PaPb* : preter
hoc autem *SR*   **23** indumenti *C* : alterius rei *I*   **23/24** murmuraverint, abstineant *C*
Cap. 23, 4 fuerit *textum antiquiorem habet I(c.13) cum Pa(3,6)Pb(3,4)*   **7** ut ... huiusmodi *textum
antiquiorem habet I(c.14) cum Pa* : om. *CSR*   **8** Si ... fuerit *C* : Si de hiis culpis proclamatus convictus
fuerit *S*, Si fuerit proclamatus et convictus *R*   **11** accipiat *C cum PaPb* : recipiat *SI*, om. *R*   **12** culpam
suam *CS* : culpam *IR, cf.* culpas suas *PaPb*

20/21 sine ... fecerint] for a similar rule, see *supra*, p. 328, note 259; — for the dating (1220-1235), see
supra, p. 410, note 241
Cap. 23, 1/59 for the dating (1216), see *supra*, p. 381   **1/42** cf. Pa, III, 6, Pb, III, 4; see *supra*, pp. 291-
292   **4** fuerit] oldest text, preserved in *Inst. S. Sixti* (cf. *supra*, p. 255, with note 65)   **7** ut ...
huiusmodi] oldest text, preserved in *Inst. S. Sixti* (cf. *loco cit.*)

Text. rec., **Cap. 23, 1** extiterit] *textum recentiorem habent CS(1,24), om. R(1,18)* sequestretur a consortio ovium Christi. In refectorio quoque ad communem mensam cum ceteris non sedebit, sed in medio refectorii super nudam mensam comedat. Et providebitur ei seorsum panis grossior et potus aque, nisi prelatus ei aliquid per misericordiam impendat. Nec reliquie prandii sui cum aliis admisceantur, ut agnoscat se ita sequestratum a consortio aliorum, quod privetur, nisi per penitentiam redeat, consortiis angelorum.   15

Ad canonicas horas ⟨et ad gratias post comestionem⟩ veniat ante ostium ecclesie et ibi, transeuntibus fratribus, prostratus iaceat,

quousque intraverint et exierint.   dum intrant et exeunt.   20

Nullus vero audeat se coniungere illi vel aliquid mandare. Ipse tamen prelatus, ne in desperationem labi possit, mittat ad eum seniores, qui commoneant eum ad penitentiam, provocent ad patientiam, foveant per compassionem, hortentur ad satisfactionem, adiuvent per suam intercessionem, si viderint in eo humilitatem cordis. Quibus suffragetur totus conventus. Nec renuat prelatus cum illo facere misericordiam. Et si videtur ei, denuo vapulet,   25

provolutus omnium pedibus,   ad pedes singulorum,

primo prelati, deinde utriusque lateris sessorum.

Talis, quamdiu erit in hac penitentia, non communicet, non veniat ad osculum pacis. Si predicator est, officium predicationis non exerceat. Non notetur ad aliquod officium in ecclesia, nec ulla committatur ei obedientia ante plenariam satisfactionem. Si fuerit sacerdos vel diaconus, his officiis non fungatur, nisi postmodum religiose fuerit conversatus.   30

Eodem modo penitere debet, qui *rem sibi collatam* receperit de hiis, que prohibentur recipi; *si collatam celaverit*, quod beatus Augustinus *furti iudicio* dicit esse *condemnandum*; vel si in peccatum carnis quis lapsus fuerit, quod gravius ceteris puniri censemus. Si quis tale quid extra monasterium commiserit, frater qui cum eo est, studeat excessum eius quam citius corrigendum prelato intimare. Correctus autem, ad locum, in quo tale quid commiserit, ulterius non redeat, nisi ita religiose fuerit conversatus, ⟨quod generale vel provinciale capitulum ipsum illuc censeat reversurum⟩. Si vero huiusmodi   40

---

14 comedat *C cum Pa* : comedet *SR cum Pb*, vescetur *I*   16 agnoscat *CS* : cognoscat *IR cum PaPb*   18 et¹ ... comestionem *textum recentiorem habent CSR* : *om. I cum PaPb*   18/19 et ibi *C* : et *S, cf.* et coram *PaPb om. IR*   20 quousque intraverint et exierint *textum antiquiorem scripsi cum PaPb* : *cf.* quousque intraverint universe *I*   24 viderit *C*   25 Et si videtur *S cum Pa* : et si videbitur *R,* et viderit *C, aliter IPb*   27 provolutus omnium pedibus *textum antiquiorem scripsi cum Pa* : *cf.* omnium pedibus advolvatur *I*   29 hac] *om. C*   non² *CS cum Pa* : nec *IR cum Pb*   34/35 Eodem ... condemnandum *CS cum Pa* : *om. IR cum Pb*   34/35 receperit ... collatam *in marg. dextr. adscr. C*   receperit *C* : recepit *S,* cf. celaverit *Pa*   35 celaverit] servaverit *C*   38 autem] vero *R*

---

20 quousque ... exierint] oldest text, preserved in *Inst. S.Sixti* (cf. *loco cit.*)   27 provolutus omnium pedibus] oldest text, preserved in *Inst. S.Sixti* (cf. *loco cit.*)   34/35 Eodem ... condemnandum] cf. Pa, III, 6; cf. also *Reg. S. Aug.,* c. 8: "Quod si aliquis rem sibi collatam celaverit, furti iudicio condemnetur" (this sentence does not occur in all manuscripts of the rule; cf. *supra,* p. 230, note 253)   36 si ... fuerit] cf. Pb, III, 4   37/38 frater ... intimare] cf. Pb, III, 4   39 nisi ... conversatus] cf. Pb, III, 4   40/42 Si ... penitentiam] cf. Pa, III, 6, Pb, III, 4; see *supra,* pp. 291-292

Text. rec., **Cap. 23, 20** dum intrant et exeunt *textum recentiorem habent CSR*   **27** ad pedes singulorum *textum recentiorem habent CSR* peccatum occultum fuerit, disquisitione secreta, secundum tempus et personam condignam agat penitentiam.

Si quis autem peccaverit et confiteri voluerit socio illud alias cognoscenti, frater confessionem eius non recipiat, nisi tali conditione ut, cum opportunitas fuerit,
45   ipsum possit proclamare. Si qui per conspirationem vel coniurationem vel per malitiosam concordiam adversus priorem vel prelatos suos manifeste se erexerint, supradicto modo peniteant et de cetero in omni vita sua extremum locum sui ordinis obtineant et vocem in capitulo nisi in sui proclamatione et accusatione non habeant, nec eis aliqua obedientia iniungatur.

50   Si qui autem fratres non malitiose sed in veritate adversus prelatum aliquid habuerint, quod tolerari non debeat nec deceat, prius eum inter se cum omni humilitate et caritate de sua correctione admoneant. Quod si frequenter admonitus se corrigere neglexerit aut contempserit,

⟨priorem provincialem⟩ ad eum admo-   ⟨priori provinciali⟩
55   nendum et corrigendum advocent vel   vel visitatoribus, cum ad eandem domum
visitatoribus, cum ad eandem ecclesiam
visitandam

venerint, causa manifeste indicetur vel ⟨capitulo generali vel provinciali⟩ significetur. Aliter prelatos suos subditi diffamare non presumant.

24. DE FRATRE QUI APOSTATAVERIT

Quicumque apostataverit, si infra quadraginta dies non redierit, excommunicabitur. Si vero misertus sui redierit, depositis vestibus in claustro, nudus cum virgis in capitulum veniet et prostratus culpam suam dicet et humiliatus veniam petet et, quamdiu prelato
5   placuerit, penis gravioris culpe subiacebit et in capitulo nudum se presentabit omnibus dominicis diebus. Infra hoc tempus penitentie ubique in conventu novissimus erit et duobus diebus in qualibet septimana per annum ieiunabit in pane et aqua. Et, peracta

---

43 cognoscenti *SR* : agnoscenti *C*   frater] habeatur *C*   **44** eius *R* : illius *S*, *om. C*   recipiat *SR* : accipiat *C*   **45** ipsum *SR* : eum *C*   **48** proclamatione et] *om. R cum* Pa(3,7)Pb(3,6)   et *S* : in *C*   **50** prelatum *CSR* : suum *add. I cum* Pa(4,7)Pb(4,8)   **54/56** priorem ... visitatoribus *restitui ex C cum* IPa : ad eam monendam et corrigendam priorem domus advocet vel curatoribus *I*, abbatem matris ecclesie ad eum admonendum et corrigendum advocent, qui ... tum demum circatoribus *Pa*   **56/** **57** ecclesiam visitandam *I cum Pa* : *cf.* ecclesiam illam *Pb*   **58** indicentur *C*   significentur *C*   **59** diffamare *CS* : infamare *R cum Pa*
Cap. 24, 1 de ... apostataverit *C* : *cf.* De his qui apostataverint *Pa(3,9)*, De apostatis *S(1,25)R(1,20) cum* Pb(3,8), *om. I*

45/49 Si ... iniungatur] cf. Pa, III, 7, Pb, III, 6   **50/59** cf. Pa, IV, 7, Pb, IV, 8   **54/57** ad ... visitandam] oldest version, preserved in *Inst. S.Sixti* (cf. *supra*, p. 255, with note 65)
Cap. 24, 1/20 cf. Pa, III, 9, Pb, III, 8; — for the dating (1216), see *supra*, p. 381

Text. rec., **Cap. 23, 54/55** priori provinciali vel visitatoribus *C* : priori provinciali et visitatoribus *S*, priori provinciali significetur vel visitatoribus *R*, *cf.* patri abbati vel domino Premonstratensi vel visitatoribus annuis *Pb*   **55** domum *CS* : visitandam *add. R*

penitentia, numquam priorem locum tenebit, sed inferiorem, secundum quod prelato
visum fuerit.

Quod si secundo fugerit et iterum redierit, supradicto modo peniteat, et priori   10
anno secundus addatur. Si tertio, tertius, si quarto, quartus. Omnibus tamen fratribus
pro huiusmodi penitentibus et humiliter in capitulo deprecantibus, prelatus, cum penitentiam eorum prospexerit, eis indulgere vel remittere poterit, secundum quod sue discretioni visum fuerit vel placitum.

Si quis in apostasia ordinatus fuerit vel post excommunicationem in ea divina celebra-   15
re presumpserit, exsecutione officii perpetuo carebit, nisi forte postea ita religiose fuerit
conversatus, ut cum eo auctoritate Sedis apostolice dispensetur.

⟨Item, qui semel apostataverit vel de lapsu carnis manifeste convictus fuerit, de
cetero non predicet nec audiat confessiones, nisi per generale vel provinciale capitulum fuerit restitutus.⟩   20

25. DE GRAVISSIMA CULPA

Gravissima culpa est incorrigibilitas eius, qui nec culpas timet admittere et penam
recusat ferre. De quo preceptum est patris nostri Augustini, ut, *etiam si ipse non abscesserit, de
vestra societate proiciatur,* secundum apostolum, qui *hereticum hominem post* prim*am et
secundam correctionem* adhibitam et incorrigibilitatem patefactam *devita*re iubet tanquam   5
*peccan*tem *peccatum ad mortem, quia subversus est, qui eiusmodi est.* Hic quidem habitu
exutus et vestibus secularibus indutus exire compellendus est, si tamen usque ad horam
illam sani capitis et integri sensus extiterit. Et nemini aliter, quod quidam indigne appe-
tunt, sub qualibet occasione umquam est danda licentia recedendi, ne ordo et canonica
disciplina in contemptum veniant, dum despicitur in indignis habitus religionis canonice.   10
Et ita, sicut a corde professionem abiecit, sic et accepta professionis insignia deponere
cogatur, nec ulli aliquo modo pro sua quantalibet importunitate aliter indulgeatur egre-
diendi licentia.

---

12 et C *cum Pa* : *om. SR*   **12/13** penitentiam eorum *CS* : eorum penitentiam *R cum Pa*   **16/17** fuerit
conversatus *CS* : conversatus fuerit *R cum Pa*   **17** eo *SR* : *om. C*   **18** Item qui] Qui vero *R*
Cap. 25, 4/5 primam et secundam *CS(1,26)* : *om.* R(1,19) *cum* Pa(3,10)Pb(3,9)   **6** submersus *C*
eiusmodi *C cum PaPb* : huiusmodi *SR*   **8** extitit *C*   **9** numquam *C*   **10** veniant *CS* : veniat *R cum
PaPb*   **11** et accepta *CSR* : *cf.* a corpore *PaPb*

11/13 Omnibus ... poterit] cf. Pa, III, 9, Pb, III, 8   **15/17** Si ... conversatus] cf. Pa, III, 9; formulated
differently in Pb, III, 8   **18/20** for the dating (1225-1235), see *supra*, p. 411, note 242
Cap. 25, 1/13 cf. Pa, III, 10, Pb, III, 9; — for the dating (1216), see *supra*, p. 381   **3/4** recusat ...
proiciatur] cf. *Reg. S. Aug.*, c. 7: "Quam si ferre recusaverit, etiam si ipse non abscesserit, de vestra
societate proiciatur"   **4/6** hereticum ... est²] cf. *Tit.*, II,10: "Haereticum hominem post unam et
secundam correptionem devita, sciens quia subversus est, qui eiusmodi est"   **6** peccantem peccatum
ad mortem] cf. I *Ioan.*, V,16: "Qui scit fratrem suum peccare peccatum non ad mortem ..."   **12/
13** nec ... licentia] cf. Pa, III, 10

INCIPIT SECUNDA DISTINCTIO

1. DE CAPITULO PROVINCIALI

Statuimus quod singulis annis i n s i n g u l i s capitulis provincialibus ⟨Hispa-
nie, Provincie, Francie, Lombardie, Romane, Hungarie, Theutonie, Anglie⟩ q u a -
t u o r fratres de d i s c r e t i o r i b u s et m a g i s i d o n e i s a provinciali capitulo per
disquisitionem prioris provincialis et prioris et supprioris eiusdem loci, ubi capitu-   5
lum celebratur, vel, si unus defuerit, per disquisitionem duorum, hoc modo eligantur. Predicti siquidem t r e s vel duo, si tertius defuerit, v o l u n t a t e s s i n g u l o -
r u m s i n g i l l a t i m et s e o r s u m aliquantulum, in eadem domo, coram oculis
omnium disq u i r a n t e t cons c r i b a n t fi d e l i t e r . Et sic incontinenti et in
eodem loco, antequam fratres discedant vel ad invicem colloquantur, s c r i p t u -   10
r a m p u b l i c e n t i n medium. Et in quibus m a i o r p a r s c a p i t u l i provincialis numero concordaverit, illi pro diffinitoribus habeantur. Si a u t e m p a r t e s
fuerint pares, tunc eodem modo disquisitionis voluntatum unus eligatur a capitulo.
Et cui parti ille consenserit, illi pro diffinitoribus habeantur. Quod si adhuc discordaverint, alius eligatur et sic deinceps, donec in parte altera maior possit numerus   15
inveniri. Capitulum autem provinciale appellamus priores conventuales cum
singulis sociis a capitulo suo electis et predicatores generales. Predicatores autem
generales sunt, qui per capitulum generale vel priorem provincialem et diffinitores
capituli provincialis fuerint approbati.

Cap. 1, 1 de capitulo provinciali *C* : De electione diffinitorum capituli provincialis *S, cf.* De electione
diffinitorum capituli provincialis et generalis *R(2,5)*   **2** singulis¹] in *praem. C*   **3** Romane] provincie
add. R   Theotonie *R*   **4** discretioribus *SR* : magis *praem. C*   **5** eiusdem loci *R* : eius loci *C,* eiusdem
conventus *S*   **7** diffuerit *C*   **8** singulatim *C*   **11/12** maior ... numero *C* : maior pars capituli numero
S, plures *R*   **13** disquisitione *C*   **17** sociis] *om. C*   electus *C*

For the titles of the chapters in the second distinctio, see *supra*, p. 373, note 9
Cap. 1, 1/16 de ... inveniri] for the dating (1220-1225), see *supra*, pp. 385-386, p. 389, note 122, pp. 395-
396   **2/14** Statuimus ... habeantur] for the affinity with Cîteaux and the Fourth Lateran Council,
see pp. 336 and 342   **2/3** Hispanie ... Anglie] for the origins of these eight provinces, see pp. 343-344
7/9 voluntates ... fideliter] for parallel texts, see pp. 354-355   **12** pro diffinitoribus habeantur] for the
origin of the *diffinitores*, see pp. 334-336   **12/13** Si autem partes fuerint pares] cf. can. 10 of the
Sixteenth Council of Carthage in 418 (*Cod. can. Eccl. Afr.*, can. 118): "Si autem partes aequales sunt ..."
(Mansi, vol. III, col. 818)   **16/17** Capitulum ... generales] for the dating (c. 1225), see pp. 408-409, with
note 229   **17/19** Predicatores ... approbati] for the presence of this rule in the earliest constitutions,
see *supra*, pp. 276-277; — for the dating (c. 1228), see p. 409, note 230

20   ⟨Nullus prior conventualis secum plures fratres ducat ad capitulum generale vel
provinciale sine causa legitima, et assumat quilibet prior socium sibi secundum
electionem capituli sui.

Accusationi vero et correctioni professi post

annum sue professionis poterunt inte- | triennium ab ingressu ordinis
25   resse.

Item, conventus qui mittit accusationes ad capitulum generale vel provinciale,
scribat de quolibet articulo numerum et nomina accusantium, et si accusant de
visu vel auditu. Et nullus accuset de auditu, nisi dicat a quo audierit. Sed utique caveat
ne malum, quod audierit de alio [fratre], referat aliquatenus, nisi dicat a quo audi-
30   verit.

Item, quilibet prior cum conventu scribat singulis annis priori suo provinciali
et diffinitoribus capituli provincialis debita domus, ponentes nihilominus causas
debitorum.

Item, nulla petitio offeratur provinciali capitulo nisi a conventu, nec generali
35   nisi a provinciali.⟩

2. DE DIFFINITORIBUS CAPITULI PROVINCIALIS

Predicti igitur diffinitores tractabunt omnia et diffinient cum priore provinciali.
Quod s i in suis diffinitionibus i n p a r t e s equales s e d i v i s e r i n t, illorum
sententia prevalebit, in quorum partem prior provincialis concordaverit. Alias
5   autem s e n t e n t i a p l u r i u m prevalebit.

20/22 Nullus ... sui *in 2,23 C* : *hic R(2,7) usque ad lin. 21* legitima *inclus., cf.* Et si commode fieri potest,
ad illud capitulum veniat unus frater discretus cum socio de voluntate prioris *S(2,1)*   Nullus] vero *add.*
R   secum ... ducat *C* : ducat secum plures fratres *R*   **24** annum sue professionis *S* : triennium ab
ingressu ordinis *corr. CR cum A(p.7)*   **26** Item conventus *C* : Conventus vero *R(2,9)*   mittit *R cum A* :
mittunt *C*   generale vel provinciale *R cum A* : provinciale vel generale *C*   **27** scribat *R cum A* :
scribant *C*   accusant *C cum A* : accusat *R*   **27/28** de² ... auditu¹ *C cum A* : de auditu vel de visu *R*
28 Et *C cum A* : Item *R(2,6), cf.* Sed *Pb(4,8)*   Sed utique *C* : Similiter *R*   caveat] quisque *add. R*
29 quod] *om. C*   fratre *textum correxi* : facto *C*, alteri *R*   audierit *R*   **31/33** Item ... debitorum *scripsi
cum A(p.7)* : Priores cum suo conventu capitulo provinciali singulis annis scribant debita domus sue et
causas etiam debitorum *R(2,7)* : *om. CS*   **34/35** Item ... provinciali *hic R(2,7)* : *in 2,34C, om. S*
provinciali capitulo *C* : capitulo provinciali *R*   **35** nisi a provinciali *C* : nisi a capitulo provinciali fuerit
approbata *R*
Cap. 2, 2 igitur *CS* : ergo *R(2,7)*   **3** suis] *om. R*   **5** autem] *om. R*   prevalebit] obtinebit *R*

20/22 for the dating (1225-1235), see pp. 407-408, with note 222   **23/24** for the dating (1225-1235),
see p. 409, with notes 231-232   **26/28** Item ... auditu¹] added in 1236 (*Acta C.G.*, p. 7)   **28/29** Et ...
audierit] for the dating (1236 or earlier), see *supra*, p. 409, note 234   **31/35** added in 1236 (*Acta C.G.*,
p. 7)
Cap. 2, 2/5 for the dating (1225), see *supra*, pp. 396-397   **3** Quod ... diviserint] cf. letter by Hincmar
of Reims to Hincmar of Laon (c. 6): "... et si in partes se eligentium vota diviserint... " (PL, vol. 126, col.
311); Leo I to Anastasius of Thessalonica (*ep. 14*, c. 5): "... ita ut si in aliam forte personam partium se
vota diviserint..." (PL, vol. 54, col. 673); cf. *Corpus iuris canonici*, vol. I, col. 247, c. 36   **5** sententia
plurium prevalebit] for the origins of this expression, see *supra*, p. 354

3. DE POTESTATE HORUM DIFFINITORUM

Isti autem quatuor diffinitores excessum prioris provincialis confessi vel procla-
mati in capitulo provinciali coram fratribus audiant et emendent, ei penitentiam
iniungentes. Si autem, quod absit, incorrigibilis extiterit, ipsum usque ad capitulum generale suspendant ab officio prioratus, priorem loci, ubi capitulum provin-   5
ciale celebratur, loco eius substituentes, et excessum eius ad capitulum referant
generale scripto communiter sigillato.

4. QUIS OBTINEAT VICEM PRIORIS PROVINCIALIS

⟨Statuimus etiam ut, mortuo priore provinciali vel amoto, prior conventualis
illius loci, in quo provinciale capitulum in sequenti anno fuerit celebrandum,
vicem eius obtineat, donec prior eiusdem provincie sit electus et confirmatus.⟩
Quod si ipsum abesse contigerit nec vicem suam alii commiserit, idem prior   5
cum diffinitoribus capituli provincialis in celebratione procedat eiusdem.
Prior provincialis etiam cum suis diffinitoribus in capitulo provinciali semper
locum determinet, u b i   s e q u e n s   c a p i t u l u m   c e l e b r etur.

5. DE ELECTIONE CAPITULI GENERALIS DIFFINITORIS

Statuimus etiam ut per duos annos in dictarum ⟨octo⟩ provinciarum capitulis
aliquis de magis idoneis a capitulo eligatur, qui sit generalis capituli diffinitor. ⟨Cui
socius competens a priore provinciali et a diffinitoribus assignetur, ut, si medio
tempore decesserit vel aliquo modo fuerit impeditus quod venire non possit ad   5
capitulum generale, ipso iure socius eius loco ipsius diffinitor habeatur.⟩

Cap. 3, 1 horum diffinitorum C : eorundem S   **6** eius² C : ipsius S, *eras.* R(2,7)   **6/7** ad ... generale
C : ad capitulum generale referant S, referant ad capitulum generale R
Cap. 4, 2 vel amoto] *om.* C   **4** vices R(2,3)   **5** ipsum] priorem provincialem *add.* R   alii CS : alicui
R(2,7)   idem prior CS : prior illius loci ubi capitulum fuerit celebrandum R   **6** capituli provincialis
C : illius capituli S, capituli R(2,5)
Cap. 5, 3 generalis capituli C : capituli generalis R(2,5)   **4** a²] *om.* SR   ut si CS : si vero R
5 impeditus fuerit R

Cap. 3, 2/7 for the dating (1225), see *supra*, pp. 395-396
Cap. 4, 2/4 interpolated between 1225 and 1235 (cf. *supra*, p. 394, note 152)   **5/6** for the dating
(1225), see pp. 395-396, with note 160   **8** locum ... celebretur] for the connection with the Fourth
Lateran Council, see pp. 342-343
Cap. 5, 2/10 for the dating (1225), see *supra*, p. 396, with notes 158-159, pp. 396-397   octo] added after
1225 (see p. 396, note 162, p. 344)   **3/6** Cui ... habeatur] added after 1225 (see p. 397, with note 163)

⟨Statuimus quod quatuor provincie, scilicet Ierosolimitana, Grecia, Polonia, Dacia, habeant singulis annis diffinitores in singulis capitulis generalibus.⟩

Tertio autem anno priores provinciales ⟨duodecim⟩ provinciarum generale
10   capitulum celebrabunt.

Item, statuimus quod priori provinciali eunti ad capitulum generale detur socius a diffinitoribus capituli provincialis.

6. DE PREIUDICIO VITANDO

Statuimus autem et in virtute Spiritus sancti et obedientie et sub interminatio-ne anathematis districte prohibemus ne priores provinciales fratribus diffinitoribus aut fratres diffinitores prioribus provincialibus per suas diffinitiones preiudicium
5   aliquod audeant generare. Quod si facere attentaverint, eadem districtione prohi-bemus ne in hoc eis aliquis presumat obedire.

Et ut multitudo constitutionum vitetur, prohibemus ne aliquid de cetero statuatur, nisi per duo capitula continua fuerit approbatum. Et tunc in tertio capi-tulo immediate sequente poterit confirmari vel deleri, sive per priores provinciales
10   sive per alios diffinitores, ubicumque illud tertium capitulum teneatur.

7. DE DIFFINITORIBUS GENERALIS CAPITULI

Isti autem ⟨duodecim⟩ diffinitores ⟨duobus annis et duodecim priores provin-ciales tertio anno⟩ cum magistro ordinis omnia diffinient et constituent et tracta-bunt. Quod s i   i n   p a r t e s   equales s e   d i v i s e r i n t, illorum sententia prevale-
5   bit, in quorum partem magister ordinis declinaverit. Si vero in partes inequales, o b t i n e a t   s e n t e n t i a   p l u r i u m. S i   a u t e m   per adiunctionem magistri p a r t e s   fiant e q u a l e s, unus eligatur, secundum quod in electione diffinitorum

---

11 Item statuimus quod C : *om. SR*   12 capituli provincialis C : provincialis capituli R, *om. S*

Cap. 6, 3 districte prohibemus CS : prohibemus districte R(2,8)   **4** aut] vel R   **6** eis ... obedire C : aliquis eis presumat obedire S, aliquis presumat eis obedire R   **7** evitetur R(prol.)   aliquid de cetero C : de cetero aliquid R   **10** teneatur] celebretur R

Cap. 7, 2 Isti C : Predicti R(2,8)   diffinitores] provinciarum *praem.* R   **3** et tractabunt] Quod ... procedant *(infra, lin. 10/11) hic inseruit C*   **6** obtineat CS : obtinebit R   plurium SR : plurimorum C

7/8 for the dating (c. 1228), see pp. 401-402   **9/10** for the dating (1225), see p. 396, with note 162   **11/12** for the dating (1225-1235), see p. 411, with note 242

Cap. 6, 2/10 for the dating (1228), see *supra*, p. 404, with note 205, p. 403, with note 196

Cap. 7, 2/12 for the dating (1221), see *supra*, p. 385, note 93, p. 390, with note 132   **2/3** duodecim[2] ... anno] added after 1225 (see p. 390, note 132)   **4** Quod ... diviserint] for similar expressions, see *supra*, under cap. 2, l. 3   **6** obtineat sententia plurium] for the origins of this formula, see p. 354   **6/7** Si ... equales] for related expressions, see *supra*, under cap. 1, l. 12

provincialium est statutum. Quod si ad capitulum aliquo casu prepediti predicti non omnes venerint, illi quos ex ipsis venire contigerit, cum magistro ordinis omnia pertractabunt. Quod si magistrum abesse aliqua occasione contigerit, nihi-   10 lominus predicti diffinitores in diffinitione procedant. Quod si non omnes in unam sententiam concordaverint, forma superius posita teneatur.

8. DE POTESTATE DIFFINITORUM

Isti autem diffinitores p l e n a r i a m habeant p o t e s t a t e m super excessum magistri ordinis corrigendum vel de eo penitus removendo. Et ipsorum sententia tam in hiis quam in aliis i n v i o l a b i l i t e r   o b s e r v e t u r, ita quod ab ipsorum sententia a nemine l i c e a t   a p p e l l a r i, et, si appellatum fuerit, frivola et nulla   5 appellatio habeatur. 〈Appellationem enim fieri i n   n o s t r o   o r d i n e sub intermi- natione a n a t h e m a tis penitus prohibemus, cum non venerimus contendere sed potius delicta corrigere.〉

9. DE EXCESSU MAGISTRI CORRIGENDO

Diffinitores predicti excessum magistri seorsum inter se corrigant et emendent. Si autem in tantum excesserit, quod removeri debeat, tunc non passim et indiffe- renter procedant, sed cautela maxima et inquisitione diligentissima. Et non depo- natur   5
nisi pro heresi | nisi pro crimine
vel pro alio criminali peccato, quod non possit sine magno scandalo ordinis tolera- ri, de quo etiam si legitime convictus fuerit vel confessus, vel si adeo f u e r i t

---

8 predicti CS : *om. R*   **10/11** Quod ... procedant *hic RS : post* tractabunt *(lin. 3)* inseruit C   Quod si CS : Si vero R   abesse aliqua occasione CS : aliqua occasione abesse R   **11** diffinitionem R
Cap. 8, 2 plenariam habeant potestatem CS : habebunt plenariam potestatem R(2,8)   **3** Et ipsorum CS : Ipsorum autem R   **4/5** ab ... appellari CS : a nemine ab ipsorum sententia liceat appellari R
Cap. 9, 2 seorsum inter se C : inter se seorsum S, seorsum R(2,8)

Cap. 8, 2/6 Isti ... habeatur] for the dating (1221), see *supra*, p. 390, with note 130 and 132   plenariam ... potestatem] for the use of this formula, see pp. 363-364   **3/7** Et ... prohibemus] for the affinity with Citeaux and the Fourth Lateran Council, see p. 341   **6/8** Appellationem ... corrigere] for the dating (1228), see *supra*, p. 404, with note 207
Cap. 9, 2/11 for the dating (1221), see *supra*, p. 390   **8/9** si² ... remissus] cf. *Eccli.*, c. 4: "Noli citatus esse in lingua tua et inutilis et remissus in operibus tuis"; letter from Innocent III to the Abbey of Subiaco (1202): "Quodsi praevaricator fuerit ordinis aut contemptor seu negligens aut remissus, ..." (*Corpus iuris canonici*, vol. II, col. 600, c. 6); letter from Honorius III to the abbeys of Lombardy: "Quod si abbas aliquis non exemptus fuerit a visitatoribus nimis negligens et remissus inventus ..." (*ed. cit.*, col. 602, c. 8); cf. also *Proc. Bon.*, no. 33: "Ego sum dignus depositione, quia sum inutilis et remissus" ; see *supra*, p. 385

Text. rec., **Cap. 9, 1** crimine C : heresi S

Text. rec., **Cap. 9, 1** nisi pro crimine] correction of 1236 (*Acta C.G.*, p. 7)

n e g l i g e n s , *i n u t i l i s e t r e m i s s u s ,* qui ordinis dissolutionem et destructio-
10   nem inducat. Et tunc, antequam deponatur, inducatur a diffinitoribus ut magistra-
tui cedat et sibi aliquem locum eligat, ubi possit honeste conversari.

Mortuo autem magistro vel a magisterio remoto, priores dictarum provinciarum in omnibus, quousque magister fuerit electus, p l e n a r i a m ipsius obtineant
p o t e s t a t e m , et eis omnes tanquam magistro teneantur obedire. Si autem inter
15   se medio tempore super aliquo discordaverint, o b t i n e a t s e n t e n t i a p l u -
r i u m . Quod s i p a r t e s fuerint pares, assumant unum de fratribus illis qui
vocem habent in electione magistri, et cui parti ille concordaverit, vigorem obtineat firmitatis. Quod si adhuc discordaverint, iterum alius eligatur, et sic deinceps
donec in parte altera maior possit numerus inveniri.

20   ⟨Precipimus autem in virtute Spiritus sancti, ut nullus ante electionem magistri
circa statum ordinis audeat aliquid immutare.⟩

10. DE ELECTIONE MAGISTRI ORDINIS

Predicti ergo priores provinciales predictarum provinciarum ⟨octo⟩ singuli
cum duobus fratribus in capitulo provinciali electis, in quos ceteri ad electionem
magistri faciendam compromittant, ⟨et quatuor priores provinciales de superaddi-
5   tis provinciis, scilicet Ierosolimitana, Grecia, Polonia, Dacia, singuli cum singulis
ad hoc idem electis,⟩ ad capitulum veniant generale. Qui postquam fuerint congre-
gati in secunda feria post Pentecosten, a prioribus conventualibus illius provincie
et fratribus presentibus in loco, in quo electio est facienda, i n uno c o n c l a v i
firmiter i n c l u d a n t u r , ita quod inde nullatenus valeant egredi nec eis ullo modo
10   aliqua alimenta ministrentur, quousque magister ordinis

| secundum formam inferius positam sit | secundum formam canonicam sit elec- |
| electus. | tus. |

11 sibi ... eligat *CS*: aliquem locum sibi eligat *R*   **14/15** inter ... tempore *C*: interim medio tempore *S*,
medio tempore inter se *R*   **15** plurium *SR*: plurimorum *C*
Cap. 10, 4 compromittant *C*: compromiserint *R(2,4)*, voces suas committant *S*   **4/6** et ... electis *C*:
om. SR   **9** inde ... egredi *C*: nullus valeat egredi *S*, inde nullatenus egredi valeant *R*

12/19 for the dating (1222-1228), see pp. 397-398, with note 169   **13/14** plenariam ... potestatem] for
the origins of this expression, see pp. 363-364   **15** obtineat sententia plurium] for the origins of this
formula, see p. 354   **16** Quod si partes fuerint pares] for similar expressions, see *supra*, under cap. 1, l.
12   **20/21** for the dating (1228), see p. 405, note 208
Cap. 10, 2/12 for the dating (1225-1227), see *supra*, pp. 398-399, with notes 171-172   **2/6** octo ... electis]
added in 1228 or later (cf. p. 402, with note 193)   **8/9** in³ ... includantur] for similar texts, see p. 357,
with note 441

Text. rec., **Cap. 10, 1** formam canonicam *CR cum A(p.8)* : canonicam formam inferius positam *S*

Text. rec., **Cap. 10, 1** secundum formam canonicam] correction of 1236 (*Acta C.G.*, p. 8)

⟨Et hoc tam ab electoribus quam a recludentibus precipimus firmiter observari, ita quod, si quis contraire presumpserit, ipso facto sit excommunicatus et penam gravioris culpe debitam sustinebit.⟩   15

11. DE FORMA ELECTIONIS

Forma electionis hec est. Electoribus supradicto modo inclusis, cum per disquisitionem vel s c r u t inium v o l u n t a t u m procedet electio, t r e s de priori- bus provincialibus, qui inter alios provinciales priores primitus habitum nostre religionis susceperunt, v o l u n t a t e s   s i n g u l o r u m   s i n g i l l a t i m e t s e o r -   5 s u m aliquantulum, tamen in eadem domo, coram oculis omnium disq u i r a n t et cons c r i b a n t. Quod si, gratia Dei i n s p i r a nte, in unum aliquem o m n e s unanimiter c o n c o r d averint, ille verus magister ordinis habeatur. S i   vero i n p a r t e s inequales s e   d i v i s e r i n t, ille in quem plures medietate omnium qui debent eligere, consenserint, ex vi talis electionis et huius constitutionis sit magi-   10 ster.

Quod si aliquem vel aliquos de electoribus contigerit non venire, nihilominus tamen per eos qui advenerint, electio celebretur. Et hoc ita fiat, ut semper in quarta feria Pentecostes magistrum habeat capitulum, antiquum vel novum, presentem vel absentem, quia tunc incipit solemniter celebrari, ne acephalum iudicetur.   15

⟨Et hec omnia, que circa electionem magistri sunt instituta, absque contradic- tione volumus et precipimus firmiter observari. Quicumque autem ausus fuerit contradicere pertinaciter vel etiam rebellare, tanquam excommunicatus et schi- smaticus et destructor nostri ordinis habeatur et, quousque satisfecerit, a commu- nione omnium sit penitus alienus et pene graviori culpe debite subiaceat.   20

Statuimus autem ut, si in anno diffinitionis priorum provincialium electio magistri celebratur, unus de fratribus electoribus de qualibet provincia, qui in suo provinciali capitulo ad hoc electus fuerit, ad diffiniendum cum eis pariter admitta-

---

15 gravioris *CS* : graviori *R*
Cap. 11, 2/3 cum ... procedet *C cum A(p.8)* : cum per ... procedat *R*, per ... procedat *S*   **3** voluntatum *SR(2,4) cum A* : *om. C*   **4** provinciales priores *C* : duodecim provinciales *R, om. S*   **6** tamen *CS* : *om. R*   **7** et conscribant *SR* : *om. C*   **8** in] *om. C*   **9** ille] *om. C*   **9/10** qui debent eligere *scripsi cum A* : qui debeat eligere *C*, eligentium *SR*   **10** ex] ille *praem. C*   **13** electio *S* : *om. C*, magistri *add. R*   **17** precipimus firmiter *SR* : firmiter precipimus *C*   **20** graviori culpe debite *C* : gravis culpe debite *S*, gravioris culpe *R*   **22** celebretur *R(2,8)*   unus *C* : illo anno *praem. R*   de¹ *C* : e *R*   suo *C cum A(p.7)* : *om. R*   **23** diffiniendum *C cum A* : diffinitionem *R*

13/15 for the dating (1228), see *supra*, p. 405, with note 208
Cap. 11, 2/10 formulated thus in 1236 (*Acta C.G.*, p. 8) using texts composed earlier (1220-1227) (cf. *supra*, pp. 398-399, with notes 172-174)   **2/10** cum ... magister] for the affinity with the Fourth Lateran Council and other texts, see *supra*, pp. 347-352 and 355 respectively   **8/9** Si ... diviserint] for similar expressions, see *supra*, under cap. 2, l. 3   **12/15** for the dating (1220-1227), see pp. 398-399, with notes 172-173   **16/20** for the dating (1228), see p. 405, note 208   **21/23** Statuimus ... admittatur] correction of 1236 (*Acta C.G.*, p. 7)

tur. Si vero in anno diffinitorum celebratur, tunc cum diffinitoribus provinciales
25   conveniant et utrorumque diffinitio sit communis.⟩

12. QUI VENIRE DEBEANT AD CAPITULUM GENERALE

Statuimus insuper quod omnes priores conventuales cum sociis suis et predicatores generales illius provincie, in qua generale capitulum celebratur, illo anno ad
capitulum veniant generale, nec eodem anno in illa provincia ad celebrandum
5   aliud capitulum teneantur.

13. DE MORTE MAGISTRI

Si ante festum sancti Michaelis magistrum mori contigerit, prior conventualis
vel provincialis, qui propinquior illi loco extiterit, ubi magister decesserit, Parisiensi vel Bononiensi conventui, sibi propinquiori scilicet, cum festinatione denuntiet.
5   Et alteruter istorum conventuum, cui primo denuntiatum fuerit, teneatur similiter
reliquis n u n t i a r e : Parisiensis provincialibus Hispanie, Provincie, Anglie, Theutonie; Bononiensis vero Hungarie, Romane provincie et aliis quibus poterit, teneatur q u a m   c i t i u s intimare. Si autem post dictum festum magister decesserit,
o b i t u s magistri nihilominus den u n t i e t u r , ut supersedeatur illo anno a capitu-
10 lo generali. Sequenti vero anno ibi capitulum celebretur, ubi prius debuerat celebrari.

Capitulum generale uno anno Parisius, alio anno Bononie celebretur.

---

24 celebretur *R*   provinciales *C* : priores provinciales *R*   **25** utrorumque *R* : utrorum *C*

Cap. 12, 3/4 ad ... generale *CS* : veniant ad capitulum generale *R(2,8)*   **5** capitulum *CS* : provinciale *add. R*

Cap. 13, 2 Si ante *C* : Statuimus ut *praem. R(2,4)*   **3/4** Parisiensi ... conventui *C* : Parisiensi conventui vel Bononiensi *R*   **4** scilicet] *om. R*   **5** Et alteruter *C* : Alterutrum autem *R*   primo *C* : prius *R*
9 magistri *C* : ipsius *R*   nuntietur *R*   **10** Sequenti ... celebrari] *om. R*

24/25 Si ... communis] for the dating (1231-1235), see *supra*, p. 410, note 237
Cap. 12, 2/5 for the dating (1231-1235), see *supra*, p. 410, note 240
Cap. 13, 2/10 for the structure and dating (c. 1222), see *supra*, pp. 400-401, with notes 178-181   **2/**
9 Si ... denuntietur] for the affinity with other statutes and the dating (1222-1225), see p. 400   **4/**
6 cum ... nuntiare] cf. bull *Inter opera pietatis* by Innocent III for the hospital of Montpellier (1204): "...
eius non differant obitum nuntiare" (PL, vol. 215, col. 378)   **8/9** Si ... denuntietur] cf. *ibid.*: "Quod si
forsan apud Montem Pessulanum obierit, ... ipsius obitus nuntietur..."   **12** stipulation of 1220 (cf.
supra, p. 384, note 85)

14. DE INFAMATIONE ORDINIS VITANDA

In virtute Spiritus sancti et obedientie firmiter precipimus observari, ne quis causam depositionis magistri vel prioris provincialis vel eius excessum vel correctionem vel secretum capituli seu dissensiones diffinitorum vel fratrum, unde ordo noster possit turbari vel infamari, audeat scienter extraneis publicare. Si quis autem   5
ex deliberatione contrafecerit, tanquam excommunicatus et schismaticus ac destructor nostri ordinis habeatur et, quousque satisfecerit, a communione omnium sit penitus alienus et pene graviori culpe debite subiaceat.

Eadem districtione precipimus ne quis verbo vel facto aliquomodo ad divisionem nostri ordinis audeat laborare. Quod si fecerit, pene subiaceat supradicte.   10

15. DE ELECTIONE PRIORUM PROVINCIALIUM

Statuimus ut provinciarum priores vel regnorum in capitulo generali a magistro ordinis et diffinitoribus, premissa diligenti examinatione, confirmentur vel amoveantur. Nam eorum electio ad provinciale capitulum pertinebit.

⟨Statuimus ut magister solus possit confirmare priorem provincialem.⟩   5

Mortuo igitur priore provinciali vel amoto, duo fratres de quolibet conventu illius provincie eligantur, qui cum suo priore conventuali secundum formam superius positam electionem prioris provincialis celebrabunt, hoc excepto quod eos includi sicut in electione magistri non oporteat.

⟨Item, priore provinciali mortuo vel amoto, prior qui locum eius obtinet,   10
teneatur convocare, quam citius commode poterit, electores. Et tunc prior provincialis eligatur et provinciale capitulum celebretur, nisi prius fuerit celebratum. Quod si modo non elegerint qui debent eligere, potestas providendi ad magistrum ordinis transferatur.

Cap. 14, 2 In C: Item *praem.* R(2,8)   firmiter precipimus CS: precipimus firmiter R   **6** ac CM(c.19): et SR   **8** gravioris MS   **9** aliquomodo CM: aliquando S, *om.* R
Cap. 15, 2 vel regnorum C: *om.* SR(2,3)   **5** Statuimus ... provincialem C: Poterit autem eum rector ordinis confirmare S(2,4), Poterit eum nichilominus magister ordinis confirmare vel amovere R   **6** unoquolibet C   **9** oporteat C: oportet R   **10** Item ... amoto *scripsi cm* A(p.8): Item provinciali priore mortuo vel amoto C, Mortuo priore provinciali vel amoto S(2,15) R   locum eius C *cum* A: eius locum SR   **11** commode C *cum* A: *om.* SR   **12** prius fuerit R: fuerit prius S, iam fuit C   **13** modo C: fratres S, tunc R, *cf.* statim A   **13/14** magistrum ordinis A: *cf.* rectorem ordinis S, magistrum C

Cap. 14, 2/10 for the dating (1228), see *supra*, p. 405, note 208   **2/8** cf. Pb, IV, 24: "Nullus professor nostri Ordinis ... destructores nostri Ordinis reputamus" (this section is the last in the constitutions of Prémontré and was apparently added later; perhaps the two orders each used a third source independently of each other)
Cap. 15, 2/4 Statuimus ... pertinebit] for the dating (1221-1225), see *supra*, p. 392, with notes 142-144   provinciarum priores vel regnorum] for the connection with the Fourth Lateran Council, see p. 343, with notes 334-335, p. 346, with note 364   **5** for the dating (1225-1235), see p. 392, with note 146   **6/9** for the dating (1225), see p. 392, with note 145   **10/17** added in 1236 (*Acta C.G.*, pp. 8 and 7)

15   Item, volumus quod electio prioris provincialis spectet tantum ad priores conventuales cum duobus fratribus de quolibet conventu ad hoc electis, omnibus
fratribus ad illum conventum pertinentibus, si commode potest fieri, convocatis.⟩

16. DE POTESTATE PRIORIS PROVINCIALIS

Provincialis autem prior eandem habeat potestatem in sua provincia vel regno
quam et magister ordinis. Et eadem sibi reverentia a provincialibus exhibeatur, que
magistro exhibetur, nisi magister presens extiterit.

5   ⟨Item, priores provinciales commissas sibi provincias curent visitare. Cum
tamen commode non valuerint, poterunt committere vices suas.⟩

Curet prior provincialis vel regnorum ut, si habuerit aliquos utiles ad docendum, qui possint in brevi apti esse ad regendum, mittere ad studium ad loca ubi
viget studium. Et in aliis illi, ad quos mittuntur, eos non audeant occupare nec ad

10   provinciam suam remittere, nisi fuerint revocati.

⟨Capitulum provinciale in festo sancti Michaelis in loco statuto in
provincia vel regno, ubi prior provinciarum vel regnorum cum consilio diffinitorum elegerit, celebretur.

Nullus religiosus alterius ordinis vel professionis nullusque

15   secularis cuiuscumque ordinis vel dignitatis vel professionis vel vite secretis
vel tractatibus capituli aliquomodo admittatur.

Et ea que dicta sunt de generali capitulo, in secunda feria post Pentecosten
debent inchoari.⟩

---

15 Item volumus S *post* amoveantur *(lin. 4)* : Volumus autem R, Item statuimus C, *om.* A*(p.7)*
16 cum duobus fratribus C : et duobus fratribus S, et duos fratres R   ad hoc SR *cum* A : *om.* C
17 illum conventum CS : conventum illum R, *cf.* illum A

Cap. 16, 5 commissas sibi provincias C *cum* A*(p.6)* : provincias suas S, provinciam suam R*(2,3)*
visitare] perpensius *add.* C   **5/6** Cum tamen A : Cum autem R, Ceterum cum C, Quod si S   **7** vel
regnorum C : *om.* SR*(2,14)*   docendum CS : discendum R   **8** esse] *om.* C   studium SR : studendum
C   **10** suam SR : *om.* C   **11/12** in¹ ... regnorum C : in loco statuto in provincia ubi priores provinciales
S, post capitulum generale ubi et quando prior provincialis R   **16** aliquomodo CS : aliquatenus R
17 Et ea C : Ea vero R*(2,9)*   dicta ... capitulo C : de generali capitulo dicta sunt R

Cap. 16, 2/4 for the dating (1221), see *supra*, p. 392, with note 142   in sua provincia vel regno] for the
connection with the Fourth Lateran Council, see p. 343, with note 335, p. 346, with note 364, p. 391,
with note 138   **5/6** added in 1236 (*Acta C.G.*, p. 6)   **7/10** for the dating (1221), see *supra*, p. 392, with
note 142   **11/13** for the dating (1224) and the connection with the Franciscans, see p. 396, note 160
11/12 in provincia vel regno] for the connection with the Fourth Lateran Council, see p. 343, with
note 335, p. 346, with note 364, p. 391, with note 138   **14/16** for the affinity with Cîteaux, see p. 338; —
for the place of this rule in the constitutions, see p. 393, note 148; — for the dating (1225-1235), see p.
411, note 242   **17/18** for the dating (1221), see p. 390, note 131

17. DE CAPITULO GENERALI

Cum autem ⟨in quarta feria⟩ fratres in capitulum venerint, primo omnium devote invocetur Spiritus sanctus, a quo *filii Dei aguntur*. Et dicatur versus *E m i t t e S p i r i t u m tuum et creabuntur* cum c o l l e c t a de Spiritu sancto. Deinde residentibus fratribus et loca sua tenentibus omnibus, ut *verbo* Dei *celi firm*entur, verbum Domini in commune fiat. Sermoni interesse possunt qui ad edificandum interesse voluerint. F i n i t o s e r m o n e, quia indigentibus quantocius subveniendum est, obitus fratrum in anno d e f u n c t o r u m in communi recitetur et f i a t eis communis a b s o l u t i o et dicatur pro eis psalmus *D e p r o f u n d i s*. Et si l i t t e r e dande sunt, dentur et recipiantur et eis cum consilio suo tempore respondeatur. 10

⟨Item, nullus de cetero petitiones diffinitoribus porrigat, que per capitulum suum non fuerint approbate.⟩

Et sic o m n e s qui non sunt de capitulo, egrediantur. Quibus e g r e s s i s, qui missi sunt ad excusandos eos qui non assunt, ad quid venerint, loquantur. D e i n - d e c u l p e audiantur. 15

18. DE VISITATORIBUS

Post hec visitatores, presentes verbo, absentes scripto, referre debent de hiis, quos visitaverint, fratribus, si in pace continui, in studio assidui, in predicatione ferventes, que de eis fama, quis fructus, si in victu et vestitu et in aliis secundum tenorem institutionum ordo servetur. Quod si alicubi minus bene invenerint, ille 5 ad quem pertinet, hec audiens, surgat sponte et veniam petat et condignam penitentiam humiliter expectet.

Cap. 17, 2 in quarta feria] post Pentecosten *add. R(2,9)*   **4** et creabuntur] et cetera *R*   **5** sua tenentibus] suadentibus *C*   **6** poterunt *R*   **8** eis communis *C* : communis eis *R*   **9** De profundis] Kyrie eleison, Pater noster cum versu A porta inferi et oratione Absolve Domine *add. R*, Quo finito ... Absolve *add. S*   Et *C* : Postmodum *R*   **10** dande sunt dentur *C* : legende sunt legantur *R, cf.* dicat prelatus : Tradant litteras quicumque habent eas ostendendas *S*   et recipiantur *CS* : *om. R*
Cap. 18, 4 et vestitu *SR(2,11)* : *om. C*   **5** bene *S* : *om. C*   **6** surgat sponte *C* : sponte surgat *S*   **6** / **7** veniam ... expectet *C* : veniam petens humiliter penitentiam expectet *S*

Cap. 17, 2 / **15** for the connection with Cîteaux and Prémontré, see *supra*, pp. 332-333; — for the dating (1220), see pp. 384-385, with note 88, p. 389, with note 122   in quarta feria] interpolated c. 1227 (see p. 390, note 131)   **3** Spiritus ... aguntur] *cf. Rom.*, VIII,14: "Quicumque enim Spiritu Dei aguntur, ii sunt filii Dei"   **5** ut verbo Dei celi firmentur] *cf. Ps.*, XXXII,6: "Verbo Domini caeli firmati sunt"   **11** / **12** for the dating (1225-1235), see *supra*, p. 407, note 222, pp. 410-411, with note 241
Cap. 18, 2 / **7** for the dating (1220), see *supra*, pp. 384-385, with note 88, p. 389, with note 122   **2** / **5** Post ... servetur] for the relationship with Cîteaux and Prémontré, see pp. 333-334

19. DE ELECTIONE VISITATORUM

⟨Statuimus quod quatuor fratres ad visitandam provinciam in capitulo provinciali predicto modo eligantur, qui excessus priorum conventualium et fratrum audiant et emendent absque constitutione et status domus mutatione. Loca vero
5 sua ubique teneant nisi in capitulo, dum ab eis sue correctionis officium exercetur, quod in tribus diebus continuis terminetur. Si qua autem gravia et periculosa invenerint, licet correcta fuerint, nihilominus cum testimonio maioris partis capituli eiusdem generali capitulo studeant denuntiare. Priores autem seu doctores in visitatores nullatenus eligantur.⟩
10 Qui vero in presenti anno visitare debuerant et non sicut oportuerit fecerint, culpam suam dicant et digne vindicte subiaceant. Tunc absentibus qui adesse debuerant, et hiis qui peccaverunt nec satisfecerunt, penitentia scripta mittatur.

20. DE IDONEIS AD PREDICANDUM

Post hec qui idonei ad predicandum ab aliquibus estimantur, capitulo vel diffinitoribus presententur, et illi qui de licentia et mandato sui prioris, necdum de licentia maioris prelati vel capituli, predicationis officium receperint. Quibus
5 omnibus diligenter seorsum examinatis ab idoneis personis ob hoc et ob alias capituli questiones institutis, et fratribus, cum quibus conversati sunt, studiose inquisitis de gratia predicationis, quam eis Deus contulerit, et studio et religione et caritatis fervore, proposito ac intentione, et hiis de eis testimonium perhibentibus, consensu et consilio maioris prelati approbabunt quicquid ipsi utilius iudicabunt,
10 utrum videlicet ipsi fratres adhuc debeant in studio morari vel cum fratribus provectioribus in predicatione exercitari vel idonei sint et utiles per se predicationis officium exercere.

21. DE QUESTIONIBUS

Tunc qui habent questiones facere sive proprias sive communes ad ordinem vel ad predicationem pertinentes, proponant ordinate unus post alium. Et ab aliquo

---

Cap. 19, 2 in CS : a R(2,11)   **10** fecerint CS : fecerunt R   **11** Tunc] etiam add. R(2,9)   **12** debuerant R : debuerint C, om. S   peccaverunt R : peccaverint C, om. S
Cap. 20, 3 presententur C : capitulo vel diffinitoribus praem. R(2,12), capitulo generali vel provinciali add. S   necdum C : nondum R   de² R : om. C   **4** receperunt R   **5** omnibus] om. R   **8** ac SR : et C
Cap. 21, 2 Tunc qui C : Fratres qui S, Qui autem R(2,9)   **3** proponant ... alium C : proponant unus post alium ordinate S, ordinate proponant R

Cap. 19, 2/9 for the dating (1225-1235), see supra, p. 410, with note 239   **10/12** for the dating (1220), see pp. 384-385, with note 88, p. 389, with note 122
Cap. 20, 2/12 for the dating (1220), see supra, pp. 384-385, with note 88, p. 389, with note 122
Cap. 21, 2/20 for the dating (1220), see supra, pp. 384-385, with note 88, p. 389, with note 122   **2/**
5 Tunc ... terminentur] for the diffinitores in the Cistercian and Dominican orders, see pp. 334-336

fratre diligenter notentur, ut suo loco et tempore ab hiis qui ad hoc statuti sunt, solvantur et terminentur. Et uno s t a n te et l o q u ente, alius non loquatur.   5

Et ut in eundo modus servetur, n u l l u s   e x e a t   s i n e   l i c e n t i a et necessitate. Egressus autem non discurrat, sed necessitate expleta citius revertatur. S i qua vero d i s s e n s i o   i n t e r fratres nostri ordinis, quod absit, e m e r s e r i t de libris vel de aliis rebus, cum preponenda sint spiritualia temporalibus, non inde agatur in capitulo, sed fratres eligantur qui in hoc periti fuerint. Et post refectionem in loco   10 competenti extra capitulum, discussa veritate, litem dirimant et inter fratres pacem restituant.

De solutione et terminatione questionum, de correctione fratrum, de modo penitentiarum et de predicatoribus et eorum sociis ob predicandum et studendum mittendis et quando et ubi et per quantum tempus moraturis, prelatus maior cum   15 aliis, qui ad hoc instituti sunt, tractabit. Et q u i c q u i d   i n d e , donante Spiritu sancto, ordinaverint, capitulum universaliter et unanimiter et devote suscipiat. N u l l u s murmuret, n u l l u s reclamet, n u l l u s   c o n t r a d i c at.

In fine communis fiat confessio et a b s o l u t i o , perseverantibus b e n e d i c -t i o , apostatis et profugis anathematis maledictio.   20

⟨Et hec eadem forma in capitulo provinciali observetur.

Magister ordinis aut priores provinciales non mutent acta capituli generalis vel provincialis, nisi forte in speciali causa necessaria et utili.⟩

22. DE CAPITULO GENERALISSIMO

Item, generalissimum capitulum non convocetur, nisi quando maior pars provinciarum petierit, vel magistro visum fuerit expedire. Provincie que petunt, scribant causas quare petunt. De hiis tamen capitulum generale non habebit iudicare, utrum sufficiant vel non, sed scribantur ut ante capitulum fratres de hiis   5 possint habere collationem. Provinciales autem cum duobus fratribus a capitulo

4 hiis C : aliis S   **6** servetur SR : observetur C   **8** nostri ordinis SR : ordinis nostri C   **9** rebus om. R **11** litem C : dissensionem R   **16/17** donante Spiritu sancto C : Spiritu sancto donante R, om. S   **22/ 23** Magister ... utili hic S(2,22)R cum A(p.6) : om. C   ordinis SR : om. A   **22/23** capituli ... provincialis S cum A : provincialis capituli aut generalis R
Cap. 22, 1/8 de ... necessitas hic R(2,10) cum A(p.7-8) absque titulo : om. CS   **2** Item] om. R **3** Provincie] autem add. R   **4** his R   **5** sufficientes sint R   sed] tamen add. R   **5/6** ut ... collationem] ut fratres de eis ante capitulum conferre valeant R   **6/7** Provinciales ... potestatem] Priores autem provinciales singuli cum duobus sociis a capitulo suo provinciali electis, tale capitulum celebrabunt R

5 Et ... loquatur] for similar rules in the Cistercian texts, see pp. 336-337, with note 299   **6** Et ... necessitate] for the connection with Cîteaux and Prémontré, see p. 337, with note 300   **7/18** Si ... contradicat] for related texts, see p. 337   **19/20** for the relationship with Cîteaux and Prémontré, see pp. 332-334, with note 279   **21** perhaps added in 1225, when the provincial chapter was organised (cf. pp. 395-396)   **22/23** added in 1236 (Acta C.G., p. 6)
Cap. 22, 2/8 added in 1236 (Acta C.G., p. 7-8)

provinciali electis tale capitulum celebrandi habeant potestatem. Et duobus annis
ante pronuntietur, nisi fuerit urgens necessitas.

23. DE CONVENTU MITTENDO

Conventus citra numerum d u o d e narium et s i n e licentia generalis capituli
et s i n e priore et doctore n o n   m i t t a t u r.

⟨Item, nulla domus concedatur, nisi a priore provinciali et diffinitoribus provin-
5   cialis capituli fuerit postulata. Nec concessa ponatur, nisi ubi predicti decreverint
expedire.

Item, statuimus ut nulla domus n o s t r i   o r d i n i s   t r a n s f e r atur de provincia ad provinciam, n i s i   per tria c a p i t u l a fuerit approbatum.⟩

24. DE ELECTIONE PRIORUM CONVENTUALIUM

Priores conventuales a suis conventibus eligantur et a priore provinciali, si ei
visum fuerit, confirmentur, sine cuius licentia de alio conventu eligendi non
habeant potestatem.

5   ⟨Item, fratres tantum post annum sue professionis admittantur ad electionem
prioris conventualis. Si vero sunt de aliena provincia, postquam per annum steterunt in domo alterius provincie ad quam missi sunt, admittantur ad electionem
prioris conventualis.

Item, priore conventuali mortuo vel amoto, conventus eligat infra mensem
10   postquam ei innotuerit. Alioquin prior provincialis eidem conventui provideat de
priore.⟩

25. DE SUPPRIORE

Prior autem conventualis de consilio discretorum fratrum instituat suppario-
rem, cuius officium erit habere diligentiam et curam circa conventum et corripere

---

7 Et] om. R   8 urgens fuerit R

Cap. 23, 2 sine C : absque R(2,1)   **4** Item] C cum A(p.6) : om. R   concedatur CR : de cetero detur A

Cap. 24, 1 priorum conventualium C : prioris conventualis S(2,23)R(2,2)   **3** confirmetur C   **5** Item
fratres C : Fratres S, Fratres autem R   tantum C cum A(p.7) : om. SR   **6** steterunt R : steterant C,
steterint S   **7** domum C   **8** prioris conventualis C : om. S, predictam R   **9** eligat CS : sibi priorem
add. A(p.8)   **10** ei S cum A : om. C   eidem C cum A : om. SR

Cap. 23, 2/3 for the affinity with Cîteaux, see *supra*, pp. 338-339; — for the dating (1220), see p. 386,
with note 101, p. 389, with note 123   **4/8** added in 1236 (*Acta C.G.*, pp. 6 and 7); — for the affinity
with Cîteaux, see *supra*, p. 339, with notes 307-308

Cap. 24, 2/4 for the dating (1220), see *supra*, p. 386, with note 102, p. 389, with note 123   **5/11** added
in 1236 (*Acta C.G.*, pp. 7 and 8)

Cap. 25, 2/6 for the dating (1220), see *supra*, p. 386, with note 103, p. 389, with note 123

delinquentes et in aliis quantum prior ei assignaverit vel permiserit. Nec in cotidia-
nis capitulis accusetur, nisi aliquando pro aliquo maiore excessu, secundum quod   5
priori visum fuerit, proclametur.

26. DE POSSESSIONIBUS NON RECIPIENDIS

P o s s e s s i o n es seu r e d d i t us nullo modo recipiantur.
Nullus fratrum nostrorum instare audeat vel rogare pro beneficiis suis consanguineis obtinendis.

27. DE CURA MONIALIUM NON PROCURANDA

In virtute Spiritus sancti et sub pena excommunicationis districte prohibemus
ne aliquis fratrum nostrorum d e   c e t e r o laboret vel procuret, ut cura vel custodia m o n i a l i u m seu quarumlibet aliarum mulierum nostris fratribus committatur. Et si quis contraire presumpserit, pene graviori culpe debite subiaceat.   5
Prohibemus etiam ne aliquis de cetero aliquam tondeat vel induat vel ad
professionem recipiat.
Item, e c c l e s i a s, quibus annexa sit cura animarum, non r e c i p i a nt. Numerum quoque missarum non admittant.

28. DE MAGISTRO STUDENTIUM

Quoniam circa studentes diligens est adhibenda cautela, aliquem fratrem
specialem habeant, sine cuius licentia non scribant quaternos nec audiant lectiones. Et que circa eos in studio corrigenda viderit, corrigat et, si vires excedant,
prelato proponat.   5

Cap. 25, 4 prior ei assignaverit C : ei prior assignaverit S(2,24), prior assignaverit ei R(2,2)
Cap. 26, 3/4 Nullus ... obtinendis om. R   Nullus fratrum nostrorum C : Nulla soror M(c.21), aliter
S(2,30), cf. Nullus frater A(p.31)
Cap. 27, 3 de ... procuret C : laboret vel procuret de cetero R(2,1), laboret vel procuret S(2,26)   4 seu
SR : vel C   aliarum C : om. R, congregationum S   5 gravioris C   6 aliquam] feminam add. S,
mulierem add. R(1,13)   8 quibus ... animarum C : quibus animarum cura sit annexa R   8/
9 Numerum quoque missarum C : Fratres vero nostri numerum missarum R(1,3)
Cap. 28, 2/3 fratrem specialem C : specialem fratrem R(2,14)   4 excedant CS(2,27) : excedat R
5 preponat C

Cap. 26, 2 ordinance of 1220 (see Jordan, Libellus, no. 87; see also supra, p. 376, with note 23); — for
the connection with Cîteaux, see pp. 338-339, with note 312   3/4 for the presence of this rule in the
oldest constitutions, see pp. 277-278; — for the dating (1220-1231), see p. 408, with note 226
Cap. 27, 2/7 for the dating (1228), see supra, p. 405, with note 209   3/4 ne ... committatur] for a
similar stipulation in the Cistercian texts, see pp. 339-340, with note 318   8 Item ... recipiant] for the
affinity with Cîteaux, see p. 339; — for the dating (1228), see p. 405, with note 210
Cap. 28, 2/9 for the dating (1220), see supra, p. 387, with notes 106-107

In l i b r i s g e n t i l i u m et philosophorum n o n studeant, etsi ad horam inspi-
ciant. S e c u l a r e s   s c i e n t i a s   n o n   a d d i s cant nec etiam artes quas liberales
vocant, nisi aliquando circa aliquos magister ordinis vel capitulum generale voluerit aliter dispensare, sed tantum libros theologicos tam iuvenes quam alii legant.

10   ⟨Statuimus autem ut quelibet provincia fratribus suis missis ad studium ad
minus in tribus libris theologie, videlicet biblia, sententiis et historiis, providere
teneatur. Et fratres missi ad studium in historiis et sententiis et textu et glosis precipue studeant et intendant.

In diebus dominicis et festis precipuis a quaternis scribendis se abstineant.

15   Cum frater de provincia ad provinciam ad regendum mittitur, omnes libros
suos glosatos et bibliam et quaternos secum deferat. Si vero mittitur et non ad
regendum, tantum bibliam et quaternos portet. Quod si in via mori contigerit,
conventus ad quem mittendus fuerit, sibi in missis et psalteriis tenebitur et ad eun-
dem libri, quos habuerit, pertinebunt. Tres fratres tantum mittantur ad studium
20   Parisius de provincia.⟩

29. DE DISPENSATIONE STUDENTIUM

Circa eos qui student, taliter dispensetur a prelato, ne propter officium vel aliud
de facili a studio retrahantur vel impediantur.

Et secundum quod magistro studentium videbitur, locus proprius statuatur, in
5   quo post disputationem vel vesperas vel alio etiam tempore, si vacaverint, ad dubi-
tationes vel questiones proponendas ipso presente conveniant. Et uno querente vel
proponente alii taceant, ne loquentem impediant. Et si aliquis inhoneste vel confu-

---

7 etiam] *om.* R   **8** circa ... generale C : magister ordinis vel capitulum generale circa aliquos R   **11** /
12 videlicet ... teneatur S : tenentur providere, videlicet in biblia, hystoriis et sentenciis R   **12** Et ...
glosis CS : et ipsi in hiis tam in textu quam in glosis R   **14** In ... abstineant *hic* R(2,14) : cf. Omnibus ...
precipimus, ne in diebus dominicis vel festivis libros vel quaternos audeant scribere, proprios vel
communes S, *in* 2,34 C   abstineant C : contineant R   **15/19** Cum ... pertinebunt *hic* R(2,14) : *in*
extrav.(2,36) C, *om.* S   **16** glosatos] et *praem.* C   et¹ C : *om.* R   **17** tantum] non tamen nisi R
18 fuerat R   sibi] *om.* R   psalteriis] in *praem.* R   tenebitur] ei *praem.* R   **19** habuit C   **19** /
20 tantum ... Parisius C : mittantur Parisius tantum ad studium R
Cap. 29, 5 disputationem S(2,28)R(2,14) : disputationes C

6/7 In ... addiscant] cf. *Statuta Ecclesiae antiqua*, c. 5: "Ut episcopus gentilium libros non legat,
haereticorum autem pro necessitate et tempore" (ed. Ch. Munier, Paris, 1960, p. 80); *Corpus iuris
canonici*, vol. I, col. 135; cf. also can. 4 of the Council of Paris (1212): "Item, statuimus ut nulli habenti
curam parochialem liceat saeculares scientias addiscere" (Mansi, vol. XXII, col. 845); for the origins
and interpretation of these rules, see G.G. Meersseman, *"In libris gentilium non studeant". L'étude des
classiques interdite aux clercs au moyen age?*, in *Italia medioevale e classica*, vol. I, 1958, pp. 1-13   **10/13** for
the dating (c. 1234), see *supra*, p. 405, with note 212   **11** biblia ... historiis] for identification of these,
see M.H. Vicaire, *Saint Dominique de Caleruega*, p. 177, note 93   **12** glosis] for the meaning and the use
of the *Glossa (ordinaria)*, see B. Smalley, *The Study of the Bible in the Middle Ages*, Oxford, 1952[2], pp.
46-66   **14** for the dating (1221-1231), see *supra*, p. 407, with note 222   **15/20** for the dating (1221-1231),
see p. 408, with note 225
Cap. 29, 2/13 for the dating (1220), see *supra*, p. 387, with notes 106-107

se vel clamose vel proterve querens vel opponens vel respondens offenderit, statim
ab illo qui tunc inter eos preest, corripiatur.

Celle non omnibus studentibus, sed quibus magistro eorum expedire videbi-   10
tur, assignentur. Quod si aliquis infructuosus inveniatur in studio, cella eius detur
alteri, et ipse in aliis officiis occupetur. In cellis legere, scribere, orare, dormire et
etiam de nocte vigilare ad lumen possunt, qui voluerint, propter studium.

30. DE DOCTORE

Nullus fiat publicus doctor, nisi per quatuor annos ad minus theologiam audierit.

⟨Item, nullus fratrum nostrorum legat in psalmis vel prophetis alium sensum
litteralem, nisi quem sancti approbant et confirmant.⟩   5

31. DE PREDICATORIBUS

⟨Statuimus ut nullus fiat predicator generalis antequam theologiam audierit per
tres annos.⟩

Ad exercitium vero predicationis, postquam prius per annum theologiam
audierint, possunt admitti qui tales fuerint, de quorum predicatione scandalum   5
non timetur. Et hii qui apti sunt, cum in predicationem exire debuerint, eis socii
dabuntur a priore, secundum quod moribus eorum et honestati iudicaverit expedire. Qui, recepta benedictione, exeuntes, ubique tanquam viri, qui suam et aliorum
salutem procurare desiderant, honeste et religiose se habeant sicut viri evangelici,
sui *sequentes vestigia* Salvatoris, cum Deo vel de Deo secum vel proximis loquendo,   10
vitabunt suspiciosi comitatus familiaritatem.

Euntes vero ad iam dictum *predicat*ionis officium exercendum vel alias itinerantes, *aurum, argentum, pecuniam* et munera, excepto victu et vestitu et necessariis
indumentis et libris, nec accipient nec portabunt.

---

13 ad lumen *SR* : *om. C*   possunt *SR* : possint *C*
Cap. 30, 2 Nullus] autem *add. R(2,14)*   nisi ... audierit *C* : nisi ad minus theologiam per quatuor
annos audierit *R*
Cap. 31, 4 theologiam] *om. C*   **5** fuerint *S(2,29)R(2,12)* : sunt *C*

Cap. 30, 2 for the dating (1221-1235), see *supra*, p. 410, note 241   **4/5** added in 1236 (*Acta C.G.*, p. 6)
Cap. 31, 2/3 for the dating (1220-1235), see *supra*, p. 387, note 109, p. 410, note 241   **4/6** Ad ... sunt]
for the dating (1220), see p. 387, note 109   **6/11** cum ... familiaritatem] for the dating (1216), see pp.
382-383   **10** sui sequentes vestigia Salvatoris] cf. I *Pet.*, II,21: "... ut sequamini vestigia eius"
11 vitabunt ... familiaritatem] cf. *Propositum Bernardi Primi*: "... suspectum mulierum consortium
prorsus evitent" (PL, vol. 216, col. 293)   **12/14** for the dating (1216), see *supra*, p. 383, with note 78
Euntes ... officium] cf. *Matth.*, X,7: "Euntes autem praedicate..."   **13** aurum argentum pecuniam] cf.
Matth., X,9: "Nolite possidere aurum, neque argentum, neque pecuniam in zonis vestris ..."

15   Omnes qui ad officium predicationis vel studium sunt deputati, nullam habeant curam seu administrationem temporalium, ut expeditius et melius iniunctum sibi ministerium spiritualium valeant adimplere, nisi forte non sit aliquis alius, qui necessaria procuret, cum in necessitatibus diei presentis oporteat aliquando occupari.

20   ⟨P l a c i t i s et causis, n i s i pro fidei negotiis, non i n t e r s i n t .⟩

32. UBI NON AUDEANT PREDICARE FRATRES

⟨P r e d i c a r e   n o n   a u d e a t aliquis i n diocesi a l i c u i u s   e p i s c o p i , qui ei ne predicet interdixerit, n i s i litteras et generale mandatum habeat summi pontificis.⟩

5   Cum fratres nostri diocesim alicuius episcopi ad predicandum intraverint, primo, si poterunt, episcopum illum visitabunt et secundum consilium eius in populo fructum faciant, quem facere intendunt. Et quamdiu in eius episcopatu fuerint, ipsi in hiis, que contra ordinem non fuerint, devote obedientes erunt.

33. DE SCANDALO PREDICATIONIS

Caveant fratres nostri, ne *ponendo os in celum* suis predicationibus religiosos vel clericos scandalizent. Sed ea, que in ipsis emendanda viderint, *obsecrando ut patres* seorsum emendare procurent.

5   ⟨Nullus assumatur ad predicationis officium extra claustrum vel fratrum consortium infra viginti quinque annos.

Statuimus ne fratres nostri in predicationibus suis dari vel colligi pecuniam admoneant pro domo vel aliqua persona speciali.⟩

---

15 ad ... studium *C* : ad iam dictum predicationis officium *R*   **16** curam seu administrationem *C* : administrationem seu curam *R*   **17** non *C* : ubi *praem. R*
Cap. 33, 2 ponendo *R(2,12)* : proponendo *S(2,31)*, ponentes *C*   **7/8** Statuimus ... speciali *hic R(2,12)* : in *2,34 C, om. S*

15/19 for the dating (1220), see *supra*, p. 387, note 109   **20** Placitis ... intersint] for a similar rule in the Citeaux text, see p. 340, with note 319; — for the dating (1221-1235), see p. 410, note 241
Cap. 32, 2/3 cf. *Reg. bullata S. Franc.*, c. 9: "Fratres non praedicent in episcopatu alicuius episcopi, cum ab eo illis fuerit contradictum. Et nullus fratrum populo penitus audeat praedicare, nisi a ministro generali huius fraternitatis fuerit examinatus..."; cf. also the letter from Leo I to Theodoret of Cyrus (*ep. 120*, c. 6): "... nullus audeat praedicare, ...qui cuiuslibet scientiae nomine glorietur" (PL, vol. 54, col. 1054); — for the dating (c. 1223), see *supra*, pp. 387-388, note 111   **5/8** for the dating (1220), see p. 387, with note 110, p. 389, note 125
Cap. 33, 2/4 for the dating (1220), see *supra*, p. 387, with note 110, p. 389, note 125   ponendo os in celum] cf. *Ps.*, LXXII,9: "Posuerunt in caelum os suum"   **3/4** obsecrando ut patres] cf. I *Tim.*, V,1: "Seniorem ne increpaveris, sed obsecra ut patrem"   **5/6** for the dating (1221-1235), see *supra*, p. 410, note 241   **7/8** for the dating (1221-1231), see p. 407, with note 222

34. DE ITINERANTIBUS

Predicatores vel itinerantes, cum in via existunt, officium suum dicant prout sciunt et possunt, et sint contenti officio ecclesiarum ad quas aliquando declinant, vel etiam agant officium vel audiant apud episcopos vel prelatos vel alios, secundum morem eorum cum quibus aliquando conversantur.   5

⟨In inclinationibus conformemur moribus eorum, ad quos declinamus.⟩

Fratres etiam viatores litteras testimoniales secum ferant et in conventibus, ad quos declinaverint, de excessibus factis ibidem corrigantur.

⟨Prior priorem supervenientem honoret. Hospes per civitatem sine consilio eius non discurrat vel moram faciat.⟩   10

Prior in ordine sit prior in via, nisi forte predicatori adiungatur vel, cum egrediuntur, aliter prelatus cum ipsis ordinaverit.

Socius datus predicatori, ipsi ut priori suo in omnibus obediat.

Fratres minores sicut et nostri caritative et hilariter recipiantur et secundum facultatem domus pie et honeste procurentur.   15

⟨Nullus fratrum vadat ad curiam nisi de licentia magistri vel capituli generalis. Sed mittatur garcio ad fratres, qui ibi sunt, vel si quis secularis voluerit procurare, ut tanquam per se et non per nos videatur facere.

Fratres non recipiant a mulieribus munuscula nec dent, et maxime confessores.⟩   20

35. DE EDIFICIIS

Mediocres domos et humiles habeant fratres nostri, ita quod murus domorum sine solario non excedat in altitudine mensuram duodecim pedum et cum solario

Cap. 34, 1 de itinerantibus] fratribus *add.* C   **3** aliquando *S(2,32)R(2,13)* : quandoque C   **6** In ... declinamus *hic S(2,32)M(c.24)* : in 1,2 R, in extrav.(2,36) C   In] *om.* C   **8** factis] *om.* R   **9/10** Prior ... faciat *hic R(2,13)* : *cf. S(2,32), in extrav.(2,36)* C   Hospes C : sed *praem.* R, et *praem.* S   **10** eius R : suo C, prioris domestici S   vel moram faciat C : nec moram faciat R, *om.* S   **12** prelatus ... ordinaverit CS : prior ordinaverit de eis R   **13** in omnibus *M(c.24)S* : eras. R(2,12), *om.* C, *cf. A(p.14,19,22)*   **16/** **18** Nullus ... facere *hic R(2,13)* : *cf. S(2,32), in extrav.(2,36)* C   **17** garcio C : nuntius R, aliquis S   **17/** **18** ad ... facere C : ad fratres qui sunt ibi, vel per aliquem alium, prout melius fieri poterit, negotium procuretur R, ad procuratorem ordinis, qui in curia commoratur S   **19** Fratres ... confessores *hic* R(2,13) : *cf. M(c.24), in extrav.(2.36)* C, in 1,4 S   recipiant CM : accipiant R   et C : *om.* R
Cap. 35, 2 domus R(2,1)   **3** excedant CR   altitudinem R   et] *om.* R

Cap. 34, 2/13 for the dating (1220), see *supra*, p. 387, with note 110, p. 389, note 125   **6** for the dating (1221-1231), see p. 408, note 225   **9/10** for the dating (1221-1231), see p. 408, note 225   **14/15** for the dating (1221-1235), see *supra*, p. 407, with note 222   **16/19** or the dating (1221-1231) see p. 408, with note 225   **16/17** Nullus ... generalis] for the affinity with Cîteaux, see p. 340, with note 320
Cap. 35, 2/5 Mediocres ... sacristiam] for the dating (1220), see *supra*, p. 387, with note 104-105

viginti, ecclesia triginta. Et non fiat lapidibus testudinata nisi forte super chorum et
5   sacristiam. ⟨Si quis de cetero contrafecerit, pene gravioris culpe subiacebit.

Item, in quolibet conventu tres fratres de discretioribus eligantur, sine quorum
consilio edificia non fiant.

Fratres non sint dispensatores alienarum rerum vel pecuniarum nec fideicommissarii. Depositarii esse possunt.

10   Item, nullus faciat sibi scribi libros de rebus domus nisi ad communem utilitatem.

Item, in diebus dominicis servilia opera, ut lapides portare, ligna aggregare et
similia, fieri prohibemus.

36. DE ANNIVERSARIIS

A festo sancti Dionysii usque ad Adventum pro anniversario fratrum clericus
psalterium, sacerdos tres missas, laici quinquaginta *Pater noster* dicant.

Idem faciat quilibet fratrum pro defuncto fratre sui conventus.

5   Idem fiat per totum ordinem pro magistro ordinis et a comprovincialibus pro
priore provinciali defuncto.

Idem etiam fiat pro visitatore a domibus, quas visitare debet, si in visitatione
moriatur. Idem etiam fiat pro diffinitoribus generalis capituli sive prioribus provincialibus sive aliis fratribus et eorum sociis, si eos in via mori contigerit, quod fit pro
10   magistro ordinis mortuo.

Item, in unaquaque provincia pro fratre illius provincie defuncto quilibet sacerdos celebret unam missam et quilibet conventus unam in communi et unusquisque aliorum septem psalmos.

Anniversarium patrum et matrum tertia die post Purificationem sancte Marie,
15   anniversarium benefactorum et familiarium tertia die post Nativitatem eiusdem
est faciendum.

5 quis] vero *add. R*   contrafecit *C*   gravioris culpe *C* : graviori culpe debite *R*   **6/7** Item ... fiant *C* :
om. SMR   **8/9** Fratres ... possunt *hic M(c.22)S(2,25)* : *in 2,13 R, in extrav.(2,36) C*   Fratres] Item *praem.*
R(2,13)   nec fideicommissarii *C* : *om. M., eras. R*   **10** Item ... utilitatem *hic M(c.22)S(2,25)* : *in 2,14 R, in
2,34 C*   **12/13** Item ... prohibemus *huc transtuli* : *in 2,34 C, cf. M(c.23), om. SR*
Cap. 36, 1 de anniversariis *CS(2,32)* : De suffragiis mortuorum *M(c.26)R(1,3)*   **3** quinquaginta *scripsi
cum M*, centum quinquaginta *S*, quingenta *CR cum A(p.18)*   dicant *MR* : *om. C*   **6** defunctis *R*
11 fratre *C* : unoquoque *praem. R*   **13** aliorum] clericorum *R*   psalmos] et conversi centum Pater
noster *add. R*, dicant vel quinquaginta Pater noster *add. M*   **14** sancte] beate *R*   **15** et *MSR* : *om. C*

5 Si ... subiacebit] for the dating (1228), see p. 405, with note 208   **6/7** for the dating (1221-1235), see
p. 410, note 241   **8/9** for the dating (1221-1231), see p. 408, with note 225   **10/13** for the dating
(1221-1231), see pp. 407-408, with note 222
Cap. 36, 2/16 for the dating (1220-1231), see *supra*, p. 408, with note 226

37. REGULA FRATRUM NOSTRORUM CONVERSORUM

Eodem tempore surgant fratres nostri conversi quo et canonici et eodem modo inclinent. Cum surrexerint ad matutinas, dicant *Pater noster* et *Credo in Deum*. Quod faciendum est ante primam et post completorium. In matutinis, dicto *Pater noster* et *Credo in Deum*, erigant se dicentes *Domine, labia mea aperies* etc., *Deus, in adiuto-* 5 *rium* etc., *Gloria Patri* etc.

Pro matutinis in profestis diebus dicant viginti octo *Pater noster* et in fine omnium dicant *Kyrie eleison, Christe eleison, Kyrie eleison, Pater noster*. Quo dicto, addant *Per Dominum* etc., deinde *Benedicamus Domino* etc. In festis novem lectio- num quadraginta *Pater noster* dicant. In aliis autem horis septem *Pater noster* dicant 10 et in vesperis quatuordecim.

Loco *Pretiosa* dicant tria *Pater noster*, pro benedictione mense *Pater noster* et *Gloria Patri*, post mensam pro gratiis tria *Pater noster, Gloria Patri* etc. vel *Miserere mei Deus*, qui sciunt. Et hoc totum cum silentio in ecclesia et ubicumque fuerint.

Conversis qui nunc habent psalteria, tantum duobus annis liceat retinere. Ab 15 inde et ipsis alia psalteria inhibemus.

Indumenta tot habeant quot et canonici preter cappas, loco quarum habeant scapularia longa et lata, que non sint alba sicut et tunice. Poterunt et brevia grisei coloris habere scapularia ad mensuram et formam scapularium canonicorum. De ieiuniis, cibis et abstinentiis et culpis et aliis omnibus sic se habeant, sicut scriptum 20 est in regula canonicorum. In labore tamen prelatus cum eis poterit dispensare.

⟨Item, nullus conversus fiat canonicus, nec in libris causa studendi se audeat occupare.

Item, priores provinciales conversos non recipiant nisi conventuum ubi fuerint induendi. Nec fratres conversi vadant extra domum soli nisi cum clerico vel con- 25 verso.⟩

Cap. 37, 2 canonici *C* : clerici *S(2,35)*, conventus *M(c.25) cum Pb(4,10)*, alii *R(2,15)*   **5** adiutorium] meum *add. C*   **9** addant *CM* : addatur *S*, additur *R*   festis] autem *add. RM*   **10/11** In ... quatuordecim *C* : In vesperis quatuordecim, in aliis autem singulis horis septem Pater noster dicant *M*, In vesperis vero quatuordecim, in aliis autem horis septem Pater noster dicant *R post lin. 9 etc.*[2], *om. S*   **12/13** Pater noster et Gloria Patri *C* : Pater noster, Gloria patri et cetera *R*, unum Pater noster cum Gloria Patri *M*, unus Pater noster cum Gloria Patri *S*   **14** Et ... fuerint *hic CS : post lin. 10* dicant *RM* fuerint *R* : fuerit *M*, *om. C*   **15/16** Conversis ... inhibemus *C* : *om. SR*   **16** aliis *C* : ceteri fratres *R*, alie sorores *M*   **18** Poterunt *C* : Possunt *R*   et[3] *C* : *om. R*   **19** et formam *C* : *om. R* canonicorum *C* : nostrorum *R*   **20/21** sicut ... canonicorum *C* : sicut et clerici *R*   **21** cum eis poterit *CM* : poterit cum eis *R*   **22/23** Item ... occupare *C* : *om. MSR*   **24/25** Item ... converso *scripsi cum A(p.6)* : *cf.* Soli non vadant, sed cum socio clerico vel converso *R*, *om. CMS*

Cap. 37, 2/21 for the dating (1220), see *supra*, pp. 388-389   **2/11** for similar rules, cf. Pb, IV, 10 and *Reg. prima S. Franc.*, c. 3   **22/23** for the dating (1221-1235), see *supra*, p. 410, with note 241   **24/ 25** added in 1236 (*Acta C.G.*, p. 6)

Comparative list of the chapters in the first *distinctio* of the Dominican text (C) and in the *Constitutiones S. Mariae Magdalenae* (M)

Missing chapters are indicated by a dash (—).

O.P.	Magd.
1. De matutinis.	1. De divino officio et de inclinationibus.[1]
2. De capitulo.	2. De capitulo.
3. De mulieribus non intromittendis.	3. De clausura claustri.
4. De horis et de modo dicendi.	4. De officio ecclesie.
5. De refectione.	5. De refectionibus et regularibus ieiuniis,
6. De ieiunio.	sicut in regula continetur…[2]
7. De prandio.	6. De modo eundi ad prandium.
8. De pulmentis.	7. De cibo.
9. De collatione et completorio.	8. De collatione.
10. De lectis.	9. De lectis.
11. De infirmis.	10. De infirmis.
12. De minutione.	11. De minutis.
13. De magistro novitiorum.	12. De instructione novitiarum.
14. De recipiendis.	13. Quomodo recipiantur novitie.
15. De tempore probationis.	—
16. De modo faciendi professionem.	14. De modo professionis.
17. De silentio.	15. De silentio.
18. De scandalo fratrum.[3]	—
19. De vestibus.	16. De vestitu.
20. De rasura.	17. De tonsura, … sicut regula continet.[4]

---

1 The words *de beata Virgine* are followed in the text by *De inclinationibus*. The words *et de inclinationibus* were also added by hand in the right margin.
2 Cf. *Instit. S. Sixti* (I), c. 2.
3 The text of this short chapter appears as the last sentence of c. 15, *De silentio* in M, but without a title.
4 Cf. *Inst. S. Sixti*, c. 10.

21. De levioribus culpis.

22. De gravi culpa.

23. De graviori culpa.

24. De fratre qui apostataverit.[6]

25. De gravissima culpa.

18. De culpis, sicut in regula continetur, firmiter volumus observari.[5]

---

5 Cf. *Inst. S. Sixti*, c. 11-15.
6 Not in *Inst. S. Sixti*.

Comparative list of the chapters in the second *distinctio* of the Dominican text (C) and in that of the Friars of the Sack (S)

Missing chapters are indicated by a dash (—).

O.P.	Friars of the Sack
1. De capitulo provinciali.	1. De electione diffinitorum capituli provincialis.
2. De diffinitoribus capituli provincialis.	2. De diffinitoribus capituli provincialis.
3. De potestate horum diffinitorum.	3. De potestate eorundem.
4. Quis obtineat vicem prioris provincialis.	4. Quis obtineat vicem prioris provincialis.
5. De electione capituli generalis diffinitoris.	5. De tempore capituli generalis et electione diffinitorum.
6. De preiudicio vitando.	6. De preiudicio vitando.
7. De diffinitoribus generalis capituli.	7. De prioribus provincialibus et diffinitoribus capituli generalis.
8. De potestate diffinitorum.	8. De potestate priorum provincialium et diffinitorum.
9. De excessu magistri corrigendo.	9. De excessu rectoris corrigendo.
10. De electione magistri ordinis.	10. De electione rectoris ordinis.
11. De forma electionis.	11. De forma electionis.
—	12. De forma decreti.
12. Qui venire debeant ad capitulum generale.	13. Qui venire debeant ad capitulum generale.
13. De morte magistri.	—
14. De infamatione ordinis vitanda.	14. De infamatione ordinis evitanda.
15. De electione priorum provincialium.	15. De electione prioris provincialis.
16. De potestate prioris provincialis.	16. De potestate priorum provincialium.
17. De capitulo generali.	17. De capitulo generali.
18. De visitatoribus.	18. De visitatoribus.
19. De electione visitatorum.	19. De electione visitatorum.
20. De idoneis ad predicandum.	20. De idoneis ad predicandum.

21. De questionibus.	21. De questionibus.
	22. De solutione et terminatione questionum, de correctione fratrum et modo penitentiarum.[1]
22. De anniversariis.[2]	
23. De conventu mittendo.	—
24. De electione priorum conventualium.	23. De electione prioris conventualis.
25. De suppriore.	24. De suppriore.
26. De possessionibus non recipiendis.	25. De paupertate.
27. De cura monialium non procuranda.	26. De cura monialium et quarumlibet mulierum non procuranda.
28. De magistro studentium.	27. De studio et magistro studentium.
29. De dispensatione studentium.	28. De dispensatione studentium.
30. De doctore.	—
31. De predicatoribus.	29. De predicatoribus.
32. Ubi non audeant predicate fratres.	30. Ubi fratres non valeant predicare.
33. De scandalo predicationis.	31. De scandalo predicationis vitando.
34. De itinerantibus fratribus.	32. De itinerantibus.
	33. De anniversariis.[3]
35. De edificiis.[4]	
36. (Extravagantes).[5]	
	34. Qualiter fieri debeant constitutiones et qualiter roborari.[6]
37. Regula fratrum nostrorum conversorum.	35. De ordinatione fratrum laicorum.

1 The text of this chapter appears in c. 21 in the Dominican text, but without a separate title.
2 This chapter appears in the text of the Friars of the Sack as c. 33.
3 This chapter appears in the Dominican text as c. 22.
4 One stipulation from this chapter appears in the text of the Friars of the Sack in c. 25: "Domorum autem et officinarum opera sint humilia et mediocria…".
5 The Friars of the Sack moved the various stipulations in this chapter to chapters with corresponding subject matter.
6 This chapter is a paraphrase of the stipulation that appears at the end of c. 6 in the Dominican text: "Et ut multitudo constitutionum vitetur…".

The ordinances of the chapter of 1236 in the texts of the constitutions

The scheme below gives the list of the textual corrections of 1236 according to the place where they appear in the *Acta*, alongside the place (with *distinctio* and *caput*) they were given in the Rodez manuscript (C), the text of the Friars of the Sack (S), and Raymond of Peñafort's edition (R) respectively. If an ordinance is missing in the edition in question, this is indicated by a dash (—).

	Acta	C	S	R
1.	P. 6 (l. 2-3)	—	II, 21	II, 9
2.	6 (l. 4-6)	II, 23	—	II, 1
3.	6 (l. 7-8)	II, 16	II, 16	II, 3
4.	6 (l. 9-11)	—	—	II, 15
5.	6 (l. 12-13)	II, 30	—	II, 14
6.	6 (l. 14-16)	I, 19	—	I, 10
7.	6 (l. 17-20)	I, 7	I, 11	I, 7
8.	6 (l. 21-23)	—	I, 11	I, 9
9.	6 (l. 24-25)	—	—	I, 7
10.	6 (l. 26-27)	I, 6	I, 6	I, 4
11.	6 (l. 28-31)	—	I, 10	I, 9
12.	6 (l. 32) – 7 (l. 2)	I, 17	—	I, 12
13.	7 (l. 3-5)	—	—	I, 14
14.	7 (l. 6-8)	—	—	II, 7
15.	7 (l. 9-11)	II, 23	—	II, 1
16.	7 (l. 12-17)	II, 11	—	II, 8
17.	7 (l. 18-21)	II, 1	—	II, 9
18.	7 (l. 22-24)	II, 1	—	II, 7
19.	7 (l. 25-26)	II, 9	—	II, 8
20.	7 (l. 27-30)	II, 15	II, 15	II, 3
21.	7 (l. 31-32)	II, 24	II, 24	II, 2
22.	7 (l. 33-34)	II, 34	—	II, 7
23.	7 (l. 35) – 8 (l. 3)	—	—	II, 10

24.	8 (l. 4-7)	—	II, 33	Prol.
25.	8 (l. 8-18)	II, 10	II, 10	II, 4
		II, 11	II, 11	II, 4
26.	8 (l. 19-21)	II, 24	II, 24	II, 2
27.	8 (l. 22-26)	II, 15	II, 15	II, 3
28.	8 (l. 27-28)	—	—	I, 15

Relationship of the various constitutions and manuscripts to the *Constitutiones Antiquae O.P.*

Legend

1. A continuous line (—) refers to the manuscripts in which the text in question was preserved.

A dashed line (-----) means that a source was adopted incompletely by another source.

A dotted line (......) means that a source was probably adopted by another source.

2. The roman titles refer to texts that are still extant, preserved in the manuscripts printed in CAPITALS.

Texts that are no longer extant or unknown are printed in *italics*.

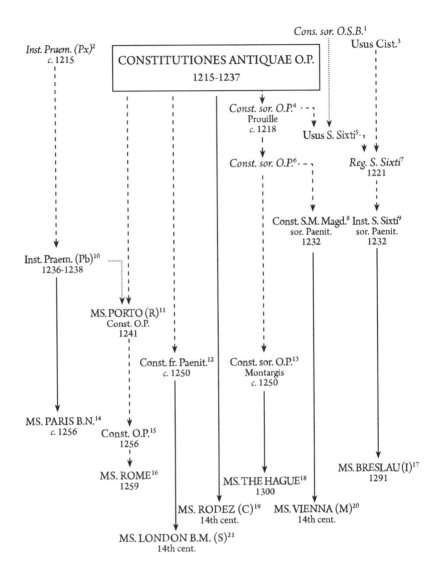

1	See *supra*, pp. 252 - 253, with footnotes 49-50.	7	See pp. 252-254.	15	See pp. 249-250.
2	See pp. 288-291, 296, 304-305, 369.	8	See pp. 256-260.	16	See pp. 249-250.
		9	See pp. 252-256.	17	See pp. 251.
3	See pp. 251, 252-253.	10	See pp. 199, 282.	18	See L. Creytens, *Les constitutions de Montargis*, p. 47.
4	See pp. 218, 252, 254-256.	11	See pp. 246-249.		
5	See p. 252.	12	See pp. 260-267.	19	See pp. 244-246.
6	See pp. 258-259.	13	See pp. 250-251.	20	See pp. 256-257.
		14	See pp. 282-283.	21	See pp. 261-263.

Comparative list of the chapters in the first *distinctio* of the Dominican text (CA) and in the *Consuetudines* of Prémontré (Pa and Pb)

Pa	O.P.	Pb
I, 1. De matutinis.	1. De matutinis.	I, 1. De matutinis.
I, 4. De capitulo.	2. De capitulo.[1]	I, 2. De capitulo cotidiano.
	3. De mulieribus non intromittendis.	IV, 13. Ne mulieres intrent officinas canonicorum.
	4. De horis et de modo dicendi.	
cf. I, 5. Quomodo se habeant fratres in estate.	5. De refectione.	cf. I,5. Quomodo se habeant fratres in estate.
cf. I, 6. Quomodo se habeant fratres in hieme.	6. De ieiunio.	cf. I, 6. Quomodo se habeant fratres in hieme.
I, 10. De refectione.	7. De prandio.	I, 9. De refectione.
IV, 12-13. De victu.	8. De pulmentis.	I, 10. De victu.
I, 13. De collatione.	9. De collatione et completorio.	I, 11. De collatione.
cf. I, 17. De dirigendis in via.		cf. I, 12. Quomodo se habeant fratres post completorium.
cf. I,14. Quomodo se habeant fratres post completorium.	10. De lectis.	
cf. I,19. De infirmis qui sunt in infirmitorio.	11. De infirmis.	cf. I, 18. De infirmis qui sunt in infirmitorio et esu carnium.
I, 20. De minutione.	12. De minutione.	I, 19. De minutione.
cf. II, 9. De magistro novitiorum.	13. De magistro novitiorum.	II, 9. De magistro novitiorum.
I, 16. De novitiis probandis.	14. De recipiendis.	I, 14. De recipiendis.

---

1 The title *De capitulo quotidiano* was added in the Rodez manuscript by a later hand in the left margin. The constitutions of Raymond of Peñafort (d. II, c. 6) have the full title *De capitulo cotidiano*.

	15. De tempore probationis.[2]	
	16. De modo faciendi professionem.	cf. I,14. De recipiendis.
cf. I, 17. De dirigendis in via.	17. De silentio.	cf. I, 16. De dirigendis in via et silentio observando.
cf. I, 9. Quomodo se habeant fratres tempore lectionis (*fin.*).	18. De scandalo fratrum.	
IV, 14. De vestitu.	19. De vestibus.	II, 13. De vestitu.
IV, 15. De rasura.	20. De rasura.	I, 20. De rasura.
III, 1. De levioribus culpis.	21. De levioribus culpis.[3]	III, 1. De levioribus culpis.
III, 2. De mediis culpis.		III, 2. De mediis culpis.
III, 3. De gravi culpa.	22. De gravi culpa.	III, 3. De gravi culpa.
III, 6. Item de graviori culpa.	23. De graviori culpa.	III, 4. De graviori culpa.
III, 9. De his qui apostataverint.	24. De fratre qui apostataverit.	III, 8. De apostatis.
III, 10. De gravissima culpa.	25. De gravissima culpa.	III, 9. De gravissima culpa.

---

2 A number of regulations from this chapter also appear in Pb (see *supra*, p. 319, footnotes 199-200).

3 This chapter in the Dominican text contains regulations from two chapters in Pa and Pb (see *supra*, pp. 255, 285-286).

The sources of the Dominican constitutions

Legend
1. For the signs and typefaces used, see the legend in Appendix V.
2. The sources and related texts in the first and the second *distinctio* appear in the left and right half of the diagram respectively.

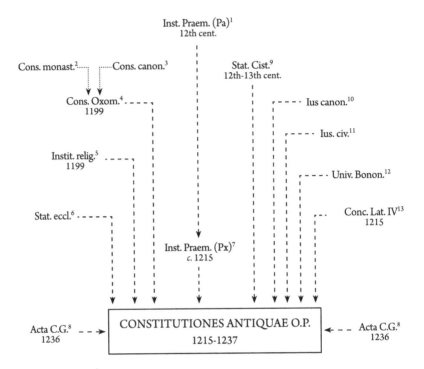

1   See *supra*, pp. 284-302.
2   See pp. 306-314.
3   See pp. 306-308.
4   See pp. 321-324.
5   See pp. 314-320.
6   See pp. 314-320, 324-328.
7   See pp. 288-291, 296-297, 303-306, 369.
8   See pp. 267-268.
9   See pp. 330-340.
10 See pp. 354-357, 366-368.
11 See pp. 357-364, 371.
12 See pp. 364-366.
13 See pp. 341-353.

Index of part II

1. The Index does not cover the introduction, the conclusions to each chapter or the appendices.
2. The names of authors and documents are included if they appear in the body of the text, but not if they are only quoted in the footnotes, except if the reference in question is of particular importance or adds additional information.